Case Studies in Comparative Politics

Case Studies in Comparative Politics

DAVID J. **SAMUELS**, ED.

University of Minnesota, Minneapolis

with contributions by

Ben Ansell and Jane Gingrich, *University of Minnesota, Minneapolis*
David Art, *Tufts University*
Erik Bleich, *Middlebury College*
Ethan Scheiner, *University of California, Davis*
Steven I. Wilkinson, *Yale University*
Cecilia Martínez-Gallardo, *University of North Carolina, Chapel Hill*
Graeme Roberston, *University of North Carolina, Chapel Hill*
Alexandra Scacco, *New York University*
Andrew Mertha, *Cornell University*
Arzoo Osanloo, *University of Washington*

PEARSON

Boston Columbus Indianapolis New York San Francisco Upper Saddle River
Amsterdam Cape Town Dubai London Madrid Milan Munich Paris Montreal Toronto
Delhi Mexico City São Paulo Sydney Hong Kong Seoul Singapore Taipei Tokyo

Senior Acquisitions Editor: Vikram Mukhija
Associate Editor: Corey Kahn
Editorial Assistants: Isabel Schwab, Beverly Fong
Executive Marketing Manager: Wendy Gordon
Senior Digital Media Editor: Paul DeLuca
Production Manager: Denise J. Phillip
Photo Researcher: Connie Gardner
Project Coordination, Editorial Services, Text Design, and Art Rendering: Electronic Publishing Services Inc., NYC
Art Rendering and Electronic Page Makeup: Jouve
Cover Design Manager: John Callahan
Cover Designer: Elina Frumerman
Senior Manufacturing Buyer: Roy Pickering
Printer/Binder: RRD-Harrisonburg
Cover Printer: RRD-Harrisonburg

Credits and acknowledgments borrowed from other sources and reproduced, with permission, in this textbook appear on the appropriate page within text or on page 465.

Library of Congress Cataloging-in-Publication Data

Samuels, David, 1967-
  Case studies in comparative politics / David Samuels.
    p. cm.
  Includes index.
  ISBN 978-0-205-74009-3
  1. Comparative government--Case studies. I. Title.

JF51.S247 2013
320.3--dc23

2011051474

Copyright © 2013 by Pearson Education, Inc.

All rights reserved. Manufactured in the United States of America. This publication is protected by Copyright, and permission should be obtained from the publisher prior to any prohibited reproduction, storage in a retrieval system, or transmission in any form or by any means, electronic, mechanical, photocopying, recording, or likewise. To obtain permission(s) to use material from this work, please submit a written request to Pearson Education, Inc., Permissions Department, One Lake Street, Upper Saddle River, New Jersey 07458, or you may fax your request to 201-236-3290.

2 16

ISBN 10: 0-205-74009-X
ISBN 13: 978-0-205-74009-3

BRIEF CONTENTS

Detailed Contents   viii

Preface   xiii

CHAPTER 1   Introduction   1
David Samuels

CHAPTER 2   United Kingdom   39
Ben Ansell and Jane Gingrich

CHAPTER 3   Germany   77
David Art

CHAPTER 4   France   114
Erik Bleich

CHAPTER 5   Japan   150
Ethan Scheiner

CHAPTER 6   India   194
Steven I. Wilkinson

CHAPTER 7   Mexico   235
Cecilia Martínez-Gallardo

CHAPTER 8   Russia   277
Graeme Roberston

CHAPTER 9   Nigeria   320
Alexandra Scacco

CHAPTER 10   China   365
Andrew Mertha

CHAPTER 11   Iran   407
Arzoo Osanloo

Glossary   449

Credits   465

Subject Index   467

Name Index   485

DETAILED CONTENTS

Preface xiii

CHAPTER 1 Introduction 1

David Samuels

CHAPTER QUESTION: Why study country cases in comparative politics?

Introduction 2
- Comparative Politics 3
- Why These Ten Countries? 6
- Chapter Framework 11

Historical Overview 12
- Early versus Late-forming States 14
- Globalization and the State 15

Institutions 17
- Democratic Regimes 19
- Non-Democratic Regimes 21
- Regime Change 24

Identities 25
- Economic and Cultural Forms of Identity 25
- Political-Identity Cleavages 26
- The Sources of Political Identity 27

Interests 28
- Social Movement 29
- Interest Groups 30
- Political Parties 30

The Contemporary Context 32
- Political Violence 32
- Political Economy 33

Conclusion 36

CHAPTER 2 United Kingdom 39

Ben Ansell and Jane Gingrich

CHAPTER QUESTION: How did limited government emerge in a country without a written constitution?

Introduction to the United Kingdom 40

Historical Overview of the United Kingdom 41
- The Establishment of the State 41
- The Gradual Emergence of Limited Government 44
- Twentieth-Century Developments 46
- The Contemporary United Kingdom 47

Institutions of the United Kingdom 49
- Institutions Promoting Effective Government 51
- Factors Supporting Limited Government 57

Identities in the United Kingdom 60
- Class Identity 60
- Regional, Religious, and Ethnic Identities 62
- Gender and Quality-of-Life Issues 65

Interests in the United Kingdom 67
- Business and Labor in the Party System 68
- "Policy Communities" in Britain 70
- Civil Society and Social Movements in the United Kingdom 71
- Mass Media 72

Conclusion 73

CHAPTER 3 Germany 77

David Art

CHAPTER QUESTION: How did Germany overcome its tumultuous history and become a healthy democracy?

Introduction to Germany 78

Historical Overview of Germany 78
- The Second Reich 79
- The Weimar Republic 82
- The Nazi Regime 83
- The Postwar Era: Division and Reunification 85

Institutions of Germany 88
- "Chancellor Democracy" 88
- The Judiciary 90

Federalism 90
International Institutions 91

Identities in Germany 94
Pre-War Identities 94
Political Culture after WWII 95
Incorporating East Germany 97
Immigration and German Identity 98

Interests in Germany 102
The Postwar Settlement 103
Political Parties 104
Challenges to the German Model 109

Conclusion 111

CHAPTER 4   France   114

Erik Bleich

CHAPTER QUESTION: Why do French citizens engage in such frequent and dramatic forms of protest?

Introduction to France 115

Historical Overview of France 118
From the Middle Ages to the Ancien Régime 118
The French Revolution and Its Aftermath 119
Regime Change in the Nineteenth Century 120
Consolidating Democracy in the Twentieth Century 120

Institutions of France 123
Semi-Presidential Democracy and the Executive Branch 124
The Legislative Branch 126
The Judicial Branch 127
Electoral Institutions 128

Identities in France 132
Class Divisions 134
Nationalism and Its Challengers 135
Religious Identities versus Laïcité 136
Post-Materialist Identities 137

Interests in France 138
Interest Groups 139
Political Parties 140
The Interests of the State 142
Examples of Protest 142

Conclusion 147

CHAPTER 5   Japan   150

Ethan Scheiner

CHAPTER QUESTION: How did a single political party dominate Japan's democracy for more than half a century?

Introduction to Japan 151

Historical Overview of Japan 154
The Tokugawa Era 154
The Meiji Era 155
Economic Growth and the Rise and Decline of Democracy before World War II 156
Rebuilding in the Postwar Era 158
The 1990s 160
The 2000s 161

Institutions of Japan 165
Unitarism 166
Parliamentarism 166
Electoral System 167
The Weak Judiciary 173
The Powerful Bureaucracy 173

Identities of Japan 175
Japanese Homogeneity 175
Class Identity 177
Status in Japan 177
Disadvantaged Position of Women 179

Interests in Japan 180
Postwar Interests 181
Environmental Interest Groups 181
Modern versus Traditional Interests 183
Koizumi's Reforms and the Fall of the LDP 187

Conclusion 189

CHAPTER 6   India   194

Steven I. Wilkinson

CHAPTER QUESTION: Why has democracy persisted in India despite its colonial legacies of ethnic and religious strife, and widespread poverty and illiteracy?

Introduction to India 195

Historical Overview of India 198
The Mughal Empire 198

The British Empire 200
The Difficult Legacy of Colonialism 203

Institutions of India 207
Federalism 208
Parliament 209
Civil-Military Relations 211
The Judiciary 211
Political Parties 212
Election Commission 214

Identities in India 216
Castes 217
Languages 219
Religion 219
The Changing Politics of Caste Identity 222

Interests in India 225
Ethnic and Minority Interests 225
Voters 226
Rural Interests 226
The Poor 227
Business Interests 227
Freedom of the Press and Mass Media 228

Conclusion 230

CHAPTER 7 Mexico 235

Cecilia Martínez-Gallardo

CHAPTER QUESTION: Why is Mexico's democratic government unable to deal effectively with persistent poverty, corruption, and drug trafficking?

Introduction to Mexico 236

Historical Overview of Mexico 237
Colonial Mexico 237
Independent Mexico 240
The 1910 Revolution 241
The Establishment of One-Party Rule, 1917–1940 242
PRI Hegemony: 1940–1970 243
The Decline of the PRI: 1970–2000 244

Institutions of Mexico 250
Executive–Legislative Relations 251
The Judiciary 252
Federalism 254
Electoral Institutions 255

Identities in Mexico 258
Forming National Identity under the PRI 258
Ethnicity Makes a Comeback 260
Political Cleavages and Electoral Behavior 262

Interests in Mexico 264
Political Parties 264
Social Movements 266
Interest Groups 269

Conclusion 272

CHAPTER 8 Russia 277

Graeme Roberston

CHAPTER QUESTION: Why has Russia failed to consolidate democracy, remaining in many ways an authoritarian regime?

Introduction to Russia 278

Historical Overview of Russia 279
Geography and the Formation of the Russian State 279
The Russian Revolution and the Rise of the USSR 283
Reform and the Collapse of the USSR 284

Institutions in Russia 287
Constitutional Crisis 1992–1993 287
The Constitution: President, Prime Minister, and Parliament 288
Federalism 290
Elections 293
The "Tandemocracy" of President and Prime Minister 296

Identities in Russia 299
Ethnic Politics 299
Chechnya and the Politics of the Caucasus 301
Russian Nationalism 302
What Happened to Class Identity? 303
Religious Identity 304

Interests in Russia 306
Economic Reform, Economic Collapse, and the Rise of the "Oligarchs" 307
Putin, the Fall of the Oligarchs, and Business Interests 309
Labor 310
Political Parties 311
Social Movements 313

Conclusion 316

CHAPTER 9   Nigeria   **320**

Alexandra Scacco

CHAPTER QUESTION: What factors account for Nigeria's poor economic and political performance since independence?

Introduction to Nigeria   321

Historical Overview of Nigeria   323
- The Pre-Colonial Period: A Diverse Territory   323
- Colonial Nigeria: Unequal Regional Development   326
- Nigeria since Independence: Political and Economic Crisis   328

Institutions of Nigeria   331
- Nigeria's Political Institutions in Theory   332
- Nigeria's Political Institutions in Practice   333
- A "Critically Weak" State   334
- Oil Dependence and State Weakness   339

Identities in Nigeria   342
- Ethnic Diversity: Is Nigeria Too Diverse to Govern?   342
- Ethnicity, Oil, and Violent Conflict   345

Interests of Nigeria   351
- Political Parties   351
- Where Is the Working Class?   354
- Economic Interest Groups   356
- Ethno-Regional Groups   357
- The Military   357

Conclusion   359

CHAPTER 10   China   **365**

Andrew Mertha

CHAPTER QUESTION: How has China's authoritarian regime managed to build and consolidate state strength in just 60 years?

Introduction to China   366

Historical Overview of China   370
- The Chinese Empire   370
- The Chinese Republic   372
- Consolidating the People's Republic of China   373
- Mao's Attack on the State   375
- The Emergence of the Contemporary PRC   377

Institutions of China   379
- China's Elite Institutions   379
- Local State Government   384
- The Military   386

Identities in China   388
- From Totalitarian to Authoritarian Identities   388
- Nationalism as a Unifying Force   391
- Ethnicity and Religion as Potentially Divisive Forces   393

Interests in China   396
- State Organizations: The Case of the Military   397
- Local Governments   398
- The Media   398
- Industrial and Professional Groups   399
- Non-Governmental Organizations   399
- Chinese Citizens   399

Conclusion   402

CHAPTER 11   Iran   **407**

Arzoo Osanloo

CHAPTER QUESTION: How does a dynamic civil society survive under repressive non-democratic governments in Iran?

Introduction to Iran   408

Historical Overview of Iran   409
- Ancient Persia: From the Achaemenids to Sassanids   409
- The Safavids and the Spread of Islam   412
- Oil and the Rise of Nationalism in the Twentieth Century   413
- The 1979 Iranian Revolution   416
- Khatami and the Limits of Reform, 1997–2005   418
- Ahmadinejad and Conservative Reaction, 2005–Present   419

Institutions of Iran   422
- Republican Institutions   422
- Islamic Institutions   425

Identities of Iran   430
- Pre-Islamic "Persian": Achaemenids to Sassanids   430
- Ethnic Identities   430

Religious Identities 431
Social Classes 433
Post-Revolutionary "Hybrid" Identities 433
Women in the Vanguard 434

Interests in Iran 436
Military Interests 436
Political Interests 437
Organized Interests 439
Nuclear and Scientific Interests 440
Examples of Protest 441

Conclusion 445

Glossary 449
Credits 465
Subject Index 467
Name Index 485

PREFACE

Comparative politics is fundamentally about constructing arguments that answer compelling questions. Teaching political science is about developing students' skills so they can be informed, engaged, and *analytical* citizens, a core element in a liberal arts education. Students should learn how to identify and contribute to questions that central to our field, recognize competing hypotheses, apply research to arguments by analyzing different sorts of evidence, and relate different perspectives to each other.

All comparative politics textbooks confront a "chicken and egg" problem: how should we as instructors teach students about how to analyze politics while also helping them learn something important about the real world around them? Thematic texts hone in on the important questions we ask as comparativists and help students learn how to analyze politics, but they sacrifice some degree of detail about different cases, details that help ground students' critical thinking. On the other hand, country study texts alone necessarily concentrate on learning about the real world at the expense of learning how comparativists ask and attempt to answer interesting questions. When used together, my thematic survey—*Comparative Politics*—with this edited collection of country cases resolves the pedagogical tradeoff.

Comparative Politics offers an intellectually coherent story of our discipline using a questions-driven approach that mirrors the process of good political science research. Each chapter frames its topic around a core question that works to foster classroom discussion, illustrates how scholars go about answering similar questions, and provides a clear reference point for students to articulate their own answers for assignments and exams.

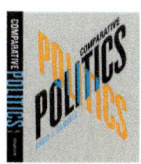

Case Studies in Comparative Politics supports the same pedagogical goals but goes one step further to bring the relationship between the countries and the questions to life. Each chapter in the casebook echoes the question-driven approach of the survey, and is organized around three main themes: institutions, identities, and interests. That is, the cases do not merely provide a bit of history and a set of facts about contemporary politics in a group of important countries. Instead, each chapter opens with a question based on a key current event in the country at hand. Then, they explore how a country's political institutions, identities, and interests are interrelated, giving students the specifics they need to more deeply engage the question raised at the start of the chapter as well as the questions raised in the survey text.

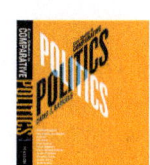

Together, the survey and accompanying casebook will appeal to instructors who want to shape their course around themes but who also want to provide students with detailed information about key countries. This casebook offers an additional pedagogical advantage: it offers instructors flexibility no matter how they organize their course. It allows instructors to find their own balance between a thematic approach and a country study approach to teaching comparative politics by allowing instructors to pick choose *when* or even *if* to present a case during a semester.

FEATURES
Approach
Each case study showcases a clear connection between country and thematic questions. Such an approach shows students how to connect the dots from the conceptual to the factual with concrete illustrations and by demonstrating how political scientists go about asking and answering interesting questions. Pedagogically, this facilitates instructors' ability to link coverage of particular countries to the important issues, questions, and themes in our field. In this way, the casebook is effective in combination with a thematic text or on its own. Furthermore, *Case Studies in Comparative Politics* introduces students to the full breadth of our subfield by exploring themes that other texts downplay or ignore entirely, particularly how political identities and interests develop through time to bridge institutions.

Each case study is structured in the same way, beginning with a question that focuses on a core aspect of what politics is in that country. For example, for France, the question is "Why do French citizens engage in such frequent and dramatic forms of protest?," and for Nigeria, the question is "What factors account for Nigeria's poor economic and political performance since independence?" Framing the chapter's subject as a question provides a narrative thread for students to follow as they read through each chapter; it also fosters classroom discussion, illustrates how scholars go about answering similar questions, and provides a clear reference point for students to articulate answers on their own that they can use for assignments and exams.

After the chapter's main question is introduced, the historical overview provides the necessary background information on each country's development. The second section describes the country's political institutions and explains why each emerged as a democracy or remained a dictatorship. Each chapter's third section focuses on the country's main forms of political identity, including ethnicity, nationalism, economic class, language, religion, and gender. The fourth section focuses on the patterns of competition over the distribution of political power and wealth between the different organized interests and identities in each society—parties, interest groups, and social movements. Each chapter concludes by reviewing how the exploration of the country's institutions, identities, and interests has helped answer the question posed at the start.

As the case study progresses, related sub-questions appear in the margins to encourage students to examine more than one facet of a main political puzzle. Every sub-question relates back to the chapter's main question and builds towards the next sub-question, and finally, each chapter concludes by returning to the chapter question and summarizing what was learned. In short, each chapter shows students how political scientists engage smaller pieces of a larger puzzle and explore, debate, and articulate plausible arguments to key questions about comparative politics.

Coverage

The ten countries in this book were chosen not just because they're big or important but because each offers a clear example of an intellectual puzzle that comparative political scientists have long sought to understand. Each chapter is written by a country expert who travels regularly to his or her region of specialty, and the order of the countries progresses from stable democracies (United Kingdom, Germany, France, Japan, India) to partial democracies (Mexico, Russia, Nigeria) and authoritarian regimes (China, Iran).

In Chapter 2, Ben Ansell and Jane Gingrich (University of Minnesota) explain how one of the oldest democracies in the world—the United Kingdom—functions without a written constitution.

In Chapter 3, David Art (Tufts University) identifies the specific ways that postwar Germany created political institutions that purposefully seek to overcome the legacy of its history and Hitler's totalitarian government.

In Chapter 4, Erik Bleich (Middlebury College) details the historical precedents of the French proclivity for political mobilization and explains how its government weathers and responds to the multitude of protests.

In Chapter 5, Ethan Scheiner (University of California, Davis) shows how a single political party dominated Japan's political system for over half a century within a democracy, only to be defeated in elections by a rival party in 2009.

In Chapter 6, Steven Wilkinson (Yale University) delves into the factors behind India's enduring democracy given its colonial legacy, ethnic and religious strife, and widespread poverty.

In Chapter 7, Cecilia Martínez-Gallardo (University of North Carolina, Chapel Hill) examines how colonial legacies and the dominance of another single-party regime laid the foundations for unstable democracy in today's Mexico.

In Chapter 8, Graeme Robertson (University of North Carolina, Chapel Hill) explains how Russia failed to consolidate democracy in the early 1990s, remaining in many ways an authoritarian regime.

In Chapter 9, Alexandra Scacco (New York University) confronts the factors that account for Nigeria's crumbling democracy: colonial legacy, ethnic violence, and the resource curse of oil.

In Chapter 10, Andrew Mertha (Cornell University) explains the astonishing rise of China's authoritarian government from extreme poverty and isolation to strong global power.

And finally, in Chapter 11, Arzoo Osanloo (University of Washington) explains the conundrum of how a dynamic civil society survives under the repression of Iran's authoritarian regime.

Pedagogy

Extensive pedagogy is also included in every chapter to help students comprehend key concepts and to apply them.

- Every chapter opens with a political map and a country comparison grid that shows the vital facts and statistics (such as Freedom House Classification, life expectancy, and literacy rate) of the ten countries side-by-side. The

comparative grid serves as a resource for critical thinking as students learn how institutions, economic development, identities, and political interests are related to country outcomes and characteristics.
- Every major section concludes with a summary table that reviews key concepts in an organized and easy-to-read format.
- Every chapter includes a marginal glossary to support students' understanding of new and important concepts at first encounter.
- For easy reference, key terms from the marginal glossary are repeated at the end of each chapter along with review questions and an annotated list of suggested readings.
- Numerous color photos and figures are integrated into the text to engage and support visual learners.

MYPOLISCILAB FOR *CASE STUDIES IN COMPARATIVE POLITICS*

The moment you know

Educators know it. Students know it. It's that inspired moment when something that was difficult to understand suddenly makes perfect sense. Our MyLab products have been designed and refined with a single purpose in mind—to help educators create that moment of understanding with their students.

MyPoliSciLab delivers *proven results* in helping individual students succeed. It provides *engaging experiences* that personalize, stimulate, and measure learning for each student. And it comes from a *trusted partner* with educational expertise and a deep commitment to helping students, instructors, and departments achieve their goals.

MyPoliSciLab can be used by itself or linked to any learning management system. To learn more about how MyPoliSciLab combines proven learning applications with powerful assessment, **visit www.mypoliscilab.com.**

MyPoliSciLab delivers *proven results* in helping individual students succeed

- Pearson MyLabs are currently in use by millions of students each year across a variety of disciplines.
- MyPoliSciLab works, but don't take our word for it. Visit **www.pearsonhighered.com/elearning** to read white papers, case studies, and testimonials from instructors and students that consistently demonstrate the success of our MyLabs.

MyPoliSciLab provides *engaging experiences* that personalize, stimulate, and measure learning for each student

- *Assessment.* Track progress and get instant feedback on every chapter, video, and multimedia activity. With results feeding into a powerful gradebook, the

assessment program identifies learning challenges early and suggests the best resources to help.
- *Personalized Study Plan.* Follow a flexible learning path created by the assessment program and tailored to each student's unique needs. Organized by learning objectives, the study plan offers follow-up reading, video, and multimedia activities for further learning and practice.
- *Pearson eText.* Just like the printed text, highlight and add notes to the eText online or download it to a tablet.
- *Flashcards.* Learn key terms by word or definition.
- *Video.* Analyze current events by watching streaming video from major news providers.
- *Mapping Exercises.* Explore interactive maps that test basic geography, examine key events in world history, and analyze the state of the world.
- *Comparative Exercises.* Think critically about how politics compare around the world.
- *PoliSci News Review.* Join the political conversation by following headlines in *Financial Times* newsfeeds, reading analysis in the blog, taking weekly current events quizzes and polls, and more.
- *ClassPrep.* Engage students with class presentation resources collected in one convenient online destination.

MyPoliSciLab comes from a *trusted partner* with educational expertise and an eye on the future

- Pearson supports instructors with workshops, training, and assistance from Pearson Faculty Advisors so you get the help you need to make MyPoliSciLab work for your course.
- Pearson gathers feedback from instructors and students during the development of content and the feature enhancement of each release to ensure that our products meet your needs.

To order MyPoliSciLab with the print text, use ISBN 0-205-88784-8.

SUPPLEMENTS

Pearson is pleased to offer several resources to qualified adopters of *Comparative Politics* and their students that will make teaching and learning from this book even more effective and enjoyable. Several of the supplements for this book are available at the Instructor Resource Center (IRC), an online hub that allows instructors to quickly download book-specific supplements. Please visit the IRC welcome page at www.pearsonhighered.com/irc to register for access.

Instructor's Manual/Test Bank

This resource includes learning objectives, lecture outlines, multiple-choice questions, true/false questions, and essay questions for each chapter. Available exclusively on the IRC.

Pearson MyTest

This powerful assessment generation program includes all of the items in the instructor's manual/test bank. Questions and tests can be easily created, customized, saved online, and then printed, allowing flexibility to manage assessments anytime and anywhere. Available exclusively on the IRC.

PowerPoint Presentations

Organized around a lecture outline, these multimedia presentations also include photos, figures, and tables from each chapter. Available exclusively on the IRC.

Sample Syllabus

This resource provides suggestions for assigning content from this book and MyPoliSciLab. Available exclusively on the IRC.

Longman Atlas of World Issues (0-205-78020-2)

From population and political systems to energy use and women's rights, the *Longman Atlas of World Issues* features full-color thematic maps that examine the forces shaping the world. Featuring maps from the latest edition of *The Penguin State of the World Atlas,* this excerpt includes critical thinking exercises to promote a deeper understanding of how geography affects many global issues.

Goode's World Atlas (0-321-65200-2)

First published by Rand McNally in 1923, *Goode's World Atlas* has set the standard for college reference atlases. It features hundreds of physical, political, and thematic maps as well as graphs, tables, and a pronouncing index.

Passport

Choose the resources you want from MyPoliSciLab and put links to them into your course management system. If there is assessment associated with those resources, it also can be uploaded, allowing the results to feed directly into your course management system's gradebook. With MyPoliSciLab assets like videos, mapping exercises, current events quizzes, politics blog, and much more, Passport is available for any Pearson political science book. To order Passport with the print text, use ISBN 0-205-24898-5.

ACKNOWLEDGMENTS

The contributors and I would like to thank the many manuscript reviewers who helped shape both *Comparative Politics* and *Case Studies in Comparative Politics*:

Dauda Abubakar, Ohio University
Janet Adamski, University of Mary Hardin-Baylor
Rebecca Aubrey, University of Connecticut
Steve Barracca, Eastern Kentucky University
Matthew Bradley, Indiana University at Kokomo
Cheryl L. Brown, University of North Carolina at Charlotte
Nic Cheeseman, Oxford University
Katy Crossley-Frolick, Denison University
Kevin Deegan-Krause, Wayne State University
Jason Enia, Sam Houston State University
Farideh Farhi, University of Hawaii at Manoa
Mark Frazier, University of Oklahoma
Lauretta Frederking, University of Portland
Daniel Fuerstman, State College of Florida
Wynford Grant, University of Warwick
Kenneth S. Hicks, Rogers State University
Jonathan Hollowell, SUNY Brockport
Debra Holzhauer, Southeast Missouri State University
Carrie Humphreys, University of Utah
Wade Jacoby, Brigham Young University
Ellis S. Krauss, University of California, San Diego
Eric Langenbacher, Georgetown University
F. David Levenbach, Arkansas State University Political Science
Yitan Li, Seattle University
Staffan Lindberg, University of Florida
Daniel Lynch, University of Southern California
Shannan Mattiace, Allegheny College
Julie Mazzei, Kent State University
Anthony O'Regan, Los Angeles Valley College
Angela Oberbauer, San Diego Mesa College
Rebecca K. Root, the State University of New York at Geneseo
James C. Ross, University of Northern Colorado
Amy Forster Rothbart, University of Wisconsin at Madison
John Scherpereel, James Madison University
Tracy H. Slagter, University of Wisconsin Oshkosh
Boyka Stefanova, University of Texas San Antonio
Tressa E. Tabares, American River College
Gunes Tezcur, Loyola University Chicago
Erica Townsend-Bell, University of Iowa
Anca Turcu, University of Central Florida
Wendy N. Whitman, Santa Fe College, Social and Behavioral Sciences
Mark Wolfgram, Oklahoma State University.

DAVID SAMUELS

Case Studies in Comparative Politics

CHAPTER 1

Introduction

David Samuels

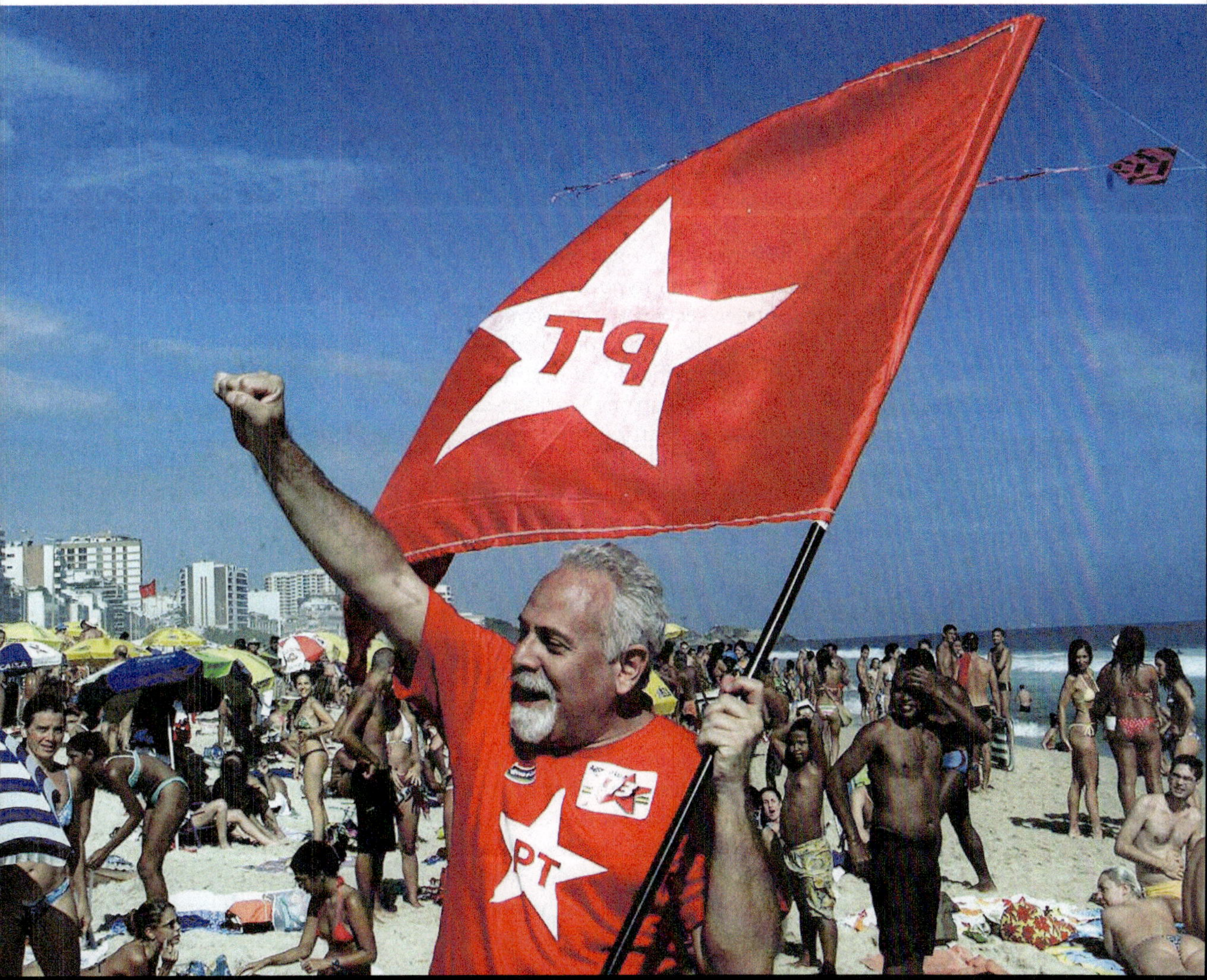

A supporter of Brazil's president Lula celebrates his 2002 election victory on Copacabana Beach in Rio de Janeiro.

Why study country cases in comparative politics?

INTRODUCTION

In June 2011, I flew to Rio de Janeiro to implement a public opinion survey. Since 1992, I have lived and worked on and off in Brazil for about four years, and on the June 2011 trip, I went to Rio to investigate a specific question. I wanted to know whether Brazilians think about political parties the same way as Americans do: do they "identify" with their parties, just as most Americans tend to associate themselves with either the Republicans or the Democrats? In the United States, a political divide exists between individuals who support one side or the other—some people just know that they're Republicans, while others sympathize just as strongly with the Democrats. Historically, relatively few Brazilians held similar sentiments about political parties compared to Americans, but certain signs in recent years indicate that more Brazilians have begun to identify with one particular party. Why? This is the question I wanted to answer.

Throughout my career, I have sought to engage colleagues and students by asking questions about politics. This is what comparativists do: we study puzzles about the political world that lack obvious answers. The question about partisanship in Brazil is specific to one country, but the answer holds broader implications. Most political scientists hypothesize that strong attachments to political parties only emerge under certain social, economic, or cultural conditions: for example, in countries where the population is divided along ethnic, religious, linguistic, or regional lines; where widespread industrialization in the nineteenth or early twentieth centuries created a strong working-class identity; or where a deep ideological divide exists about the nature and purpose of government, as in the United States.

Brazil has none of these sorts of characteristics: it is culturally diverse, but political parties have never formed along its ethnic or racial lines. As for religion, most Brazilians remain at least nominally Roman Catholic, but faith has never served as the basis for party formation. Everyone speaks Portuguese, ideological divides are relatively weak, and although Brazil has a complex and diverse economy, industrialization created a relatively small working class. Given these conditions, scholars expect parties to have only shallow roots in society.

Given that these country characteristics that make partisanship unlikely (at least in theory), I and others like me find it surprising that in recent years one party—the *Partido dos Trabalhadores* (PT, or Workers' Party)—has captured popular attention to the point where almost one in four Brazilians now identify with it—a proportion just less than that of Americans who consider themselves either Democrats or Republicans. Is this emerging attachment superficial—a short-term result of the PT's charismatic leader and successful reduction of poverty and unemployment? Or does Brazilians' affinity with the PT represent something deeper—an attachment that will endure through good times as well as bad, and long after these particular politicians have vanished from the scene?

Having spent a good bit of time in Brazil—but also broadening my perspective by studying comparative politics for some years—I saw that the narrow question about Brazilian political identity might have broader implications—after all, if partisanship in Brazil is "real," then it has emerged where few would expect it. Yet this intuition has more than academic importance: political parties are crucial instruments of representation—and democracy cannot survive without parties to channel its citizens' interests. Brazil has a long history of political instability and military rule. If the Workers' Party is growing, it signals an important transformation in Brazilian politics—one that may solidify democracy in that country for the foreseeable future.

In my quests to combine my in-depth knowledge of Brazil with a broader understanding of comparative politics, I flew to Rio to study changing partisan sympathies. Just as I did on that trip, when the contributors to this textbook travel to their country of expertise, they go with big questions in mind and a desire to offer practical insight to students and policymakers. However, each of us started out in an introductory course like the one you are currently taking, knowing relatively little about any country in particular and even less about comparative politics. We all soon learned that in order to understand what counts as an important question—as well as how to develop answers to those questions—we needed to gain in-depth understanding of how politics works in a few key countries.

This book provides you with an introduction to comparative politics that brings to life this relationship between countries and questions—between the depth of knowledge that comes from knowing particular cases and the breadth of perspective that comes from comparing and contrasting cases against each other. The authors of the chapters in this volume are experts not just about their particular countries, but in knowing how to ask and answer the questions that relate to comparative politics. The questions they raise are interesting because they are counterintuitive: that is, each author recognizes something surprising or unexpected about politics in their country; and in answering those questions, each author seeks to show you how to shed light on how politics works in that country. When read together, you may begin to recognize patterns among characteristics and outcomes in these ten country cases. And before you know it, you are doing comparative politics.

Comparative Politics

Comparativists travel the world to develop our research and teaching, yet what is the goal of a course in comparative politics? **Comparative politics** is the systematic search for answers to political questions about how people around the world make and contest authoritative public choices. In contrast to a course in international relations, comparative politics tends to focus on politics *within* different countries—both in terms of their similarities and their differences—while international relations concentrates on the interactions *between* countries.

A comparative approach to understanding politics around the world asks questions about unexpected events or patterns of events—such as why some countries are rich while other similar countries remain poor, or why conflict plagues some societies while other similar societies remain peaceful. A comparative approach also generates hypotheses that offer potential explanations for such

comparative politics ■ the systematic search for answers to political questions about how people around the world make and contest authoritative public choices.

THE WORLD

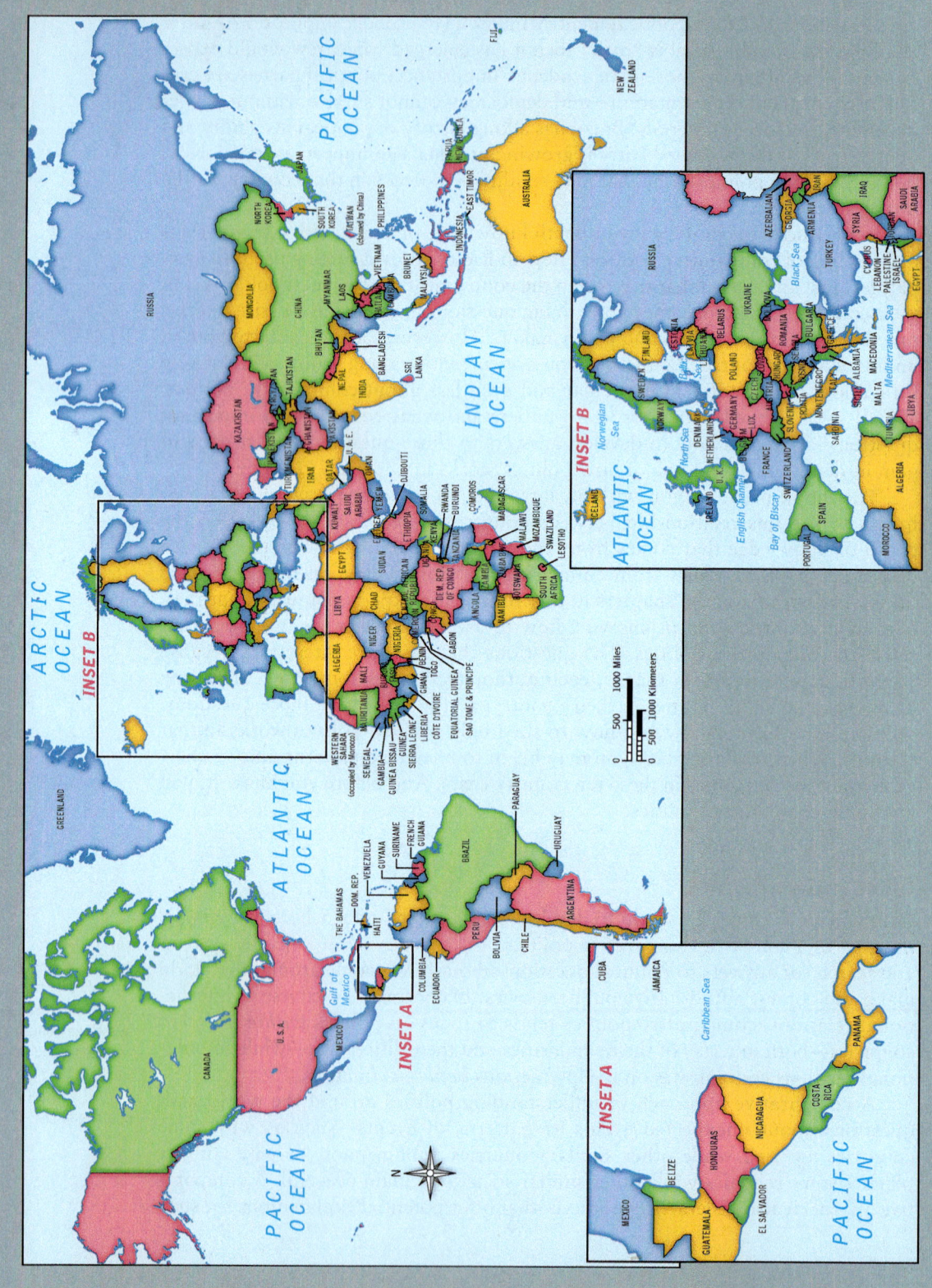

THE WORLD IN COMPARISON

	United Kingdom	Germany	France	Japan	India	Mexico	Russia	Nigeria	China	Iran
Freedom House Classification	Democracy	Democracy	Democracy	Democracy	Democracy	Partial democracy	Partial democracy	Partial democracy	Non-democracy	Non-democracy
Land Size (sq km)	243,610	357,022	643,801	377,915	3,287,263	1,964,375	17,098,242	923,768	9,596,961	1,648,195
Land Size Ranking	79	62	42	61	7	15	1	32	4	18
Population (July 2011 Estimate)	62,698,362	81,471,834	65,312,249	126,475,664	1,189,172,906	113,724,226	138,739,892	155,215,573	1,336,718,015	77,891,220
Population Ranking	22	16	21	10	2	11	9	8	1	18
Life Expectancy (Years)	80.1	80.1	81.2	82.3	66.8	76.5	66.3	47.6	74.7	70.1
Life Expectancy Ranking	28	27	13	5	51	72	162	220	95	146
Literacy Rate	99%	99%	99%	99%	61%	86.1%	99.4%	68%	91.6%	77%
GDP Per Capita (2010 Estimate)	US$35,100	US$35,900	US$33,300	US$34,000	US$3,500	US$13,800	US$15,900	US$2,500	US$7,600	US$11,200
GDP Ranking	22	32	39	38	163	85	71	178	126	100

comparative method ■ an approach to building arguments that involves comparing and contrasting cases that share attributes or characteristics but differ on the outcome you're exploring—or that have a variety of attributes but experience the same outcome.

puzzling patterns, and tests those hypotheses against evidence we gather from the real world to develop arguments using what we call the comparative method. The comparative method involves comparing and contrasting cases (a set of countries, for example) that share attributes or characteristics but differ on the outcome you're exploring—or that have a variety of attributes but experience the same outcome. The goal of comparing countries in this way is to generate convincing answers to our questions about what politics is all about.

To answer questions about politics, a comparativist searches for patterns—whether similarities or differences—across countries, and undertakes a systematic effort to understand why different outcomes occur in similar places, or similar outcomes occur in different places. This helps us make sense of complex patterns, offering simpler yet convincing answers to the questions that concern real-world political events.

All good comparative politics research begins with a question. Additionally, the only truly convincing explanations in comparative politics actually involve comparing several countries against each other. However, in doing such cross-national comparisons, we often lose sight of what is specific to each country—and in doing so, we may miss crucial details that also help explain the events we find interesting in each country. The cases in this book leverage detailed information about a set of cases to help you understand how scholars develop answers to the questions they pose about politics.

Why These Ten Countries?

Any country could be interesting in some way—for both scholars and students—so why focus on these ten countries in particular? A country casebook for an introductory comparative politics course cannot explore every country—or even every "important" country. The ten countries in this book were chosen not just because they're big or important—and the chapters do not simply describe the main contours of politics in each country. Instead, I chose these cases because each offers a clear example of an intellectual puzzle that comparative political scientists have long sought to understand. My goal is to explain the relationship between the broad questions that comparativists ask and how we choose which countries to research to help answer those questions.

One of the most enduring and intriguing of all political science questions is *how do we achieve a balance between limiting government's power over individuals while simultaneously empowering the government to "get things done?"* Every country in the world confronts this fundamental problem. The more power the government accrues, the less liberty individuals possess. Yet the more that government power is fragmented, weakened, and reined in, the harder it is for governments to effectively resolve pressing economic or political crises, whether domestic or international. This is certainly not the only question that motivates the ten cases in this book, but the way in which power is distributed—within the institutions of government and between government and the people—is typically the first question that political scientists ask when they study any country.

To start, consider the bizarre fact that the United Kingdom (UK) has no written constitution. How do political players know what the rules of the game are if there is no rule book? We often assume that politicians will try to leverage any opportunity to enhance their power. If that is the case, how did Britain's absolute monarchy evolve into a democracy, without a set of guidelines that codify individual rights and set limits on government power? In Chapter 2, Ben Ansell and Jane Gingrich explain the answer to this question by detailing the historical evolution of democracy in the UK, the development of effective legislative and executive institutions, and the nature of British political identities and interests which hold abuse of power in check.

Like the UK, Germany today is considered a stable democracy. Yet, unlike the UK, German democracy did not evolve gradually. It suffered through tremendous setbacks, the most traumatic being Adolf Hitler's totalitarian regime, the Holocaust, and defeat in World War II. Given its tumultuous history, few observers believed democracy would survive in Germany after the war. How has Germany overcome its legacy of dictatorships and militarism? In Chapter 3, David Art explains how Germany has enacted political institutions that purposefully seek to avoid a repetition of its past. The success of its political system contains powerful lessons for other countries that endeavor to overcome traumatic histories.

There exists a stereotype (often unfair) that Germans prefer powerful governments that get things done. In Chapter 4, Erik Bleich confronts a very different stereotype about the French: that *nothing* gets done because the French will drop everything to protest at the slightest provocation. Historical patterns actually support this impression. In 1789, French citizens instigated a violent revolution that toppled their country's king and queen, and, ever since, France has swung from dictatorship to unstable democracy, back to monarchy, then occupation by the Germans during World War II, until *finally* a stable democracy took root. Why do the French enjoy such a proclivity for protest—and doesn't such constant mobilization threaten to hobble government completely? The answer to this puzzle lies in the fact that, despite a history of revolution and protest, French government remains more centralized than does American government. The combination of centralized power with frequent mass mobilization characterizes French democracy to this day. Street protests allow French citizens to blow off steam and warn leaders when the government has gone too far.

French people engage in street protest far more commonly—and with much greater effect—than do the British or Germans, but the Japanese seem particularly reluctant to take to the streets to publicly express their political views. Like Germany, Japan has been a stable democracy only since its defeat in World War II. Yet since the late 1800s, Japan has sought to model its government and economy after several Western countries, among them France. However, Japan's citizens not only have less of a tradition of popular protest, but their country's postwar stability raises a profound question about the very definition of democracy, and what differentiates it from non-democratic forms of rule.

Control over government in wealthy democracies such as France, the UK, and the United States is defined in part by alternation between political parties. In Chapter 5, Ethan Scheiner explains how one political party has dominated Japan's democracy for nearly the entire period since the end of World War II. Can a system in which the same people stay in power for decades really be called a democracy? According to Scheiner, although the rules of Japanese politics formally allow limits on government power, political institutions that centralized politics combined with a highly homogenous culture made it hard for the political opposition to win elections. As in France, cultural norms and practices in Japan interact with the formal institutions of politics—but in this case, produce a very different outcome—a less contentious way of balancing out limited and effective government.

Learning about the UK, France, Germany, and Japan helps us understand how wealthy societies balance limits on government power with effective governance—an ability to get things done. The way we do things in the United States is, as these cases reveal clearly, hardly the only way. Yet the other cases in this book consider the nature of politics in societies with very different characteristics. For instance, Steven Wilkinson's chapter on India (Chapter 6) raises the question of the conditions that give rise to and sustain democracy itself. India gained independence from the UK in 1948, and immediately became a democracy. Yet, like with Germany, few observers had much faith that democracy would survive. India was abysmally poor, it had been exploited for centuries by British colonial authorities, and its population was deeply divided in countless ways along ethnic, religious, and class lines.

Despite these conditions, India continually confounded those who predicted civil war or government collapse. What makes democracy possible in a society divided in so many ways? Wilkinson explains how in 1948, India's fledgling democracy adapted what was effective from British colonial government institutions but opened up participation to ever-larger segments of the population. The country decentralized and distributed power to state governments and grounded India's national identity in the idea of a diverse and pluralistic society in which no single ethnic or religious group would ever dominate. In recent years, the Indian economy has begun to grow rapidly, and although Indian society is far from conflict free, this recipe for balancing effective government with limited government offers lessons for other societies that are struggling to establish a stable government that gets things done while not trampling on individual liberties.

The difficulty of finding and following a formula that generates stable and effective government has challenged Mexico since it transitioned to democracy in 2000. Mexico managed to transition from a single-party regime in which election results were a foregone conclusion to a system in which elections are highly competitive and multiple parties compete to hold power; yet, since that time, its government has been unable to deal effectively with persistent poverty, corruption, and drug trafficking. Why? In Chapter 7, Cecília Martínez-Gallardo explains that democratization has frustrated Mexicans, because increased competition and individual freedoms that serve as "limits" on government power have resulted in deadlock within the country's political institutions. Many now believe that Mexico's government is less effective than it was under the single-party, non-democratic regime in performing essential tasks.

The case of Mexico illustrates how the price of democracy can be too steep for some countries. Other cases in this volume echo this insight, including Russia, Nigeria, and China. Like Mexico, Russia initiated a transition to democracy in the early 1990s. For several years, government effectiveness declined as the economy collapsed and civil conflict emerged in outlying regions. To many, the Russian government was in a downward spiral and out of control. In Chapter 8, Graeme Robertson details how Russia's recent leaders have reconsolidated power so successfully that many now worry that the government has gone too far in centralizing authority, and that a return to full-fledged dictatorship is increasingly likely.

Is there a tradeoff between effective government and limited government? Although India's relative success in recent years at keeping the peace and growing its economy in the face of widespread poverty, inequality, and deep ethnic and religious divides might lead one to dismiss such a question, the Russian and Mexican cases force us to think about whether democracy can thrive only in certain conditions. The persistent problems Nigeria has faced since independence in 1960 deepen this doubt about whether a balance between limited and effective government can be achieved in difficult conditions.

India and Nigeria share several similarities, such as widespread poverty, diversity, and a history of British colonial exploitation. However, unlike India, Nigeria is situated over massive petroleum deposits, which ought to provide the country and its people with a reliable source of wealth. However, as Alexandra Scacco explains in Chapter 9, Nigeria's economic performance has remained poor, and its governance ineffective. Why has Nigeria failed while India has succeeded? Scacco suggests that military meddling in Nigeria's politics tends to delegitimize its civilian institutions, and oil wealth makes disputes over government control all the more volatile. As a result, ethnic and religious conflicts have been frequent and widespread, and governments have been highly unstable. This combustible mix of factors has made Nigeria highly unstable—although the country has recently returned to elected government from military rule, its future remains unclear.

Given its conditions, it is possible that democracy will never thrive in Nigeria. Two other countries in this collection—China and Iran—have zero experience with democracy, and the leaders of both countries are explicit in making the case that that democracy's tradeoffs are too costly. China's one-party regime has consistently touted the advantages of non-democratic rule as more "effective" than democracy—and given its astounding economic growth since the 1980s, some who wish to strengthen democracy around the world fear that other countries will seek to emulate its path. In 1960, China was one of the poorest countries on earth. It had suffered from devastating war and revolution that had left cities in ruins and millions dead, and caused widespread famine. Controlling and providing for its massive and diverse population imposed severe challenges.

The question that has attracted scholarly and media attention in recent years is, "How has the Chinese government found the elusive recipe to establish effective government under such difficult conditions?" In the last 30 years, the Chinese government has helped hundreds of millions of people emerge from absolute poverty, a feat that many other countries around the world would love to duplicate. In Chapter 10, Andrew Mertha explains how China's rulers have combined centralized "control when necessary" with "decentralization when possible" of political power to local government authorities. Given the country's massive population, China's rulers have concluded that local decision making frequently results in more effective government than would centralized control. Yet China has remained solidly non-democratic—its ruling party insists that democracy would endanger the country's economic success.

Finally, consider the case of Iran (Chapter 11), a country ruled by Muslim religious leaders. Iran illustrates the hardships imposed on average people under non-democracy. Yet, like democratic France, civil society has flourished under non-democracy in Iran. How is this possible? How does a dynamic civil society survive under a repressive regime? We expect non-democratic rulers—perhaps especially those who claim divine inspiration—to demand both cultural and political conformity. Iran confounds this stereotype, and given recent events in other Muslim countries in the Middle East and North Africa, protests and mass mobilizations in Iran—often in the face of grave threats from the government and its supporters—can teach us a great deal about the possibilities for political change.

This collection introduces readers to just a sampling of the possible questions in comparative politics. Each chapter starts with a question that engages a theme—such as the evolving balance of limited and effective government in each country—but each question is specifically tailored to apply to the politics of each country. The body of the chapter presents the nuts-and-bolts necessary to understand how the basics of politics work in that country, but also provides an answer to the chapter's core question. By framing the coverage around a question and its answer, readers learn about the process of doing political science research. This, in turn, presents readers with opportunities to build and strengthen useful skills, particularly in terms of learning how to marshal evidence and construct arguments that will withstand scrutiny and critique.

By focusing on this fundamental relationship between questions and countries, this book also helps answer the "So what?" question. Why should anyone care about these far-off people and places? Why do protest and repression, state sovereignty, and election results halfway across the world matter to us? Comparative politics helps us see more clearly that in our increasingly interconnected world, both stability and chaos "over there" impact what happens "over here"—and not just in Washington, D.C., but in our cities and even our homes.

A focus on politics in other countries also illustrates—for example—how economic stagnation and drug violence in Mexico might influence the rate of immigration into the United States; how governance in India is partly a function of its relationship with Pakistan—and how stability in that neighborhood has implications for U.S. foreign policy in neighboring Afghanistan; and how violence in Nigeria or Russia and instability in Iran cause oil price spikes. We also learn how our economy's health is tied to China's ability to continue to politically manage its own massive economic expansion, and how an inability to address pressing political and economic challenges in the UK, France, Germany, and Japan could sink the prospects for a return to economic growth in the United States.

Finally, a key purpose of a comparative politics course is to acquire a sharper perspective on the emerging and evolving challenges our own country confronts. By focusing each chapter in part around the success and/or failure of effective and limited government in ten key cases, we gain both an appreciation for democracy's successes as well as insight into why we sometimes see government inaction when confronted with pressing challenges, and why our government takes one path and not another. In sum, this book's focus on the relationship between countries and questions provides knowledge about particular cases, practical insight into the way scholars build arguments in comparative politics, and a critical perspective both on how politics elsewhere shapes and constrains our own political and economic welfare, and on how politics works right here at home. Let us now detail the organizational structure of each chapter.

Chapter Framework

As noted, this book differs from other country case-study comparative politics texts. The authors are not merely providing pertinent and relevant information about a set of ten countries—our goal is to give you a feel for the sorts of important questions that got us interested in doing political science research, and to show you how we go about answering those questions. This approach balances learning about particular countries with an effort to reveal how political scientists develop arguments about how politics works in the countries that interest them. Because each chapter begins with a question—and the body of the chapter then answers that question—this book provides you with examples to use in developing your own arguments.

Each chapter poses a question right off the bat, and then briefly explains how the material in the chapter will answer that question. Although every chapter takes on a different country and, thus, asks a different question, they all follow the same basic structure: first, an introductory section offers background information on each country's historical development. The second section describes the country's political institutions, and explains why each country has emerged as a democracy or remained a dictatorship. The third section focuses on the main forms of political identity in each country, such as ethnicity, nationalism, economic class, language, religion, or gender. The fourth section focuses on the patterns of competition over the distribution of political power and wealth between the different organized interests and identities in each society—parties, interest groups, and social movements. Each chapter concludes by reviewing how the exploration of the country's institutions, identities, and interests has helped answer the question posed at the beginning of the chapter.

The end of each chapter provides material for you to review and deepen your understanding of what you've just learned. After the chapter conclusion ties everything together, you'll find a list of the chapter's key terms—which are in any case highlighted and defined at first mention throughout each chapter. You'll also find a set of review questions to help you assess whether you've digested the chapter's main points (and to help you study for exams), and several annotated reading suggestions, if you want to learn more about a particular country.

This book provides the tools for you to learn how comparativists leverage deep knowledge and understanding of a particular case to answer pressing questions about politics. Although the book is organized around countries, it uses interesting questions to demonstrate how to build comparative politics arguments. Yet, before diving into the details of each case, it is important to lay down a conceptual and terminological foundation. The next four sections of this chapter are structured just like the body of each of the country-case chapters, as described above: we explore the political importance of whether a country gained independence centuries ago or in recent decades; the impact of political institutions on the relationship between government and citizens; the relationship between political identities and political mobilization; and the key ways in which organized political interests shape politics in different countries around the world.

HISTORICAL OVERVIEW

1.1 How do historical patterns of state development impact contemporary politics?

The fundamental problem of politics is establishing a stable and orderly society out of a collection of individuals who often have conflicting interests. When individuals do not necessarily want to participate in an action that would benefit all members of a group, a **collective action problem** results. For example, nobody likes paying taxes—but everyone likes the benefits governments provide, such as national defense, a highway system, or primary and secondary education. The **state** is the political-legal unit that solves this problem by establishing sovereignty over a particular territory and the population that resides in that territory. Once established, **sovereignty** is authority over the conduct of internal affairs within a set of borders, including a claim to a monopoly on the legitimate use of physical force within those borders.

collective action problem ■ a situation wherein each individual has incentives not to participate in an action that benefits all members of the group.

state ■ a political-legal organization with sovereign power over a particular geographic territory and the population that resides within that territory.

sovereignty ■ supreme legal authority over people within a certain territory.

◉ Watch the Video "Kenya's Developmental Challenge" at **mypoliscilab.com**

◉ Watch the Video "Global Food Prices and Changing Diets" at **mypoliscilab.com**

Soldiers of China's People's Liberation Army take part in a 2009 celebration commemorating the 60th anniversary of the Chinese Revolution—illustrating the connection between control over both territory and people and the concept of sovereignty.

States in comparative politics are not like one of the 50 U.S. states—states are countries. States also differ from governments—governments are comprised of leaders who administer the institutions of the state, and they change frequently. For example, Prime Minister David Cameron of the Conservative Party is the current head of government—the chief officer of the executive branch of government, usually a president or a prime minister—of the UK. When Cameron eventually steps down, a new government will bring in different personnel and perhaps change some policies—but the UK will remain as a sovereign state. Once formed, states tend not to disappear from the map. However, sometimes, former colonies gain independence (or new states break off from existing ones).

It is also important to distinguish the state from society and from the idea of a nation. Society is a term for all formal and informal organizations, social movements, and interest groups that attempt to (1) remain autonomous from state control and (2) articulate their own economic, cultural, and/or political identities and interests. In turn, while the state is a political-legal abstraction, a nation is a form of political identity—a cultural grouping of individuals who associate with each other based on collectively held political identity. Sometimes, states and nations overlap perfectly, but this is not always the case. In Japan, the two overlap almost exactly—after all, the country is very homogeneous. However, in culturally divided societies, the coincidence between state and nation can be much looser. In countries such as Iran, India, and Nigeria, some cultural groups are split between two or more states, meaning that a group of individuals who consider themselves to be part of one nation can be citizens of more than one state. For example, ethnic Kurds are found in Turkey, Iran, and Iraq. Table 1.1 highlights the terminological distinctions between state, government, nation, and society.

government ■ the organization that has the authority to act on behalf of a state, and the right to make decisions that affect everyone in a state.

society ■ all formal and informal organizations, social movements, and interest groups that attempt to (1) remain autonomous from state control and (2) articulate their own economic, cultural, and/or political identities and interests.

nation ■ a form of political identity—a cultural grouping of individuals who associate with each other based on collectively held political identity.

TABLE 1.1

Distinctions among State, Government, Nation, and Society

Concept	Definition	Example
State	A *political-legal* unit with sovereignty over a particular territory and the population that resides in that territory.	The United Kingdom
Government	The organization that has the authority to act on behalf of a state and the set of individuals who act within the state's institutions.	British Prime Minister David Cameron, his appointees, and bureaucrats accountable to his leadership
Nation	A *cultural grouping* of individuals who associate with each other based on collectively held political identity.	Scottish and Welsh—groups that live in the UK but identify with a regional cultural identity, including different accent or language, dress, food, customs, and, perhaps, religion

(Continued)

TABLE 1.1 (CONTINUED)		
Concept	**Definition**	**Example**
Society	The formal and informal organizations, social movements, and interest groups that attempt to (1) remain autonomous from the state and (2) articulate their own identities and interests independently from the influence of the state and its authorities.	British environmental, feminist, sports, or religious organizations

Early versus Late-Forming States

The fact that a map of the world's states can change from time to time raises the question of where states come from. As the ten cases in this book illustrate, the historical factors that drive state formation vary widely—and the timing of state emergence has important political consequences. Some states—particularly those in Western Europe, such as France and UK—emerged as unified political entities centuries ago. Today, these early-forming states tend to be wealthier, more effective at providing order and stability, and they enjoy relatively widespread popular support.

In contrast, the ability of many late-forming states to exert sovereignty varies with states that formed in earlier eras. In large part this is because a few early-forming European states grew so powerful that they managed to colonize much of the rest of the world; colonized territories gained independence as sovereign states more recently. These late-forming states have to deal with a colonial legacy—a history of state weakness and illegitimacy that derives at least in part from the fact political institutions were initially set up by foreigners not for benevolent purposes, but to politically repress and economically exploit the locals. Upon independence, such institutions had scant legitimacy to provide a basis for effective rule by locals.

We draw a distinction between early- and late-forming states because this difference in timing is important for understanding variation in patterns of politics around the world today. Early-forming states tend to be relatively stronger in terms of their ability to exercise sovereignty, maintain political stability, and implement public policies, while late-forming states tend to be relatively weaker. For example, India and Nigeria—both former British colonies—tend to face greater contemporary challenges in terms of establishing legitimate political order, eradicating corruption, and ensuring economic development for all citizens.

At the extreme, the world's weakest states—such as Afghanistan or Somalia—are sometimes called failed states, because they provide no order, have no legitimacy as unified political entities, and cannot protect their own borders. In a failed state, violence rather than law and order may be the norm. However, timing is not everything. For example, after 300 years as a Spanish colony, Mexico gained

early-forming state ■ a state that managed to consolidate sovereignty centuries ago.

late-forming state ■ a state that only consolidated sovereignty in recent decades.

failed state ■ a state where sovereignty has collapsed or was never effectively established.

independence in the 1820s—yet it still struggles to establish effective authority. Meanwhile, Germany formed as a unified state only around 1870—yet today ranks among the most orderly and legitimate of all contemporary states. Each chapter in this book pays particular attention to the factors that drove a country's experience with state formation. This investigation provides insight about why government legitimacy and effectiveness vary so greatly—from strong on both elements in the UK, for example, to quite weak in Nigeria.

Globalization and the State

In the contemporary era, many observers believe that a second factor beyond the timing of state formation influences states' ability to exercise sovereignty: globalization. Globalization works at the intersection of comparative politics and international relations, and refers to the increase in the scope and extent of political, economic, and cultural connections between governments, organizations, and individuals across state borders. Because it has proceeded so rapidly in recent decades, the impact of globalization on the world's states has become contentious. Debate focuses on its political and economic consequences.

Politically, globalization involves the growth in the number and scope of transnational political and economic issues, and the increasingly transnational responses to such issues. In the contemporary world, states are increasingly interdependent—they cannot solve the problems that affect their territory or citizens on their own. Interdependence has deepened in recent decades, although some countries have opened up to the world faster than others. Figure 1.1 provides the "level" of

globalization ■ the increase in the scope and extent of political, economic, and cultural connections between governments, organizations, and individuals across state borders.

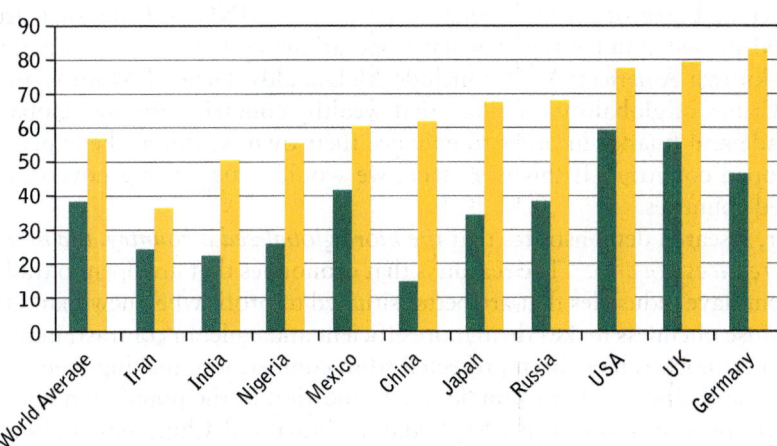

FIGURE 1.1
Globalization: 1970 and 2010

This figure shows the different levels of globalization for selected countries in 1970 and 2010 (except for Russia, which uses 1990 and 2010, due to unavailability of data). Some countries opened up more than others.

Source: Calculated from the KOF Swiss Federal Institute of Technology "Index of Globalization," data downloaded from http://globalization.kof.ethz.ch, accessed June 5, 2011.

globalization since 1970 for the countries in this volume. The scale ranges from 0–100, with higher numbers indicating greater extent of openness, and integrates measures of countries' openness to foreign trade and investment; extent of international tourism; number of Internet users; participation in international organizations, and even the number of McDonald's and Ikea stores per capita—a rough indicator of lifestyle similarities across countries.[1]

Debate about the political consequences of such interdependence centers on the questions of whether the growing number of international governmental organizations (IGOs) and international non-governmental organizations (INGOs) undermine states' hard-won sovereignty. IGOs include such agencies as the United Nations (UN), the World Trade Organization (WTO), and the European Union (EU). INGOs include organizations like Amnesty International, the International Red Cross, or Greenpeace. Some suggest that IGOs and INGOs are increasingly replacing states' political functions and binding states' hands to unaccountable international organizations, limiting their autonomy to control their own territory and people. However, although the traditional boundaries between domestic and international politics are weakening, one should not exaggerate globalization's political consequences. Evidence does not suggest that increased international cooperation means the end of state sovereignty, but merely that states must increasingly work with other states, IGOs, and INGOs to address political and economic challenges.

Global trade and financial flows have both expanded rapidly in recent decades, deepening countries' economic interdependence, as well. The internationalization of global commerce has been accompanied by a dramatic rise in **foreign direct investment**—the purchase or creation of assets in one country by an individual, firm, or government based in a different country—and by the growth in the number and size of **multinational corporations** (MNCs)—firms that are headquartered in one country but that have operations and employees in many others. Well-known American MNCs include McDonalds, General Motors, and Coca-Cola. Critics of globalization allege that wealthy countries promote globalization of trade and finance in order to enhance their own wealth at the expense of less-developed countries. If this were true, we would expect rising poverty in less-developed countries.

However, research demonstrates that *the more globalized a country, the more it grows and reduces poverty*.[2] The reason is that economies that are open to trade and investment have industries that are better situated to profit when new markets open up, because openness makes them more efficient and agile. In contrast, industries in closed economies have been protected from competition, making them far less innovative and efficient. For example, the proportion of the population living at the absolute poverty level of just $1.25/day in India and China has declined substantially over the last 30 years, and as a result hundreds of millions of people have emerged from destitution. As Figure 1.1 shows, both India and China have opened up to world markets. As a result, their economies have grown, helping to reduce poverty. In 1977, 94 percent of China's 792 million rural residents subsisted at the rate of only $1.25/day—that's more than 750 million people, or about three times the total U.S. population at the time! Yet by 2005, only 26 percent of China's rural population of 760 million subsisted at the absolute poverty level.[3] In short, although globalization does bring rapid change, which means social disruption

---

foreign direct investment ■ the purchase or creation of assets in one country by an individual, firm, or government based in a different country.

multinational corporations (MNCs) ■ firms that are headquartered in one country but that have operations and employees in many others.

and economic instability, greater and more open trade and financial flows have benefited hundreds of millions of poor people around the planet.

States exert sovereignty—supremacy of political authority and a monopoly on the legitimate use of physical force within a given territory. They organize the institutions, interests, and identities of governments, nations, and societies. Where did all these states come from? The historical factors that drove state formation vary widely, but a key factor is timing. States that consolidated sovereignty early tend to be more effective, and citizens regard them as more legitimate sources of political authority. In contrast, many late-forming states have limited effective and legitimate sovereignty over their territory. This is partly because many inherited institutions from former colonial authorities—institutions that were not set up to provide effective and legitimate government, only to extract resources. Governance tends to be relatively ineffective and illegitimate in late-forming states. And although some observers suggest that political and economic globalization has made establishment of effective and legitimate governance more difficult, the evidence supporting such a hypothesis is ambiguous at best. Let us now turn to the different ways in which the institutions of the state shape the relationship between the government and citizens, whether as individuals or groups.

INSTITUTIONS

Institutions structure the rules of the political game. One of the most fundamental rules has to do with who gets to participate in choosing and removing rulers—the difference between democracy and non-democracy. As Figure 1.2 illustrates, **democracy** is a system in which the rulers are accountable to the ruled. Under democracy, citizens have regular and realistic opportunities to remove rulers from office, through institutionalized political participation and contestation: everyone must have equal ability to participate in the political process in ways of their own choosing—they cannot be forced to vote for or against particular parties or candidates—and competition for power cannot be manipulated or controlled by the incumbent government. Even more concretely, democracy requires fair and frequent elections to install a government, and civil liberties such as freedom of speech, the press, and assembly. Finally, democracy requires that there must be at least one alternative group of potential rulers willing and able to replace the incumbents. By way of contrast, **non-democracy** is a system in which the rulers are not accountable to the ruled, because the rulers restrict political participation and contestation, often by using violence and other coercive tactics.

1.2 How do political institutions shape the relationship between governments and citizens?

democracy ■ a political regime that allows for government accountability to all citizens through institutionalized participation and contestation.

non-democracy ■ a system in which rulers are not accountable to the ruled because rulers restrict political participation and contestation.

Explore the Comparative "Violence and Civil War" at mypoliscilab.com

Elected Government, Civil Liberties, and Fair and Frequent Elections → Participation + Contestation → Democracy: Accountability of the Rulers to the Ruled

FIGURE 1.2
Democracy
A set of political institutions is necessary to support participation and contestation, which are required for democracy.

Voters cast their ballots in a legislative election in the state of Mexico, which surrounds Mexico City.

The countries in this book vary in terms of both whether they are democratic or not, and when they became democratic. Iran and China have no experience with democracy at all (see Table 1.2). In contrast, France and the UK were among the first countries in the world to adopt democracy; India, Germany, and Japan became democracies right after World War II. Nigeria, Russia, and Mexico have all had some experience with democracy since about 1990—but each has taken a different political trajectory. Russia has reverted to non-democracy, Nigeria has oscillated between regime types, and Mexico has remained democratic, but with serious problems with violence and maintaining the rule of law.

TABLE 1.2

Democracies and Non-Democracies

\multicolumn{3}{c	}{Democracies}	Partial or Non-Democracies
Parliamentary	Presidential	Semi-Presidential	
UK	Mexico	France	Iran
Germany			China
India			Nigeria
Japan			Russia

Democratic Regimes

Democracies can institutionalize participation and contestation in many different ways. The core difference in the design of democratic political institutions is whether they concentrate power in the hands of the central government and in the hands of a single majority party that controls the central government, or disperse power to subnational governments and to different minority groups in proportion to their size. There are four main ways in which democratic constitutions concentrate and/or disperse political power.

First, some constitutions—such as those of France or Japan—are **unitary systems**, which means that the central government has veto power over the decisions of subnational (regional or municipal) governments. Yet other countries' constitutions, such as those of Germany, India, Mexico, and Nigeria, are **federal systems**. In federal systems, the constitution grants two or more governments—for example, a state or provincial government as well as the national government—overlapping authority over the same group of people or the same piece of territory. Federal constitutions tend to disperse political power away from the central government, while unitary constitutions tend to concentrate political power in the hands of the national government of the day.

Second, the balance of power between the executive and legislative branches of government varies with different democratic constitutions (see Table 1.3). The legislature is typically the body charged with making laws, while the executive is responsible for implementing the laws. **Presidential systems** fragment political power by having voters directly elect a legislature as well as an executive, the president. Examples of presidential systems include Mexico and—when it is operating as a democracy—Nigeria.

In contrast to presidential systems, in which citizens directly elect both the executive and the legislative branches of government, **parliamentary systems** tend to concentrate political power because voters only elect a legislature. Under this system, the legislature (parliament) itself elects the executive to head the government—a **prime minister**—from among its members. The UK, Germany, and India are examples of parliamentary systems.

unitary system ■ a state in which the constitution grants the central government exclusive, final authority over policy-making across the entire national territory.

federal system ■ a state in which the constitution grants two or more governments overlapping political authority over the same group of people and same piece of territory.

presidential system ■ a democratic constitutional design in which voters directly elect a legislature as well as an executive.

parliamentary system ■ a democratic constitutional design in which voters only elect a legislature, and in which the legislature (parliament) itself elects the executive to head the government.

prime minister ■ the chief executive in a parliamentary system, elected by the members of parliament.

TABLE 1.3

Democratic Constitutional Formats

Type of Government	Direct Election of Both Branches	Concentration of Power in Theory
Presidentialism	Yes	Low
Semi-Presidentialism	Yes	Medium
Parliamentarism	No	High

semi-presidential system ■ a democratic constitutional design in which the president and prime minister share executive authority.

judicial review ■ the ability of a country's high court to invalidate laws that the legislature has enacted by declaring them unconstitutional.

parliamentary supremacy ■ a democratic system in which the legislature holds supreme political authority—no court can overrule legislation that it passes.

electoral system ■ the political institutions that translate citizens' votes into legislative seats and/or control of a directly elected executive.

plurality rule ■ an electoral system in which the candidate who receives the largest share of the votes in the electoral district wins the seat, even if that share is less than a majority of 50 percent +1 of the votes.

majority rule ■ an electoral system which requires candidates to win an actual majority of 50 percent +1 of the votes in an electoral district to win.

Finally, in semi-presidential systems, voters elect both a president and a legislature, but the legislature then also elects a prime minister, who is accountable both to the parliamentary majority as well as to the president. In such systems, the president and prime minister must share executive authority. France and Russia (if it were to become democratic) are examples of semi-presidential systems. As the name implies, semi-presidential systems combine attributes of both parliamentary and presidential systems. The formal distribution of power in such systems can vary a great deal, but semi-presidential systems tend to concentrate power in the hands of the president.

Third, democratic constitutions can also vary in terms of the role of the judiciary—the branch of government that administers justice and decides whether laws the legislature passes conform to the country's constitution. Most democracies today give the judiciary the power of judicial review, the power to invalidate bills the legislature has passed and the executive has signed into law. For example, the constitution of Germany establishes a separate Federal Constitutional Court that can declare legislative acts unconstitutional. This system tends to impose a brake on the power of the parliamentary majority of the day. In contrast, countries that lack judicial review embody the principle of parliamentary supremacy. As the name implies, in countries such as the UK that lack judicial review, the parliamentary majority of the day holds supreme political authority. If a country does not have judicial review, the political system tends to concentrate political power with the legislature.

Finally, the design of the electoral system can shape the relative concentration or dispersion of political power. Electoral systems translate citizens' votes into legislative seats and/or control of a directly elected executive. Electoral systems tend to either (1) give one party control or (2) promote proportional representation in the legislature, giving ethnic, religious, or other political minorities some power. Electoral systems that give one party control tend to emphasize the benefits of effective government, and promote easy voter identification with the group of leaders responsible for governing the country.

Two electoral systems tend to give one party control: plurality rule and majority rule. Under plurality rule, the candidate who receives the largest share of the votes in the electoral district wins the seat, even if that share is less than a majority of 50 percent +1 of the votes. This system is used for elections to the U.S. House of Representatives—and it is also used in the UK and India. In contrast to plurality rule, majority rule requires that candidates obtain an actual majority of 50 percent +1 of the votes in an electoral district to win. Sometimes—in a three-way race, for example—no candidate obtains 50 percent +1 of the votes. When this occurs, countries that use majority rule then have a second round of elections that pit the top two vote-getters from the first round against each other. This necessarily results in a majority winner.

Majority rule and plurality rule both employ what are called single-member districts (SMDs), in which voters cast a ballot for a single representative from their electoral constituency. In systems where only one candidate can win in each district, the person with the most votes eventually gets the seat. This means that citizens who cast votes for losing candidates ultimately get no representation at all—a highly disproportional result. For this reason, SMD systems tend to discriminate against small parties—as is the case in both the UK and France, in which elections tend to be dominated by two large parties. Plurality rule or majority rule systems,

TABLE 1.4
Power in Government Institutions

Tendency to Concentrate Power	Tendency to Disperse Power
Unitary systems	Federal systems
Parliamentary systems	Presidential systems
No judicial review	Judicial review
Plurality or majority rule	PR or mixed electoral rule

which both use SMDs, only allow small parties to flourish when they concentrate their support in just a few constituencies—as is the case in Nigeria and India, where small ethnic and religious parties frequently gain most of their support in a relatively small number of electoral districts.

In contrast, electoral systems that give groups proportional representation tend to emphasize limiting a single party's authority, and value representation of diversity as much or more as accountability. Proportional representation (PR) gives parties seats in proportion to the number of votes each receives. Unlike SMD systems, PR systems use multi-member districts (MMDs), in which more than one person is elected within each electoral constituency. In some countries, such as Israel, the entire country is a single electoral district—in this case, electing all 120 members of Israel's parliament. Because multiple candidates are elected in each constituency, PR systems tend to favor smaller parties, and allow a greater number of parties to win some degree of representation in the legislature. Of the cases in this book, only Russia uses a PR system—but because its elections are not entirely free and fair, one party tends to dominate.

About a third of the world's democracies use systems that promote majoritarian outcomes (plurality or majority rule), and a third use systems that promote proportional outcomes. The remainder use what are called mixed electoral systems, which combine elements of both SMD and PR rules, typically by giving voters two ballots—one for a representative from a single-member district, and one for a list of candidates elected in a multi-member PR district. Japan, Germany, and Mexico use mixed electoral systems, which tend to generate outcomes in between SMD and PR systems, in terms of balancing out the desire for a clear majority with some degree of minority representation.

The design of democratic institutions always implies a tradeoff: concentrating power might enhance government effectiveness and accountability, but it tends to eliminate checks and balances. In contrast, dispersing power might reduce government effectiveness, but it offers greater checks on majority rule and guarantees of minority rights. Table 1.4 highlights the key differences across the world's democracies.

Non-Democratic Regimes

Unlike democracies, all non-democratic regimes limit citizens' rights to participate, thwart contestation for power, and concentrate power in the hands of government

proportional representation ■ an electoral system that gives legislative seats to parties in proportion to the votes they receive in each district.

mixed electoral system ■ an electoral system that combines a plurality or majority electoral rule to elect some members of the national legislature, while a proportional representation electoral rule is used to elect the remainder.

CHAPTER 1 Introduction

electorate ■ citizens eligible to participate in electing government leaders.

selectorate ■ small subset of the national population that chooses and removes the leader or leaders.

totalitarian regime ■ a non-democratic regime that attempts to shape the interests and identities of its citizens through the use of ideological mobilization, coercion, and limiting pluralism.

authoritarian regime ■ a non-democratic regime that focuses on controlling political pluralism through coercion.

fascism ■ a totalitarian ideology based in racist principles that glorified militarism, violence, nationalism, and the state over individuals; and that emphasized charismatic individual leaders.

communism ■ a political doctrine which holds that the wealthy exploit the poor under capitalist economic systems; that wealth should be redistributed; and that a single political party should control the state.

monarchy ■ a non-democratic system in which rulers assume power via birthright and are not removed until they die.

authorities. Today, about one in four countries in the world today are non-democratic. These include China, Iran, and Russia. In a non-democracy, the electorate has no or a very limited role in choosing national leaders. Instead, a selectorate of some small subset of the national population exists that dominates the choice of selection and removal of the leader or leaders.

Two key features distinguish types of non-democratic regimes from each other: (1) the nature of the relationship between the state and society; and (2) the institutions of leadership selection. First, non-democratic regimes can be categorized as either totalitarian or authoritarian, based on the way rulers establish authority over citizens and society. In a totalitarian regime, the government attempts to shape the interests and identities of its citizens by articulating a coherent ideology, employing extensive efforts to coercively mobilize support for the regime, and imposing tight restrictions on both social and political pluralism. In contrast, in an authoritarian regime, rulers concentrate on using coercion to limit political pluralism in order to remain in power, but they tend to permit some social pluralism. Moreover, authoritarian regimes do not make extensive use of ideology or coercive mobilization.

Few totalitarian regimes exist in today's world; the best contemporary example is North Korea. However, historical examples include Nazi Germany (1933–1945) and Soviet Russia (1917–1991). Totalitarian ideologies can vary dramatically. Hitler's Nazi regime in Germany drew upon fascism, which is based on racist principles that glorify militarism, violence, nationalism, and the state over individual interests and identities—and is typically led by a charismatic political leader. In contrast, Russia's Soviet regime was based originally on communist economic principles, which hold that under capitalist economic systems, the wealthy exploit the workers and the poor. Communists believe that efforts should be made to redistribute economic wealth as much as possible, and that a single political party should direct the government and control the state. Some non-democratic regimes today—such as contemporary China—started out as totalitarian communist regimes, but have cast aside most of the ideological justification for their rule and evolved into authoritarian systems.

Non-democratic regimes can also be compared and contrasted based on the selectorate's relationship to the ruler or rulers. The key issues are the size of the selectorate; criteria for admission to the selectorate; rules for the selectorate's selection of leaders; and whether the relationship between the selectorate and the leader(s) is based on formal rules and procedures including lines of succession, party rules, and military chain of command, or whether this relationship is based on informal personal connections or networks including friends and family members.

Based on these four characteristics, we can distinguish six types of non-democratic systems (see Table 1.5): monarchy, single-party regimes, military regimes, oligarchy, theocracy, and personalistic regimes. Monarchies are non-democratic systems in which rulers assume power via birthright and are removed from power when they die. Russia and China were monarchies until the early twentieth century, as was Iran until 1979. Very few such systems exist in the world today; examples include Brunei and Saudi Arabia. (Some non-democratic monarchies have undergone regime change and evolved into democratic constitutional monarchies. In such systems, a king, queen, or emperor serves as head of state—the symbolic embodiment of the culture and values of a state's citizens and history. However, the monarch is not the head of government—the chief officer of the executive branch of government—and has little political authority. Instead, elected politicians rule the government and make all day-to-day decisions. The UK and Japan are examples of contemporary constitutional monarchies.)

In an oligarchy, which means "rule by the few," the selectorate consists of a small social, economic, or political elite, which selects a leader to represent its interests. Criteria for membership are often informal, as are the group's rules for selecting the leader. No oligarchies exist in a formal sense in today's world, although several non-democratic systems can be informally classified as oligarchies, such as Russia.

Single-party regimes are political systems in which one political party dominates all government institutions and restricts political competition to maintain

constitutional monarchy ■ a system in which a monarch serves as head of state, symbolically embodying the culture and values of a state's citizens and history, yet operates under the constraints imposed by a written constitution.

head of state ■ the symbolic embodiment of the culture and values of a state's citizens and history, typically a monarch or appointed honorary president.

oligarchy ■ a non-democratic system of "rule by the few." The selectorate consists of a small social, economic, or political elite.

single-party regime ■ a non-democratic system in which one political party dominates all government institutions.

TABLE 1.5

Characteristics of the Selectorate in Non-Democratic Regimes

Type of Non-Democracy	Size	Membership Criteria	Rules for Leadership Selection	Relationship between Leader and Selectorate	Examples as of 2011
Monarchy	Ruler's family	Family relationship	Family descent	Institutionalized limited reciprocal accountability	Saudi Arabia
Single-Party Regime	Variable	Party membership; rise through ranks	Determined by party rules	Institutionalized reciprocal accountability	China, Mexico until 2000
Military Regime	Typically limited to high officer corps	Military member; rise through ranks	Determined by military high command	Institutionalized reciprocal accountability	Myanmar
Oligarchy	Small	Informal	Unclear and informal	Informal reciprocal accountability	1990s Russia
Theocracy	Variable	Member of a religious order; rise through the ranks	Variable	Variable	Iran
Personalistic Regime	Limited to ruler's cronies	Leader handpicks	Unclear and informal	Reciprocal accountability, but unclear & unstable	Libya under Muammar Qaddafi (until 2011)

itself in power. China is a prominent contemporary example of a single-party regime: by the country's constitution, the Communist Party is the only party allowed to run candidates and hold power.

In **military regimes**, the selectorate is limited to a small group of the highest-ranking officers, who select and remove the leader or **junta** (pronounced HUN-ta, meaning a group) of leaders. Selection of the national leader is typically a function of military protocol, meaning that the relationship between the leader and the selectorate is highly institutionalized. Although military regimes have been quite common historically—including in Nigeria, until 1998—relatively few exist today. A recent example is Myanmar, in Southeast Asia.

Theocracies are non-democratic regimes in which leaders who claim divine guidance hold the authority to rule. Such leaders acquire their positions by rising through a religious clerical hierarchy. Thus, in a theocracy, the selectorate consists of high religious authorities. In today's world, religious authorities exert considerable power in several Islamic states—for example, Saudi Arabia. However, religious authorities do not *rule* in those states. Instead, monarchs or other secular authorities do. Only the Vatican City (where the pope rules) is a true theocracy, while Iran—where religious authorities hold the top positions—comes close.

Finally, in a **personalistic regime** politics revolves around the glorification and empowerment of a single individual. Most non-democratic regimes have elements of personalistic rule, but what distinguishes a truly personalistic regime from other kinds of non-democratic regimes is a lack of institutionalization—that is, the absence of clear rules governing politics and, in particular, governing the transfer of political power. In a personalistic regime, rulers arbitrarily intervene in individuals' lives, and their whims decide government policy. Sometimes personalistic leaders are popular, but more often they rule through cunning, guile, and a willingness to use violence. Belarus is a contemporary example of a personalistic regime.

Regime Change

As of 1974, only 26 percent of the world's states were democratic regimes. However, by 1995, 48 percent were.[4] This important dynamic turns our attention to the question of **regime change**—transitions between democratic and non-democratic forms of government. Why are some countries democratic, while others remain non-democratic? For some countries, such as the UK and France, the process of democratization was gradual and took place literally over centuries. Historical factors related to culture and economic development are most important in these examples. In contrast, India, Mexico, and Japan democratized very rapidly, meaning that long-term background factors are less important. In more recent cases of regime change, what seems critical to shaping the number of democracies and non-democracies in the world are global factors such as the foreign policy interests of major global powers, as well as **neighborhood effects**, which are the positive effects on the probability of a regime change to democracy of having geographic neighbors that are democracies. In the contemporary world, one of the most pressing questions is whether democracy can survive in countries, like Mexico, that have limited experience with free and fair elections and that confront serious challenges to state authority; and whether democracy can emerge in cases such as China and Iran, which have no experience with democracy at all.

Institutions shape the distribution of power. This section began with the most fundamental institutional distinction across countries, between democracy and non-democracy. Within democracy, the key issue is the degree to which institutions either concentrate or disperse political power, through federalism or unitarism, the nature of the separation of powers, whether there is judicial review of legislation or not, and the electoral system. In non-democracies, where the electorate has no role in holding governments accountable, the core issue is, therefore, the nature of the selectorate and its role in choosing and removing government leaders. The section concluded by exploring one of the key questions facing students of comparative politics, the sources of regime change between democracy and non-democracy. In recent decades a number of non-democracies—such as Mexico before the year 2000—have transitioned to democracy. However, some countries—such as Russia and Nigeria, for example—have oscillated between one regime and the other, while others—such as Iran and China—remain firmly non-democratic. In the next section, we begin to consider the sources of pressure for and against limits on government power, noting the ways that identities can influence politics.

IDENTITIES

After providing background information and a description of the country's main political institutions, each chapter then turns to the main ways in which political identities are mobilized into politics. We all have political identities—the ways that we categorize others and ourselves as members of different groups, and how we subjectively understand the power relationships of domination and oppression that exist between groups. Identity becomes politicized when large numbers of people mobilize to advance political interests they believe derive from attachment to a particular group. Most of the time, different identity groups live together peacefully—even in countries marked by considerable diversity. Ethnic or religious conflict, for example, is not a simple function of a diverse population within a country's borders. Yet, when instigated, such conflicts can be particularly divisive and explosive.

1.3 Why are political identities important?

Explore the Comparative "Civil Societies" at mypoliscilab.com

Economic and Cultural Forms of Identity

There are two general ways to think about political identity: economic and cultural. The first originates with the ideas of Karl Marx and suggests that **class-consciousness**, self-awareness of the particular economic and political interests that derive from one's economic position in society—for example, as a farm laborer, an industrial worker, or a financier—is the primary way in which people think about individual and collective political identity. Marx believed that workers' collective identity as an economic class would facilitate their ability to form unions and advance their interests—for better wages and working conditions, for example—against the interests of wealthier members of society.

class-consciousness
■ an individuals' self-awareness of the political implications of belonging to a particular economic class.

cultural identity ■ attachments based on non-economic associations, based on a understanding of common heritage.

ethnicity ■ a group of people who share an understanding of a common heritage based on religion, language, territory, or family ties.

But economic class offers an incomplete answer to understanding political identity. Around the world, many relatively poor people vote for conservative parties, and many wealthier people vote for left-leaning parties. And in many poorer countries, economic status explains relatively little compared to other forms of political identity. This brings us to the second main form of political identity, cultural identity rooted in the ideas of German sociologist Max Weber, who suggested that the strongest political identities form along non-economic lines, among groups of people who share an understanding of a common heritage based on different forms of culture—particularly racial or ethnic ties, religion, language, territory, or family ties.

Weber understood that non-economic forms of identity can serve as powerful engines of political mobilization. For example, individuals in an ethnic group may share communal attitudes, values, and knowledge, and they may recognize and understand the political significance of cultural symbols. Such symbols include flags; forms of music; food, or art; particular phrases or terms; a mode of dress or of wearing one's hair or beard; religious icons; local, regional, or national festivals; or the deliberate use of a regional accent. Any of these characteristics might mark individuals as members of a particular ethnic or national group. Weber's argument suggests that political mobilization along non-economic lines tends to be easier than mobilization of economic classes, because non-economic groups share both cultural orientations and lived experiences such as religious observance or family and community history, practices, and traditions. Table 1.6 summarizes the core differences between Marx and Weber in terms of political identities.

Political-Identity Cleavages

A central concept for understanding differences in the nature of competition and conflict based on identity groups across different societies is that of a political cleavage—a deep and lasting source of political conflict based on identity which pits one group against another or several others. In some societies, an economic class cleavage emerges, pitting the relatively poor against the relatively well-off. For example, the chapter on the UK highlights how, historically, a strong economic class cleavage has divided British society. The Industrial Revolution emerged in

political cleavage ■ a salient dimension of political conflict and competition within a given society, such as religion, ethnicity, or ideology.

▸ TABLE 1.6

Political Interests and Identity: Marx versus Weber

	What defines interests and identity?	What drives mobilization?
Marx	Political identity and interests are a function of economic status.	Mobilization will occur along *economic class* lines, for example rich versus poor.
Weber	Political identity and interests are a function of non-economic group differences.	Mobilization will occur along *non-economic* status group lines, for example, one ethnic group versus another.

the UK early on, driving the formation of a strong working class, which mobilized to fight for voting rights and economic welfare through the Labour Party.

Yet those same societies could also see the emergence of political cleavages based on non-economic forms of identity—for example, pitting ethnic groups against one another or adherents of one religion against adherents of another. And in fact, the class-cleavage in the UK is weakened by the fact that people in Scotland, Northern Ireland, and Wales are citizens of the UK, but view themselves as culturally distinct from the dominant English. As a result, relatively small regional parties have emerged in those territories, competing with both Labour and its archrival, the Conservative Party, for votes.

Most countries are divided by several political cleavages, which helps us understand why political identity based on economic interests only weakly explains the main forms of political conflict around the world. For example, the chapter on India seeks to explain why, given the country's deep and widespread poverty, democracy has survived despite the existence of intense rivalries between literally dozens of religious and ethnic groups. Each chapter in this casebook describes the main identity cleavages that have gained expression in politics, such as ethnicity, nationalism, religion, class. However, we have emphasized that this book is not merely engaged in description. We also seek to explain why certain forms of identity are politicized in one country—but not in another similar country, and why similar forms of identity might be politicized in two very different countries.

The Sources of Political Identity

There are two main approaches to understanding the politicization of identity: primordialism, which assumes political identities are innate and largely unchanging, and constructivism, which assumes that individuals have some choice over their political identities, but that such choice is constrained by the social context.

Primordialism emphasizes kinship bonds—a connection to others formed by blood, marriage, or other family relations—as the fundamental building blocks of collective political identity. The glue that cements kinship bonds need not literally be based in biology. Kinship bonds can also be metaphorical, based in cultural and historical connections to an imaginary "extended family." Primordialism suggests that identity becomes politicized as a result of deep emotional and/or psychological attachments individuals feel toward members of a broader community. It also suggests that collective mobilization occurs when groups perceive a threat to the continued practice of their collective identity. They react just as they would if their family were threatened.

This approach seems intuitive—but the fact is that it remains unsatisfactory. Contrary to the notion that identity is ancient and timeless, many forms of identity are, in fact, not that old. For example, the idea of nationalism only emerged about two centuries ago; many supposedly ancient groups such as "French people" or "German people" have only come to think of themselves as nations in the relatively recent past. To the extent that *any* form of identity emerged only relatively recently, primordialism offers no help in answering this chapter's main question, because it cannot explain what caused that form of identity to emerge in the first place.

primordialism ■ assumes that identity is something people are born with or that emerges through deep psychological processes in early childhood.

constructivism ■ assumes that political identities are malleable, even if they often appear to be primordial, and suggests that we think of identity as an evolving political process rather than as a fixed set of identity categories.

gender ■ a concept used to distinguish the social and cultural characteristics associated with femininity and masculinity from the biological features associated with sex, such as male or female reproductive organs.

For this reason, the chapters in this volume tend to offer a constructivist approach, which assumes that the forms, meaning, and salience of different sorts of political identities can change over time. To explain why identities are politicized in certain ways and not others, constructivism focuses our attention on the historical evolution of the political context. For example, long-term social, economic, or technological change can politicize identity. Karl Marx correctly noted that industrialization tends to create an urban working class, members of which may come to understand the political implications of their economic status differently from their ancestors who had worked the land. Rapid economic development can also dramatically alter how people perceive the proper roles for men and women inside and outside of the home, thereby changing the nature of gender identities. The spread of religions can also politicize differences about morality and ethics between communities. Oftentimes, slow, long-term change in the social context shapes how individuals conceive of themselves and their community, which in turn influences the politicization of identity as whole.

Both primordialism and constructivism recognize that identity shapes people's political priorities—what they believe is worth defending or advancing in politics. However, the former takes both identity and its political salience as given, while the latter assumes that political identities evolve even if they appear to be primordial and seeks to uncover the historical processes that shape the emergence and politicization of different forms of identity. Each chapter explores the interplay between broad historical processes and leaders' efforts to mold history themselves to understand the politicization of different forms of identity. Explaining the formation and politicization of identity remains a difficult challenge. Yet, given that questions of political identity drive many forms of contention and conflict in the contemporary world, you can understand why it is important to do so. Constructivism points us toward the importance of comparing and contrasting the historical context to explain why identities are politicized in different ways in different countries—that is, how identities combine with political interests to shape citizens' involvement in politics.

INTERESTS

1.4 How are political interests evident in the political process in different countries?

Explore the Comparative "Political Campaigns" at mypoliscilab.com

The final section of each chapter in this book explores the major political interests that are active and organized in each society. This is where each chapter brings together institutions and identities to explain who gets what and how groups compete for advantage in the political arena. The chapters consider both peaceful and violent ways that group interests are mobilized in politics. All countries—even non-democratic societies—see peaceful mobilization of organized political interests. Some countries—such as France or Mexico—experienced extremely violent revolutionary levels of mobilization decades or even centuries ago. Other countries—such as Russia, India, and Nigeria—continue to experience varying levels of inter-group violence.

Each chapter explores the prominent forms collective political action takes—whether sporadic protests or social movements, interest groups, and political parties—the different ways individuals and organizations attempt to mobilize people on the basis of their identities or their interests, or both. The reasons people get involved politically vary widely. Some people hold liberal political interests (an attitude favoring gradual political change), while others are conservative (an attitude that favors preserving things the way they are, or even reversing recent political changes). Sometimes people wish to influence broad issues, while others act on very narrow interests. Individuals can mobilize at the local, national, or even at the transnational level.

Social Movements

Social movements are organized, sustained, and collective efforts that make claims on behalf of members of a group. They challenge the power of government authorities or other groups in society, contest the legitimacy of established ideas or practices, and foment political change. Social movements are often referred to as a "grassroots" form of political mobilization, because they are the main way that ordinary people participate in politics.

Social movements differ from other forms of collective action such as interest groups and political parties in three ways. First, relative to other forms of collective action, social movements attempt to attract followers by making broad, abstract appeals, and are less likely to offer concrete enticements to get people to participate. Relative to interest groups, social movements' appeals seek to resonate with individuals' political identities rather than with narrower and more concrete political interests.

Second, compared to interest groups and political parties, social movements are relatively informal organizations, and tend to have less hierarchical and more fluid structures. This does not mean that social movements are spontaneous, such as riots or protests. Even though they may not be as highly institutionalized as an interest group or political party, social movements can and do often endure, whereas riots and protests are typically ephemeral, even if they occur frequently.

Third, compared to interest groups and political parties, social movements tend to concentrate their activities to the sphere of civil society rather than in the formal institutions of the state. Some social movements even *distance* themselves from the government and engage in "consciousness-raising" or educational activities designed to change the way people think about an issue rather than directly lobbying the government to change a policy.

Why do we see the social movements we do in different societies? To explain patterns of political mobilization, two key factors are the degree to which existing organizations already "cover all the bases" in terms of contentious issues, interests, and identities, and the receptiveness of the state to challenge through mobilization from civil society. If, for example, there are many women's rights groups, it will be more difficult to successfully organize yet another. In addition, the chances of success depend on whether the state allows mobilization or seeks to repress it. A civil rights movement might be easier to form in a democracy, while a pro-democracy movement might face surveillance and police repression in a non-democratic state.

liberal political interests ■ an attitude favoring gradual political change.

conservative political interests ■ an attitude that favors preserving things the way they are, or even reversing recent political changes.

social movement ■ organized, sustained, and collective efforts that make claims on behalf of members of a group.

Interest Groups

Interest groups are organized groups of citizens who seek to ensure that the state enacts or follows particular policies. Although the lines between the one and the other are not always clear, interest groups differ from social movements in that they tend to focus their mobilization efforts on obtaining concrete benefits for their supporters; they also tend to be more formally organized, with a professional rather than activist membership; and they tend to concentrate their energies on influencing the formal sphere of institutional politics, by lobbying legislators and bureaucrats or engaging in lawsuits, rather than focusing on grassroots mobilization in civil society.

Although the line between political parties and interests groups is sometimes unclear; unlike political parties, interest groups tend to focus on a single issue or a narrow set of issues, whereas parties must present and campaign on a platform that covers more political terrain. They also do not present candidates for elections. Finally, because they do not need to win votes as parties do, interest groups do not require as extensive a formal organization or membership base. Instead, they often rely on a relatively narrow base of supporters who provide labor and/or funding. Of course, the more members in an interest group, the more likely that it will gain credibility and attract attention to its cause.

What influences interest group formation? First, unlike social movements, which tend to focus their appeals around questions of identity or abstract political goals, interest groups may form because a group of people shares a common, concrete political interest. Yet perhaps more important is the political context. Just as with social movements, the nature of the state's engagement with society is critical. Interest group mobilization tends to follow one of two patterns. First, under **pluralism**, interest groups mobilize and organize societal interests freely, in a decentralized fashion. A pluralist pattern of interest group formation can only thrive in a democracy, because it requires that the political opportunity structure be wide open. Thus, when we see a pluralist pattern, we know that the state plays relatively little role in fostering or impeding interest group formation.

Most democracies do not have such "free markets" in interest group formation. Instead, they exhibit a pattern of interest group mobilization known as **corporatism**. Corporatism is a pattern of interest group mobilization in which the state plays an active role in organizing and mediating between groups. The idea is that because different groups in society all perform necessary functions, each should have institutionalized channels of representation in the state. In theory, such institutionalized representation levels the political playing field and promotes social peace—in particular, between labor and business interests.

Political Parties

Finally, each chapter will describe the main **political parties** that exist in each country. A political party is a group of people who have organized to attain and hold political power. Note that parties can exist in both democratic and non-democratic settings. Parties differ from interest groups and social movements because even though both of the latter try to *influence* policy, neither tries to *take* political

---

interest groups ■ organized groups of citizens who seek to ensure that the state enacts or follows particular policies.

pluralism ■ in which interest group mobilize and organize societal interests freely, in a decentralized fashion.

corporatism ■ a pattern of interest group mobilization in which the state plays an active role in organizing and mediating between groups.

political party ■ a group of people who have organized to attain and hold political power.

power. In their pursuit of political power, parties recruit and socialize potential leaders, nominate candidates, mobilize the electorate, represent different social groups, aggregate political interests, structure political issues under consideration, and form and sustain governments. Parties can also inject energy into the process of collective mobilization. To the degree that parties succeed at forming a coherent notion of what they stand for, they can also promote a particular form of political identity.

Each chapter will then take care to describe the main basis for political competition between parties—what issues drive elections, and why some parties tend to remain in power while others struggle to win. Political parties emerge and evolve in competition with other parties, in what we call a *party system*—the typical pattern of political competition and cooperation between parties within a state. We are interested in comparing patterns of party competition for two reasons: because they tell us whether a country qualifies as a democracy or not, and because they tell us about government stability and the nature of interest representation in a given country. When comparing party systems, we're interested in the main competitors—the parties that can credibly compete to hold at least a portion of government power. Given this definition, we can identify four types of party systems, as shown in Table 1.7.

One-party systems, like China's, that actually prohibit political contestation are non-democratic. As this book's chapter on Japan highlights, for decades debate existed as to whether Japan should be classified as a democracy or not because one party, the Liberal Democrats (LDP), almost always won. The government did not prohibit contestation, and, in fact, in 2009, another party finally beat the LDP. This means that one-party systems can be democratic even if a single party retains power for considerable time—just so long as contestation is permitted and elections remain free and fair.

Party systems also reflect the tradeoff between limited and effective government: one-party systems embody effective government by concentrating power in a single party. Two-party systems tend to give one party temporary control over

party system ■ the typical pattern of political competition and cooperation between parties within a state.

TABLE 1.7

Patterns of Party-System Competition

Type of Party System	Main Pattern of Competition	Examples
One-party (non-democratic)	Participation without contestation	China
One-party (democratic)	Participation with limited contestation	Japan 1950–2009
Two-party	Participation with contestation largely limited to the two largest parties	UK (until 2010), France
Multi-party	Participation with contestation between more than two parties	Mexico, India, Germany

government, but also check that party's influence because both major parties tend to alternate in power. By contrast, multiparty systems embody limited government, because in such systems a single party rarely controls a majority of legislative seats. As a result, even the largest parties must usually share power with other parties. Under such conditions, **coalition governments**—governments comprised of more than one political party, each of which holds at least one cabinet ministry—often arise. Coalitions disperse power by forcing parties that represent different interests and identities to work together. Because no party holds a majority, multiparty systems can be chaotic and even prone to deadlock. Although most democracies around the world have multiparty systems, highly fragmented party systems may sacrifice effective government in the name of enhancing representativeness.

Political institutions shape the nature of interest representation in the formal realm of politics—and political identity is often the raw material from which individuals and groups construct their political interests. Each chapter in this book explores how political interests and identities are mobilized collectively, through peaceful forms of collective action such as social movements, interest groups, and political parties, or sometimes through violent forms of political mobilization such as protests, riots, civil war, and even revolution, which can overturn the entire political order. The study of institutions, identities, and interests provides the foundation for understanding how politics works in each country, allowing us to make sense of current events—and even to consider potential future political trajectories.

coalition governments governments comprised of more than one political party, each of which holds at least one cabinet ministry.

THE CONTEMPORARY CONTEXT

1.5 What are the key issues confronting comparative politics today?

After describing the historical evolution of the state and the institutions, interests, and identities that interact within the political system, each chapter in this volume explores recent political events and trends, focusing particularly on how the main organized interests and identities cooperate and compete with each other, particularly in terms of whether political competition turns violent or remains peaceful, and questions of political economy.

Political Violence

Political violence is defined as the use of force by states or non-state actors to achieve political goals. Governments frequently perpetrate political violence upon their citizens in order to consolidate power by repressing, imprisoning, or even murdering individuals or entire groups. Headlines are filled with news of insurgent groups that seek to weaken state authority with riots, bombings, or assassinations. Some countries—such as Japan and the UK—see relatively little political violence. Yet, political violence can plague both democratic and non-democratic regimes. For example, Russia has been attempting to repress separatist rebellions in its southern regions for years, and in India and Nigeria, conflict between ethnic and religious groups frequently results in bloodshed.

The chapters on Russia, France, Mexico, and China will also discuss the contemporary relevance of **revolutions**—armed conflict between insurgents and forces of a state in which the insurgents win and impose wholesale political change.

political violence the use of force by states or non-state actors to achieve political goals.

revolutions armed conflict between insurgents and forces of a state in which the insurgents win and impose wholesale political change.

Meanwhile, chapters on Nigeria, Mexico, and India will consider the causes of contemporary violence—whether due to criminal activity or to inter-group conflict based on political identities and interests, which can result in civil war, armed combat within the boundaries of a sovereign state between parties that are subject to common authority at the start of hostilities.

Political Economy

The countries in this volume differ greatly in terms of their wealth and rates of economic growth. A useful indicator of average income is per capita gross domestic product (GDP), the average citizen's yearly income. As Figure 1.3 indicates, on average, citizens in the countries in this volume range from poor to wealthy.

Each chapter considers the main issues of political economy—the study of the relationship between economics and politics—that each country confronts. Political economy concerns day-to-day issues of policymaking and governance, such as the ways in which politicians respond to economic crises; what economic policies governments attempt to implement; and how governments seek to pay for those policies—usually through taxation. Those who study political economy also consider important questions of political philosophy, such as the tension between individual freedom of choice and communal goals such as equality of economic opportunity.

Each chapter addresses two key political economy questions. The first is how governments work to promote economic development—sustained increases in the

civil war ■ armed combat within the boundaries of a sovereign state between parties that are subject to common authority at the start of hostilities.

per capita gross domestic product (GDP) ■ the average citizen's yearly income.

political economy ■ the study of the relationship between economics and politics.

economic development ■ sustained increase in the standard of living of a country's population.

Political violence has marked recent protests around the world. Here, a police officer in Teheran, Iran, sprays tear gas at a protester during riots following a disputed presidential election in June 2009.

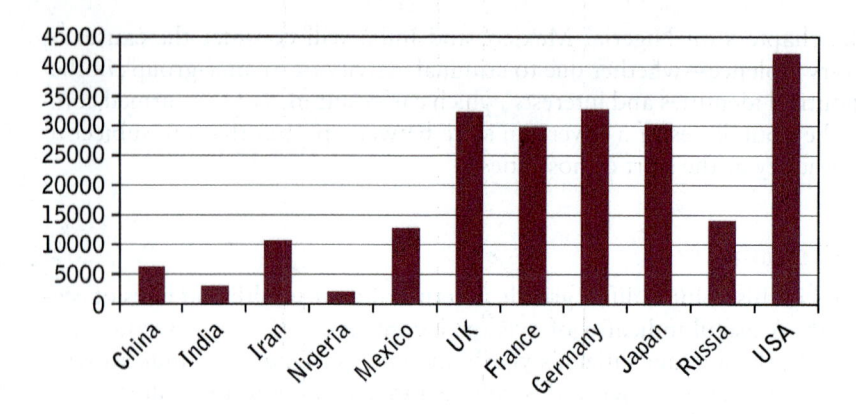

FIGURE 1.3

GDP per capita in 2009 (In Constant 2009 US Dollars)

This figure shows average per capita income in the countries included in this volume, compared against the United States. Note that despite China's fantastic growth in recent years, the average Chinese person remains far poorer than the average Mexican.

Source: The World Bank "World DataBank," http://databank.worldbank.org/, accessed June 17, 2011.

standard of living of a country's population, resulting from changes and improvements in education, infrastructure, and technology. As Table 1.8 shows, India and China, for example, have in recent years experienced fantastic economic growth rates. However, as Figure 1.3 shows, citizens in those two countries remain relatively poor on average compared to the average American or even Mexican. Some countries—such as the UK, France, and Germany—have seen slow growth over the last 20 years, while Japan and Russia's economies have largely stagnated.

Relatively poor countries, of course, seek an answer to the question of how to promote economic development. Scholars and policymakers hotly debate the extent and ways governments should intervene in the economy. The main line of debate pits those who advocate **free market principles**—an economic system in which private individuals and firms (rather than the government) own and have rights to make all decisions about buying and selling property—against an **interventionist state**, in which the central government allocates resources, sets prices, makes investment decisions, and owns most of the country's productive industries and/or resources. Figuring out what "recipe" might best spark economic development for each country inspires students of political economy, because a definitive answer could improve the lives of hundreds of millions of people around the world.

The second key question of political economy focuses on why some governments engage in relatively more or less economic redistribution of wealth than do others. Economic development usually produces some degree of economic inequality—the extent of the wealth gap between rich and poor. Most governments redistribute some wealth among their citizens. When a state intervenes to protect the economic and social interests of both the rich and the poor, it is called a **welfare state**—the term used to describe the role states play in protecting the economic and social well-being of all its citizens through redistributive taxing and spending programs.

---

free-market principles ■ an economic system in which private individuals and firms (rather than the government) own and have rights to make all decisions about buying and selling property.

interventionist state ■ the central government allocates resources, sets prices, makes investment decisions, and owns most of the country's productive industries and/or resources.

welfare state ■ describes the role states play in protecting the economic and social wellbeing of all its citizens through redistributive taxing and spending programs.

TABLE 1.8

Average Yearly GDP Growth Rate (Percent), 1990–2009

Country	Average Yearly GDP Growth Rate (Percent), 1990–2009
China	10.1
India	6.4
Iran	5.0
Nigeria	4.6
Mexico	2.6
UK	2.0
France	1.6
Germany	1.6
Japan	1.2
Russia	0.2
USA	2.6

Source: The World Bank "World DataBank," http://databank.worldbank.org/, accessed June 17, 2011.

Politicians—whether in a democratic or non-democratic regime—have strong incentives to redistribute wealth. Doing so enhances their legitimacy as capable leaders; doing nothing can have the opposite effect. Even politicians who favor minimal government intervention in the economy often find it hard to resist supporting some redistribution and social insurance programs, because that is what their constituents—both rich and poor—usually want.

Still, the extent of redistribution varies a great deal across the countries in this volume. Consider just the wealthy democracies: Table 1.9 shows that government spending on social welfare programs—which include old age, survivors, and disability pensions; publicly provided health care; family support such as child-care subsidies; job training and retraining programs and unemployment compensation; public education; and housing subsidies—varies widely. Countries like France and Germany have generous welfare states, while the United States and Japan redistribute relatively less. Several factors explain why some states spend more than others, including the country's overall level of development and the relative strength of organized labor and big business. A final factor said to influence the extent of welfare state spending is globalization.

Politics is about "who gets what." That is, politics is inevitably about competition over scarce resources. Will one group dominate, or will resources be shared out relatively equally? Each chapter in this volume explores competition between organized identities and interests, exploring the conditions under which political competition remains peaceful or turns violent—resulting in civil war or even revolution, and considers the two key questions of political economy—how governments

TABLE 1.9

Extent of Redistributive Welfare-State Spending, 2007 (Percent of GDP)

Country	Extent of Redistributive Welfare-State Spending, 2007 (Percent of GDP)
UK	20.5
France	28.4
Germany	25.2
Japan	18.7
USA	16.2

Source: Organization for Economic Cooperation and Development, "StatExtracts,". http://stats.oecd.org/Index.aspx?datasetcode=SOCX_AGG, June 17, 2011.

promote economic development and why some governments engage in relatively more or less generous economic redistribution.

CONCLUSION

Why study comparative politics? By the end of this book, you'll have gained an introduction to how politics works in ten key countries. Yet, unlike with other country casebooks, because this book employs a distinct pedagogy consistently throughout, you'll have gained a lot more than that. Although the book is organized around countries, it uses interesting questions to demonstrate how to build comparative politics arguments.

The sections in each chapter are structured like this introduction, exploring the political consequences of early or late state formation, the impact of political institutions on the relationship between citizens and their government, the dynamic interplay between political identities and political mobilization, and the ways organized political interests shape politics.

Yet, the real payoff for using this textbook comes from each chapter's effort to answer a difficult question about contemporary politics in an important country. By framing the empirical material about each country around a question and its answer, you learn how political scientists conduct research. This gives you experience you can use later to develop your own arguments about topics that interest you. The book's approach also provides practical insight into how and why politics elsewhere shapes politics closer to home, and gives you a critical perspective on the society we live in. Focusing on the relationship between countries and questions provides practical knowledge about particular cases, as well as practical insight into the way politics works.

KEY TERMS

comparative politics   3
comparative method   6
collective action problem   12
state   12
sovereignty   12
government   13
society   13
nation   13
early-forming state   14
late-forming state   14
failed state   14
globalization   15
foreign direct investment   16
multinational corporation (MNCs)   16
democracy   17
non-democracy   17
unitary system   19
federal system   19
presidential system   19
parliamentary system   19
prime minister   19
semi-presidential system   20
judicial review   20
parliamentary supremacy   20
electoral system   20
plurality rule   21
majority rule   21
proportional representation   21
mixed electoral system   21
electorate   22
selectorate   22
totalitarian regime   22
authoritarian regime   22
fascism   22
communism   22
monarchy   23
constitutional monarchy   23
head of state   23
oligarchy   23
single-party regime   23
military regime   24
junta   24
theocracy   24
personalistic regime   24
regime change   24
neighborhood effect   24
class-consciousness   25
cultural identity   26
ethnicity   26
race   26
political cleavage   26
primordialism   27
constructivism   27
gender   28
liberal political interests   29
conservative political interests   29
social movement   29
interest groups   30
pluralism   30
corporatism   30
political party   30
party system   31
coalition governments   32
political violence   32
revolutions   32
civil war   33
per capita gross domestic product (GDP)   33
political economy   33
economic development   33
free-market principles   34
interventionist state   34
welfare state   35

REVIEW QUESTIONS

1. What are the advantages of studying country cases in comparative politics?
2. What are the key factors shaping historical patterns of state development, and why do they matter for contemporary politics?
3. What are the principal ways political institutions shape the relationship between governments and citizens?

4. What are the main forms of political identity?
5. What are the main forms of organized political interests?

SUGGESTED READINGS

Fearon, James. "Counterfactuals and Hypothesis Testing in Political Science." *World Politics* 43 (1991): 169–196. Describes an important way to test arguments for which there is little or not direct empirical evidence—counterfactuals, or "thought experiments."

Geddes, Barbara. "How the Cases You Choose Affect the Answers You Get: Selection Bias in Comparative Politics." *Political Analysis* 2 (1990): 131–150. Explains why the challenges of comparative research frequently impede the development of convincing explanations for important events or processes.

Lijphart, Arend. "Comparative Politics and the Comparative Method." *American Political Science Review* 65(3) (1971): 682–693. A classic explanation of how to employ the comparative method.

Munck, Gerardo. "The Past and Present of Comparative Politics." In Gerardo Munck and Richard Snyder, *Passion, Craft and Method in Comparative Politics*. New York: Cambridge University Press, 2007. Details the evolution of the comparative politics subfield.

Wood, Elisabeth Jean. "Field Research." In Carles Boix and Susan Stokes (eds), *The Oxford Handbook of Comparative Politics*. New York: Oxford University Press, 2007, 123–146. A discussion of why it is crucial for comparative political scientists to spend extended periods of time in the paces where they conduct their research.

NOTES

1. These figures are based on data from the "KOF Index of Globalization," available at http://globalization.kof.ethz.ch.
2. See e.g., Xavier Sala-i-Martin, "The World Distribution of Income: Falling Poverty and…Convergence, Period." *Quarterly Journal of Economics* 121(2) (2006): 351–397.
3. The World Bank, "Databank" online resource, available at http://data.worldbank.org.
4. To calculate the number of democracies and number of countries, I used the cutoff of "6" on the POLITY IV scale, which ranges from –10 (least democratic) to 10 (most democratic). See http://www.systemicpeace.org/polity/polity4.htm.

CHAPTER 2

United Kingdom

Ben Ansell and Jane Gingrich

Conservative Prime Minister David Cameron takes questions during the regular Prime Minister's Questions (PMQs) session in the House of Commons. PMQs are often rowdy and adversarial, with the opposition party directly attacking government

> **?** How did limited government emerge in a country without a written constitution?

INTRODUCTION TO THE UNITED KINGDOM

The United Kingdom was perhaps the first modern "nation state," with a unified England emerging in the tenth century AD, although the conquest of Wales, Scotland, and Ireland took place later. The unification of the UK was largely achieved through warfare, conquest, and the consolidation of an absolute monarchy. While the UK is now fully democratic and the British monarch—the king or queen—no longer exercises substantial political power, the British prime minister and his or her Cabinet still make policy with very few checks and balances.

This highly centralized form of rule embodies *effective government*—politicians in the majority can get things done without worrying about obstacles placed in their way. Yet, despite this centralization of power with few checks and balances, the UK is also the home of *limited government*. Principles of political and civil rights and limits on government power familiar to contemporary Americans originated as early as 1215, and were gradually extended in the subsequent centuries.

Despite these important reforms, and in contrast to almost every other democracy on the planet, *the UK has no written constitution*. No single document defines the limits on government power or the rights citizens enjoy, as do the U.S. Constitution and its Bill of Rights. The absence of a written constitution means that the rules of British politics are informal rather than formally defined. Indeed, for centuries, politicians have "followed the rules" even though there are no clear rules to follow! This tension between effective and limited government in the UK raises a question: *How did limited government emerge and survive in a country without a written constitution?*

This chapter answers this question by starting with an historical analysis detailing the emergence of effective yet limited government in Britain. We then turn to the institutions of British government, looking at how Britain's unwritten constitution, the organization of Parliament, and the electoral system allow British governments to rule with few formal constraints. Yet the sheer historical age of British institutions means that parties respect the informal traditions of government. British political identities and the UK's two-party system further this pattern. In contrast to many other countries, Britain's two main parties have incorporated most of the important political divisions in British society, limiting opposition to the government. But the two-party system also means that all governments know that an eager opposition party is waiting to win the next election, forcing leaders to remain responsive to the British public. Finally, the chapter looks at how interest groups promote both effective and limited government. It argues that the incorporation of key interest groups in the political parties has helped strengthen government power, but the existence of social movements and citizen participation outside of government has also created a check on it.

A variety of names exist to describe the United Kingdom, which includes the 'countries within a country' of England, Wales, Scotland, and Northern Ireland.

Read and Listen to **Chapter 2** at **mypolscilab.com**

Study and Review the **Pre-Test & Flashcards** at **mypolscilab.com**

monarch ■ the king or queen of England. Before 1688, had near absolute power to collect taxes, raise armies, and dissolve Parliament. Their powers today are negligible.

We will use 'United Kingdom' or 'UK' to refer to the state and 'British' as the adjective form throughout the text.

HISTORICAL OVERVIEW OF THE UNITED KINGDOM

The history of the United Kingdom is paradoxical. The UK was perhaps the first modern global military and imperial power, and has long had a powerful central government. Yet, it was also the first country to formally grant individual political rights and to develop representative government. Today, the paradox remains of a centralized *effective* government that behaves in a strikingly *limited* fashion. In this section we explore the historical development of the combination of effective and limited government in the United Kingdom.

2.1 How did Britain's balance between effective and limited government develop historically?

Watch the Video "Margaret Thatcher Ousted" at **mypoliscilab.com**

Explore the Comparative "Political Landscapes" at **mypoliscilab.com**

The Establishment of the State

In 1066, Normans from Northern France successfully invaded England. Before this time, Britain had gradually been unified by a series of conquests, invasions, and mergers led by warring Anglo-Saxon and Viking kings. The king of the Normans, William the Conqueror, attempted to further centralize control over English territory. His efforts provoked resistance from local nobles, who sometimes constructed castles with their own money to defend their independence from the king. In response, the king sought to strengthen the central government and expand the power of his military. To do so, he sought to increase taxes. These actions provoked further resistance by the nobles, who ultimately forced King John (1199–1216) to agree in 1215 to limits on his power in the famous **Magna Carta**. The Magna Carta limited the power of the king by granting rights such as *habeus corpus*, which protected ordinary citizens against unlawful imprisonment, and created a Great Council of nobles that the king did not control and that had some power over taxation.

The basic principles found in the Magna Carta evolved over the following centuries. The Great Council eventually evolved into the English Parliament, which had two chambers: the **House of Commons**, with a limited voting franchise, and the **House of Lords**, whose members inherited their seats. Yet at the same time, the Tudor monarchs of the sixteenth century strengthened the central government substantially by bringing Wales and Scotland under central control and developing the state's war-making powers by building England's famed Royal Navy. The Tudors also strengthened the authority of the central government by establishing the Protestant Church of England, which removed the influence of the powerful Catholic pope in Rome over domestic English politics.

The strengthening of the central government under the Tudors and their successors the Stuarts produced a backlash in Parliament. This conflict came to a head under the Stuart king Charles I (1625–1649), who arbitrarily dissolved Parliament and levied additional taxes, producing a conflict that resulted in the bloody Civil War in 1642. Charles lost the war and was beheaded, and Oliver Cromwell—a commoner—declared the end of the monarchy and the creation of the Commonwealth of England, to be run by Parliament.

Magna Carta ■ the original "constitutional" document of British government. Signed in 1215 between King John and the nobility, setting out limits on the monarch and establishing civil rights.

House of Commons ■ the lower chamber of Parliament. Currently comprised of 650 members. Has power to legislate, amend, and pass bills. The party with the most seats in Parliament forms government.

House of Lords ■ the upper chamber of Parliament. Comprised of appointed and hereditary members. Has lost power to veto bills and now can only delay legislation.

UNITED KINGDOM

UNITED KINGDOM IN COMPARISON

	United Kingdom	Germany	France	Japan	India	Mexico	Russia	Nigeria	China	Iran
Freedom House Classification	Democracy	Democracy	Democracy	Democracy	Democracy	Partial democracy	Partial democracy	Partial democracy	Non-democracy	Non-democracy
Land Size (sq km)	243,610	357,022	643,801	377,915	3,287,263	1,964,375	17,098,242	923,768	9,596,961	1,648,195
Land Size Ranking	79	62	42	61	7	15	1	32	4	18
Population (July 2011 Estimate)	62,698,362	81,471,834	65,312,249	126,475,664	1,189,172,906	113,724,226	138,739,892	155,215,573	1,336,718,015	77,891,220
Population Ranking	22	16	21	10	2	11	9	8	1	18
Life Expectancy (Years)	80.05	80.07	81.19	82.25	66.8	76.47	66.29	47.56	74.68	70.1
Life Expectancy Ranking	28	27	13	5	51	72	162	220	95	146
Literacy Rate	99%	99%	99%	99%	61%	86.1%	99.4%	68%	91.6%	77%
GDP Per Capita (2010 Estimate)	US$35,100	US$35,900	US$33,300	US$34,000	US$3,500	US$13,800	US$15,900	US$2,500	US$7,600	US$11,200
GDP Ranking	36	32	39	38	163	85	71	178	126	100

MAGNA CARTA

The Magna Carta was drawn up between King John and English nobles who wanted to constrain the ability of the monarch to tax. This document provided the foundation for the gradual emergence of the balance between effective and limited government in the UK.

The Gradual Emergence of Limited Government

The Civil War marked the end of absolute monarchy and the divine right of kings in the UK. Cromwell's Commonwealth lasted until 1660, when the monarchy regained power. However, the monarchy's power did not survive Charles's son James II, whose Catholic faith threatened the established position of the Anglican Church and offended many prominent figures in British politics. James's Protestant opponents in Parliament invited William, the king of Holland, to invade England to overthrow James II. James abdicated, resolving the crisis peacefully. Parliament followed this "Glorious Revolution" of 1688 by passing a Bill of Rights in 1689. The Bill marked a major step towards limited government in the UK. It ended kings' direct authority over the military, taxation, and the judiciary, and ensured that the monarchy would not interfere in elections. Parliament also passed an Act of Toleration, which granted religious freedom to certain non-Anglican Protestant sects. By 1689, England had managed to keep a monarch while giving Parliament real power, creating a constitutional monarchy.

The UK was still far from a modern democracy at this time. Parliament in the eighteenth century was run by and for the elite few—the landowners and wealthy merchants in the cities. Nonetheless, the early 1700s saw the development of

Bill of Rights ■ drawn up in 1688 following the "Glorious Revolution"—restricted the monarch and granted English citizens right to elect representatives, carry arms, and be free of royal taxation.

Britain's two-party system, although one party, the Whig Party, held the office of prime minister for most of the 1700s. Nonetheless, rivalry between and within the Whigs and the opposition Tory Party meant that Whig prime ministers had to rely on negotiation and providing favors to stay in power. By the 1800s, the Whigs and Tories would commonly alternate control over the government every few years, ensuring that all sections of elite society felt incorporated.

The Act of Union in 1707, which joined the kingdoms of Scotland and England and merged their parliaments, created further political stability. In 1801, union with Ireland followed. While the rise of Parliament contributed to more limited government, the incorporation of Scotland and Ireland led to greater centralization and more effective government. This combination of effective and limited government served to limit political tensions. In contrast to France in 1789, for example, the UK experienced no violent social revolution against the dominance of the wealthy elite.

Foreign turmoil in the late eighteenth century contrasted with this domestic peace. The British Empire began in earnest in the eighteenth century. However, the government faced rebellion in its American colonies after 1776, and became embroiled in 25 years of war with France in the aftermath of the French Revolution: the Napoleonic Wars. The demands of war promoted further centralization of the state, with the introduction of an income tax in 1801 and with efforts to limit political opposition to the wars. Even so, the UK retained many elements of limited government: control of government rotated among the parties and the king remained politically marginalized.

The defeat of France in 1815 left the UK as one of Europe's predominant powers. The global prominence of the UK grew further as a consequence of the Industrial Revolution, which made the country the wealthiest in the world. Beginning with the development of steam engines, a system of factory production emerged producing hitherto unimaginable quantities of manufactured goods like cotton shirts and metal tools. The UK maintained a lead of several decades over its European rivals. The wealth generated by this rapid industrial growth allowed an enormous increase in population—England's population nearly tripled from 6 million in 1750 to 18 million by 1850—and, eventually, in living standards.[1] Throughout this time, industrialists and merchants demanded a laissez-faire policy from government—that is, to be left to their own interests. For the most part, this is exactly what they received: *limited* government.

British economic growth led to a tremendous demand for raw materials and for new markets for British exports. The expansion of the British Empire met both needs. Although the UK had lost its American colonies, it retained valuable colonies in the Caribbean, Canada, and West Africa. The empire's chief expansion, however, occurred in India. India's great supply of precious gems, silks, teas, and cotton provided both luxuries and raw materials to British firms and consumers, and India's enormous population provided a captive market for British exports. The UK effectively maintained control over its vast empire, but British colonial rule also reflected the country's tradition of limited government, by entrusting local control to traditional indigenous rulers. This flexibility enabled Britain to expand its empire more rapidly than its rivals, and to largely avoid large-scale colonial revolts.

In domestic politics, nineteenth-century Britain also reflected a balance between effective and limited government, with a gradual liberalizing trend in British politics. The First **Reform Act** in 1832 expanded the voting franchise in the

Reform Acts ■ a series of acts between 1832 and 1928 that increased the voting franchise of the UK from less than 5 percent of men to all adults over the age of 18.

Conservative Party
■ emerging from the Tory Party in 1834, the Conservative Party has long been associated with supporting the monarch and the Church of England. It generally advocates lower taxes and smaller government.

Liberal Party ■ emerging from the Whig Party in 1859, the Liberal Party represented urban interests and the middle classes. It advocated social reform and the extension of political rights. It is a predecessor to the contemporary Liberal Democrats.

Labour Party ■ founded in 1895, the Labour Party advocated on behalf of the newly enfranchised working classes and the poor. By 1945, it had replaced the Liberals as the main opposition party to the Conservatives. It advocates extensive social policies and a powerful role for government.

decolonization ■ the process of peaceful abandonment of the British Empire, permitting colonies to become independent states. Most immigrants to Britain post–1945 came from these colonies.

House of Commons from about 5 percent to about 15 percent of adult men.[2] The Second Reform Act in 1867 expanded the franchise further to about 35 percent of adult men, and the Third Reform Act of 1884 expanded the franchise to about two-thirds of all men.[3] The 1911 and 1949 Parliament Acts eliminated the House of Lords' power to veto legislation, putting legislative power once and for all in the hands of the people's elected representatives. Universal male suffrage would come in 1918.

Along with these voting reforms, successive parliaments also implemented a series of civil rights reforms, including the legalization of trade unions in 1825, granting Catholics political and civil rights in 1829, providing property rights to women in 1870, and introducing the secret ballot in 1872. These reforms constituted a uniquely British "gradual democratization," with Parliament slowly implementing reforms that limit the state's power. Yet, the reforms also strengthened the government. By removing the power of the unelected House of Lords and by expanding the voting franchise, the House of Commons was able to act without constraints and with the backing of the voting public. Throughout the 1800s, politics in the UK became more and more a function of debates between the parties, instead of being hashed out in backroom deals between a few select members of the political elite. By the mid-nineteenth century, the Tories and Whigs had given way to the Conservative Party and the Liberal Party, out of which emerged the arrangement that continues to this day between the Conservatives and the Labour Party, which grew out of the gradual enfranchisement of the working classes.

Twentieth-Century Developments

The United Kingdom entered the twentieth century as the world's most powerful country. Yet, by the end of World War II, the United States and the Soviet Union would become the world's superpowers. The UK's important role in both world wars provoked the collapse of British power and the abandonment of its empire. Between 1914 and 1918, the UK fought in the World War I. Nearly one million British citizens were killed during the war—around 2 percent of the population. While the UK emerged victorious, the costs of war forced it to sell foreign investments and borrow heavily from the United States, flipping the two countries' roles as creditor and debtor. The UK retained its empire, but within two decades, its important colonies in Australia, Canada, New Zealand, and South Africa were effectively independent.

The Second World War between 1939 and 1945 proved even costlier to the UK financially, though casualties were fewer. The successful but expensive war devastated the British economy and forced Prime Minister Winston Churchill's government to rely on American loans. In the immediate postwar years, the UK relied economically, politically, and militarily on the United States, and both American pressure and changing goals in the British government led it to relinquish control of its empire.

Britain abandoned the empire in haste—a process called decolonization—with the "jewel in the crown" of India, the first to gain independence in 1947. Britain's Southeast Asian and African colonies followed the path to independence in the 1950s and 1960s. In France, the abandonment of empire created a nationalist backlash and the threat of government collapse. In contrast, Britain took these losses in stride. Postwar British politics involved regular changes in the party in power—even the victorious Churchill lost the General Election of 1945—and both political parties followed through on promises to decolonize, preventing recriminations against one party for "losing" the empire. The broad incorporation of most British citizens into politics through the two-party system helped the UK make the transition away from a global empire.

The consensual nature of foreign policy was also reflected in domestic policy, as the UK moved away from limited state intervention in the economy to the effective provision of a wide array of services. Prime Minister Clement Attlee's Labour government (1945–1951) developed the modern British welfare state: the National Health Service, which provided free universal public health care, public housing, expanded public secondary and higher education, and greater spending on pensions and unemployment insurance. The government also nationalized several key industries, including steel, telecommunications, and the railroads. Although the Conservative governments of the 1950s could have stripped away the welfare state, they largely chose to retain it.

This consensus endured through the 1960s. However, the women's rights movements and the growth of a large immigrant population generated social tensions. Trade unions became increasingly powerful in terms of securing their wage demands, and public spending increased rapidly. Following the oil shock in 1973, inflation spun out of control and trade unions engaged in massive strikes, generating a fear that the UK was becoming ungovernable—that it could no longer balance both limited and effective government. Britain's entry into the European Economic Community in 1973 offered further change, integrating Britain into the growing European internal market that would in 1992 become the modern European Union (EU).

The Contemporary United Kingdom

The election of Conservative Prime Minister Margaret Thatcher in 1979 marked the end to the UK's consensus politics. Thatcher saw the UK's economic decline in the postwar era as a symptom of an overbearing state, and she proposed that the government reduce its intervention in the economy in order to promote the interests of private firms and consumers. Her policies to control inflation served to increase unemployment, hurting the working class. She also lowered income tax rates, cut public spending, and sold off many of the industries that previous Labour governments had nationalized, such as British Petroleum, British Steel, British Telecom, and British Airways. Outside of economic policy, Thatcher also took strident steps, responding militarily to Argentina's invasion of the British controlled Falkland Islands.

Thatcher's reforms were controversial, yet she was the longest-serving British leader of the twentieth century. She was successful because many voters agreed that Britain needed "strong medicine" to reestablish the balance between limited and effective government, and because she was able to use the freedom of action granted to her by Britain's parliamentary system, which lacked the checks and balances of the American system of separation of powers, to introduce many controversial reforms that limited government intervention in the economy.

By 1997, the UK public had grown weary of Conservative leadership. The Conservative Party, governed by John Major from 1990–1997, lost the 1997 election to Labour, leading to a new prime minister, Tony Blair. Blair came to office promising a "third way" between Conservative economic policies and those of Labour's more radical past. This move involved a return to more socially aware policies than Thatcher, and yet Blair also moved Labour away from policies favoring government intervention in the economy, abandoned Labour's commitment to nationalizing industry, reduced the influence of labor unions in the party, and promised not to raise taxes. That is, although he could have reversed many of Thatcher's policies, he chose to continue down the path of limiting the power of the British state. For example, he granted political autonomy to the Bank of England—Britain's equivalent of the U.S. Federal Reserve—which limited his government's ability to politically manipulate interest rates in emergency situations. He also passed a Freedom of Information Act, legalized gay civil unions, and limited the number of hereditary members of the House of Lords. To further restrict the power of the central government, he also began the process of **devolution**, granting the regions of Scotland, Wales, and Northern Ireland their own parliaments. Finally, Blair continued to integrate UK into the European Union, although he opted not to join the single European currency.

Controversies over war and national security, though, ultimately defined Blair's premiership. Early in Blair's premiership, he achieved notable successes in foreign policy, including the Good Friday Accord, which ended most conflict between the UK and Irish nationalists in Northern Ireland. The attacks of 9/11 in the United States led to Blair's rise as a high-profile global leader. His support of U.S. president George W. Bush at first gained him international acclaim, but his decision to send British troops in support of the invasion of Iraq eventually became a domestic political burden. In 2005, homegrown Islamic terrorists attacked London's transport networks, killing 56 people. As in the United States, protecting British citizens against future terrorist attacks presented a serious challenge to maintaining limited government in the UK.

Tony Blair was succeeded by his longtime Chancellor of the Exchequer (the British finance minister) Gordon Brown in 2007. Brown's tenure coincided with the global credit crisis of 2008 and the ensuing recession, the worst in Britain since 1945. As the recession wore on, Brown's popularity collapsed and Labour lost power in the General Election of 2010. However, while the Conservative Party under David Cameron won the most seats, it did not have a parliamentary majority and was forced to form a coalition with the smaller Liberal Democrat Party. The challenge facing the coalition government mimics that of British politics more broadly—the coalition faced few limits on its ability to make unprecedented cuts to public spending in the wake of the recession, but its effectiveness in doing so was limited somewhat by the fragility of the coalition. The Cameron government's actions have prompted opposition from the Labour Party, and popular demonstrations, particularly among students who opposed sharp rises in university tuition fees, and among teachers and civil servants who engaged in the first major strikes since the 1980s.

This brief history shows that effective and yet limited government have developed together in Britain. At times, these principles have been in

devolution ■ the process of creating parliaments in Scotland, Wales, and Northern Ireland, with their own elections, and some tax-setting powers. Can legislate in all areas not reserved to the UK Parliament.

> **SUMMARY TABLE**
>
> **Historical Overview: A Gradual Development of Government Power and Democracy**
>
> | | | |
> |---|---|---|
> | 1066–1215 | Norman Conquest | Unification of England under Norman king William the Conqueror |
> | 1215–1641 | Rise of the English monarchy | Signing of Magna Carta limits monarch but monarchy strengthens under Tudors and Stuarts |
> | 1642–1651 | English Civil War | War between King Charles I and Parliamentarians led by Oliver Cromwell |
> | 1651–1660 | Commonwealth | Rule by Cromwell and his son Richard as a republic |
> | 1660–1688 | Restoration | The return of the Stuart monarchy, ended by the Glorious Revolution |
> | 1688–1832 | Constitutional monarchy | Period of growing parliamentary power and limits on the monarch |
> | 1832–1918 | Expansion of suffrage | Gradual emergence of British democracy through series of Reform Acts; limits on House of Lords |
> | 1918–present | Modern democracy | Full enfranchisement of men and women (in 1928); parliamentary sovereignty of House of Commons |

tension, but for the most part, British history demonstrates the peaceful co-evolution of both forces.

INSTITUTIONS OF THE UNITED KINGDOM

In this section, we explore how the mix of institutions in the UK both grants considerable formal autonomy to the government of the day while simultaneously informally constraining politicians' actions. This interplay between enabling and constraining institutions strikes a stable balance, avoiding the perils of weak government, yet securing citizens' rights.

The history of the Poll Tax illustrates this interplay between limited and effective government. In 1987, Prime Minister Margaret Thatcher proposed replacing the system of local property taxes with a fixed charge per person—the so-called Poll Tax. This change would have greatly reduced taxes for people who owned expensive houses, but would have increased taxes on people who owned no property. The Conservatives held a parliamentary majority and, thus, easily passed legislation creating the Poll Tax, which went into effect almost immediately. The relative speed and ease of passing this important reform reflects the freedom that the UK's political institutions provide to the ruling party to act as an *effective* government.

2.2 How do Britain's formal political institutions concentrate power in the central government? Which institutions limit government power?

Watch the Video
"The Problem of Party Discipline"
at mypoliscilab.com

Watch the Video
"Reforming the House of Lords"
at mypoliscilab.com

The Poll Tax, however, was deeply unpopular with the public. In Scotland, Anti-Poll Tax Unions quickly developed, calling for mass nonpayment. This movement spread into England and Wales, and in 1990, some 200,000 citizens demonstrated in central London in the Poll Tax Riots. Members of the Labour Party seized on the Conservatives' unpopular policy with glee. Facing this public and parliamentary pressure, the Conservative party abandoned the Poll Tax by 1993, moving to a more limited local tax. These events demonstrate how a series of factors forced the government to reverse itself, illustrating ways in which government power is limited in the UK. The opposition party encouraged public protest, which was fed by strong popular opposition to the new tax and to abandoning a long-standing property tax dating back 1601. And even within the Conservative Party, the prime minister was unable to maintain the support of the majority of her colleagues, weakening her political position and contributing to her eventual ouster by her own party.[4] All of these factors combined to limit the government's authority.

POLL TAX RIOTS
Protesters challenge the Poll Tax, forcing the government to back off its plans to introduce it. Although the UK's strong government could impose the tax without formal restraints, it was limited by popular discontent and opposition from the regions and other political parties, forcing it to back down.

In this section we explore in greater detail how the UK's political institutions create this combination of effective and limited government. We begin by setting out those institutions that appear to grant the government with wide-ranging powers before turning to the institutional constraints that limit that power.

Institutions Promoting Effective Government

Perhaps the most striking contradiction in the politics of the UK is that although its informal constitution dates back to 1215, this constitution does not look like that of any other state. In contrast to the United States and many European countries, where such rights as freedom of speech, religion, and assembly are written plainly and simply into a bill of rights, such important questions of civil liberties do not have a clear written basis in the British constitution. Instead of a set of formal rules, procedures, and rights written in a single document, the informal constitution of the UK really amounts to a set of ancient documents, legal precedents, and informal traditions. Moreover, even when such rights are written into UK law, they remain formally vulnerable to change or abandonment via a simple majority vote in Parliament. The absence of a formal written constitution suggests that the government is able to act with few legal restrictions—a hallmark of *effective* government. In this section, we examine the institutions that support effective government in the UK: the principle of parliamentary supremacy, prime ministerial government, and the majoritarian electoral system.

informal constitution ■ the collection of statute law, treaties, precedent, custom, and legal interpretations that constitute the UK's equivalent of the formal legal constitution.

Parliamentary Sovereignty

Britain's informal traditions and constitutional law have evolved to focus political authority in Parliament. In the UK, parliamentary sovereignty means that the legislature has supreme decision-making power. In contrast to other ways of organizing democratic institutions, parliamentary sovereignty tends to concentrate political authority in a single institution.

parliamentary sovereignty ■ principle that all power in the UK comes from Parliament. In actuality, this means that the majority party in Parliament can legislate and execute policies at will.

The evolution of British democracy meant that each reform empowering Parliament took away power from the monarchy. Today, the monarch serves more as a symbol of national unity and retains little real power, although formally it is the monarch who calls Parliament to session. In theory, the monarch also has the authority to conduct foreign affairs, appoint judges, and assign honors. In practice, the monarch now defers to the prime minister on these issues, effectively delegating power to the government of the day. Indeed, today, the monarch even pays taxes like other British citizens.

Formally, Parliament—the House of Commons and the House of Lords—has the central policymaking role. The House of Commons is a directly elected legislature, composed of 650 Members of Parliament (MPs) who represent geographic constituencies through the UK. The upper chamber of Parliament, the House of Lords, is an unelected body, consisting of both appointed members (life peers) and hereditary members. Technically, bills may originate in either the Commons or the Lords, but in practice, the Commons dominates the policy process. Both houses must debate, scrutinize, and approve all legislation before it becomes law. In the case of an impasse between the two chambers, the Commons can override the Lords. This leaves the House of Lords with only the power to delay rather than prevent legislation from being enacted.

Members of Parliament (MPs) ■ typically, refers to members of the House of Commons, each elected as the single representative of a geographical constituency through "first past the post" voting.

Parliamentary sovereignty is also reflected in the fact that the UK has a highly centralized unitary system of government. Unlike subnational units in a federal system, local governments and the regional assemblies in Scotland, Northern Ireland, and Wales do not have a formal constitutional role. Indeed, the Thatcher government of the 1980s abolished several local governments through simple legislative acts. Reforms in 1999 devolved power to the British regions. Although these moves have created a "quasi-federal" system in the UK, where the devolved regional parliaments have control over health, education, and judicial policies and some aspects of taxation, the power of these assemblies depends on legislation, not on a constitutional guarantee. The central government has maintained control over internal and external security, and most public spending and taxation. Moreover, the prime minister and Cabinet have full autonomy in negotiating and signing treaties with foreign powers, and engaging in warfare, although membership in international organizations such as the North Atlantic Treaty Organization (NATO) and the European Union (EU) limits this flexibility.

Finally, the traditions of the British constitution do not provide for a strong judicial "check" on parliamentary power. Traditionally, judges in the UK have had little authority to judge the constitutionality of legislation, and until recently the highest court in the UK was drawn from the House of Lords. That is, the high court of the judiciary emerged from within a part of the legislature, and had no formal autonomy as a separate branch of government. In October 2009, the UK introduced a Supreme Court, which acts as the highest court in the land for civil and criminal cases. However, in contrast to the U.S. Supreme Court, this court does not have the right to strike down parliamentary legislation. Thus, although this reform appears to limit parliamentary sovereignty by removing the high court from the legislature, in practice the laws of Parliament remain supreme. Oversight from the European Court of Justice (ECJ) does present a more direct challenge to parliamentary sovereignty, as the ECJ is able to enforce EU law over those of member states. This influence is important, but nonetheless more limited than many constitutional courts, as EU competencies are less comprehensive than many national governments and the UK has opted out of the Charter of Fundamental Rights (which outlines individual rights) in the European Union.

On the one hand, parliamentary sovereignty over other institutions of government in the United Kingdom embodies the notion of limited government, because it empowers representatives of the people to control the government. In the UK, the historical alternative to parliamentary sovereignty was monarchy—the sovereignty of an unelected ruler. Yet parliamentary sovereignty most clearly embodies effective government, because it concentrates power in a single institution and means that there are no formal institutional "checks and balances" on Parliament's power to enact new policies or to change the rules of the political game. This absence of restrictions on parliamentary sovereignty is a hallmark of *effective* government.

Prime Ministerial Government Several informal institutional features serve to concentrate political power *within* the sovereign Parliament, thereby enhancing the capacity for effective government. In practice, parliamentary sovereignty means that the political party that wins a majority of the seats in legislative elections gains temporary yet near-absolute control over government decisions. After an election, the leader of the largest party in the House of Commons becomes the prime minister (PM) for a term of up to five years. That is, in the UK, as in other parliamentary democracies, the chief of the executive branch is not elected directly but is drawn from the members of the legislative branch. This indirect selection of the executive branch stands in stark contrast with the United States, where the executive and legislative branches of government are elected separately.

After becoming chief executive of government, the PM selects a **Cabinet** of ministers, and together the PM and his or her Cabinet form the executive branch. Cabinet ministers head the different bureaucratic departments of government such as Defense, Foreign Affairs, Justice, Health, and the like. The Cabinet meets weekly, and makes policy decisions collectively. The PM can also shuffle the Cabinet by promoting or demoting Cabinet members or changing their portfolios. The PM also has his or her own staff, which works at the PM's official residence at Number 10 Downing Street in downtown London, to assist in managing the government.

Even though they form the executive branch of government, the prime minister and all Cabinet ministers remain sitting legislators—usually from the House of Commons. However, this does not mean that ordinary members of Parliament play key roles in proposing and formulating policy proposals. Instead, the informal evolution of parliamentarism in the UK has led to the emergence of prime ministerial government—a concentration of power not merely within the majority party in Parliament, but within the executive branch that emerges from that majority party. This informal concentration of power within the British Parliament places few checks and balances on the use of government power in the path of the PM and his or her Cabinet, creating an environment for highly effective government.

Prime ministerial government means that most individual members of Parliament play at best secondary roles in the legislative process. The PM and Cabinet ministers set the agenda and largely determine the content of policy proposals, and when they send a bill to the floor for a final vote they expect their party to provide close to unanimous support. Individual MPs are free to vote against any piece of legislation, but, in practice, most members of the governing party follow the leadership of their prime minister.

The prime minister controls key tools that generate such unity. As noted, if the government loses an important vote, elections may follow. In order to avoid frequent elections—and avoid the possibility of being booted from office—individual MPs in the governing party have strong incentives to toe the party line.

Within Parliament, the relationship between party leadership and their **backbenchers** furthers this emphasis on effective government. Both major parties have parliamentary whips, legislators whom the PM appoints to cajole, convince, and twist arms to ensure that MPs from the government party vote with the PM's proposals. Whips use the information they gather on the relative loyalty of each backbencher MP to advise the PM on future promotions to the ministerial or junior ministerial level. Control over such plum political jobs empowers the PM and Cabinet vis-à-vis the backbenchers. These powers give individual MPs additional incentives to follow the government's line. In the end, the governing party is usually guaranteed to pass its proposed legislation.

This system concentrates policymaking power in the hands of a select few elected representatives, and differs from the policymaking process in the United States by substantially curtailing legislators' ability to propose, block, or amend legislation. This holds as well for members of the opposition, who are almost completely

Cabinet ■ the ministers of the government, chosen by the prime minister from Members of Parliament. The Cabinet takes collective responsibility for all decisions of government.

backbenchers ■ the rank and file Members of Parliament who do not have a position in the government or a leadership role in an opposition party. Backbenchers literally sit on the back benches in the House of Commons, with the government and lead opposition members sitting in the front benches.

excluded from the legislative process—but it also holds for most members of the government party.

The secondary status of the House of Lords further weakens Parliament's role as a check on prime ministerial power. Unlike other upper chambers like the U.S. Senate, for example, the House of Lords rarely exerts its legislative authority—and even where it does, the House of Commons can override it. In the nineteenth century, the House of Lords could veto legislation coming from the House of Commons. However, the Parliament Act of 1911 limited the power of the House of Lords to debating and delaying legislation. In all, the concentration of power in the Cabinet and the weak power of the House of Commons and the House of Lords combine to provide the prime minister of the day with tools for highly *effective* government.

One key check on prime ministerial government exists: the requirement that the Cabinet and prime minister maintain parliamentary confidence, which means that the government of the day must always be able to win a majority of votes of all Members of Parliament. For example, if an important bill is defeated in Parliament, the government will call a vote of confidence, explicitly asking Parliament whether it retains confidence in the government. If this vote does not pass, the government must resign and call new elections. On particularly controversial bills, sometimes members of the governing party decide that they prefer to topple the prime minister and risk new elections than support the proposal in front of them. When enough members of the governing party decide to vote against their leader, the government may be forced to resign. Although most votes on the floor of Parliament reflect strong support for the prime minister, six of thirteen British prime ministers between 1945 and 2010 resigned without an election, due to ill health or internal party dissent—the other seven left office because their party lost an election.

vote of confidence
■ a vote held in Parliament to discover whether the government of the day has the confidence of Parliament. If the government fails, it must hold new elections.

Majoritarian Electoral System In addition to parliamentary sovereignty and prime ministerial government, the concentration of power in a single political party further enhances effective government in the UK. Unlike most other European countries, single-party majority governments are the norm in the UK. Coalition government, in which several relatively small parties formally ally to achieve a majority and control Parliament, is rare. Indeed, since 1945, the UK has had just one coalition government, the current Conservative–Liberal Democrat coalition headed by David Cameron.

Single-party majority government is a byproduct of the UK's majoritarian electoral system. The country is divided into 650 electoral constituencies, each of which sends one MP as its representative to Parliament. In order to win the constituency, a candidate only needs to receive a plurality of votes, not an absolute majority. This electoral system is familiar to Americans because it is used in elections to the U.S. House of Representatives.

This electoral system has two consequences. First, the party that wins the most votes often receives a disproportionately large number of the seats. That is, the largest party tends to win a higher percentage of all the seats than of the popular vote. Smaller parties, such as the Liberal Democrats and regional parties such as the Scottish National Party have been greatly disadvantaged by the disproportional way votes are translated into seats. Table 2.1 shows this disjuncture between the popular vote and seats in the UK, which Figure 2.1 also shows visually. Because the electoral system often produces disproportionality in the allocation of seats, allowing a single party to dominate government by manufacturing a majority of seats from a smaller proportion of votes, the electoral system is a key element of *effective* government in the UK.

Second, the electoral system has encouraged a strong two-party system, maintaining the dominance of the Labour and Conservative parties. While the Liberal Democrats have gained strength in recent years, they have had less electoral success

TABLE 2.1

Election Results in the UK 1945–2005

	Labour		Conservatives		Liberal Democrats*		Other	
	Percent of Vote	Percent of Seats	Percent of Vote	Percent of Seats	Percent of Vote	Percent of Seats	Percent of Vote	Percent of Seats
2010	29.0	39.6	36.1	**47.2**	23.0	8.8	11.9	4.3
2005	35.3	**55.0**	32.3	30.0	22.1	9.5	10.3	4.6
2001	40.7	**62.6**	31.7	25.2	18.3	7.84	9.3	4.25
1997	43.2	**63.6**	30.7	25.0	16.8	7.0	9.3	4.4
1992	34.4	41.6	41.9	**51.6**	17.8	3.1	5.4	3.7
1987	30.8	35.2	42.2	**57.8**	22.6	3.8	4.4	3.5
1983	27.6	32.2	42.4	**61.1**	25.4	3.5	4.6	3.2
1979	37.0	42.4	43.9	**53.4**	13.8	1.7	5.3	2.5
1974	39.3	**50.2**	35.7	43.6	18.3	2.0	6.7	4.1
1974	37.2	47.4	37.8	46.8	19.3	2.2	5.8	3.6
1970	43.0	45.7	46.4	**52.4**	7.5	0.95	3.1	0.95
1966	47.9	**57.6**	41.9	40.2	8.5	1.9	1.7	0.3
1964	44.1	**50.3**	43.3	48.3	11.2	1.4	1.4	0.0
1959	43.8	40.9	49.4	**57.9**	5.9	0.95	1.0	0.15
1955	46.4	43.9	49.6	**54.8**	2.7	0.95	1.3	0.3
1951	48.8	47.2	48.0	**51.4**	2.6	1.0	0.7	0.5
1950	46.1	**50.4**	43.3	47.7	9.1	1.4	1.5	0.5
1945	47.7	**61.4**	39.7	32.9	9.0	1.9	3.6	3.8

*For the 1983 and 1987 elections, this column shows the data for the Social Democratic Party–Liberal Alliance, and for the 1979 election the Liberal Party, both precursors to the Liberal Democrats. Bolded numbers indicate the majority party in Parliament.

Source: http://news.bbc.co.uk/2/shared/vote2005/past_elections/html/

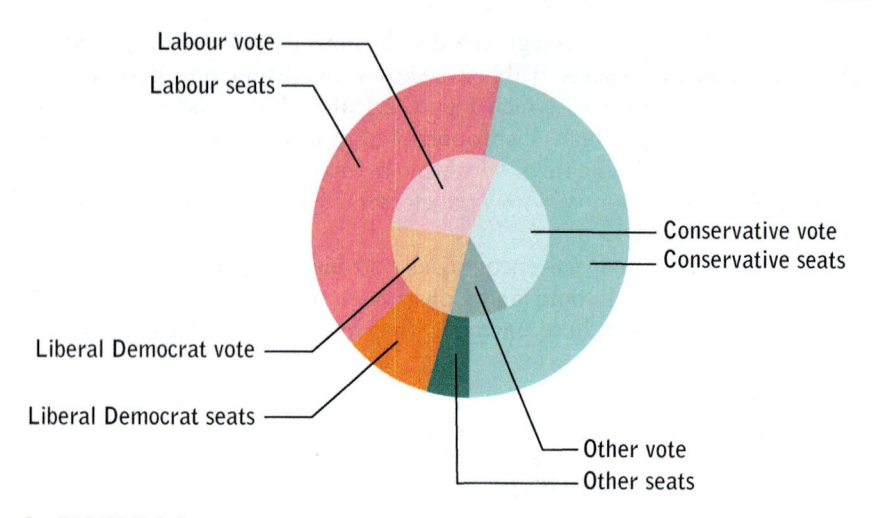

FIGURE 2.1

The Relationship between Votes and Seats in the 2010 General Election

Britain's majoritarian electoral system creates a disconnect between votes cast and the seats in Parliament parties win, which disadvantages smaller parties.

than smaller parties in other European countries that use a proportional electoral system. In the UK, voters are concerned that they will "waste" their vote on uncompetitive candidates, so they tend to favor the two major parties. As Table 2.1 shows, the Labour and Conservative parties consistently alternate control of government. Even the 2010 election, which produced a coalition government between the Conservative Party and the Liberal Democrats, did not break this pattern, as Labour quickly took on the form of a "shadow government," attacking the coalition's proposed spending cuts. For their part, Prime Minister David Cameron's Conservative Party was the senior partner in the coalition, drafting an array of policies that reflected little impact from the Liberal Democrats and staffing the Cabinet with a predominance of Conservative MPs. Although the rise of the Liberal Democrats is increasingly changing Britain's political landscape, historically it has been a two-party system. This two-party system improves *effective* government because—in contrast to other European countries where coalition governments dominate—it typically avoids the need for power-sharing across a coalition of smaller parties.

We have identified three factors that underpin effective government in the UK: parliamentary sovereignty, prime ministerial government, and the majoritarian electoral system. The absence of a written constitution means that the governing party faces few checks and balances: it has strong executive privileges, controls the legislature by virtue of its parliamentary majority, and faces a weak judiciary. Concentration of power means that central government operates without strong subnational actors such as the U.S. states and that the prime minister and the Cabinet take sole responsibility for policy. Finally, the majoritarian electoral system generates cohesive parliamentary majorities and allows the government party to ignore the demands of minority parties.

Factors Supporting Limited Government

The institutions promoting effective government concentrate political power in the UK in the hands of the leader of the majority party in Parliament. Because the UK lacks a written constitution, much of this concentration of power is informal. This returns us to the chapter's main question—why do politicians follow the rules, if there are no clear written rules to follow? How does the UK maintain limited government, despite such a great concentration of power? We now explain this puzzling phenomenon, pointing to institutions that help support limited government: institutional longevity; oppositional politics; the UK's regions; and the impact of membership in the European Union.

Institutional Longevity The sheer historical age of British institutions provides them with a solidity and seriousness that provides a large obstacle to any government wishing to alter them. Many of the traditions in British political life appear anachronistic, such as the enormous white wig sometimes worn by the Speaker of the House—the non-partisan presiding officer of Parliament, who decides who gets to speak during debates. However, behind these traditions lies a fundamental commitment to democracy and a respect for the historic limits of government power. For example, unlike France and other European countries, by the late 1700s some of these checks on government power were already emerging in Britain. While these constitutional limits never became formalized in a single document, they nonetheless served to constrain the expansion of central-government authority in the British state. Politicians are loath to violate this long tradition of limited government, even given the opportunities provided to them by the informality of existing institutions. The UK's slow evolution has nurtured these norms of political restraint.

Oppositionalism Although prime ministerial government and majority rule tend to concentrate power within Parliament, the opposition does have a key tool to hold the government's feet to the fire: the process of parliamentary debate. The House of Commons is a "debating" legislature, in contrast to the "working legislatures" in the United States and Germany. As such, Parliament provides a public forum for both the government and for opposition to express their policies and views. This debate limits the government's power in two ways. First, debate forces the government to publicly defend its positions against the opposition's most difficult inquiries. For example, by tradition, each week the prime minister must address the House of Commons for **Prime Minister's Questions (PMQs)**, during which time the PM answers questions from other MPs on any issue. PMQs are largely a spectacle, rather than a genuine place for information gathering. Nonetheless, they provide the media and the public with a weekly window into the legislative process.

Second, the adversarial dynamic of public debate concentrates accountability for policy with the government and gives the voters a clear alternative to the government. British parliamentary politics has long been oppositional. Since the early eighteenth century, Parliament has almost always been divided into two parties of similar size and power. This feature has meant that whenever one party is in

Prime Minister's Questions ■ a weekly occurrence while Parliament is in session during which prime ministers must face questions on policy from both the opposition and their own party.

government, the other forms a large and coherent opposition ready to criticize the incumbent government and replace it at a moment's notice. Indeed, opposition parties in the UK usually organize a "shadow Cabinet," an alternative government lying in wait. Debate gives the opposition the opportunity to attempt to paint the government as out of touch with public preferences.

In short, the intense competition between the two major parties generates incentives for each party to rein in the temptation to pursue power after winning an election. For most of the twentieth century, the Conservative and Labour parties have been evenly sized, rotating in and out of power. Both parties maintain strong links to their traditional support bases—Labour tends to draw support from the less wealthy, while Conservatives count on votes from wealthier citizens. However, to win an electoral majority, both parties need to compete for the large group of middle-class voters, who tend to be relatively uncommitted to either party. Over time, the need to appeal to these crucial swing voters has pushed both parties to moderate their own political positions. Thus, the Conservatives accepted social programs Labour had created that became quickly popular with voters such as the National Health Service, while Labour has come to accept the move towards less economic regulation that the Conservatives enacted in the 1980s. Frequent alternation in power has furthered this moderate approach to politics. Although each party has different governing priorities, as long as the other party remains lying in wait, neither ever has an incentive to completely reinvent the British state after each election.

Britain's Regions The incumbent party in power also faces limits on its power from governments in the semiautonomous regions of Scotland, Wales, and Northern Ireland. Traditionally, British regions had a weak constitutional role, though Scotland has long had a separate legal and educational system from England's. However, the recent process of devolution of political power to the regions has made them a relatively stronger check on centralized government.

Since 1801 Wales, Scotland, and Ireland (the entire island until Ireland's independence in 1922; only the northern part that remained part of the UK since then) have had constituencies in Parliament. Some regional parties advocate independence from the UK, including the Scottish Nationalist Party and Sinn Féin, a Catholic party that favors unification of Northern Ireland with the rest of Ireland and had links to the Irish Republican Army. Other regional parties—such as Plaid Cymru in Wales and the Ulster Unionists (a Protestant party in Northern Ireland)—advocate for particular regional interests. Due to their small size and the dominance of the two main parties, however, regional parties have rarely held political power nationally, although they have scored success in regional elections.

Political reforms in the late 1990s—referred to as devolution—more substantially limit central governmental power by providing Scotland, Wales, and Northern Ireland with their own regional parliaments and some degree of political autonomy. Regional parliaments now have authority to legislate in all matters outside of foreign affairs, migration, internal security, and national taxation. To date, the regional parliaments have gained limited tax-levying powers, as well as control over natural resources. Devolution in Northern Ireland has been implemented more slowly due to the difficulty of power-sharing between Sinn Féin and the Unionist parties. Yet overall, the process of devolution has served to grant regions a certain degree of autonomy, thereby serving to limit the central government's power.

The European Union Finally, the institutions of the European Union (EU) have limited the power of the British government in a number of areas. Britain was not a founding member of the European Economic Community, the predecessor to the EU, but joined it in 1973. Since this time, the EU's influence over a number of policy areas has expanded substantially. While Britain has opted out of some areas of EU policy, most prominently the euro currency, the EU nonetheless represents a constraining influence. For example, the EU limits Britain's autonomous control over trade policy decisions about tariff and subsidy levels. Moreover, the EU has laws governing economic and, increasingly, civil, political, and social rights across all European countries. With these laws, the EU limits the power of all member-states to legislate in important areas. While this process increasingly provides UK citizens with rights under EU law, particularly economic rights, it also limits government power in the UK.

On the one hand, Britain's informal constitution has allowed for substantial centralization of political power. Parliamentary sovereignty, prime ministerial government, and a majoritarian electoral system appear to enable effective government with few checks and balances. However, several other features of British

SUMMARY TABLE

Institutions of British Government

Executive Branch	Has near total control over the legislative agenda. The power of the prime minister and Cabinet combined with Britain's largely majority governments mean that the executive has few institutional constraints on introducing its preferred legislation.
Parliament	The House of Commons is directly elected by the people, while the House of Lords consists of appointed and hereditary peers. The House of Commons is the more powerful legislative body, but its role in actually legislating is limited by strong executive power.
Judiciary	Historically there was little judicial oversight over the executive and the House of Commons. The Law Lords in the House of Lords—part of the legislature—had final legal authority. The UK now has a Supreme Court but this cannot overturn legislation.
Electoral Institutions	Members of Parliament are elected through a "first past the post" electoral system, which favors larger parties.

politics balance out this concentration of power, limiting government authority: historical tradition, oppositionalism, and the existence of regional governments and the EU. This combination produces a pattern where governments often announce ambitious far-reaching policies, such as the Poll Tax mentioned earlier, but face powerful opposition groups and institutions that, in practice, can foil the aims of even the strongest majority parties.

IDENTITIES IN THE UNITED KINGDOM

2.3 How has a political system built around class identities helped shape effective but limited government?

Watch the Video "Contesting Political Cultures in Britain" at mypoliscilab.com

In the United Kingdom, powerful divides between identity groups have always shaped political life. In this section, we explore how class identity helps answer the question of how the UK balances limited and effective government. Class identity has fueled the creation of the two broad yet coherent political parties, which helps sustain effective government. However, frequent rotation between these same dueling parties has also supported limited government, because rotation ensures that few identity groups are permanently excluded from politics. We begin this section by examining the importance of class identity in British politics and its relationship to the two-party system. We then examine regional, ethnic, and religious identities and show how—except for the case of Irish identity—these are less contentious bases for political mobilization. We conclude by noting that British citizens have recently identified more with non-economic values such as gender equality and environmentalism, potentially weakening the role of class in British politics.

Class Identity

From the Norman Invasion of 1066, membership in the upper class in the British Isles was defined by the ownership of land. The king created the British aristocracy by granting land to favored families, which passed ownership of this land down from generation to generation. The vast majority of citizens never owned any land. Instead, they worked the field as feudal peasants, which meant that they had no right to leave the land and were obligated to provide the aristocratic feudal lord with food and military service. Thus, in the medieval era, Great Britain was already divided into a class system split between the wealthy aristocrats and the poor peasants. The former dominated politics, and the latter could only express themselves politically through occasional, bloody rebellions.

Over the centuries, cities and towns emerged, and prominent urban citizens became rivals to the landed aristocrats. The common people who lived in these towns owed nothing to the feudal lords. Moreover, the political interests of urban dwellers often differed from those in the countryside, because their income was based on trade and industry rather than on agriculture. This difference between urban and rural political interests began to influence political life during the era of King Charles I. Rural areas favored the king, while urban areas favored the king's enemies in Parliament. From this split emerged England's first two political parties, the Whigs and the Tories. The Whigs supported parliamentary liberty, while the Tories were royalists, and drew support from large landowners.

Although these two parties also diverged over religious issues, the split between urban and rural economic interests provided the foundation of Britain's two-party political system.

The Industrial Revolution greatly strengthened this class-based political divide. Beginning in the mid-eighteenth century, the United Kingdom became the world's first industrialized economy, and its manufacturing and financial centers grew massively while land and agriculture became less important in generating wealth or status. By the early nineteenth century, politicians fought over free trade: industrialists and merchants demanded that restrictions on imports be eliminated to lower commodity prices, while landowners argued in favor of trade restrictions that would close the British market to imports, thereby artificially inflating prices. Industrialists also demanded parliamentary reform to enfranchise voters in the rapidly growing cities, many of which lacked even a single seat in Parliament due to the ancient dominance of landholding aristocrats.

This fierce split between industry and agriculture mapped into parliamentary politics, first between the Whigs and Tories, and after mid-nineteenth-century name changes, into the modern Liberal and Conservative parties. The Liberals favored free trade, enfranchisement of the urban middle classes, and minimal government involvement in business and industry. In contrast, the Conservatives favored protection of agriculture from foreign competition, the maintenance of traditional political institutions that favored rural over urban political interests, and deference to the wishes of the monarch and aristocracy regarding the economy.

As time passed, the importance of agriculture and the landed aristocracy declined in both the economy and in politics. Between 1700 and 1870, the proportion of the labor force working on the land declined from 61 percent to 20 percent. During this period the vast majority of the population moved to and began working in industrial cities, beginning the formation of the great English working class.[5] The working class was made up of the poorer urban industrial laborers, who toiled in the factories owned by the wealthy urban commercial elite. As the working class grew in size and the importance of rural areas declined, the nature of class politics in Britain shifted to the cities.

Neither the Liberals nor the Conservatives could effectively represent the interests of the new urban working class. By the late nineteenth century, a new political party would emerge out of workers' efforts to mobilize for higher wages, workers' pensions, workplace safety laws, and the legalization of trade unions. As the twentieth century began, working class voters found a political voice in the Labour Party. By the mid-1920s, the Liberal party had faded, and parliamentary politics was split between Labour and Conservatives. Labour retained the support of the working classes and the Conservatives that of the "middle classes," meaning small businesses, managers, and professionals. (The aristocratic upper class was now too small to retain any political power.) Labour advocated higher taxes and greater state involvement in the economy, to fund unemployment insurance, government-funded public health care, state ownership of major industries, and universal public education. The Conservatives tended to support a more limited role for the government, lower taxes, and private education.

CLASS POLITICS IN THE UK

Two upper-class boys attending Harrow private school stand next to working-class boys from London. Class has long been the key political divide in the UK, enabling the formation of effective class-based parties but also limiting the importance of regional, religious, and ethnic divisions.

Class remains an important element shaping party politics today, although less so than in the past. When it took power in 1979, the Conservative Party moved quickly to reduce the role of government in the economy and to cut taxes on the wealthy. When Labour returned to power in 1997, however, it did not attempt to return to the pre-1979 situation. Instead, Labour retained many of the Conservative Party's policies, leading observers to comment Labour's leaders had brought an end to the UK's tradition of class-conflict politics.[6] Even following the collapse of the British financial system and a major recession in 2008–2010, class politics have not re-emerged strongly. Neither, however, have other forms of political identity—such as those based on religion, region, or ethnicity—replaced class as a key organizing principle of British politics.

Regional, Religious, and Ethnic Identities

In this section, we discuss why class remains more politically salient in the UK than regional, religious, and ethnic forms of identity, and why the case of Irish identity has been so distinct in its political salience. In contrast to the strength of nationalism in many other countries, "British" nationalism is not strong in the contemporary UK, because the UK is comprised of the union of several nations, each of which has a better-defined nationalist identity. Even so, with the notable exception of Ireland, regional identity has been relatively unimportant in modern UK politics. And again in contrast to many other European countries, religion has never been a key mobilizing factor in UK politics. Finally, despite the arrival of millions of non-white immigrants from former British colonies in recent decades, race and ethnicity have also never been important divides in British party politics at the national level, although they are important social issues. Instead, class politics have either overwhelmed or overlapped identity politics.

The Decline and Reemergence of Regional Identity   The United Kingdom took many centuries to unite. Scotland had its own monarch until 1601 and an independent Parliament until 1701. Until 1284, Wales existed only as a set of battling principalities. While England controlled Ireland from the 1200s, its inhabitants retained a fierce sense of national identity and Ireland was not fully integrated into the UK until 1801. Scottish, Welsh, and Irish regional identities were politically important up through the 1700s as different from English identity. Yet, with the exception of the Irish, the subnational identities of England, Scotland, and Wales became politically unimportant in the nineteenth and twentieth centuries.

Two processes explain the decline of subnational identity. First, subnational identity tended to disappear because of the way class and regional identities overlapped. By the late nineteenth century, Scotland and Wales were substantially poorer than southern England, and as a result they became Labour Party strongholds. This incorporation of "regional" identity into the Labour Party's electorate helps explain why no powerful regional parties exist in the UK today, in contrast to the party systems of Belgium, Spain, or India, for example.

Second, the expansion of the British Empire in the nineteenth century also strengthened British nationalism at the expense of regional forms of identity. As the empire expanded in size and wealth, it drew English, Scottish, Welsh, and Irish alike to the colonies, as both administrators and emigrants. The great ports that harbored Britain's navy, which protected trade within the empire, were spread throughout the entire UK: not only English London and Liverpool but also Scottish Glasgow, Irish Belfast, and Welsh Cardiff. Imperialism bound the regions together, giving individuals from across the kingdom the opportunity to share in the growing national wealth and in the unapologetic pride in holding an empire that spanned the globe.

This nationalistic glue that held the UK together began to dissolve in the 1940s as the UK began to disband its empire, and by the 1980s there were renewed demands in Wales, Scotland, and Northern Ireland for greater political decentralization. The 1999 devolution of autonomy to the regions once more placed regional identity on the political agenda. Even so, regional parties have as yet been unable to reshape the two-party system, which continues to dominate national politics. At the regional level, however, regional parties have made important gains.

Church of England
■ the established state church, with the monarch as its head. Created by Henry VIII in a split from the Roman Catholic Church. In contrast to the separation between church and state in the United States, in Britain there is an official Church.

The Decline of Religious Identity Like regional identity, religious identity in the UK was once a powerful political cleavage, but it has long been dormant. The critical political divide emerged when King Henry VIII split the **Church of England** in 1534 from the authority of the Roman Catholic Church. This effectively united church and state in England. However, the Scots and Irish remained Catholic or developed their own Protestant sects separate from the Church of England. Still, the religious unity within England itself eliminated much of the religious conflict that would define politics in France and Germany, for example. As the British party system emerged in the 1800s, support for the king became identified with support for the Church, and opposition to the king was associated with support for greater religious tolerance. Yet, as with regional identities, religious divides took a back seat to class conflict in British politics.

The population of the UK is now highly secular. Church attendance declined throughout the twentieth century, and recent surveys have found that only 17 percent of the population attend a religious services once a week or more.[7] This has meant that religion has little importance in terms of driving the principal political divides in the contemporary UK.

Only in one case—Ireland—have religious and regional identities remained important in British politics into recent years. The southern areas of Ireland remained Catholic after the formation of the Church of England, even though Ireland was eventually incorporated into the UK. By the end of the 1800s, an Irish Home Rule movement had emerged, demanding independence. Debates over home rule divided British politics, with the Liberals arguing in favor and the Conservatives strongly opposed. Irish independence followed the First World War, but Northern Ireland remained part of the UK. The population of Northern Ireland is split between Protestants and Catholics, with a slight majority of the former.[8] The region was for almost the entire twentieth century a site of violent conflict between independence-minded Catholic groups such as the Irish Republican Army, and police and military forces from the UK as well as Protestant pro-union paramilitary organizations. Irish politics retained considerable significance until 1998, when a series of peace agreements were signed that have partially defused the situation. As of 2007, the Northern Ireland Parliament began functioning, establishing regional government, just as in Wales and Scotland. The religious divide between Catholics and Protestants has been an important element in perpetuating the salience of regional identity in Northern Ireland. In the rest of the UK, religion has not played an important role in politics for almost 200 years. This has simplified the party system, further enabling effective government by a single majority party—but also ensuring that a single opposition party always faces the governing party, ready to jump into office if the voters decide to throw the incumbents out of power.

Ethnicity, Immigration, and Politics Ethnic politics have also been less important in the United Kingdom than in other European countries, such as France or Germany. Decolonization in the 1940s and 1950s led to unprecedented levels of immigration from former British colonies in South Asia (India, Pakistan, and Bangladesh), the Caribbean (Jamaica, Barbados, and Trinidad and Tobago), and Africa (Nigeria, Uganda, Kenya, Tanzania). In recent years, many immigrants have also arrived from China and southern and eastern Europe. The percentage of foreign-born citizens in the UK grew from 4 to 9 percent between 1951 and 2001.[9] The reason that immigration has been relatively non-contentious in the UK, at least compared to several of its European neighbors, is because the two-party system has been able to incorporate immigrants and their interests. For the most part, Labour has benefited from immigrants' votes, as immigrants tended to be poorer than average British citizens.

Immigration has caused some political tensions, however, largely because it has changed the country's religious profile: the Muslim population rose from negligible in 1945 to 3 percent of the population by 2001.[10] These changes have sometimes spurred a backlash, prompting the creation of the anti-immigrant United Kingdom Independence Party and the electoral growth of the whites-only British National Party. Anti-immigrant sentiment has forced the two main parties to address the issue, particularly following the terrorist attacks in London committed by British Muslims. Yet despite these heightened tensions, ethnicity has not yet reshaped the party system. The size of the immigrant population remains too small and ethnically diverse for immigrant groups to form their own parties, and explicitly anti-immigrant parties have not won representation in the national Parliament.

Regional, religious, and ethnic divisions have been relatively unimportant in the UK compared to the persistent strength of class politics, largely because Labour was able to attract voters in Wales and Scotland due to the relative poverty of those regions, and because the rise of the British Empire in the nineteenth and early twentieth centuries gave individuals in Britain's regions a stake in the success of the United Kingdom and strengthened British national identity. Recent incorporation of immigrants has not been without difficulty, but has been less painful than in other European countries because the immigrant population is highly diverse and because Labour has successfully included minorities in its support coalition. The only exception to the relatively low salience of region, religion, or ethnicity has been Northern Ireland, where the religious divide between Catholics and Protestant runs deeper even than the class divide.

Gender and Quality-of-Life Issues

In recent years, new political cleavages have emerged in the UK that do not follow traditional class lines. Gender relations, the environment, and other quality-of-life issues have become important in British politics, putting a range of non-economic issues on the political agenda. These issues have led to both expanded state involvement in parts of society but have also called state power into question and demanded more limits on government.

British women have long been involved in political life. The franchise was first extended to women over 30 in 1918, and to all adult women in 1928. However, women had pushed for legal and political rights since the mid-1800s. Women's organizations were advocates of both voting rights and social reforms to improve maternal and child health.[11] By mobilizing to lobby the central government, women gained political rights. However, British women were less successful than their

European counterparts in obtaining social welfare benefits. British government policy eventually provided only meager benefits to widows, new mothers, and single parents, leading to comparatively high levels of female and child poverty.[12]

The emergence of women as members of the voting public had important implications for party politics. As elsewhere, female enfranchisement first produced a "traditional gender gap" in voting, in which women tended to favor the Conservative party while men were more likely to vote for Labour. However, by the 1990s, women's preference for the Conservatives had disappeared. Today, roughly equal numbers of women and men vote for both parties.[13]

The pressure to respond to women's concerns has shattered both parties' traditional "old boy networks." Labour in particular has faced heavy pressure to promote female candidates in recent elections. In 1997, Labour's efforts nearly doubled the number of female MPs in Parliament—from 9.2 percent to 18.2 percent.[14]

At the same time, as both major parties sought to win women's votes, a number of new issues emerged. Many women, particularly, demanded greater state involvement in family and welfare policy. Labour took the lead in advocating expanded social programs that would benefit women and children, such as paid maternity leave and early childhood education. Both efforts contributed to Britain's effective state, funding new policy initiatives and expanding its legislative role in areas of gender equity.

However, the rise of women's issues is part of the broader shift in British politics away from the mobilizing power of economic class identity, and this broader movement has also politicized Britain's effective state. Since the mid-1970s, the Labour and Conservative parties have faced a more volatile electorate and challenges from third parties such as the Liberal Democrats. New social issues that cut across traditional party lines have partly driven this electoral volatility. For example, both parties have had to engage in debate about what policies Britain should adopt vis-à-vis immigration, membership in the European Union, environmental degradation, and civil liberties in the post–9/11 era.

In response to these new concerns, to attract voters both parties have begun to consider new policies—such as devolution to regional governments, constitutional reform limiting unelected bodies such as the House of Lords and giving citizens more rights, further engagement with the EU, and tighter laws for asylum seekers. Many of these issues address the question of whether the British state should become more effective or more limited in its exercise of power. For instance, policymakers have heeded calls for a more active state, creating new legislation on environmental protection, and limits on immigration. At the same time, calls for a more participatory political system, and subsequent constitutional reforms, have limited governing powers in new ways. As the issues British citizens care about change, it is likely the British state will continue to reshape itself along new lines.

Class identity has long dominated status-based identities such as religion, region, and ethnicity in British politics. The UK's two-party system has long reflected a basic divide between those who identify or ally with the working class and its political interests versus those who do not. In contrast, religious, regional, and ethnic identities have never formed the basis for substantial political mobilization with the British party system. This pattern of political competition has meant that

> **SUMMARY TABLE**
>
> **Identities in the United Kingdom**
>
> | | |
> |---|---|
> | Class | The UK has long had a well-defined class structure, with a landed aristocracy, urban middle classes, and by 1900, a large working class. These class splits were crucial to the emergence of first the Tory and Whig parties and later the Conservative, Liberal, and Labour parties. Class has been less crucial in recent years. |
> | Religion | Religion has largely been incorporated in the two-party system, with Conservatives strongly supportive of the Church of England and Liberals and Labour more supportive of religious minorities |
> | Region | Region has also been incorporated into the two-party system, with Scotland and Wales support bases for Labour, and England more Conservative. The status of Ireland, however, proved more difficult to incorporate politically and produced major party splits before Irish independence in 1922. |
> | Ethnicity | Ethnic minority integration into British politics has been fairly smooth compared to other European states, with Labour generally more representative of ethnic minorities. Nonetheless immigration and home-grown terrorism have made ethnicity more political recently. |
> | Gender | Women remained unable to vote until 1918 (1928 fully) but since then have been incorporated into the two-party system. However the British "gender gap" has changed from women voting for the Conservatives to equal voting across parties. Women's issues have become increasingly important as parties compete for their votes. |

the UK has suffered relatively little from grievances based on political identity that have caused bloodshed elsewhere in Europe. The relative unimportance of identity politics in Britain has also allowed effective government to flourish, because the central government does not have to worry about regional interests, and it does not have to work with subnational regional governments on most policies. However, the influence of class-based identity has recently weakened, and issues like gender, the environment, and regional independence have emerged on the agenda. These issues may potentially limit the effectiveness of Britain's central government in new and so far unknown ways.

INTERESTS IN THE UNITED KINGDOM

Despite declining party identification, political parties remain the dominant form of interest expression in the United Kingdom. Political institutions and the salience of class identity have combined to produce an oppositional form of two-party politics, allowing the UK to combine effective with limited government. Within this political system, organized groups do play an important role. Unlike in the United States, organized groups are not as important for electoral politics: they rarely directly advertise to the public and are limited in financing campaigns. However,

2.4 Are interest groups able to limit Britain's effective government?

Explore the Comparative "Political Parties" at mypoliscilab.com

groups do have important links to both the political parties and the bureaucracy and form an important part of the policy process. These links give the government leeway to govern effectively, without fear of chaotic street protests or intense independent lobbying pressures in Parliament blocking change. Yet on the other hand, the influence of outside groups and the existence of a vibrant civil society also tend to limit governmental power.

In this section, we examine the role of organized interests such as business associations and trade unions and key social groups such as the mass media. Doing so reveals that interest groups have focused on building links to the political parties and the bureaucracy. Britain's two-party system has co-opted major economic interests into its oppositional structure. That is, unions and business associations have often identified with one or the other political party. Even the news media is divided along partisan lines. At the same time, interest groups linked to specific issue areas, like health and agriculture, have cultivated close links to bureaucrats and other executive actors creating narrower "policy communities" where the politicians, bureaucrats, and interest groups work together in developing policy. Close cooperation with interest groups by the executive and party actors strengthens their legitimacy, thereby supporting effective government. Nonetheless, because these interest groups reflect different perspectives, including those at odds with the government of the day, they also help sustain limited government.

Business and Labor in the Party System

In many countries, private actors in the economy such as business associations and trade unions are highly influential in the policymaking process. In the United States, for example, industry lobby groups frequently convince politicians to legislate in their interest. Trade unions in the United States, while less powerful than elsewhere, also exert influence in the legislative process on issues from education to trade policy. Organized interests also coordinate campaign contributions to both parties, to ensure that their voices are heard, whichever party is in office. This kind of system of interest groups is called pluralism, a system in which societal interests must organize by and for themselves, and must compete for political influence.

In countries such as Germany, interest groups are organized differently, in a type of system called corporatism. Under corporatist arrangements, both business and labor associations are formally involved in the political process. In contrast to the system in the United States, in corporatist systems the government actively supports the organization of both business and labor—meaning that neither industrial associations nor unions have to compete for influence and both are free from the need to constantly seek new members and private financial support. Instead, both sides are guaranteed a seat at the negotiating table on a host of important economic issues, including employment policies, wage-setting, and decisions about regulation.

When we turn to the UK, we find elements of pluralism and corporatism, but neither model adequately describes it as a whole. Although lobbying and pressure groups have long played a role in British politics, unlike the United States, campaign contributions are a relatively unimportant aspect of party politics. For example, although there is a British equivalent to PhRMA, the American pharmaceutical lobby, it wields less power than in the United States, even though Britain is home several major multinational pharmaceutical companies. Interest groups invest resources and time in lobbying MPs, but given their more restricted legislative role, this lobbying is on smaller scale than in the United States. Equally, unlike Germany, there are no formal mechanisms to involve important interest groups in national policymaking.

Instead, the two main political parties have essentially co-opted both businesses and labor unions within the party system. The Conservatives remain the party of business, and Labour is the party of unions. For example, many key firms join the Confederation of British Industries (CBI), a business lobby, which advocates lower taxes and looser regulation of business and industry. The leaders of this group and of a similar organization for business owners, the Institute of Directors, for example, were particularly influential in the Conservative Party during the leadership of Margaret Thatcher in the 1980s. Thus, British business groups have been most successful at achieving their policy aims when the Conservative Party has been in power. However, during the government of Tony Blair, the Labour Party had unprecedented success in courting the CBI, even appointing its former chairman as a government minister in 2007. Thus, the traditional ties between the Conservatives and business have weakened in recent years.

Whereas businesses traditionally lobbied government through their contacts in the Conservative Party, the Labour Party has long represented labor unions. Labour traditionally relied on union funds for organizational support, and unions still provide the bulk of the party's funding. Britain's key labor unions select 12 of the 30 members of Labour's National Executive Committee, and elect 50 percent of the delegates to the party's national conference. This gives unions tremendous influence within the Labour Party. Moreover, most large British trade unions are "affiliated unions," which means individual workers who are members of an affiliated union also pay a membership fee to the Labour Party. Even more than with the relationship between the Conservatives and British business, this explains why Labour has long had a symbiotic relationship with trade unions. This relationship between Labour and the unions did change under Tony Blair's leadership, as Blair limited links to the unions, retained much of anti-union legislation of the preceding Conservative government, and expanded his contacts with the business world. Yet, following Gordon Brown's resignation in 2010, the unions played an important role in the Labour Party leadership election victory of his successor Ed Miliband, the current Leader of the Opposition.

The relationship between organized interests of business and labor and the two main political parties in the UK appears to strengthen effective government, giving key elements of British society access to the halls of power when the party they support is in power. Moreover, the tight relationship between business and the Conservatives and unions and Labour means that parties do not have to deal with countless independent lobbies when they are in power. This facilitates the efficient operation of government.

The relationship between organized interests and parties in the UK also works to promote limited government, precisely because of this tight relationship between key elements of civil society and the agents of state authority. When key interest groups have a voice within the political parties, this prevents party leaders from acting as they please, without input from their supporters. Both business and labor unions retain considerable influence over the provision of campaign contributions and in internal party voting in the parties they support. Political parties can buck the preferences of their supporters on occasion, but party leaders may be vulnerable to interest groups' withdrawal of funds or support. The two-party system, by incorporating interest groups into the parties themselves, often allows interests to prevent governments from legislating in ways that they find unattractive.

However, the situation of business and labor unions in the UK also has drawbacks for each. Each group only has influence when the party each supports is in power. For example, unions are empowered when Labour holds the government, but unions' power is greatly reduced when the Conservatives are in power, simply because they have little sway within the Conservative Party. Moreover, in recent years, unions have been unable to use their influence to prevent Labour from moderating its political stances and from initiating links to some business groups. Labour's leaders understand that unions have nowhere else to go. Since the Conservatives remain unfriendly toward trade unions, the unions are stuck attempting to defend their interests within the Labour Party.

"Policy Communities" in Britain

Scholars have noted that British interest groups often form "policy communities," where groups representing specific economic or professional interests, like doctors and farmers, have developed close, regular relationships with the government.[15] Through the 1950s–1970s, groups such as the British Medical Association and the National Farmers Union regularly participated in decision making in the Department of Health and Agriculture, respectively. Politicians and civil servants consulted these groups when drafting legislation, and their opinions were highly respected. Although these groups frequently lobbied Parliament and had close contacts with MPs, they focused their efforts on the executive branch, where much policy is made.

When Margaret Thatcher was elected as prime minister in 1979, she critiqued the role of these groups in the policy process. The Thatcher government tried to limit contact between politicians and interest groups, excluding them from the policy process. For instance, when reforming National Health Service in 1989, the Thatcher government excluded the British Medical Association from the reform process, something that had not happened since the founding of the NHS in 1948. Nonetheless, these groups retained close links to the bureaucracy, regularly communicating with civil servants. Today, some organized interest groups retain close links to the government, and remain important players in the policy process.

The financial sector—referred to as the "City" (of London) much like financial interests are referred to as "Wall Street" in the United States—is one of the most important of such interests. Although not as formally organized as doctors or farmers, financial interests have long had important links to bureaucratic agencies like the Bank of England and the British Treasury. Finance has been the UK's most important industry since the nineteenth century. Financial firms tend to have the ear of government, and have been successful at fighting off regulation of financial markets. Although the financial crisis of 2008 would appear to weaken the "City," these firms remain politically influential.

Policy communities help make the policy process work smoothly, by incorporating powerful social interests into it. However, not all groups have the same access to the policy process, leaving some as "outsiders" with more limited power.[16] Consequently, outsider groups often are forced to mobilize their members through public protests.

Civil Society and Social Movements in the United Kingdom

While business and unions are largely co-opted into one or the other main political party, and "policy communities" have developed close links with the executive branch, the UK has a long tradition of strong civic culture, which creates an autonomous sphere for political debate outside of Parliament and provides a channel for popular dissatisfaction with government. The main organized interests in British civil society act as a powerful social bulwark against the power of the state. Indeed, because of Britain's long tradition of electoral politics, the country also has a tradition of large but peaceful protest that has produced government responsiveness to popular concerns without sparking repression, supporting Britain's balance of effective but limited government.

By civil society, we mean the networks of private actors who exist outside of government. Many scholars believe that a strong civil society is an important part of democracy, because it gives citizens a way to channel their political, economic, and religious views up to parties and thus into the policy process. Peter Hall argues that even as membership in voluntary associations and groups fell in the United States, these groups remained important in Britain.[17] While political scientists debate whether this claim remained true through the 1990s and 2000s, there is evidence that Britons continue to join clubs, donate money, and volunteer at high levels. These organizations may not be explicitly political—for instance, the Royal Society for the Protection of Birds boasts 1 million members—but they demonstrate strong involvement by Britons in collective organizations, many of which lobby the government and participate in political life. Thus, even as British electoral turnout has fallen and Britons are less likely to join political parties, they remain involved in social and political organizations in the community.

More obviously political movements have also developed. Mass opinion has a long history of influencing government in the UK. The modern era of protest dates to the early nineteenth century and the Chartist movement, which demanded expanded voting rights and social reforms from government. The Third Chartist petition of 1848 gathered several hundred thousand signatures. Even though the government of the day did not enact its demands for expanded suffrage, the peaceful mass demonstrations in support of the Chartist Movement set the stage for the Second Reform Act of 1867.

Chartist movement ■ a nineteenth-century social movement demanding political and social rights for workers that engaged in peaceful mass protest.

A similar pattern occurred with the expansion of the vote to women. The suffragist movement of the early twentieth century used non-violent mass protest to highlight women's political rights. Again, it took several decades, but British women were eventually granted the vote in 1918. In more recent times, mass peaceful social movements have developed against nuclear power and U.S. nuclear missiles on British soil (in the early 1980s), against the Poll Tax on property introduced by Margaret Thatcher in 1990, against the Labour government's ban on fox hunting, and against the Iraq War in 2003. More recently, students mobilized against proposed increases in tuition fees, and unions and other groups have protested the austerity measures of the Cameron government.

In each of these cases, the pattern of political reaction has been similar. Peaceful mass protests rarely lead to immediate government reaction, but over the subsequent years, politicians usually incorporate the demands into electoral and parliamentary politics, finally resulting in the desired reform. The peaceful nature of the revolts has meant that government has not had to act immediately to stave off violent protest—as in France, for example. However, the peaceful protests have also been important in dissuading the government from violent repression of mass movements. Consequently, the right to protest has usually been untrammeled and the government has not developed large police or intelligence forces to undermine these groups. Peaceful social movements, even though they do not immediately appear to constrain effective British government, have actually limited it in the long run.

Mass Media

Although the main radio and television broadcaster in the UK—the British Broadcasting Corporation (BBC)—is government owned, this state-sponsored institution has not crowded out private alternative sources of information. Several other television channels exist on both broadcast and cable, and one can find multiple choices—including political talk shows—along the radio dial. National newspapers are more explicit in their political viewpoints: from the left-wing *Mirror* and *Guardian* newspapers to the right-wing *Sun* and *Telegraph*, for example. Altogether, there are ten major national newspapers with significant readerships. Although most of these papers articulate a clear political view, they rarely consistently support the government, even when the party they favor is in power.

The mass media market reflects Britain's oppositional political culture. Politicians must constantly face hard questions from the press, which follows and publicizes all sorts of scandals. Unlike the case of the American press and the U.S. president, journalists show very little deference to the British prime minister and his or her Cabinet colleagues, often directly asking them pointed and harsh questions in interviews. The media also cover Prime Minister's Questions closely, exposing citizens to the oppositional nature of Westminster politics. The media also serves as an important link between mass politics and elite debate. For example, lower-income citizens of many different political persuasions can read one of the so-called "tabloid" newspapers, which have readerships of millions. These newspapers cover electoral politics in depth and are known for developing their own political positions—such as on immigration and the European Union, for example—that the government cannot afford to ignore.

> **SUMMARY TABLE**
>
> **Interests in the United Kingdom**
>
> | | |
> |---|---|
> | Business and Labor | Business and labor have largely been incorporated into the two-party system, with business often supporting the Conservatives and trade unions supporting Labour. However, in recent years, business associations have developed close contacts with both parties. |
> | Policy Communities | Britain has many well-developed associations, among doctors, farmers, banks, etc., that have close connections to both politicians and civil servants. |
> | Civil Society | Britain, in contrast to other European countries, has a long history of peaceful mass protest and large voluntary organizations that have served as an important "safety valve" for public interests and grievances. |
> | Mass Media | British newspapers mirror the two-party system with openly partisan allegiances. In contrast, the British Broadcasting Corporation (BBC) is state owned and is obliged to remain politically neutral. |

The primary way that political interests are expressed in the UK is through the two main political parties. This means that elected governments are highly effective, since other interest groups cannot be sure their voices will be heard. In particular, business and labor interests have been co-opted into the political parties and are reliant on their good graces. However, the British government is nonetheless limited by the broad array of actors in the UK's thriving civil society, who have a long tradition of publicly criticizing government policy. Social movements too have often emerged to limit government behavior, though their impact tends to be gradual and indirect.

CONCLUSION

We began this chapter with an intriguing puzzle—why does the British government follow rules if it lacks formal constraints? The first section of the chapter demonstrated that the slow and peaceful development of democracy through British history allowed for the simultaneous emergence of *effective* government—where government can legislate and execute policies quickly—and *limited* government—where the government is constrained by outside forces—to explain this puzzle.

To further understand this balance, the chapter examined the institutions of British government. The formal British institutions appear to grant the government considerable discretion to act as it wishes. In the UK, Parliament is sovereign, meaning that legally it can make legislation without oversight from the Courts or a written constitution. These features combine with a heavy concentration of power within the executive branch, as the prime minister and his or her Cabinet have a near monopoly on introducing legislation. The British electoral system, which tends to produce single-party government, further empowers the government, reducing the likelihood of power-sharing across parties.

However, the sheer age of British institutions and respect for precedent, combined with the "two-party" system in which the Conservative and Labour parties rotate in power regularly, have long limited government. When in power, each party is able to legislate as it sees fit, but under the constraint that a ready-made replacement lies in wait. Oppositional politics prevents the government from acting without criticism and reminds it that its power is not permanent. More recently new limits from both below—in the regions—and above—in the European Union—have emerged.

The nature of British political identities furthers this mix of effective and limited government. The core expression of identity in Britain is class, or economic interests, represented by the Labour and Conservative parties. These parties have been successful in incorporating both diverse identities—like regional, religious, and ethnic identities. This move both concentrates power in the political parties, but also limits their reach, requiring them to make broad appeals to diverse groups.

Finally, we discussed the role of political interests in shaping the system. The incorporation of business and labor groups within the major parties has long strengthened government action. However, the United Kingdom also has a series of long-standing independent actors in civil society who monitor and cajole government effectively. Put simply, while any one government *could* operate highly effectively, in practice it faces several powerful sources of potential opposition within and outside of politics.

How stable is the United Kingdom's balance between effective and limited government? Since that balance has been maintained successfully for several centuries, we should not read too much into recent events. Nonetheless, contemporary challenges have emerged. In recent years the threat of terrorism, particularly following the attacks in London in 2005, has raised new questions about British civil liberties. Here the government must balance liberty and security in a changing world. Economic events have also presented new challenges—particularly the collapse of the UK's housing and financial sectors in 2008. It is not yet clear how the UK will reconcile its tradition of limited regulation with demands for more effective control over banks and investors.

Study and Review the Post-Test & Chapter Exam at mypoliscilab.com

KEY TERMS

monarch   40
Magna Carta   41
House of Commons   41
House of Lords   41
Bill of Rights   44
Reform Acts   45
Conservative Party   46
Liberal Party   46
Labour Party   46
decolonization   46

devolution   48
informal constitution   51
parliamentary sovereignty   51
Members of Parliament (MP)   51
Cabinet   53
backbenchers   53
vote of confidence   54
Prime Minister's Questions   57
Church of England   64
Chartist movement   71

REVIEW QUESTIONS

1. What are the key factors that permit the UK to maintain a balance between limited and effective government?
2. How important do you think the age of British institutions are to the success of democracy in the United Kingdom?
3. What effect has class had on British politics and society?
4. How do labor unions, policy communities, and the media affect British politics and society?
5. Why does the UK have a two-party system and how does that help retain limited government?

SUGGESTED READINGS

Bale, Tim. *The Conservative Party: From Thatcher to Cameron*. London: Polity, 2010. Routledge, 1998. An overview of recent developments in the Conservative Party.

Birch, Anthony. *The British System of Government*. London: Routledge, 1998. A classic text on the institutions of British government.

Driver, Stephen, and Luke Martel. *New Labour*. London: Polity, 2006. An overview of the policies and strategies of Blair's Labour government.

Hall, Peter. "Policy Paradigms, Social Learning, and the State: The Case of Economic Policymaking in Britain." *Comparative Politics* 25(3) (1993): 275–296. A detailed examination of changes in economic policymaking in the postwar years through the Thatcher government.

Hefferman, Richard, Philip Cowley, and Colin Hay. *Developments in British Politics 9*. London: Palgrave MacMillan, 2011. An overview of current issues and developments in British politics.

Peston, Robert. *Who Runs Britain?: And Who's to Blame for the Economic Mess We're In?* London: Hodder Paperbacks, 2008. A readable overview of the financial crisis by a key financial journalist.

Wickham-Jones, Mark. "Signalling Credibility: Electoral Strategy and New Labour in Britain," *Political Science Quarterly* 120(4) (2005): 653–673. A theoretically motivated analysis of Labour's electoral strategy in the 1990s.

NOTES

1. E. A. Wrigley and R. S. Schofield. *The Population History of England 1541–1871: A Reconstruction* (New York: Cambridge University Press).
2. John A. Phillips and Charles Wetherell. "The Great Reform Act of 1832 and the Political Modernization of England," *The American Historical Review*, vol. 100 (1995), 411–436.
3. Neal Blewett. "The Franchise in the United Kingdom 1885–1918." *Past & Present*, No. 32 (Dec. 1965): 27–56.
4. Eric Evans. *Thatcher and Thatcherism* 2nd ed. (London: Routledge, 2004).
5. Nicholas Crafts. *British Economic Growth During the Industrial Revolution* (Oxford: Clarendon Press, 1985).
6. Martin Elff. "Social Structure and Electoral Behavior in Comparative Perspective: The Decline of Social Cleavages in Western Europe Revisited." *Perspectives on Politics*, 5(2) (2007): 277–294.
7. *World Values Survey*. Great Britain, 2006.

8. *Census* (April 2001), Northern Ireland Statistics and Research Agency.
9. Michael Rendell and John Salt. "The Foreign Born Population," *Focus on People and Migration* (2005), Office for National Statistics.
10. *UK Census* (April 2001), Office for National Statistics.
11. Seth Koven and Sonya Michel. "Womanly Duties: Maternalist Politics and the Origins of Welfare States in France, Germany, Great Britain," *The American Historical Review*, Vol. 95, No. 4 (Oct., 1990): 1076–1108.
12. Janet Gornick, Marci Meyers, and Katherin Ross. "Supporting the Employment of Mothers: Policy Variation Across Fourteen Welfare States," *Journal of European Social Policy*, 7 (1) (1997): 45–70.
13. Pippa Norris. "Gender and Contemporary British Politics," in *British Politics Today*, Colin Hay, ed. (Cambridge: Blackwell, 2002).
14. Norris. 2002.
15. Wyn Grant. *Pressure Groups in British Politics* (New York: St. Martin's Press, 2000).
16. Grant, 2000.
17. Peter Hall. "Social Capital in Britain," *British Journal of Political Science*, 29 (1999): 417–461.

CHAPTER 3

Germany
David Art

Chancellor Angela Merkel places a rose on a memorial plaque during a visit to Buchenwald, a former Nazi concentration camp. President Barack Obama and Holocaust survivors Elie Wiesel (left) and Bertrand Herz look on.

> **?** How did Germany overcome its tumultuous history and become a healthy democracy?

INTRODUCTION TO GERMANY

Consider the modern political history of Germany: the country entered the First World War in 1914 as a monarchy, and by the time it capitulated in 1918 it was close to civil war. Germany's first experience with democracy during the **Weimar Republic** lasted only 15 years, much of it marked by economic collapse, fear of communist revolution, and political deadlock. In 1932, Hitler's Nazi Party won more votes than any other party, and less than a year later Hitler had destroyed the Weimar democracy and created a fascist dictatorship. With the goal of dominating first Europe, and eventually the world, Hitler led Germany into World War II and launched the Holocaust, causing untold suffering and destruction across the continent.

After its defeat in World War II, the victorious Allied Powers (the United States, Russia, France, and the UK) occupied Germany with hundreds of thousands of military troops. Shortly afterwards, Germany became a symbolic battleground in the Cold War between the United States and the Soviet Union (Russia today). The country was divided into two states: the United States established West Germany with a democratic, capitalist regime, whereas the Soviet Union established East Germany with a non-democratic, communist regime. Clashes over the divided capital city of Berlin brought the United States and the Soviet Union to the brink of nuclear war in 1949 and 1961.

Despite Germany's chaotic and bloody history in the first half of the twentieth century, for the last 50 years German politics has been remarkably stable and peaceful. When the East German government collapsed in 1989, the two halves of Germany were peacefully reunited—much to the surprise of many observers. Germany now has the largest population and economy in Europe, yet in contrast to its recent modern history, Germany's neighbors no longer fear its strengths but look to it for leadership in the process of peaceful integration in the European Union.

This leads us to ask *how did Germany overcome its tumultuous past and become a healthy democracy?* Contemporary German politics is not without its problems and challenges: incorporating formerly communist East Germany into the country has not been easy. The process of reforming the German welfare state has been contentious, and immigration and integration have raised difficult questions about what it means to be German. But the conflicts that characterize German politics today pale in comparison with those of its past. Indeed, given the tension and violence in Germany's twentieth-century history, one might think that German politics would remain highly contentious to this day. Before we can begin to answer the chapter question, we need to briefly survey Germany's political history with the goal of understanding why Germany failed for so long to develop a stable democracy.

HISTORICAL OVERVIEW OF GERMANY

Germany's political development from the decline of feudalism to the eve of the World War I differed from that of both the United Kingdom and France in three respects. First, Germany is an example of late state formation. By the early nineteenth

---

Weimar Republic ■ Germany's first democratic regime that was founded in 1919 after World War I and lasted until 1933, when it was destroyed by the Nazis.

▶─ Read and Listen to Chapter 3 at mypoliscilab.com

✓●─ Study and Review the Pre-Test & Flashcards at mypoliscilab.com

3.1 What types of regimes did Germany experience before it became a stable democratic state?

century, both the UK and France were largely established as modern states, but there was no "Germany" as we know it today. Instead, the area that would become Germany was comprised of more than 300 small territories. Only after 1871 were these territories united into a state called Germany.

Second, whereas both the UK and France were emerging democracies by the late 1800s, Germany remained a fully authoritarian regime until 1919. The largest of Germany's component states—Prussia—developed a military-bureaucratic regime that would block efforts at democratization and make militarism an essential element of German political culture until the end of World War II.[1]

Third, the legacy of the Protestant Reformation divided the inhabitants of the German-speaking lands into Catholics and Protestants. Unlike in Britain and France, where religious wars in earlier eras led to the victory of one side or the other by the 1800s, a religious cleavage persisted in Germany. This division hindered both the unification of the German state and the unification of German national identity. It also divided Germany's liberal middle class into Protestant and Catholic groups that refused to ally, making the middle class a much weaker organizing force for democracy than elsewhere in Western Europe.[2]

The Second Reich

The prime minister or chancellor of Prussia **Otto von Bismarck** unified Germany through a series of wars, culminating with the defeat of France in 1871. The political regime he created is referred to as both the German Empire and the Second Reich (the First Reich was the Holy Roman Empire) and lasted until 1919. During the late nineteenth century, Germany underwent rapid economic growth and became one of the wealthiest countries in the world. Yet unlike most other countries, economic development did not lead to democracy, a fact that has puzzled many scholars.

It is true that the Second Reich did possess some democratic features. For example, there was universal male suffrage and free and fair elections for the **Reichstag**, the lower chamber of Germany's two-chamber legislature. Multiple parties also contested these elections, including the **Social Democratic Party** (SPD), which represented the interests of Germany's rapidly growing industrial working class, and the Centre Party, which represented the interests of Catholics.

However, contestation was often suppressed: Bismarck tried to undercut the growing strength of the SPD by limiting its freedom to organize and shutting down some of its newspapers. Moreover, in terms of accountability, the Second Reich was truly non-democratic. Real power lay less in the Reichstag than in the Bundesrat, the Senate or upper chamber of the legislature. Germany's chancellor appointed the members of the Bundesrat—and the emperor appointed the chancellor. Members of the Bundesrat were drawn mostly from the Prussian nobility and military establishment, which was, therefore, able to remain in political control of Germany from 1871 to 1918.

Several underlying factors explain the persistence of this non-democratic system in Germany. First, Bismarck is recognized as one of history's most skillful politicians.[3] He built a political coalition that united industrial and land-owning elites in what was known as the "marriage of Iron and Rye." This coalition opposed granting democratic rights to workers and peasants. Bismarck also cleverly co-opted

---

Watch the Video "Germany's Anschluss of Austria" at **mypoliscilab.com**

Watch the Video "The Berlin Blockade" at **mypoliscilab.com**

Otto von Bismarck ■ Prussian leader who first unified Germany and served as chancellor for more than two decades in the Second Reich.

Reichstag ■ The term for the legislative assembly under both the Second Reich and the Weimar Republic.

Social Democratic Party ■ One of Germany's largest political parties, founded in 1860 to represent the interests of the working class.

GERMANY

GERMANY IN COMPARISON

	United Kingdom	Germany	France	Japan	India	Mexico	Russia	Nigeria	China	Iran
Freedom House Classification	Democracy	Democracy	Democracy	Democracy	Democracy	Partial democracy	Partial democracy	Partial democracy	Non-democracy	Non-democracy
Land Size (sq km)	243,610	357,022	643,801	377,915	3,287,263	1,964,375	17,098,242	923,768	9,596,961	1,648,195
Land Size Ranking	79	62	42	61	7	15	1	32	4	18
Population (July 2011 Estimate)	62,698,362	81,471,834	65,312,249	126,475,664	1,189,172,906	113,724,226	138,739,892	155,215,573	1,336,718,015	77,891,220
Population Ranking	22	16	21	10	2	11	9	8	1	18
Life Expectancy (Years)	80.05	80.07	81.19	82.25	66.8	76.47	66.29	47.56	74.68	70.1
Life Expectancy Ranking	28	27	13	5	51	72	162	220	95	146
Literacy Rate	99%	99%	99%	99%	61%	86.1%	99.4%	68%	91.6%	77%
GDP Per Capita (2010 Estimate)	US$35,100	US$35,900	US$33,300	US$34,000	US$3,500	US$13,800	US$15,900	US$2,500	US$7,600	US$11,200
GDP Ranking	36	32	39	38	163	85	71	178	126	100

potential opposition. To win the support of German workers, in the 1880s he laid the foundations for what would become the world's first welfare state—offering forms of health, accident, and disability insurance, as well as retirement pensions. Bismarck also proved adept at dividing Germany's liberal middle class, keeping Protestants and Catholics divided and politically weak.

Second, just like many countries that have experienced non-democratic rule in recent years, Germany's military retained an extraordinary amount of influence in German politics during the entire Second Reich. The German military—and its allies in the political elite—felt extremely insecure on the global political stage. This insecurity was one factor that led it to join other European countries in the scramble for colonies in Africa. The German military also felt surrounded by Britain and France to its west and Russia to its east, and constantly pressed for greater military spending.

Germany's conservative ruling establishment, comprised of the military, the agricultural and industrial elites, and the emperor himself, also felt constant threat due to internal political pressures. By 1912, the SPD had become the largest political party in the Reichstag. Even though it wielded little real power, its popularity gave it considerable legitimacy, making it difficult for the regime's rulers to simply control what the SPD leaders said and did. Germany's rulers felt threatened by the rise of this new, socialist party. Given this, several military commanders and politicians suggested that a war against Germany's European rivals—one which they imagined they would win quickly—would not only improve Germany's international situation but would generate patriotic support for the emperor and the regime.[4] Thus, both international and domestic pressures led German leaders to launch World War I. However, rather than stabilizing Germany's authoritarian regime, Germany's eventual defeat in World War I led to the rapid collapse of its monarchy and the creation of a democratic regime.

The Weimar Republic

Named after the town in which the constitution was written, the Weimar Republic lasted from 1919 to 1933. This period was Germany's first experience with democracy. Yet the Weimar system would prove unstable. Germany during this period witnessed repeated political crises, and was unable to weather the economic disaster of the global Great Depression, which began in 1929. The Weimar Republic's political system lurched from one crisis to another, eventually collapsing entirely at the rise to power of Adolf Hitler and his Nazi Party.

As in the case of Germany's failed democratization in the nineteenth century, there are many reasons for the Weimar Republic's failure. The first is timing. Germany's first attempt at democracy began under very inauspicious circumstances—defeat in a major global war. Many Germans accused Weimer leaders of "stabbing Germany in the back" for signing too much away in the Versailles Treaty that ended the First World War. The Versailles Treaty accepted German responsibility for the war and forced Germany to pay huge amounts of war damages to the countries like France that had defeated Germany. Many Germans viewed the treaty as an affront to national honor, and equated democracy with national weakness and humiliation.

A second reason for the Weimar Republic's eventual political collapse has to do with the system's democratic institutions. At the time, the Weimar Constitution was hailed as the most democratic document in the world: it included universal adult suffrage; proportional representation; a semi-presidential executive composed of both a prime minister (chancellor) and a president; provisions for referenda; and many civil liberties. However, the Weimar Constitution also contained two flaws that contributed to the republic's demise. First, its proportional representation system was so proportional that parties could win less than 1 percent of the vote to get a seat in parliament. This led to the proliferation of dozens of small parties, some of which never won more than 1 percent in national elections. Germany's legislature became divided into many relatively small political parties, which meant that parliamentary majorities were often made up of unstable coalitions of several parties. Given the diversity of political interests in each government, it is perhaps not surprising that German governments of this period proved extremely short-lived: Germany had 22 different prime ministers between 1919 and 1933! The second flaw in the Weimar's Constitution was the notorious Article 48, which gave the president of the republic the right to declare states of emergency and to issue decrees unilaterally—that is, without having to wait for the parliament to pass proposed legislation. Article 48 robbed the Weimar Republic of functioning checks and balances, and would provide the mechanism through which Hitler would come to power.

Article 48 ■ the article in the Weimar Constitution that allowed the president to bypass the Reichstag and rule by decree during "emergency situations," the nature of which were never properly defined.

The third factor contributing to the Weimar democracy's collapse was economic crisis. The Weimar Republic was born under conditions of massive unemployment, with millions of soldiers returning from war to find themselves unemployed. The reparations that the Versailles Treaty imposed made it harder for Germany's economy to recover from the devastation of the war, and helped cause high rates of inflation throughout the 1920s. Many middle-class Germans lost their savings during this period, and they blamed the Weimar system. When the Great Depression began in 1929, it hit Germans particularly hard, given their already weakened economic situation. Germany's unemployment rate skyrocketed to 30 percent, leading to street protests and generalized dissatisfaction with democracy.

By the early 1930s, the Weimar Republic had become essentially ungovernable. Anti-democratic parties—that is, political parties that publicly campaigned to end the Weimar democratic constitution—garnered popular support on both the fascist right and the communist left. In the elections of 1932, pro-democracy parties won 35 percent of the vote while the Nazi Party captured 32 percent of the vote. The German Communist Party won 17 percent, which terrified many upper- and middle-class Germans, who feared a communist revolution along the lines of the one that occurred in Russia in 1917.

The Nazi Regime

Founded in 1920, Nazi is actually a sort of nickname for the National Socialist German Workers Party (NSDAP). Adolf Hitler—who had served Germany in World War I and blamed Jews, socialists, and communists for Germany's defeat—did not help found the party, but he soon took control of it. Had it not been for the Great Depression, the Nazis probably would have remained one of the Weimar Republic's numerous and insignificant political parties: the party won only 2.6 percent in the elections of 1928. Yet, Hitler's message of national pride and his rabid anti-socialism and anti-communism not only attracted many ordinary voters, but also convinced many German political and business elites to ally with him. Some of these elites believed that they could control Hitler and use him for their own purposes. This proved to be a disastrous miscalculation.[5]

Hitler came to power through democratic means after the 1932 elections. In January 1933, German president Paul von Hindenburg appointed Hitler as chancellor. Hitler wasted no time in dismantling the Weimar democracy. On February 27, 1933, a fire broke out in the house of parliament (Reichstag). Although the exact cause of the fire remains unclear to this day, Hitler claimed that the communists were behind it and convinced President Hindenburg to invoke Article 48 and restrict civil liberties through the Reichstag Fire Decree. This was a key step in Hitler's takeover of the German state. By the summer of 1933, the Nazis had banned all other political parties and had begun to create a totalitarian regime.

Totalitarian regimes differ from authoritarian regimes like the Second Reich in three respects.

1. Totalitarian regimes develop systematic and dogmatic ideologies, whereas authoritarian regimes do not;

HITLER APPOINTED CHANCELLOR

Throngs of supporters gather in Berlin outside of the residence of the German president to greet the new chancellor of Germany. The date is January 30, 1933, and President Hindenburg has just appointed Adolf Hitler as chancellor. Members of the crowds are extending their right hands towards Hitler's car in the Nazi salute.

2. Totalitarian regimes engage in mass mobilization of their societies, whereas authoritarian regimes more often *demobilize* ordinary people; and
3. Totalitarian regimes seek to erase the border between the public and private sphere, normally through coercion, whereas authoritarian regimes leave this division intact.

The Third Reich (1933–1945) clearly exhibited all the characteristics of a totalitarian regime. Nazism was a form of fascist ideology that glorified German nationalism, suggested that Germans and other so-called "Aryans" were racially superior to other races, and demanded greater "living space" (*Lebensraum*) for Germans at the expense of other nationalities in Europe, especially Slavic peoples in Eastern Europe. Nazi racial doctrine also led to the internment and forced sterilization of Germans who were considered threats to the purity of the Aryan race, such as the mentally ill and the handicapped, as well as "asocial" types, such as prostitutes, vagrants, orphans, petty criminals, and homosexuals. It led to the Holocaust, the rationalization of the deliberate murder of millions of Jews and other "undesirables" during World War II.

In terms of mobilization, the Nazis organized mass demonstrations and used emerging technologies such as radio and film to spread their propaganda. The party replaced all types of civic organizations—such as youth groups, women's organizations, neighborhood associations, and even choral societies—with "Nazi" versions of the same groups. And it exerted absolute control over other aspects of German society, such as education, the media, and arts and culture.

Finally, the Nazis set up an elaborate system of monitoring and coercion that invaded personal and family life. Concentration camps were set up to hold political prisoners, even people who were merely suspected of not supporting the Nazi regime. A "Malicious Gossip" Law made it a crime to say—even in private conversation—that the Nazis were suppressing freedom, that prisoners were beaten in concentration camps, or that the Nazis were corrupt. As a result, ordinary Germans settled personal scores by denouncing their neighbors, friends, and even family members to the Gestapo, the Nazi regime's secret police.[6]

Despite its systematic violation of human rights, the Nazi regime enjoyed considerable popular support—up to the point where it was clear that Germany would lose World War II. This suggests that Hitler's reign did not rest merely on cowing the population into submission. Politically, Hitler succeeded in ending the chronic instability of the Weimar democracy, and virtually eliminated unemployment within a few years of taking power, primarily through military spending. He also reestablished Germany's national pride by repudiating the Versailles Treaty and by invading and conquering territories on Germany's borders. Many, if not most, Germans cheered these moves, up through the first years of World War II, which witnessed an unbroken set of German victories in both Western and Eastern Europe. Support for the Nazi regime diminished only at the very end of the war—but even then, active resistance was rare.

Nazism ■ The ideology of Adolf Hitler and the Nazi Party. A racial version of fascism that places the "Aryans" at the top of the racial hierarchy and demands that they conquer and eliminate lesser races in their quest for more living space.

The Postwar Era: Division and Reunification

In 1945, Germany was once again a defeated country. Recall that within 30 years, Germany had experienced tremendous political instability, going from a non-democratic monarchy (the Second Reich) to a democracy (the Weimar Republic), and then to a brutal totalitarian regime (the Nazi regime). After losing World War II, Germany was occupied by the military forces of Britain, France, the United States, and the Soviet Union, and between the years of 1945–1949 it was not, technically, an independent, sovereign state.

Germany would remain divided for more than 40 years. The western zones occupied by American, French, and British forces regained sovereignty in 1949 as the Federal Republic of Germany (FRG, also known as West Germany) and became a democratic state with a capitalist economy. The eastern zones occupied by the Soviet Union became the German Democratic Republic (GDR, or East Germany) in the same year, and became a communist one-party state. The GDR was formally an independent sovereign state, but in reality its politics were heavily influenced from the Soviet Union.

The Nazis had implemented a fascist totalitarian regime. In contrast, East Germany's leaders implemented a communist totalitarian regime. The government mobilized society through mandatory membership in mass organizations, and the Ministry of State Security, known as the Stasi, monitored individuals in order to identify political dissenters. At one point, the Stasi consisted of 500,000 employees and informers for a total population of around 16 million. At the time of its dis-

Federal Republic of Germany (FRG) ■
The official name for both West Germany during the period of German division, and for unified Germany after 1990.

German Democratic Republic (GDR) ■
The official name of East Germany, the communist state that existed from 1949 to 1990 before the fall of the Berlin Wall.

CHECKPOINT CHARLIE TODAY

Checkpoint Charlie in Berlin is now a tourist attraction, and the U.S. and Soviet "border guards" in this photo are actually German students. But between 1961, when the Berlin Wall was built, and 1989, when the wall fell, Checkpoint Charlie was the most famous crossing point between East and West Berlin. It was a symbol of both the Cold War and the division of Germany.

solution, it had collected "intelligence" files on two-thirds of the adult population of East Germany.

In 1961, the GDR also constructed a physical border around the city of West Berlin, which was part of West Germany but geographically surrounded by East German territory. Usually, when countries put walls or barbed wire on their borders, they are attempting to keep people *out*. Yet, the Berlin Wall was actually designed to keep East Germans *in* and to prevent the massive emigration of its population to West Berlin's enclave of democracy. East German border guards were ordered to shoot to kill any East Germans attempting to flee.

During the 1960s and 1970s, the GDR managed to stabilize and grow its economy. Yet, still it lagged behind that of West Germany. Indeed, West Germany's democratic and capitalist system became one of the world's wealthiest societies. Many East Germans were able to watch West German TV, and saw with their own eyes how poor they were in relation to citizens on the other side of the border. In 1989, when the Soviet Union made it clear that it would no longer prop up the communist regimes of Eastern Europe, the GDR's communist regime crumbled. The Berlin Wall—the symbol for division of Germany—fell on November 9, 1989. Within just a year, the GDR ceased to exist and the two Germanys reunified under the institutions of West Germany.

This chapter's main question focuses on what was West Germany—how and why it proved to be so successful and stable, not only in contrast to previous German political systems, but also in contrast to the East German communist regime. Unlike East Germany, the FRG recovered from the devastation of World War II relatively quickly. Germany had experienced periods of prosperity in the past but this time economic growth and democratic stability coincided. Given the country's history, this was surprising. Remember that in 1949, it was hardly a foregone conclusion that the FRG would grow into a stable democracy, particularly given the effects of 13 years of Nazi propaganda on a society whose support for democracy was weak to begin with.

Even so, by the late 1950s, democracy was taken for granted in West Germany—to the point that it exhibited greater democratic stability even compared against some of its democratic neighbors. One might even say that politics in the FRG had become an unremarkable fact within just two decades after the collapse of Hitler's regime—a notable achievement given the violent instability in Germany's recent past. The FRG was so strong and stable that it was able to integrate another entire country—the GDR—even though the GDR government had spent more than 40 years indoctrinating the population about the supposed evils of capitalism and democracy. Today, Germany anchors the European Union, a group of democratic states that unites former enemies into the largest economic bloc in the world. How did Germany go from being the erratic bully on the block to a leader in promoting peaceful cooperation among states? How did democracy succeed in West Germany? And how did it become so stable and successful that it could incorporate East Germany without significant trauma or instability? This transformation is all the more remarkable given the history of authoritarianism and totalitarianism in Germany that this section has highlighted. In the next sections, we explore how the institutions, identities,

> **SUMMARY TABLE**
>
> **Historical Overview: Germany's Regime Changes, 1871–present**
>
> | | |
> |---|---|
> | **Second Reich (1871–1918)** | Non-democratic regime with substantial participation but controls on contestation, high military influence in politics, as well as political control by agricultural and industrial economic elites |
> | **Weimar Republic (1919–1933)** | Unstable democratic regime with little popular support, a highly fragmented party system, and a too-powerful presidency. Ultimately done in by the impact of the Great Depression |
> | **The Nazi Regime (1933–1945)** | A totalitarian non-democratic system that nonetheless enjoyed considerable popular support |
> | **The Postwar Era (1945–present)** | Germany initially divided into two sovereign states—the capitalist and democratic West Germany and the communist and non-democratic East Germany, from 1945–1990, and then reunified |

and interests that emerged in Germany after the Second World War created a stable democracy for the first time.

INSTITUTIONS OF GERMANY

3.2 How did postwar political institutions contribute to democratic consolidation and avoid the problems of the past?

Germany's constitutional document is called the **Basic Law** (*Grundgesetz*) and dates from 1949. Less than a year before, Allied powers had instructed the West German authorities to draw up a constitution for what would become their sovereign state. The authors of the Basic Law wrote the document with the goal of preventing the breakdown and collapse of democracy. Indeed, the first sentence of the Basic Law makes it clear that its central purpose is to protect individuals from the abuse of state power: "The dignity of man shall be inviolable: To respect and protect it shall be the duty of all state authority." The Basic Law does a very good job of striking a balance between limited and effective government: while it *disperses* power, it prevents the concentration of power that occurred under the Nazi regime. It also ensures that German governments possess enough power to be *effective* in order to avoid the chronic instability that contributed to the collapse of the Weimar Republic. The Basic Law functions so well that it was simply amended in 1990 to incorporate the territory of the former East Germany.

Basic Law ■ West Germany's founding constitutional document, as well as the constitutional document of contemporary Germany.

Explore the Comparative "Judiciaries" at mypoliscilab.com

"Chancellor Democracy"

Beginning with the executive branch, the Basic Law called for a parliamentary democracy in which the chancellor, or prime minister, is the most powerful figure and the official head of government. The chancellor is elected by the lower house of the legislature, the **Bundestag**, and has always been the leader of the largest political party of that body. As in other parliamentary systems, the chancellor has considerable power, which enhances effective government. The chancellor appoints the members of the cabinet, and is able to create or eliminate cabinet ministries altogether. Chancellor also possesses their own ministry—the Federal

Bundestag ■ the lower house of the German parliament. Its members elect the chancellor.

Chancellery (*Bundeskanzleramt*)—which is staffed by several hundred civil servants. The Federal Chancellery helps to coordinate, and monitor, the actions of the other ministries and ensure that the chancellor's policies are carried out. It is the government, rather than the legislature, that initiates most legislation.

Although a chancellor is ultimately responsible to the Bundestag, the framers of the Basic Law also sought to enhance effective government and avoid the instability of the Weimar Republic by creating rules to promote government stability. The Basic Law contains a provision called a **constructive vote of no confidence**, which requires the Bundestag to first agree on a person to replace the chancellor before voting to oust the chancellor. Many other countries with parliamentary systems do not require the simultaneous approval of a new prime minister when parliament ousts the old prime minister in a no-confidence vote. This procedure has only been used successfully once in the history of postwar Germany, in 1982.

These institutional rules tend to enhance effective government. Because the Basic Law centralizes policymaking authority in the office of the prime minister, postwar Germany has been referred to as a "chancellor democracy." Germany still has a president, but the presidency is now largely ceremonial, somewhat like the queen of England. The president is elected by the parliament, and is expected to act in a non-partisan manner in conducting what are mainly symbolic tasks, such as signing treaties, hosting other heads of state, and asking the leader of the largest party in the Bundestag to form a government. This is clearly a far cry from the Weimar Republic, where the president possessed emergency powers and could dismiss governments and appoint new prime ministers at will.

The Basic Law also created a bicameral legislature composed of the lower house (the Bundestag) and the upper house (the **Bundesrat**). The Bundestag is more important than the Bundesrat (see below on Federalism), because it has the sole authority to elect or remove the chancellor and to pass national legislation. That being said, individual Bundestag members have little power, because the body normally approves bills drafted by the chancellor and his or her ministers. Still, because a majority vote in the Bundestag determines which parties get the chancellorship, Bundestag elections are extremely important to the functioning of German democracy.

Germany uses a complicated electoral system that combines elements of majoritarian and proportional systems. In contrast to elections in the United States or the UK, German citizens cast *two* votes in Bundestag elections: the first is for a specific candidate in their electoral district, and the second is for a party that is running in the same district. Half of the seats in the Bundestag go to the individual winners in the single-member constituencies, while the other half are divided proportionally among the parties, based on the percentage of the vote that the party received across the entire country. The proportionally elected seats, thus, ensure that the overall distribution of seats in the Bundestag is proportional to the national distribution of party votes. This system thus embodies elements of both the majoritarian and the proportional visions of representation.

An important feature of the system—and one that seeks to avoid a repeat of the Weimar experience with both ineffective government and a proliferation of antidemocratic parties on both the political left and right—is a relatively high hurdle for parties to gain a seat in the Bundestag. To prevent the proliferation of small parties and instability in the legislature, the Basic Law requires that political parties win three individual seats outright (on citizens' first vote) or receive at least 5 percent of

constructive vote of no confidence ■ parliamentary vote that can withdraw confidence in, and thereby terminate, a government only if a prospective successor has majority support.

Bundesrat ■ the upper house of the German parliament that represents the interests of the 16 federal states.

the proportional vote at the national level (on citizens' second vote) to be allowed to sit in the Bundestag at all. This system has been particularly effective in preventing extremist parties from winning representation and using the Bundestag as a national stage.

The Judiciary

The Basic Law was not solely concerned with promoting effective government. After all, the Nazi regime was "effective" in getting things done. A major concern of the occupying powers was also in promoting *limited* government in postwar Germany. Under Hitler, the German judiciary had actually *upheld* the legality of many Nazi laws, so the power to declare laws unconstitutional was deemed particularly important in postwar Germany. The 1949 Basic Law established a judicial system that endowed the Federal Constitutional Court, the most important actor in the legal system, with the power of judicial review. Judicial review is a key way that institutions can be designed to check and balance executive power.

One way that the judiciary's design works to enhance democratic stability is that the Federal Constitutional Court has the final word on whether political parties and organizations are considered anti-democratic or not. A special Office for the Protection of the Constitution under the Ministry of the Interior collects information on such parties to help the constitutional court decide whether they should be banned according to a provision in the Basic Law. That provision outlaws parties that "seek to abolish or impair the free democratic order." The Federal Court has upheld two such government bans: one against the fascist Socialist Reich Party in 1952 and another against the German Communist Party in 1956. Germany is, thus, known as a "militant democracy"—one that actively protects itself from anti-democratic elements. Again, this is clearly a protective measure learned from the failure of the Weimar Republic.

Federal Constitutional Court ■ The highest court in Germany, established by the Basic Law and responsible for judicial review.

Federalism

The Basic Law established Germany as a federal system. West Germany was composed of 11 Länder (or states), and five more were formed from the former East Germany to bring the total to 16 after unification. Federalism in Germany was not instituted to protect minorities, as in Canada or India, or because citizens preferred limited government, as in the United States. Rather, federalism was viewed as yet another check on the power of the executive branch and the central government. The 16 German states control many key policy areas, such as education, justice, the media, and law enforcement. In fact, aside from defense and foreign policy, which are the exclusive domains of the federal government, the states control most aspects of administration. Each has its own parliament and its own state prime minister who, as in the Bundestag, is elected by the state parliament.

Länder ■ the 16 political units, or states, that form the Federal Republic of Germany (FRG).

The German states are also represented in the upper house of the German legislature (the Bundesrat). The 69 members of the Bundesrat are appointed by the state governments, and each state, depending on its population, is allowed to appoint between three to six members, each of whom are required to vote in a block. In practice, this means that the prime minister of a German state heads a delegation of his party in the upper chamber of the federal government, making him or her far more powerful than the governor of an American state, for example.

The Bundesrat's main power is to vote on bills that would require implementation by the states. In contrast to the Bundestag, where the chancellor can normally count on the passage of his or her government's bills, it is entirely possible—and in fact even probable—that the opposition can form a majority and, hence, veto the bill in the Bundesrat. German voters, like voters in the United States, sometimes vote differently in state elections than in national elections. Moreover, since state elections are not held at the same time as national elections, anti-government sentiment can build and opposition parties can capture control of the Bundesrat. Thus, while Germany is a "chancellor democracy," the existence of federalism and the Bundesrat serves to check the chancellor's power. Although it may be less powerful as an institution than the Bundestag, and membership in it is less desirable for an ambitious politician than membership in the lower house of parliament, the Bundesrat still has a major role to play in the functioning of German democracy.

International Institutions

German power is not only dispersed within its domestic institutions: Germany is a member of both the North Atlantic Treaty Organization (NATO) and the European Union (EU). NATO is a military alliance that was founded in 1949 by the United States, Canada, and numerous states in Western Europe to defend one another from the Soviet Union. The European Union originally began as a free trade union but has increasingly taken on political functions. Membership in these international institutions serves as an additional guarantee that Germany will not repeat its destructive behavior of the first half of the twentieth century, because it ties German politics to the interests of neighboring countries.

NATO West Germany became a member of NATO in 1955, which essentially meant that its security was guaranteed by the United States. Until unification in 1990, West Germany was happy to play the role of an "economic giant and political dwarf" and bind itself closely with the United States and its allies in foreign policy questions. This has shifted somewhat over the last decade. For example in 2002, the German government of Gerhard Schroeder (SPD) criticized the United States's war against Iraq. The Germans have also begun to deploy troops in places like Afghanistan, East Timor, and Bosnia in what are described as humanitarian missions. This marks a departure from the first four postwar decades when Germany never sent troops abroad and only conceived of using military force for self-defense. Still, given its history, Germany remains extremely reluctant to use military power and only does so in cooperation with its allies through multilateral institutions.

The European Union Germany was one of the original members of the European Economic Community (renamed the EU in 1993 after the signing of the Maastricht Treaty) in 1957. The origins of the EEC date back to the European Coal and Steel

Community, an organization designed to coordinate the production of these materials in the aftermath of the Second World War. Although its purpose might appear banal, one must remember that coal and steel provided the foundations for war-making, and European leaders felt that binding Germany in this organization would act as a precaution against any future German militarization.

The EEC began as an economic organization, charged with the task of creating a free trade zone among its members. Over the years, however, the EEC (and later the EU) acquired a great degree of political power, and the members of this institution have agreed to give up a fair degree of their sovereignty. Most of the laws that affect German citizens, and indeed citizens of any country in the European Union, are written in Brussels, Belgium (the "capital" of the EU), rather than in their home countries. Members of the EU are constrained in setting their own economic policies, particularly those that (like Germany) use the euro as their currency. The EU, in short, has eroded the sovereign power of all European states, including the large ones like Germany.

By and large, Germany has supported the growing power of the EU over the last five decades. Like NATO, German leaders have often viewed the EU as another potential check on the abuse of state power. EU membership also allowed Germans a venue to pursue their economic interests without appearing too threatening toward their neighbors.[7] As one of the world's largest exporters, free trade has always been in Germany's interest.

German leaders were initially less interested in giving up their cherished currency—the Deutschmark—in return for a common European currency. Given Germany's remarkable economic recovery after the war, the Deutschmark had become a symbol of national pride in a society where such symbols were in short supply. German leaders also placed great trust in their own central bank—the Bundesbank—which had done an outstanding job of avoiding the financial crises of the past. Yet, in the end, the timing of German reunification and acceptance of the euro were deeply linked. In 1989, the president of France, François Mitterrand, agreed to not stand in the way of German reunification so long as Germany could be tightly bound to the EU by giving up the Deutschmark and adopting the euro. Helmut Kohl, the chancellor of Germany at the time, agreed to this historic bargain, which helped smooth the incorporation of East Germany into Germany.

In contrast to the Weimar system, the Basic Law has forged stability. Yet, in contrast to the Nazi regime, the Basic Law also created multiple checks and balances on state power. No single politician, and no single political party, can have a decisive influence on politics and policymaking. Furthermore, Germany must now cooperate with the 26 other members of the European Union to craft and implement many policies that used to be handled domestically.

One might imagine that this system is a recipe for gridlock, and it is true that policies in Germany change slowly and incrementally in comparison to some other advanced industrial democracies. The tremendous policy changes that occurred in the early 1980s under Margaret Thatcher in Britain or Ronald Reagan in United States would have been inconceivable in the context of German politics. Yet recall

SUMMARY TABLE

Institutions: Balancing Limited and Effective Government

Chancellor Democracy	Parliamentarism enhances effective government by giving the prime minister considerable power and allowing only "constructive" votes of no confidence.
Parliament	The upper chamber represents the states or *Länder*, while the lower chamber represents the people. Members of the lower chamber are elected both by proportional representation and single-member districts. Parties must receive at least 5 percent of the proportional vote to win any seats, helping to preserve effective government.
Judiciary	Helps preserve limited government by establishing judicial review of parliamentary laws.
Federalism	Helps preserve limited government by checking the power of the national government.
International Institutions	Germany's membership in institutions such as NATO and the European Union also help limit the power of the German central government.

that stability was one of the primary goals of the authors of the Basic Law, and in this sense the system has functioned exactly as designed.

Moreover, it is more accurate to say that German political institutions are designed to produce—and actually do produce—consensus rather than paralysis. The chancellor may be able to set the guidelines of policy, but that individual also knows that he or she may face opposition in the Bundesrat and needs to plan accordingly. Moreover, except for one brief period, all postwar German governments have been coalitions of political parties. Given the difficulty that the "constructive vote of no-confidence" imposes on swapping out the chancellor, in contrast to the Weimar experience these coalitions have actually promoted compromise rather than conflict. In fact, between 1966 and 1969 and again from 2005 to 2009, Germany was governed by a so-called Grand Coalition between its two largest parties: one on the right (the Christian Democratice Union [CDU])/Christian Social Union [CSU]) and one on the left (the SPD)—as if the Democrats and Republicans had explicitly agreed to govern the United States together. Clearly, in such situations as these, a reasonable degree of cooperation between parties that normally view one another as opponents was essential to getting anything done.

Institutions help us to understand both why Weimar Republic Germany was so unstable, and why postwar West Germany—and later united Germany—successfully balanced limited and effective government. The Basic Law avoided the pitfalls of the Weimar Republic by creating a strong chancellor, albeit one whose power is checked by the judiciary and the Bundesrat, and by defining the electoral rules in such a way as to produce a small number of strong parties that represent the interests of voters, without putting democracy itself at risk. Germany's membership in international institutions act as further insurance against the destructive behavior of the past. Yet, institutions are only part of the story. For Germany to escape from its authoritarian and totalitarian history, political attitudes needed to change as well, and it is to them that we now turn.

IDENTITIES IN GERMANY

3.3 How did change in German political identities both reinforce democracy and confront contemporary challenges?

Watch the Video "Germany Reunification" at mypoliscilab.com

At the end of World War II, many people within the Allied countries believed that Germans were incapable of becoming good democrats. U.S. Secretary of the Treasury Henry Morganthau, Jr. believed that Germans were inherently militaristic and devised a plan—which was partially implemented before being overturned—that would strip Germany of all its heavy industry after World War II and turn it into a purely agrarian economy. According to Morgenthau, Germans were incapable of changing their political identities, and only by returning them to the pre-industrial age could the peace of Europe be secured.

Today, support for democracy in Germany is nearly universal. Germans are less nationalistic than any other European country, and they attend anti-war protests and demonstrations against racism instead of fascist rallies. The German experience demonstrates just how malleable political identities are, and how democratic values can be fostered and consolidated over time. Yet, this does not mean that Morgenthau and others did not have cause to believe that German political culture was anti-democratic and threatening. The first part of this section highlights some of the attitudes that contributed to German aggression and authoritarianism in the first half of the twentieth century. We will consider how and why German political attitudes became more democratic and less nationalistic in the decades following World War II, and with these changes in mind, we will then examine the extent to which East Germans have adopted democratic attitudes, and how immigration has raised new questions about the defining features of German national identity.

Pre-War Identities

There were four elements of German political identity in the first half of the twentieth century that contributed to its aggressive foreign policy, the persistence of authoritarianism, and to the rise of Nazism. First, many Germans were intensely nationalistic under the Second Reich. The late nineteenth and early twentieth centuries were a time of intense nationalism across Europe: industrialization, the rise of mass education, military conscription, and the battle for colonies all contributed to rising patriotism that often devolved into jingoism. This was true in France and Britain, as well as in Germany. Yet these trends were clearly exaggerated in the latter. Otto von Bismarck's wars of unification created a burst of nationalism, and he appealed to this sentiment frequently in order to legitimize his authoritarian regime. Germans' perceptions that they had been denied their rightful place in the scramble for colonies contributed to the rise of many army and naval leagues that were intensely nationalistic.[8] Furthermore, German national identity was defined in ethnic terms, meaning that only those who possessed German blood could become German citizens.[9] This was a different conception of citizenship than in the UK and France, where citizenship could be acquired at birth, regardless of whether the parents were English or French. The Nazis would obviously take notions of racial purity to the extreme, but it is important to note that such ideas were prevalent before their rise.

Second, many Germans under the Second Reich held political activity in low esteem. They drew a distinction between serving the state, which was one's patriotic duty, and serving political parties or other narrow interest groups, which they viewed as a base and demeaning activity. The general feeling was that those with any talent should not waste their efforts on politics. This attitude persisted during the Weimar Republic, and contributed to low levels of support for democracy.

Third, militarism pervaded German politics and society. The German army and navy had a great deal of political influence under the Second Reich, a situation not unlike that in many developing countries today. Ordinary Germans accorded the military a great deal of respect, so much so that citizens were expected to automatically make way for an army officer walking down the street. Moreover, since non-commissioned officers were guaranteed state employment when they left the army, many state organizations (such as the police, post office, and the railways) were filled with former military men imbued with a martial ethos.

Fourth, there was little respect for minority rights. For example, ethnic minorities—particularly Poles—were subjected to "Germanization" policies that prohibited the use of non-German languages in public affairs. Anti-Semitism was also an undeniable element of German political culture before the rise of Nazism, but here one must be careful not to draw a direct line between it and the Holocaust. Anti-Semitism was no more deeply rooted in Germany than it was in other European countries, such as France and Russia. Jews were well integrated into German society under the Second Reich and the Weimar Republic. To be sure, there were political movements that were virulently anti-Semitic before the rise of Hitler, but these views did not find wide acceptance in German society. Even the Nazis did not widely advertise their anti-Semitism to potential voters, and often deliberately downplayed it.[10] Of course, the presence of some deeply rooted anti-Semitic impulses combined with Nazi socialization efforts meant that many ordinary Germans acquiesced to, or agreed with, Nazism's persecution of Jews. Yet, to claim that the Holocaust was somehow pre-programmed into Germany's DNA is misguided. The Nazi regime is a good example of how political leaders can exploit and cultivate pre-existing ethnic identities for their own purposes.

Political Culture after World War II

In 1947, the Allensbach Institute for Public Opinion Research, the first of its kind in West Germany, was founded and began tracking German attitudes toward democracy and Nazism. The initial results were not encouraging. For example, in 1951, 32 percent of West Germans still favored the restoration of the pre-Weimar Republic monarchy, while only 36 percent were against it. Also in 1951, 25 percent of Germans believed that it was better for a country to have only one political party, as opposed to multiple parties. In 1955, 48 percent of Germans agreed with the statement that Hitler would have been Germany's greatest statesman had it not been for the Second World War. Well into the 1950s, nearly half of all West Germans believed that "Nazism was a good idea, badly carried out." It was clear that although the Basic Law had grafted a set of democratic institutions onto German society, it was an open question whether West German democracy would become a "republic without republicans" like the Weimar Republic and subject to collapse if threatened.

Surprisingly, by the 1960s, attitudes began to change. When asked the same question about the restoration of the monarchy in 1965, only 11 percent of Germans were in favor. When asked about Hitler in 1964, only 29 percent of Germans believed he would have been Germany's greatest statesman without the war. And by 1967, only 8 percent of Germans supported having a single party instead of multiple ones.

There were other changes in German political culture, as well. Militarism plays virtually no role in contemporary German politics and support for military action of any sort is very low in Germany. For example, in the early 1980s, hundreds of thousands of West Germans participated in demonstrations against the deployment of American medium-range nuclear missiles, and the peace movement was instrumental in bringing down the government of Helmut Schmidt in 1982.

Nationalism has also been tamed and transformed. Germany went from being a country with high levels of national pride to the one with far and away the lowest levels in Europe. A *Eurobarometer* survey (conducted by the European Union) in 2003 found that while 71 percent of Irish people were "proud to be Irish," only 20 percent of Germans were "proud to be German." This does not mean that Germans have not found other sources of national pride: in 2000, 60 percent answered that they were proud of the country's constitution and democratic political institutions, leading many observers to claim that "constitutional patriotism" had become a new form of German national identity.

What led to these changes? Why did German political culture shift so dramatically within a relatively short period of time? Although there is no single answer to this question, the malleability of German political identity argues against a primordial view of identity construction. Germans, it seems, are no more predisposed to authoritarianism and genocide than they are to democracy and pacifism. To understand why German political identities could change so profoundly within two decades, we need examine the deliberate efforts of postwar policy to shape those identities.

Education Both the Allied powers and the new leaders of West Germany made ideological reeducation a priority, and every German student was required to take courses in the theory and practice of democracy. Whereas German schools and universities had taught nationalist and anti-democratic ideas to generations of Germans from the mid-nineteenth century to 1945, the postwar German education system deliberately tried to turn young Germans into active democratic citizens. The generation born immediately after the war directly challenged the political and social values of their parents. The late 1960s were a time of massive student unrest in which the so-called "generation of 1968" accused their parents, teachers, and leaders of authoritarian tendencies and challenged Germans to "dare more democracy."

Confronting the Holocaust The 1960s also marked the beginning of public debates about the Nazi past. In the immediate postwar years, German politicians portrayed Nazism as the creation of a small number of fanatics and a system under which Germans had suffered. When Germans remembered the victims of World War II in the late 1940s and 1950s, they thought primarily of German soldiers who had died at the front, or of German civilians who had died during bombing raids or during forced expulsions from the east. The victims of the Holocaust were rarely mentioned. This began to change in the 1960s and 1970s, when the complicity of ordinary Germans in the Holocaust—and not just Hitler and the small clique around him—became the subject of successive waves of national discussions.

These debates were contentious. Some politicians and intellectuals argued that the Nazi past should be allowed to pass away, that other countries had committed massive violations of human rights, as well, and that constantly referring back to one's own crimes prevented the development of a healthy national identity. On the other side were those who argued that Germans had a duty to remember the victims of the Holocaust and continue to critically examine Nazi crimes. Doing so was not only a moral imperative, they argued, but also a means of insulating themselves against the destructive impulses of the past. In the end, the second perspective became the dominant one in German politics, and no country has made remembrance of its own crimes a more central part of its contemporary identity.

The presence of this "culture of contrition" has served as a further check on nationalism and militarism.[11] Monuments and memorials to the victims of the Holocaust are prominently displayed in many German cities. In Berlin, Germany's capital, the gigantic Monument to the Murdered Jews of Europe stands directly across from the Reichstag. German students learn about the Holocaust at multiple points in their educations, and visits to museums at the site of former concentration camps have become standard school excursions. German politicians are expected to continually remind their fellow citizens of the duty to remember the Holocaust, and if they deviate significantly from this line they are often labeled extreme right-wingers and pressured to resign. All this does not mean that every German has the same views about the Holocaust—indeed, some students are no doubt tired of learning about the Holocaust and many ordinary Germans resent being held accountable for the actions of previous generations. But remembrance of the Holocaust has become such an accepted part of German political culture that it is difficult to imagine it waning anytime soon.

Incorporating East Germany

Germany has had to overcome the legacies of communism as well as fascism. Although none of the major political institutions of East Germany were preserved after unification, Germany after 1990 still needed to integrate 16 million citizens whose political values had been shaped entirely under communism or, if they were old enough, Nazism.

Some commentators began to speak of a "**wall in the head**" after the initial euphoria over unification dissipated and the attitude differences between

wall in the head ■ refers to the difference in mentalities between people living in Western and Eastern Germany.

Easterners (*Ossis*) and Westerners (*Wessis*) became apparent. Helmut Kohl initially promised Ossis "blossoming landscapes" of economic growth, but disenchantment soon followed as it became clear that East German industries were not very competitive and many Ossis lost their jobs. In a 1991 survey among East Germans, support for democracy as the best form of government stood at 70 percent, but support for democracy as practiced in unified Germany stood at only 31 percent. Corresponding figures among West Germans in the same year were 86 percent and 80 percent, respectively.[12]

These differences have persisted since reunification: Easterners remain far less satisfied with democracy than are Westerners. However, attitudes toward democracy among younger Ossis and Wessis have converged, suggesting that those who come of political age in a democratic system are more likely to express satisfaction and trust in it. Yet the persistence of unemployment and the failure of living standards in the east to "catch up" with those in the west have contributed to a general sense of grievance among many Ossis. East Germany did not undergo an "economic miracle" in the 1990s, as West Germany did in the 1950s, and democratic attitudes have been more difficult to create and sustain under such circumstances. Even so, attitudes in both the former GDR and FRG are strongly pro-democratic, while anti-democratic movements and attitudes are confined to the political fringes.

Immigration and German Identity

As if absorbing an entire society that developed along a separate path for four decades were not enough, Germany has also been faced with the challenge of integrating a foreign population that topped 8 percent of its total population in 2008. Unlike the United States, which is a "melting pot" of immigrants, and Britain and France, which experienced immigration from their overseas colonial empires, Germany remained an ethnically homogenous society for far longer. Until very recently, German citizenship was restricted to ethnic Germans. This principle of *ius sanguinis* (citizenship through blood) meant that even non-ethnic Germans who had been living in the country for generations could not acquire citizenship.

What implications would rapid transformation from a homogenous society to a diverse one have for German politics? What sorts of social tensions has immigration brought out, and how has German democracy dealt with them? How has it changed notions of what it means to be German?

To answer these questions, we need to begin by understanding who these immigrants were and why they came to West Germany. For the first several decades of the postwar period, the largest groups of immigrants were the 8 million ethnic Germans who had been expelled from the eastern territories and the 3 million East Germans who escaped to the West before the construction of the Berlin Wall in 1961. But the period from 1953 to 1973 marked a major change. To keep up with the demands of Germany's booming economy, the government invited 9.5 million so-called **guestworkers (*Gastarbeiter*)** into the country, most of whom came from Turkey, Spain, and Italy. These guestworkers were supposed to be temporary, but nearly 4 million remained in the country when the recruitment program ended in

ius sanguinis ■ policy of determining citizenship through ancestry rather than through birthplace (**ius soli**).

guestworkers (*Gastarbeiter*) ■ Workers from southern Europe and Turkey who, as part of government policy, were invited to settle temporarily during the economic boom of the 1950s and 1960s. Many stayed permanently, and thereby changed the ethnic complexion of German society.

TABLE 3.1

Percentage of Foreign-Born Population of Germany* for Selected Years

1960	1.2
1973	6.7
1980	7.2
1988	7.3
1990	8.4
2000	8.9
2007	8.9

* Germany refers to West Germany until 1990 and united Germany thereafter.

Source: Organization for Economic Co-operation and Development (OECD)

1973. Their numbers increased as they had children and other family members from their home country settled in Germany.

Toward the end of the 1980s, immigration rates increased suddenly and led to a perception among some Germans that their country was being overrun by foreigners. Hundreds of thousands of ethnic Germans who had been living in Eastern Europe and the Soviet Union were able to resettle in Germany after the Cold War ended. Most of these people spoke no German whatsoever, and their only tie to the country was perhaps a grandparent of German origin. Yet, since German citizenship was defined in ethnic terms, they were able to become full members of the political community, whereas the children of the guestworkers who were born and raised in Germany were not.

Waves of asylum seekers from the Balkan wars, the former Soviet Union, and elsewhere in the world added to the non-native population. Article 16 of the Basic Law guaranteed the right to asylum and generous social benefits for those fleeing racial or political persecution. The combination of this liberal asylum law—which was a form of atonement for the Nazi past—and Germany's large economy made it far and away the most popular destination for asylum seekers in Europe. Although less than 10 percent of these individuals actually received asylum—because many were, in fact, not politically persecuted but seeking a better quality of life—their influx led many Germans to claim that their country could not handle any more immigration and that "the boat was full."

In the early 1990s, immigration was arguably the most important topic in German politics and the subject of many debates among politicians and ordinary citizens. Politicians from parties on the right (such as the CDU/CSU) argued that Germany's liberal asylum law needed to be changed, while politicians from parties of the left (such as the SPD and the Greens) retorted that Germany's Nazi past required that it remain a refuge for the politically persecuted. At the same time as these debates were occurring, anti-immigrant parties began to do well in state elections, and a series of violent attacks on foreigners by neo-Nazis drew international attention and led to further tortured discussions about whether Germans

PROTESTS AGAINST NEO-NAZISM

Turks protest an arson attack by neo-Nazis that killed a Turkish family in the German town of Solingen in 1993. Many of these protestors were probably born in Germany, yet until 1999 they were denied a path to citizenship. The integration of foreigners remains an important issue in German politics today.

had actually absorbed the lessons of history. These incidents were concentrated in Eastern Germany, where both xenophobia and general frustration ran higher than in the West. Hundreds of thousands of Germans took to the street to protest these attacks, and politicians created public organizations charged with combating racism. Still, public skepticism toward unchecked immigration was running high. In 1992, the government passed a reform that dramatically reduced both the number of asylum seekers and the number of ethnic Germans from the east who could claim German citizenship. This served to defuse the immigration issue for a while.

When the SPD–Green government of Gerhard Schroeder took power in 1998, one of their first major pieces of legislation was a reform of Germany's outdated citizenship law. The conservative parties, which had been in power since 1982, had refused to acknowledge the fact that Germany had become a country of immigration, and clung to the law from the nineteenth century that effectively prevented 8 percent of Germany's population from becoming citizens. Conservative politicians tried to mobilize the public against reforming citizenship, and did so with some success in several state elections. Yet, the law passed in 1999 and introduced elements of the principle of *ius soli* which means "citizenship through birth," meaning that people who were born in Germany could, under certain circumstances, become citizens. Over the long run, this will open the path to citizenship to

ius soli ■ Policy of determining citizenship by birthplace, rather than through ancestry.

> **SUMMARY TABLE**
>
> **Identities: Constructing Support for Democracy**
>
> **Pre-War German Identity** German culture seemed anti-democratic, as identity included an aggressive foreign policy, low interest in engaging in politics, high support for the military, and little respect for minority rights.
>
> **Postwar German Identity** German culture evolved away from anti-democratic tendencies due to changes in education, a deliberate effort to confront German culpability for the Holocaust, and a relatively successful incorporation of East Germany. However, immigration currently presents a new challenge to German identity.

millions of people who would never have been able to acquire it when citizenship was wholly determined by the principle of *ius sanguinis*.

Since the turn of the twenty-first century, the debate about immigration has shifted from whether Germany is a country that supports immigration to how immigrants should be integrated into German society. This issue has raised questions about the defining features of contemporary German national identity. In 2000, Friedrich Merz, a conservative politician, argued that immigrants should conform to what he called Germany's *Leitkultur*, or "leading culture." Many wondered exactly what Merz meant by this term—should all immigrants don *Lederhosen* and guzzle beer during Oktoberfest? Others expressed outrage at the term and argued that the Nazi past precluded any attempt to impose German cultural norms on others.

Although Merz and the CDU eventually retracted the idea of Leitkultur, the issue of integration remains quite important in German politics, for several reasons. First, there are concerns that if foreigners do not learn to speak fluent German, they will be permanently confined to low-paying jobs. Second, conservatives, in particular, are afraid that foreigners will not develop strong connections to the society in which they live, and succeeded in introducing a citizenship test in 2008 that includes questions about German history and German political institutions. Third, there are fears that foreigners—and Muslims in particular—will not respect the core values of German society, such as the promotion of gender equality and non-discrimination on the basis of sexual orientation. Fourth, German politicians from across the political spectrum often link the failure to integrate with the rise of fundamentalism and terrorism.

These are important issues, and there is no doubt that German politicians will continue to debate immigration and integration policy. Yet, it must be emphasized that these debates will occur in a political culture that is radically different from that of the first half of the twentieth century. Although both immigration and the incorporation of the former East Germany have made it more difficult to define the core features of German national identity, we can confidently say that democratic norms are deeply embedded in German society, and that nationalism and militarism are truly marginal positions. German identities have changed fundamentally since the end of World War II and, like Germany's postwar institutions, constituted a rejection of the destructive features of the past. The combination of reeducation, critical examination of the Nazi past, and the experience of growing up in a stable and wealthy state have created political attitudes that help underpin German democracy.

INTERESTS IN GERMANY

3.4 How have historic conflicts over economic, religious, and class interests been successfully regulated in postwar Germany?

To this point, we have analyzed the role of institutions and identities in stabilizing postwar German politics. The Basic Law, we have seen, created an institutional architecture that avoided the pitfalls of the Weimar Republic. As the West German state began to function smoothly, and as the economy led to a rapid increase in the standard of living, the attitudes that had helped undermine democracy in the past began to disappear. German political culture became among the most democratic and least nationalistic in all of Europe.

But to fully account for the remarkable transformation of German politics from chaos and violence to predictability and harmony, we must consider the role of interests. How have the interests of central political actors in German politics changed over time? How have the relations between these actors changed? How have the ways in which their interests have been represented—what political scientists often refer to as patterns of *interest articulation*—mattered? And how have these patterns of interest articulation helped to stabilize German democracy?

It is helpful to begin by considering how two key historic cleavages or divisions in German politics contributed to the persistence of authoritarianism and the rise of Nazism. The first was a class cleavage: the seemingly irreconcilable conflict of interest between labor and capital. The rise of the labor movement and the SPD created enormous fear among the upper classes before the outbreak of World War I. Under the Weimar Republic, both the upper and middle classes worried about the possibility of a communist revolution like the one that had occurred in Russia in 1917. It was this fear that led many of them to support the Nazis, who declared themselves the arch-enemies of the communists and the socialists. The second was the religious cleavage: the split between Protestants and Catholics. Religion divided Germany's middle class and prevented it from mounting the type of challenge that could have potentially led to democratization in the nineteenth century.

The Postwar Settlement

postwar settlement ■ collection of tacit and official agreements between labor and capital that were designed to ameliorate the class cleavage and that underpin postwar Germany's economic system.

The two postwar German states tried to resolve the class cleavage in different ways. East Germany sought to eliminate it by replacing capitalism with communism, while West Germany tried to make capitalism itself less conflictual and more compatible with democracy. This central idea underpinned the so-called "postwar settlement" between business and labor. This settlement does not refer to any particular agreement, but rather to a more or less general understanding between the representatives of Germany's classes that their adversarial relations had contributed to Germany's disastrous recent history. Both labor and business had an interest in avoiding a repeat of the Weimar Republic. The question was whether they could find some form of historical bargain.

The first element of the postwar settlement was the creation of a generous welfare state to cushion the blows of capitalism.[13] Bismarck laid the foundations of the welfare state in the Second Reich to co-opt Social Democrats and solidify authoritarian rule. Some social welfare policies were expanded under both the Weimar Republic and the Third Reich. Yet, the postwar welfare state involved a massive expansion of benefits, including universal healthcare, generous pensions, and unemployment insurance for the entire population. Postwar leaders of Germany reasoned that workers who do not fear for their livelihoods are less likely to support communism or other extremist political ideologies. In turn, businesses would not fear organized labor or be tempted to undermine democracy to preserve their property. In return for this welfare state, which the upper classes pay for through high tax rates, labor unions agreed to play by the rules of the capitalist economy and not work toward a socialist revolution.

Yet another part of the settlement was that capitalism itself was to function differently from countries like the United States. The leaders of postwar Germany spoke of a "social market economy," whose central element was cooperation between business and labor. For example, German law recognizes the right of workers to have an influence on management decisions and the law on co-determination (*Mitbestimmung*) means that workers have a greater degree of representation on the board of directors of all German companies with more than 500 employees.[14] Although labor never has the deciding vote in decisions, employers do need to consider the interests of labor under this system and they are motivated to seek mutually beneficial solutions. This pattern of business–labor relations is very different from that of the United States or the United Kingdom, in which labor has much less influence on decision making and often needs to resort to strikes to protect its interests. As a result of co-determination, strikes are not common occurrences in Germany, and relations between labor and capital are nothing like they were during the Weimar period.

The third major element of the postwar settlement is the active involvement of the state in mediating the relationship between labor and capital—a system that is often called neo-corporatist. The state has always played a relatively large role in Germany's economy. This is because Germany, like Japan, developed a modern industrial economy later than did countries like Great Britain and the United States. In order to compete internationally, the German state did not have time to allow private companies to develop on their own, but rather invested directly in certain heavy industries and devised economic policies that would help create large industrial conglomerates.[15]

Germany's postwar economy was characterized by a system of "tripartite bargaining" in which the state set broad guidelines for negotiations between the peak interest groups of labor and capital. The German state does not seek to micromanage economic activity as under communism, but rather seeks to organize and coordinate capitalism. This has been one of the defining features of what some scholars have referred to as *Modell Deutschland*, or the German model of capitalism.[16]

These features are not unique to Germany, and other scholars have argued that other continental European countries have adopted a "variety of capitalism" that is closer to that of Germany than to that of the United States.[17] One can argue about whether one variety of capitalism is preferable to the other, yet it is undeniable that the postwar settlement has been a central factor in making postwar German politics far more stable and predictable than in the past.

co-determination ■
German law requiring that companies with more than 500 employees allow workers to be represented on their board of directors.

Whether Germany can continue to maintain this economic system in its current form, however, is uncertain. The globalization of economic activity now means that German companies can locate their operations outside of the country, and avoid paying taxes that help fund the welfare state. The German population is also ageing, meaning that there are fewer young and middle-aged workers to fund the pensions of elderly retirees. Since these retirees are also living longer than in the past, the costs of providing and caring for them are rising, as well. For these reasons, some scholars have claimed that the German model of capitalism is broken and that it will be forced to pare back the welfare state and introduce less protection for workers. Others argue that the basic model is sustainable and only needs to be reformed at the edges. Still others maintain that even if the German model is no longer viable, it is unlikely to converge on a more laissez-faire, American-style model, because Germans strongly support their own version of capitalism and will come up with their own solutions. While it is difficult to say which position is correct, it is clear that debates about the social market economy and the welfare state will characterize German politics in the future.

Political Parties

Political parties have also played an important role in overcoming, as opposed to solidifying and magnifying, Germany's historic political cleavages. Article 21 of the Basic Law explicitly recognizes the importance of parties in "forming the will of the people," and we have already seen how electoral laws have helped limit their number. Only five political parties have ever been represented in the Bundestag since 1945, as opposed to the dozens that made it into parliament under the Weimar Republic. Yet, the reasons for the stability of German party politics are not simply institutional: its political parties have also made explicit choices with the intent to avoid past mistakes.

The Christian Democratic Union
Consider first the Christian Democratic Union (CDU) and its sister party the Christian Social Union (CSU), which exists solely in the state of Bavaria. The CDU/CSU was founded after World War II by former leaders of the Centre Party. Yet, rather than appealing only to Catholics as the Centre Party had, the CDU/CSU targeted Protestants as well and was, therefore, designed to overcome Germany's historical religious cleavage. The Weimar Republic experience had demonstrated how divisions among democratic political parties had been exploited by the Nazis, and the founders of the CDU/CSU argued that a union of religiously oriented parties would help stabilize the new democracy. Although the party identified with Christian values and was conservative in terms of social values, it strongly supported the expansion of the welfare state and the idea of the social market economy. The party's ideology was explicitly loose in order to attract as wide a voter base as possible.

The party has also benefited from strong leaders. Konrad Adenauer was the first leader of the party and served as West Germany's first chancellor from 1949 until 1963. Referred to as the "old man" because he did not step down until the age of 85, Adenauer's central goal was to win back Germany's sovereignty and to anchor West Germany in the Western alliance. In this, he was remarkably successful. Helmut Kohl was another important CDU party leader, serving as chancellor from 1982 to 1998, and he is best known for presiding over German unification. In 2005, Angela Merkel (CDU/CSU) became Germany's first female chancellor and the first chancellor to come from the former East Germany. In sum, the CDU/CSU has been an anchor of postwar German democracy and it helped dissolve some of the pre-existing political tensions between Catholics and Protestants.

The Social Democratic Party The other major political party in Germany is the Social Democratic Party (SPD). Unlike the CDU/CSU, the SPD was not a new party. In fact, its founding in 1860 makes it one of the oldest political parties in the world. Bismarck and his successors in the Second Reich tried, unsuccessfully, to stymie the growth of the SPD through repression and co-optation. During the Weimar Republic period, leaders of the SPD were identified with both the "stab in the back" legend and the weakness of German democracy. During the Nazi era, the SPD was banned and many of its leaders were killed or sent to concentration camps. When West Germany regained its independence and held its first elections in 1949, everyone expected the SPD would defeat the CDU/CSU and become the dominant party. After all, it was the one political force in Germany that had not collaborated with the Nazis. However, the CDU/CSU narrowly defeated the SPD in 1949, and the SPD would not win an election until 1966.

These years of electoral loss produced soul-searching by SPD leaders and members. A consensus emerged that the party had failed to win because it had been unable to win support beyond the working class, and that its adherence to some radical economic positions prevented it from expanding its vote base. In 1959, the party dropped its outdated ideology to appeal more to the middle class. Like the CDU/CSU, the SPD chose to water down its ideology in the hopes of becoming a party that could attract voters from all classes and backgrounds.

With both parties adopting this strategy, the ideological distance between the two major parties narrowed considerably and German politics became much less charged than it had been during the Weimar Republic period. In fact, in 1966 the SPD and the CDU/CSU formed their first "grand coalition" and worked together to guide Germany through its first major economic downturn in the postwar period. In 1969, the SPD prevailed over the CDU/CSU in elections for the Bundestag under the leadership of Willy Brandt, and would govern in a coalition with the Free Democratic Party (FDP) until 1982. In 1998, Gerhard Schroeder led the SPD to victory and formed a coalition government for the first time with the Green Party (see below). From 2005–2009, neither the CDU/CSU nor the SPD had enough votes in the Bundestag to lead a coalition government, so once again they formed a grand coalition. In sum, since 1966, the SPD has been in government several times, and formed a coalition with both its major competitor on its right as well as with two other smaller parties (see Table 3.2).

The Free Democratic Party Until 1983, the only three parties represented in the Bundestag were the CDU/CSU, SPD, and the FDP. Between them, the first two parties regularly accounted for close to 90 percent of the seats won. Germany, thus, possessed a "two and a half party system" in which the FDP played the pivotal

TABLE 3.2
Chancellors of the Federal Republic of Germany

Chancellor	Governing Coalition	Years
Konrad Adenauer (CDU)	CDU/CSU, FDP, DP	1949–1953
Adenauer	CDU/CSU, FDP, DP, G	1953–1957
Adenauer	CDU/CSU, FDP, DP/FVP	1957–1961
Adenauer	CDU/CSU, FDP	1961–1963
Ludwig Erhard (CDU)	CDU/CSU, FDP	1963–1966
George Kiesinger (CDU)	CDU/CSU, SPD	1966–1969
Willy Brandt (SPD)	SPD, FDP	1969–1974
Helmut Schmidt (SPD)	SPD, FDP	1974–1982
Helmut Kohl (CDU)	CDU/CSU, FDP	1982–1998
Gerhard Schroeder (SPD)	SPD, Alliance 90/Greens	1998–2005
Angela Merkel (CDU)	CDU/CSU, SPD	2005–2009
Angela Merkel (CDU)	CDU/CSU, FDP	2009–

role between the two major parties of the right and left. The FDP is a liberal party, which in the European context means that it is generally conservative on economic issues (it is, for example, more supportive of a free market and less supportive of the welfare state than is the CDU/CSU) but liberal on social issues. Founded in 1949, the FDP has won between 5 and 10 percent of the seats in the Bundestag and has been the junior coalition partner with both the CDU/CSU and SPD. The structure of the German party system allowed this small party far more influence than its vote share would suggest: by custom, the junior coalition partner receives the important cabinet position of foreign minister, as well as other important posts.

The Greens From the late 1940s until the early 1970s, the core issues in German domestic politics were economic. Political parties competed over who was best able to manage the economy, and the system of tripartite bargaining managed to depoliticize potential conflicts over the distribution of resources. This began to change in the 1970s and 1980s as a series of new political issues arose, and new political actors rose to prominence to represent new types of interests. The economic crises of the 1970s did not pass Germany by, but its system of cooperative capitalism allowed it to weather the crises better than countries like Great Britain or the United States. The SPD and the CDU/CSU continued to compete over which party could best manage the German economy. Yet, most of these new issues had less to do with material resources than they did with quality-of-life and cultural issues. Germans born after the war, who never had to worry about securing their livelihoods, had different political motivations than did the older generation of voters and political activists. New political parties on the left and right formed to represent these interests.

Of the many social movements that formed on the left of the political spectrum in the 1970s and 1980s, the environmental and the peace movements were the most important.[18] The participants in these movements often overlapped, and the two interests became intertwined in their opposition to nuclear power plants and to the stationing of medium-range nuclear weapons on German soil. Of these social movements, the Green Party emerged to become the only party besides the SPD, CDU/CSU, and FDP to enter the Bundestag in 1983, with 5.6 percent of the vote. The Chernobyl disaster of 1986 raised the salience of environmental issues and the dangers of nuclear power, and the Greens raise their vote share to 8.3 percent in the 1987 elections. The party was split between a radical fundamentalist wing that refused to work with other political parties, and a realist wing that was willing to form coalitions with the SPD. In the end, the realists won the inner-party struggle and the Greens joined a German government for the first time as the junior coalition partner in the Schroeder government from 1998 to 2005.

Politicians from the Green Party tried to cut a different profile from their counterparts in other parties. They refused to wear ties and demonstratively rode bicycles to parliamentary sessions. Their emphasis on peace and the environment appealed largely to the highly educated, younger, urban sector of the electorate, and they were considered to be a fairly radical leftist alternative to the SPD when they first appeared.

Over the years, mainstream parties have largely adopted much of the Green's environmental program, forcing the party to adopt other issues in order to remain competitive. One of these issues has been protecting the rights of minorities and militating against the rise of xenophobia, a cultural issue that Germany had obviously experienced before.

Far-Right Parties When immigration became a salient political issue in the late 1980s and early 1990s, several anti-immigrant parties emerged to capitalize on a growing perception among some Germans that foreigners were draining the welfare state, taking jobs from natives, engaging in criminal activity, robbing their country of its cultural unity, or some combination of the above. These views were most prevalent among the least educated segment of the population, as well as among eastern Germans. These anti-immigrant parties attracted enormous domestic and international attention when they won representation in several state parliaments beginning in the late 1980s.[19] International observers warned that Germany was returning to its dark past, and many Germans feared that perhaps they were right. However, none of these parties has ever surmounted the 5 percent hurdle to enter the Bundestag, and there is little sign that they will in the near future.

This is not to downplay the significance of these parties in local politics. The National Democratic Party (NPD) has built strong organizations in some towns in eastern Germany, and cooperates with violent neo-Nazi networks that have attacked and killed foreigners in the past. Yet the legacy of the Nazi past, as well as the monitoring activities of the Office for the Protection of the Constitution, has served as a check on the electoral growth of these far right, anti-immigrant parties.

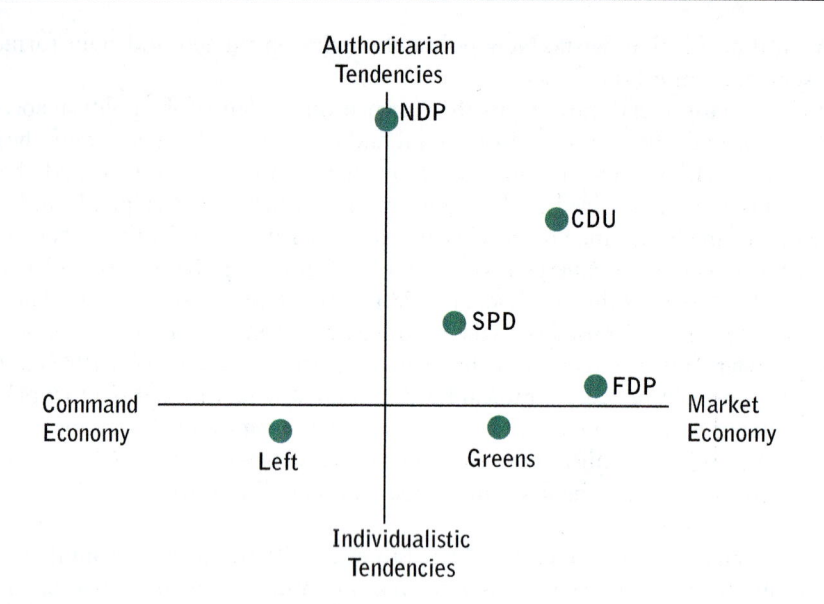

FIGURE 3.1
General Orientations of German Political Parties along Two Dimensions
The positions of German political parties can be represented along two different dimensions: positions toward individual liberty and toward the economy.

Whereas similar parties receive somewhere between 10 to 25 percent of the vote in national parliamentary elections in other European countries, such as in neighboring Austria where the far-right Austrian Freedom Party won nearly 27 percent in 1999 and became a member of the national government, their highest total in an election for the German Bundestag since 1990 has been less than 2 percent. In this sense, the legacy of the Nazi past serves as an additional constraint on extremist politics in Germany and has contributed to the country's political stability.

Far-Left Parties In addition to the Greens and the various far-right parties, the emergence of the left-wing populist party *Die Linke* (the Left) has added further complexity to the German party system. This party was formed through a merger of the Party of Democratic Socialism (PDS) and a splinter group from the SPD (the Labor and Social Justice Alternative or WASG, according to the German acronym), who felt that their former party had betrayed its leftist roots. The PDS was the heir to the East German Communist Party, and the majority of its support came from the former East German provinces in which voters were disillusioned by German unification or were otherwise nostalgic for the old communist regime. More than any other party, it marketed itself as the representative of East German interests and identity. But by merging with WASG, the PDS was able to extend its base beyond former East Germany and Die Linke was able to win almost 12 percent of the vote in the 2009 Bundestag elections. All the other political parties currently treat it as a pariah because of its connection to left-wing extremism and ambiguous relationship to the communist past. Still, its strong recent performance

> **SUMMARY TABLE**
>
> **Creating Domestic Peace after the War**
>
> | | |
> |---|---|
> | **The "Postwar Settlement"** | A set of agreements between business and labor to cooperate on wages and other work-related issues, and support government intervention in markets. |
> | **Political Parties** | Major parties such as the Christian Democrats and Social Democrats reached out beyond their traditional bases, ending the pre-war political polarization. Extremist parties on the left and right are treated as political pariahs, further promoting centrist outcomes. |

suggests that it will remain the fifth member, after the CDU/CSU, SPD, FDP, and Green Party, in Germany's five-party system.

Challenges to the German Model

The last two decades have seen important changes in the German party system, and challenges to the German economic model. As Table 3.3 reveals, while only three political parties won representation in the Bundestag between 1949 and 1983, the fact that five parties can be expected to regularly surmount the 5 percent threshold today means that coalition formation is less predictable than in the past. Yet, this is still a long way from the instability of Weimar democracy.

Economic globalization, particularly competition from countries in which labor costs are cheaper, have placed strains on the German model of coordinated capitalism. Yet, there is little sign that Germany is converging on the United States's model of capitalism, or that its generous welfare state is no longer sustainable.[20] If anything, the financial crisis of 2008 and the resulting recession—the worst since the Great Depression—is helping to reinforce the view that Germany's system allows it to weather economic downturns while minimizing social pain and manifestations of political extremism. The social dislocations produced by the crisis were far less severe in Germany than they were in the United States, or in other advanced industrial countries with a less generous welfare state and a less coordinated model of capitalism. Thus, while economic crisis led to the collapse of the Weimar democracy, there is virtually no possibility of a similar threat to German democracy today. It is even possible that the German model—a model that we have seen arose precisely to save Germany from the trauma of its past—will emerge even stronger from the latest economic challenge.

This section has argued that the social, religious, and partisan conflicts that undermined German democratization in the past have been much better managed since the end of the Second World War. The postwar settlement smoothed relations between owners and workers and gave them both a strong interest in building and preserving a social market economy. The two major political parties (the SPD and the CDU/CSU) have succeeded in attracting a broad spectrum of voters, thereby making the ideological conflicts of the past less intense. Although

TABLE 3.3
Percentage of Second Votes (List Votes) by Party in Bundestag Elections

Year	Christian Democratic Union/Christian Social Union *Christlich Demokratische Union Deutschlands/ Christlich-Soziale Union in Bayern (CDU/CSU)*	Social Democratic Party of Germany *Sozialdemokratische Partei Deutschlands (SPD)*	Free Democratic Party *Frei Demokratische Partei (FDP)*	The Greens *Bündnis 90/ Die Grünen*	Left Party of Democratic Socialism** *Partei des Demokratischen Sozialismus/Die Linke (PDS)*	Others
1949*	31.0	29.2	11.9			27.8
1953	45.2	28.8	9.5			16.5
1957	50.2	31.8	7.7			10.3
1961	45.4	36.2	12.8			5.7
1965	47.6	39.3	9.5			3.6
1969	46.1	42.7	5.8			5.5
1972	44.9	45.8	8.4			0.9
1976	48.6	42.6	7.9			0.9
1980	44.5	42.9	10.6			2.0
1983	48.6	38.2	7.0	5.6		0.5
1987	44.3	37.0	9.1	8.3		1.4
1990	43.8	33.5	11.0	5.0	2.4***	4.2
1994	41.5	36.4	6.9	7.3	4.4	3.6
1998	35.1	40.9	6.2	6.7	5.1	5.9
2002	38.5	38.5	7.4	8.6	4.0	3.0
2005	35.2	34.2	9.8	8.1	8.7	3.9
2009	33.8	23.0	14.6	10.7	11.9	6.0

Source: The Federal Returning Officer of the Federal Republic of Germany. http://www.bundeswahlleiter.de/en/

* Voters only cast a first vote in the 1949 elections.

** The results are for the PDS from 1990–2002, and for the Left thereafter.

*** The results for the PDS in the 1990, 1994, and 2002 elections are reported because although the party did not overcome the 5 percent threshold, it won enough first votes in these elections to win seats in the Bundestag.

other political parties now compete for voters, and although changes in the international economy may reshape the German model of capitalism, the ways in which interests have been defined and represented since the end of World War II have helped democracy work in Germany.

CONCLUSION

We began this country study with a central question: how did Germany overcome its turbulent history to become a strong and stable democracy? We developed our answer by looking at how Germany reacted to the experience of Nazism in particular, and how institutions, identities, and interests were reshaped in order to prevent any type of political extremism from coming to power.

The Basic Law was a clear response to the deficiencies of the Weimar Republic. Although it was originally conceived as provisional, the institutional architecture that it created has served Germany extraordinarily well. It allows for the formation of a government that is effective, in the sense that it is likely to serve out its entire term in office and have its legislation approved by the Bundestag. Yet, the power of the government is limited by the institutions of German federalism, the constitutional court, and by general patterns of interest representation that all serve to favor coordination and incremental change over decisive action.

The smooth functioning of German institutions, combined with the economic prosperity of the 1950s and 1960s, helped to reshape German political attitudes and collective identities. Whereas German political culture helped undermine the Weimar Republic, one cannot say that contemporary Germany is a "democracy without democrats."

Finally, the central political cleavages that produced instability and contributed to democratic breakdown in the 1920s and 1930s have been transformed through the actions of political parties and through the postwar settlement. The major political parties of left and right dropped their rigid ideologies of the interwar period and tried to appeal to as many voters as possible. The German model of coordinated capitalism represents a compromise between business and labor. The interests of major groups in German society may not be identical, but they have been brought closer together than at any point in German history.

Although contemporary German politics may be far less dramatic than it was in the past, it still raises a number of intriguing questions for students of comparative politics. To what extent are international economic pressures, as well as the process of European integration, forcing changes in Germany's economic model? How might we measure how well Germany is integrating its immigrant population, and what might the consequences of successful versus unsuccessful integration be for German politics and society? Will German voters continue to vote against political parties that represent extremist positions, or will economic hardship, lingering resentment over unification, and cultural tensions between immigrants and natives bolster the types of movements that have succeeded in other countries of Western Europe? These and other questions will continue to make Germany a fascinating laboratory for political scientists.

✓ Study and Review the Post-Test & Chapter Exam at mypoliscilab.com

KEY TERMS

Weimar Republic　78
Otto von Bismarck　79
Reichstag　79
Social Democratic Party　79
Article 48　83
Nazism　85
Federal Republic of Germany (FRG)　86
German Democratic Republic (GDR)　86
Basic Law　88
Bundestag　88
constructive vote of no confidence　89
Bundesrat　89
Federal Constitutional Court　91
Länder　91
wall in the head　98
ius sanguinis　99
guestworkers (*Gastarbeiter*)　99
ius soli　101
postwar settlement　103
co-determination　104

REVIEW QUESTIONS

1. Explain why the Second Reich underwent rapid economic growth, yet failed to liberalize politically. Consider the characteristics of Germany's identity, institutions, and interests at the time.
2. What were two important flaws of the Weimar Constitution?
3. How has Germany's history, specifically the Weimar Republic and the Holocaust, influenced the provisions of the Basic Law?
4. Compare and contrast Germany's attitude toward immigration to that of the United States. How do its history and present attitudes differ from that of the United States? How are they similar?
5. In what ways is capitalism in Germany organized differently than in the United States? Is this model sustainable in a more globalized world? Why or why not?

SUGGESTED READINGS

Ash, Timothy Garton. *The File*. New York: Vintage, 1998. In this investigative memoir, a well-known British scholar of Germany examines the file that the Stasi kept on him.

Berman, Sheri. "Civil Society and the Collapse of the Weimar Republic." *World Politics* 49, 3 (1997): 401–429. This article argues that German clubs and voluntary organizations were captured by the Nazis and helped them to gain power in Weimar Germany.

Craig, Gordon. *The Politics of the Prussian Army*. Oxford: Oxford University Press, 1955. The classic study of the rise of militarism in Prussian politics and society.

Elo, Kimmo. "The Left Party and Long-Term Developments in the German Party System." *German Politics and Society* 26, 3 (2008): 50–68. Argues that the SPD will need to rethink its strategy in dealing with the left.

Hamilton, Richard. *Who Voted for Hitler?* Princeton: Princeton University Press, 1982. This book examines which social groups voted for Hitler, and why.

Wiliarty, Sarah Elise. "Chancellor Angela Merkel—A Sign of Hope or an Exception That Proves the Rule." *Politics and Gender* 4 (2008): 485–496. This article traces the political rise of Merkel and argues that her success is the product of a very specific set of circumstances.

NOTES

1. Gordon Craig, *The Politics of the Prussian Army* (New York: Oxford University Press, 1955).
2. Gregory Luebbert, *Liberalism, Fascism, or Social Democracy* (New York: Oxford University Press, 1991).
3. A. J. P. Taylor, *Bismarck: The Man and the Statesman* (New York: Vintage Books, 1955).
4. John Moses, *The Politics of Illusion: The Fischer Controversy in German Historiography* (London: Prior, 1975).
5. Henry Ashby Turner, *Hitler's Thirty Days to Power* (New York: Addison-Wesley, 1996)
6. Robert Gellately, *The Gestapo and German Society* (Oxford: Clarendon Press, 1990).
7. Peter Katzenstein, ed. *Tamed Power: Germany in Europe* (Ithaca: Cornell University Press, 1997).
8. Geoff Eley, *Reshaping the German Right* (New Haven: Yale University Press, 1980).
9. Rogers Brubaker, *Citizenship and Nationhood in France and Germany* (Cambridge: Harvard University Press, 1992).
10. William Sheridan Allen. *The Nazi Seizure of Power: The Experience of a Single German Town* (Danbury, CT: Children's Press, 1984).
11. David Art, *The Politics of the Nazi Past in Germany and Austria* (New York: Cambridge University Press, 2006).
12. David P. Conradt. *The German Polity* (New York: Pearson Longman, 2005)
13. Sheri Berman, *The Primacy of Politics* (New York: Cambridge University Press, 2006).
14. See Kathleen Thelen, *Union of Parts: Labor Politics in Postwar Germany* (Ithaca, NY: Cornell University Press, 1991).
15. Alexander Gerschenkron, *Bread and Democracy in Germany* (Berkeley: University of California Press, 1943).
16. Andrei S. Markovits, ed. *The Political Economy of Germany: Modell Deutschland* (New York: Praeger, 1982).
17. Peter Hall and David Soskice, eds, *Varieties of Capitalism: The Institutional Foundations of Comparative Advantage* (Oxford: Oxford University Press, 2001).
18. Andrei Markovits and Philip Gorski, *The German Left: Red, Green and Beyond* (Cambridge: Polity Press, 1993).
19. David Art, *Inside the Radical Right: The Development of Anti-Immigrant Parties in Western Europe* (New York: Cambridge University Press, 2011).
20. Jonas Pontusson, *Inequality and Prosperity: Social Europe vs. Liberal America* (Ithaca: Cornell University Press, 2005).

CHAPTER 4

France

Erik Bleich

A French Muslim woman wearing a *niqab* protests the 2010 ban.

> **Why do French citizens engage in such frequent and dramatic forms of protest?**

INTRODUCTION TO FRANCE

In 1789, just as the United States was putting the finishing touches on its Constitution, France went through a violent revolution against monarchical rule. Since then, the French have maintained a strong tradition of collective action and aggressive protest. For example, in May 1968, the entire country ground to a halt for weeks as students and workers went on strike. In 1986, hundreds of thousands of high school and college students marched to oppose the government's suggested changes to the education system. A 1995 protest against proposed reductions in government welfare benefits brought millions to the streets to resist the government's plans. And in 2009, a one-day strike against the government's approach to the economic crisis mobilized over 1 million workers. France has also repeatedly experienced a wide variety of smaller strikes, marches, blockades, and other forms of political protest that have disrupted daily life and upset the political sphere.

These events raise the question: *why do French citizens engage in such frequent and dramatic forms of protest?* The logic of collective action suggests that it can be difficult to mobilize people for a cause, especially when the undertaking is risky, illegal, or has uncertain hope of success. France is a functioning democracy, with the world's eighth-largest economy, generous government-provided social welfare benefits, and a leadership role in the European Union—so why the recurrence of mass strikes, clashes with police, and dramatic symbolic anti-government activities? France is not a society constantly in tumult, nor is it alone among developed democracies in dealing with protest. But given the profile and intensity of such events, France provides an excellent site for examining the causes of such extreme forms of political participation.

This chapter explores several possible explanations for French protest dynamics. We begin by reviewing France's turbulent history to demonstrate that upheavals have been part of French politics for centuries. We examine how France's political institutions—which are more centralized than those of the United States or Germany—focus protestors who feel excluded from the political process on a clear target. Next, key political identities in France such as class divisions, nationalistic tendencies, principles of church–state separation, and a general sympathy for protest serve as foundations for agitation. And finally, French interest groups such as unions, student organizations, and anti-racist groups bring protestors together in both coordinated and spontaneous ways to fight for their goals. It is the combination of French history, institutions, identities, and interests that produces a distinctive French way of "doing protest" that sets the country apart from other liberal democracies.

FRANCE

FRANCE IN COMPARISON

	United Kingdom	Germany	France	Japan	India	Mexico	Russia	Nigeria	China	Iran
Freedom House Classification	Democracy	Democracy	Democracy	Democracy	Democracy	Partial democracy	Partial democracy	Partial democracy	Non-democracy	Non-democracy
Land Size (sq km)	243,610	357,022	643,801	377,915	3,287,263	1,964,375	17,098,242	923,768	9,596,961	1,648,195
Land Size Ranking	79	62	42	61	7	15	1	32	4	18
Population (July 2011 Estimate)	62,698,362	81,471,834	65,312,249	126,475,664	1,189,172,906	113,724,226	138,739,892	155,215,573	1,336,718,015	77,891,220
Population Ranking	22	16	21	10	2	11	9	8	1	18
Life Expectancy (Years)	80.05	80.07	81.19	82.25	66.8	76.47	66.29	47.56	74.68	70.1
Life Expectancy Ranking	28	27	13	5	51	72	162	220	95	146
Literacy Rate	99%	99%	99%	99%	61%	86.1%	99.4%	68%	91.6%	77%
GDP Per Capita (2010 Estimate)	US$35,100	US$35,900	US$33,300	US$34,000	US$3,500	US$13,800	US$15,900	US$2,500	US$7,600	US$11,200
GDP Ranking	36	32	39	38	163	85	71	178	126	100

HISTORICAL OVERVIEW OF FRANCE

4.1 What are the historical precedents for French protest?

Watch the Video "Anglo-French Union" at mypoliscilab.com

To begin to answer the chapter question, it is helpful to examine France's history because it provides a common point of reference and inspiration for groups engaged in contentious politics. Pushing back against the authority of the state and overturning the established political order has been far more common in France since the late 1700s than in the United States. For example, Americans have lived under one constitution since that time, but France has cycled through a dozen or more regimes, ranging from monarchies to constitutional democracies. This history of dramatic revolution, revolt, and protest helps shapes the context of politics in France today, and it helps French citizens justify the contentious forms of political participation that often grab world headlines.

From the Middle Ages to the *Ancien Régime*

In the 1400s, France was not much more than a mishmash of overlapping political entities, with local authorities loosely controlling their own claimed territories. By the 1500s, however, the territory we think of today as "France" began to take shape, especially under the rule of Henri IV (1589–1610). In 1598, Henri IV ended internal conflict by issuing the Edict of Nantes, which granted Protestants limited religious freedoms in what remains a largely Catholic country.

France subsequently flourished in the 1600s and 1700s as a military, cultural, and economic powerhouse. Sovereignty was also consolidated under the leadership of kings such as Louis XIV (1643–1715), who forged a relatively efficient government bureaucracy to administer the whole country. This marked a significant departure from the previous norm of allocating high offices to friends, relatives, and wealthy nobility, who would often abuse their powers by mixing bribery with tax and duty collection according to whim.

In the 1600s, France's central government administration was, by comparison, much more stable and powerful than that of its closest rival, Great Britain, but this did not mean that the French state had fully modernized. Prior to the 1789 Revolution—referred to as the *Ancien Régime*, or the old regime—political power was divided among three core groups: the monarchy, the aristocracy, and the clergy. In addition to the authority of the king, land-owning aristocratic nobles continued to dominate France politically and economically, leaving rural peasants, urban workers, and the rising middle class largely powerless. During this time, the Catholic Church held substantial tracts of tax-exempt property that also limited farmers' access to tillable land and greatly reduced the central government's tax revenue.

Adding to the challenges of the time, kings Louis XIV and Louis XV (1715–1774) involved France in a series of colonial wars and European campaigns that lasted from the mid-seventeenth to the mid-eighteenth century. This led to mounting state debts that generated pressure for unsustainable new taxes. Eventually, in an effort to open the door for extracting even more tax from his subjects, Louis XVI (1774–1792) was forced to call the first meeting in over 150 years of the Estates-General—a meeting of representatives from the clergy, the nobility, and the middle classes. But by 1789, any additional burdens

Ancien Régime ■ a term coined during the French Revolution to refer derisively to the "old regime," or the time prior to 1789 when kings ruled with absolute power and when the clergy and nobility were also strong forces in French society.

Estates-General ■ a meeting of representatives from the clergy, the nobility, and the middle classes on the common people and middle class seemed unbearable, and the calling of the Estates-General served to launch debates about completely overhauling the monarchical regime.

The French Revolution and Its Aftermath

The assembly of the Estates-General in 1789 occurred against the backdrop of the Enlightenment, a period of time during which French thinkers such as Descartes, Montesquieu, Diderot, Rousseau, and Voltaire advocated the concepts of democracy and individual freedom over the traditional authority of kings. News of the success of the American Revolution, also based on the ideals of the Enlightenment, sparked further debates about the future of the French monarchy. Combined with the terrible economic stresses of the era, the French middle class began to demand greater access to political power and change.

As tensions rose between groups assembled at the Estates-General, a mob stormed the Bastille prison in Paris on July 14, 1789. With the fall of the medieval fortress, the citizens of Paris dealt a symbolic blow against the king's authority and the established elites of the *Ancien Régime*. The event represented a turning point between parliamentary debate and open insurrection, and it marked the beginning of the French Revolution. Within the next decade, the country would experience a tumult of changing political systems:

- From 1789–1792, a **constitutional monarchy**, which constrained the previous absolute authority of the monarch with a set of rules embodied in a written constitution that granted primary power to the National Assembly, which represented the middle classes;
- From 1792–1795, a **republic**, which deposed the king and granted all power to representatives chosen by universal male suffrage, but which eventually degenerated into a dictatorship when confronted with counter-revolution at home and invasion from abroad;
- And from 1795–1799, a **constitutional dictatorship** (known as the Directory) run by a small committee of leaders who deposed the previous authorities in an effort to restore order and which eventually culminated in a 1799 *coup d'état* by Napoleon Bonaparte, a popular and successful general who crowned himself emperor in 1804 and ruled until 1814.

The rapidly shifting and extremely unstable governing structures during this time period were often determined by mass mobilization against perceived oppression and by leaders who imposed their will by force.

It is impossible to underestimate the importance of this era for France. The French Revolution and its aftermath marked European and world politics for decades. Unlike the American Revolution, France had been ruled for centuries by kings. Its citizens did not just overthrow a king and anoint another in 1789—they overthrew an entire system of government, along with the only political and social culture the people had ever known. The ideas of "Liberty, Equality, and Fraternity"—the motto of the revolution that remains France's national motto to this day—replaced long-held values associated with monarchy such as

constitutional monarchy ■ a democratic system in which a monarch serves as head of state, symbolically embodying the culture and values of a state's citizens and history, yet operates under the rules and constraints imposed by a written constitution.

republic ■ a form of government that relies on rule by the people through their representatives.

constitutional dictatorship ■ strong rule by one or more leaders who are nominally constrained by a written constitution approved by the people through their representatives.

obedience to one's supposed social betters. In the process of protecting their interests, the French people were redefining their institutions as well as their identity. The wrenching process of the French Revolution generated widespread violence across the country, as various factions vied to control the reins of power. Yet, the revolution firmly established the notion in France that political protest can be a powerful tool for changing the world.

Regime Change in the Nineteenth Century

Political unrest followed the revolution and endured in France over the next 150 years (see the summary table on the following page). After Napoleon's downfall, first in 1814 and ultimately in 1815 following his defeat at Waterloo, the Bourbon monarchy was restored to power. However, in 1830 an uprising replaced the Bourbon-ancestral line of monarchs with another, the Orleans. In 1848, another revolution overthrew the Orleans monarchy and led to the brief rule of the Second Republic. In 1851, Louis Napoleon (the nephew of Napoleon Bonaparte) staged a coup d'état to end the Second Republic and declared himself emperor the following year. In 1870, he was captured by German forces during the Franco-Prussian War and deposed. In the early 1870s, French factions jockeyed with each other for the power to decide what regime should come next. The French Third Republic emerged out of this turmoil in 1875, described unenthusiastically at the time by head of state Adolphe Thiers as "the form of government that divides France the least." As is obvious, protest, upheaval, and big political changes were integral to French history from the late eighteenth to the late nineteenth century.

Consolidating Democracy in the Twentieth Century

The French people did not immediately embrace the Third Republic, but it endured from 1875 until 1940—the longest-lasting French form of government since the *Ancien Régime*. The Third Republic ended with France's sudden and catastrophic defeat at the hands of Nazi Germany in 1940. At that time, the Nazis took direct control of the northern portion of France and set up the puppet **Vichy regime** (named after its capital) in the south of the country. The Vichy leadership preached authoritarian values and collaborated with the Nazis; it deported Jews to concentration camps and provided supplies and workers for the German war effort. Although most French citizens did not stand up to the regime, some did. Within France, small bands of resistance fighters did their best to undermine the fascist system. From abroad, General Charles de Gaulle organized the Free French Forces and led the effort to discredit the Vichy regime.

After the war, de Gaulle was appointed the provisional leader of the transition government. France would revert to a democracy, but not without another heated debate over the form it should take. De Gaulle was unable to convince his fellow citizens that the fragmented institutions of the Third Republic had directly contributed to France's vulnerability in the face of the Nazi onslaught, yet given the Vichy years, many remained leery of strong centralized political power. In the end, French voters narrowly approved the constitution of the **Fourth Republic** which essentially

Vichy regime ■ the Nazi-sympathizing puppet state set up in the southern part of France from 1940–1944.

Fourth Republic ■ the French political regime that lasted from 1946–1958. It was characterized by great political instability.

SUMMARY TABLE

Historical Overview: Political Turbulence and Regime Change in France Since the Late Middle Ages

Late Middle Ages–1789	*Ancien Régime*	Ended with onset of French Revolution
1789–1792	Constitutional monarchy	Ended with deposing of Louis XVI
1792–1795	First Republic	Ended with the execution of its radical leaders
1795–1799	The Directory	Ended with the a coup by Napoleon Bonaparte
1799–1814	Consulate and First Empire (Napoleon Bonaparte)	Ended with foreign invasion toppling Napoleon
1814–1830	Bourbon Restoration	Ended with domestic uprising overthrowing the monarch
1830–1848	Orleans monarchy	Ended with demonstrations and protests by Parisians
1848–1852	Second Republic	Ended with coup d'état by Louis Napoleon
1852–1870	Second Empire (Louis Napoleon)	Ended with Louis Napoleon's capture in the Franco-Prussian War
1870–1875	Provisional governments	A transition period toward the Third Republic
1875–1940	Third Republic	Ended with defeat by Germany in World War II
1940–1944	Vichy France	Ended with Allied invasion of Europe
1946–1958	Fourth Republic	Ended due to crisis of Algerian War
1958–present	Fifth Republic	

reestablished institutions similar to those of the Third Republic: a parliamentary democracy in which power rested in the lower house of parliament. The Fourth Republic was successful in putting France on a path toward economic recovery, especially through its state-led economic policies known as *dirigisme* (pronounced dee-ree-jhee´-smuh). It also fostered a healthy relationship with Germany in the aftermath of World War II and helped launch the European Economic Community (which later became the European Union) as one of the six original signatories of the 1957 Treaty of Rome. However, because most mainstream political parties lacked broad popular support, the Fourth Republic witnessed a seemingly endless string of fragile coalition governments that fell apart more than 20 times in just 12 years.

The constant political turnover generated significant instability during this period, which the country could never quite surmount. In particular, the Fourth

dirigisme ■ an economic strategy that involves the state providing significant leadership in the capitalist economy through policies such as indicative plans and selective support for favored industries.

France tried but failed to keep control of Algeria during a war that lasted from 1954 to 1962. France's failure in this war led to the collapse of the Fourth Republic and to the birth of the Fifth Republic under the initial leadership of General Charles de Gaulle.

Republic proved unable to cope with uprisings against French colonial authority in Indochina (Vietnam) and in North Africa. Like other European powers, France had acquired these territories—and many others around the world—in the eighteenth and nineteenth centuries. Yet unlike neighboring Britain, which ceded control of most of its overseas empire without a fight after World War II, France considered its possessions integral to its national interests and was determined to hang on to them.

Chief among its colonies was Algeria, which lay just across the Mediterranean Sea from the southern French coast. From 1848 until 1962, Algeria was officially part of France, much in the same way Alaska is part of the United States. Yet, its inhabitants were primarily Muslims of North African origin who did not all have the same rights as the European colonizers. Frustrated with these long-standing inequalities, resistance groups launched a revolutionary war for independence in 1954. The French government responded to unrest in Algeria by fighting back, even though divisions within the army and within the French government about whether and how to maintain France's overseas empire meant that by 1958 French politics had deadlocked over how to proceed. The political situation grew so uncertain that elements within France's military forces threatened a coup d'état against the democratically elected civilian government. This outcome was averted only when civilian leaders called de Gaulle out of retirement to lead the country. De Gaulle accepted on the condition that he be granted extraordinary political powers in the short term and that he be allowed to rewrite the French constitution. By October 1958, he had done just that, giving birth to the French **Fifth Republic**, whose institutions have lasted through today.

French history has involved considerable political turmoil—more so than many of France's neighbors, especially Great Britain. Revolutions, political protest, coups d'états, rebellions, and threats of greater unrest have been integral to French politics since the French Revolution in 1789. Protest has sparked significant changes to French politics, including complete changes in political regime. This sets France apart from most other European countries and has imbued its citizens with a sense of the importance of political action. It is too simple to say that this history is the sole explanation for collective action, or that history dictates protest in modern France. But the legacy of these protests provides encouragement to protestors in France, who see themselves as part of a long-standing national tradition of standing up to their leaders in an effort to enact important change.

Fifth Republic ■
the current political regime of France, established by the Constitution of 1958.

INSTITUTIONS OF FRANCE

If we want to know why the French engage in such frequent and dramatic forms of protest, we also have to examine France's institutions. State institutions have a direct bearing on which people are represented, how loudly different voices are heard, and how citizens' interests are transformed into concrete policy outcomes. These aspects of political institutions can impact the likelihood of intense protest. For example, if groups of citizens can achieve their goals by voting for political parties or by lobbying influential spokespeople, they are much less likely to burn cars, blockade highways, or march on government ministries. On the other hand, if some segments of society feel that they cannot get within earshot of their leaders, they may turn to more disruptive politics to express themselves and capture attention.

France is a clear-cut example of a democracy that consistently receives a "Free" rating from Freedom House. Moreover, French government institutions for the most part successfully balance limited and effective government. The government has strong legitimacy, stability, efficacy, and efficiency when it comes to getting things done, and it permits high levels of popular sovereignty, participation, contestation, civil rights, and accountability—the central ingredients of limited government. However, more than in many other democracies, French political institutions tend to concentrate decision-making power in the hands of a few and they tend to deflect or ignore input from a number of societal groups. Because some groups feel frozen out of the traditional political process, they frequently turn to contentious forms of political participation—at times including violent protest—to make their views known and to force the government to take them into account.

To get a better sense of how France's political institutions concentrate power, restrict decision-making access, and help generate protest, we will examine how the French constitution allocates political power in the Fifth Republic, how its

4.2 How responsive is the French government to its people's protests?

Explore the Comparative "Chief Executives" at mypoliscilab.com electoral institutions work, and how its leaders and citizens connect to the political process. Examining the distribution of political power sheds light on why some social groups feel left out, and why resorting to protest and other forms of contentious politics has become so common.

Semi-Presidential Democracy and the Executive Branch

In 1958, Charles de Gaulle created a new constitution that ushered in the Fifth Republic, a semi-presidential system of government. The system features separation of origin, in that voters cast one vote to directly elect members of the lower house of parliament, known as the **National Assembly**, and, as of 1962, another for the president. The semi-presidential system involves a dual executive, which means that there is both a president and a prime minister, each with real power in the political process. The president selects the prime minister, but the prime minister must also have majority support in the National Assembly. The National Assembly cannot remove a sitting president, but it can remove a sitting prime minister through a majority vote of no-confidence.

National Assembly ■ the lower house of parliament in France; its members are directly elected by the citizens; it supports but can also vote to remove the prime minister.

In most circumstances, the majority in the National Assembly is from the same political party as the president. In this case, the president has complete control over who becomes prime minister. This principle was confirmed in 1962 when the parliament voted no-confidence on President de Gaulle's choice for prime minister. In response, de Gaulle used his presidential power to dissolve the National Assembly, forcing its members to stand for reelection. When the election resulted in an outcome favorable to the president, he simply reappointed the prime minister whom he had initially selected. Although the prime minister in the Fifth Republic has many important tasks, such as navigating legislation through the parliament, in normal times it is the president who has the principal authority and power to lead the executive branch.

However, the Fifth Republic constitution left open the possibility that the National Assembly majority and the president would represent different political parties. Until 2002, the president served a seven-year term, whereas the National Assembly members stood for election at least once every five years. In 1986, five years into François Mitterrand's presidency, the voters rejected his Socialist Party in legislative elections and returned an opposition coalition to power in the National Assembly. This inaugurated the first period of **cohabitation**, in which the left and right shared executive power—one party held the presidency while the other held the majority in the National Assembly. In these instances, the National Assembly had the power to choose the prime minister, while the president influenced who was appointed to lead the foreign affairs and defense ministries. As a result, the president retained primary responsibility for representing France and its interests at the international level while the prime minister controlled domestic affairs.

cohabitation ■ when the president and the majority in the National Assembly (and, thus, the prime minister) come from political parties on opposite sides of the political divide.

Since the creation of the Fifth Republic in 1958, there have been three periods of cohabitation, amounting to approximately nine years. This means that executive power has been concentrated in the hands of one person (the president), and one political party most of the time. In 2000, parliament amended France's constitution to reduce the presidential term by two years to align it with the five-year term of the National Assembly, a change that took effect starting with the 2002 presidential and parliamentary elections. This dramatically decreased the likelihood of future episodes of cohabitation. The effect of this reform is to further concentrate political power in the hands of the French president, who will preside over a National Assembly that almost certainly will always contain a majority of members sympathetic to the president's party.

Whether under unified government or cohabitation, the Fifth Republic's constitution concentrates political power in the executive branch. By executive branch, we mean the president and his prime minister and cabinet. This skewed distribution of power was an intentional response to the relatively weak executive branch under the Fourth Republic, which many blamed as the source of the regime's political instability and ineffectiveness. Most of the major decisions of the French government are put on the agenda by the executive branch.

The strength of the executive branch is reflected in France's policymaking process. The president or prime minister typically launches an initiative by proposing a bill for parliamentary review. The legislature has the opportunity to debate the bill and to suggest amendments, and though it can delay the legislation, there are institutional provisions that make it difficult for the parliament to stop legislation deemed critical by the government. For example, Article 44 of the constitution enshrines the right of the government to force a vote on any piece of legislation that contains only the amendments approved by the government. This blocked vote provision prevents excessive or unfriendly amendments by legislators. Article 45 allows the government to shape the final form of a bill whenever the lower and upper houses cannot agree on a common text. Perhaps most dramatically, Article 49-3 of the constitution permits the government simply to declare legislation as officially adopted into law unless the National Assembly passes a resolution of no-confidence against the government. These powerful governmental tools are not deployed frequently, but the mere threat of their use constrains the legislature and strengthens the government's hand in negotiations over legislation. Once a bill has been passed by the legislature, there is a brief window before it enters into force during which the president, the prime minister, the leaders of the National Assembly and the Sénat, or 60 members of either the upper or lower chamber can appeal the outcome to the Constitutional Council if they feel that the law violates the constitution. This overall policymaking process contrasts sharply with the American system, where members of Congress have a much greater ability to initiate, amend, and influence legislation.

Within the executive branch, elite government bureaucrats also help craft key policies. The upper echelon of the national bureaucracy has considerable influence in France. Its members are the cream of the crop of students trained at highly selective institutions of higher education known as the *grandes écoles*. These students undertake a rigorous academic program and once they graduate, the most highly ranked recruits leapfrog over many of their elders to top positions in the Ministries of Finance, Foreign Affairs, or other critical posts. Some make their careers in the civil service, while others become political leaders or executives at large firms. Around half of all prime ministers of the Fifth Republic and several presidents attended the *grandes écoles*. This system produces highly capable leaders, but it can also serve to limit input from new or different voices.

Sénat ■ the indirectly elected upper house of parliament; it can delay but cannot block legislation and cannot remove either the president or the prime minister.

grandes écoles ■ the elite, highly selective, specialized universities in France that train many of the country's upper echelon of civil servants, politicians, and business leaders.

The Legislative Branch

The bicameral legislature is composed of the directly elected lower house, the National Assembly, and the indirectly elected upper house, the Sénat. Like presidents, National Assembly members serve five-year terms although the president has the power to dissolve the body and call for early elections. The electoral institutions for other French representative bodies—such as the upper house of parliament, as well as regional, district, and local governments—differ substantially from the system for the presidential and National Assembly elections. Most of the nearly 350 members of the Sénat, for example, are indirectly elected—primarily by local elected authorities—for six-year terms, with one half elected every three years.

Members of the National Assembly and the Sénat play an important role in discussing legislation, and they can at times suggest amendments to bills passing through their chambers. At least until a constitutional amendment that took effect in 2009, however, their ability to set the agenda by initiating proposals was relatively limited. The National Assembly is not simply a rubber stamp, but if you are

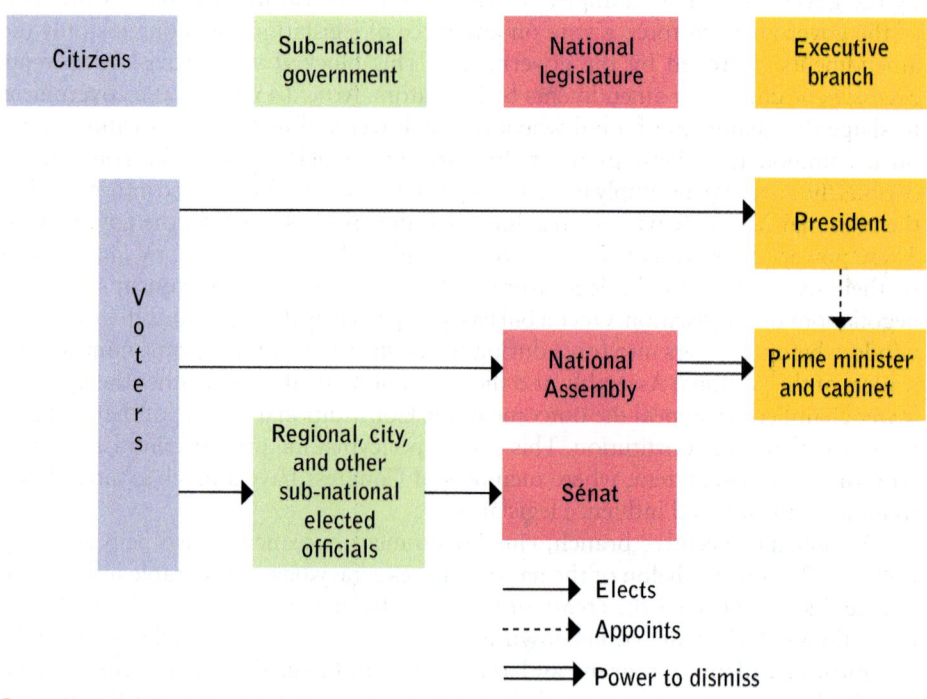

FIGURE 4.1
France's Structure of Government

French voters are linked to their national-level political leaders through three separate pathways. They directly elect the president and their representatives in the National Assembly. But the prime minister is appointed by the president and is ultimately responsible before the National Assembly, and senators are elected primarily by local officials.

a French citizen considering a career in politics and your ambitions are to hold the reins of power, a term in the legislature is at best a way-station while you wait to be called up to the major leagues of the executive branch, and especially to one of the most powerful ministries such as Interior, Foreign Affairs, Finance, or Economy.

The Judicial Branch

The third branch of government—the judiciary—acts as modest brake upon executive power. Most importantly, the Constitutional Council has some authority to review legislation. Every three years, the president of France and the leaders of the upper and lower houses of parliament choose one distinguished public figure each, appointing three Council members for nine-year terms. The result is a nine-person Council, although this number can grow because former French presidents are also entitled to membership. The Constitutional Council is empowered to rule on whether legislation conforms to the constitution, and has become an important part of the policymaking process in the past few decades.

Constitutional Council ■ the body of the judiciary tasked with reviewing legislation, to ensure that it conforms to the constitution.

From 1958 until the early 1970s, the Constitutional Council was virtually impotent, since only the president, the prime minister, and the leader of the National Assembly or Sénat had the ability to submit legislation for review. This meant that the Council was not very active, as none of those actors has any particular interest in having unelected judges review the legality of bills already passed. In 1974, a constitutional reform allowed 60 members of either house of parliament to appeal legislation to the Constitutional Council. This made it possible for opposition parties to send any controversial item to the Council for review, and it significantly increased the independence and influence of this arm of the judicial branch. Currently, approximately 10 percent of all legislation—and particularly any controversial law—is sent to the Council for review, and almost half of the statutes it scrutinizes are found at least partly incompatible with the Constitution and must be amended before being enacted into law.

However, the power of the Constitutional Council remains limited in important ways compared to that of the U.S. Supreme Court. In the United States, any citizen can appeal a case to the Supreme Court. In France, until 2010, only politicians could initiate the review process, and they could only do it during the brief window between parliamentary approval of a law and the president's promulgation of the law into force. The Constitutional Council has, therefore, acted primarily as a partial brake on the government, but it is hardly the powerful counterweight that judiciaries have become in some other democracies. This situation is currently evolving, however, as a constitutional revision enforced as of 2010 allows other French judicial bodies to submit constitutional questions to the Council after the statute has gone into force. Whether this change will have a significant effect on the functioning of the Constitutional Council is not yet clear.

The concentration of power in the executive branch and in the central government is striking when compared to the system of the Fourth Republic and compared to federal countries like the United States or Germany. Even so, it would be wrong to view France as completely dominated by the central government in Paris. In the 1980s, the government decentralized some authority to regions, districts, and localities, granting elected bodies of these sub-national areas greater power over policies pertaining to local economic development, transportation, the environment, consumer protection, and workplace health and safety.

France's participation in the European Union has also encroached upon the central government's ability to do as it pleases. As an EU member, France must conform to legislative, bureaucratic, and judicial decisions taken at the transnational level at EU headquarters. The French government has a strong hand in many of those outcomes, but EU decisions are not always exactly what the French government prefers. These domestic and international changes have chipped away at France's image as a highly centralized state. However, Paris still retains a lot of power. In some democratic countries, such as the United States, citizens take complaints to the city council, or the state legislature, or other local government bodies. Yet in France, the central government still calls the shots for most important policy decisions.

Electoral Institutions

majority rule ■ a political institution that requires candidates obtain a majority of 50 percent + 1 of the votes in the district to win.

France has a two-round **majority rule** system for presidential and National Assembly elections. Candidates need 50 percent + 1 of the votes to be elected to office in the first round. Because it is not typical for a politician to assemble a majority of votes in a field of many candidates, there is usually a second round runoff election that

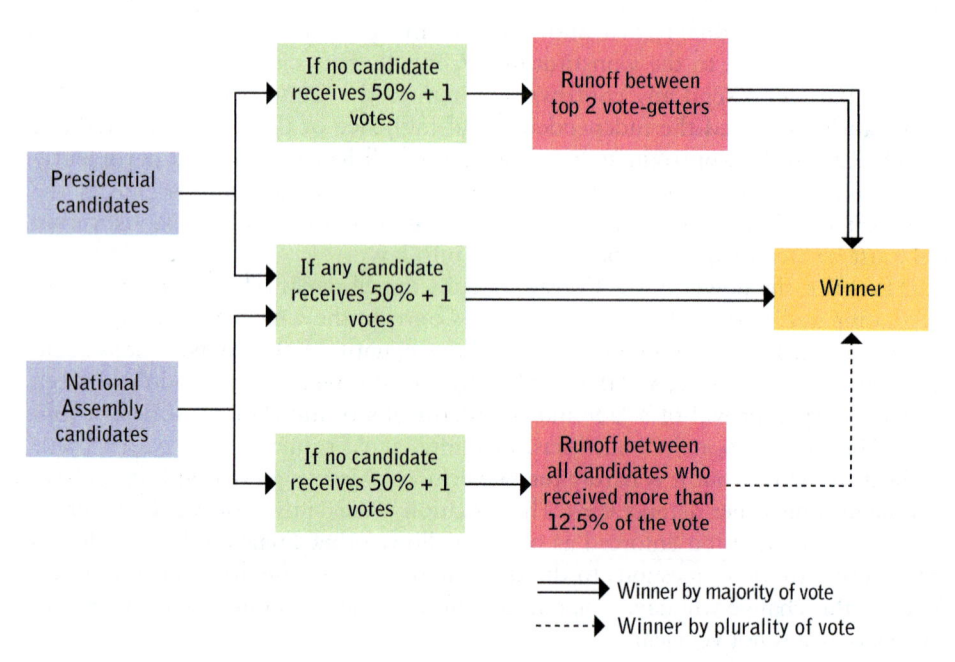

FIGURE 4.2

The Two-Round French Electoral System

Any candidate who receives over 50 percent of the vote in the first round of the election is the winner. If no candidate surpasses this hurdle, there is a second round runoff election. For presidential elections, the top two vote-getters move on. For the National Assembly, any politician who receives more than 12.5 percent of the first-round vote is eligible to run in the second round.

decides a winner between the top two vote-getters from the first round in presidential elections, or between any candidate receiving more than 12.5 percent of the vote for National Assembly elections. This system lets voters express their true first preference in the first round and it offers fringe parties an opportunity to appeal to relatively narrow segments of the population. However, because most unpopular politicians are forced out or marginalized after the first vote, it also makes it easier for centrist candidates to win in the second round. To further maximize their chances of winning the second round, main parties of the left and right usually agree to nominate only one candidate each.

For example, the first round of the April 2007 presidential election pitted 12 candidates against each other. Eight of those candidates received less than 10 percent of the vote each. The top four candidates were the center-right Nicolas Sarkozy with 31 percent of the vote, the center-left Ségolène Royal with 26 percent, the centrist François Bayrou, with 19 percent, and the far-right Jean-Marie Le Pen, with 10 percent. Had this been a National Assembly election, Sarkozy, Royal, and Bayrou all would have passed to the second round, having each obtained more than 12.5 percent of the vote. But because this was the presidential election, only the top two candidates moved on. In the second round of the election, held two weeks later, Sarkozy topped Royal by 53 percent to 47 percent to become president of the Republic.

Such an electoral system provides French voters with more extensive party choices than in the United States or Great Britain, yet it also generates relatively

THE 2007 PRESIDENTIAL CANDIDATES
The final round of the 2007 presidential election pitted Ségolène Royal against eventual winner Nicolas Sarkozy.

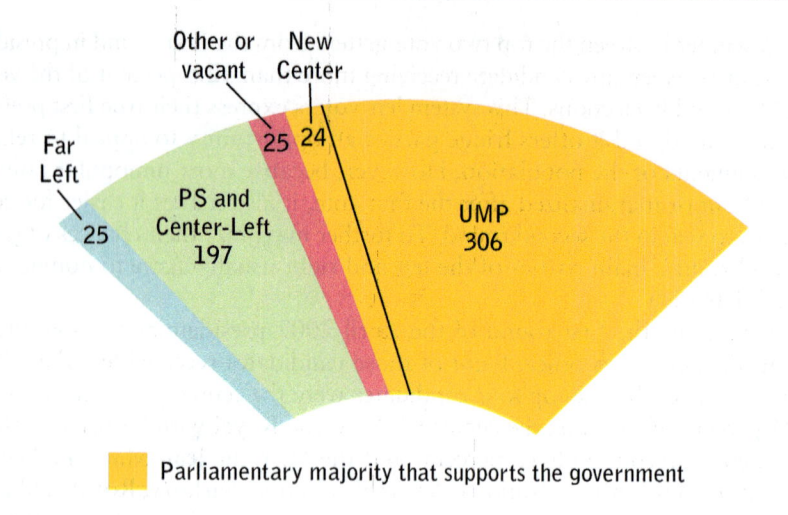

FIGURE 4.3

Composition of France's National Assembly, 2011

Following the 2007 election, parties of the center-right won a sizable majority of the seats in the National Assembly. This allowed them a comfortable margin for governing the country.

*Numbers represent seats in the 577 member-National Assembly as organized into four official parliamentary groups for the XIII legislature of the Fifth Republic.

Source: http://www.assemblee-nationale.fr/13/tribun/xml/effectifs_groupes.asp, accessed 29 November 2011.

Far Left: 25
PS and Center-Left: 197
Other or vacant: 25
New Center: 24
UMP: 306

Parliamentary majority that supports the government

cohesive governing majorities. For example, upon election in 2007, Nicolas Sarkozy immediately dissolved the National Assembly and called parliamentary elections, which took place a month later. The two rounds of voting yielded 345 seats for the center-right and 227 seats for the left, giving Sarkozy a comfortable governing majority in the 577-member house. When compared against the instability of the Fourth Republic, the history of Fifth Republic presidents and prime ministers reflects the stability and centrism provided by the electoral institutions of contemporary France.

The French state is democratic to the core, but democratic in a particular way. The institutions of the Fifth Republic, while providing some checks and balances, place considerable power in the hands of the executive branch. Well-trained, self-assured, and imbued with a sense of purpose, the president, prime minister, cabinet, and top members of the bureaucracy take the lead in the policy process. They are more insulated from the legislative branch, the judicial branch, and from average citizens and interest groups than many of their counterparts in countries such as the United States or Germany. Moreover, there are no powerful, constitutionally autonomous sub-national governments, as in many federal democracies.

France's institutions make for efficient government, but they also help account for the intensity and frequency of protest. When French citizens feel that their interests are not being taken seriously because they are excluded from the policymaking process, they take their case to the streets. Because they believe the executive branch

TABLE 4.1

Presidents and Prime Ministers of the French Fifth Republic

President		Prime Minister	
Charles de Gaulle (center-right)	1958–1969	Michel Debré (center-right)	1959–1962
		Georges Pompidou (center-right)	1962–1968
		Maurice Couve de Murville (center-right)	1968–1969
Georges Pompidou (center-right)	1969–1974	Jacques Chaban-Delmas (center-right)	1969–1972
		Pierre Messmer (center-right)	1972–1974
Valéry Giscard d'Estaing (center-right)	1974–1981	Jacques Chirac (center-right)	1974–1976
		Raymond Barre (center-right)	1976–1981
François Mitterrand (center-left)	1981–1995	Pierre Mauroy (center-left)	1981–1984
		Laurent Fabius (center-left)	1984–1986
		Jacques Chirac (center-right)	1986–1988
		Michel Rocard (center-left)	1988–1991
		Edith Cresson (center-left)	1991–1992
		Pierre Bérégovoy (center-left)	1992–1993
		Edouard Balladur (center-right)	1993–1995
Jacques Chirac (center-right)	1995–2007	Alain Juppé (center-right)	1995–1997
		Lionel Jospin (center-left)	1997–2002
		Jean-Pierre Raffarin (center-right)	2002–2005
		Dominique de Villepin (center-right)	2005–2007
Nicolas Sarkozy (center-right)	2007–	François Fillon (center-right)	2007–

decides policy behind closed doors and then pushes decisions through parliament or sidesteps the legislature altogether, they also believe that they have no other options.

On the other hand, institutions are not the only answer to the question of why the French so often engage in political protest. Great Britain also has a strong executive branch and relatively limited opportunities for public participation in

> **SUMMARY TABLE**
>
> **Institutions of the Fifth Republic: Democratic with a Strong Executive**
>
> | | |
> |---|---|
> | Executive Branch | Sets most of the legislative agenda and has powerful tools to push outcomes in the direction that it prefers; its semi-presidential nature places real power in the hands of both the president and the prime minister appointed by the president. |
> | Parliament | The National Assembly is directly elected by the people while the Sénat is indirectly elected and has less power. As of 2002, the National Assembly majority has always had the same political orientation as the President and thus acts as more of a conduit for than as a brake on government initiatives. |
> | Judiciary | The Constitutional Council interprets whether legislation conforms to the dictates of the highest law of the land, but it is not as powerful as the Supreme Court of the United States. |
> | Electoral Institutions | French presidents and members of the National Assembly are elected through a two-round majority rule system. If a candidate receives a majority in the first round, he or she obtains the seat; if not, the second round constitutes a runoff between the top candidates. |

policymaking. And while the British have staged significant periods of protest—some of which are also due to their centralized institutions—French protests tend to be more intense and more common. Moreover, since the 1970s, France has decentralized power to a limited degree by increasing the power of the Constitutional Council, regional and local governments, and even the legislature, but this has not significantly reduced the levels or strength of dissent. In other words, to answer the question of why contentious protest is such a common part of French politics, the answer cannot lie *only* with the highly centralized nature of French institutions. What other factors help explain the prominence of protest in France?

IDENTITIES IN FRANCE

4.3 What kind of political identities contribute to the frequency of French protest?

Recent evidence confirms that a particularly French approach to protest exists. Surveys conducted between the early 1980s and late 1990s reveal French respondents to be much more likely to have taken part in lawful demonstrations, unofficial strikes, and building or factory occupations than their counterparts in similar developed democracies (see Table 4.2). This stands in contrast to the tradition of signing a petition or participating in a boycott, which are much more common in Sweden and the United States. French citizens are simply more likely to participate

TABLE 4.2

Percentage of Respondents Saying They Have Participated in Various Forms of Protest, 1981–1999

	Attending Lawful Demonstrations	Joining Unofficial Strikes	Occupying Buildings or Factories
France	33%	11%	8%
Germany	22	3	1
Great Britain	12	9	2
Italy	32	5	7
Netherlands	22	3	3
Spain	24	7	3
Sweden	26	4	1
United States	16	4	2
Average	23	6	3

Source: The World Values Survey, Four Wave Aggregate of the Values Studies, at http://www.wvsevsdb.com/wvs/WVSAnalize.jsp, "Political Action," E027–E029.

in active, collective forms of contentious politics than most of their neighbors. Protest is, thus, a ritual that is intimately linked to a French identity.

Is there something distinctive about French identity when it comes to contentious politics? French history provides many examples of what political sociologist Charles Tilly has called **repertoires of collective action**, forms of mobilization that are ingrained in the public consciousness and that recur at regular intervals because the public intuitively understands what the form of mobilization is supposed to accomplish. French protestors and the French public alike tend to be relatively sympathetic to dramatic kinds of mobilization, and this helps increase the frequency of contentious politics. It is important not to overstate this point—it is easy to believe that history dictates present day events, or to reduce France to a caricature of a society in permanent upheaval—but it is also true that "doing protest" and "being French" have a lot in common.

This section explains how four critical social cleavages in French society help generate much of the country's unrest. First, economic class divisions have been a source of friction for more than 200 years, and political parties on the left such as the socialists and communists have frequently used the divide between haves and have-nots to mobilize protest. Second, appeals to nationalism have also spurred conflict, especially when leaders on the political right have tapped into a yearning for what they view as a bygone era of "Frenchness" that has been undermined by

repertoire of collective action ■ the most common type of protest actions undertaken within a country in a given time period.

France's joining the multinational European Union and by the entry of millions of immigrants from overseas.

Religion is a third long-standing form of identity that generates political mobilization in France. However, in contrast to many other countries, it is not so much that different religions divide the French people from each other. Instead, the French are divided to a greater extent between those who believe religion should have a role in public life and those who believe in a strict separation of church and state, known in France as *laïcité* (pronounced ly-ee´-see-tay´). The final identity-based division in France revolves around what University of Michigan political scientist Ronald Inglehart calls post-materialism. Inglehart argues that individuals who do not worry about food, shelter, and other basic material necessities of life tend to express greater concern for values of individual autonomy, self-expression, and lifestyles of their own choosing. In contrast, people who adhere to "materialist" values focus on obtaining and maintaining their own and their families' day-to-day physical and economic security. At root, Inglehart argues that material prosperity tends to change people's values. In France, post-materialists are differentiated from materialists partly by education levels and partly by generation—with younger and better-educated citizens tending to have post-materialist political interests, while older and less well-educated citizens remain focused on materialist concerns. Together, these four cleavages create political friction that drives many waves of social protest.

laïcité ■ secularism, or the principle of separation of church and state in France.

post-materialism ■ a set of values that emphasizes goals such as personal freedom, environmental preservation, aesthetics, and anti-racism over material values such as economic and national security.

Class Divisions

Class identity has long divided French society. Industrialization on the outskirts of major cities began in the early nineteenth century and drew large number of peasants off the land into urban areas. As industry spread, working-class consciousness developed and gained intensity during the unrest of 1848 and in widespread protests in Paris in 1871. By the end of the nineteenth century, the French working class was highly mobilized. Yet, as a group, workers' sympathies were divided between two main political groups: the communists and the socialists.

After World War II, France had one of the strongest communist parties in Western Europe, reflecting the continuing importance of class identities and of the working class movement. In the founding postwar legislative election of November 1946, the French Communist Party received 28 percent of the popular vote, the highest percentage of any political party in the country. In subsequent elections of the Fourth Republic, the Communist Party regularly garnered more than 25 percent of the vote. Yet, starting in the 1970s, French citizens' identification with the working class began to decline. This is consistent with trends across Europe, as factory work has been outsourced to developing countries and as ideologies of class struggle were dealt a blow by the demise of the Soviet Union in 1991. Still, perceived class differences have not disappeared. Tensions between workers and employers or between workers and the state—when it is perceived to oppose workers' rights, job security, or the welfare state—create ongoing opportunities for mobilizing protest in France. In 2009, for example, more than 1 million workers participated in a one-day strike to protest the government's handling of the economic crisis. Given France's population of 63 million, this would be the equivalent of a strike involving the entire population of the state of Minnesota.

Nationalism and Its Challengers

As with class identities, French nationalism is deeply rooted in the country's history. Yet, support for nationalism can be found across the entire political spectrum in France. All strains of French nationalism call for strong central government and for France to retain independence from international commitments seen as limiting national sovereignty. Nationalists on the political left emphasize the global political, intellectual, and artistic leadership France has exhibited since the Revolutionary era. On the center-right of the political spectrum, Charles de Gaulle's resistance to the Nazi-imposed Vichy regime has inspired what are known as "Gaullist" nationalists.

Yet it has been nationalists on the far right that have captured international media attention. They are by far the most numerous and vocal nationalists in contemporary French politics, tracing their roots back to nineteenth-century monarchist or Napoleonic imperial sympathies, or even to the twentieth-century Vichy regime. Although these historical forms of political organization are typically not held up as models for the future, many far-right nationalists hearken back to an era of "strong leadership," and call for limiting the influence of "external" forces within French society, in particular immigrants and the supra-national European Union. The National Front Party exemplifies this type of far-right nationalism, mobilizing voters that tend to have less education and, thus, fewer skills with which to compete in a competitive global marketplace.

In large part, these voters and their far-right leaders are focusing their frustrations on the large-scale immigration from France's former overseas colonies that literally changed the face of the country in the post–World War II era. Millions of non-white immigrants came from the Caribbean, from sub-Saharan Africa, and from South, Southeast, and East Asia. Many of these newcomers brought different cultures and religions—in particular, Islam. They have settled in France, they have had children and grandchildren, and many of these families have become citizens and have integrated themselves into French society.

Unlike in the United States, France keeps no official census data on ethnic minorities. However, estimates of France's immigrant or immigrant-descendant population is placed as high as 25 percent of the total, if all French citizens with at least one immigrant grandparent are included. These French immigrants and their descendants are not anti-nationalist in any organized way: indeed, many are proudly French. However, their presence has created tensions between far-right nationalists who want them to "go home," and immigrant leaders and non-immigrant French citizens who are adapting more easily to the new face of France. This cleavage, thus, divides nationalists who value centralized authority and a more unified notion of French culture, and multiculturalists or regional forces that have a more pluralistic or decentralized vision of France.

National Front (FN) ■ France's most significant far-right party. It is staunchly anti-immigrant.

Religious Identities versus *Laïcité*

France is a predominantly Catholic country, sometimes called the "eldest daughter of the Church" for its long-standing official ties to Catholicism. Yet, the Catholic Church lacks the political and social influence it possesses in countries such as Italy or Ireland. This is partly because while a majority of respondents in a recent poll self-identified as Catholic, only about 5 percent of France's Catholics attend Church services regularly.[1] There are also important non-Catholic minorities in the country that have become meaningful actors in negotiations over religious issues. France's 2 million Protestants have played a prominent role in the country's history as far back as the *Ancien Régime*. France also has the largest populations of Muslims (estimates range from 2.5 to 5 million) and Jews (600,000) in Europe, and one of the largest and most active Buddhist communities in the West. As with Catholics, not all of these minority religious adherents attend services regularly.

In fact, this disjuncture between those who practice religion and those who do not is reflected in the extremely important political divide between people who believe there is a role for religion in public affairs and those who demand a strict separation of Church and State. As in the United States and Turkey, and unlike in most other Western European countries, in France there exists strong support for the political principle of secularism known as *laïcité*. This principle emerged out of the Revolutionary and Republican traditions, which saw the Church as an ally of the hated monarchy and nobility. In the late nineteenth and early twentieth centuries, French politicians enacted a series of reforms that ended government support of Catholicism as the official state religion. For example, following a 1905 law, the government could provide no religion with financial or political support. Although the concept of *laïcité* has been hotly debated, it is also officially enshrined as a core concept in the French constitution, Article 1 of which reads, "France shall be an indivisible, secular, democratic, and social Republic."

There are a number of exceptions to this principle of political secularism. In all parts of France, the government negotiates with leaders of religious groups over matters of importance to them, even though it does not officially recognize religions. For example, the government provides financial support to private religious schools that agree to conform to the state's official educational curriculum, a fact that has been contentious for advocates of *laïcité*. On the other hand, the state has also gone further than many of its European counterparts to publicly distance itself from expressions of religion in the public sphere, for example by forbidding the wearing of Muslim headscarves and other visible signs of religion in public schools and by banning the *burqa* and *niqab*, full-face and body covers worn by a very small percentage of Muslim women in France.

In short, a divide between religious adherents and advocates of *laïcité* have been the poles around which many protests have been organized. This is true not only of the painful and prolonged national debates about the place of Muslim headscarves in public schools (which culminated in a ban in 2004), but also in protests in the 1980s surrounding state funding of religious schools. Tensions over church–state relations have cropped up numerous times in Fifth Republic France in ways that have few or no parallels in other developed democracies.

Post-Materialist Identities

In the 1970s, political scientist Ronald Inglehart argued that citizens' values in wealthy democratic societies were changing. He called this transformation a shift from "materialism" to "post-materialism."[2] Materialists were interested first and foremost on obtaining economic prosperity and security, while post-materialists turned their focus to values such as freedom from authority, individualism, aesthetics, and maintaining the environment. Post-materialist values emerged most clearly in Western Europe starting in the 1960s, after Europe had recovered from the devastation of World War II. With prosperity widespread, citizens in Western Europe began changing their attitudes towards the use of government authority.

Although this value system was not unique to France, it has formed the basis of a number of protest movements in France over the years. In particular, many French citizens grew weary of the influence of the powerful centralized state on their individual lives. Such anti-authoritarian ideas motivated students and workers in the late 1960s to protest the hierarchical nature of French society. In recent years, post-materialist values have fed protest against government policies that appear to favor economic growth at the expense of values like preserving the environment.

For example, protest leaders such as farmer José Bové gained fame for challenging the influence of large multinational corporations in French life. Bové led a 1999 march that ransacked a McDonald's construction site. His actions—and the fact that he then had to spend a few weeks in jail—brought attention to his movement's complaint that multinational companies were making money selling mediocre products that displaced the higher quality, more natural foods produced by French farmers. Another group, known as ATTAC (Association for the Taxation of Financial Transactions for the Aid of Citizens), crystallizes many of these same concerns. ATTAC describes itself as working toward "social, environmental, and democratic alternatives in the globalization process," and its members call themselves *altermondistes* (other worlders), to reflect their thinking that "another world is possible."[3] Tensions between citizens with a post-materialist identity and a state they view as too focused on exercising its authority or promoting economic growth have resurfaced with regularity in France and underpin a number of large contemporary protests.

As the summary table on the following page highlights, a variety of important political identities exist in France, based around class, nation, religion, and post-materialism. At times, individuals may embrace multiple identities, such as a "working-class Muslim immigrant student," or "middle-class Catholic nationalist retiree." While these identities are not sufficient to explain the French propensity to engage in protest, they are the raw material that political leaders can mold into successful political action. This is especially true in France, where certain repertoires of collective action have long existed, and continue to remind citizens that their friends, neighbors, and fellow-citizens frequently attempt to make a political statement by engaging in demonstrations, strikes, or even by occupying a building. However, even if political identity helps account for the greater likelihood of protest in France, it still cannot explain when and why particular protest events take place. For that, it is important to turn to the concrete interests that mobilize actors.

> **SUMMARY TABLE**
>
> **Identities: The Raw Material for Protest**
>
> | | |
> |---|---|
> | Repertoires of Collective Action | More than in comparable liberal democracies, French citizens are willing to participate in or to tolerate relatively radical forms of protest. This is rooted in long-standing traditions and histories of protest that are part of the normal repertoire of political participation in the country. |
> | Class | French society has long been divided between the haves and the have-nots. In recent years, vulnerable groups have mobilized to fight unemployment and to defend the welfare state. |
> | Nationalism | Far-right nationalism has become a staple of French politics and society, with the National Front party routinely receiving approximately 10% of the vote. This party is often mobilized against immigrants and minorities. |
> | Religion/*Laïcité* | While there are some divisions and tensions across religious lines in France, the main axis of difference is between religious adherents and proponents of a secular state that conforms to the principles of *laïcité*. |
> | Post-Materialism | Post-materialists seek "higher order" values, like freedom, support for the environment, organic food, and beautiful public spaces. In France, they often square off against what they argue is a rapacious or uncaring capitalist state. |

INTERESTS IN FRANCE

4.4 What kinds of interests are involved in France's recent protests?

Watch the Video "Sarkozy's Winds of Reform" at mypoliscilab.com

French political institutions provide a target for protest and political identities define many of the axes along which protest develops. However, it usually takes political interests to mobilize people to action. Most scholars of contentious politics argue that groups are not just expressing their identities when they act collectively; rather they are trying to achieve specific goals. What do French groups want when they strike, march, or burn things down? At least in part, students want money for schools; workers and the unemployed want jobs or benefits; and those who live in run-down neighborhoods want economic opportunities. Organized interests in French society help coordinate these political actions.

In order to understand the role of interests in French politics, it is vital to survey the key French interest groups, political parties, and the state itself (which is an actor with its own interests during moments of protest). These groups are especially important for answering this chapter's question. Then we will look at three watershed moments in the recent history of protest in France, including the dramatic events of May 1968, protests over education policy in the 1980s, and conflicts over urban and economic policy in the 2000s. Each of these moments involved the substantial influence of concrete interests or interest groups. By examining the broader context, however, we see that interests by themselves are also not sufficient to explain instances of contentious politics in France.

Interest Groups

As in most democracies, France has a vibrant community of interest groups that seek to further their members' goals in politics. Some of these groups are powerful by virtue of their close ties to the national-government bureaucracy or to political leaders. This is true, for example, of the National Federation of Farmers' Unions (FNSEA) and of the employers' organization Movement of French Enterprises (MEDEF), both of which meet regularly with state representatives to discuss policy decisions affecting their interests and also play a role in administering state-sponsored programs. While the MEDEF does not have much experience leading disruptive strikes, the FNSEA has been more active when agricultural interests have been at stake. In September and October 2009, to protest falling revenues, its members stopped traffic by driving tractors onto highways and through towns and dumped truckloads of dirt in local streets and town squares, including on the Champs-Elysées in Paris.

Although workers' unions such as the General Labor Confederation (CGT), the Workers' Force (FO), and the French Democratic Confederation of Labor (CFDT) have a high profile, their membership and influence has dwindled over the past few decades. They now organize fewer than 10 percent of the workforce, which is the lowest unionization rate of any industrialized democracy in Europe. Yet, they continue to play a prominent role in protest movements, as they often succeed in mobilizing non-union members when they stand up for issues that benefit all workers. In March 2010, the unions helped sponsor a day-long public sector strike that brought tens of thousands of people to the streets to protest economic and social cuts by the government, crippling train service and prompting many teachers to leave their classrooms.[4]

Unlike in the United States, many French university students participate in student unions that have at times played leading roles in organizing protests. The influential National Students Union of France (UNEF), for example, organizes its members to shape central government policies that affect university students across the country. It has been active in all major episodes of protests involving young people, mobilizing in 1968 to oppose restrictive university policies and in 2006 to help overturn the employment law that weakened protections for first time jobseekers.

In the early 1980s, these traditional groups were supplemented by the emergence of ethnically based groups, including some that grew to national proportions and contributed to protest actions. This rise was thanks in part to a 1981 law permitting non-citizens to organize associations and to early 1980s legislation that provided incentives for cities and towns to support local associations. One group of second-generation North Africans capitalized on these changes in the mid-1980s to organize massive demonstrations calling attention to the problems of racism and the uncertain legal status of many immigrants. Their efforts were complemented by anti-racist groups such as the influential *S.O.S. Racisme*.

Political Parties

Political parties traditionally represent society's identities and interests, channeling citizens' concerns and aspirations into parliamentary and governmental discussions and policies. Yet, French political parties in the Fifth Republic are not as strong or cohesive as parties in many other liberal democracies. Ideological and personal differences have created splits on the left and the right that have often undermined the formation of stable, successful parties. Although their numbers, names, and philosophies have shifted over time, parties in France can be understood as divided between center-right, center-left, far-right, and far-left tendencies.

Center-Right: The UMP, the UDF, and the UDF Successor Parties The Union for a Popular Movement (UMP) is the major center-right party. It was formally founded in 2002, but it evolved out of earlier incarnations (such as the long-standing Rally for the Republic Party, RPR), and in its various forms has held power in the Fifth Republic longer than any other party. It rose in the early years of the Republic as the party that supported President de Gaulle, and represents the conservative segments of society such as business leaders, shopkeepers, professionals, farmers, and retirees. It succeeded in electing Jacques Chirac and Nicolas Sarkozy as presidents in 2002 and 2007.

Historically, the other major center-right party was the Union for French Democracy (UDF), which was formed in the 1970s to support President Valéry Giscard d' Estaing. In its early years, the UDF (itself a coalition of small center-right parties) differed from the Gaullist parties in that it favored less government intervention in the market economy, but it typically worked with the Gaullist party in parliament. In 2007, the UDF split into the New Center Party, which is allied with the UMP, and the Democratic Movement, which tacked toward the center and does not support Sarkozy or the UMP. Center-right parties have had a National Assembly majority since the 2002 elections.

Center-Left: The Socialists The Socialist Party (PS) has been the dominant center-left party in France's Fifth Republic. By the late 1970s, it had grown in strength and had emerged as the primary vote-getter on the political left, pulling ahead of the far-left Communist Party. In 1981, François Mitterrand was the first socialist elected president, and the subsequent legislative elections brought the left to power in the National Assembly as well. This momentous transition has been termed *l'alternance*, to mark the shift across the right–left political divide. It was particularly significant because in the early years of the Fifth Republic, Mitterrand had referred to de Gaulle's 1958 constitution as a "permanent coup d'état," raising questions about whether the institutions would survive under leftist leadership, or whether the Constitution would be rewritten yet again. Once in power, however, Mitterrand decided that the strong state and strong executive branch suited him just fine. The Fifth Republic had survived another potential crisis.

Union for a Popular Movement (UMP) ■ the main center-right party in France. It evolved out of the Gaullist Rally for the Republic Party (RPR) in 2002.

Socialist Party (PS) ■ the biggest center-left party in the country.

l'alternance ■ literally "the alternation" in French; the shift in power from the right to the left that took place for the first time after the 1981 elections; left parties accepted the political institutions of the Fifth Republic once they came to power.

When the socialists took control of the government, they acted as a traditional leftist party, by nationalizing banks and insurance companies, increasing workers' wages and taxes on businesses, reducing working hours, and ramping up public spending. However, these measures failed to reverse the widespread economic problems of the day, and by 1983 the PS leadership decided to turn away from its socialist platform and to engage in policies that were friendlier to the free market. Since that time, the socialists have moved even further towards the political center and away from their leftist roots. The party still draws support from civil servants, lower income groups, and educated professionals, but the Socialist Party and its allies have not held a majority in the National Assembly since 2002.

Far Right: The National Front Founded in 1972 and led by Jean-Marie Le Pen until he was succeeded by his daughter Marine Le Pen in 2011, the National Front (FN) is the major far-right party in France. It represents the most conservative elements in society and, increasingly, the down-and-out working class that used to support the far-left Communist Party. The FN grew rapidly in the 1980s by appealing to anti-immigrant sentiment, employing such campaign slogans as "France for the French." It also appeals to those who oppose French membership in the European Union, and those who favor stronger law and order.

The FN has never won many seats in the National Assembly. However, since 1988 Jean-Marie Le Pen and the FN have consistently appealed to millions of voters during presidential elections and during the first round of legislative elections. For example, in 2002, Le Pen received almost 5 million votes in the first round of the presidential election, enough to obtain a spot on the ballot for the runoff against Jacques Chirac. This was the first time since the Vichy era that a politician of the far right had been within striking distance of holding power in France, and the result shocked the country and the world. Although Le Pen garnered 4.5 million votes in the second round of the election, all of the other parties—from the far left to the center-right—threw their support behind the center-right candidate. Chirac was re-elected with more than 25 million votes, or more than 80 percent of the ballots cast.

Far Left: The Communists and Others The French Communist Party (PCF) has been in decline for the past 30 years. It was one of the strongest parties in the country after its prominent role in the resistance against the Vichy regime during World War II, and it maintained a leading position on the political left well into the 1970s. However, its hard-line leftist appeal eventually wore thin for French voters, and its traditional support base of young voters, workers, and the less educated began to shift towards other parties. Some shifted allegiance to the socialists, while others moved in the direction of the National Front. Today, the PCF has little electoral appeal, even though it has reformed its political platform to be less dogmatic. In the 2007 legislative elections, the party won only 15 seats in the 577-member National Assembly, and its

French Communist Party (PCF) ■
France's main party of the far left.

candidate garnered less than 2 percent of the vote in the presidential election held that same year.

There are a handful of other far-left parties on the French political scene that are represented in the first round of presidential elections. Parties like The Greens (which sometimes appeals to far-left sentiments, but at others times is more centrist), Workers Struggle, and the Revolutionary Communist League have each polled more than 1 million votes in at least one election since 1988. These parties are mostly a symbolic presence, drawing support from post-materialist voters attracted to their themes of environmentalism, anti-racism, and anti-capitalism. But they sometimes help translate these identities into extra-parliamentary protest actions.

The Interests of the State

To understand protest dynamics, it helps to think of the state itself as an actor with its own motivating interests. One key function of the modern state is to manage political conflict to keep the peace. When hundreds of thousands of protestors stream out onto the streets, the state has failed in this task. Social scientists Daniel Béland and Patrik Marier have identified two strategies that French governments have deployed to reduce the likelihood and the extent of social mobilization against the state. First, governments seek to divide the groups that are likely to protest—particularly labor unions—by cutting deals with some to undermine their resistance to controversial reforms. Second, they have tended to launch their most divisive initiatives during or just before the summer holiday season, when most French people are on vacation and are, thus, less likely to protest.[5]

When these strategies do not work, the state is faced with a choice: stand firmly behind its policies and weather the storm of protest, or back down on its initiatives to appease the protestors. Staying the course is difficult. Given the French propensity and sympathy for mobilizing against the state, demonstrations can go on for weeks, crippling the economy and destroying the legitimacy of the government in power. Backing down gets the people off the streets, but it means that important changes the government seeks to implement are not enacted. It also provides an incentive for mass mobilization the next time around, since the state has shown itself to be weak. In practice, the state often grants significant concessions to the protestors. However, it typically does not give them everything they want, nor does it usually deliver on all of its promises, scaling them back once the initial heat has subsided. The French state is, thus, an independent and calculating actor during prominent cycles of protest.

Examples of Protest

Massive demonstrations of 100,000 or more people are not everyday occurrences in France, yet they do occur with a certain regularity. Let us look more closely at three major protest events in recent decades to see what role interests, identities, and institutions have played in explaining protest. The French institutional setting has created frustrations and tensions that encourage outsiders to mobilize. Underlying identities provide the raw material for action and increase the likelihood that people will use protest to express themselves. And, in most cases, specific actors pursuing their interests ultimately catalyze the protest movement.

The Events of May 1968 France experienced a baby boom after World War II, and students in this generation began arriving at universities in the 1960s. In response, the French state hastily constructed several new campuses across the country. However, the central authorities' top-down approach to education had not changed. There were restrictions on visitation rights between men's and women's dormitories, professors were distant, and university authorities were losing their patience with the squatters, drug dealers, and other minor troublemakers who were populating their dormitories. When administrators enforced what seemed to the students to be hidebound and irksome rules and regulations, they drew attention to the symbolic distance between the government and the people. When about 300 members of the general student movement, the student union UNEF, and the more radical Revolutionary Communist Youth group gathered at the Sorbonne—France's premier university—on May 3, 1968, to protest against these rules and regulations, the university rector ordered the police to arrest them, in spite of their having agreed to leave. Other students quickly arrived on the scene and leveled verbal abuse at the authorities, surrounded the police vans, and threw stones. The police responded with tear gas and further arrests.

Students organized a second wave of protests on May 6, with more than 60,000 people taking part. During the so-called "night of the barricades" on May 10–11, students felled trees and turned over cars to block the police, who overran the students with a stronger type of tear gas and dragged them out of cafés and buildings. Soon, teachers and workers struck out of sympathy for the students and frustration with the system of strict, top-down authority that rubbed them the wrong way in their own workplaces. There was a pervasive sense that French society was tightly controlled by employers and a few leading politicians, and that the rules they set were too confining and irritating for the times. By mid-May, automobile manufacturing plants were closed, air traffic was impossible, and rail travel had been suspended. At the height of the events of May 1968, between 7 and 10 million students and workers were protesting and the country was at a standstill.[6]

The dynamics of this massive and prolonged protest illustrate the points made throughout this chapter. First, the fact that French political institutions tend to concentrate power and freeze workers, students, and other interest groups out of policy discussions contributes to widespread discontent. Because they feel that traditional political channels will fail to address their interests, citizens express themselves in more confrontational ways. Second, the wealth and stability of French society in the postwar era incubated anti-authority post-materialist values, especially among younger French citizens. Finally, organized interests channeled these growing sentiments into active protests. Student groups such as the UNEF and the Revolutionary Communist Youth mobilized their members, and labor unions joined in with workers' strikes. The government responded by granting universities greater autonomy to set rules, and with pay hikes for workers, including half-pay for strike days lost. However, the protests only ended when President de Gaulle dissolved the National Assembly at the end of May, called for snap elections in June, and threatened to impose a state of emergency if the unrest continued. The demonstrations subsided after a resounding majority of voters re-elected the Gaullist party to power in parliament.

1986 Education Reform Protests

If the students of 1968 wanted to relax the restrictions placed on them by authority figures, by 1986, they wanted jobs. When the new conservative government of that year proposed an overhaul of the higher education system, it triggered a massive response. University and high school students were leery of the government's plans to increase university fees and to identify on a diploma which particular university had granted the college degree. Students felt that higher education had to be accessible to all, regardless of their ability to pay, and that all universities had to be equally good. Raising the cost would financially squeeze some prospective students, and identifying the university on the diploma—a common step in most countries—would disadvantage students who did not attend what most informally regarded as the best universities.

From the government's perspective, higher education reform aimed to promote economic development, and it calculated that since university campuses had been relatively quiet since 1968, serious opposition to proposed reforms was unlikely. But by 1986, youth unemployment was running around 39 percent, so the government underestimated students' anger at proposed policy changes that might threaten their ability to attend university or to get a job once they graduated. Teacher and student unions voted to participate in a one-day strike on November 23 and to create an ad hoc committee to coordinate a series of demonstrations. They also received support from the anti-racist group *S.O.S. Racisme*, which helped to mobilize hundreds of thousands of high school students to attend the December 4 and 10 demonstrations that amounted in total to more than a half million students.[7]

During the protests, police and right-wing youths were caught on film attacking some of the participants. One student lost a hand, another lost an eye, and one student was clubbed to death. Public support quickly turned against the government and shifted squarely behind the students, who responded to the brutality by blocking traffic, erecting barricades, and breaking windows. In an effort to quell the violence and to shore up its flagging popularity, the government withdrew its proposed reforms.[8]

In this case of mass protest, organized interest groups played a leading role in generating protest, drawing on materialist, post-materialist, and anti-racist identities to oppose state institutions that had not taken their perspective into account.

Urban Protests and the Backlash to Reforms of 2005–2006

The term "suburb" conjures up an image of a leafy, placid neighborhood in the United States, but French suburbs (called *banlieues*) are more like what Americans think of when they hear the term "inner cities"—areas of poverty, joblessness, and, at times, lawlessness, especially for young people. A wide range of ethnic groups populate France's suburbs, including immigrants from France's former colonies. Although many of these immigrants and their descendants are French citizens, they are often perceived as outsiders in France, including by the police who have a tense relationship with the inhabitants of the *banlieues*.

When two immigrant origin youths died fleeing the police in a Paris suburb in September 2005, it lit a powder keg of nationwide discontent. Over the

banlieues ■ literally "suburbs" in French, but more accurately, a shorthand for depressed zones on the peripheries of major cities that have high rates of joblessness and lawlessness, and that are often associated with an elevated population of ethnic minorities.

ensuring weeks, young men of predominantly Arab and African descent set fire to more than 9,000 cars and damaged dozens of schools, day-care centers, public buildings, and private businesses, causing approximately $300 million in damage and resulting in one death and more than 200 injuries. These protests, unlike the student protests of 1968 and 1986, were not organized by any central body. They occurred across the country, but were spontaneous and local, mostly involving forms of vandalism (like burning cars) that had been common for decades in these neighborhoods. The participants clearly shared an identity of feeling isolated and alienated from society, but they also shared interests in prompting the state to provide more concrete economic opportunities for the residents of these down-and-out neighborhoods.

The government responded with a mix of policies. It cracked down on the protestors, instituting a curfew and invoking state of emergency powers not used in mainland France since the early years of the Fifth Republic when Algerian decolonization still roiled the country. They also reached out to residents of the *banlieues* with a series of policy proposals encapsulated in a March 2006 law on equal opportunities. This law proved incredibly controversial, especially a provision called the First Employment Contract, designed to relax protections for young workers looking for their first job. The proposal was meant to encourage employers to hire young workers—particularly those from the suburbs—by granting them more flexibility to dismiss new employees than is available under France's restrictive labor laws, where firing people after the three-month probationary period is difficult and costly. However, the government used a series

First Employment Contract ■ the 2006 proposal to make it easier for employers to fire workers during the first two years of their employment.

This 2006 protest actually comprised hundreds of thousands of students—and such protests are fairly frequent in France.

of legislative maneuvers to pass the law that gave members of the National Assembly little time to debate it or power to amend it. Parties on the left appealed to the Constitutional Council, but to little avail, since it approved the First Employment Contract dimension of the law.

While the bill was working its way through parliament, the left parties, labor and student unions, and other groups ramped up opposition to the plan both inside and outside of parliament. Opponents of the law feared that it would place young people in an especially vulnerable position, with bosses able to pressure them and then to fire them for no good reason. They dubbed it the "Kleenex contract," because it allowed employers to use and discard young employees.[9] Protests against the law began in February and came into full force in March and April. Hundreds of thousands and then millions of university students, high school students, and workers jammed the streets, blockaded universities, and disrupted transport and mail services—all to show their massive rejection of the government's plan. Although the prime minister at first would not back down, saying that the government refused to "capitulate to the logic of ultimatums,"[10] President Chirac began to hedge on his support for the law at the end of March, and by mid-April the government withdrew the First Employment Contract, giving in to the overwhelming pressure of nationwide protest. In these cases, therefore, immigrant and class identities combined with concrete economic and social interests in the context of an exclusive institutional structure to produce one of the most intense sequences of protest events in contemporary French history.

To the casual observer, demonstrations involving millions of citizens may seem like a spontaneous outpouring of anger. Yet, these protests are most often organized events with a specific set of goals in mind. As the summary table below indicates, interest groups such as labor unions, student unions, and anti-racist groups play an important role in mobilizing members into the streets. They also represent their particular interests in demanding more freedom in the dorms, no university names on diplomas, or the preservation of workers' rights for young people entering the job market. Concrete interests and the leadership of interest groups are almost always central to mas-

> **SUMMARY TABLE**
>
> **Interests: Mobilizing, Channeling, and Opposing Protest**
>
> | | |
> |---|---|
> | Interest Groups | Unions, non-governmental associations, and other groups often take the lead in mobilizing people to pursue their concrete interests. |
> | Political Parties | Parties seek to represent different interests in society, and they can also be a conduit for channeling particular interests to minimize (or sometimes to maximize) contentiousness within French society. |
> | The State | The state strategically decides when and how to implement controversial reforms, and negotiates with protestors who oppose its initiatives. |

sive demonstrations. However, they are not always of primary importance, as we saw in the 2005 riot events. Moreover, even when they are critical, they are not enough to explain protest. In France, understanding interests has to be combined with a grasp of institutions and identities in order to comprehend the many instances of high-profile protest that have rocked the country during the decades of the Fifth Republic.

CONCLUSION

The urban protests of 2005–2006 epitomize the intricate relationship between institutions, identities, and interests that characterizes many protest events. As an actor with interests, the government responded to the 2005 wave of suburban disturbances by repressing the violence and by introducing legislation aimed at preempting further unrest in the *banlieues*. However, it used the strength of the executive branch to push its plan through with little debate and excluded input from workers, students, or other groups relatively isolated from power. Labor unions, student unions, and high school students mobilized along class lines and student identities to fight for their interest in preserving protections for young people. Participants in the 2006 protests stood up for workers' rights, even though protecting those rights may mean fewer jobs for young people as a group. The government responded by quickly using the strong institutions to repeal the objectionable law.

Why do French citizens engage in such frequent and dramatic forms of protest? The evidence suggests that we need to analyze how history, institutions, identities, and interests have interacted to produce France's particular circumstances. Historically, French citizens have a long track record of participating in intense protests. Dating back to the French Revolution that toppled the *Ancien Régime* and stretching through the popular uprisings of the nineteenth and twentieth centuries, revolts have formed part of the fabric of French history. They provide an understandable "repertoire of collective action" that allows today's French citizens to sympathize with many protests when their Americans counterparts might not.

The institutions of the Fifth Republic also play a significant role. Since 1958, France's political structure has tended to insulate top-level decision-makers from the input of average citizens. In response, people have to make their case in other ways. While protest is far from ubiquitous in France, it is more frequent and intense than in many other advanced democracies, partly because French political institutions force the hand of those who are discontent with state policies. Since they feel they cannot be heard through more institutionalized channels of participation, they have a greater tendency to march through Paris by the thousands, blockade highways with their trucks, burn cars in the *banlieues*, or use their tractors to dump tomatoes in town centers.

Protesters often mobilize around important group identities within France. The unemployed, far-right anti-immigrant activists, proponents of the separation of church and state, and anti-globalists draw on class, nationalist, secular, and post-materialist identities to rally their troops to action. These identities divide groups within society and are, therefore, the seed beds from which dramatic protest can grow. They are not permanent, nor are they the only salient identities within

France's borders, but in their various and evolving forms they have constituted the main axes of conflict within the country since the inauguration of the Fifth Republic.

Without concrete interests at stake, however, these identities are much harder to mobilize. Students want jobs and job security, workers want to preserve their pensions, nationalists want to protect France from the influences of immigration or the European Union. These interests often bump up against those advocated by other domestic groups, such as employers who seek a more flexible labor market or openness to foreign trade, or even against the interests of the state in trimming the welfare state to lower its budget. The public clashes between groups and the state that so often dominate international headlines typically revolve around the distribution of key economic or social resources.

In sum, France's track record of revolution, revolt, and turmoil has laid the groundwork for popular understanding of the power of protest and has shaped the country's repertoires of collective action. The centralized and insulated institutions of the Fifth Republic help the state take relatively decisive action, but they also tend to freeze some voices out of the discussion. This increases the incentive for marginalized actors to take to the streets to make their opinions heard. Long-standing cleavages across dimensions of class, nation, religion and post-materialism provide the raw materials for many political conflagrations. And concrete interests and organized interest groups help funnel action in specific instances of strikes, marches, and violence. Although there is no iron law of social protest, understanding how these factors interact provides a much clearer picture of why a stable, rich democracy like France continues to experience so much disruptive contentious politics.

KEY TERMS

Ancien Régime   118
Estates-General   118
constitutional monarchy   119
republic   119
constitutional dictatorship   119
Vichy regime   120
Fourth Republic   120
dirigisme   121
Fifth Republic   122
National Assembly   124
cohabitation   124
Sénat   125
grandes écoles   125

Constitutional Council   127
majority rule   128
repertoire of collective action   133
laïcité   134
post-materialism   134
National Front (FN)   135
Union for a Popular Movement (UMP)   140
Socialist Party (PS)   140
l'alternance   140
French Communist Party (PCF)   141
banlieues   144
First Employment Contract   145

REVIEW QUESTIONS

1. What are the most important reasons why protest is so common in France?
2. Have institutions, identities, and interests been equally important in all cases of French protest?
3. Is being a student a class identity, a post-material identity, or both?

4. Should states negotiate with protestors to take their opinions into account, or does this only invite more protest in the future?
5. What do lessons from France imply about protest in other countries?

SUGGESTED READINGS

Baumgartner, Frank. *Conflict and Rhetoric in French Policymaking*. Pittsburgh: University of Pittsburgh Press, 1989. This book traces the dynamics of French policymaking, with a particular focus on episodes of tense interactions.

Béland, Daniel, and Patrik Marier. "Protest Avoidance: Labor Mobilization and Social Policy Reform in France." *Mobilization*, 11(3)(2006): 297–311. An article that highlights the strategic calculations of the state when trying to cope with the challenges of citizen mobilization.

Kedward, Rod. *France and the French: A Modern History*. Woodstock, NY: Overlook, 2006. An introductory overview of contemporary France, with an excellent chapter on the events of May 1968.

Kriesi, Hanspeter, et al. *New Social Movements in Western Europe: A Comparative Analysis*. Minneapolis: University of Minnesota Press, 1995. Places French social movements in a European comparative perspective.

Tilly, Charles. *The Contentious French*. Cambridge, MA: The Belknap Press of Harvard University Press, 1986. Examines the concept of repertoires of collective action with a particular focus on France.

NOTES

1. U.S. Department of State Religious Freedom Country Report: France (http://www.state.gov/g/drl/rls/irf/2008/108446.htm).
2. Ronald Inglehart, *The Silent Revolution: Changing Values and Political Styles among Western Publics* (Princeton: Princeton University Press, 1977).
3. See the ATTAC website at http://www.attac.org/.
4. BBC News, "French National Strike Disrupts Transport," March 23, 2010.
5. Daniel Béland and Patrik Marier, "Protest Avoidance: Labor Mobilization and Social Policy Reform in France," *Mobilization*, 11(3)(2006): 297–311.
6. See Tony Judt, *Postwar: A History of Europe since 1945* (New York: Penguin, 2005), 407-413; and Rod Kedward, *France and the French: A Modern History* (Woodstock, NY: Overlook, 2006), 416-431.
7. Scott S. Bryson, "France Through the Looking Glass: The November–December 1986 French Student Movement," *The French Review*, 60(2) (1987): 251.
8. Cyrus Ernesto Zirakzadeh, "Traditions of Protest and the High-School Student Movements in Spain and France in 1986–87," *West European Politics*, 12(3)(1989): 220–237.
9. *New York Times*, March 18, 2006.
10. *Le Monde*, March 21, 2006.

CHAPTER 5

Japan

Ethan Scheiner

Liberal Democratic Party Prime Minister Jun'ichiro Koizumi paints in the first eye of the *daruma* doll for good luck at the outset of the 2005 election. The second eye is left to be filled in after victory. But little did anyone know that the 2005 election would be the last in an unbroken string of LDP victories. Four years later, in 2009, the Democratic Party of Japan would end the LDP's political dominance in Japan.

> **?** How did a single political party dominate Japan's democracy for more than half a century?

INTRODUCTION TO JAPAN

In August 2009, the Democratic Party of Japan (DPJ) crushed the Liberal Democratic Party (LDP) at the polls, winning an overwhelming majority in Japan's lower house of parliament. It was a historic election in Japan that signified an end to more than half a century of LDP dominance. The LDP had once before briefly lost its place in the government—for nearly 11 months in 1993–1994—but in that case it remained easily the largest party in Japan, and soon was able to form a coalition government with two much smaller parties. However, the 2009 election marked the first time any single party had bested the LDP. Indeed, minus the brief 1993–1994 exception, the LDP had controlled Japan's government throughout the entire 54 years since the party's formation in 1955—first through many years of economic success, but also, after 1990, through two decades of economic stagnation. By most measures, Japan is a democracy. But multiple decades of LDP dominance confound the conventional definition of democracy, and implies that in some sense Japanese politics resembled a one-party non-democratic state.

For many years, the LDP won elections because it could take credit for impressive economic growth. After the devastation of World War II, the LDP helped restore the Japanese economy. Between 1950 and 1973, Japan's gross national product grew more than 10 percent per year.[1] Through the 1980s, Japan's growth rates exceeded the average for other wealthy democracies. Yet, beginning in 1990, the economy came to a screeching halt, as growth slowed to less than 2 percent annually in the 1990s, and even lower in the first decade of the 2000s. Combined with this economic stagnation, numerous corruption scandals generated widespread voter disillusionment with the LDP. In the 1990s and first decade of the 2000s, polls indicated that the LDP had only about a 25 percent approval rate, on average.[2] Disdain for the LDP grew so high that in one poll in the early 2000s, for instance, 44 percent of respondents said that the LDP was the party they most disliked.[3] Still, it was not until 2009 that the LDP finally lost power to the DPJ.

How did a single political party dominate Japan's democracy for over half a century? This chapter seeks to answer this question and, in the process, illustrate how Japanese democracy functions. In a democracy, participation and contestation offer the possibility of holding government accountable. When a party loses support, we expect it to be voted out of office. The Japanese case confounds this expectation, and brings into question the very definition of democracy. What prevented party alternation in power for so long after Japan's economy began to stagnate and the LDP acquired an image as corrupt and out of touch?

Democratic Party of Japan (DPJ) ■
Japan's leading opposition party after 1997. Defeated the LDP in the 2007 House of Councillors election and the 2009 House of Representatives election.

Liberal Democratic Party (LDP) ■
political party that dominated Japan's government for all but 11 months from 1955 until 2009.

Read and Listen to **Chapter 5** at **mypoliscilab.com**

Study and Review the **Pre-Test & Flashcards** at **mypoliscilab.com**

JAPAN

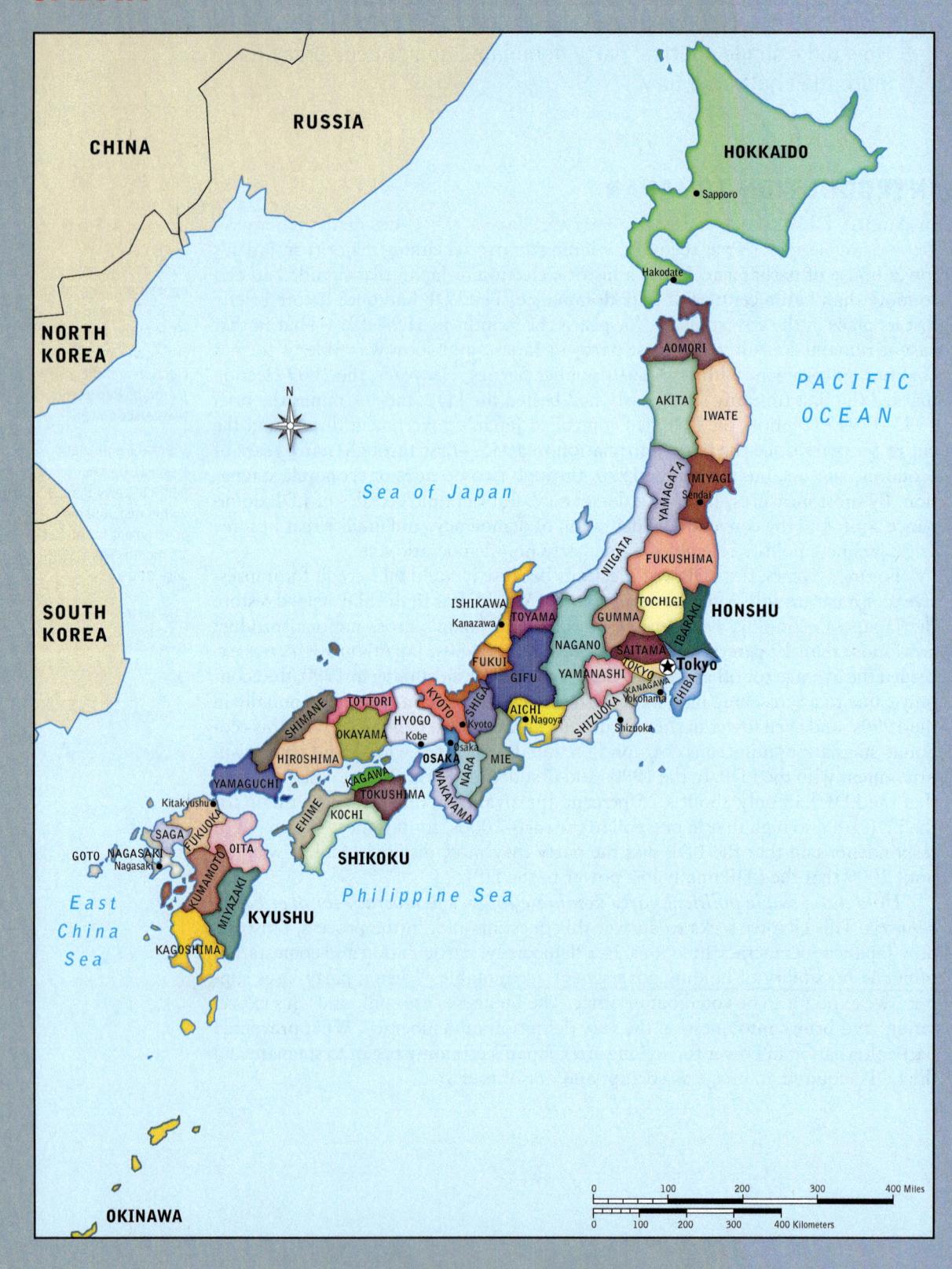

JAPAN IN COMPARISON

	United Kingdom	Germany	France	Japan	India	Mexico	Russia	Nigeria	China	Iran
Freedom House Classification	Democracy	Democracy	Democracy	Democracy	Democracy	Partial democracy	Partial democracy	Partial democracy	Non-democracy	Non-democracy
Land Size (sq km)	243,610	357,022	643,801	377,915	3,287,263	1,964,375	17,098,242	923,768	9,596,961	1,648,195
Land Size Ranking	79	62	42	61	7	15	1	32	4	18
Population (July 2011 Estimate)	62,698,362	81,471,834	65,312,249	126,475,664	1,189,172,906	113,724,226	138,739,892	155,215,573	1,336,718,015	77,891,220
Population Ranking	22	16	21	10	2	11	9	8	1	18
Life Expectancy (Years)	80.05	80.07	81.19	82.25	66.8	76.47	66.29	47.56	74.68	70.1
Life Expectancy Ranking	28	27	13	5	51	72	162	220	95	146
Literacy Rate	99%	99%	99%	99%	61%	86.1%	99.4%	68%	91.6%	77%
GDP Per Capita (2010 Estimate)	US$35,100	US$35,900	US$33,300	US$34,000	US$3,500	US$13,800	US$15,900	US$2,500	US$7,600	US$11,200
GDP Ranking	36	32	39	38	163	85	71	178	126	100

HISTORICAL OVERVIEW OF JAPAN

5.1 What is the historical background for democracy in Japan?

Watch the Video "Hiroshima, 1945" at mypolscilab.com

shogun ■ generalissimo or supreme military ruler who led Japan (1603–1868).

Japan does not have a long tradition of democracy. Prior to World War II, except for a brief period in the 1920s, Japan had long been ruled by non-democratic regimes. In a sense, therefore, the LDP's loss in 2009 was an important step in the development of a Japanese democracy that is founded on not only participation, but also fully competitive party contestation.

Early-modern Japan (1600–1853) is described as a period of peace in which the central government exerted substantial influence throughout the country but did not maintain the same sort of strong state that was emerging in countries such as France, England, and Germany at the time. During this period, Japan was essentially a military dictatorship, led by the shogun (generalissimo or supreme military ruler).

But from the mid-1850s, Japan entered a period of warfare and constant change. Beginning in 1868, Japan developed a centralized state focused on the country's monarch, the emperor. This centralized state, led by a new bureaucratic elite, pushed economic and military growth, which ultimately led the country into World War II. Japan lost the war, but arose to become the second largest economy in the world. After World War II, Japan became a democracy, but one dominated by a single political party, the LDP, which used the strong economy to its great advantage. In the 1990s, the economy soured, and 20 years later the economy still had not improved. Nevertheless, until 2009, the LDP did not lose its position as the predominant party in Japan.

The Tokugawa Era

samurai ■ warriors who ultimately became bureaucrats during the Tokugawa era.

In the fifteenth and sixteenth centuries, Japan faced constant civil war, with no central state. Regional warlords led samurai (warriors) against each other in battles over land, leaving Japan socially and economically devastated and politically unstable. Beginning in the 1570s, three warlords in succession pulled order from the chaos. These leaders ruthlessly put down their enemies, but rewarded those who joined them. By 1591, they consolidated control over all of Japan. Rifts remained, but after the battle of Sekigahara in 1600, Japan became unified under Ieyasu Tokugawa, the last of the three powerful warlords. In 1603, Tokugawa had Japan's monarch, the emperor, declare him to be shogun.

Tokugawa era ■ period in which Japan's central government was led by the shogun.

bakufu ■ the central government led by the shogun during the Tokugawa era.

The Tokugawa era (1603–1868) was largely peaceful and stable, and saw the introduction of central control by the government. Led by the Tokugawa shogunate, the country was controlled by the central *bakufu*, or military government. During this period, the emperor largely held a symbolic role. Although Japan was unified, its system during this period is often referred to as "centralized feudalism," since each local domain and its ruler, the *daimyō*, held considerable independence as long as it remained loyal to the bakufu and offered various required tributes. Because the bakufu did not have a strong daily influence on the domains, and because there was a lack of unified national Japanese identity, the Japanese state was nowhere near the strong, centralized force that it was to become after the Tokugawa period or that Western European countries like France or England were during this period.

Travel into Japan was forbidden for most foreigners except the Dutch (who were relegated to a small trade outpost), and Japanese were largely prohibited from travel overseas. In order to create stability and an economy where each person had a specific role, Japan's leaders sharpened the hierarchical distinctions among the people according to their inherited status. Samurai were at the top—they had moved from being warriors to elite bureaucrats who received a salary for running the business of the government and their home domain. Most people were commoners, with the greatest respect given to farmers, then artisans (craftsmen), and then, at the lowest status level, merchants.

The Meiji Era

In the mid-nineteenth century, Japan faced a series of domestic and external threats that led to the Meiji Restoration, a revolution led by samurai who "restored" power to the emperor—specifically the Emperor Meiji—and created a new governmental system centralized around him that exerted power throughout the country.

Meiji Restoration ■
1868 revolution led by samurai who "restored" power to Emperor Meiji and created a new governmental system centralized around him that exerted power throughout the country.

The Fall of the Tokugawa Regime

Over time, the revenue sources of the Tokugawa bakufu dried up. Much of the problem was complacency on the part of the leaders of the state. Because status was hereditary, many high-ranking samurai who oversaw the administration of the state and the domains made relatively little effort to attend to emerging problems of the time. The Tokugawa leaders rarely carried out land surveys, which made it hard to tax subjects fully. Meanwhile, commerce modernized and a thriving merchant class emerged, but for the most part the bakufu did not bother to tax merchants' wealth. At the same time, many samurai grew disenchanted with their place in the economic and social order. Lower-ranking samurai who did not receive the plum government positions grew increasingly resentful. And as the *bakufu* and *daimyō* grew poorer, these lower-level samurai received smaller stipends. Samurai found the decreased wealth galling, as they watched socially inferior merchants grow increasingly wealthy.

Against this backdrop of a weakened and resource-poor central government, the Western powers forced Japan to open up to the outside world. In 1853, U.S. navy ships arrived in Japan and, threatening military force, forged trade agreements. The Western powers instituted a series of "unequal treaties," that favored the West, infringed on Japanese sovereignty, and forced Japan to forfeit its legal power over foreigners who stepped on Japanese soil. Unable to protect Japan from outside "barbarians," the *bakufu* lost credibility. Domains that had long quietly opposed the *bakufu* from afar sought to take a greater leadership role. They developed their own armies and, led by samurai who sought to improve their positions, defeated the forces of the *bakufu*. In 1868, the victorious forces brought an end to the Tokugawa *bakufu* and "restored" power to the Meiji emperor.

The Meiji System

The growth of the Japanese state matches many classic notions of state development founded on war-making capacity and tax extraction.[4] The Meiji state was in large part a response to the decline of the legitimacy of traditional forms of authority, but also designed to develop a stronger Japanese military and economy to catch up to the West.

The Meiji system did not merely replace the shogun with the emperor; it created a wholly new structure. Meiji leaders ended status distinctions between samurai and commoners—all Japanese people became equal under the emperor. With the entrance of foreign "barbarians," Japanese developed national pride and desire to protect themselves from Western colonialism. By 1889, the reformers instituted a national constitution, with the emperor at the center. In reality, though, the emperor was largely directed by 10 to 20 leaders of the restoration—that is, former samurai of the Tokugawa period—who are often known as the **Meiji oligarchs**. The restoration instituted a centralized state in which national bureaucrats served as the principal policymakers. The constitution gave a small number of wealthy people the right to vote, and established a parliament. But for more than a decade the oligarchs chose the leaders of the cabinet, and the imperial bureaucracy dominated policymaking.

Meiji oligarchs ■ small group of men who directed the emperor and played the central role in the Japanese government in the aftermath of the Meiji Restoration.

The reformers believed their best chance of removing the yoke of the unequal treaties was to catch up to the West economically. So they instituted a systematic land tax, a national currency, and a new infrastructure that included a government-led railroad. But above all, it was the land taxes from the agrarian sector that supported Japan's economic growth.

The government leaders did not believe the free market would allow a late-developing country like Japan to succeed economically. Therefore, government leaders deliberately financed likely industry and corporate winners, which they supported with public funds. They created huge transportation networks, such as major railroad lines, and they placed tariffs on potentially competitive imports. Most of all, from 1895 the government used state funds to develop heavy industry. In this way, although the private sector played a part, the government led the way to organizing and financing Japan's late nineteenth century development.

The reformers also changed society. Official status distinctions were eliminated. In 1887, employment in the highly esteemed government bureaucracy became dependent on merit-based civil service examinations rather than personal connections and social status. By 1873, Japan instituted a military draft. Although unpopular at first, the draft made military service a tool to instill Japanese patriotism and loyalty. Simultaneously, the government introduced compulsory education, which promoted patriotism and developed an educated citizenry that helped develop Japan's economy.

Economic Growth and the Rise and Decline of Democracy before World War II

Japan's economy grew rapidly from 1880 to 1900. Monopolies or *zaibatsu* (financial cliques) led much of the economic development process. These companies had a hand in nearly every part of the economy—mining, refining, production, trading, transportation, and banking—and maintained close ties to the government, through which they received favored treatment.

The Japanese leadership sought to build up its military, partly as a tool to keep order at home, but also to start to create its own empire. In turn, especially beginning in the 1890s, Japan faced major tensions with its neighbors, which ultimately led to armed and bloody conflict—much of it focused on Korea. Japan, China, and

Russia all sought control over Korea, for strategic security reasons, because of Korea's natural resources, and generally as part of their efforts to build empires. Conflict turned to war with China (1894–1895), which Japan ultimately won. The victory established Japan as a regional power in Asia and stoked greater nationalism at home. Before long, Japan and Russia engaged each other in battle in the Russo–Japanese War (1904–1905). Both sides were badly bloodied, but Japan was widely viewed as the victor—a shocking result at the time for a "non-white" nation to defeat a major "white" power (although the Western powers were reluctant to reward Japan for its victories in the war). Thereafter, Japan colonized Korea beginning in 1905, occupying the peninsula until the end of World War II. With its success in these battles, Japan gained both international esteem and the resentment of its Asian neighbors. This resentment grew as Japan took on an increasing presence in China beginning in the 1930s.

As Japan's power and prestige grew, so did its economy. This meant that more groups clamored for political representation—and for favors from the government. Thus, from the early 1900s, with the co-optation of some of the more liberal oligarchs, political parties began to play a more positive role in the parliament (called the Diet). Particularly in the late 1910s, parties began to play such a significant role that we can see the beginning of what was to be called Taisho Democracy, named after the new emperor of the time (who reigned 1912–1926). Beginning in the 1890s, the parliament asserted some of its own will through its ability to reject budgets put forward by the oligarchs. Political parties began to organize more seriously for elections, and started to mobilize voters. Over time, workers gained greater rights and, in 1925, universal male suffrage was instituted.

However, the decline of the economy in the 1920s helped drive Japan towards authoritarianism. Economic decline led to a backlash against the government and business leaders. Many Japanese viewed their leaders as corrupt, greedy, and weak in the face of a perceived political threat from socialist and communist parties and trade unions. This backlash was matched by disenchantment with the West, which many Japanese believed continued to place Japan in an inferior position in military and trade agreements. Against this backdrop, support for military buildup grew, and militaristic nationalism increased in Japan. The Japanese military instigated war in China, effectively beginning World War II in Asia. In 1937, Japan began the war in China in earnest. As the United States and Britain condemned Japanese aggression, Japan formed an alliance with Germany and Italy in 1940. When the United States froze Japanese assets and blocked oil supplies to Japan, the Japanese attacked Pearl Harbor in Hawaii in 1941, bringing the United States into the larger world war.

At first, Japanese forces found military success, but over time the Allied forces fought back successfully. In its occupations in Asia, Japanese forces committed atrocities against many civilians and forces they captured. The Japanese military also forced many civilian women from East and Southeast Asian countries to work as prostitutes in "comfort stations" for Japanese forces near the front lines. As a result, to this day, citizens of many Asian countries resent Japan. People living in Japan also faced hardships. Food was hard to come by and Allied bombing devastated the country. Nevertheless, Japan did not surrender until August 1945, when American forces dropped two atomic bombs on the Japanese cities of Hiroshima and Nagasaki—the only time nuclear weapons have ever been used in warfare.

Taisho Democracy ■ growth of democracy—in the form of greater political and social rights and emergence of political parties—in the first decades of the twentieth century. Named after the Emperor Taisho who reigned from 1912–1926.

Rebuilding in the Postwar Era

In the aftermath of the war, the American occupation of Japan, led by the U.S. military and General Douglas MacArthur, the Supreme Commander of the Allied Powers (SCAP), instituted a sweeping reorganization of Japanese institutions. The American occupation focused on demilitarization and democratization. Most dramatically, **Article 9** of the new **1947 Constitution**—written under the guidance of American authorities—eliminated Japan's military and renounced Japan's right to wage war. Japan later established **self-defense forces**, which ultimately grew into a military in everything but name. However, partly because the United States still retains about 35,000 U.S. military personnel on Japanese soil, with the largest percentage on the island of Okinawa, and has virtually guaranteed Japan's national security since the end of the war, Japan still spends a smaller proportion of its economy on defense relative to other wealthy democracies.[5]

The constitution also wholly transformed Japan's non-democratic system. The new constitution reduced the emperor to a mere figurehead symbol of the Japanese state, like the UK's monarch. Meanwhile, the constitution listed civil liberties for Japan's citizens, established a democratically elected bicameral parliament, which would determine the prime minister, gave women the right to vote, dispersed the power of the *zaibatsu*, and eliminated the emphasis on nationalism in primary and secondary education.

Nevertheless, there was also substantial continuity from the pre-war era. American occupation authorities needed locals to run the Japanese government on a day-to-day basis, so they left the bureaucracy largely intact. This permitted the Japanese bureaucracy to continue its major involvement in running the country's economy. Prior to the war, government bureaucrats had provided advantages to particular firms in industries that it wanted to succeed. This meant that after the war, the Japanese government adopted democracy, but not American-style free-market capitalism. Instead, it continued to protect and promote key domestic industries (although more indirectly) and eventually, the *zaibatsu* were re-established as what were called *keiretsu*—a network of interlocking firms that share their own central bank.

In 1952, the United States formally ended its military occupation of Japan. At that time, conservative politicians from the Liberal and Democratic parties dominated. However, in 1955, two smaller socialist parties joined together to form the **Japan Socialist Party (JSP)**. The JSP's base of support was organized labor, and the party devised an "us versus them" mode of appeals designed to attract voters fed up with the dominance of big business in government and politics and Japan's partial rearmament and alliance with the United States. This cohesion on the political left emerged as a serious threat to conservatives' dominance of the system. Soon thereafter, the Liberals and Democrats merged into a single party. Offsetting the JSP's strength among workers, the new Liberal Democratic Party especially appealed to voters in rural areas, and among both small and big business owners.

Many observers expected that the emergence of party alternation in power in Japan would eventually drive policymaking, but instead the LDP ultimately remained the dominant party in Japan for decades. With the exception of a few elections for

---

Article 9 ■ article in Japan's postwar constitution that eliminated Japan's military and renounced Japan's right to wage war.

1947 Constitution ■ the constitution that the Western powers imposed on Japan after World War II and that has governed Japan ever since.

self-defense forces ■ Japan's de facto military.

keiretsu ■ a network of interlocking firms that share their own central bank.

Japan Socialist Party (JSP) ■ Japan's largest opposition party from 1955 through 1993.

the less important upper chamber of parliament known as the House of Councillors, the LDP was the top vote-getter in every election for roughly the next 50 years. And, except for an unusual period in 1993–1994, the LDP and its typically politically conservative allies would control the majority in the House of Representatives until 2009.

Japan's strong postwar economy was a big part of the LDP's success for many years. In the years after World War II, Japanese leaders focused on rebuilding the country and growing the economy. The government promoted specific industries and firms, which it protected against foreign competitors. Most notably, the government pursued a strategy of industrial policy, whereby, especially in the 1950s and 1960s, the Japanese government bureaucracy shifted resources and provided regulatory advantages to specific firms in industries in which it wanted Japan to become internationally competitive. However, at the same time, in some areas, business entrepreneurs launched companies such as Sony and Honda without much government help. High rates of education meant that companies had a skilled and disciplined workforce. And Japanese citizens saved much of their income in government-run postal savings banks, which gave the government funds it could lend out at low interest rates to support small and medium-sized businesses. The result was what many call the Japanese "economic miracle." From 1950 to 1973, Japan's gross national product grew by an average of more than 10 percent a year, far greater than the 4 percent rate of annual growth in the United States for the same period.

During this time, the LDP dominated politics. In 1960, it appeared the Socialists might be able to mount a challenge to the LDP, after the LDP had forced through a renewal of the U.S.–Japan Mutual Security Treaty, which maintained the close alliance between the two countries. Protests grew in the streets against the treaty, which appeared to offer hope for parties opposing the LDP. But, ultimately, the Socialist Party's platform had little appeal for most Japanese, who benefitted from Japan's fantastic economic growth. To be sure, the LDP lost votes from its peak in 1958, and never won a majority of the vote after 1963. But it continued to win nearly 60 percent of seats throughout the 1960s, in part because of the tremendous economy and the party's strength in rural areas, which had more seats than they deserved by population.

Although the LDP's performance stagnated in the 1970s, it improved in the 1980s, again due in large part to rapid Japanese economic growth. By the 1980s, Japan was seen throughout the world as an economic superpower. The country's rapid growth caused some consternation in the United States, where some began to fear America's decline as an economic powerhouse. Some Americans resented seeing "Made in Japan" on cars, electronics, and other consumer goods, and believed that Japanese investment in U.S. government bonds, American factories, and famous American properties such as the Pebble Beach Golf Course and Rockefeller Center represented a Japanese takeover of the U.S. economy.

The 1980s proved to be Japan's high point in the postwar period. The country impressed the world with its stunning economic growth, which also helped the LDP dominate Japanese politics. Indeed, the party had one of its most successful House of Representatives elections in 1986. Although more Japanese began to complain about corruption within the LDP during the 1980s, the party always managed to maintain control of the government.

industrial policy ■ Japan's governmental approach to promoting economic growth and internationally competitive businesses. Especially in the 1950s and 1960s, the Japanese government bureaucracy shifted resources and provided regulatory advantages to specific firms in industries in which it wanted Japan to become internationally competitive.

The 1990s

The connection between strong economic growth and LDP success at the polls made the 1990s more puzzling. Beginning in 1990, Japan's economy began to decline. Yet, despite economic stagnation and increasing reports of LDP corruption, the party somehow managed to maintain its hold on power.

In the 1980s, property values in Japan skyrocketed. Some estimated that the value of land just in the Tokyo region exceeded the value of all land in the entire United States. Government economists grew worried that in this climate, real estate and stocks had become over valued and that such rapid increases in prices would fuel inflation. Over 1989–1990, the government took steps to slow this growth, but it was too aggressive in its efforts and, instead of halting price increases, caused real estate and stock prices to plummet. The Tokyo stock market lost the equivalent of $2 trillion dollars, or 38 percent of its total value, by the end of 1992, and real estate prices fell by two-thirds—a far worse drop than what occurred when the property bubble burst in the United States between 2006 and 2008.[6]

The decline in stock market and property values left many investors high and dry, unable to repay their bank loans. This, in turn, left many major Japanese banks insolvent. Bureaucrats in Japan's Ministry of Finance hid the true extent of the problem for years, so the government did not take serious action until 1998. By then, there were nearly $1 trillion in bad loans on the banks' books. When the Japanese government finally resorted to a bailout program to save the big banks—as the United States did in 2008—financial assistance covered roughly half of the bad loans or about 15 percent of GDP.[7] By comparison, the 2008 American bank bailout will likely cost less than 1 percent of U.S. GDP.[8]

Meanwhile, in the late 1980s and early 1990s in Japan, the media regularly revealed scandals surrounding the exchange of money for favors between business and politicians, and illegal ties between organized crime and the LDP. For example, in 1988 many major LDP leaders were caught accepting stocks in exchange for political favors; a similar scandal led to the bribery arrest of an LDP leader in 1993. Exposing these scandals caused increasing public outrage.

Given the economic decline and the succession of major scandals, the opposition had a great opportunity to oust the LDP from power in the 1993 elections. By then, a number of high-profile politicians had left the LDP to form new parties, partly out of frustration with the party's unwillingness to reform the political system. In the election that followed, the LDP remained the largest party, but for the first time in its history—and only time prior to 2009—did not win enough seats to form a majority in the House of Representatives. The new parties formed an anti-LDP coalition with longtime opposition parties such as the JSP and managed to pass electoral reform in 1994. However, the anti-LDP coalition would not last, and broke up after less than 11 months when the LDP convinced the Socialists—its longtime enemy!—to join it in a coalition government.

As time passed, Japan's economy continued to stagnate—so much so that the 1990s became known as the "lost decade"—and the country was afflicted by other major problems, as well. Huge corporations went belly up, bankruptcies rose, and major firms such as Nissan, NEC, and Sony had to fire thousands of workers. Japan had been ranked the most internationally competitive economy in the world in 1990, but by 1997 it had fallen to fourteenth.[9] By the end of 2002, unemployment hit a then-record 5.5 percent—unheard of in a country where large firms are known for guaranteeing workers lifetime employment—over two to three times what it had been at the height of Japan's economic growth, and the Tokyo Stock Exchange dropped to its lowest levels in more than 15 years. Adding insult to injury, in 1995, a massive earthquake hit the city of Kobe and killed thousands of people. Government gaffes appeared to slow relief efforts—and to make things worse, in 1996, it was revealed that government ministries covered up negligence that had led to the transfusion of HIV-tainted blood to many Japanese citizens.[10]

Except for 1993–1994, the LDP maintained control over the Diet, but remained unpopular. In the 1990s, new parties—most notably, the Democratic Party of Japan (DPJ)—took up the mantle as Japan's leading opposition. Tapping into anger with the LDP, the DPJ first emerged in 1996, but was unable to seriously challenge the ruling party for more than a decade.

The 2000s

In 2001, the LDP put forward Jun'ichirō Koizumi as its new prime minister. Koizumi was different from previous LDP leaders. His long wavy hair and fashionable clothes appealed to many Japanese, and he talked about genuine change. Known as a "maverick," he challenged his own party to reform many of its inefficient programs that advantaged rural parts of the economy, even though such changes might undermine the party's strongest base of support. Koizumi was wildly popular with the public, and utilized television coverage to help create his own base, independent of the party. Under his leadership, the LDP had one of its most successful elections in history in 2005. His policies also seemed to have positive effects: by 2006, the last year of Koizumi's prime ministership, the economy was growing, unemployment was dropping, wages were rising, and stock and land prices were increasing.

Unfortunately for the LDP, the Koizumi premiership did not permanently reverse the LDP's decline. When the world economy crashed in 2008, Japan's economy entered into another recession. In 2009, unemployment reached 5.7 percent and Japan faced negative economic growth. The LDP proved incapable of reversing the economic slide, corruption scandals continued to plague the party, and its leaders appeared increasingly out of touch with average voters' concerns and stopped talking about reform. In the 2009 elections, the DPJ finally swept the LDP out of power in the lower house of parliament.

However, the DPJ soon wondered what it had gotten itself into. The party proved unable to address a number of important issues—such as the relocation of American military bases in Japan—and started losing popularity quickly. More difficult, still, on March 11, 2011, the country was hit by a 9.0 magnitude earthquake, which immediately led to devastating tsunami that crushed vast portions of northeast Japan. Perhaps most overwhelming, the tsunami destabilized nuclear reactors, which led substantial radiation to leak into the air, ground, and water. At first, popular support for the government grew in response to the crisis. And the Japanese government acted swiftly in a number of areas, immediately mobilizing more than 100,000 troops and accepting assistance from countries around the globe.[11] The government also provided more than 27,000 temporary housing

"MAVERICK" PRIME MINISTER KOIZUMI

Known as a "maverick," LDP Prime Minister Jun'ichirō Koizumi used the mass media to develop a base of support, independent of the party. He talked about genuine change and challenged his own party members to reform many of the government's inefficient programs that advantaged rural parts of the economy, even though such changes might undermine the party's strongest base of support.

units to the devastated areas within ten weeks of the earthquake.[12] But popular sentiment held that neither the power company in charge of the reactors nor the government was totally open about the extent of the problem, and the public grew impatient with the slow pace of shutting down the reactors. Public frustration with the government grew, as the DPJ prime minister put forward inconsistent and unclear statements about the implementation of safety measures involving the reactors and the future of nuclear power in Japan. The government's handling of the response to the disaster became a political issue, as the LDP and opponents of the prime minister even within the DPJ criticized the government, in part in the hopes of gaining electoral advantage—although few high-profile politicians offered meaningful alternative proposals. The result was a badly weakened DPJ government, but still clear signs that Japan had become a competitive party system.

We should be careful not to let the DPJ's problems distract us from how significant the new party's rise has been: if we focus too much on the new volatility in Japanese politics, we overlook what a dramatic shift it is away from decades of LDP dominance. Indeed, LDP dominance was the defining feature of Japanese politics for more than a decade, holding on even when there was little reason to think that it should. Probably the most significant question to understanding the way Japanese politics functions is, how was the LDP able to hold on to power for so many years, despite almost 20 years of economic stagnation and popular discontent over the party's economic policies, compounded by party corruption and overall ineffectiveness?

SUMMARY TABLE

Historical Overview: From Tokugawa to the Fall of the LDP

1603–1868	Tokugawa era	Largely peaceful and stable period that saw the introduction of central governance by the government.
1853	U.S. warships "open" Japan	In 1853, U.S. navy ships arrived in Japan and, threatening military force, forged a series of unequal trade agreements that favored the West and infringed on Japanese sovereignty.
1868	Meiji Restoration	A revolution led by samurai who "restored" power to the emperor and created a new centralized monarchy that exerted power throughout the country.
1868–1912	Meiji Era	Period in which Japan sought to modernize Japan and "catch up" to the West by means of economic and military development. The Meiji leaders promoted strong government, an educated populace, a thriving economy, and a powerful military.
1894–1895	Sino–Japanese War	War with China. Japan's victory established itself as a regional power in Asia and stoked greater nationalism at home.
1904–1905	Russo–Japanese War	Bloody war with Russia. Japan was widely viewed as the victor—a shocking result at the time for a "non-white" nation to defeat a major "white" power.
1912–1926	Taisho era	Period (associated with the Emperor Taisho) in which Japanese democratic institutions began to thrive. Marked by the development of political parties, and the enactment of universal male suffrage.
1926–1937	Lead up to WWII	Increasing conflict between Japan and other countries in East Asia. Marked by efforts by the Japanese military to gain influence and control in portions of the continent.

(Continued)

SUMMARY TABLE (CONTINUED)

1937–1945	Japan's participation in WWII	Japan initiated war with China in 1937 and engaged the U.S. in 1941 by bombing Pearl Harbor. Japan did not surrender until August 1945 when American forces dropped two atomic bombs on Hiroshima and Nagasaki—the only time nuclear weapons have ever been used in warfare.
1945–1952	American Occupation of Japan	American military forces occupied Japan, restructuring its government and society. In 1947, occupation authorities introduced a new constitution to Japan, the same document that still governs Japan today.
1955	Birth of LDP and JSP	Both the Japan Socialist Party and the Liberal Democratic Party are born.
1950s–1970s	Japan's "Miracle Economy"	From 1950–1973, Japan's gross national product grew by an average of more than 10% a year.
1950s–1970s	Environmental movements	Upset over significant pollution and declining social welfare, Japanese citizens began to organize for change. In an effort to regain support, the LDP implemented anti-pollution measures.
1970–1980s	Japan as an "economic superpower"	Japan's economic growth continues and Japanese products spread throughout world markets.
1980s	Bubble economy	Period in which Japanese stocks and real estate became grossly overvalued.
Late 1980s–early 1990s	Bursting of the bubble	The Japanese government raised interest rates, which led to a sell-off of stocks and property, thus leading to dramatic drop in the value of both. The result was numerous unrepayable bank loans and a stagnant economy.
1990s	Lost decade	Japan's economy stagnates.
1993	Lower house election that costs the LDP control of government	Several high-profile politicians leave the LDP to form new parties. In the election that follows, the LDP remains the largest party, but for the first time in its history—and only time prior to 2009—fails to win enough seats to form a majority in parliament.
1993–1994	Anti-LDP coalition government	New parties form an anti-LDP coalition with longtime opposition parties such as the JSP.

(Continued)

SUMMARY TABLE (CONTINUED)

1994	Electoral reform		Led by the anti-LDP cabinet, the government reforms the rules by which lower house elections are held.
1994–1996	LDP-Socialist Party coalition		The LDP convinces the Socialist Party to join it in a coalition government, thus ending the anti-LDP coalition's hold on power.
1996–1998	Birth of the DPJ		The Democratic Party of Japan forms in 1996 as a relatively small center-left party. A new version of the party forms in 1998, as the 1996 DPJ merges with others who seek to create a consolidated challenge to the LDP.
2000–present	Continued economic stagnation		Japan's economy continues to stagnate.
2001–2006	Prime Minister Koizumi		Koizumi takes over as president of the LDP and prime minister. He promises "reform without sanctuary." He is among Japan's most popular leaders, but once he leaves office the LDP faces much greater difficulty.
2009	DPJ wins the lower house election		The election marks the first lower house poll in which the LDP is not the largest seat winner. DPJ controls the government and position of prime minister.
2011	Triple disaster		On March 11, 2011, Japan is hit by a 9.0 magnitude earthquake, which quickly leads to a devastating tsunami. The tsunami pounds a handful of nuclear reactors, which then leak radiation. The DPJ quickly mobilized troops and built temporary housing to respond to the crisis, but the public was frustrated by the poor quality of information provided about the crisis, unclear government nuclear plans, and the slow pace of halting radiation leaks.

INSTITUTIONS OF JAPAN

Japan's democratic institutions promote limited government by offering citizens extensive rights and privileges. The constitution guarantees numerous individual freedoms, such as equality before the law; freedom of thought, conscience, and religion; freedom of assembly and association; and universal suffrage. Free and fair elections are held regularly, and candidates' and parties' right to contest those elections is protected.

Yet, despite all these individual freedoms and the formal apparatus of democracy, for decades Japanese politics was dominated by a single party—a dynamic

5.2 How have Japanese institutions helped promote and maintain LDP dominance?

that is more consistent with non-democratic rule. Japan's political institutions helped perpetuate the LDP in power by centralizing political authority in a unitary, parliamentary system. Its electoral rules helped governing parties like the LDP that could channel state resources to the districts of their candidates. In addition, Japan's powerful bureaucracy worked in support of the ruling party, and for years, Japan's weak judiciary failed to stand up to the ruling government party. In this section, we will explore the ways that Japanese institutions favored one-party rule for so long.

Unitarism

Unlike federal countries, such as the United States, that give substantial political authority to sub-national units, Japan places most power in the hands of the central government. Japan is divided into 47 **prefectures**, which are Japan's largest administrative subunits—something like the states in the United States, but with much less independent authority. While prefectures are gaining somewhat greater tax and regulation discretion today,[13] Japan's central government has long restricted localities' revenue raising ability. Most prefectures and lower-level municipalities still rely upon the central government to fund projects, and in this way, the central government can push its own priorities at the local level by providing or denying subsidies. As a result, the party that controls Japan's central government has power over the prefectures that rely upon state resources. And, because of LDP central governments' power and control over resources that local governments need, large numbers of local voters and politicians grew to support the LDP. In this way, the LDP developed a very strong local base of support that cemented its national dominance.[14]

Parliamentarism

Japan's postwar constitution provides democratic accountability through elections to its **Diet** or bicameral parliament. Members of the lower chamber of parliament, the **House of Representatives (HR)**, serve for four-year terms. However, like most parliamentary systems, the HR can also hold early elections at any point before the term is up. Members of the upper house, the **House of Councillors (HC)**, serve fixed six-year terms.

Like unitarism, parliamentarism in Japan tends to centralize political power. Because it lacks the checks and balances of a presidential system, Japanese politics has narrowed the possible arenas in which an opposition can gain power. Moreover, a parliamentary system does not formally separate the executive and legislative branches of government, so a single party can more easily wield power without constraint. When parliamentarism is combined with single-party government, we have a recipe for effective government. However, such a combination also tends to constrain opposition parties' ability to limit government power.

In theory, opposition parties can use no-confidence motions to check the authority of the ruling party. For example, in 1993, opposition parties joined with several defectors from the LDP to pass a no-confidence motion that led to the dissolution of the lower house and new elections. However, no-confidence motions have rarely passed in Japan, simply because during the postwar era, the LDP typically had an overwhelming majority in the House of Representatives.

A majority in the House of Representatives determines Japan's prime minister, who, in turn, selects the cabinet. For years, Japan's prime minister has been a particularly weak leader: in order to maintain party stability, the LDP spread important government posts roughly evenly throughout all factions in the party. In addition, "iron triangles" developed on most major issues, with small groups of LDP politicians (who were not necessarily in the cabinet), government bureaucrats, and key interest groups working together to determine policy. As a result, Japanese prime ministers have typically had far less centralized power than their counterparts in other countries, such as the UK. However, since the 1980s, Japanese prime ministers have gained power. Beginning in the 1980s, some prime ministers took advantage of the opportunities provided by the media—especially television, as larger numbers of news and opinion shows have emerged since the 1980s—to create a mass base of support that they could use to go over the heads of powerful party members. In the 1990s, the government passed legislation that centralized governing power more thoroughly in the cabinet (which is led by the prime minister). Finally, as we will see in our discussion of Japan's electoral system, changes in the way Japanese Diet members get elected promoted a shift to more centralized parties.[15]

The key way that opposition parties can exercise some check on government power is by winning control of the upper chamber of the Diet. The House of Representatives passes the budget and ratifies foreign treaties, without any input from the House of Councilors (although the HC can briefly delay the passage of the budget and/or treaties). But in all other policy areas, both houses of parliament must approve bills for them to become law. Since 1989, no party has held a majority in the upper house, but prior to 2007, the LDP was always the largest party in that house. Overall, as long as a single party holds a majority in both chambers of the Diet, parliamentarism in Japan tends to promote centralization of power. Since the formation of the LDP, single-party government has been the norm. However, bicameralism has at times given the opposition greater power to check the prime minister's party. By winning a majority in the upper chamber, opposition parties were able to block legislation passed by the lower in the following cases: in 1998, the majority held by non-LDP parties in the upper house forced the LDP to address the banking crisis. From 2007 to 2009, the LDP controlled the lower house, but the DPJ was the largest party in the upper house and, therefore, held off some LDP legislation.

In short, at times in more recent years the opposition has been able to block LDP power by holding a substantial number of seats in the Diet's upper house. But, in general, parliamentary government controlled by a single party in Japan has allowed the LDP to centralize power in the cabinet with few checks and balances from outside forces.

Electoral System

The rules used to elect politicians to seats in the Diet provided the LDP a number of advantages that helped it maintain its dominance. In the 1990s, reform of the rules used to elect politicians to the lower house led to significant changes in political behavior in Japan, but did not lead to the LDP's fall for many years.

Japan's 1947–1993 Lower House Electoral System Through most of the postwar period, the main electoral system used to elect politicians to both houses of Japan's Diet was the single non-transferable vote (SNTV) system: as used in elections to the House of Representatives from 1947–1993, Japan was composed of more than 100 districts, with each typically electing three, four, or five candidates to office. In each district, each voter cast a single ballot for an individual candidate, and whichever candidates (up to the number of seats in the district) received the most votes were awarded the seats.

single non-transferable vote (SNTV) ■ Japan's House of Representatives electoral system from 1947–1993. Voters cast ballots for individual candidates in electoral districts. Most districts held three, four, or five seats. In each district, those candidates (up to the number of seats in the district) who received the most votes were awarded the seats.

Elections to Japan's Upper House House of Councillors elections elect half of the upper house every three years—so each member of the upper house is up for election every six years—and treat each prefecture as an SNTV district—each with between two and ten seats (but only half of these seats are up for grabs in any given election). In upper house elections, Japanese voters cast two ballots. The first is for a candidate in an SNTV race. The rules governing the second ballot have changed more than once over the years. In 2010, with this second ballot voters had a choice of casting their vote either for a party or for an individual candidate. That year, 73 seats were allocated via prefectural SNTV districts, and 48 were allocated to parties and candidates according to their share of the second ballot votes cast across the country.

Personalistic Elections The SNTV electoral system encourages politicians to emphasize their own individual personalities and ability to bring benefits back to their districts. Elections in Japan long turned on politicians' individual qualities rather than on parties' policy positions or ideological stances. LDP politicians in particular focused on developing a personal vote—building up electoral support through their individual efforts to aid constituents—rather than on ideological or policy appeals. There were two major ways in which LDP politicians attempted to build up a personal vote.

personal vote ■ for years, most politicians (especially from the LDP) in Japan drummed up electoral support through their personal popularity and individual efforts to aid constituents, rather than on ideological or policy appeals.

First, Japanese politicians—from all parties, but particularly those from the LDP—spent a great deal of time, energy, and money dealing with constituents' individual concerns. Conventional depictions of Japanese electoral politics highlight politicians' appearances at countless weddings, funerals, and parties to pass out cash and other sorts of gifts. Japan's electoral rules forced politicians to compete not only with candidates from other parties but also other candidates from *their own* party as well, thus making it absolutely essential that they consolidate their electoral support based on the personal vote. Moreover, extensive personal contact with voters was essential because Japanese campaign laws restricted candidates' and parties' access to TV, radio, and print, making it difficult to rely on mass appeals channeled through the media.[16] Election campaigns are officially only about two weeks long, and campaign activities outside of that period are prohibited. This means that candidates had to constantly campaign informally by meeting with their constituents. Because there are few methods available to appeal to voters and little time to campaign, it is difficult for new candidates to attract attention—thus, providing a major advantage to incumbents, most notably candidates from the LDP.

To develop a personal vote base of support, candidates in Japan long relied on *kōenkai*, personal support organizations through which candidates create close ties to voters. Politicians provided their *kōenkai* members with employment, helped their children with school placement, and sometimes even provided marital matchmaking services. Politicians also frequently donated bottles of expensive *sake* to local organizations that *kōenkai* members led, and often gave money for small-scale community construction projects that *kōenkai* members pushed.[17] In turn, during non-campaign periods, *kōenkai* members organized on behalf of their politicians (and got around many of the campaign restrictions by avoiding referring to the politicians as a candidate in an election), and mobilized the campaign get-out-the-vote effort during the official campaign.

kōenkai ■ Japanese politicians' personal support organizations that mobilize support for individual candidates.

Second, Japanese politicians—again, especially those from the LDP—attempted to develop a personal vote based on their ability to bring government benefits back to constituents in their district. Such spending focused on direct benefits, such as price subsidies for farmers or massive construction projects, which both generated jobs and improved infrastructure. For decades, Japan has spent far more money than did similar countries on public works projects, such as bridges, roads, and irrigation. In 1996, for example, public works spending in Japan amounted to 8.7 percent of GDP, compared against 3.2 percent in France, 2.2 percent in Germany, 1.4 percent in the UK, and 1.7 percent in the United States.[18]

Government spending was particularly important in rural and less-wealthy constituencies, where LDP candidates tended to perform best. The emphasis on channeling government spending back to their districts brought both benefits and costs to LDP candidates. On the one hand, many voters supported LDP candidates precisely because of their pragmatic, relatively non-ideological approach to politics, and many LDP politicians made long careers out of their ability to obtain benefits for their constituents and districts. Japanese voters typically have had weak attachment to political parties and voted for politicians whom they liked personally or who showered their districts with benefits—an attitude that served to benefit the LDP and helps explain its long grip on power. In a recent study, Japan ranked fourth lowest among wealthy democracies in terms of the proportion of voters who list themselves as "partisans" of a particular party,[19] and since the 1970s, the number of independent voters has grown dramatically. Since the mid-1990s, about 50 percent of the electorate has claimed to prefer no party at all.[20]

On the other hand, some voters—especially those in relatively wealthy urban areas where infrastructure such as roads, bridges, and subways is already world-class—have not benefited from additional government spending and see public works projects as wasteful. Moreover, many Japanese citizens believe that such spending encourages government corruption. Construction projects often go to political supporters who jack up the price of the contracts in order to provide politicians with kickbacks. Thus, while government spending on public works projects helped the LDP win elections in poorer and rural areas, it hurt LDP support among urban voters, who were far more likely to vote for opposition parties in the postwar era.

Malapportionment The LDP did not win a majority of votes in a House of Representatives election after 1963, but it still typically won a majority of seats. A key way that political institutions helped the LDP maintain its position of power was through **malapportionment**, in which certain rural and underpopulated legislative districts tended to have many more seats per share of the population than certain urban and over-populated districts. Put differently, many rural districts got more representation than they deserved according to population, and other urban districts got less representation than they deserved. When Japan's electoral districts were created in the early postwar period, there were roughly equal numbers of voters per seat in each. Over time, millions of Japanese moved from the countryside to the cities, but the cities were not given enough additional seats to compensate for their rising populations.

This meant that rural areas became overrepresented and cities were underrepresented. For example, just as the U.S. Senate gives equal weight to Wyoming and California, malapportionment in Japan gave rural districts relatively greater weight within the Japanese legislature. In the United States, the malapportionment of the Senate is counterbalanced by the equally apportioned House of Representatives, but in Japan both houses of the Diet are malapportioned in favor of the countryside.

As Figure 5.1 shows, the LDP won a much larger share of seats in rural areas than in cities: between 1958–1990, the LDP and conservative independents

malapportionment ■ in Japan, many rural districts got more representation than they deserved according to population while many urban districts got less representation than they deserved.

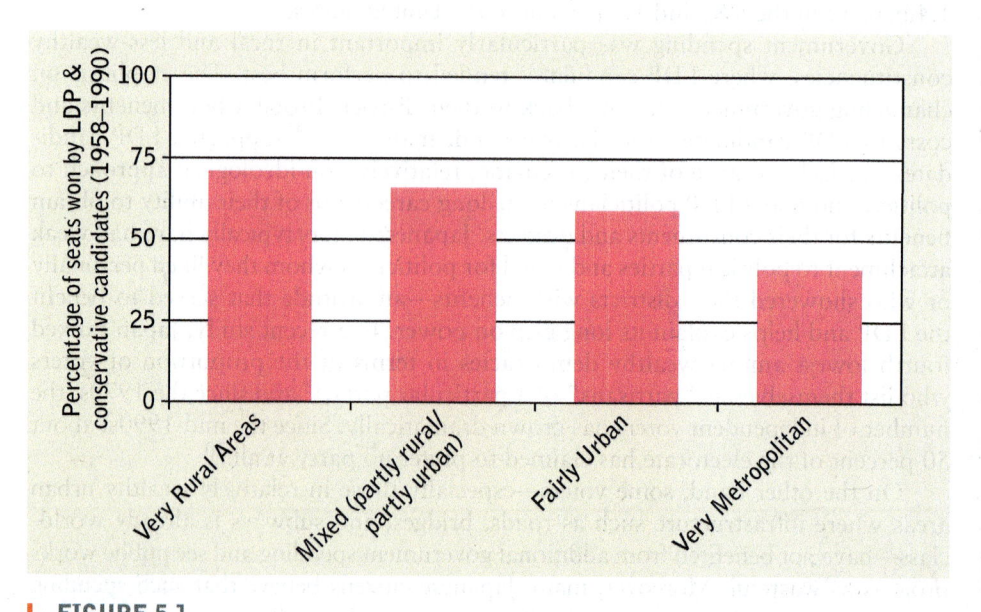

FIGURE 5.1

Percentage of Seats Won by the LDP and Conservative Independents by Level of Urbanness (1958–1990)

The more urban the districts, the smaller the share of seats that the LDP wins.

(who often joined the LDP immediately after winning office) won 71 percent of all seats in the most rural districts in the country, but only 41 percent in the most urban districts, thus giving the ruling party an advantage over other parties. Its candidates in rural districts could win seats with a relatively small number of votes. In contrast, in the urban districts, candidates required many more votes to win. The United States had the same problem until 1964 when the U.S. Supreme Court decided that anything less than "one person, one vote" was unconstitutional. The Supreme Court in Japan, however, has never forced the Diet to completely reapportion according to population, even when it has sometimes declared malapportionment unconstitutional, so the problem remained. In this way, malapportionment helped the LDP retain power. However, in 1994, Japan dramatically reduced malapportionment when it introduced the new electoral system, which we will discuss in the next subsection. Still, the LDP did not lose power until 2009, meaning that malapportionment only partly explains the persistence of LDP dominance.

Japan's New Electoral System and Changes in Campaign Behavior As noted, after a series of corruption scandals involving LDP politicians, Japan reformed its electoral system in 1994 in an effort to de-emphasize the personal vote. Japan's electoral rule today focuses somewhat less on candidates' personal qualities and pushes voters to consider candidates' partisan attachments. Today, Japan uses a mixed electoral rule similar to what is used in Germany. Under the mixed system, each voter casts two ballots for elections to the lower chamber of the Diet: one for a party in proportional elections and one for a candidate in a single-member district election using the plurality rule.

There are 480 total seats in the lower house of parliament. Three hundred seats are allocated using the plurality rule in single-member districts (SMD). Here, voters cast a vote for a candidate; whichever candidate receives the most votes in that district wins the seat, like in the U.S. House of Representatives elections. The other 180 seats are divided into 11 regional districts ranging from six to 29 seats each. In these districts, parties win seats based on proportional representation rules (PR)—that is, in proportion to the percentage of votes they receive in that district. Once the votes are counted, the election authorities tell each party how many seats it won in each PR constituency. If a party wins three seats in a given constituency, for example, the first three candidates on its PR list in that constituency get the seats. This part of the electoral system gives the party considerable authority over candidates, and forces all candidates to cooperate rather than compete against each other for attention, because the more votes the entire party wins, the better are each candidate's chances of winning a seat.

After this system went into effect in 1994, elections became somewhat more focused on parties as organizations and less on individual candidates. In the single-member districts, voters cast ballots for individuals rather than parties, meaning candidates still must highlight their personal qualities. However, with only one representative per district, what party the candidates belong to has become more important to voters. And for both the single-member and PR districts, all candidates must appeal to the party leaders in order to obtain nomination. Even more, in the case of the PR list, they must demonstrate loyalty and effective work on behalf of the party to obtain one of the top spots, which virtually guarantee election.

In addition, the post-1993 electoral system helped centralize parties and also pushed Japan's opposition to consolidate into a single stronger party. Under the old rules, the LDP needed to run many candidates—all of whom had their own personal bases of support—in each district in order to win a majority, but the new rules allowed the party to centralize power more in the hands of the leaders who could choose the single party candidate in each SMD and the candidates who would go on the party PR list.

The rule change also helped the opposition centralize as well—by pushing the opposition parties to consolidate around a single option, ultimately the DPJ—which helped create a more viable challenge to the LDP. This consolidation occurred because to win a sizeable number of single-member district seats, the opposition could not afford to fragment its vote among several candidates in each district: dividing the opposition vote would virtually hand the election to the LDP candidate in every district, since the candidate with the most votes wins. After 1993, the opposition consolidated around a smaller number of parties. And after 1993, politicians focused less on their own personal agendas, politics centered more on parties, and the system consolidated around two large parties rather than one government party and several small opposition parties. Although the 1994 reform did not immediately end the LDP's political dominance, it did serve to weaken the party, in part by undermining its traditional strength and its personal-vote-based appeals, and alter one area of the opposition's traditional weakness, its fragmentation. The combination of Japan's relatively centralized political institutions—created in the aftermath of World War II—and its emphasis on personalistic politics (especially until 1994) is key to understanding the LDP's long dominance.

Local politicians and voters believed that LDP politicians used political criteria to distribute government funding—the LDP made a big show of awarding government contracts to its friends and to districts where voters would support the party in elections, and threatened to send few projects to districts where the party received little electoral support. Given this dynamic, municipal- and prefectural-level politicians faced considerable pressure to join the LDP, and they in turn would pressure local voters to support the LDP. Not surprisingly, the LDP always dominated elections to prefectural assemblies, often doing better than it did in national parliamentary elections. In contrast, opposition parties typically performed worse in local elections than they did in national elections.

The LDP used its local strength to maintain its national level success. Subnational politicians proved to be great help to LDP candidates running for national office, because they knew the districts' concerns and worked on a daily basis with locals, even more than the most locally-oriented national politicians—most of whom, of course, spend considerable time in Tokyo. Many national and sub-national politicians developed a symbiotic relationship: the national politicians help bring funding to the district on behalf of the local politicians, and the local politicians organize voters for the national politicians.

This situation particularly helped the LDP, given the candidate-focused elections. Until 2009, the LDP continued to outperform its rivals in the single-member district elections in Japan's lower house mixed electoral system, where voters cast ballots for individual candidates. In contrast, opposition parties (including the DPJ) have tended to perform better in the PR elections, where voters cast their ballots for parties, not individual candidates. In the single-member district elections, the most successful candidates are typically incumbents—those who already hold office and, therefore, have greater name recognition and ability to use government resources to attract support. Thanks to its success in sub-national elections, the LDP had a huge pool of local-level office holders that it ran for national elections. These candidates often did well in national races.[21] In contrast, because opposition parties typically did poorly in local or prefectural elections, they had fewer competitive candidates to run for national office. In short, the LDP used Japan's highly centralized political system to its advantage for several decades, cultivating candidates who knew their districts and who had developed a strong personal vote support base. In this environment, the more ideologically oriented opposition parties tended to struggle. As we will see later, it was only once elections became at least as much about parties as they were about individual candidacies that the opposition was able to topple the LDP finally.

The Weak Judiciary

Formally, Article 76 in Japan's constitution provides for an independent judiciary, and Article 81 grants it the authority to determine the constitutionality of any law parliament passes. However, elected leaders—most notably those from the LDP—have long held considerable sway over judges. Throughout the postwar era, the LDP appointed Supreme Court judges who were sympathetic to the party's views. As of 2007, the Supreme Court had ruled that official acts were unconstitutional only nine times,[22] thus passing decisions that favored the LDP's wishes. Most striking, the Supreme Court typically overturned lower court decisions that went against LDP electoral interests. For example, the Court overturned lower court efforts to ban campaign rules—such as limits on politicians' ability to engage in electoral canvassing—that worked to the LDP's advantage. In addition, the LDP even managed to influence which corruption cases the judiciary would pursue, shielding many of its key members and supporters from indictment.[23]

The Powerful Bureaucracy

The national civil service bureaucracy also played a significant role in helping the LDP retain power. Since the early twentieth century, government bureaucrats have taken a leading role in policymaking in Japan. For example, in the postwar era, the Ministry of Finance and Ministry of International Trade and Industry set many of the policies that shaped Japan's economic success story. Jobs in the bureaucracy were prestigious, in part because bureaucrats had such tremendous influence over the direction of important national policies. And the bureaucracy's success helped the LDP, as well: because of the bureaucracy's apparent mastery of the economy, the LDP could focus on issues of specific local concern to their different constituents, while taking credit for economic growth.

However, the bureaucracy's public image and reputation has changed dramatically in the last 20 years, from fair and effective to corrupt and incompetent. The LDP's slow response to the 1990s financial crisis and economic decline has ruined the bureaucracy's reputation for skillful economic policymaking. The bureaucracy's cover-up of blood suppliers' distribution of HIV-infected blood, its loss of millions of citizens' pension records, and the widespread practice of *amakudari* (descent from heaven), whereby bureaucrats retire from government work to take on high-paying jobs in the industries they had regulated, have all served to dirty the bureaucracy's formerly clean image.

In part because the bureaucracy was long associated with the LDP, and helped it maintain its grip on power, the recently elected DPJ put bureaucratic reform at the center of its campaign pledges, and in early 2010 began public oversight hearings designed to expose the roots of corruption and bureaucratic malpractice. In addition to many examples of bribery, government investigations uncovered thousands of cases of businesses and local governments taking central government bureaucrats out to lavish meals in the hopes of receiving favorable regulations in exchange.

In sum, as the table below indicates, the unitary system in Japan served to concentrate authority in the central government. The system of parliamentary rule, the weak judiciary, and a powerful bureaucracy also helped limit the opportunities for opposition groups to assert themselves into the policymaking process. The relative absence of checks and balances in Japan's institutional structure, combined with single-party governments for nearly the entire postwar era, gave the LDP the opportunity to use its control of the national government to create major advantages for itself—especially in an electoral system that seemed to favor individual LDP candidates and the rural areas that supported the party.

amakudari ■ practice in which bureaucrats retire from government jobs to high-paying jobs in the industries they had regulated.

SUMMARY TABLE

Institutions of Japan: Centralizing Political Authority in a Unitary, Parliamentary System

Unitarism	Unlike federal countries such as the U.S. that give substantial political authority to subnational units, Japan places most power in the hands of the central government.
Parliamentarism	Japan's legislature is the Diet, a bicameral parliament. Members of the lower chamber of parliament, the House of Representatives (HR), serve for four-year terms. However, like most parliamentary systems, the HR can also hold early elections at any point before the term is up. Members of the upper house, the House of Councillors (HC), serve fixed six-year terms.
Prime Minister	The head of government, usually the leader of the largest party in the House of Representatives. Typically, the Japanese prime minister has been relatively weak, but has gained power in recent years.

(Continued)

SUMMARY TABLE (CONTINUED)

SNTV Electoral System	The single non-transferable vote (SNTV) electoral system in multi-member districts was used to elect members of Japan's House of Representatives from 1947 to 1993. Voters cast ballots for individual candidates in electoral districts. Most districts held three, four, or five seats. In each district, whichever candidates (up to the number of seats in the district) received the most votes were awarded the seats. The electoral system is still the used to elect members of the House of Councillors.
Japan's New Electoral System	In 1994, Japan changed its system to elect members to the House of Representatives. Under the new mixed system, each voter casts two ballots for elections to the lower chamber of the Diet: one for a party in proportional elections and one for a candidate in a single-member district election using the plurality rule.
Judiciary	Japan's constitution provides for an independent judiciary, but in practice the judiciary has not tended to act independent of the LDP's wishes.
Government Bureaucracy	Japan's government bureaucracy has been extremely powerful, and has played a major part in policymaking, especially with respect to the economy. For many years, Japanese held the bureaucracy in high esteem, but in recent years a variety of failures—most notably, economic stagnation—have led to public displeasure and distrust of the bureaucracy.

IDENTITIES OF JAPAN

Japan is a relatively homogenous society in comparative perspective; it lacks the religious, racial, ethnic, or economic class cleavages that exist in many countries. This high degree of socio-cultural homogeneity made it difficult to form a political opposition to the LDP. This contrasts with the ethnic divisions in India and Nigeria's party systems, and the class divisions in the UK and Germany's party systems, for example. In Japan, status—usually derived from one's age or length of service within a hierarchy—plays an important part in shaping political identity. However, this emphasis on seniority status in Japan did not provide a division that challengers to the ruling party could use to their advantage, and even helped maintain LDP dominance.

5.3 How do the Japanese identify themselves and how do these identities shape Japanese politics?

Watch the Video "Royalty and Politics in Japan" at **mypoliscilab.com**

Japanese Homogeneity

In many ways, Japan is extremely homogeneous. About 95 percent of the population is ethnically Japanese, nearly everyone speaks Japanese, and religion is not a major cleavage—only about 1 percent of Japanese are Christian. Most of the population is

Buddhist, Shinto, or both. Shinto is Japan's indigenous religion, involving informal prayer to multiple gods at tiny shrines, and focusing on the preservation of purity and life in human society and nature.[24] However, being Shinto does not preclude a person from also being a part of other religions. In recent decades, "new-new religions"—often founded on some combination of Buddhist principles and millenarian beliefs—have emerged, attracting a small but devout following, particularly in urban areas.[25] Nevertheless, on the whole, such groups remain relatively small, and religion is not central to the daily lives of most Japanese.[26]

Growing out of the country's homogeneity, many Japanese rightfully take pride in many unique aspects of Japanese heritage and culture—but some leaders stretch this view to absurd lengths. For example, in the 1980s, Japanese policymakers justified restrictions on the importation of foreign beef by claiming that Japanese have unusually long intestines.[27] At other times, some Japanese leaders stated a belief that both Japan's homogeneity helped promote economic success and in the United States racial and ethnic heterogeneity slowed down economic growth.[28] Of course, this does not explain why Japan's economic growth stagnated or the United States's boomed in the 1990s to mid-2000s. Still, it remains true that homogeneity—and especially Japanese *perceptions* of homogeneity—has meant that few social, cultural, or economic identity groups exist that can divide Japanese from each other politically.

Japan is not totally homogeneous. Roughly 5 percent of Japan's 125 million people can be classified as members of minority groups.[29] Japan's largest minority group is the Burakumin (approximately 2–3 million people). Burakumin look exactly like other Japanese, but their ancestors were categorized as inferior members of society in the Tokugawa period. Somewhat like the old "untouchable" castes in India, in the Tokugawa period, Burakumin were tasked with "dirty" jobs involving the slaughter and use of animals (like leather making).

Although discrimination against Burakumin is now illegal, Burakumin still experience prejudice. For example, status-conscious parents sometimes hire private detectives to investigate the family background of their children's potential spouses, and oppose marriage to a Burakumin. Some companies also purchase secretly published information on Burakumin, and deny employment to anyone believed to have these ancestors. Burakumin remain more likely than other Japanese to be employed in low-paying, physically demanding jobs and to have lower levels of education.[30]

Perhaps the most complicated situation in Japan exists for ethnic Koreans, who may account for up to 1 million people in Japan. During Japan's colonization of Korea, many Koreans came to Japan, often unwillingly as forced laborers. Most returned to Korea after the war, but many remained in Japan and have faced discrimination ever since. Ethnic Koreans—even if they or their parents were born in Japan—are not considered Japanese citizens, but remain classified as "resident aliens" who must carry an alien registration card with them at all times. Korean resident aliens can become naturalized Japanese citizens, but the government does not make the process easy. Japanese Koreans also face discrimination in other areas, including housing, employment, and education.[31]

Finally, since the 1980s, a growing number of foreign workers have come to live in Japan's major cities, especially individuals from the Philippines, China, Brazil, Peru, and Thailand. Japan's population is shrinking as a result of the country's

Burakumin ■
Japan's largest minority group (approximately 2–3 million people). Somewhat like the old "untouchable" castes in India, Burakumin—despite looking exactly like other Japanese—tend to face significant discrimination.

low birthrate, so there aren't enough native workers to fill positions that open up as the workforce ages. Moreover, there is a persistent shortage of workers for jobs that most Japanese don't want, such as in difficult and dangerous construction jobs. Estimates suggest that there are at least 1.3 million foreign workers in Japan, some illegally.[32]

Despite these exceptions, Japan remains a relatively homogenous society, especially in political terms. No politically important ethnic, religious, linguistic, or racial cleavages exist that could divide Japanese society and potentially generate the formation of identity-based movements or political parties.

Class Identity

Japan is not a classless society. Labor unions have existed since the pre-war era,[33] and for years the LDP's leading opponent was the Japan Socialist Party, which represented Japan's public sector unions. However, class divisions are less important than in some other wealthy democracies, such as England or Germany. In most countries, labor unions emerged to protect workers' rights, employment, and wages. Yet, in Japan's prewar period, the government managed to shift labor unions' attention away from protecting the rights of workers, and toward promoting national unity behind the government's imperial aims. Using political pressure and propaganda, the government highlighted nationalism and denigrated class-consciousness, which was portrayed as traitorous because it divided Japanese people from each other.

After the war, class-consciousness remained relatively weak, primarily because Japan's economy grew so rapidly that even the working class and the relatively poor saw their incomes grow. Moreover, inequality was never an obvious problem—in fact, up through the 1980s, Japan ranked among the world leaders in terms of relative income equality between the upper and lower classes. One survey taken in the 1980s found that 90 percent of Japanese categorized themselves as middle class.[34] This positive economic performance limited the JSP's ability to attract voters. Japan's relative wealth helped dampen a sense of class-consciousness. Moreover, the organization of labor in Japan further contained potential class identity. In many countries, unions are organized at the industry level—such as automotive workers or steelworkers. In Japan, labor was encouraged to organize at the company level, so that there would be only one union representing all workers at the Toyota Corporation, for example. As a result, workers developed solidarity with others from their own company, but gained a much less deep sense of class-consciousness. Moreover, Japan's large firms maintain a policy of "lifetime" employment, in which workers could expect to be employed by a single company for their entire working lives. In this system, wages were tied to seniority—a worker's wages went up simply by remaining in the job for a long time, thus further linking workers to their company.

Status in Japan

In contrast to other forms of political identity, social status—relationships based on some sort of hierarchy within society—has long played an important role in shaping Japanese society and politics. This emphasis on social status does not mean that Japanese are culturally predisposed to follow orders, just that relationships are often structured hierarchically, between acknowledged superiors and inferiors.

During the Tokugawa era, social status classified everyone hierarchically: samurai warriors ranked above farmers, who stood above artisans (craftsmen)—such as the makers of clothes, furniture, and even swords—who outranked merchants.[35] The Meiji Restoration eliminated this status system and ended the privileges of the samurai. Many samurai were devastated as they were forced to cut the topknot—the symbol of their privileged role—from their hair.

Social hierarchies today differ greatly from those in the Tokugawa era. Today, nearly any Japanese can rise in social status. There are few restrictions on the type of people who can become a part of the elite. To gain access to the top, educational achievement is paramount. To be sure, just as is the case anywhere, wealth and prestige provide many advantages. For example, Japanese kids attend *juku*, or cram-schools, after school to prepare for their college entrance exams, and more successful *juku* tend to be pricey. And attending prestigious schools helps Japanese get good jobs. Nevertheless, there are few restrictions on the type of people who can become a part of the elite.

Not all status is related to where one goes to college; in Japanese schools and corporations, hierarchy is based on seniority. More senior students, as well as employees who have been in the company longest, receive the highest rank and respect. In this way, anyone can move up in the hierarchy if they do well on the required tests (which get them into top schools), or stay in an organization long enough.

To illustrate how Japanese can acquire high social status, consider the example of career patterns in Japan's government bureaucracy. For decades, the most prestigious jobs in Japan have been in the central government bureaucracy. Children who did well on high school entrance exams would get into the top high schools; those who did best on the college entrance exams would then get into the top colleges; and college graduates with the highest scores on the civil service exams would get accepted into the most prestigious government ministries. Once a person obtained a job in a government ministry, it was extremely rare to shift into a different ministry. Instead, most bureaucrats would gradually work their way up the hierarchy until retirement. The emphasis on seniority-based status meant stability, but it tended to discourage bureaucrats from promoting creative ways to address pressing government problems.

The emphasis on status hierarchy helped maintain the LDP in power. Political divisions based on class, ethnicity, or religion tend to generate political debate between groups who benefit from the status quo and those who wish to change politics to their advantage. In the case of social status, relatively few people have strong incentives to change the status quo. After all, if virtually anyone can acquire high status, but doing so takes years and years, everyone understands what is expected and few people have incentives to rock the boat. Social status does not offer a basis for challenging the current political order. The emphasis on social status helped preserve the political status quo because it did not promote a cultural cleavage the LDP's opponents could exploit.

Disadvantaged Position of Women

Although in theory anyone can rise up the social hierarchy in Japan, women continue to confront obstacles to social, political, and economic advancement as individuals. Scholars note that gender equality is associated with country wealth and low religiosity. Japan is both wealthy and a fairly irreligious society. However, in contrast to other countries that share these characteristics, such as Sweden or the Netherlands, we do not see gender equality in Japan. For example, more than 40 percent of Japanese agree with the statement that "men are better political leaders," compared with fewer than 20 percent of respondents in places like Germany, the UK, and even Italy.[36] Although Japanese men tended to do well as the country's economy grew rapidly in the postwar era, the traditional salary gap between men and women never narrowed as it did in other advanced industrial democracies. Women still find it difficult to break out of jobs seen as "for women" such as office clerical and support staff, including simply serving tea to assembled male executives. Indeed, instead of entering the workforce, women are typically expected to raise children, handle the household, and take care of their (and their husbands') parents, who commonly live with the family. Given this view, although many married women work in Japan, the general expectation is that women need only work full time until they are ready to have children.[37] Women have challenged this condition, and laws have been passed to promote equality in the workplace, but most legislation did not legally prohibit many forms of discrimination.[38]

Given cultural opposition to gender equality, it should not be surprising that few women get elected to political office in Japan. About 10 percent of all members of Japan's Diet are women, ranking the country at 105th place in terms of female representation—one of the worst records among democracies.[39] The emphasis on politicians' personalities and their constituency service in Japanese elections limits women's advancement in politics. Emphasizing personality and how well a politician provides service to voters means that Japanese elections typically do not turn on social issues, as is sometimes the case in the United States, for example. In addition, politicians traditionally depend heavily on long-standing networks of supporters to channel government funds to their districts. Given their weaker position in society and the expectation that they should stay home and take care of the family, relatively few women have established the support networks necessary to become viable candidates. For these reasons, gender equality has never become an important campaign issue that an opposition party could use to challenge the LDP.

In short, as the table on the following page summarizes, differences in social identity don't much help us understand the contours of Japanese politics. Japan's homogeneity and the lack of emphasis in Japan on divisions based on things such as class, ethnicity, and gender have left few openings for opposition parties to undercut the LDP's base of support or to develop a new challenge to the long-time ruling party. And Japan's emphasis on status—status that most people can achieve if they persevere long enough—provides incentives for many people to support the status quo, something that only served to help maintain LDP dominance. That being said, in a society of great homogeneity, other types of divisions—based on things such as political interests—may be more likely to become key issues that can underpin the workings of a party system.

> **SUMMARY TABLE**
>
> **Identities: Relatively Homogeneous Society**
>
> | | |
> |---|---|
> | **Homogeneous Society** | About 95% of the population is ethnically Japanese, nearly everyone speaks Japanese, and religion is not a major cleavage—only about 1% of Japanese are Christian. |
> | **Burakumin** | Japan's largest minority group is the Burakumin (approximately 2–3 million people). Burakumin look exactly like other Japanese, but their ancestors were categorized as inferior members of society during the Tokugawa period. Somewhat like the old "untouchable" castes in India, in the Tokugawa-period Burakumin were tasked with "dirty" jobs involving the slaughter and use of animals (like leather making). |
> | **Koreans** | Perhaps the most complicated situation in Japan exists for ethnic Koreans, who may account for up to 1 million people in Japan. During Japan's colonization of Korea, many Koreans came to Japan, often unwillingly as forced laborers. Most returned to Korea after WWII, but many remained in Japan and have faced discrimination ever since. |
> | **Foreign Workers** | Estimates suggest that there are at least 1.3 million foreign workers in Japan, some illegally. Since the 1980s, a growing number of foreign workers have come to live in Japan's major cities, especially individuals from the Philippines, China, Brazil, Peru, and Thailand. |
> | **Class** | Labor unions have existed in Japan since the pre-war era, but class divisions are less important in Japan than in some other wealthy democracies such as England or Germany. |
> | **Social Status** | Relationships based on some sort of hierarchy within society have long played an important role in shaping Japanese society and politics. |
> | **Gender** | Women in Japan continue to confront obstacles to social, political, and economic advancement as individuals. |

INTERESTS IN JAPAN

5.4 What are the most influential interests in Japan and how have they contributed to LDP dominance and then its decline?

Political interests play an important role in explaining this chapter's main puzzle, the LDP's lengthy hold on power. Most notably, differences between Japan's wealthy cities and relatively poorer countryside generated distinct political interests between urban and rural areas. For years, the LDP maintained power especially by catering to the interests of rural voters. However, with the rural part of the economy increasingly dragging down the economy, in 2005, the party put forward an electoral platform that undercut much of its rural base. In doing so, the LDP sowed the seeds of its own 2009 destruction.

Postwar Interests

In the first decades after World War II, sustained economic growth tended to mute any political divisions in Japanese politics. Opposition parties found it difficult to rally voters behind opposition to the LDP, simply because the LDP could point to such obvious success in delivering effective government. In the 1950s and 1960s, the LDP enjoyed a broad support base. It received support from small business, big business, and agricultural interests—groups that benefited from the party's policies and the country's economic growth.

Opposition parties tried, but found it very difficult to convince voters that the LDP should be voted out of office. For example, few middle-class voters took seriously the Socialist Party's claim that workers were being exploited, given that nearly everyone's income grew every year. The Japan Socialist Party (JSP), the largest opposition party, received the support of public sector labor unions (public school teachers, for example). However, its performance in elections peaked in 1958, with 33 percent of the vote and 36 percent of the seats in the House of Representatives. After 1967 the JSP never won more than 24 percent of the vote and 27 percent of the seats in the lower house (see Table 5.1).[40]

Other opposition parties managed to attract a small proportion of voters. The Democratic Socialist Party (DSP) represented private sector unions, such as those of Toyota workers. The Clean Government Party (CGP) or *Kōmeitō* was the political wing of Sōka Gakkai, a lay Buddhist organization. *Kōmeitō* did not usually emphasize religious issues, but instead focused on promoting the interests of urban working class. And the Japan Communist Party (JCP) had a small but consistent base of support among intellectuals and others opposed to the economic and political status quo.

In large part, we can see a sharp divide between specific interests in postwar Japan, and these interests played out in the party system. Farmers and (both big and small) business supported the LDP, while labor unions backed the opposition—especially the JSP and DSP in earlier years, and the DPJ more recently. But again, in an era in which the economy was growing and workers' unions were tied to their companies—rather than workers, in general—the interests of workers were not necessarily at odds with those of business. As a result, it was hard for the opposition to use this base of interests to develop a powerful challenge to the LDP.

Environmental Interest Groups

By the 1970s, cracks began to appear in the LDP's hegemony, especially after Japan was rocked by environmental crises. At the time Japan had extremely lax environmental laws, and in some regions, pollution—caused by the negligence of businesses such as chemical plants—was devastating. In the town of Minamata, for example, mercury dumped into the local water supply water caused many otherwise healthy people to grow gravely ill, lose the ability to think clearly, lose control over bodily functions, and ultimately die.[41] Local governments were slow to respond to the pollution even after the source of the problems became apparent. Traditionally, small-town Japanese usually avoided public protests, but with their livelihood and health threatened, the ordinarily quiet citizens organized and pushed back in ways that

TABLE 5.1
Percentage of HR Seats Won by Japan's Major Parties in Each Election: 1958–2009

	1958	1960	1963	1967	1969	1972	1976	1979	1980	1983	1986	1990	1993	1996	2000	2003	2005	2009
LDP	61.5	63.3	60.6	57.0	59.2	55.2	48.7	48.5	56.0	48.9	58.6	53.7	43.6	47.8	48.5	49.4	61.7	24.8
DPJ														10.4	26.5	36.9	23.5	64.2
NFP														31.2				
JSP/SDPJ	35.5	31.0	30.8	28.8	18.5	24	24.1	20.9	20.9	21.9	16.6	26.6	13.7	3.0	4.0	1.2	1.5	1.5
Komeito						5.9	10.8	11.2	6.5	11.4	10.9	8.8	10.0		6.5	7.1	6.5	4.4
JCP	0.2	0.6	1.1	1.0	2.9	7.7	3.3	7.6	5.7	5.1	5.1	3.1	2.9	5.2	4.2	1.9	1.9	1.9
NLC							3.3	0.8	2.3	1.6	1.2							
DSP	3.6	4.9	6.2	6.4	3.9	5.7	6.8	6.3	7.4	5.1	2.7	2.9						
Shinsei													10.8					
Sakigake													2.5					
JNP													6.8					
Other														2.4	10.5	3.5	5.0	3.3

were unusual for Japan. Beginning in the late 1950s with the residents of Minamata, many Japanese organized local "citizens' movements," large-scale protests by previously apolitical citizens. Citizen's movements were unlike most political behavior in Japan to that point. Rather than focused on a particular candidate, party or ideology, the movements sprouted from the grassroots level and highlighted specific issues, usually in particular regions or localities: for example, the residents of Minamata petitioned the polluters and government to address the problems and compensate them for their lost wages and health. They recruited support from across Japan and staged sit-ins at the polluters' headquarters, even creating tent settlements outside the company in Tokyo. Most famously, the citizen's movements instigated several successful lawsuits against the companies responsible for the pollution and, by creating a new channel to express displeasure with the political system, offered one of the strongest challenges to the status quo that the LDP represented.[42]

Environmentalism and demands for greater regulation of pollution provided a political issue that the opposition could leverage against the LDP. Until the 1970s, economic growth had benefited nearly everyone, but during that decade many Japanese began to consider the costs of relatively unregulated industrialization. However, the growth of environmentalism did not bring an end to LDP dominance. Based in large part on the environmental movements, opposition parties were able to gain control over an increasing number of local governments, and, as a group, held nearly as many seats as the LDP in the Diet. Nevertheless, the opposition was not able to fully take advantage of the increasing support for environmental movements—opposition parties with strong support among labor unions actually shared industry's interests in promoting economic growth, and were reluctant to support citizens groups' calls for limits on industrial expansion.[43] Moreover, many environmental groups limited their activities to finding practical solutions to pollution, rather than broader political concerns. With the opposition largely unwilling to take a strong stance against businesses' activities, the LDP undercut the political impact of environmentalism by implementing its own environmental policies, thereby forestalling the formation of a sizeable Green Party such as later came to exist in countries like Germany.

Modern versus Traditional Interests

Up through the 1980s, economic growth bolstered the LDP, and the unchecked environmental consequences of that growth would fail to undermine it. However, the consequences of Japan's rapid economic development would eventually come back to haunt the LDP. On the one hand, development made Japan one of the most technologically advanced societies in the world, with internationally competitive multinational vehicle, electronics, and computer manufacturing companies such as Honda, Mitsubishi, Toyota, and Sony. Yet, despite these companies' global prominence and the image many foreigners have of Japan as a country of glittering cities, outside of these urban areas much of Japan remains relatively underdeveloped and rural. In these areas, many businesses could not survive without government support. Japan's "modern" and "traditional" sectors have divergent economic and political interests. This division caused constant tension within the LDP even during the party's greatest popularity, and the difference in political interests between "traditional" and "modern" Japan ultimately proved to be the LDP's downfall.

During its heyday, the LDP particularly cultivated the political interests of Japan's rural sector, the party's most consistent and core base of support. As mentioned, the LDP did this by channeling government spending to the less-developed areas of Japan. In exchange, it received political support from local politicians and voters. A well-known example was the allocation of the equivalent of U.S. $6.3 billion to extend a high-speed bullet train line to the sparsely populated rural prefecture of Niigata—not a major travel destination—by former Prime Minister Kakuei Tanaka.[44] There was no rational reason to spend this money in Niigata, but the government did so anyway, on the request of this powerful LDP politician, who wanted to shower his home district with rewards.

The LDP did not only rely on public works spending. It also designed government policies to keep rural business alive and support an increasingly dependent rural population. In contrast to the competitiveness of many familiar Japanese multinationals, many of Japan's rural businesses are not internationally competitive. Rural residents tend to be older and less educated, and, therefore, are often employed in less technologically advanced industries that rely on government support. The problem of supporting such groups has become increasingly important as Japanese society has aged: one of Japan's greatest problems is its low birthrate, combined with the fact that each year a larger share of the population is elderly.

THE "MODERN" JAPANESE CITY

The modern globalized Japanese city—its economy is made up of consumers looking to buy the latest goods from abroad and internationally competitive companies that could survive without government assistance.

THE "TRADITIONAL" JAPANESE COUNTRYSIDE

An LDP campaign sign and two traditional Japanese farmers—undoubtedly beneficiaries of government subsidies that protect domestic production of rice and keep out imports from countries such as the United States.

In 1950, 4.9 percent of Japan's population was over 65 years old. In 2009, the number was 22.7 percent. By 2050, 39.6 percent of the population is projected to be over 65.[45]

In contrast, urban firms tend to be more internationally competitive and city dwellers are on average younger and more educated.[46] Given this difference in education and skill levels, many rural industries—especially those related to the agricultural sector—survive on a combination of government subsidies and regulations that constrain the ability of foreign firms to enter the Japanese market. Most notably, the Japanese government subsidized rural farmers by keeping Japan closed to foreign rice producers and by selling rice to consumers at very high prices. Even after the rice market opened up slightly in 2000, the price of rice in Japan was four times higher than its price in California.[47]

The difference between Japan's internationally competitive urban industry and its uncompetitive rural sector resulted in what we can "parallel party systems" existing within Japan: a "rural" party system completely dominated by the LDP and an "urban" party system in which opposition parties were much more competitive. Figure 5.2 illustrates these two party systems. Recall that Japan is made up of 300 single-seat electoral districts; Figure 5.2 divides these constituencies based on population density into the 100 most rural, 100 most urban, and the 100 "mixed" districts that fall in between urban and rural, and indicates how many seats the LDP and the opposition DPJ each won in these different categories of districts from 1996–2009.

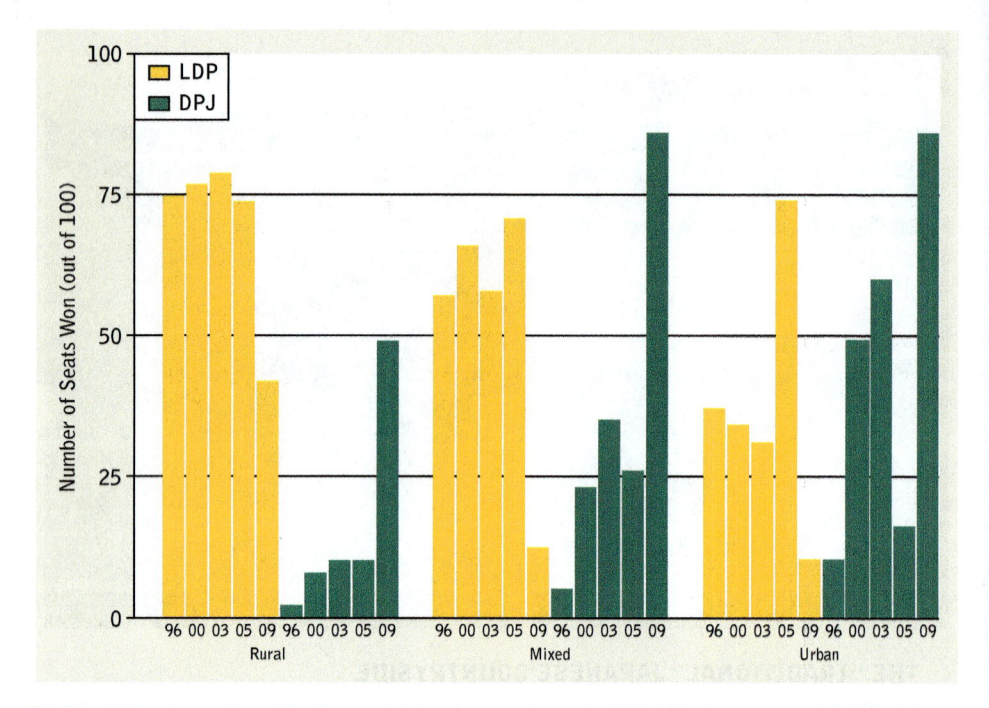

FIGURE 5.2

LDP and DPJ Single-Member Seat Wins in the 100 Most Rural Districts, the 100 Most Urban, and the 100 In-Between Districts

From 1996–2005, the LDP continued to dominate elections in the countryside, while the DPJ found lots of success in Japan's cities. For example, in 2003, the LDP won 79 out of Japan's 100 most rural districts, but only 31 out of Japan's 100 most urban districts—whereas the DPJ won only 10 rural districts, but 60 urban districts. However, in 2009 everything changed. The DPJ not only won the most urban seats, it even won more seats in the countryside than the LDP. In 2009, the DPJ won 86 out of the 100 most urban seats in the country—far more than the 10 won by the LDP. And the DPJ won 49 rural seats, as compared with only 42 for the LDP!

The bars on the left-hand side of the figure indicate the number of seats the LDP and DPJ won in Japan's 100 most rural districts in each election. On the left, you can see that the LDP won 75 out of Japan's 100 most rural seats in 1996, while the DPJ won only two of those 100 most rural seats that same year. On the right, you can see the number of seats won by the LDP and DPJ in Japan's 100 most urban districts. In 2000, for example, the LDP won 34 of those seats, whereas the DPJ won 49. The pattern is clear: the LDP was weakest in urban areas, won more than half of the seats in "mixed" areas, and did best in rural areas, winning about three out of every four seats in countryside elections through 2005.

The LDP's political reliance on rural voters meant that it could win control of parliament while doing relatively little on behalf of urban political interests. As long as Japan's economy continued to grow rapidly, this was not a politically sensitive issue, simply because neither rural nor urban voters had much to complain about. However, starting around 1990, Japan's declining economy began to create political tension between urban and rural political interests, because it grew more difficult to satisfy both groups of voters once the economy grew sour. Moreover, the rural sectors became more and more of a drain on the taxpayers who worked in the more competitive urban sectors of the economy. However, because it had invested so much politically in maintaining the support of rural voters, the LDP found it difficult to reduce its economic support of the countryside. This challenge plagued the LDP for almost two decades—and it ultimately proved insurmountable.

The division between rural and urban political interests drove transformations in Japan's party system in the 1990s and 2000s. In the early 1990s, the declining economy and a series of LDP corruption scandals inspired voter anger, splits within the LDP, and several new parties to emerge. It was this split that led to the LDP's brief period out of power in 1993: a few dozen members of the LDP grew unhappy with the party's inability to enact electoral system reform and left the LDP to form the Shinsei party and the Sakigake party. In the 1993 lower house elections that followed, voters who favored reform supported these LDP defectors and the LDP had its worst lower house election ever (at least until 2009) with only 36.6 percent of the vote (which got the party 43.6 percent of the seats). This gave the opposition the opportunity to form the government for the first time since the founding of the LDP. However, this coalition was made up of a wide array of diverse parties that proved unable to work together. Within a year, the government collapsed and the LDP returned to power.

After the collapse of this first non-LDP government, the opposition remained fragmented for several years. Meanwhile, the LDP remained relatively unified, thanks in part to its control over state resources. Only in 2003 did the DPJ finally complete its consolidation, when a former LDP leader, Ichirō Ozawa, merged his own small party with the DPJ to create a more unified opposition front against the LDP. The DPJ and LDP are today Japan's main parties.

Urban political interests drove the opposition's ferment in the 1990s and 2000s. For example, the Japan New Party (JNP), which jump-started the formation of new parties in the 1990s, drew its support overwhelmingly from large cities.[48] Many of the LDP politicians who were dissatisfied with their party's inability to address Japan's problems represented urban districts.[49] These LDP politicians realized that urban voters increasingly believed LDP politicians to be generally corrupt. Politicians with bases in urban areas began to offer new policy prescriptions for Japan's pressing problems, such as deregulating Japan's economy. Rural politicians opposed these measures because regulations tended to shield uncompetitive industries from imports. Leading opposition politicians also railed against the LDP's profligate spending on "bridges to nowhere" type public works projects in the countryside. In addition, urban voters increasingly supported the new policies that opposition politicians were advocating, first supporting the New Frontier Party (NFP)—which was born from a merger of former LDP members and politicians from opposition parties—and then especially the DPJ when it emerged in its current form in 1998.[50]

Koizumi's Reforms and the Fall of the LDP

In 2001, Jun'ichirō Koizumi became head of the LDP and prime minister. At that time, the declining economy meant that the LDP had less money to spend on rural interests. Koizumi also saw a connection between high levels of government spending on weak sectors and Japan's sluggish economy, and he knew that he would have to convince members of his own party—many of whom relied on rural voters—to change their ways. Koizumi sought to change the LDP's image by emphasizing the modern side of Japan's economy and reducing spending on rural construction projects.

Most famously, Koizumi sought to privatize Japan's postal savings system. For more than a century, the government-owned Japanese postal service had provided not only letter and package delivery, but also life insurance and even banking services. Japanese famously save a great deal of their earnings, and many older and rural voters never put their money in private-sector banks that offer competitive interest rates. Instead, they would deposit their money in the low-interest post office savings accounts. In turn, the government used this money to make loans to favored economic interests, especially in the rural sector. Not surprisingly, postmasters—whose very business was protected by the government—have traditionally served as key vote-mobilizers for LDP candidates.[51]

Privatization would have meant significant job cuts in the postal service, and, thus, an end to postmasters' political influence. In addition, the LDP used the money kept in the postal savings banks as cheap loans to small and medium-sized businesses that supported the party. For these reasons, a number of LDP members did not support Koizumi's postal privatization bill when he initially proposed it in 2005. Koizumi then called for an election, managed to expel from the LDP those who opposed his reforms,[52] and directed financial and other party support to new LDP candidates. He then sold the election as a referendum on his reform program and leadership. Because Koizumi was wildly popular in Japan's cities, he won a landslide election for the LDP.

The LDP allows its leaders to serve only two terms as party president, the position that also makes them prime minister (assuming that the LDP controls a majority of the lower house seats). This meant that Koizumi had to leave office in 2006, even though he had just led his party to a smashing victory. Conservative LDP politicians who had opposed Koizumi managed to regain control of the party, and they replaced him with leaders who sought to undo many of Koizumi's policies. The post-Koizumi LDP prime ministers invited most LDP members who had opposed postal service privatization back into the party. The question of Japan's stagnating economy remained unanswered, and the party's decision to undermine Koizumi's reforms alienated urban interests, especially those who had flocked to the LDP to vote for Koizumi.

As summarized by the table on the following page, the division between traditional rural and modern urban interests in Japan played a major part in shaping the LDP's longtime dominance and finally its failure in 2009. The LDP's reliance upon these rural interests initially made it hard for the party to cut them off. However, Koizumi's decision to reduce support for these interests and, thus, attack his own party in its most important and economically vulnerable constituency had destabilized long-standing patterns of Japanese politics. In the 2005 election, rural political leaders were no longer willing to support the LDP without question. They did not shift *en masse* to the opposition, but rural LDP candidates in 2005 lost votes when compared with 2003.

At the same time that Koizumi was courting urban interests to support the LDP, opposition politicians saw their chance to finally capture some portion of

> **SUMMARY TABLE**
>
> **Interests: A Key Foundation of Japan's Party System**
>
> | | |
> |---|---|
> | **Rural Interests** | Much of Japan remains relatively underdeveloped and rural. Many of Japan's rural businesses are not internationally competitive. Rural residents tend to be older and less educated, and many rural industries—especially those related to the agricultural sector—survive on a combination of government subsidies and regulations that constrain foreign firms' ability to enter the Japanese market. |
> | **Urban Interests** | City dwellers are on average younger and more educated, and urban firms tend to be more internationally competitive. |

the rural electorate. Thus, when Ichirō Ozawa joined the DPJ in 2003, his party made greater efforts to court rural voters by promoting policies more sympathetic to rural interests. The DPJ won the 2007 upper house election partly because it did well in both urban and rural areas. In its campaign for the 2009 lower house election, the DPJ advocated scaling back postal privatization and spending more money in rural areas. To illustrate how much things had changed in less than ten years, in 2009 groups of postmasters worked on behalf of the DPJ!

Rural interests were no longer bound to the LDP, and, as a result, the DPJ won the 2009 lower house election in a landslide, taking the largest share of seats by any party in Japanese postwar history. As shown above, the LDP all but disappeared in urban areas where voters were turned off by the party's inability to address economic decline, and by its reversing course on its promises to reduce support for rural interests. Yet, in the countryside, the LDP had proven unable to regain the support it enjoyed prior to Koizumi's tenure, and for the first time ever it did not win a majority of rural seats.

CONCLUSION

In hindsight, it seems inevitable that the LDP would finally lose power. For nearly two decades, Japan had suffered from economic stagnation and corrupt and incompetent politicians. Yet, what is so remarkable is that the LDP held onto power for so long, despite becoming so unpopular. This chapter has sought to explain the LDP's ability to dominate Japanese politics for more than 50 years. Until the 1990s, the LDP benefited from Japan's successful economy. But Japan's relatively centralized government institutions also gave it control over government spending without many checks and balances, and the party used this control to favor rural political interests. Because centralization made them highly dependent on the LDP, Japan's subnational politicians had a strong incentive to become members of the LDP, which could help them access the central resources they needed to deliver to their districts. These subnational politicians then mobilized votes for national-level LDP candidates and ran as attractive LDP candidates for national office. This symbiotic relationship between the LDP and its rural support base proves to be a key element in explaining the LDP's long hold on power.

However, this same dynamic also helps us understand why the LDP ultimately lost power. The LDP provided poorer rural areas with financial support and government subsidies. This helped it win enough seats to offset its lack of popularity in wealthier urban areas. As long as Japan's economy was growing, urban opposition to the LDP was fairly weak. But as Japan's economy stagnated, new opposition parties emerged, with strong urban vote bases. Meanwhile, the electoral reform of the 1990s created incentives for the opposition to consolidate around a single party, which it did in the DPJ starting in the late 1990s. As a result, the opposition was better primed than in the past to tap into unhappiness with the LDP. In the early 2000s, LDP prime minister Koizumi sought to capture the urban political interests by forcing the LDP to reduce its inefficient spending on rural areas and cater more to urban political interests. His policies succeeded in alienating rural voters from the LDP, and his successors' policies succeeded in alienating urban voters even more. The result was the 2009 landslide that brought the party down.

However, in many ways the new DPJ government may have wished that it could allow the LDP to continue governing longer. Japan continues to face economic stagnation. Most seriously, the 2011 earthquake/tsunami/nuclear disaster introduced a whole new set of problems. Party alternation in power may have raised the quality of Japan's democracy, but the next step is to deal with the major problems confronting Japanese society.

Study and Review the Post-Test & Chapter Exam at mypoliscilab.com

KEY TERMS

Democratic Party of Japan (DPJ) 151
Liberal Democratic Party (LDP) 151
shogun 154
samurai 154
Tokugawa era 154
bakufu 154
Meiji Restoration 155
Meiji oligarchs 156
Taisho Democracy 157
Article 9 158
1947 Constitution 158
self-defense forces 158
keiretsu 158

Japan Socialist Party (JSP) 158
industrial policy 159
prefecture 166
Diet 166
House of Representatives (HR) 166
House of Councillors (HC) 166
single non-transferable vote (SNTV) 168
personal vote 168
kōenkai 169
malapportionment 170
amakudari 175
Burakumin 176

REVIEW QUESTIONS

1. To what extent was LDP dominance simply a result of Japan's successful economy?
2. How did Japan's electoral rules help promote the LDP's control of the government?
3. This chapter suggested that the LDP held many advantages because of its control over the central government budget. Is there reason to think that the DPJ would begin its own long run of electoral dominance once it took control in 2009?
4. How has the homogeneity of the Japanese people helped deny opposition parties chances to challenge the LDP?
5. How did the LDP balance "traditional" and "modern" interests? How did its failure to continue to balance them cost it control of the government?

SUGGESTED READINGS

Curtis, Gerald. *The Japanese Way of Politics*. New York: Columbia University Press, 1988. Provides a detailed description of the way Japanese politics worked through the 1980s.

Green, Michael J. "Balance of Power," in Steven K. Vogel, ed., *U.S.–Japan Relations in a Changing World*. Washington, D.C.: The Brookings Institution, 2002. An article-length work on Japanese security policy.

Johnson, Chalmers. *MITI and the Japanese Miracle*. Stanford: Stanford University Press, 1982. A classic discussion of how Japan's government bureaucracy utilized industrial policy.

Schoppa, Leonard J. *Race for the Exits: The Unraveling of Japan's System of Social Protection*. Ithaca: Cornell University Press, 2006. A discussion of the effects of Japan's inability to reform in recent years.

Vogel, Steven K. *Japan Remodeled: How Government and Industry Are Reforming Japanese Capitalism*. Ithaca: Cornell University Press, 2006. Describes the ways in which Japan's economy has changed in recent years.

NOTES

1. Andrew Gordon, *A Modern History of Japan: From Tokugawa Times to the Present* (New York: Oxford University Press, 2003), 245–246.
2. These figures are commonly seen in monthly reported results of public opinion surveys in Japan. See, for example, *Daily Yomiuri*, June 8, 2009 (http://www.yomiuri.co.jp/dy/national/20090608TDY01304.htm).
3. Ethan Scheiner, *Democracy Without Competition in Japan* (New York: Cambridge University Press, 2006), 34.
4. See, for example, Charles Tilly, "War-Making and State-Making as Organized Crime," in Evans et al., eds., *Bringing the State Back In* (New York: Cambridge University Press, 1985), 169.
5. The *CIA Factbook* lists countries according to the share of their GDP that they spend on defense. Out of 174 countries on this list, Japan (2006 figures) is number 149. See https://www.cia.gov/library/publications/the-world-factbook/rankorder/2034rank.html. In contrast, the Stockholm International Peace Research Institute (SIPRI) lists countries according to their absolute spending on defense. According to these measures, Japan ranks in the top 5–10 of all countries. See the data available at http://www.sipri.org/databases/milex.
6. For the statistics, see the following: On the Japanese stock market decline in value, see, for example, T.J. Pempel, *Regime Shift: Comparative Dynamics of the Japanese Political Economy* (Ithaca, NY: Cornell University Press, 1998), 201. On the decline in the value of Japanese real estate, see for example, "Published Land Prices," listed by the Japanese Ministry of Land, Infrastructure, Transport, and Tourism at http://tochi.mlit.go.jp/h20hakusho/chapter7/chapter07_eng.html. On the decline in American real estate value, see, for example, the Standard & Poor's/ Case-Shiller Home Prices Indices, such as is listed at http://www2.standardandpoors.com/spf/pdf/index/CSHomePrice_Release_022445.pdf.
7. Jennifer A. Amyx, *Japan's Financial Crisis: Institutional Rigidity and Reluctant Change* (Princeton, NJ: Princeton University Press, 2004), 2; and Paul Krugman, *The Return of Depression Economics and the Crisis of 2008* (New York: W. W. Norton & Co., Inc., 2009), 73.
8. See Deborah Solomon, "Estimated TARP Cost Is Cut by $200 Billion," *Wall Street Journal*, December 7, 2009, online at http://online.wsj.com/article/SB126015764384079549.html.

9. T. J. Pempel, *Regime Shift: Comparative Dynamics of the Japanese Political Economy* (Ithaca, NY: Cornell University Press, 1998), 139.
10. For discussion of the scandals and other problems faced by Japan in the 1990s, see Pempel, *Regime Shift*, chapter 5.
11. See Eric Talmadge, "Japan's Troops Play Major Role in Tsunami Relief," Associated Press, March 31, 2011.
12. The 27,200 units were just short of the 30,000-unit goal of the government, but falling short led to criticisms of the government. See "Evacuee Housing Units Shy of Target," *Japan Times Online*, May 31, 2011, available at http://search.japantimes.co.jp/mail/nn20110531a3.html.
13. See especially Linda Hasunuma, "Restructuring Government: Party System Change and Decentralization in Japan" (Unpublished doctoral dissertation, UCLA, 2010). For the most part, these changes have not yet born fruit in most expected ways, but in some cases local governments have begun to make efforts to change policies to do things such as create greater incentives for private business to work in their prefecture. On this shift, see Kay Shimizu, "Private Money as Public Funds: The Politics of Economic Downturn" (Unpublished doctoral dissertation, Stanford University, 2008).
14. Ethan Scheiner, *Democracy Without Competition in Japan* (New York: Cambridge University Press, 2006), chapter 5.
15. On the changes in Japan's prime minister, see, for example, Ellis S. Krauss and Robert J. Pekkanen, *The Rise and Fall of Japan's LDP: Political Party Organizations as Historical Institutions* (Ithaca: Cornell University Press, 2011), chapters 8 and 9.
16. Ray Christensen, "The Effect of Electoral Reforms on Campaign Practices in Japan: Putting New Wine into Old Bottles," *Asian Survey*, 38 (1998): 986–1004.
17. Gerald Curtis, *Election Campaigning Japanese Style* (New York and London: Columbia University Press, 1971), 145–150.
18. Scott R. Seaman, "Crumbling Foundations: Japan's Public Works Policies and Democracy in the 1990s" (Unpublished doctoral dissertation, Duke University, 2003).
19. Pippa Norris, *Electoral Engineering: Voting Rules and Political Behavior* (New York: Cambridge University Press, 2004).
20. Herbert F. Weisberg and Aiji Tanaka, "Change in the Spatial Dimensions of Party Conflict: The Case of Japan in the 1990s," *Political Behavior*, 23 (2001): 75–101.
21. Scheiner, *Democracy Without Competition in Japan*, chapter 6.
22. Yasuo Hasebe, "The Supreme Court of Japan: Its Adjudication on Electoral Systems and Economic Greedoms," *International Journal of Constitutional Law*, 5 (2007): 296–307.
23. David Johnson, "A Tale of Two Systems: Prosecuting Corruption in Japan and Italy," in Frank J. Schwartz and Susan J. Pharr *The State of Civil Society in Japan* (New York: Cambridge University Press, 2003), 257–277.
24. Gordon, *A Modern History of Japan*, 6.
25. For more on the "new-new religions," and especially *Aum Shinrikyo*, see Helen Hardacre, "After Aum: Religion and Civil Society in Japan," in Frank J. Schwartz and Susan Pharr, eds., *The State of Civil Society in Japan* (New York: Cambridge University press, 2003), 135–153.
26. Ellis S. Krauss, "Politics and the Policymaking Process," in Takeshi Ishida and Ellis S. Krauss, eds., *Democracy in Japan* (Pittsburgh: Pittsburgh University Press, 1989), 58.
27. See J. A. A. Stockwin, *Governing Japan: Divided Politics in a Major Economy* (Oxford: Blackwell Publishing, 1999), 239.
28. See, for example, Michael Doan, "A Slip of the Lip Heard across the Pacific," *U.S. News & World Report*, October 6, 1986.

29. John Lie, *Multiethnic Japan* (Cambridge: Harvard University Press, 2004), 4; and Yoshio Sugimoto, *An Introduction to Japanese Society* (New York: Cambridge University Press, 2003), 185.
30. Sugimoto, *An Introduction to Japanese Society*, 189–193.
31. Sugimoto, *An Introduction to Japanese Society*, 193–202.
32. Sugimoto, *An Introduction to Japanese Society*, 204–207.
33. On labor in Japan, see especially Andrew Gordon, "Contests for the Workplace," in Andrew Gordon, ed., *Postwar Japan as History* (Berkeley: University of California Press, 1993); Andrew Gordon, *Labor and Imperial Democracy in Prewar Japan*, (Berkeley: University of California Press, 1992); and Andrew Gordon, *Wages of Affluence: Labor and Management in Postwar Japan* (Cambridge: Harvard University Press, 1998).
34. Margaret A. McKean, "Equality," in Takeshi Ishida and Ellis S. Krauss, eds., *Democracy in Japan* (Pittsburgh: Pittsburgh University Press, 1989), 218.
35. People could not officially change social status in Tokugawa Japan, but at times, often through trickery, they did so. See David L. Howell, "Territoriality and Collective Identity in Tokugawa Japan," *Daedalus*, 127 (1998): 105–132.
36. See the latest World Values Surveys at http://www.worldvaluessurvey.org/.
37. Gordon, *A Modern History of Japan*, 261.
38. Frank Upham, "Unplaced Persons and Struggles for Place," in *Postwar Japan as History*, Andrew Gordon, ed. (Berkeley: University of California Press, 1993).
39. Inter-Parliamentary Union (www.ipu.org).
40. The Socialists did win the unusual 1989 upper house election, but the election was only for half the members of the House of Councillors.
41. See, for example, Upham, "Unplaced Persons and Movements for Place," 338.
42. See Upham, "Unplaced Persons"; and Margaret McKean, *Environmental Protest and Citizen Politics in Japan* (Berkeley and Los Angeles: University of California Press, 1981).
43. See McKean, *Environmental Protest and Citizen Politics in Japan*.
44. See Louis D. Hayes, *Introduction to Japanese Politics* (Armonk, NY: M.E. Sharpe, Inc., 2005), 107.
45. See the Ministry of Internal Affairs and Communications report at http://www.stat.go.jp/english/data/handbook/c02cont.htm#cha2_2.
46. Pempel, *Regime Shift*; and Scheiner, *Democracy Without Competition in Japan*, chapter 3.
47. See, for example, information provided by the United Nations Conference on Trade and Development at http://www.unctad.org/infocomm/anglais/rice/ecopolicies.htm#japon.
48. Ethan Scheiner, "Urban Outfitters: City-based Strategies and Success in Postwar Japanese Politics." *Electoral Studies* 18 (1999): 179–198.
49. Steven R. Reed and Ethan Scheiner, "Electoral Incentives and Policy Preferences: Mixed Motives behind Party Defections in Japan," *British Journal of Political Science*, 33 (2003): 469–490.
50. Scheiner, *Democracy Without Competition*, chapter 8.
51. Patricia L. Maclachlan, "Storming the Castle: The Battle for Postal Reform in Japan," *Social Science Japan Journal*, 9:1 (2006), 1–18.
52. A small number of politicians who left the LDP around this time formed small new parties. One of these new parties ultimately created an alliance with the DPJ.

CHAPTER 6

India

Steven I. Wilkinson

Although many doubted whether democracy would survive after independence in 1947, opinion polls show that Indians of all communities and classes remain deeply committed to democratic values. Indians also vote in greater proportions than citizens in many Western democracies. Above, Congress Party supporters celebrate their 2009 national election victory with

> **?** Why has democracy persisted in India, despite its colonial legacies of ethnic and religious strife, and widespread poverty and illiteracy?

INTRODUCTION TO INDIA

In August 1947, after nearly two centuries of colonial rule, the British government granted India its independence. In doing so, however, it split its vast colony of 390 million people into two new states: Hindu-majority India and Muslim-majority Pakistan. Expectations were high. Both countries inherited the legal and governmental institutions established by the British. And both countries appeared to have strong political leaders, each of whom—Jawaharlal Nehru of the Indian National Congress and Mohammad Ali Jinnah of the Muslim League—had won an overwhelming electoral majority from their country's territory in the 1946 elections. Nehru reflected the massive enthusiasm for the new states in his speech on the eve of Indian independence, August 14, 1947: "At the stroke of the midnight hour, when the world sleeps, India will awake to life and freedom."[1]

But both states also faced huge challenges. Several decades of Hindu–Muslim political competition and regional tensions during the independence movement had led to the 1947 partition. So how could each country now successfully unify its population around a new national identity? The problem was especially acute in Pakistan, which joined two ethnically different Muslim-majority areas out of India, one in the west and one in the east, with 1,100 miles of India between them. Both India and Pakistan also faced the challenge of establishing full sovereignty over each country's share of the 562 semi-autonomous "princely states" that had existed alongside the parts of India that the British had ruled directly. Both new countries were extremely poor, and illiteracy was widespread. Only 15 percent of the Indian population in 1941 could read—and that proportion was far smaller among women than among men.

Despite the hope that partition would prevent conflict, it resulted in massive ethno-religious violence. Six million Muslims fled from India to Pakistan, while 7.5 million Hindus and Sikhs fled the other way. In the accompanying chaos, hundreds of thousands of people died, and after independence, both India and Pakistan continued to witness significant ethnic tensions within and across their borders. Even after this massive migration, millions of Hindus and Muslims were left on the "wrong" side of the border, with each nation concerned about the treatment of "its" group within the neighboring state. In this case, as in many others, partition caused as much conflict as it prevented by creating new minorities within each of the supposedly homogenous new states.

Endemic ethnic violence, lack of effective sovereignty, and widespread poverty and illiteracy are hardly the sorts of things we tend to associate with successful democracies. Yet India has successfully held together as a country and as a democracy, in contrast to Pakistan, which has suffered civil war and the resulting secession of half the country in 1971 as the new country of Bangladesh, as well as three long periods of military rule. India's political institutions enjoy wide legitimacy among the population, and politicians are frequently voted out of office for poor

Read and **Listen** to **Chapter 6** at **mypolscilab.com**

Study and **Review** the **Pre-Test & Flashcards** at **mypolscilab.com**

Jawaharlal Nehru ■ one of the major Congress Party leaders in the fight for freedom, and independent India's first prime minister from 1947 to his death in 1964.

Mohammad Ali Jinnah ■ the dominant leader of India's Muslim community from the early 1930s, the president of the All India Muslim League, and the first leader of Pakistan, which he led until his death.

INDIA

INDIA IN COMPARISON

	United Kingdom	Germany	France	Japan	India	Mexico	Russia	Nigeria	China	Iran
Freedom House Classification	Democracy	Democracy	Democracy	Democracy	Democracy	Partial democracy	Partial democracy	Partial democracy	Non-democracy	Non-democracy
Land Size (sq km)	243,610	357,022	643,801	377,915	3,287,263	1,964,375	17,098,242	923,768	9,596,961	1,648,195
Land Size Ranking	79	62	42	61	7	15	1	32	4	18
Population (July 2011 Estimate)	62,698,362	81,471,834	65,312,249	126,475,664	1,189,172,906	113,724,226	138,739,892	155,215,573	1,336,718,015	77,891,220
Population Ranking	22	16	21	10	2	11	9	8	1	18
Life Expectancy (Years)	80.0	80.0	81.1	82.2	66.8	76.4	66.2	47.5	74.6	70.1
Life Expectancy Ranking	28	27	13	5	51	72	162	220	95	146
Literacy Rate	99%	99%	99%	99%	61%	86.1%	99.4%	68%	91.6%	77%
GDP Per Capita (2010 Estimate)	US$35,100	US$35,900	US$33,300	US$34,000	US$3,500	US$13,800	US$15,900	US$2,500	US$7,600	US$11,200
GDP Ranking	36	32	39	38	163	85	71	178	126	100

performance. India has also outperformed Pakistan in terms of raising literacy rates (now 65 percent in India and 44 percent in Pakistan) and citizens' overall welfare—even though poverty remains widespread.

In this chapter, we will focus on the question of *why democracy has persisted in India, despite its colonial legacies of ethnic and religious strife, and widespread poverty and illiteracy*. Why has India succeeded at establishing a stable democracy, where Pakistan has failed? Both countries inherited the same government structure from pre-1947 British India, so the institutional legacy seems unlikely to be the only answer. The key, we will argue, is that India inherited a strong well-institutionalized political party, one that had already encouraged broad representation from different regions and social groups and robust internal contestation for several decades before independence. This broad-based and democratic Congress Party, under the leadership of Jawaharlal Nehru and a strong and talented layer of national and provincial leaders, allowed more participation within the party and created much better institutions to manage conflict than those in Pakistan. The Congress also ensured—through land reform, social programs, and subsidies for farmers and the poor—that democracy worked, at least some of the time, for the majority and not just for the elite.[2]

HISTORICAL OVERVIEW OF INDIA

6.1 How has India's colonial legacy influenced its democracy today?

In some parts of Asia and Africa, the colonial power completely demolished the indigenous state that existed, and replaced it with its own officials and practices. In India, however, the British East India Company wanted to easily and cheaply establish its own control and raise revenue during the wars and great insecurity of the late eighteenth century. This led to the British rulers initially adapting local law and order institutions, and land and tax collection practices, rather than getting rid of them. The result was that the British Raj relied on pre-existing state-building capacity and local practices more than most empires, and also that Indians had a larger role in staffing the colonial administration in India than did local people in many other colonized areas.

Raj ■ literally rule, administration, but often used as a general term for the period of British rule in India from 1757–1947.

The Mughal Empire

When European traders first descended upon India in the sixteenth and seventeenth centuries, they encountered a sophisticated state at the height of its power. The Mughal Empire (1526–1720) included most of the territory of present-day India, Pakistan, and Bangladesh, and about half of modern-day Afghanistan. Led by Muslims, the state's elite always included some Hindus, some of whom eventually converted to Islam out of genuine religious conviction or to gain access to wealth, position, or land. The Mughal emperor in 1700 governed a population of roughly 150 million people through a huge bureaucracy that operated throughout his empire's 22 provinces and 4,350 districts. Administrators and clerks kept detailed accounts in Persian, the language of administration, reported regularly on money owed and received, and audited the accounts of nobles to try to ensure no one cheated the state.[3] The Mughal Empire used much of this revenue to fight wars against other major powers and put down rebellions, as well as finance a lavish

Mughal Empire ■ founded by Babur in 1526, the Mughal territories included most of South Asia. The empire reached its peak from the mid-sixteenth to the late seventeenth centuries, before breaking up in 1720.

court culture, and build great architectural achievements like the city of Fatehpur Sikri and the Taj Mahal. The empire created lasting institutions: it regulated trade, maintained communications and irrigation systems, created an early postal system, and enforced law and order through locally appointed police officials.

The Mughal Emperor Aurangzeb (1658–1707), whose father Shah Jahan had built the Taj Mahal at Agra in 1653 as a mausoleum for his beloved wife, was determined to extend his kingdom's territory and also emphasize its Islamic character. Soon after he deposed his father in 1658, he launched campaigns to conquer the wealthy independent Hindu- and Muslim-ruled states of central and southern India. He also passed various laws and regulations, such as a poll tax upon non-Muslims that emphasized a more narrowly Islamic view of the Mughal state, in contrast to previous rulers. Despite early successes, Aurangzeb's increasing centralization, his costly military campaigns and his measures against non-Muslims led to internal rebellions and external resistance that cost a great deal of money to put down. The resulting instability and increased taxes reduced support for the regime. After Aurangzeb's death there were several succession struggles, and the lack of strong leadership led to several successful rebellions. The Mughal Empire lost power in the next two decades to several large successor states, like the Marathas in the west, Bengal in the east, and Hyderabad in the south.

These successor states had to deal with the increasing influence and threat posed by the East India Company (EIC). The company was founded by British merchants in 1600 to monopolize trade with India, and it made enormous profits selling Indian products, such as silk and cotton textiles, to Europe as well as (in the nineteenth century) selling Indian opium to China. The company had always protected its major trading stations at Surat, Bombay, and Madras with forts and detachments of British and local troops, permitted by treaties with the Mughals and local rulers. But the company found itself increasingly forced to enlarge its armies and ambitions in the mid-eighteenth century in order to defend its commercial interests from the French and from various Indian states in the unstable environment that followed the decline of the Mughal Empire. The company's conquest in 1757 of one of the largest and richest of the Mughal successor states, Bengal, established it as the major military power in India.

Why, as the Mughal Empire crumbled, did none of the indigenous successor states manage to effectively replace it? The main reason is that they lacked the ability of the Mughal Empire to tax land, trade, and people, which left them unable to raise the money to assemble effective armies against the British East India Company. The efficiency with which the EIC taxed the territories it conquered in the late eighteenth century gave it an income more than *17 times* that of its strongest rival Indian state, the Maratha Confederacy.[4] This enabled the Company to field larger and better armed forces, and to bribe enemy generals and states to switch sides or remain neutral. This greater state-building and military capacity allowed the Company to defeat all its most important rival states over the next few decades: Mysore in 1799; the Marathas by 1819; and the Sikhs by 1849. By 1857, the East India Company, now acting under the direction of the British government, had taken over two-thirds of India directly and forced the remaining "independent Indian states,"—often termed "princely states"—such as Hyderabad, Bhopal, and Baroda, to acknowledge British supremacy.

East India Company (EIC) ■ private trading company established in 1600, which expanded through conquest and British military support after the 1750s to administer most of India. As a result of the 1857 mutiny and rebellion, its charter was ended and Indian administration was taken over directly by the British government.

But the East India Company was not invulnerable. In 1856–1857, a series of political and military missteps—including the annexation of the independent state of Awadh from which many of the company's soldiers came, and the issuing of ammunition which offended both Hindus and Muslims by allegedly being greased with a mix of cow and pig fat—led to a mutiny of most of the northern army's soldiers as well as a mass rebellion throughout the north. It took a year and a half for the British to finally end this revolt, with the aid of 60,000 troops rushed to India from around the world, as well as from southern, western, and northwestern India who had remained loyal. After 1857, having run up massive debts putting down the rebellion, the British government abolished most functions of the Company and took over the administration of India directly, ruling from then on through a British Viceroy in India, responsible to a British Cabinet minister, the Secretary of State for India in London.

The British Empire

The fact that the British Empire in India began as an explicitly commercial and private enterprise, rather than one directed by the crown, was very important to India's state-building. The East India Company was determined to administer territories as cheaply as possible, and to make colonies pay for themselves. In the absence of some key commodity like gold or silver that could be exploited, this meant building effective administrative and tax raising bureaucracies, and using as many elements of the existing Mughal and Indian state bureaucracies as possible, while trying to make sure that local people served the British interests rather than their own. The British, therefore, only employed as few (expensive) Europeans in a colony as were necessary in order to safeguard their rule.

This approach to colonial rule meant that by the time of independence, government in India, unlike in the Spanish Empire in the early nineteenth century, the Belgian Congo, or French colonies in Africa in the mid-twentieth century, was already largely run by a well-educated and indigenous elite and middle class. In the Belgian Congo, for instance (now the Democratic Republic of Congo), *none* of the 1,000 army officers or senior 6,000 civil servants were Congolese in 1958, two years before independence, and there were fewer than two dozen Congolese university graduates in a country of 14 million. The upper levels of the state, hospitals, and universities in India by contrast were staffed by locals, who flocked to the numerous English-language schools, many of them established by Christian missionaries in the nineteenth and twentieth centuries. For example, in 1857, the British created three major universities at Madras, Bombay, and Calcutta, and these produced 60,000 graduates in the following three decades, a third of whom went into government service. By 1936, there were 334 colleges and universities in British India, with more than 110,000 students enrolled, almost all of them Indian. Even in those branches of the 1.5 million-strong colonial administration that were still overwhelmingly European-dominated at the upper levels because of British security concerns, such as the army, police, and intelligence services, there was a large number of well-trained Indian subordinates ready and able to take over. The British began to employ a small number of Indian officers in the army in 1920 and then trained 14,000 Indian officers as part of the massive army expansion in World

War II. As a result, there were more than enough officers to staff India's army after independence. By 1947, 54 percent of the 939 officials in the elite Indian Civil Service, which staffed all the highest positions in the provinces and in the central government, were Indian.[5]

The British also created a more unified India. They established a consistent system of district and provincial administration, with elite all-India civil and police services—recruited through professional competitions—to run these administrations. Geographically, the British unified the country through a large-scale government-backed program of railway and road building. The Grand Trunk Road stretched all the way from Calcutta in the east to Peshawar near the Afghan border, and 25,000 miles of railway had been built by 1900 and 43,000 miles by 1943.[6] The country was unified linguistically, as well, at the elite level, by the use of English as the common language of government and business. Of course, the British took these steps to cement their own rule, but nonetheless the institutions and common elite language they created, as well as Indians' common experience of exploitation and oppression at British hands, gradually allowed them to develop a sense of themselves as part of a larger Indian nation.

Thanks in part to shared communication and media, India also developed a vibrant civil society, which is important for democracy. Civic improvement organizations, artists, and writers provided forums for discussion and culture. Associations of lawyers and businessmen existed to push particular interests before the British administration, such as the Madras Native Association founded in 1852. Some of these groups existed only to maintain a particular ethnic identity, but many other groups incorporated people from diverse linguistic and caste backgrounds, linking them as equals in associational and political life for the first time. A host of new magazines and newspapers were founded to link both the English-speaking national elite and the literate classes in the provinces, such as the *Modern Review*, *Hindustan Review*, and Mohandas Gandhi's publication *Harijan*. In the last decades of British rule, these associations and publications helped to create a growing sense of Indian national identity. By 1947, India had a wide variety of the strong civil society organizations that bridged many of the country's most important caste and regional divides. These organizations, in India as elsewhere, have acted as a powerful watchdog over the actions of the state since independence, and as powerful defenders of the democratic process during the rare occasions when democracy seemed in danger.

The most important of these associations was the Indian National Congress (INC or Congress), founded in 1885. By the early twentieth century, the Congress had established itself as the leading nationalist organization representing India's middle and upper classes. In the late 1920s and early 1930s, as the nationalist movement radicalized, Gandhi pushed the Congress to transformed itself into a better organized political party, with more than a million members. Under the moral and tactical leadership of Mohandas K. Gandhi and the organizational leadership of Jawaharlal Nehru and Sardar Vallabhbhai Patel, the Congress committed itself to largely non-violent opposition to colonialism, by means of symbolic demonstrations and non-cooperation with the state, designed to show the inequities of colonial rule. For instance, in 1930, Gandhi marched to the sea to make salt from evaporated seawater, which was banned because the British got revenue from a government salt tax monopoly. In doing this, Gandhi not only denied the British

caste ■ the hierarchical Hindu social and religious system, through which Hindus are split up into broad categories of priests, warriors, merchants, and those who serve them, as well as hundreds of smaller occupational and ritual castes (*jati*) within each of these categories.

Mohandas K. Gandhi ■ the inspirational architect of non-violent resistance to colonial rule, he helped transform Congress into a mass party in the 1920s, and was the conscience of the nationalist campaign until his assassination by a Hindu nationalist militant in January 1948.

Indian National Congress (INC) ■ the dominant political party in India from 1885 until the present.

THE FATHER OF NON-VIOLENCE

Mohandas K. Gandhi (center) leads the 1930 salt march, in which he led Indians in making salt from seawater to symbolically challenge the colonial state's legitimacy. The non-violent tactics Gandhi pioneered, such as sit-downs and hunger strikes to demand justice, are still widely used.

revenue, he also challenged the moral authority of the colonial state that would deny ordinary Indians the right to do something as simple as make salt for their food.

From the 1880s to 1935, the British colonial government in India gradually extended electoral institutions in order to boost its own legitimacy and the effectiveness of government. The town councils introduced after the 1870s and 1880s had few real powers, but began to draw talented Indians into politics and administration. Provincial parliaments introduced in 1919 were, for the first time, given control of some important areas such as education and local self-government, which encouraged even more Indians to enter politics, though only a few million people could vote due to property requirements for the franchise (women were 5–10 percent of the electorate). Mass protests led by Gandhi throughout the 1920s and early 1930s convinced the colonial administration and the British Parliament in London to take the risk of devolving real power to Indians or else risk losing their most important colony completely. The **1935 Government of India Act** was by far the most significant devolution of power. It created a federal structure, and decentralized control of such crucial areas as police, agriculture, and local taxation to elected provincial governments. The 1935 structure greatly enlarged the size of provincial electorates, which were now 13–15 percent of a province's

1935 Government of India Act ■ the last and most substantial decentralization of power by the British administration before Indian independence.

population. In the first elections under this new structure, in 1936–1937, the Congress won unexpected victories in all of the Hindu-majority provinces, defeating some British-supported parties. Congress leaders decided, after extracting promises from the Viceroy that he and the Governors would not abuse their emergency and veto powers, that they would take the risk of "working the system" from within rather than boycotting it.

By their independence in 1947, Indians had several decades of experience with political parties, elections, and running local and provincial governments, albeit in a colonial state that was certainly far from free. The Indian National Congress Party had more than 4 million members by the late 1930s, and many other Indians participated in politics through meetings, associations, political campaigns, and by voting. The system was one with high degrees of contestation and participation compared to most other Asian and African colonies. Indians shaped the laws and government framework they were to inherit upon independence, which made these institutions more legitimate and effective compared to those in other colonies, where the colonized inherited rules and regulations which had been created and run entirely by Europeans.

The Difficult Legacy of Colonialism

There were, of course, many bad legacies as well. The good legal and government institutions and transport the British left behind were offset by deep ethnic divides, poverty, illiteracy, and a culture in which many government officials thought themselves masters, rather than servants. Perhaps the worst legacy the British left behind was the deep ethnic imbalances and conflicts. Like most multi-ethnic empires throughout history, the British had practiced *divide and rule*, in which they kept control by pitting different groups and regions against each other. For example, the British disproportionately recruited soldiers from particular ethnic groups such as the **Sikhs** and Muslims from the province of Punjab, where most people had stayed loyal to the British in the 1857 rebellion, rather than from the areas of north India, where troops had mutinied. The result was that by 1930, the colonial Indian Army recruited over half of all its troops from Punjab, which comprised only 7 percent of India's overall population. Despite protests from other regions, there were hardly any troops from the United Provinces, Bihar, Bombay, and Madras, with a combined 39 percent of India's population; and there were none at all from Bengal, the province that the British regarded as most politically troublesome, and which had 16 percent of India's total population.

In politics, too, the British encouraged religious conflicts. The British had encouraged Muslim–Hindu divisions to undercut opposition to their rule, and the institutions they established "protecting" Muslims were attractive to some from the minority community who worried what Hindu majority rule might bring. In 1906, the British encouraged the foundation of a new association to represent the Muslim elites, the **Muslim League**, as a counterbalance to the predominantly Hindu Indian National Congress. In 1909, the British created separate representation for Muslims in new provincial councils. And in 1919 and 1935, they preserved the principle of separate Muslim representation—separate seats in which only Muslims

Sikhism ■ founded by Guru Nanak (1465–1539) in the Punjab, Sikhism is a monotheistic religion that combines elements of Hinduism and Islam, and whose male adherents typically signify membership through practices such as wearing their hair uncut (under a turban), and carrying a small knife (*kirpan*).

Muslim League ■ established in 1906, this association and later political party promoted Muslim interests and, from the early 1940s under its leader M. A. Jinnah, the formation of the state of Pakistan as a solution to the problem of how to protect Muslim interests in a Hindu-majority country.

could vote and be elected—in the expanded provincial elected assemblies. In 1932 the government also guaranteed the Muslim minority a fixed share of central government jobs and overrepresentation in Hindu-majority provinces.

By encouraging Muslims and Hindus to see themselves as directly competing over a whole range of policies, the British weakened a cross-religious national identity that might have kept the country together. Instead, despite centuries of social, political, and linguistic intermixing between India's Hindus and Muslims, political polarization was so far advanced by 1947 that Jinnah could argue that only a separate state could provide Indian Muslims with the guarantees against Hindu domination. He gave an exaggerated cultural justification for his political project when he argued, "The Hindus worship the cow, we Muslims eat it, how can we live together?"

Throughout the 1930s and 1940s, there were two central political issues in India. First, when would the British leave? Second, when they left, which kind of political system would take their place? The Muslim League under Jinnah wanted to protect their interests in a loose federation in which Muslims and/or Muslim-majority provinces would have maximum autonomy, and in which Muslims would have a "minority veto" in the national government at the center. The League was prepared to delay the date of independence and work with the British in order to protect Muslim interests. It wanted parity of representation with the Congress and recognition as the sole voice for India's Muslims, and it demanded a three-quarters majority vote on controversies such as land and education policy where it felt Muslim interests were most threatened. Jinnah made these demands in part because of Muslims' negative experiences in Congress-controlled provincial governments from 1937–1939, when many Muslims felt that their views and interests had been ignored. The Congress, on the other hand, wanted independence sooner rather than later, and most of the party wanted to abolish what they saw as the "divide and rule" aspects of the British system, including the separate seats for Muslims and the minority veto that the Muslim League regarded as vital protections. In the last elections before independence, in 1945–1946, Congress won an overwhelming majority in all the Hindu majority provinces, as well as in the Muslim-majority North West Frontier province. The Muslim League, which had failed to win Muslim support in many areas in previous elections, achieved an equally dominant position among Muslim voters by promising to protect Muslim interests at the bargaining table, winning all the Muslim seats in the central assembly and 439 out of 494 Muslim seats in the provincial assemblies.[7]

After this strong electoral performance, Jinnah felt that the League had a mandate to demand a loose federation with the right for Muslim regions to secede later, failing which he wanted an independent state of Pakistan immediately. While the Congress initially seemed to agree to a loose federation, this concession was ultimately too much for Nehru and many senior Congress leaders to take, and in the end they preferred the partition of the country to a weak federation in which Jinnah and the league would exercise a veto power over important legislation. In February 1947, a new British viceroy, Lord Mountbatten, was appointed to oversee independence and what turned out to be the bloody partition of the country into two new states.

After the partition of the country in August 1947, the Congress leaders were free to carry out policies such as land reform (which would affect many Muslim landlords) and the abolition of separate seats for Muslims without the interference of the League. Most of the Muslim League's senior leadership left India for Pakistan, together with a large proportion of the Muslim middle and upper classes, attracted by good options in Pakistan and worried about discrimination and economic challenges if they stayed behind. In India's states, and in the central assembly that now had to draft a new national constitution, Nehru and a group of important leaders now had freedom to build new institutions to realize their goal of a democratic and secular state. From 1947–1949, India's Constitutional Assembly debated the kind of society it wanted, and the pros and cons of different kinds of constitutional arrangements used throughout the world (these debates are all online, at http://parliamentofindia.nic.in/ls/debates/debates.htm). In the end, the model they chose in the 1950 constitution owed a lot to the structure India had inherited from the British.

We should not overstate the similarities, however. Although the 1950 constitution adopted many of the measures the British had implemented in the 1935 Government of India Act, Congress *did* alter the institutional structure of the government it inherited in several important ways. First, Congress dramatically widened participation, instituting universal suffrage for both men and women. Despite the fact that the Indian electorate was initially overwhelmingly illiterate—only 27 percent of men and 9 percent of women could read according to the 1951 Census—Indian voters have proved themselves to be increasingly sophisticated and engaged with politics. Illiteracy and lack of modernization, it turned out, were not huge obstacles to democracy, especially given the efforts the Indian state made to reach out to illiterate and poor voters, such as putting party symbols as well as words on ballots.

And in economic policy, too, the new government also differed significantly from the British. There were initial debates over whether to adopt more socialistic or capitalistic models. But in a series of decisions after 1948, and especially in the second five-year plan (1957–1962), the Congress Party nationalized many of the key industries in the country, and highly regulated most of the others.

SUMMARY TABLE

Historical Overview: India From Colonialism to Democracy

1200–1526	Sultanate period	Growth of Muslim-ruled states in northern India while important Hindu-ruled kingdoms in south.
1526–1720	Mughal Empire	Powerful empire with great wealth and sophisticated administrative and military capacity.
1720–1755	Post-Mughal fight for dominance	The rise of powerful Muslim- and Hindu-ruled successor states, and the growth of British and French interests in the subcontinent.
1755–1803	Rise of East India Company as a land power	The East India Company (EIC) defeats its rivals, and conquers and administers much of east, south, and north India.

(Continued)

SUMMARY TABLE (CONTINUED)

1803–1857	Extension of EIC power	Establishment of central, provincial, and district EIC administrations and conquest of more Indian states.
1857–1909	Post–1857 reforms	After defeat of 1857 rebellion, British solidify their rule through army and civil service reforms and building of roads and rail links, but make fewer attempts to interfere with "traditional society."
1909–1919	Weak legislative reforms	1909 and 1919 reforms create weak provincial governments in response to Congress demands for Home Rule. Reforms entrench religious divide through separate electorates.
1919–1945	Nationalist campaign for independence	Despite state repression Gandhi and Congress press for home rule and independence. British introduce major legislative reforms in 1935 in failed effort to preserve power and put off demands for independence. Muslim League emerges as main political voice for Muslims and presses for "Pakistan."
1945–1947	Negotiations with Congress and Muslim League over independence and subsequent partition of India	A post–1945 weakened Britain grants independence to new states of Pakistan and India, in bloody partition process.
1947–1950	Constitution making	India debates and writes its new constitution as a secular and federal democracy.
1950–1964	Nehru's India	Congress the dominant party under Prime Minister Nehru. Government led attempts to industrialize through nationalized industries.
1964–1977	Post-Nehru crises	After Nehru's death, a struggle for control of Congress which Indira Gandhi wins, but she imposes emergency rule 1975–1977 to crush opposition to her policies.
1977–1990	Gradual loss of Congress dominance	Increasing challenges to Congress at center, beginning with 1977 victory of Janata coalition that ended the emergency.
1991–	Era of coalitions	Congress can no longer win a majority on its own. But is a return to single-party government even desirable any more in a country as diverse as India?

INSTITUTIONS OF INDIA

India and Pakistan both inherited the same government structure from the 1935 Government of India Act. But India took only two years to debate and pass a new constitution, paving the way for the new republic's first universal franchise elections in 1951–1952. Pakistan, meanwhile, took nine conflict-ridden years to pass its first constitution, and that lasted only two years before the country's first military coup took place in 1958. In contrast, India's 1950 Constitution remains in place today.

India's constitution preserved many core aspects of the British structure, particularly a parliamentary system with the Prime Minister as head of the government. However, instead of a monarch, India has a President as the constitutional head of state. This system is replicated in each of the states, where a Chief Minister is the head of a state's government and a governor is the state's constitutional head of state. In addition, the 1950 Constitution enshrined an independent judiciary. The central government also maintains the right to impose emergency **President's Rule**, in which a state's government is temporarily suspended—with the permission of parliament and the president—and the state ruled from New Delhi. The constitution also maintains national unity through its all-India civil service and police forces, which continue to staff the most important central and state government positions.

The new constitution also imposed some major changes, such as abolishing **untouchability** and other forms of ethnic discrimination, permitting land reform, abolishing forced labor, introducing village governments, and suggesting public ownership of some important sectors of the economy. But the formal structure of the 1950 Constitution alone, with its many similarities to the 1935 Government of India Act and to unsuccessful Pakistani institutions, provides few clues to why it has fostered a successful democracy. That success is explained better by the way the Congress Party and Prime Minister Nehru democratically worked the constitution in India's first 15 years, and the willingness of the Congress Party to amend the document and compromise when faced by regional and social opposition rather than rely on the emergency clauses in the constitution to crush dissent, as Jinnah and his successors did in Pakistan.

Many in Congress wanted to dismantle British state institutions completely after 1947. There was a fierce debate between followers of Gandhi (who was assassinated in January 1948) who wanted to develop a decentralized authentically Indian system of devolved government, built on traditional **panchayat** village assemblies; and others who felt that the new state could not afford to get rid of a strong and effective central government, as well as strong national civil service, military, and police forces, at a time of real instability and danger. In this struggle over different visions of state-building the latter approach won out over Gandhi's. In large part because Indians had several decades of working and running the colonial institutions they inherited, they had much more legitimacy than might have been expected: much more, for instance, than colonial institutions in Indonesia or Congo, where the locals had been almost completely excluded from power.

6.2 How has India developed into a stable representative democracy?

Explore the Comparative "Legislatures" at mypoliscilab.com

President's Rule ■ emergency clauses in the Indian Constitution giving the central government the right to suspend state governments and administer states in case of financial or security emergencies.

untouchability ■ discrimination against members of the traditionally "unclean" Hindu castes who dealt with animal and human death or waste. Although made illegal by the 1950 Constitution, many discriminatory practices survive today.

panchayat ■ previously referred to representative village assemblies, now refers both mainly to elected local governments, to which many development tasks have been decentralized since the passage of constitutional amendments in the 1990s.

Federalism

The 1950 Constitution preserved much of the federal system introduced by the British, with nine states in 1950, as well as several centrally run union territories. This total increased to 28 states in 2010 as a result of subdividing existing states and making some centrally ruled union territories into states. The central government appoints a governor to each state, which has an elected state assembly (called *Vidhan Sabha*) and sometimes also an upper house. The constitution establishes a list of policies that only the central government in New Delhi controls, such as defense, foreign affairs, central banking and currency; a mixed list where there is joint authority between the center and the states; and a list of the areas under the control of the elected state governments, which includes such important subjects as education, agriculture, law and order, and local taxes.

In emergencies, a centrally appointed governor can dissolve the state government as long as his or her actions are approved by the president of India and subsequently by the national parliament in New Delhi. The appointed governor typically acts on the direct instructions of the prime minister and ruling party in Delhi. This imposition of President's Rule, which has happened more than 100 times since 1950, has always been controversial, with critics seeing each imposition as a violation of the democratic and federal spirit of the constitution; and as something that, especially in the 1970s and 1980s, was often done for partisan political reasons—such as to kick opposing parties out of state office—rather than because of a genuine emergency.

After independence, the Congress Party reorganized colonial territorial units in order to break up princely state–British province distinctions as well as recognize new regional aspirations. Within a decade, all the states except Tripura and Jammu and Kashmir had been merged with former British provinces, which diluted their separate identities. The Congress also created many new linguistic states in response to regional demands to break up the larger multi-ethnic states. There were debates about whether creating these new states would lead to the collapse of the country or help to save it. In the aftermath of partition, Nehru and the Congress Party were so worried that giving in to regional demands would encourage separatism and even more conflicts that they abandoned the party's pre-independence pledge to create linguistic states—that is, states that are meant to be, as far as possible, linguistically homogenous. These states were meant to replace the many multi-language states that existed before 1947: for instance the state of Madras had large populations of Telugu, Tamil, and Malayalam speakers, as well as many other languages. The center eventually reversed course, however, because its refusal to create linguistic states caused widespread violent protests. It thought that the certainty of large-scale violence and protests if it refused to create the new states was much more of a threat than the possibility that in the long run creating the new states might increase regionalism.

In the following three decades, there were several major waves of state creation: after a fatal hunger strike by a Telugu activist demanding a Telugu-speaking state of Andhra in December 1952, which sparked off large-scale riots, the government created Andhra and examined the possibility of creating more linguistic states. This sparked the initial wave of linguistic state-making, with the carving out of Andhra, Kerala, Tamil Nadu, Mysore (now renamed Karnataka) Gujarat, Maharashtra,

Jammu and Kashmir ■ India's only Muslim-majority state. Delayed joining India or Pakistan in 1947, precipitating a Pakistani attempt to take the state by force and leading to the first India–Pakistan conflict. India has held on to most of the state since then, but it has faced periodic political unrest and militant campaigns, supported by Pakistan. Conflicts between India and Pakistan over the state have led to three declared wars and frequent fighting.

Punjab, and Haryana by the mid-1960s; This was then followed by a second wave in the late 1960s and early 1970s that created a whole host of (economically not very viable) small states in the politically troubled northeast. This was followed by a third wave in 2000, when the three new states of Chhattisgarh, Uttaranchal (now renamed Uttarakhand) and Jharkhand were carved out of undeveloped regions of larger states. The process looks likely to continue, as a regional leader's hunger strike (not fatal, this time) and subsequent riots that began in Andhra Pradesh in late 2009 looked likely to lead in the next few years to the creation of a new state of Telangana, formed from a region of Andhra that feels it has been neglected within the new state carved out from Madras in 1953.

Despite the decentralization to the states, the central government can use its control of resources, its governors, and, in the last resort, its emergency powers to influence the states. The country is also unified by a national administrative cadre. There was a debate after independence over whether to abolish the elite national civil service and police forces, the Indian Civil Service (ICS) and Indian Police (IP), which occupied virtually all the senior positions at both the federal and state level. Many Congressmen saw these services as stooges of the British, and as representatives of a "colonial" style of government that could not be reformed. However, Congress ultimately decided that these services had to be kept as a unifying influence, even though the ICS and IP were renamed the Indian Administrative Service (IAS) and the Indian Police Service (IPS). The higher positions in each state's police force and civil service must be members of these nationally recruited forces, who alternate between posts at the center and in the states, and who cannot be fired by the state governments without the permission of the Indian president.

Parliament

At the federal level, India has a bicameral parliamentary system with a lower house, the *Lok Sabha* (House of the People), elected for a term of no more than five years; an upper house, the *Rajya Sabha* (House of the States); and a largely ceremonial president elected jointly by members of the national and state legislatures. The 543 elected members of the Lok Sabha are elected through single-member plurality districts, meaning that the candidate with the largest number of votes wins the seat. Lower caste and tribal representation is ensured by the requirement that 22.5 percent of the seats may be contested only by members of the Scheduled Castes (15 percent) and Scheduled Tribes (7.5 percent)—the "Schedule" refers to the official list of disadvantaged castes that were traditionally regarded as untouchable, the lowest rung of the Hindu castes, and the list of indigenous tribal peoples. In addition to these elected members, two members may be appointed to the Lok Sabha by the president to represent the small Anglo-Indian minority.

The Rajya Sabha has 250 members, 12 nominated by the president and 238 of whom elected indirectly for six years by the state assemblies and union territory assemblies, with a third of members up for re-election every two years, as in the U.S. Senate. Each state's number of representatives is broadly proportionate to its population, but according to a constitutional rule that overrepresents the smaller states: one seat minimum per state and "One seat per million for the first

Indian Administrative Service (IAS) ■ the most elite and prestigious all-India civil service, the IAS staffs virtually all the most senior positions in state and central governments, as well as many state enterprises. It is recruited mainly through a national and very competitive annual examination.

Lok Sabha ■ lower house of parliament

Rajya Sabha ■ upper chamber of parliament

scheduled castes ■ those castes included on central and state "schedules" (lists) of the most discriminated against castes, those traditionally treated as "untouchable" by upper-caste Hindus. Castes listed are eligible for reserved places in government employment, schools, and colleges.

scheduled tribes ■ tribal peoples recognized by the government in schedules similar to those for the scheduled castes, and, like the SCs, eligible for special reserved places in government employment, schools, and colleges.

THE LOK SABHA

Newly elected Congress MPs meet in parliament after their victory in the 2009 elections to formally select Manmohan Singh as prime minister of India. Prime Minister Singh, a member of the country's 2 percent Sikh community, symbolizes India's relative success at integrating its religious and linguistic minorities. Most Indian cabinets represent a rainbow coalition of castes, religious groups, and regions.

five millions and one seat for every additional two millions or part thereof exceeding one million."

The Lok Sabha has more power than the Rajya Sabha. Only a vote of no-confidence in the Lok Sabha can force the government to resign. And while the Rajya Sabha can send most bills back with amendments to the lower house, it does not have the power to do this for the all-important money bills, which only the Lok Sabha can initiate and amend. Even in the case of the other bills, it has much less power than, for instance, the U.S. Senate: competing bills are reconciled not through a Senate-House committee process as in the United States, but instead though "joint sittings," in which the 545 members of the Lok Sabha greatly outnumber the 250 representatives from the Rajya Sabha. Cabinet ministers may, as in the UK, be drawn either from the lower or the upper house.

Civil–Military Relations

The relationship between civil and military authorities established soon after independence also served to strengthen India's democracy. Congress acted very quickly to establish civilian control over the military, something that was much easier to do because of its huge mandate and unquestioned legitimacy in the country.[8] One of the first letters Nehru wrote after independence was to tell army officers that the rules of the game had fundamentally changed, and that he was not prepared to allow any army interference or obstruction with Congress policy. When officers interfered with the planning for Independence Day celebrations in August 1947, Nehru wrote to the head of the army to remind him that, "In any policy that is to be pursued, in the Army or otherwise, the views of the Government of India . . . must prevail. If any person is unable to lay down that policy, he has no place in the Indian Army, or in the Indian structure of Government."[9]

Congress also downgraded the army commander-in-chief from his previous cabinet-level status, where he was daily involved in setting policy, and to further emphasize the new hierarchy Prime Minister Nehru moved into the imposing mansion near parliament that had formerly been the house of the army's commander-in-chief. Even the order of precedence at state dinners was changed to make sure that cabinet ministers, senior judges, and other important political leaders now came before the generals.[10] Congress also broadened the army's ethnic composition, making sure that new units raised were open to all Indians, not just the "martial classes" from the north and west that had dominated the Indian Army under the British, and that still dominate the Pakistani Army. The "martial classes" are still important (30 percent of the Indian armed forces), but unlike in Pakistan, they are far from a majority of the army, and, therefore, do not pose a threat to the stability of the country.

The Judiciary

Judicial autonomy has also contributed to India's democratic survival, and acted as a check on executive power and a defender of federalism. Since independence, India's courts, especially at the higher levels, have largely retained their independence and resisted interference from elected officials. The Supreme Court in particular has displayed considerable independence. Its chief justice and 28 justices are appointed directly by the president of India in consultation with a committee of judges already on the court, on the basis of legal seniority and reputation, as well as regional representativeness, rather than because of partisan backing. Though justices can be removed by parliament with a two-thirds vote for wrongdoing, parliament plays no role in their initial appointment, which is until the retirement age of 65, not for life as in the United States. Justice may not always be sure and swift, but belief in the neutrality of the courts does act as a check on corrupt politicians and business interests who know that even if their friends will not allow the administration to bring charges against them, their enemies might. The Supreme Court has also over the years placed several important limits on the power of the central government to interfere with India's federal structure. Most importantly, in the 1994 *Bommai* decision, the Supreme Court restricted the government's ability to impose President's Rule on a state, allowing for judicial review of future cases where emergency rule was imposed. Since that decision, there have been relatively few controversial cases of President's Rule, outside of its frequent imposition in the troubled state of Jammu and Kashmir, which faces a long-term insurgency.

The Supreme Court also entertains public interest litigation launched by concerned citizens and by organizations that complain of violations of their constitutional rights. The number of Public Interest Litigation (PIL) cases filed in the High Courts has greatly increased since the first case was heard in 1979, leading to better protection for people charged with crimes, better protection for women, and the release of many bonded laborers working as virtual slaves in rural areas and in the mining industry. Women's rights groups—of which there are a huge number and variety in India—have also successfully pushed for a ban on the use of amniocentesis centers to allow families to find out the sex of their child, which they then often use to selectively abort female fetuses because of the widespread social preference for sons, and because of the large costs involved in paying dowries to marry daughters off. Despite formal restrictions, however, selective abortion continues, leading to increasingly sharp gender disparities in many states as the numbers of males increases relative to females.

Political Parties

From 1952 to 1977, the secular and left-leaning Congress Party won more than 50 percent of the seats at every election, and often closer to two-thirds of the seats, easily defeating the main communist, socialist, and regionally based opposition parties. But Congress was always so broad a party in terms of its internal regional, religious, and caste diversity, that it never seriously tried to use this massive majority to rig the political game in its favor, even when it lost power in a particular state election. The openness and competitiveness of the system reduced the threat posed by the opposition, because challengers could join Congress and try to win the election rather than having to compete by forming separate parties. Only when there was a serious split in the Congress Party in 1969 between **Indira Gandhi** (Nehru's daughter, and no relation to Mahatma Gandhi) and "The Syndicate" of strong regional Congress party leaders, did this competitive and broad-based "Congress System" begin to break down. First, Indira Gandhi excluded these important regional leaders from the party and then, when she won the national parliamentary elections in March 1971, stopped holding internal Congress Party elections in order to prevent future challenges to her power. Since that time, the Congress has been a dynastic party, in which power flows downwards from the Nehru–Gandhi family in New Delhi rather than up from the districts and states. Before elections in the 1970s and 1980s, for instance, there were huge gatherings of hopeful candidates from all over India gathered outside the Nehru family residences in New Delhi, hoping for the nod from a family member or advisor that would mean a "ticket": permission to run for a seat in some faraway constituency.

Gandhi sought to marginalize her political opponents outside the party, as well as within it. The banks and insurance companies and some other large companies opposed her socialist economic policies in the 1960s and donated to opposition parties. Former princely rulers were also active in opposition politics. So the Congress neutralized these landed and business elites by nationalizing the banks and major insurance companies, and by abolishing the annual grants that the former princely rulers had received since giving up their thrones at independence, as well as by regulating more

Indira Gandhi ■
daughter of Jawaharlal Nehru, she became prime minister in 1966, two years after her father's death. She led the Congress Party and the country from 1966–1977 and from 1980 until her assassination in 1984.

and more of the economy under a plan to "abolish poverty." Congress politicians now had the discretion to grant loans, permits to businessmen to produce or import things, and also to control prices. This discretion was granted on what was jokingly referred to as a "case by case basis," which referred to the suitcases of money necessary for businessmen to get the decision they wanted.

Indira Gandhi also used the emergency clauses of the constitution to throw out state governments on trumped-up charges whenever she thought this would be politically advantageous for her own Congress Party. From 1966–1977, the Congress declared President's Rule on a state 39 times (an average of 3.25 times per year), compared with only six impositions in total during the Nehru years from 1950–1964 (0.4 per annum) and two during Prime Minister Lal Bahadur Shastri's government from 1964–1966 (1 per annum). Throughout the mid-1970s, despite her initial personal popularity and support for her promise to abolish poverty, the party's centralization and misuse of state power generated increasing opposition. From within the party, she was opposed by Congress politicians who had not received high wealth or office and from idealist "Gandhians," who felt the party had lost its values. From outside, she was confronted by opposition parties. And within the broader society, she was opposed by those who disliked the creeping authoritarianism of her rule, and, in particular, by Muslims and other groups who felt victimized by Congress slum clearance and family planning sterilization policies, which hit minorities and the poorest the hardest.

Fortunately, these attempts to rig the democratic system came 20 years too late to be successful. Ther independence of the judiciary and popular support for democracy were too well ingrained by the mid-1970s to be subverted by Gandhi's brief period of emergency rule from 1975–1977, which she imposed in reaction to losing a High Court electoral malpractice case that would have removed her from parliament. She decided in 1977 to call snap elections, believing her advisors that the opposition was too weak and uncoordinated to stand a chance. But the depth of popular opposition to the emergency rule and abuses of the mid-1970s was so strong that even with only six weeks to campaign, the Janata (People's) coalition that had been hastily assembled defeated the Congress overwhelmingly, in a triumphant reassertion of India's democratic will.

Janata Party ■ the loose coalition of parties that came together to defeat Indira Gandhi in a massive rebuke to her "emergency" rule after elections were called in 1977.

The Janata coalition was too diverse (it included everyone from communists to Hindu nationalists) to hold together for more than a couple of years, and when it collapsed, Gandhi was swept back into power at the head of a new Congress government in 1980. She had to contend, however, with growing regional tensions in the northeast as well as from Sikh militants in Punjab. Her fateful decision in June 1984 to send the army in to dislodge militant Sikhs from that religion's holiest site, the Golden Temple in Amritsar, led to a massive increase in violence in the state, and also to her own death when two of her Sikh bodyguards shot her while she was walking in the garden of her official residence in New Delhi. This assassination sparked off a huge and bloody anti-Sikh riot in Delhi in November 1984, in which some Congress politicians were clearly involved, and also led to the promotion of Indira Gandhi's surviving son Rajiv, a former airline pilot.

Rajiv Gandhi's term as prime minister started very well with peace settlements with regional movements in Assam and new initiatives to resolve the Punjab crisis.

Backward Castes ■ castes in between the upper castes and the untouchables, with around 40–45 percent of the Indian population.

reservations system ■ the proportional system through which lower castes and tribals are allocated jobs and educational positions in government employment.

Sonia Gandhi ■ current president of the Congress Party and the chairperson of the United Progressive Alliance (UPA) coalition, which Congress leads.

Manmohan Singh ■ Oxford-trained economist who initiated India's economic reforms as finance minister in the 1990s, and was chosen by Sonia Gandhi after Congress' victory in 2004 to become prime minister. Re-elected as a result of the Congress–UPA victory in 2009.

Rajiv also took the first tentative steps towards relaxing the system of economic regulations and state ownership that had become associated with what critics called India's low 4 percent "Hindu rate of growth." But corruption within the Congress, opposition from regional parties, and the rise of the Backward Caste parties which pushed for greater social equity and caste reservations for lower castes led to Congress' defeat in the 1989 elections and to a Janata Dal coalition. When this government fell in 1991, Rajiv was murdered at a campaign meeting by a Sri Lankan Tamil suicide bomber in revenge for Indian military intervention in the Sri Lankan civil war. This second murder of a prime minister from the Nehru–Gandhi family suddenly catapulted Rajiv's widow, the Italian-born Sonia Gandhi, to the informal leadership of India's major party. Sonia Gandhi wisely recognized that her Italian heritage would create serious complications for her own candidacy for prime minister, so since 1991, she has moved only gradually to positions of formal leadership in the Congress, becoming leader of the party in 1998. She has let other leaders, such as P. V. Narasimha Rao (prime minister 1991–1996) and Manmohan Singh (2004–) occupy the highest government positions, while her own children Rahul (born 1970) and Priyanka (born 1972) gain the age and experience that will enable them later to run for the highest offices.

The growth of Backward Caste parties, regional parties, and the Hindu nationalist Bharatiya Janata Party (BJP) which headed a coalition government in New Delhi from 1998–2004, have meant that Congress now exists in a very different world from the 1950s and 1960s, when it could routinely win 50–65 percent of seats in the Lok Sabha. As Figure 6.1 reveals, in every election since 1996, no single party has been capable of winning more than a third of the parliamentary seats. Initially, parties failed to adjust to this new reality, and failed to form pre-election coalitions that stood a chance of winning a majority, leading to a series of weak minority governments from 1990–1998 (see Table 6.2). But since 1998 both the Congress and its main challenger, the BJP, have accepted that no single party can win on its own, and both parties now spend a lot of time building up stable alliances, the UPA alliance headed by Congress and the NDA backed by the BJP. India has in the past two decades entered an era of permanent coalition politics, in which the BJP, Congress, or "Third Front" parties all need the support of at least several regional parties to win a majority of the seats at the center. In the 2009 elections, for instance, the Congress-led UPA coalition included Congress and *nine* regional coalition partners, such as the Trinamool Congress from the state of West Bengal and the Dravida Munnetra Kazhagam from the state of Tamil Nadu.

Election Commission

India has a central Election Commission (EC) charged with ensuring clean and fair elections. Unlike in the United States, where districts are drawn in most states by partisan state legislatures, India's election commission draws seat boundaries in a way that is widely regarded as neutral and fair. The commission has also introduced cheap and reliable electronic voting machines. In the last few years, the commission has also tried to shine a light upon the high levels of criminality and

FIGURE 6.1

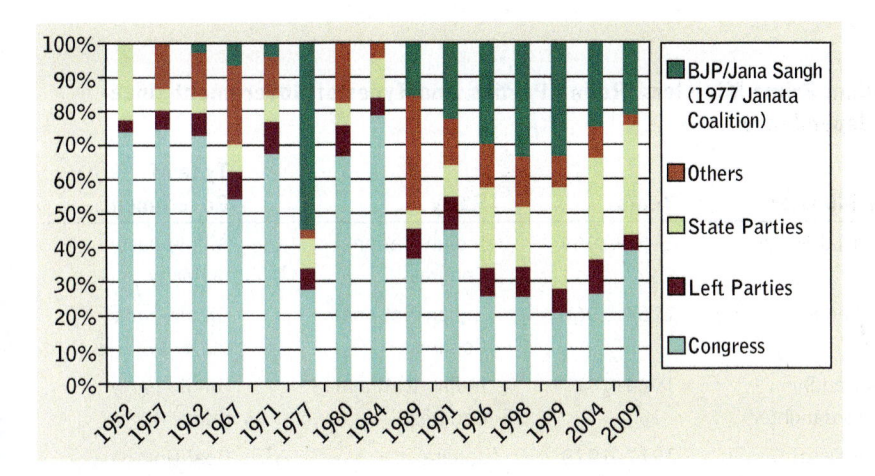

Party Balance in the Indian Parliament, 1952–2009

Before 1989, the Congress Party was generally dominant in national elections, typically winning two-thirds or more of the seats. Since 1989, however, India has entered an era of coalitions. The BJP and Congress each get around 25–30 percent of the seats, and who wins or loses national power, therefore, depends on whether the BJP or Congress makes better pre-election alliances with regional parties.

Bharatiya Janata Party ■ successor party to the Hindu Nationalist Jana Sangh, which opposed Congress from the 1950s until it entered the Janata coalition in 1977. The BJP was founded as a separate party in 1980. It stands for a strong, assertive policy of emphasizing *Hindutva*, or "Hinduness" in politics, and is often seen as hostile to minorities.

corruption in Indian politics. In 1997, the EC published data revealing what many already knew: large numbers of MLAs (members of the state legislative assemblies) and MPs were criminals, or at least had had criminal cases lodged against them. While some of these cases are deliberately lodged by political rivals, making it difficult to assume that all politicians with cases against them are actually criminals, the study showed that 40 out of 545 sitting MPs and around 700 of the 4,072 members in the various State Assemblies had a criminal record.[11] Additional studies suggested that many MPs and MLAs were personally corrupt, with many "rags to riches" stories of politicians born in poverty who have somehow accumulated vast wealth after gaining office.

Over the past decade, the Election Commission has tried in several different ways to end this corruption. In 2002 and 2003, in measures ultimately sustained by the Supreme Court, the Election Commission forced candidates for office to (1) declare whether they had been charged or convicted with any crime; and (2) declare all their assets and their family's fixed and liquid assets when they file for election. Neither of these measures is a panacea, but there is growing hope that these measures are at least placing limits on the scope of illegality. And as the "clean" proportion of politicians grows, these people have every incentive to try to limit the ability of their corrupt peers to outspend them in elections, by pressing for further reforms. The commission has also proposed that the count from individual voting machines be totaled at a constituency level, to make voters from individual polling stations less vulnerable to retaliation if they vote heavily against powerful politicians.

TABLE 6.1

Indian Prime Ministers, Ruling Parties, and Types of Government since Independence

Prime Minister	Years	Party	Type of Government
Jawaharlal Nehru	1950–1964	Indian National Congress	Single-party majority
Lal Bahadur Shastri	1964–1966	Indian National Congress	Single-party majority
Indira Gandhi (Nehru's daughter)	1964–1977	Indian National Congress	Single-party majority
Morarji Desai	1977–1979	Janata	Coalition
Charan Singh	1979–Jan. 1980	Janata	Minority government
Indira Gandhi	1980–1984	Indian National Congress	Single-party majority
Rajiv Gandhi (Indira's son)	1984–1989	Indian National Congress	Single-party majority
V. P. Singh	1989–1990	Janata Coalition	Coalition
Chandra Shekhar	1990–1991	Janata Coalition	Minority government
P. V. Narasimha Rao	1991–1996	Indian National Congress	Minority government
H. D. Deve Gowda	1996–1997	Janata	Minority government
I. K. Gujral	1997–1998	Janata	Minority government
Atal Bihari Vajpayee	1998–2004	Bharatiya Janata Party (NDA Alliance)	Coalition
Manmohan Singh	2004–	Indian National Congress (UPA Alliance)	Coalition

Excludes two very short terms as interim PM served by Gulzarilal Nanda in 1964 and 1966, and the 13-day government of Atal Bihari Vajpayee (BJP) in May 1996.

6.3 How has India prevented regional and ethnic movements from destabilizing the country?

IDENTITIES IN INDIA

India is one of the most ethnically diverse countries in the world, divided by caste, language, and religion. Scholars have long wondered whether diversity of identity groups sustains or harms democracy—and in this regard India has long puzzled scholars, many of whom believed that democracy in a country as diverse as India could never survive. There is no question, for example, that divisions between religious or ethnic groups sometimes results in violence, even civil war. As noted in the chapter's introduction, India and Pakistan emerged as separate countries precisely because of a fear that the Hindu–Muslim divide would result in massive conflict. And despite the partition, India and Pakistan have fought three major international wars since independence, and relations between the two countries remain tense. Even in India, inter-group conflict sometimes breaks out. Yet, in contrast to Nigeria for example, or Russia, India's democracy has never been seriously threatened by inter-group conflict. In some ways, identity group diversity has strengthened India's democracy. The decisions that Nehru made in the early 1950s to institutionalize linguistic and caste identities through government policy allowed India to defuse the dangerous macro-regional and religious cleavages (such as Hindus versus Muslims, or Southerners versus Northerners) that could have endangered the stability of Indian democracy.

Explore the Comparative "Identity" at mypoliscilab.com

Castes

A Hindu is typically born into a caste which reflects his or her region and position in the Hindu hierarchy (high, low, or outcaste), and which in the old days at least, also functioned as an occupational category, with castes of potters, herders, barbers, merchants, priests, etc. These days, however, a large proportion of people do not practice their traditional occupations. Although non-Hindus typically say they do not practice caste, in reality Christians (2 percent), Sikhs (2 percent), and Muslims (13 percent) also have caste divisions that in many ways parallel those of the Hindus. At the top of the broad Hindu caste hierarchy are the "upper caste" *Brahmins* (the priestly caste), *Kshatriyas* (warriors), and *Vaishyas* (merchants), who together are around 10–15 percent of the population. (Exact numbers are difficult because there has been no caste census since 1931.) In the middle are the *Sudras*, a broad range who traditionally labored and performed services for the other castes, and who constitute maybe 40–45 percent of the population and include many groups now officially designated as "Backward Castes" or "Most Backward Castes." And at the bottom of the caste hierarchy are the Dalits or "Scheduled Castes," a name now applied to the lowest castes whose occupations were traditionally regarded as the dirtiest (e.g., leather work, cremation, disposal of animals), and who were treated as "untouchable"—whose touch and, in some cases, even presence could "pollute"—by the higher castes. Somewhat outside this caste hierarchy are India's tribal peoples, often displaced to remote mountain and forest areas by a succession of invasions over the centuries, and who practice a mix of Hindu, Christian, and traditional religions.

The caste system has many local and regional variations. In addition, Indians are further divided along jati lines, and for most people these *jati* caste identities have much more meaning than broad categories such as Brahmin and Kshatriya, or upper or lower caste. There are perhaps 7,000 *jati*, or sub-castes, in India, most of which are regionally based. Most families marry only within their own *jati*, or to members of a closely related *jati*. Every year, there are cases, especially in conservative rural areas, of young men and women being punished or even murdered for wanting to marry outside their caste, or wanting to marry

Hinduism ■ majority religion in India, with 81 percent of the population. Thousands of years old, this religion is polytheistic and highly diverse in terms of its leadership and regional differences in theology and practice.

Dalits ■ literally, "the oppressed." A modern and more politically acceptable name for the ex-untouchable Scheduled Castes, this term is used especially by SC activists and politically aware scholars and activists.

jati ■ a sub-caste group, typically based in a relatively small region.

someone other than their family's choice. Even among those individuals who are most inclined to make their own marriage choices, caste preferences run strong. A 2008 survey using an Internet marriage site found that a lower-caste prospective groom's income would need to increase eight times before it would generate the same number of responses from higher caste women compared to the number of responses from women of their own caste.[12]

This is not to say that caste is not changing. Some caste practices do seem to be diminishing, as a result of modernization. Caste restrictions on alcohol and food seem to be lessening in urban areas, for instance, as meat eating and alcohol consumption have become more widespread among the prosperous Indian middle classes. It has become unacceptable in many areas to tolerate caste discrimination in access to restaurants and tea stalls, where formerly lower castes would not be served or served only in separate dishes. And the form of the traditional arranged caste marriage, in which the bride and groom did not meet or else met only a few times under close family supervision is also changing. A higher proportion of prospective brides and grooms are now allowed input into the decision than in the past, with the right to veto partners who are clearly incompatible, and even in some cases to go on supervised dates. Some men and women are taking the initiative themselves to identify suitable partners, through newspaper advertisements or by placing ads on popular marriage websites. Despite the growth of dating in urban areas and the entry of more women into workforce environments where they can meet potential partners on their own, probably more than 80 percent of marriages even among the urban middle and upper classes are still arranged, and arranged marriages are nearly universal in rural areas.

Caste does not just affect family life, but also still plays a role in where people live, in their employment chances, and also in people's political preferences. Lower castes and non-vegetarians, for instance, will find it tough to rent accommodation from upper-caste vegetarians. And they may also find it difficult to get interviews for jobs. An experiment in 2006, for instance, in which equally matched "applicants" applied for jobs advertised in the leading national newspaper *The Times of India*, found that applicants with stereotypically lower-caste names were only two-thirds as likely to be called back as applicants with stereotypically upper-caste names, and that people with Muslim names were even worse off, with only one-third as likely to be called back.[13] This study, the method for which was based on an important study of discrimination in hiring in the United States titled "Are Emily and Greg More Employable than Lakisha and Jamal?" seems to show that there are still many significant challenges to social and employment equality in India.[14]

Own-caste preferences also play out in the political realm, especially when a *jati* is large enough to constitute a major chunk of a state's electorate. The Bahujan Samaj Party in Uttar Pradesh, for instance, tends to be associated with the *Jatav* or *Chamar* community, a large *jati* of former leatherworkers from the lowest Hindu castes, who constitute more than 10 percent of this mega-state's population of 190 million. People often vote for parties which promise social policies that will benefit their caste, such as reserved government jobs, places in higher education, and special infrastructure and loan programs for members of the "backward classes."

Languages

As we can see in Figure 6.2 on the next page, Indians also speak many different languages. The 22 most important languages are given "official" national status in the eight schedule of the constitution: the value of a banknote is listed in Hindi, English, and (in smaller type) a further 15 of these official languages. There are also dozens of smaller languages with a million or more speakers. Moreover, each of the largest languages has several major regional variations (such as Rajasthani, Bhojpuri, and Maithili within Hindi) that we could also consider as separate languages, depending on how the term "language" is defined. The big division is between the northern Indo-European languages, such as Hindi, Urdu, and Punjabi, and the various southern languages, such as Tamil, Malayalam, and Telugu, which are from the completely separate Dravidian language group. People from the south have long protested against anything that smacks of an attempt to impose Hindi on them, or to make Hindi rather than English the language of higher government and commerce. As well as these, there are also smaller tribal languages spoken by Scheduled Tribes and by groups in the northeast that don't fit within the larger language families. Because of the enormous diversity of languages, as well as high levels of internal migration, it is very common to meet Indians who speak two or three major languages: Tamils who speak Tamil, Malayalam, and English, or Bengalis who speak Hindi, Bengali, and English. Despite various attempts over the years to downgrade the position of English, the recent market liberalization has made acquiring it as well as Hindi even more attractive in the past decade, and even in poor neighborhoods there are lots of signs advertising English tutoring and classes. (Most Indians even in non-Hindi-speaking areas also learn Hindi as a compulsory language at school, as well as through the ubiquitous Bollywood films and television.)

Religion

As we can see in Figure 6.3 on the next page, India is primarily Hindu, but there are also very substantial communities of Muslims (13 percent), Sikhs (2 percent), Christians (2 percent), and Buddhists (1 percent), as well as a very small Jewish community. India is also home to the world's last significant community of Zoroastrians (Parsis), members of an ancient religion from Iran whose members have achieved great professional success. Despite fears at independence that India would continue to suffer from the same high levels of Hindu–Muslim strife as it had in the colonial period, this has generally not happened, though there have been some severe communal riots over the years. The reason why is because first thing India did after independence was to reform those elements of the colonial state that made religion a legitimate *political* identity. In the aftermath of partition, Prime Minister Nehru and other senior Indian leaders viewed religion as an illegitimate identity in politics, and while the new constitution protected freedom to practice any religion, it banned all government discrimination on the basis of religion. In 1949, during debates over the new constitution, the Constituent Assembly decided to abolish the reserved separate electorates for religious minorities, such as Muslims and Sikhs, that had been such an important part of British policy before 1947. The assembly and various state governments also stopped reserving

India's Linguistic Diversity

- Hindi
- Bengali
- Telugu
- Marathi
- Tamil
- Urdu
- Gujarati
- Kannada
- Malayalam
- Oriya
- Punjabi
- Maithili
- Others

India's Religious Diversity

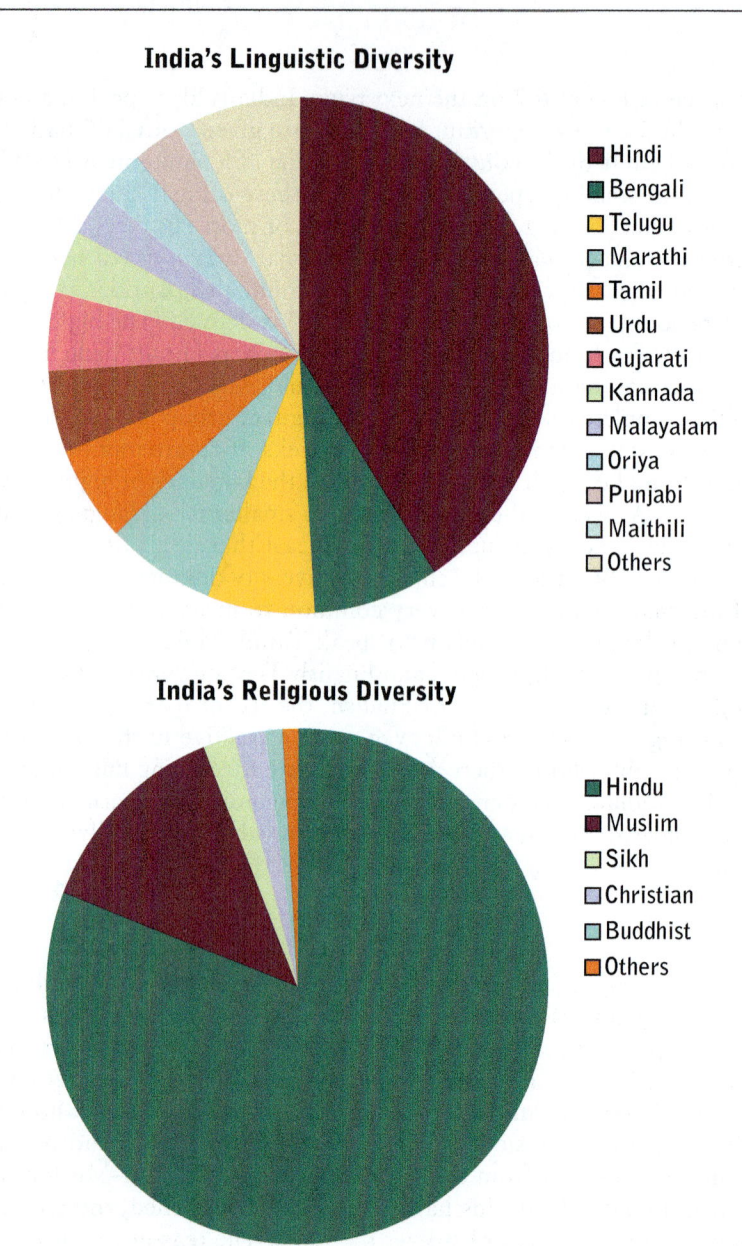

- Hindu
- Muslim
- Sikh
- Christian
- Buddhist
- Others

FIGURE 6.2 and 6.3
Cross-Cutting Cleavages: India's Religious and Linguistic Diversity

government jobs and places in educational institutions for members of particular religious groups. Delegitimizing religion as a valid political identity, together with measures that increased the political importance of caste and language, was very important in explaining why, despite occasional attempts by the BJP and other parties to reassert the importance of religion, India has not suffered from sustained national-level Hindu–Muslim political cleavages since independence.

Prime Minister Nehru would have liked to further downplay the importance of ethnicity by ending the state recognition of linguistic and caste identities, as well. He opposed regional demands to create linguistic states in the years from 1947–1952, on the basis that these were a threat to the newly independent country's hard-won national unity, as well as very hard to implement because they would create new minorities within each of the new states. And he opposed demands for caste "reservations" (a more rigid style of affirmative action in which positions are formally reserved for members of different groups if they meet certain minimum requirements) as well, on the basis that they promoted "casteism" and that they also downplayed merit. The caste system, he complained to a senior Congress leader in 1954, was "the biggest weakening factor in our society."[15]

However, Nehru, when confronted with serious movements around caste and linguistic identities, was willing to compromise when faced with large-scale opposition, rather than turn to the emergency powers used by his peers in Pakistan. This was partly because he was inclined to compromise rather than confrontation, but also because Congress had long operated as a democratic party with many important regional leaders, whose opinions had to be taken seriously. In the case of caste, in 1950 large-scale riots erupted in the southern state of Madras, where "Backward Caste" reservations had been in place since the 1920s. Rioters were protesting against a High Court decision that seemed to place reserved government jobs for these castes in jeopardy. Led by the Dravida Kazhagam, a Tamil-language opposition party identified with the Backward Castes, the issue was to be used against Congress in the first parliamentary elections due to be held in early 1952. Nehru backed down and Congress passed a new provision to the constitution in 1951 that allowed reserved jobs and other benefits in favor of the "Backward Classes" (i.e., castes), notwithstanding the constitution's general anti-discrimination clauses. Nehru also backed down when large-scale linguistic protests exploded in 1950–1952, when Telugu speakers were campaigning to carve out a new state of Andhra Pradesh from Tamil-dominated Madras. In 1953, Nehru allowed the creation of a new Telugu-speaking state called Andhra Pradesh and also appointed a new committee, the States Reorganization Committee, to look into the whole question of whether other new linguistic states ought to be created.

These two decisions, in response to short-term threats of violence and instability, were to have long-term and important consequences. By enshrining the legitimacy of caste and language as Indian political identities, the central government showed that it was prepared, in some cases, to concede to the threat of violence at the state level. Over the subsequent five decades, groups that have wanted things in Indian politics have frequently mobilized around either language or caste because the state has tacitly declared language and caste identities as valid through its policies and constitutional clauses. Politicians have responded in kind, offering to provide more advantages to Backward Castes, or even to declare relatively prosperous castes "backward," in return for votes. In Rajasthan, for instance, the Meena community was reportedly recognized as a Scheduled Tribe in return for 13 state representatives' support for the chief minister during a party leadership contest in 1957.[16]

In 1994, the powerful Vokkaliga and Lingayat *jatis* in the state of Karnataka were recognized as "Other Backward Classes" in return for their support of the chief minister's party in the state elections.[17] As a result of this kind of political horse-trading, the number of backward castes has shot up: in 1955, there were 2,394 officially recognized Backward Castes in India, but by 1980 there were 3,743.[18]

The Changing Politics of Caste Identity

The political incentive to widen the number of backward classes sometimes causes serious conflict. In the late 1980s, India was rocked by a massive upper-caste and urban backlash against caste job and educational reservations, as upper-caste students protested the central government's decision to implement the Mandal Commission report, which recommended a substantial increase in central government reserved positions for the Backward Castes. In the campuses of elite universities, several students tried to burn themselves to death in protest at the increase in job quotas for middle castes; several succeeded. But though several politicians initially seemed to consider reining in reservations, they have largely backtracked because of the very large share of the electorate from the groups that benefit from reservations. In an opinion poll in 2004, 61 percent of the Indian population supported reservations, and only 22 percent opposed them. These percentages seem to suggest that what people think about reservations depends very much on where they sit: the percentage who support job and educational reservations is very similar to the percentages of Dalits and Backward Castes in the population, while the proportion opposed is similar to the proportion of (non-eligible) upper castes in the country.[19] In a "first past the post" system, no politicians can afford to ignore 61 percent of the electorate, so upper-caste opponents drag their feet on implementation, rather than oppose the policies openly. Much of the political conflict over caste, in fact, is between groups that are already included in the reservations system, but who feel they are not getting their fair share of benefits, those who want a "quota within a quota." In 1998, for instance, demands by one Dalit group in the south that it should get its own separate caste quota within the Scheduled Caste reservation led to ten attempts at self-immolation (one ending in death), 1,100 arrests, several large-scale strikes, and the burning of 86 buses.[20]

The number of regional movements demanding new states has also escalated, as not just linguistically separate regions, but also rich or poor regions within states argue that they would be better off as a separate state than as part of a larger unit. In 2000, three new states, Chattisgarh, Jharkhand, and Uttarakhand, were carved out of the larger states of Madhya Pradesh, Bihar, and Uttar Pradesh. The number of India's states, 28 as of 2009, looks likely to increase. In December 2009, in a symbolic repeat of the December 1952 hunger strike that had forced Prime Minister Nehru to grant the state of Andhra Pradesh, another regional politician started fasting to force the center to carve a new state of Telangana out of Andhra Pradesh. Telangana is an economically underdeveloped area, though it contains the thriving state capital of Hyderabad, whose elite educational institutions and recent tech boom have given it the nickname "Cyberabad." In response to this fast and the threat of violence, the central government announced that it would support the

CONFLICT OVER RESERVATIONS

Upper-caste medical students undertake a silent march to protest the expansion in lower-caste reservations to places on postgraduate medical courses announced in 2005. National and almost all state governments now implement widespread caste reservations in employment and higher education. Supporters of caste reservations want to extend them to the booming private sector, traditionally dominated by upper castes, as a way of reducing economic and social inequality, while opponents argue that they undermine merit and benefit mainly the better-off lower castes.

creation of the new state. This sparked a violent backlash from the other areas of Andhra Pradesh, as well as a renewed wave of demands from state creation movements in backward regions of other states, such as those wanting "Gorkhaland" from West Bengal, and "Bundelkhand" and "Harit Pradesh" from the 190 million-inhabitant mega-state of Uttar Pradesh.

Although in some ways these caste and language movements have had negative consequences, often causing large-scale protests and violence in some states, on the whole they have played a valuable role in two ways. First, the creation of so many new linguistic states helps break up the conflicts over larger religious or regional identities that might otherwise emerge in national politics. The growing importance of regional politicians from these new states in national coalition politics has also stopped the center from doing things like frequently imposing President's Rule, which might have endangered Indian democracy as a whole. The creation of new states seems also to have helped their inhabitants, because the evidence shows that the new smaller states do better on most development and growth measures than the larger states they are carved out of, despite being less economically developed.

Since 2000, the new states of Uttarakhand, Jharkhand, and Chattisgarh have done much better than the states they left, and their growth rates have exceeded even the most optimistic estimates.[21]

Second, because both caste and language are *local* identities, they have helped to undercut larger and potentially much more damaging religious or north–south cleavages from becoming dominant in Indian politics. Divides over caste seem much more meaningful to many people than divides over much larger and potentially more divisive identities, such as who speaks which language or who is a Hindu and who is a Muslim. Politicians have tried, from time to time, to polarize people around national anti-Muslim or anti-Christian appeals, but these have little appeal to most people because they don't deal with the economic and social issues most voters care about, which are more closely related to caste inequality. The BJP, for instance, ever since serious state election losses in November 1993, has been forced to mix its appeals to Hindu nationalism with more local caste appeals in order to win at the state level.

Caste, language, and religion are very important in Indian politics, but most Indians still list their main electoral concerns as things like jobs, inflation, and the availability of *bijli, sarak, pani* (electricity, roads, and water), rather than ethnic issues. In a major 2009 election poll, the top five issues mentioned by voters were: drinking water (18 percent), unemployment (13 percent), electricity (9 percent), price rises (8 percent), and poverty (7 percent). And most Indians, although their regional identities may be important, still strongly identify as "Indians," which is a testament to the success of 60 years of Indian state-building. In a 2006, 89 percent of Indians declared themselves to be "proud" or "very proud" of their Indian identity, with Muslims, Sikhs, and Christians just as proud as members of the majority communities.[22] These development and national issues are very important in elections, and increasingly so now that Indians see evidence through internal migration and the mass media of development progress in other areas.

SUMMARY TABLE

Identities in India

Language	The identity that seemed likeliest to rip India apart in the 1950s. The creation of new linguistic states after 1952, and the promises in the mid-1960s not to impose Hindi on the southern states, successfully defused these conflicts.
Caste	India's thousands of *jati* group together in different caste coalitions in politics, such as Backward Castes or Most Backward Castes. But India is so diverse that usually no single caste can win election on its own, which lessens the divisiveness of these identities.
Religion	The identity that led to the partition of India in 1947. Religion has not been as divisive since independence, despite periodic attempts to polarize Indians around it, in large part because of the strength of language and caste identities.

INTERESTS IN INDIA

Federalism can, if well designed and flexible, play a very valuable role in promoting political stability and defusing ethnic conflicts. India's federal system has done very well at moderating ethnic conflicts. There are so many separate ethnic, caste, and economic interests within each of the 28 states—identities encouraged by India's political institutions—that they make it virtually impossible for national politics to revolve around a single, damaging cleavage such as religion. But all these state identities and cross-cutting cleavages also have their downside. The fact that national politics is now dominated by unwieldy coalitions of 10 to as many as 20 different parties representing very different interests can slow down speedy and decisive national policy-making. The Indian nuclear deal with the United States, for instance, was significantly delayed by ideological opposition from the Communists, the Congress's coalition ally from 2004–2009. Attempts to further liberalize the Indian economy have also been slowed down by opposition from the Communists, the Trinamool Congress (which blocked moves to open access for foreign retailers and supermarkets in late 2011), and other regional parties that are ideologically opposed to liberalization or have major industries that might suffer if there is further deregulation. And attempts to improve the efficiency of the sclerotic Indian public sector, by better-targeted fertilizer, food, electricity subsidies, and social programs, and by rationalizing the many inefficient public sector units, have been slowed down by the large number of voters who depend on these programs.

6.4 Does the great diversity of interests in India and the country's federal structure make economic and political reforms more difficult, and is that a good thing or a bad thing?

Watch the Video "India's New Middle Class" at mypoliscilab.com

Ethnic and Minority Interests

When India became independent in 1947, the country's politics appeared likely to divide along language and religious identity, given the long struggle between the Muslim League and the Indian National Congress. In the 1946 elections for the legislature that would write India's new constitution, an overwhelming majority of Hindus voted for the Congress, and an overwhelming majority of Muslims voted for the Muslim League. Lurking in the background were tensions over language, as Congress turned its back on decades of promises to establish linguistic states because of concerns over national unity.

These issues have not gone away. Periodically, politicians have tried to create a national Hindu movement, though these have never succeeded in permanently replacing other issues for Indian voters. In the 1950s and 1960s, Hindu nationalists protested against the Hindu Code bill (which integrated much of Hindu law, but not Muslim law, within the civil legal framework governing divorce and inheritance), and in support of bans on cow slaughter, which was a thinly veiled attack on Muslims. Politicians have also often fomented violence against Muslims in order to solidify electoral majorities. For example, in the 2002 riots in Gujarat 1,000 people were killed, the BJP state government of Narendra Modi received a huge electoral boost from the violence in the subsequent state elections.[23]

The largest and temporarily most successful campaign to make religion a central issue in Indian politics was from 1989–1992, when the Bharatiya Janata Party achieved significant electoral successes by campaigning, together with conservative Hindu organizations, for the destruction of a mosque in the town of Ayodhya that was allegedly built over the birthplace of the Hindu god Ram. The BJP leader L. K. Advani toured India in a motorized Hindu "chariot," building support for his party and for the new temple at Ayodhya to be built on the site of the mosque after its hoped-for demolition, and the movement raised money and support by selling bricks for the new building across the country. The incumbent Congress government of Narasimha Rao, like many governments confronted with populist Hindu mobilizations, feared creating sympathy for the BJP. It acted only after Hindu activists succeeded in destroying the mosque on December 6, 1992, an event that set off large-scale Hindu–Muslim riots across the country.

But national elections that revolve around one single theme—such as the 1977 election that was a referendum on Gandhi's imposition of emergency rule—are rare in India. The great diversity of India means that the story of most Indian national elections is that *there is no national story.* Some state elections are won on governance issues, others on caste, still others on issues such as water and electricity availability, or the prevalence of farmer suicides. Each state has a different story to tell. In the 2009 national elections, the Congress did well ultimately because it was more skilled than its main rival, the Bharatiya Janata Party, at estimating which seat-sharing and coalition deals would be likely to deliver the largest number of seats, based upon its reading of which parties were stronger for all these different reasons at the state level. The BJP did badly in the state of Orissa, for instance, because it demanded too many seats from its regional ally, the Biju Janata Dal (BJD). The BJD realized that it could win unaided, so it pulled out of its alliance with the BJP and won a huge electoral victory on its own. In a "first past the post" electoral system, especially one with India's great social and party heterogeneity, small changes in vote share can make huge differences to seat shares. In this environment the Congress cut the right deals and the BJP did not, which explains why the Congress increased its majority and won 11 percent more seats (27 percent in 2004 to 38 percent in 2009) in the national parliament despite its vote share remaining basically unchanged (26 percent to 28 percent).

Voters

In the 2009 parliamentary elections, 59 percent of all eligible Indian voters voted (compared to 57 percent of self-registered voters in the U.S. election that elected President Obama), and turnout was, if anything, slightly higher among poorer groups such as Dalits, Muslims, and Tribals than it was among the upper castes. This makes India highly unusual compared to most countries, where the poor consistently vote less frequently than the rich. Indians were also very active participants in election campaigns, with 19 percent of people attending election meetings and 13 percent election attending processions and rallies.[25] Some of this participation may be because the votes of the poor are bought off or coerced, but much of it is voluntary and highly engaged, and survey research shows that the Indian poor care a great deal about democracy.

Rural Interests

India is still, despite increasing industrialization and urbanization, a predominantly rural society, with around 60 percent of the population relying on agriculture to some extent (many workers live some months in the city and some in the country, or commute from farms to the city for daily employment). Before independence, much of the country was dominated by large landlords called *zamindars* (literally one who has *zamin*, land), but in the late 1940s and early 1950s, the Congress state governments carried out politically very popular large-scale land reforms that broke up the largest estates, and redistributed land to many middle peasants who had previously been smallholders or rented land from the zamindars. These middle peasants, not the very poorest farmers and landless laborers, were generally the main beneficiaries of the land reforms.

The next significant transformation in rural India came in the 1960s, as a product of the technological **Green Revolution**, in which Indian farmers adopted new high-yielding varieties of rice and wheat and more modern methods of production, with chemical fertilizer and electric pump irrigation replacing the cow dung and hand and animal power that had been used previously. These changes radically increased agricultural productivity: India had to import food in the early 1960s from the United States and elsewhere to avert famine, but since the Green Revolution India has been self-sufficient.

Farmers are an effective pressure group in Indian politics, and their huge political influence has been able to win them a large number of concessions. In most states, the major agricultural inputs, such as electric power and fertilizer, are heavily subsidized by the government. Farmers are also exempt from many taxes, something that has led some of India's growing number of ultra-rich to try to set up lavish "farms" on the outskirts of major cities to try to take advantage of tax exemptions. These farm subsidies (now $20 billion a year) have had political and social benefits, generating the solid support for incumbent parties that has enabled them to carry out other economic reforms, and encouraging Indians to stay on the land rather than emigrate to cities. But they have also had negative effects, especially on the environment, because farmers have been encouraged to overuse fertilizer and water because of their low cost. In many areas, the soil is becoming exhausted and the water table is sharply declining, forcing farmers to dig ever-deeper wells.

Green Revolution ■ term used to describe the introduction of High-Yield Varieties (HYVs) of wheat and rice, which helped India become self-sufficient in these important foods.

The Poor

For the Indian poor, their votes are perhaps their most valuable possession. The poor do not constitute an all-India lobby and they have a wide variety of regional and community interests. Some want job reservations for members of their castes, others want broader job opportunities, while others, depending on their particular region, want employment, housing, farming, and other programs. As Indian politics has become more competitive since the 1970s, politicians have promised the poor a bewildering variety of social programs. The current government has spent more than $50 billion on such programs since it was elected in 2004, focusing particularly on a program, the National Rural Employment Guarantee Act (NREGA), which provides work for the rural poor in a way that reduces the possibility of corrupt officials skimming all the money.

Business Interests

From the mid-1950s until the 1980s, the Indian government tried to achieve economic growth and development through a series of socialist-inspired central plans that focused on building up heavy industries under state ownership, rather than focusing on private industry. Private enterprises were not abolished, but the state took over the "commanding heights" of the economy in areas such as steel, aviation, mining, transportation, and later on in banking and insurance. State and private enterprises were heavily regulated under what was termed "License Raj," a system where the government tightly regulated the businesses in which they could compete, and how much they could invest or produce. Businesses spent a great deal of time trying to influence politicians and administrators to try to keep their businesses afloat and keep competition down in the sectors in which they operated, leading to a huge undersupply of basic consumer goods such as cars and televisions. Overall, the system became associated with corruption, poor quality, and low growth, though it did also minimize the sort of income inequality that has become so apparent in India over the past decade.

There were some minor attempts at liberalization under Rajiv Gandhi in the mid-1980s, who opened up some new sectors of the economy, such as computers and telecommunications, to private business. But the real change only came about because of a major balance of payments crisis in India in 1991, after which the newly elected Narasimha Rao Congress coalition had to go to the World Bank for a $500 million loan. The Bank demanded reforms in exchange for its help, and the crisis provided the excuse domestic reformers needed to start to begin to dismantle the most costly elements of the License Raj. Progress since then has been steady, though never as much as international investors and India's trading partners would have liked.

The Indian government has gradually deregulated many areas of the economy, without, however, dismantling the social safety net (in terms of food and fertilizer subsidies and employment programs) on which many of the poor rely, and which politicians also rely on to generate votes. The dividend has been economic growth levels that are much higher than the 4 percent "Hindu rate of growth" enjoyed under the regulated system, with growth levels of 9 percent before the economic crisis hit in 2008, after which they dropped back a percent or two. The economic growth has led to the rise of a sizeable new middle class, perhaps 300 million people, working in the new car factories of the south; the software services centers of Pune, Bangalore, and Hyderabad; and the call centers of Gurgaon and Mumbai. This growing wealth has not trickled down to everyone, to be sure, and it has created losers as well as winners. Growth in states such as Bihar and Madhya Pradesh has often been half the 10 percent level seen in Gujarat, Maharashtra, and Delhi. But even in the poorest parts of Indian villages, there are people who have gained from the economic expansion, and are using the salaries they get themselves, or the money they receive from relatives working in the booming cities, to fund education for their children, new brick houses to replace the mud houses of the past, and consumer items such as phones and televisions that link their lives much more directly to people in New Delhi and the world beyond.

Freedom of the Press and Mass Media

India's free press and vibrant civil society organizations act as an important check upon executive power. India now has dozens of civic organizations dedicated to defending civil liberties and cleaning up government, such as the veteran Peoples Union for Civil Liberties (www.pucl.org) founded in 1976, as well as newer groups such as "The Campaign for No Criminals in Politics" (www.nocriminals.org). One NGO, the Mazdoor Kisan Shakti Sangathan (Farmers and Laborers Together) (http://www.mkssindia.org/) works in Rajasthan to shine a light on corruption at the local level by allowing villagers to compare what's actually being spent in their villages with the money that officials tell their superiors is being spent. Individuals who have not received payments suddenly get paid once MKSS holds public meetings to discuss the issue. The oxygen of publicity helps to clean up the bureaucratic corruption that thrives on private discretion and secrecy.

India also has a dynamic and expanding press and mass media, especially since the reforms and economic boom of the 1990s substantially deregulated both sectors. In the 1990s, India had what one observer called a "newspaper revolution," a massive expansion in readership of the vernacular (i.e., non-English) press, linking the local world of the town and village with the news of the metropolis and beyond. For every 1,000 Indians, 58 daily papers were sold in 2001, more than three and a half times the figure in the mid-1970s, and this figure underestimates the scale of the change as many more people share their newspapers with others in India than they do in the West. By comparison, the corresponding recent readership figure in Pakistan is 23 per 1,000; in the Philippines, 79; and the United States, 215.[26]

In the last 15 years, there has also been a huge rise in private satellite and cable television penetration, a massive contrast to the situation in the early 1990s, when Indians could only watch the official (and often *very* boring) Doordarshan channel, where the news was read in very stilted high Hindi and a few other languages. Fifty-seven percent of Indians now own a TV, and around two-thirds of these subscribe to a bewildering selection of entertainment and private news channels, for a monthly fee of around $3.50.[27] Several of the new channels have launched important investigative television programs, and they also pick up the anti-corruption and political scoops of the major news and Internet media sources, such as www.tehelka.com. There is a definite connection between the openness of the market for new media and pressure to deal with India's major problems of corruption, development, pollution, and social inequality.

The mobile phone revolution has also been very significant in India. In 1990, only one in a hundred households had a phone, and to get one from the expensive state monopoly required a wait of a year or more, and often a bribe. If the phone went dead, it often required payments to the local "lineman" to get it working again, leading to great speculation that the linemen sabotaged phones deliberately to increase their income. The massive expansion in private cellphones after the late 1990s deregulation has completely revolutionized things, and more than 50 percent of Indians now have a cell phone. Major cell phone companies sell inexpensive phones for less than $20, with pay-as-you-go plans from companies such as Bharti Airtel and Vodafone are now within the reach of many poor villagers. With the new phones, farmers can even obtain text messages with information on prices in local grain markets and other information that helps them extract better deals from middlemen. The government is now exploring pilot projects that let people

> **SUMMARY TABLE**
>
> **Interests in India**
>
> | | |
> |---|---|
> | **Farmers–Rural Interests** | More than 50% of the electorate and very powerful politically. Governments provide them with massive power and fertilizer subsidies. |
> | **The Poor** | Not as effective an interest as farmers, but parties try to win these groups over with subsidies and health, education and employment programs. |
> | **Business** | Increasingly effective interest groups with the gradual dismantling of license raj since 1991. Not all "pro-reform": some business groups benefit from retaining regulations while others do not. |
> | **The Media** | The growth of the non-English press and cable television since the 1990s, together with investigative journalism of corruption scams, has been effective in increasing pressure for government reforms. |

receive government payments through mobile phones, to cut out the often-grasping government bureaucracy.

The increase in political competition, combined with the growing support among the press and reformist organizations and NGOs, has created a very healthy trend in recent years for the reinvigoration of government institutions charged with fair and honest elections and anti-corruption efforts. The success of the Mazdoor Kisan Shakti Sangathan (MKSS) in Rajasthan, for instance, which organized on behalf of villagers to demand documentation from officials on all the government goods and services that ought to have been provided to them, has played an important role in the passage of the 2005 national Right to Information Act (RTI), which is gradually helping citizens to exert pressure on an often-unresponsive bureaucracy.

CONCLUSION

More than 60 years after independence, India still has enormous challenges: too many of its citizens remain poor and illiterate, gender inequality is high, and the quality of many government services is bad. But India also has much to be proud of. Most impressively, unlike the other two states that were carved out of former British India (Pakistan in 1947 and Bangladesh after it split off from Pakistan in 1971), India remains vibrantly democratic and free, with high levels of both political competition and popular participation.

India inherited parliamentary institutions from the British, but these institutions, many of which were retained in the 1950 Constitution, are not the main explanation for India's success. Pakistan, which inherited the same institutions, has had huge problems in consolidating its democracy. Instead, much of the credit has to go to the role played by the Indian National Congress, a broad, internally democratic party that had gained legitimacy and cohesion through the long struggle for independence. This party and its leaders had developed habits of compromise and moderation that were vital in determining how it would respond successfully to the various ethnic, regional, and economic challenges India faced in the 1950s.

Perhaps the country's greatest success was in dealing with the challenge of mobilizations around ethnic identities. In Pakistan, weak political parties worried that government negotiation and compromise with such movements would weaken and destroy the state. So they met regional movements with increased centralization and, when that failed, the Muslim League used its emergency constitutional powers to attack the opposition and dismiss opposition governments in the provinces. In India, the much stronger Congress Party internally openly debated its best response to opposition and was prepared to negotiate with caste and language movements. In the 1950s, the party agreed to redraw India's internal state boundaries and allow caste reservations, even though Nehru and some other senior leaders were skeptical about whether these steps would make things worse or not. India's risk taking in the 1950s has paid off: the country has retained a central government and institutions strong enough to hold the country together, while devolving enough fiscal and political power to the regions to prevent ethnic and regional movements from demanding independence.

Despite the frustratingly slow pace of Indian government, there are many positive signs for the future. Interest groups representing business are pushing for policies that will lead to higher levels of overall economic growth, while movements representing farmers, lower castes, and the poor are working to ensure that the interests of these groups are not forgotten in the push for growth. There is also a growing focus on good governance and development performance. Parties that had performed well in cleaning up government and improving the quality of services, regardless of which caste or ideology they allegedly represented, were rewarded very well by voters in the 2009 parliamentary and state elections. Citizens' movements in Bangalore, Mumbai, and other towns are putting increasing pressure on politicians to improve government performance. These movements can take a long time to be effective: the first citizens' anti-corruption and reform movements in New York state were founded in the late nineteenth century, and no one would say that the work of these organizations in the USA is complete! But India's economy is still growing quickly. The extra wealth and tax revenue created by this growth, most of which comes from increases in India's own consumption and investment, not from abroad, will make it easier to solve India's social and economic challenges in the years ahead.

✓• **Study** and **Review** the **Post-Test & Chapter Exam** at **mypoliscilab.com**

KEY TERMS

Jawaharlal Nehru   195
Mohammad Ali Jinnah   195
Raj   198
Mughal Empire   198
East India Company (EIC)   199
caste system   201
Mohandas K. Gandhi   201
Indian National Congress   201
Sardar Vallabhai Patel   201
1935 Government of India Act   202
Sikhism   203
Muslim League   203
President's Rule   207
untouchability   207
panchayat   207
Jammu and Kashmir   208
Indian Administrative Service (IAS)   209
Lok Sabha   209
Rajya Sabha   209
Scheduled Castes   209
Scheduled Tribes   209
Indira Gandhi   212
Janata Party   213
Backward Castes   214
reservations system   214
Sonia Gandhi   214
Manmohan Singh   214
Bharatiya Janata Party   215
Hinduism   217
Dalits   217
jati   217
Green Revolution   227

REVIEW QUESTIONS

1. What advantages did India have at independence, compared to some other states with a long history of colonization?
2. How has India been able to deal with significant religious, linguistic, and regional challenges to national integration?
3. How have federalism and the creation of new states helped India to moderate ethnic conflicts?
4. How important was the Congress Party in consolidating Indian democracy in the 1950s?
5. Why did India adopt and then start to reform the economic policies known as "License Raj"?
6. When did Indian politics change to an "era of coalitions"?

SUGGESTED READINGS

Brown, Judith. *Gandhi: Prisoner of Hope*. New Haven: Yale University Press, 1991. The best biography of the man whose non-violent tactics and emphasis on the immorality of an unjust colonial system defeated the British, and later inspired Dr. Martin Luther King in his struggle for civil rights in the United States.

Das, Gurcharan. *India Unbound: From Independence to the Global Information Age*. New York: Penguin, 2000. An analysis of the reasons for, and a celebration of, India's recent economic reforms.[28]

Guha, Ramachandra. *India after Gandhi: The History of the World's Largest Democracy*. New York: Harper Collins, 2007. A beautifully written and comprehensive overview of modern Indian history, which also provides lots of detailed suggestions for further reading.

Jadhav, Narendra. *Untouchables: My Family's Triumphant Journey out of the Caste System in Modern India*. New York: Scribner, 2005. The successful struggles of one family against the massive caste prejudice against India's "untouchables," told by a man who rose to be the first Dalit chief economist of the country's central bank.

Wilkinson, Steven I. "Reading the Election Results." *Journal of Democracy* (January 2005). An overview of India's politics in the current "era of coalitions."

NOTES

1. Sarvepalli Gopal, *Jawaharlal Nehru: A Biography* (Oxford University Press, 1995), 178.
2. See Weiner (1989).
3. Richards, *The Mughal Empire*, 70, 138.
4. Rajat Kanta Ray, "Indian Society and the Establishment of British Supremacy, 1765–1818," in P. J. Marshall, ed. The *Oxford History of the British Empire: The Eighteenth Century* (Oxford University Press, 2001), 508–529.
5. Judith Brown, *Modern India: The origins of an Asian Democracy* (Oxford: Oxford University Press, 1984), 31.
6. Brown, *Modern India: The origins of an Asian Democracy* (Oxford: Oxford University Press, 1984), 101–102.
7. Brown, 1984, 325.
8. Ramachandra Guha, *India after Gandhi: The History of the World's Largest Democracy* (New York: Harper Collins, 2007), 748–749.
9. Guha, 2007, 748.
10. Pakistan started off with a similar strategy, putting the chiefs of staff at #14 (compared to #12 in India) in the 1950 Warrant of Precedence. But the Pakistan chiefs of Staff were upgraded during the military regime of Ayub Khan in the 1960s, to sixth place, where they have remained ever since. Shuja Nawaz, *Crossed Swords: Pakistan, Its Army and the Wars Within* (Karachi: Oxford University Press, 2008), xl.
11. Election Commission "Discussion Document," National Commission to Review the Workings of the Constitution September 2000, 17.
12. Subhasish Dugar, Haimanti Bhattacharya, and David Reiley, "Can't Buy Me Love: A Field Experiment Exploring the Tradeoff Between Income and Caste in the Indian Matrimonial Market." Paper presented at the Annual Meeting of the American Economic Association, January 2009.
13. "The Legacy of Social Exclusion: A Correspondence Study of Job Discrimination in India," by S. Thorat and P. Attewell, *Economic and Political Weekly* (India) (October 13, 2007), 4141–4145.
14. Marianne Bertrand and Sendhil Mullainathan, "Are Emily and Greg More Employable than Lakisha and Jamal? A Field Experiment on Labor Market Discrimination," http://www.economics.harvard.edu/faculty/mullainathan/files/emilygreg.pdf.
15. Sarvepalli Gopal, *Jawaharlal Nehru: An Anthology* (Delhi: Oxford University Press, 1983), 324–325.
16. "Racketeering in Quotas," *India Today* (November 15,1994), 36–42.
17. "Racketeering in Quotas," 36–42.
18. Srinivas, M.N., *Caste: Its Twentieth Century Avatar* (New Delhi: Viking 1996), xxviii.
19. A poll of 17,885 voters conducted 26 July–5 August 2004. "Mood of the Nation-Poll," *India Today*, International Edition (New Delhi) (August 30, 2004), 16–23.
20. S. Ramakrishna, "Reservation Wars," *Indian Express* (June 20, 1998).
21. Amarnath K. Menon, "Dividends of Division," *India Today* (December 28, 2009).

22. *State of Democracy in South Asia* (Oxford/CSDS, 2008), Table 5.3.
23. See Wilkinson, *Votes and Violence: Electoral Competition and Ethnic Violence in India* (New York: Cambridge University Press, 2004).
24. http://www.hinduonnet.com/nic/howindiavoted2009/howindiavoted2009.htm.
25. CSDS National Election Survey, 2009, *Economic and Political Weekly* (September 26, 2009), 49.
26. Robin Jeffrey, *India's Newspaper Revolution: Capitalism, Politics, and the Indian Language press* (Oxford, 2010), xi.
27. Sue Taylor, "The Indian Pay-TV Market Evolution," *Card Technology Today*, 20 (August 2008), 10.

Mexico

Cecilia Martínez-Gallardo

CHAPTER 7

"No more blood!" Drug- and crime-based violence dominates Mexico's political scene, giving rise to social movements and protests. Here, a protest at Zócalo Square ends a four-day caravan for peace from the city of Cuernavaca to Mexico City

> **?** Why is Mexico's democratic government unable to deal effectively with persistent poverty, corruption, and drug trafficking?

INTRODUCTION TO MEXICO

Partido Revolucionario Institucional (PRI) ■ founded in 1929 in the aftermath of the Mexican Revolution and dominated Mexican politics throughout the twentieth century. Although it lost the presidency in 2000, it remains an important player in state and national politics.

Read and Listen to Chapter 7 at mypoliscilab.com

Study and Review the Pre-Test & Flashcards at mypoliscilab.com

On July 2, 2000, Mexicans voted the **Partido Revolucionario Institucional** (Institutional Revolutionary Party, PRI) out of office after 71 years in power. Excitement about the prospects for democracy was high, because democracy would bring not just political change but social and economic improvements, as well. Such optimism was not unfounded. Mexico had no previous experience with democracy, but by the 1990s, it had developed a strong civil society and a culture of political contestation and participation. Mexico's transition to democracy also involved a process of gradual political liberalization, and by 2000, several institutions—such as the Federal Electoral Institute and the Supreme Court—had sufficient autonomy to stand up to the ruling party. Moreover, Mexico's per capita income in 2000 was around $12,000 per year, which is well above the world average and higher than democracies in the region like Costa Rica and Brazil. Finally, by 2000, Mexico had established a close trade partnership with the United States and Canada, which generated incentives for Mexico to match those countries' democratic political systems in order to provide the conditions of stability sought by international investors.

However, a decade after the end of one-party rule, hope has given way to dissatisfaction with democracy and to pessimism about the capacity of Mexico's political institutions to solve the problems that Mexicans care about. Political institutions have been strengthened by political competition but pluralism has not translated into lower poverty rates or less corruption. Consequently, many Mexicans have lost faith in democracy's ability to provide *effective* government; in the 2010 Latinobarometer survey, only 49 percent of Mexican respondents answered that democracy is preferable to any other government type (the regional average was 61 percent). Moreover, in recent years, Mexico has been plagued by an unprecedented wave of violence related to drug trafficking and, to many Mexicans, the state appears incapable of solving the most pressing issues.[1] So, *why is Mexico's democratic government unable to deal effectively with persistent poverty, corruption, and drug trafficking?*

In this chapter, we will see how the gradual process of change that culminated in 2000 improved political contestation and participation and increased the opportunities for accountability. Elections are now highly competitive and, for the most part, considered free and fair. The centralization that marked the non-democratic period has given way to a stronger system of checks and balances, in which the legislature and the judiciary have an enhanced role in the political process. As a result of a more open political environment, independent organizations and interest groups have been able to organize collectively to press their demands on the state. However, increased political competition has also brought conflict and deadlock and has led many Mexicans to think that the government is less effective than before in performing essential tasks.

We begin with an overview of Mexico's history from colonial times through the twentieth century. Then we examine Mexico's main institutions and assess their contribution to limited and effective government. In the third section we turn our attention to the formation of a national identity in Mexico and to current cleavages and forms of identity. The fourth section examines the role of different interests—political parties, social movements, and interest groups—in Mexico's economic and political development. The last section concludes with some thoughts about Mexico's democratic development and the challenges that it faces in going forward.

HISTORICAL OVERVIEW OF MEXICO

Much of the history of Mexico has been marked by efforts to create an effective government within contexts of conflict and great decentralization of power. This was the most important task facing the newly created Mexican government after independence in 1810, and it was also the main challenge for the ruling elite a century later, after the 1910 Revolution. In this section, we explore how the creation of the Partido Revolucionario Institucional (PRI) and the consolidation of one-party rule contributed to the centralization of political authority, but in doing so undermined limited government in Mexico. We will also see how the gradual process of reform that culminated in 2000 contributed to the development of more limited government but has hurt the ability of the government to act effectively to solve people's problems.

7.1 What are the historical precedents for the creation of a single-party regime in Mexico?

Explore the Comparative "Economic Policy" at **mypoliscilab.com**

Colonial Mexico

In 1519, Hernán Cortés led a Spanish colonial expedition to Tenochtitlán, the site of Mexico City today, which was at that time the heart of the Aztec Empire. Through a mixture of violence and persuasion, the Spanish subjugated the Aztecs and the other civilizations of the region. They created an entirely new political, economic, and social system that was designed with the interests of the Spanish Crown in mind. Spanish colonialism had several features that in the long run have harmed efforts at combining limited and effective government in Mexico.

First, the colonial political system reflected the Spanish Crown's need to extract the maximum profit from its colony at the lowest possible cost. Spain built a highly centralized bureaucracy that ruled the colony from Mexico City, but that gave regional landowners considerable autonomy from central government rule. This combination of centralized authority in principle with weak authority in practice remains problematic in Mexican politics to this day.

Second, economically, the Spanish colonial system focused on exporting silver and other valuable raw materials back to Spain. This system relied heavily on the exploitation of indigenous labor for mining and farming, and discouraged colonial authorities from developing programs that would help lift the indigenous population out of poverty. Instead, the system generated vast economic inequalities between the tiny elite and the great mass of the population. This economic inequality has also remained a hallmark of Mexican life to this day.

Tenochtitlán ■ city-state founded in what is now Mexico City; capital of the Aztec Empire.

MEXICO

MEXICO IN COMPARISON

	United Kingdom	Germany	France	Japan	India	Mexico	Russia	Nigeria	China	Iran
Freedom House Classification	Democracy	Democracy	Democracy	Democracy	Democracy	Partial democracy	Partial democracy	Partial democracy	Non-democracy	Non-democracy
Land Size (sq km)	243,610	357,022	643,801	377,915	3,287,263	1,964,375	17,098,242	923,768	9,596,961	1,648,195
Land Size Ranking	79	62	42	61	7	15	1	32	4	18
Population (July 2011 Estimate)	62,698,362	81,471,834	65,312,249	126,475,664	1,189,172,906	113,724,226	138,739,892	155,215,573	1,336,718,015	77,891,220
Population Ranking	22	16	21	10	2	11	9	8	1	18
Life Expectancy (Years)	80.1	80.1	81.2	82.3	66.8	76.5	66.3	47.6	74.7	70.1
Life Expectancy Ranking	28	27	21	5	51	72	162	220	95	146
Literacy Rate	99%	99%	99%	99%	61%	86.1%	99.4%	68%	91.6%	77%
GDP Per Capita (2010 Estimate)	US$35,100	US$35,900	US$33,300	US$34,000	US$3,500	US$13,800	US$15,900	US$2,500	US$7,600	US$11,200
GDP Ranking	36	32	39	38	163	85	71	178	126	100

criollos ■ word used to describe those born in New Spain or Mexico, from Spanish parents.

mestizo ■ word used to describe those of mixed Indigenous and Spanish descent.

Finally, life in colonial Mexico was marked by a hierarchical social order based on ethnicity. At the top of the pyramid sat a small group of native-born Spaniards, who had a near monopoly on prestige and political power. Below the Spanish-born were the Mexican-born white *criollos*, who had a weaker political attachment to Spain and who resented the privileges of the Spanish-born elites. Beneath the *Criollos* in the social order were the *mestizos*, people of mixed European and Indian ethnicity, who soon grew to be the largest group. At the bottom of the social hierarchy stood indigenous peoples and Africans. Traces of this ethnic hierarchy are still evident in Mexican society today.

Independent Mexico

In 1808, events in Europe precipitated Mexico's independence from Spain. That year, French ruler Napoleon Bonaparte invaded Spain and overthrew the Spanish monarchy. This event threw Spain's colonies into chaos. *Criollos* in Mexico (and elsewhere in Latin America) regarded Spain's new rulers as illegitimate, and on September 16, 1810, Miguel Hidalgo, a *criollo* priest, called his parishioners to arms against Spanish authority in the **War of Independence**. After 11 years, Spain signed the Treaty of Córdoba in 1821, recognizing Mexico's independence.

War of Independence ■ in 1810, the people of Mexico took arms to fight for their independence from Spain. The War of Independence lasted until 1821, when Spain recognized Mexico's independence.

caudillos ■ the name given to strongmen whose power was based on control of a personal army.

Mexican–American War ■ armed conflict between Mexico and the United States over the territory of Texas, which was annexed by the United States in 1845.

Treaty of Guadalupe Hidalgo ■ this treaty, signed in 1848, put an end to the Mexican–American War, recognizing Mexico's loss of Texas and other territory to the United States.

After the war, Mexico's new leaders confronted the challenge of state-building. Prolonged and extensive fighting had destroyed Mexico's economy and had left the country's infrastructure heavily damaged. Poverty was widespread, especially in rural areas where most of the population resided. Politically, life was marked by chaos, instability, and the absence of effective and legitimate government institutions. Efforts to centralize authority and form a state would dominate the following 60 years of Mexican history. The creation of a stable central government was hindered by continued civil conflict between different regional political groups. The first 40 years after independence saw 50 different presidents take office, and six constitutions were enacted between 1814 and 1857. During this period, the central government never managed to monopolize control over the use of force. Instead, a series of strongmen, or *caudillos*, emerged who controlled portions of the country and defended them through force using their own personal armies.

The challenge of consolidating state authority was made more difficult by international conflict. Mexico had a tenuous hold over all its territory, particularly in the northern areas. In the wake of the declaration of independence by Texas in 1835 and its formal annexation to the United States in 1845, disputes over the territory led to the **Mexican–American War** of 1846. The treaty that would end the war in 1848 (**Treaty of Guadalupe Hidalgo**) recognized the loss of Texas and ceded territory that corresponds to present-day California, Nevada, and Utah, as well as most of Arizona, New Mexico, and Colorado, to the United States, leading to the loss of nearly half of Mexico's original territory. An extremely weak central government would continue as the normal state of affairs, until the election of President Porfirio Díaz, who took office in 1876 and managed to finally bring a measure of stability to the country. To enhance the state's capacity, he built up the federal army, enhanced the government's ability to collect taxes, and invested in infrastructure projects such as railways and irrigation.

This stability, however, came at a high price. Although Díaz was initially elected legitimately, his rule became progressively more dictatorial. Díaz eventually excluded from politics all but his small circle of allies. After his re-election in 1884, he eliminated competitive elections and stayed in power until 1911. Under his rule, most Mexicans were excluded from the benefits of economic development, and the gap between rich and poor widened even further. By 1900, less than 1 percent of Mexican families controlled 85 percent of the nation's wealth.

The 1910 Revolution

Díaz's rule brought stability, but after 35 years, many Mexicans had grown weary of his dictatorship. In 1910, opposition to his regime erupted into a violent revolt that would eventually become the Mexican Revolution. A diverse array of groups arose against the Díaz government, including workers, peasants, and disenfranchised elites, who realized that the only way to gain access to political and economic power would be to get rid of Díaz. However, although all these groups wanted to throw Díaz out of power, their goals differed widely. The upper classes of industrialists, landowners, and merchants wanted reforms that would give them greater say in the political process. They also demanded term limits for politicians, limits on the influence of the Catholic Church, and restrictions on the power of foreign investors. Workers, miners, and peasants, on the other hand, wanted land and better working and living conditions.

The **Mexican Revolution** began in 1910 when one of Díaz's opponents, Francisco I. Madero, called for an armed revolt. Madero's call to arms drew widespread support and the revolution spread rapidly. By 1911, Díaz had resigned and Madero had been elected president. However, Madero was never able to unite the revolutionaries behind his government, and conflicts between rival groups quickly led to a civil war over which group would play the leading role in constructing the post–Díaz political system.

In an attempt to end the conflict, a new constitution was proposed in 1917 that formally established limited government. In theory, this new constitution created a federal system, checks and balances between the executive and legislative branches of government, and an independent judiciary. Moreover, to prevent a repeat of the concentration of political power in the hands of one individual, re-election was prohibited for the president and governors—and this prohibition was later extended to cover positions at all levels of government. For workers and peasants, Article 27 of the new constitution allowed for land redistribution, while Article 123 guaranteed better working conditions and protections for labor. And for those who had fought to limit the power of the Catholic Church, the constitution banned priests from participating in politics, limited their role in education, and limited the Church's ability to own property.

These reforms sought to establish both limited and effective government in Mexico—avoiding a repeat of Díaz's dictatorship and at the same time promoting equitable development for all Mexicans. However, not everyone was satisfied with the path of the revolution, and civil war continued until 1920. By then, Mexico's economy was in shambles, and there was widespread starvation and riots.

Mexican Revolution ■ after Porfirio Díaz reneged on his promise to hold free elections in 1911, Francisco I. Madero led a revolt against his dictatorial rule.

The economic chaos and political conflicts that followed the revolution meant that the principles of the 1917 Constitution would not be implemented for several decades. Instead, what came next was not democracy, but one-party rule.

The Establishment of One-Party Rule, 1917–1940

One hundred and ten years after Mexico's independence, the question facing the country remained the same: how to consolidate state authority in a context characterized by chaos, violence, and decentralized political authority. To create a strong central government, politicians knew that they had to take power away from the military generals and regional political bosses who had gained power in the aftermath of the collapse of Díaz's centralized rule.

To do this, Plutarco Elías Calles, who became president in 1924, proposed the creation of a single political party that would allow the different factions that had helped overthrow Díaz to coexist peacefully instead of deciding their political disputes through force of arms. Although it was formally founded in 1929, the process of creating and consolidating this party took place between 1917 and 1940, and it involved two main strategies: (1) incorporating the interests of workers and peasants into the political system, and (2) consolidating the institutions that allowed for peaceful transitions from one president to another. Additionally, a series of electoral reforms also weakened and eventually abolished regional parties, effectively incorporating thousands of local leaders and regional bosses into the new party.

Incorporating Workers and Peasants   The logic behind Calles's desire to incorporate workers and peasants into the new party was to manage the potential political threats that the vast numbers of peasants and the growing working class posed for political elites. During the revolution, many peasants had acquired arms, and political elites feared that if peasants' demands for land to farm were not at least partially met, they could resort to violence. In addition, the numbers of industrial workers in urban areas was increasing rapidly, especially after the discovery of oil in Mexico in the first years of the twentieth century. As in other countries, Mexico's workers were becoming more important for the country's economy and were starting to organize to demand political rights and better working conditions.

The threat of peasant and worker revolt was not exclusive to Mexico at the time. In 1917, the Communist Revolution overthrew the Russian monarchy, and in the civil war that followed many Russian elites lost property, went into exile or lost their lives. In Mexico, the leaders of the Mexican Revolution took several steps to incorporate workers and peasants to the party, reasoning that a stake in the regime and its stability would eliminate their incentives to oppose it. The most important steps were taken in the 1930s by president Lázaro Cárdenas (1934–1940).

Cárdenas sought to secure the support of workers and peasants through a series of political concessions, including:

- Considerable redistribution of land from the wealthy to peasants
- Naming workers to important posts in the government
- Promoting socialist ideals in the school system
- Nationalizing oil and the railway system

1917 Constitution created a federal system, checks and balances between the executive and legislative branches of government, and an independent judiciary. It also included extensive labor rights and a system of communal land ownership.

Cárdenas implemented a series of reforms that created **corporatist** governance structures within the party—that is, membership in the government party was based on an individual's occupation: (1) the military; (2) labor; (3) peasants; and (4) the "popular" sector, which was a collection of diverse interests such as teachers, youth, and small business owners. Each sector participated in party decisions, such as the selection of candidates for office. The corporatist structure of the party gave workers, peasants, youth and other groups a stake in the government's stability. Its broadly inclusive nature also generated considerable legitimacy and helped consolidate support for the emerging party, which would dominate Mexican politics for most of the twentieth century.

corporatism ■ a pattern of interest group mobilization in which the state plays an active role in organizing and mediating between groups.

Solving the Problem of Presidential Succession Post-revolutionary governments also faced the challenge of how to successfully manage the competing factions within the party. Because the leaders of the revolution disagreed about the direction the country should take, transfers of presidential power after 1917 seldom happened through an election and often involved violence. To consolidate power in the hands of the party while simultaneously reducing the likelihood that individuals would attempt to take power through violence, a series of institutional reforms passed between 1929 and 1940 created a system of rotation of political positions that sought to defuse elite conflict by assuring members of the government party that if they remained loyal they would get a chance to participate in governing.

The president of Mexico—who was also head of the government party—stood at the head of this system. In this dual role, the president appointed party members to the bureaucracy and nominated the party's candidates for other government offices, such as governors, senators, and members of the lower house of the legislature. The key to the system was the **no-re-election clause**: re-election to every political office was prohibited, which meant that politicians had every incentive to be loyal to the president, who could be very helpful in getting them a job beyond their term in office. For example, because legislators could not be reelected, and depended on the party and the president for their next job, they were extremely unlikely to dissent from the president's legislative proposals. And although the president could not run for re-election, beginning with Cárdenas, the president gained the ability to handpick his successor. Because presidents kept their choice secret until the last minute, this practice also engineered loyalty to the president among members of the cabinet and other important politicians who thought they might be chosen to succeed the president.

no-re-election clause ■ the 1917 Constitution prohibited the re-election of the president and a reform in 1933 extended this prohibition to include members of the legislature and elected officials at the state and local levels.

Of course, to make the promise of future rewards credible, the party had to consistently win elections. This was done both by using the resources of the state to provide peasants, workers, and average citizens with benefits in exchange for their support, and by coercion—typically by employing different methods of electoral intimidation and fraud.

PRI Hegemony: 1940–1970

The first name of the government party Calles founded was the National Revolutionary Party (*Partido Nacional Revolucionario,* PNR). Cárdenas renamed it the Party of the Mexican Revolution (*Partido de la Revolución Mexicana*, PRM), and Cárdenas's successor, Manuel Ávila Camacho, decided on the party's current name, the Institutional Revolutionary Party or *Partido Revolucionario Institucional* (PRI), in 1946.

By 1940, the main elements of the PRI regime were in place: key elements of society were incorporated into the party's governance structures, and rules were put in place to ensure rotation of political elites in office. This political system, it should be noted, did not reflect the principles of democracy written into the 1917 Constitution. Instead of a system of separation of powers that would ensure limited government and accountability, by 1940 the system was highly centralized in the office of the president. Federalism offered little autonomy to states and local governments; the legislature became a rubber-stamp assembly, and the same was true of the judiciary.

Such centralization meant that for the first time in Mexican history, the political system did manage to generate highly effective government. However, this effectiveness came at a cost: the system placed few limits on the authority of public officials and made accountability by individual citizens very difficult. Moreover, although citizens could participate in politics through elections, contestation was constrained, as the PRI dominated elections from the presidency down to the local level. PRI leaders co-opted most political opposition to the regime, and where this strategy failed repression was employed to eliminate threats—for example, from striking workers, peasant revolts, or communist guerrillas. However, repression was used relatively infrequently when compared against other non-democratic systems in Latin America and elsewhere.

The stability of the PRI regime was supported by its economic performance. In the absence of meaningful elections, the PRI placed a great importance on its claim to provide economic benefits to all Mexicans. Between 1940 and the early 1970s, the government implemented an economic policy of state-led development, in which the government rather than the private sector decides where to direct investment resources, and in which the government owns key elements in the national economy, such as natural resources and major industries. The Mexican government used this policy to promote rapid industrialization and, like other countries that implemented similar policies in these years, it managed to produce high rates of growth. These decades became known as the Mexican Miracle, and the government's capacity to provide economic stability provided an important source of state legitimacy (see Table 7.1).

state-led economic development ■ strategy of economic development that gives the government a central role as the promoter of capital formation. The government rather than the market decides where to direct investment resources.

Mexican Miracle ■ term used to refer to the years between 1940 and 1970 when the Mexican economy grew at 6 percent annually on average, based on a strategy that called for heavy state intervention in the economy.

The Decline of the PRI: 1970–2000

Unlike regime change in many other non-democratic regimes—such as the collapse of Chile's military dictatorship in 1990 and the collapse of the Soviet Union in 1991—the decline of the PRI's dominance and the transition to democracy in Mexico occurred gradually. The same factors that helped the party hold onto power for decades—its economic performance and a series of institutional reforms—help explain why the party's support began to decline in the 1970s.

Change in the Economic Model The first nail in the PRI's coffin was the economy. Until the early 1970s, the government's ability to take credit for strong economic growth and the political stability it brought gave the government con-

TABLE 7.1

Economic Growth and Mexican Presidents, 1934–2009

President	Years	Growth
Lázaro Cárdenas	1934–1940	4.55
Manuel Ávila Camacho	1940–1946	6.15
Miguel Alemán Valdés	1946–1952	5.95
Adolfo Ruiz Cortines	1952–1958	6.43
Adolfo López Mateos	1958–1964	6.42
Gustavo Díaz Ordaz	1964–1970	6.25
Average	**1940–1970**	**6.08**
Luis Echeverría Álvarez	1970–1976	5.97
José López Portillo	1976–1982	6.60
Miguel de la Madrid Hurtado	1982–1988	0.23
Carlos Salinas de Gortari	1988–1994	3.08
Ernesto Zedillo Ponce de León	1994–2000	3.50
Vicente Fox Quesada	2000–2006	2.41
Felipe Calderón	2006–2009	0.78

siderable legitimacy and meant that opposition to the government's authoritarian practices remained minimal. However, support for the PRI began to erode in the 1970s as the economy stalled. To counter the slowdown, which generated both increasing unemployment and greater economic inequality, the PRI used government spending in an attempt to spur economic growth. In addition to a growing government debt, by the early 1980s, Mexico's external debt had also soared, reaching 49 percent of GDP in 1982.[2] Moreover, Mexico had grown highly dependent on the petroleum industry and when oil prices crashed, the country found itself with no money to pay its debts. On August 12, 1982, Mexico's minister of finance informed its debtors abroad that Mexico would be unable to pay its bills—setting off the most serious economic crisis that the nation had faced in decades.

After the debt crisis, Mexico fell into deep recession—with rising unemployment, plummeting real wages, and high inflation. Economic growth dropped from an average of 6.3 percent per year between 1970 and 1982 to 0.23 percent per year between 1983 and 1988, and inflation jumped from an average of 17.6 percent to 88.4 percent in the same periods.[3] The government was forced to turn to the International Monetary Fund (IMF) for help. In exchange for a large loan, the Mexican government agreed to a series of economic reforms, including privatization of many state-owned companies, deregulation of several key industries, and reduction of foreign trade and investment barriers. Under President Carlos Salinas in the early 1990s, Mexico's government privatized several huge corporations, including the telephone company (*Teléfonos de México,* TELMEX) and

North American Free Trade Agreement (NAFTA) ■ an agreement signed in 1994 that sought to remove most barriers to trade and investment, including tariffs, quotas, and licensing requirements, between Mexico, the United States, and Canada.

large state-owned banks. Salinas' government also signed the North American Free Trade Agreement (NAFTA) in 1994 with Canada and the United States, which sought to remove most barriers to trade and investment between the three countries.

Despite the reforms, the 1980s and 1990s saw continued economic crisis and growing popular dissatisfaction with the PRI's ability to govern. The economic reforms were especially tough on the groups that most loyally supported the PRI: peasants and workers. For example, in an effort to stimulate investment and competitiveness in the agricultural sector, Salinas reformed Article 27 of the 1917 Constitution. Article 27 had given peasants access to *communal* land (known as *ejidos*), but did not give them the right to buy and sell land as *individuals*. Salinas's reform allowed peasants the right to buy and sell their land, but instead of spurring peasant families to invest in their farms, it made them vulnerable to competition from large export-oriented agro-business corporations, which snapped up the best land and converted it to mechanized agriculture. Wages in rural areas dropped and jobs dried up, forcing many peasants off their lands and into the already-crowded cities.

Industrial and government workers also experienced losses of hard-won gains: privatization of many state-owned enterprises resulted in extensive layoffs (nearly one in four government employees were laid off between 1986 and 1990), reduced wages, and the loss of union privileges. As part of the reforms, the government changed its approach to the allocation of social benefits from one based on the corporatist structure of the party to a program of targeted benefits channeled through the federal bureaucracy. This change bypassed the party and the sectors, greatly weakening the PRI's ability to use patronage to maintain voters' loyalty. Perhaps the most obvious sign that dissatisfaction was growing was the performance of the PRI in the 1988 presidential election. The PRI candidate managed to get only 50.4 percent of the votes (20 points less than his predecessor) in an election marred by claims of fraud and marked by a split in the PRI that was caused in part by disagreements over economic reforms.

Electoral Reforms Another source of stability for the PRI regime had come from its ability to legitimize its rule through the ballot box. Regular elections were held since the end of the revolution, and opposition parties were permitted to participate. Very quickly, these opposition parties perceived that they had no real chance to win power. To maintain the façade that the PRI government was "revolutionary" but not authoritarian, in the 1970s the PRI began to institute a series of electoral reforms that gradually increased the opposition's ability to win. At that time the PRI's support was already declining, especially after protests in 1968 ended with the killing of several students by government forces.[4] To restore their support and legitimacy, party leaders calculated that if they allowed opposition parties more opportunities to compete they would demonstrate that the PRI truly had the full support of the Mexican people.

Chamber of Deputies ■ lower house of the legislature. It is composed of 500 members directly elected by the citizens; 300 of them are elected in single-member districts and 200 are elected through proportional representation.

The first major reform came in 1977 when the PRI agreed to expand the lower chamber of the legislature, the Chamber of Deputies, by 100 seats and to introduce the principle of proportional representation for legislative elections. This reform served its purpose by helping the opposition win a larger number of seats: from 42 in 1976 to 104 in 1979 (see Figure 7.1). Further reforms came in the 1990s, after serious allegations of fraud clouded the results of the 1988 presidential election. In 1990, the Federal Electoral Institute (*Instituto Federal Electoral*, IFE) was created and by 1994 it was completely autonomous, with extensive ability to ensure transparency and accountability in the organization of elections and the tally of votes.

In the short term, these reforms suited the PRI's interests. The electoral reforms allowed spaces for political opposition *within* the system, drawing potential dissenters towards non-violent expression of their demands. Although violent revolutions were raging in several neighboring Central American countries such as Guatemala and El Salvador in the 1980s, Mexico did not experience comparable levels of political violence. The reforms also helped the PRI to reassure foreign investors that the country was becoming democratic and, thus, would remain stable. However, the reforms benefited the opposition in the long run. Over the years, the opposition gained experience running campaigns and governing. By the mid-1990s, the main opposition parties had captured several state governments and, in 1997, they surpassed the PRI as the main force in the Legislature (see Figure 7.1). The slow process of political liberalization culminated in the 2000 election, when Vicente Fox, a former governor from the conservative

Federal Electoral Institute (IFE) ■ institution created in 1990 that is in charge of organizing elections in Mexico and guaranteeing their fairness.

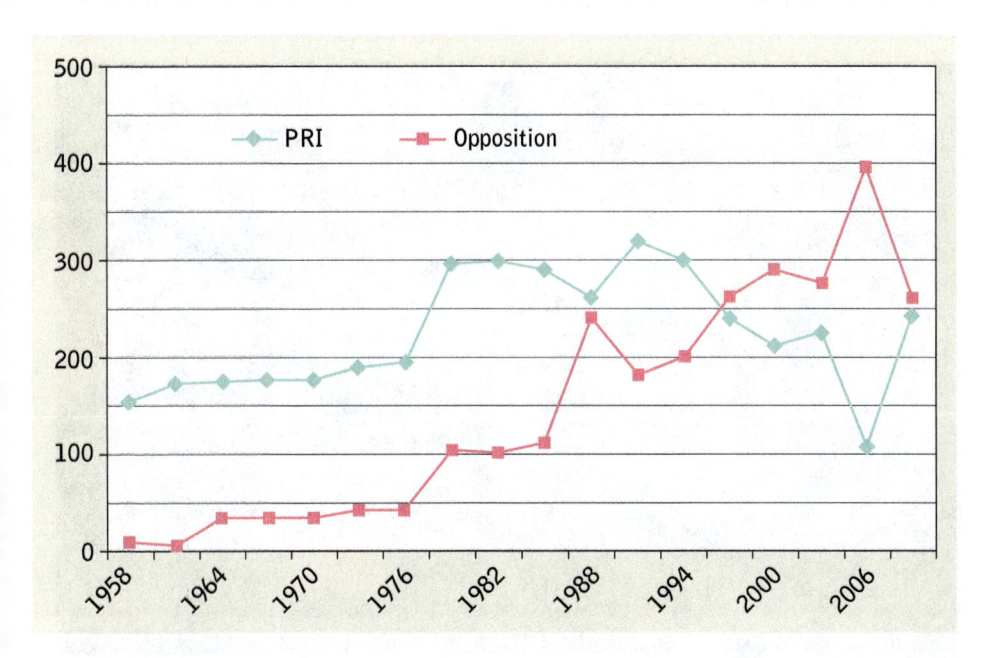

FIGURE 7.1
Number of Seats in Chamber of Deputies, 1958–2009
This figure shows the evolution of support for the PRI and the opposition in Mexico's legislature. Note the steady opposition gains and the decline of PRI support from the 1980s to the 2000s. Currently the legislature is fairly evenly split between the three largest parties.

National Action Party (PAN) ■ founded in 1939 by a group of conservative businessmen and intellectuals, in part as a reaction to the left-wing policies of President Lázaro Cárdenas (1934–1940).

opposition National Action Party (Partido Acción Nacional, PAN), captured the presidency. This was the first time that Mexico had ever experienced a peaceful transition of presidential power from one party to another, and the change signified that Mexico had moved away from a single-party state and closer to a democracy.

By 2000, many Mexicans were optimistic about the future of their county. Yet, although the country peacefully adopted limited government, many of the problems that hampered effective and legitimate government throughout Mexico's history remained. The PRI had accomplished much in its first decades in power. However, its efforts to establish effective government had had perverse consequences. Instead of focusing on developing effective government for all Mexican citizens, the PRI concentrated on providing benefits to its core supporters in the party. Although the party did have many supporters, this approach bred corruption and meant that problems such as poverty, inequality, and crime were never fully dealt with. Further, economic reforms that might hurt the party's support were not implemented. Mexico's reliance on oil revenue, for example, meant that the government had never fully implemented an effective tax system, because taxing the wealthy proved too sensitive a political issue for even the single-party PRI regime to tackle. Today, Mexicans remain among the least-taxed citizens in the Western Hemisphere.[5]

In short, the PRI created a government that for many decades was organized around the central goal of maintaining control of government. When that system

VICENTE FOX'S INAUGURATION

After more than 70 years of one-party rule, in July 2000, Vicente Fox, of the conservative PAN, was elected president of Mexico. The election marked the culmination of a long process of political liberalization and gave Mexicans great hope for the future of the country.

SUMMARY TABLE

Historical Overview: From Spanish Colony to Democratic Transition

AD 200–900	Classic era	Emergence of first city states, including Teotihuacán, El Tajín, and Monte Albán.
AD 900–1521	Post-classic era	Growth of city states including establishment of the Aztec Empire and its capital, Tenochtitlán, in what is now Mexico City.
1519–1521	Spanish conquest of Aztec Empire	Led by Hernán Cortés; Mexico became part of Spanish Empire as the Viceroyalty of New Spain, which included the western United States, Mexico, most of Central America, and most of the West and East Indies.
1521–1810	Spanish colony	Characterized by an economy based on exporting raw material back to Spain, a highly centralized political system, and a very hierarchical social structure.
1810–1821	Mexican independence	Revolt against Spanish rule led by Miguel Hidalgo and, after his death, by José María Morelos. Mexico proclaims its independence from Spain in 1821.
1836	Texas independence	Texas declares independence and in 1846 becomes part of the United States.
1846–1848	Mexican–American War	After Mexico's defeat, the Treaty of Guadalupe Hidalgo cedes half of Mexico's territory to the United States.
1876–1910	Porfiriato	Porfirio Díaz is president (1876–1880, 1884–1910). Although elected, his rule becomes progressively authoritarian.
1910	Mexican Revolution	Revolt against the dictatorial rule of Porfirio Díaz. Revolt grew to include demands for social and economic reform, including labor and peasant rights, as well as political reforms.
1929	Creation of PRI	Government party is founded under the name PNR (National Revolutionary Party); renamed PRI in 1946.
1940–1970	PRI hegemony	Period of dominance of the PRI over Mexican politics, including all branches of government as well as local and state institutions.

(Continued)

SUMMARY TABLE (CONTINUED)

1968	Student Movement and Tlatelolco Massacre	A series of student mobilizations protest government brutality. On October 2, 1968, government forces fire on a group of students, killing several and wounding many others.
1982	Debt default and debt crisis	Mexico defaults on its debt, setting off the most serious economic crisis that the nation had faced in decades.
1988	Presidential election of 1988	President Carlos Salinas (PRI) is the official winner in an election that is widely believed to have been manipulated.
1994	NAFTA goes into effect; EZLN Uprising	On the eve of the start of the North American Free Trade Agreement, the EZLN, an armed group, rises in the state of Chiapas to demand respect for the rights of indigenous communities.
1997	First instance of divided government	Opposition parties win more seats than the PRI in the legislature, making it necessary to negotiate policy reforms.
2000	Election of Vicente Fox	First member of opposition elected to the presidency.

proved incapable of responding to global economic shocks and the debt crisis in the 1970s and early 1980s, the PRI lost even the ability to effectively maintain its hold on power. Thus, even though Mexico has transitioned to democracy, the government remains unable to effectively deliver law and order, to provide education and health care in many regions, and to deal effectively with the economic and social inequalities that have persisted since the colonial era. In the next three sections, we see how these problems express themselves in relation to institutions, identities, and interests in contemporary Mexican politics.

INSTITUTIONS OF MEXICO

7.2 Why did the institutions provided for in the 1917 Constitution not contribute to the establishment of limited and effective government?

On paper, Mexico's political institutions resemble those in the United States. There is a directly elected president, a bicameral legislature, an independent judiciary, and a federal system. Yet, in contrast to the United States, these institutions have not promoted limited government in practice. Instead, although the checks and balances enshrined in the 1917 Constitution were never suspended or changed significantly, for most of the twentieth century the PRI dominated all government institutions and was able to govern in a very centralized way. Within this context, Mexico's 1997 legislative elections were historic. For the first time, the opposition won more legislative seats than did the PRI. This was a major advance towards accountability in Mexican politics—towards limited government. The opposition's electoral gains meant that the 1917 Constitution would finally come into play; the legislature and the judiciary could exercise oversight of the executive; and federalism could offer a check on the central government's power rather than provide a façade that masked a highly centralized political system.

Unfortunately, decades of PRI rule have left Mexican institutions ill adapted to the task of providing both limited *and* effective government. The lack of a majority party that controls both the executive and legislative branches of government—a **divided government**, a situation that has characterized Mexico since 1997—has brought pluralism to politics, but also legislative deadlock that has prevented the adoption of necessary economic and social reforms. The judicial system has started to exercise more oversight, but it is slow and inefficient and threatened by endemic corruption. And because several different parties are now in power at the state level, federalism has thus far proven incapable of facilitating cooperation across levels of government on issues such as revenue sharing and crime prevention. Finally, the electoral system, though reformed to promote democratic contestation, needs additional reforms to eliminate electoral corruption. As we will see, the challenges remain great and have led to considerable disenchantment with democracy.

divided government
■ a situation in which the legislature and the executive are held by different parties, making agreement across party lines necessary in order to pass any legislation.

Executive–Legislative Relations

A first obstacle in the establishment of limited and effective government in Mexico has been that since 1997 no party has captured both the presidency and a majority of seats in the legislature, making it difficult to pass reforms or new proposals. This affects the quality of democracy in Mexico because it makes it difficult for the government to act on many of the challenges facing the country, including drug trafficking, the administration of justice, corruption, and economic stagnation.

The legislature in Mexico is composed of two chambers, the Chamber of Deputies and the Senate. The Chamber is composed of 500 deputies, elected for three-year terms. Three hundred deputies are elected in single-member districts by majority rule, and 200 are elected through proportional representation. The Senate is composed of 128 members, three for each of the 31 states and the federal district (Mexico City), and 32 members elected by proportional representation. The term for senators is six years. Prior to 1997, the legislature did not present a political obstacle to presidential initiatives, because the PRI always held a majority of seats. For decades, the executive saw nearly 100 percent of its proposals approved and was subjected to little oversight from the legislative. PRI dominance gave the president tremendous *de facto* autonomy and made it unnecessary to change the formal rules provided for in the 1917 Constitution. Yet, since 1997, divided government has become the defining feature of executive–legislative relations, and the relationship between the president and the legislature has changed as a result—even if the formal rules that govern that relationship actually changed very little. For example, 98 percent of the president's proposals were approved in the 1994–1997 legislature, but only about 85 percent of his initiatives were approved in the legislatures beginning in 1997 and 2000. In addition, prior to 1997, presidents proposed about 80 percent of legislation ultimately passed by the Legislature, but since 1997, presidents have proposed only about 20 percent of all legislation the Legislature approves. Instead, most legislation now originates with opposition parties.

Since 1997, legislation no longer reflects a single party's vision of the direction in which the country should be moving. Democracy has brought a multiplicity of views to the legislature and has made the legislature a much more active participant in the policymaking process; the number of laws approved in the Chamber of Deputies increased from 108 in the 1994–1997 legislature to 137, and 275 in the following two legislatures. But divided government makes *effective* government more difficult. When no single party wins a majority of seats, one party can block the other parties' initiatives. Thus far, Mexico's three main parties have been unable to come to an agreement about how to meet pressing national challenges. Between 2000 and 2006, for example, opposition parties blocked most of President Fox's reform proposals, including efforts to reform the energy sector, labor laws, and the tax code. President Felipe Calderón, elected in 2006, has done a bit better, managing to get opposition support for some electoral reforms in 2007, justice system reform in 2008, and tax reform in 2009, but each reform required major concessions to opposition parties, and the need for further reforms in all these areas is still a point of contention in the Legislature. Further, agreement on other issues, like reforming the energy sector, continues to elude political parties. Legislative paralysis has eroded voter support for democracy and increased the view that democracy is dysfunctional and an obstacle to effective government, rather than a means to achieve it.

The Judiciary

A second challenge in the consolidation of democracy in Mexico is the judicial system. Throughout the decades of PRI hegemony, the judicial branch, like the legislative, was subordinated to the executive. PRI leaders handpicked judges—including those on the Supreme Court—whose political independence was minimal. As a result, the legal system grew riddled with corruption, and failed to develop mechanisms to guarantee citizens' rights, equality before the law, and limits on government power. With the transition to democracy, reforms have made the judiciary more independent and given it stronger powers of oversight. However, the system is still characterized by corruption and inefficiency.

The first effort to reform Mexico's judicial system came in 1994, under PRI President Ernesto Zedillo. The reform reduced the executive's role in the appointment of judges, increased the court's ability to settle intergovernmental disputes between state and national governments, and gave the court enhanced powers of judicial review—that is, it gave the court the authority to declare unconstitutional any legislation passed by the legislature and signed by the president. This reform greatly enhanced the "checks and balances" in the Mexican system. As part of Mexico's process of regime change to democracy, the reforms worked to enhance limited government.

However, reforms have thus far fallen short in terms of improving the judiciary's ability to provide effective government for Mexican citizens, particularly in terms of providing the state's most important service: law and order. The legal system is marked by impunity for criminals and corruption at all levels. In recent years, corruption has been an obstacle in the government's efforts to fight drug cartels and to control the spread of violence related to organized crime. In 2001, 45 percent of Mexicans polled believed that corruption was on the increase, but by

Supreme Court ■ the head of the judicial branch. It is made up of 11 judges (*ministros*) whose terms last 15 years. Judges are elected by the Senate from a list of names proposed by the president.

2009 this percentage was 73 percent. In the same survey, 90 percent of respondents said there was a lot of corruption in the government.[6] These numbers are confirmed in the 2010 survey done by Transparency International, which measures levels of corruption around the world and gives Mexico a score of 3.1, on a scale where 10 represents no corruption.[7]

Given the pervasive sense that corruption is endemic to the system, most Mexicans lack confidence that the police or judicial institutions can solve problems they experience with crime. For example, in contrast to the United States, where it is estimated that citizens report about 50 percent of crimes to the police, in Mexico only around 16 percent of crimes are reported—and of these, only a very small percentage are prosecuted, and less than 1 percent are punished.[8]

Criminal impunity and corruption are costly to society. Property rights are insecure when crooks do not fear the police but instead can buy them off easily. As a result, economic investment and productivity suffer. And when the government cannot guarantee citizens' safety, citizens pay the consequences, literally. In 2008, it was estimated that Mexicans invested more than $3 billion in personal security measures, ranging from guard dogs to private security guards.[9]

Mexicans are paying for private security because public security is inadequate, particularly to confront the recent increase in violence related to organized crime and drug trafficking. Although concentrated in certain areas of the country, the increasing violence—more than 12,000 deaths due to crime in 2011—has come as a shock (see Figure 7.2). More Mexicans in 2010 placed crime above the economy as

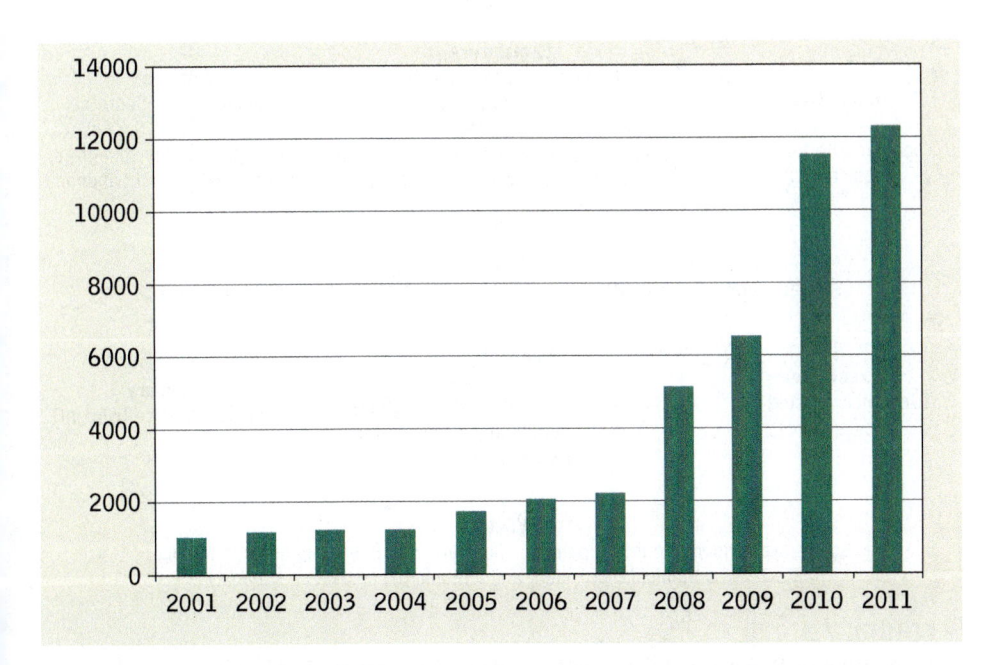

FIGURE 7.2

Drug-related deaths in Mexico, 2001–2011

Many Mexicans view the increase in drug-related violence in Mexico as evidence that the government is ineffective, and that the government cannot eliminate powerful drug cartels.

the top issue facing the government, and more Mexicans believe that the criminals are winning the "war" on organized crime, not the government.[10] In Mexico today, the government's strategy against the drug trade—which has included an expanded role for army troops and a renewed effort to capture drug cartel leaders—is one of the main topics of discussion. While some Mexicans are supportive of President Calderón's efforts to curb the power of drug cartels, others place blame for the increased violence on the government's confrontational approach.

The widespread perception of corruption and criminal impunity undermines the legitimacy of the judiciary and tarnishes its reputation, eroding support for democracy. Recent polls also show that, despite dogged efforts to improve police and judicial performance, Mexicans still do not trust their legal system: 71 percent of people surveyed say judges are very corrupt, and 80 percent of respondents described the legal system as very corrupt.[11]

Federalism

The authors of the 1917 Constitution made Mexico a federal system because they believed that federalism would impede a repeat of the political centralization of the Díaz era (see Figure 7.3). Despite this effort, the *de facto* political centralization of the PRI era curtailed the impact of formal federal institutions and gave state and local governments little political autonomy relative to the central government.

Federal

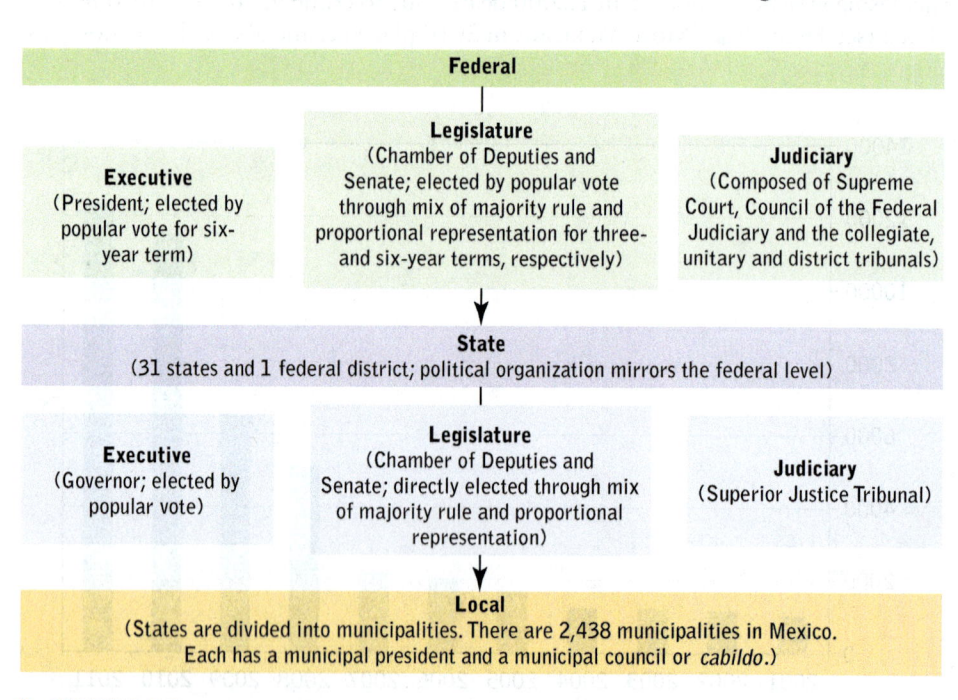

- **Executive** (President; elected by popular vote for six-year term)
- **Legislature** (Chamber of Deputies and Senate; elected by popular vote through mix of majority rule and proportional representation for three- and six-year terms, respectively)
- **Judiciary** (Composed of Supreme Court, Council of the Federal Judiciary and the collegiate, unitary and district tribunals)

State (31 states and 1 federal district; political organization mirrors the federal level)

- **Executive** (Governor; elected by popular vote)
- **Legislature** (Chamber of Deputies and Senate; directly elected through mix of majority rule and proportional representation)
- **Judiciary** (Superior Justice Tribunal)

Local (States are divided into municipalities. There are 2,438 municipalities in Mexico. Each has a municipal president and a municipal council or *cabildo*.)

FIGURE 7.3

Separation of Powers and the Three Levels of Government in Mexico

Mexico's political system resembles the United States', with the separation of executive, legislative, and judicial power, and a federal system that empowers state governments. In theory, this system should generate limited government. However, many Mexicans believe it provides neither limited nor effective government.

Beginning in the 1980s, a process of decentralization has sought to reverse decades of political centralization and make federalism a reality in Mexican politics, enhancing limited government. As a response to the economic crisis of the 1980s, the PRI transferred much of the responsibility for education and infrastructure upkeep to state governments. However, the central government tended to transfer responsibility without transferring sufficient revenue to meet the new policy obligations. In the 1990s, the PRI did transfer some revenue, increasing state and municipal governments' political autonomy to a limited degree. However, resource allocation remains highly centralized in comparison to other federal systems: because most states lack the ability to bring in their own tax revenue, most states depend on the central government for an average of 60 percent of their revenue.

Moreover, divided government hurts the delivery of public services to Mexican citizens at the local and state levels, just as it does at the national level. At all levels of government in Mexico today, the three main parties must share political power. For example, more than half of state governors are from the PRI, but in many states other parties control the state legislatures. Democracy has made inter-party cooperation both within state and local governments and between levels of government essential to effective government.

Electoral Institutions

Elections have been held in Mexico at regular intervals since the end of the Revolution in 1920. However, between 1940 and the mid-1990s, these elections did

THE IFE

The Federal Electoral Institute has played a central role in the transition from one-party to democratic rule in Mexico, organizing the elections and guaranteeing their transparency. Today, however, the Institute faces important challenges; chief among them are the regulation of campaign finance and the role of the media in elections.

not really offer the possibility of democratic accountability. Instead, they merely served to rubber-stamp PRI candidates for office. This changed in the mid-1990s, particularly with the creation and consolidation of the IFE's ability to oversee the electoral process. As a result of these changes, by 2000, international organizations such as the Carter Center regarded elections in Mexico as free and fair.[12] However, serious questions remain about the IFE's ability to guarantee the transparency of the electoral process, which is central to electoral accountability. Three particular features of elections present the largest challenge to effective democratic governance.

The first major issue is the reform of the system of campaign finance. In an effort to level the playing field for all parties, reforms in the 1960s and 1970s implemented public financing of party organizations and election campaigns. Today, donations from private individuals can only amount to 10 percent of a party's total annual revenue.[13] Public financing is meant to eliminate the influence of large donors and give all parties a fighting chance to win. However, critics argue that Mexico's system gives parties too much money. Campaigns in Mexico are expensive, at least in part, because they are longer than in many countries. On average, legislative campaigns last 109 days, almost five times as long as they do in France and more than three times as long as in Chile. The average cost of a winning campaign has also increased dramatically in recent years, from 49 pesos per vote in 1991 to more than 400 in 2003.[14] Critics also suggest that the IFE does a poor job preventing illegal private contributions to parties and candidates, a particularly important threat to democratic accountability in a context of increased influence of criminal organizations.

A second aspect of elections that is central to accountability is the issue of whether politicians should be allowed to run for re-election to their current post. One of the rallying cries of the Mexican Revolution was "No re-election!" because many believed re-election led to dictatorship. As a consequence, legislators are not allowed to run for two consecutive terms. While prohibiting re-election may indeed prevent one person or party from growing too comfortable in power, it also may impede effective government. Even if someone is doing a good job in office, he or she cannot run again. Moreover, without the possibility of running for re-election, politicians are more responsive to the people who can offer them another political job—the leaders of their party—rather than to voters, who might return them to office.

A third question is whether electoral rules should do more to allow the formation of effective governments. Since 1988, three parties have run competitive candidates in all presidential elections. But because Mexico uses the plurality rule for presidential elections, no winning candidate has obtained a majority—and the legitimacy that accompanies such a victory (see Table 7.2). Mexico's presidential elections have raised questions about the strength of the president's mandate and the extent of popular support for his initiatives and agenda. In most presidential systems, this issue is solved with a second-round runoff election between the two top vote-getters, which means that ultimately one candidate wins a majority.

Since it began its democratic transition, Mexico has tried to adapt its electoral institutions. Thus far, reformers have not discovered an ideal recipe to balance the principles of accountability, transparency, and effective government. In recent years, the government and the political parties have submitted a set of proposals

TABLE 7.2

Vote for President (percentage), 1988–2006*

Party	1988	1994	2000	2006
PRI	*50.36*	*48.69*	36.11	22.72
PAN	17.07	25.92	*42.52*	*36.69*
PRD (FDN)	30.80	16.59	16.64	36.11
Other	1.77	8.00	4.73	4.48

*Percentage obtained by winner in italics.

Source: IFE and Political Database for the Americas

to give the IFE more autonomy, to allow for re-election up to four terms, and to reform both the presidential and legislative electoral systems. However, as of this writing, no major changes can be reported.

As the table below suggests, although on paper the institutions provided for in the 1917 Constitution laid out a system of checks and balances, in reality these institutions worked very differently; throughout the twentieth century the PRI managed to dominate every branch of government, centralizing power and hindering accountability. Since the end of one-party rule in 1997, however, much progress has been made in making the separation of powers delineated in Mexico's constitution a reality. However, important challenges remain. The constitution has brought better limitations on government power through the separation of powers, improved judicial independence, genuine federalism, and more electoral accountability.

However, these same institutions have made it difficult for the Mexican state to provide effective governance. In a context of divided government, the very strength of the separation of powers and federalism have become a barrier to adopting needed reforms. The judiciary and electoral institutions need further reform to reduce corruption and impunity. The lack of movement on such reforms has increased public discontent with democracy. Without more effective government performance, discontent with the political system is likely to grow, and with it the difficulty of consolidating Mexico's young democracy.

SUMMARY TABLE

Institutions of Mexico: Separation of Powers with a Weak President

Executive Branch	The Mexican president has weak formal powers. For example, in contrast to executives in other presidential systems, the Mexican president cannot legislate by decree and cannot call a referendum.

(Continued)

SUMMARY TABLE (CONTINUED)

Legislature	The Chamber of Deputies and the Senate are directly elected by the people for 3- and 6-year terms, respectively. Although the legislature was dominated by the PRI after 1929, since 1997 no single party has controlled both the legislature and the executive. Divided government has contributed to a more active legislature and to better oversight of the president but has also lead to legislative paralysis.
Judiciary	The Supreme Court is the head of the judicial branch and is in charge of interpreting the constitution and protecting the separation of powers. It is composed of 11 judges (*ministros*) who are elected by the Senate, from a list drawn up by the president.
Electoral Institutions	The Mexican president is elected by plurality rule. In the Chamber of Deputies, 300 members are elected by plurality in single-member districts and 200 are elected by proportional representation. In the Senate, each of the 31 states and the federal district (Mexico City) elects two senators through plurality rule; an additional seat is allocated in each state to the "first minority" or second place party. An additional 32 senators are elected through proportional representation.

IDENTITIES IN MEXICO

7.3 How do Mexicans identify themselves and how do these identities shape Mexican politics?

Mexicans define their identity based on many different categories; religion, ideology, geographical region, ethnicity, and economic class are all important. However, the extent to which one or another form of identity gains political salience changes with time. For example, as the PRI regime developed in the 1940s, it sought to downplay some forms of identity and emphasize the importance of economic class, which was the key principle around which the "revolutionary family" was organized. The PRI's success over several decades was due to its ability to bring people from all walks of life—workers, peasants, business, youth—into one political party. Yet, as the dominance of the PRI weakened, other forms of identity became more salient.

Watch the **Video** "The Zapatista Rebellion" at mypoliscilab.com

Explore the **Comparative** "Political Cultures" at mypoliscilab.com

In this section we will describe the main sources of political identity in contemporary Mexico and study how their salience has evolved over time. Some forms of identity—such as nationalism—provide glue that holds all Mexicans together. Yet other forms of identity are sources of political conflict. With democratization, ethnicity in particular has emerged as an important source of conflict that has at times threatened national unity and has posed an important challenge for effective governance.

Forming National Identity under the PRI

Mexico is an ethnically diverse country. The broadest ethnic distinction is between the majority *mestizo* population—of mixed white and indigenous descent—and the indigenous population. However, this basic division masks enormous diversity. On one hand, *mestizos* are a very heterogeneous group and, as we will see, they rarely act on a common ethnic identity and instead describe themselves in terms of region of origin, gender, ideology, or occupation. On the other hand, although the indigenous population is also characterized by enormous diversity, groups organized around issues common to indigenous communities have grown in number and importance, especially since the 1970s. As of the 2005 census, 7 percent of Mexicans considered themselves indigenous; this community is comprised of 62 different ethno-linguistic groups (defined on the basis of common use of a language other than Spanish) and is located primarily in Mexico's southern states.

Indigenous people are vastly outnumbered by the *mestizo* population. As far back as the pre-independence colonial era, *mestizos* grew to outnumber the indigenous population (see the table on the following page). By the end of the nineteenth century, most Mexicans believed that ethnicity was not primordial but was instead a mutable category that could be changed through education and upward mobility. Nevertheless, Mexico's indigenous population remained the poorest group in the country and was a frequent target of discrimination.

At the end of the Revolution, politicians in what would become the PRI faced the challenge of consolidating power and building a strong state. One of the threats they faced was the potential for renewed violence from disgruntled indigenous people who, although they joined the Revolution in large numbers, had seen few changes in their living conditions. In order to neutralize this potential threat and build the regime's legitimacy, PRI leaders built a national discourse around the idea that every Mexican shared an ethnic identity. This project, called *mestizaje*, promoted the integration of Mexico's Indians into national life and suggested that *all* Mexicans belonged to a single race—a *mestizo* race—rooted in the mixture of Mexico's Aztec past with more recent Spanish and European blood. In promoting this idea, PRI leaders aimed to unify the country and reduce the importance of ethnicity as a factor that separated Mexicans from each other. In the process, it was hoped that the Indians, who at the time were around 15 percent of the population, would be lifted out of poverty and integrated into the economy.[15]

mestizaje ■ project espoused by the Mexican government that promoted the integration of Mexico's Indians into national life and suggested that all Mexicans belonged to a single, *mestizo* race.

To support the cultural and economic integration of Indians to the *mestizo* mainstream, the government established institutions such as the Department of Indigenous Affairs and the National Indigenous Institute. Through these institutions, the government actively promoted a sense of pride in the country's indigenous past, but also emphasized the *mestizo* identity as the key to the country's development.[16] In the 1940s and 1950s, intellectuals, writers, and artists also promoted *mestizaje*, arguing that the mixture of races enhanced national strength. Perhaps the most famous example is José Vasconcelos, a noted writer, education minister, and president of the National University, who popularized this view of *mestizaje* in his book *The Cosmic Race*.

The structure of the PRI also served to weaken the salience of ethnicity in politics. The corporatist structure of the party meant that voters were mobilized in terms of class rather than ethnicity. Indigenous Mexicans were not formally included in the PRI as a group. This created incentives for those who identified as indigenous to organize instead as peasants in order to receive benefits from

> **SUMMARY TABLE**
>
> **Identities: The Indigenous Population in Mexico**
>
> | Year | Total | Indian | (Percent) |
> |------|-------|--------|-----------|
> | 1570 | 3,380,000 | 3,366,800 | 98.7 |
> | 1646 | 1,712,600 | 1,269,600 | 74.6 |
> | 1742 | 2,477,200 | 1,540,200 | 62.2 |
> | 1793 | 3,799,500 | 2,319,700 | 61.0 |
> | 1810 | 6,122,300 | 3,676,200 | 60.0 |
> | 1895 | 12,632,000 (approx.) | * | 16.1 |
> | 1900 | 13,607,259 | * | 15.3 |
> | 1910 | 15,160,000 (approx.) | * | 12.9 |
> | 1920 | 14,500,000 (approx.) | * | 12.7 |
> | 1930 | 16,552,722 | * | 16.0 |
> | 1940 | 19,653,552 | * | 14.8 |
> | 1950 | 25,791,017 | * | 11.2 |
> | 1960 | 34,923,129 | * | 10.4 |
> | 1970 | 48,225,238 | * | 7.8 |
> | 1980 | 66,846,833 | * | 9.0 |
> | 1990 | 81,249,645 | 5,282,347 | 7.5 |
> | 2000 | 97,014,867 | 6,300,000 | 7.1 |
> | 2005 | 106,306,438 | 7,016,224 | 6.6 |
>
> *Information unavailable.
>
> Source: Data from 1895–2000 from the INEGI yearly census (first column includes all Mexicans; % Indigenous in the last column only includes speakers of an indigenous language who are five years and older).
>
> Data from 1570–1810 comes from Gonzalo Aguirre Beltrán, *La población negra de México 1519–1810; estudio etno-histórico*, Mexico, Ediciones Fuente Cultural, 1946, 234.

the government. However, because indigenous communities had different sorts of demands—for protection of age-old communal customs and education in indigenous language, for example—the PRI's structure tended to discriminate against indigenous peoples.[17] As a result, for most of the twentieth century, indigenous people saw little improvement in their living standards, and they remained marginalized and isolated from the rest of Mexican society.

Ethnicity Makes a Comeback

Starting in the 1970s, indigenous communities increasingly began to reject the integrationist ideas of *mestizaje*, and started calling for greater indigenous autonomy. They also began pushing the idea that ethnicity was a relevant form of political identity. This change was driven by changes in the national political and economic context, as well as in the international environment.

Although the political and economic issues facing Mexico's indigenous population have existed for centuries, the uprising in 1994 of the Ejército Zapatista de Liberación Nacional brought national and international attention to their plight. Despite the attention, however, this population remains one of the most marginalized in the country.

In terms of the political context, in the 1970s, the PRI sought to more explicitly incorporate emerging indigenous organizations in an effort to sustain its legitimacy. The PRI created the *Consejo Nacional de Pueblos Indígenas* (National Council of Indigenous Communities), organized the First National Indigenous Conference in Chiapas, and increased expenditures on indigenous peoples' most pressing demand: land reform. Although these organizations had only limited impact in representing indigenous peoples' interests, over time the process of political liberalization gave indigenous groups opportunities to mobilize politically in ways that had previously been foreclosed. More independent indigenous organizations gradually emerged, further increasing pressures on the PRI for land reform and for greater input from indigenous people into local and national politics.

However, the economic context in the late 1980s and the economic reforms implemented after the 1982 debt crisis undermined the government's ability to provide resources to its supporters, including labor, peasants, and indigenous groups. Cuts to government expenditures reduced or eliminated many social programs and agricultural subsidies—programs that had generated considerable support for the PRI. In particular, efforts at land reform were stopped or even reversed, and President Salinas's reform of Article 27 of the constitution weakened the communal land-owning system at the heart of indigenous communities, putting them at a considerable disadvantage against large agribusiness corporations.

As public expenditures declined and communal land rights were eliminated, more groups mobilized around indigenous peoples' rights issues. Such calls also came in the context of growing international support for abandoning the idea of assimilation in favor of multiculturalism—the recognition of ethnic and cultural diversity.[18] In Mexico, the most important indigenous mobilization has been the *Ejército Zapatista de Liberación Nacional,* or the Zapatista Army of National Liberation (EZLN). On January 1, 1994, the Zapatistas, an armed movement based in the southern state of Chiapas, took control of several towns and issued a declaration demanding better health care, education, and housing for indigenous communities, as well as their right to freely elect their leaders. The timing of the uprising—the day NAFTA entered into effect—was meant to emphasize the Zapatistas' disapproval of the PRI's economic policies and to publicize the negative effects of these policies on indigenous peoples' livelihoods.

Zapatista Army of National Liberation (EZLN) ■ insurgent armed group based in the state of Chiapas and organized in defense of the rights of indigenous communities. After an uprising in January 1994, the group has mostly pressed its demands through nonviolent means such as marches and protests.

The government initially sent army troops and aircraft to force the rebels to retreat or surrender. However, under increased media coverage and pressure from national and international human rights organizations, the government proposed a cease fire, and peace talks started in February 1995. In September 1995, the government and the EZLN signed the San Andrés Larrainzar agreements, but it was not until 2001, after the PRI had left power, that a constitutional amendment was passed recognizing the right of indigenous peoples to self-determination and autonomy. These rights include the right to decide how to organize their communities economically, politically, and socially, and to apply traditional mechanisms to solve disputes within their communities rather than use the judicial system. The reform, however, did not include the Zapatistas' demands for collective land rights or control of natural resources, and the Zapatistas have continued to press their views and demands through media campaigns and protest marches.

In short, despite these reforms, indigenous communities remain marginalized; their influence in the political process remains limited. Today, indigenous peoples are poorer than the rest of the country on average; they have lower levels of education and higher rates of illiteracy; and they have less access to health services, electricity, or clean water. The Zapatista movement has brought much-needed attention to the issues of indigenous communities, but the project of making Mexico a more inclusive society remains incomplete. Given their exclusion, Mexico's indigenous people remain dissatisfied with the performance of the government under democracy.

Political Cleavages and Electoral Behavior

Ethnicity is not the only important form of political identity in Mexico today. After all, more than 90 percent of the population does not consider themselves indigenous. In this section, we look more closely at electoral behavior and see how geography and ideology are becoming important cleavages in Mexican politics.

Party of the Democratic Revolution ■ left-wing party founded in 1989 by a group of dissident members of the PRI. Although it has never won the presidency, the party governs several states and is, with the PRI and the PAN, one of the three largest parties in the Legislature.

In contrast to many other countries around the world, since elections became competitive in Mexico, citizens do not base their votes on ethnic, class, or religious identity. It is true that the PAN tends to gain support from relatively wealthier, religious, and white Mexicans; the PRI performs best in rural areas, among Mexicans with less education, and among older voters; and the Party of the Democratic Revolution (*Partido de la Revolución Democrática*, PRD) tends to attract support among the indigenous population, and young, secular urbanites. However, these differences are not large enough to constitute the kinds of stable political cleavages that we find in other countries. This is due in part to the fact that over the last quarter of the twentieth century, Mexicans of many different backgrounds were united in attempting to oust the PRI from power.

In the decade since the PRI lost power, however, we see evidence of political cleavages beginning to emerge. One key potential divide is regional. In the 1990s, a clear pattern emerged, with the PAN developing strong support in Mexico's northern states, while the PRD performed best in the southern states and in Mexico City. This regional pattern is still evident in presidential elections but in state-level elections it has become less clear. In the 2009 midterm legislative elections, the PRI made up much lost ground at the expense of both the PAN and PRD, which lost support in every region. In the context of the global economic crisis and increased criminal activity, the midterm election served as a referendum on PAN President Felipe Calderón's performance. It is, therefore, too soon to tell whether the regional political cleavage that emerged in the 1990s will become a permanent divide in Mexican politics.

A second potential cleavage is ideological. In order to compete with the PRI before 2000, opposition parties downplayed ideology in their effort to appeal to a wide swath of the population. Even the PAN, which was founded on conservative and religious principles, tried to capitalize on the anti-PRI sentiment to win elections by broadening its appeal. However, the end of the PRI regime in 2000 meant that parties could now try to carve out an ideological niche on the political spectrum. During the 2006 presidential election, for example, the two top contenders, Felipe Calderón from the conservative PAN and Andrés Manuel López Obrador from the leftist PRD presented policy programs rooted in ideologies at opposite ends of the political spectrum. Analyses of the election show that voters could both distinguish between these two candidates and that voters' ideology was also strongly correlated with their vote choice.[19] However, as with regional voting, it is presently too early to tell whether ideology will permanently shape voting behavior in a democratic Mexico.

Scholars hold that forging a common national identity is a key to consolidating an effective and legitimate state. In Mexico today, the expression of political identities offers both grounds for optimism and words of caution. Perhaps the most promising facet of political identity in Mexico today is the high level of national identity. Mexican nationalism manifests itself in a variety of ways, from the enormous enthusiasm for the national soccer team to the enthusiasm for celebrating national holidays such as Independence Day. Popular support for Mexican national identity helps consolidate a stable democratic polity. Indeed, the strength of Mexican nationalism makes fears of Mexico becoming a "failed state" highly exaggerated.

Nevertheless, consolidating democracy will also require integrating indigenous people into the economy and the polity. Because they were not seen as part of the national identity, Indians remained underrepresented and lacking in mechanisms to press their political and economic demands. Despite a constitutional amendment recognizing some indigenous rights, they have remained marginalized. The failure of the state to provide economic security for a large segment of the population, and to effectively integrate indigenous communities, is damaging to its legitimacy and to the consolidation of the democratic regime. Unless these problems are resolved, Mexico's democratization will remain incomplete.

INTERESTS IN MEXICO

7.4 What are the most influential interests in Mexico and how have they contributed to the development of a more democratic country?

Watch the Video "Drug Policy in Mexico" at mypoliscilab.com

A defining feature of a strong democracy is the existence of independent organizations that allow citizens to organize and mobilize to press their demands on the government. By 2000, Mexico had an electoral democracy—a system in which the opposition is free to contest elections, and in which citizens are allowed to participate freely. In the second half of the twentieth century, Mexico also saw the development of an increasingly autonomous and lively civil society. However, the ability of these organizations to represent and effectively channel citizens' interests into the political system is still variable and remains one of the challenges to democratic consolidation in Mexico.

As described previously, during the years of PRI hegemony, the party used corporatist methods to incorporate major societal groups into the structure of the party, including peasants, labor, women, and youth. Because the party distributed jobs and other political favors in exchange for political support, members of such groups had few incentives to organize outside of the party—and the party was the only viable channel through which these organized interests could channel their demands. Organizations developed to help the PRI control society, but groups had few opportunities to independently lobby the government and keep public officials accountable.

Ties between organized interests and the state weakened with the increase in political pluralism in the 1990s, and these groups found new ways to mobilize collectively. For example, interests that had traditionally been associated with the PRI such as business groups and labor unions saw independent rivals emerge and were forced to compete for membership. As the PRI loosened its political control, new interest groups and social movements gained legitimacy as avenues for the expression of people's needs and demands.

In this section, we explore how this process has unfolded in the last 20 years or so. We will see how changes in the political context—in particular the opening of the political system to non-corporatist, autonomous forms of collective action—has affected political parties, social movements, and interest groups. The gradual liberalization of the Mexican political system in recent decades has led to new groups gaining access to the political system and to a considerable increase in political competition. However, despite the growth of a diverse array of autonomous organizations in civil society, important challenges remain. Although political competition now focuses on three main parties rather than just on the PRI, public trust in the party system is declining as parties prove unable to devise a set of policies to address Mexico's economic and social challenges. Outside of the party system, social movements have proliferated. Although this is a positive development for democracy, the kinds of groups that have emerged indicate deep dissatisfaction with the state's ability to fulfill its basic functions such as providing law and order. Last, economic reforms since the early 1990s have highlighted the relative weakness of labor and the strength of business—but have also encouraged Mexican governments to integrate the millions of emigrants to the United States into Mexico's political system.

Political Parties

Since the 1990s, Mexico's party system has evolved from a non-democratic one-party system dominated by the PRI to a competitive multi-party system in which competition takes place largely between three major parties—the PRI, the PAN, and the PRD. This is clear evidence of a core element of a functioning democracy. However, in recent years, the inability of these parties to form effective governing coalitions has led to a decline in trust in political parties in general and to discontent with the operation of the party system.

The PRI Between 1929 and 2000, Mexico had a non-democratic one-party system in which there was substantial electoral participation but no effective interparty contestation. During these years, the only real opposition came from the rightist PAN and from the Mexican Communist Party (*Partido Comunista Mexicano,* PCM). However, both of these parties remained relatively small, and neither ever truly had a chance of stripping the PRI of its hold on power. Between its creation in 1929 and the start of its decline in 1970, the PRI won 88 percent of the presidential vote, on average.

The PRI has long been a mixture of a mass and an elite party. Although it was designed to incorporate mass groups such as peasants and labor, the PRI was also very hierarchical, with the president at the top. Cabinet members and governors of important states shared in the party's important decisions, as did labor and peasant leaders when their support was necessary for the issue at hand. Further down the pyramid were members of the Legislature, state legislators, leaders of unions, and other peasant and labor organizations.

This hierarchical system was held together by the PRI's ability to distribute political jobs and other perks to key elements of its support base. Because the president was central to this system of rewards, observers predicted that the PRI would disintegrate after it lost the 2000 presidential election. However, the party has adapted by becoming less hierarchical and transferring authority within the party to PRI state governors.[20]

The PAN Until 1988 the most important opposition to the PRI came from the PAN. The PAN was formed by a group of business leaders and activist Catholics who opposed the extent to which the PRI had involved the government in the economy since the presidency of Lázaro Cárdenas. Although the party was founded around a Catholic doctrine, religious ideology was often put aside in order to attract voters who opposed the PRI. The party was very important in demanding electoral reforms and was a key participant in the process of reforms that started in the 1970s and culminated in the formation of the IFE in the 1990s. It won its first state governorship in 1989 (Baja California) and won the presidency in 2000 and 2006.

The PRD The other major source of opposition to the PRI has come from the PRD. This party emerged as a result of a split within the PRI. In 1988, Cuauhtémoc Cárdenas—son of president Lázaro Cárdenas—left the PRI to head a coalition of left-wing parties, which later merged to form the PRD. Cárdenas led this rebellion due to widespread opposition to the PRI's economic policies in the 1980s and to dissatisfaction with the way that the incumbent president got to choose his successor with no input from average citizens or even average party members. Cárdenas believed that the PRI's policies were abandoning the party's revolutionary ideals and would damage the economic prospects of its core constituencies, labor and peasants.

The PRD has struggled to consolidate its support after its strong performance in 1988.[21] It is divided internally between multiple factions, all of which fight to determine nominations for office. These internal divisions tend to hurt the party's image as a viable alternative for governing the country. In the 2009 elections, the party was left governing only five states, one of which is Mexico City, and it received only 12 percent of the legislative vote, losing more than 50 seats.

Party Competition since 2000   Mexico now has a three-party system: together, the three major parties win around 90 percent of the vote. These three parties also structure competition ideologically, because voters know that the PRD is on the left, the PRI is centrist, and the PAN is more conservative.[22] A few smaller parties such as the environmentalist Green Party or the left-wing Workers' Party exist, and these parties sometimes play an important role because they run in coalition with larger parties. Since none of the major parties has obtained a legislative majority since 1997, smaller parties can also play an important role in building alliances in the Legislature.

The increase in political competition, however, has had a negative side effect: because no party has been able to capture a majority of the votes in a legislative election, divided government has become a normal state of affairs. This has tended to frustrate supporters of *all* the parties. For example, in a 2009 poll by the newspaper *Reforma,* 86 percent of respondents said that they thought parties were very corrupt.[23] In addition, there has also been a sharp increase in the proportion of people who do not vote or nullify their ballot: in the 2009 election, 5.4 percent of voters invalidated their ballot, as compared against an average of 3 percent in previous elections. Sixty percent of those who annulled their vote said they did so because the existing parties do not listen to voters.[24] In sum, although Mexico's party system reflects thriving inter-party contestation, the change from a non-democratic one-party system has not increased citizens' satisfaction with government. In fact, quite the opposite has been the case.

Social Movements

In recent years, Mexico has developed a broad array of social movements, reflecting economic, social, and cultural interests and identities, such as environmentalism, labor rights, the rights of peasants and indigenous people, gay rights, religious conservatism, and anti-crime groups. As in most democracies, hardly a day goes by without some large-scale protest taking place, especially in the capital Mexico City. However, it was not always so. In the years of PRI hegemony, there were few such movements and little large-scale protest. By incorporating peasants, workers, and others groups into the party, the PRI gave these groups a channel for pressing their demands upon the state. Making these groups a part of the party was an effective way to ensure that leaders of such groups had few incentives to take their demands to the streets. The regime preferred incorporation to repression, but it would also actively prevent large-scale anti-government mobilization when it considered it necessary. Because there are far too many social movements in Mexico to mention, in this section we focus on two major movements that helped force open the political system: students in the late 1960s, and groups that organized in the aftermath of the economic crisis of 1982 and a major earthquake in 1985. These two broad movements forced the PRI into a defensive position and opened opportunities to far wider civil society mobilization in later years.

The Student Movement The first instance of significant mobilization against the PRI government in several decades was the large anti-government student mobilization in 1968. The movement originated when the police used what many saw as unnecessary force to break up a fight between two groups of students, and grew over the summer of 1968 to include students protesting across the country against government repression. On October 2, a rally in a housing development called *Tlatelolco* ended with the death of a number of unarmed students at the hands of the army and the secret police. The number of casualties is still contested, ranging from 44 individuals identified by the National Security Archive, a non-governmental research institute based at George Washington University, to numbers as high as 200 or 300, in most sources.[25] After the massacre, several student leaders were sent to prison and many others went into hiding to avoid detention. In consequence, the movement itself faded.

However, though the student movement failed to achieve its immediate goals, it was very important for the development of social movements in contemporary Mexico because it was the first movement clearly directed at the state itself. In the short term, the protests demonstrated that there was significant demand for change that the government was not addressing. The student movement also had long-term effects. Many Mexicans consider the 1968 movement as the beginning of the end for the PRI, and the start of Mexico's long transition to democracy. Some of the movement's participants remained politically active, planting the seeds for organized opposition to the regime. After the protests, PRI leaders realized that they had to work hard to restore the legitimacy of their regime, and tried to do this by allowing greater expression of discontent. As noted, in the 1970s the PRI passed a series of electoral reforms that leveled the playing field somewhat in favor of opposition parties, and it eased censorship, allowing the formation of several opposition newspapers and magazines.

The 1985 Earthquake and Beyond A second important moment in the evolution of social movements in contemporary Mexico came in the 1980s. In the aftermath of the 1982 debt crisis, Mexicans had started to show clear signs of discontent at the slowing economy and the marked increase in unemployment. This was obvious, for example, in the midterm elections in 1985 that saw the PRI losing important ground to the PAN and other opposition parties. In this context, the 1985 earthquake caused both immense physical damage, especially in Mexico City, as well as damage to the PRI government's reputation and legitimacy. More than 1,500 buildings were destroyed or damaged and an estimated 10,000 people died in the earthquake.[26] The government's response was slow, prompting accusations of corruption and inefficiency in the delivery of aid. Citizens took the initiative and organized much of the rescue effort themselves. Many of these groups of citizens had already staged mobilizations against worsening economic conditions and now they came together to protest government inefficiency. These groups—which included neighborhood associations and other grassroots organizations—remained active in the months and years after the earthquake and extended their demands beyond the government's inability to deliver better services, to include demands for cleaner elections and a more democratic political system.[27]

The presidential elections of 1988 provided an opportunity for many of these groups to rally around the newly formed Frente Democrático Nacional, a federation of small parties that supported the presidential candidacy of Cuauhtémoc Cárdenas and that would become the PRD. The PRI candidate won, but many Mexicans believed he did so only by manipulating the electoral results. Mexicans across the country took to the streets in the aftermath of the election to protest, organizing events that included a protest in Mexico City with more than 200,000 participants. In contrast to 1968, years of economic stagnation and the disastrous response to the earthquake had so undermined the PRI's legitimacy that by 1988 the government could no longer afford to simply repress the protests. Social movements had grown in size and organization, making it harder for the PRI to control the expression of dissent. Increased political competition at home and scrutiny from abroad further tied the PRI's hands in dealing with growing discontent.

In short, by 1988 citizens felt much more capable, and had more opportunities to mobilize autonomously from the state. Since that year social movements have proliferated. And as the variety of groups has increased, so have the tools that groups use to effect change. For example, in October 2009, a group of Twitter users organized a protest against a proposed tax on Internet usage, and managed to stop the proposal in its tracks. Yet as is the case with political parties, such creativity in organizing and mobilizing in civil society reflects both the advances and challenges facing democracy. On the one hand, the vibrancy of Mexican civil society reflects the end of the era of PRI dominance where formal and informal opposition was minimal. Yet on the other hand, as is the case around the world, social movements mirror the concerns Mexican citizens feel that their government is not meeting: issues of gender equality, environmental degradation, and government accountability, for example. In particular, as citizens have grown increasingly concerned with crime and personal security in recent years, they have organized groups such as Mexico United against Crime (*México Unido contra la Delincuencia*), the National Council for Public Security and Justice (*Consejo Ciudadano para la Seguridad Pública y la Justicia Penal*) formed in 2002, and SOS (*Sistema de Observación para la Seguridad Ciudadana*), formed in 2008 to bring attention to the issue and propose solutions. These and other organizations have been very active, organizing forums, informative sessions, and protests. The fact that citizens can mobilize is a plus, but the fact that they are drawing attention to their lack of faith in the government's effectiveness also highlights the continued challenges to effective and legitimate government in Mexico.

Frente Democrático Nacional (FDN) ■ coalition of left-wing parties and movements that got together to support the candidacy of Lázaro Cárdenas in the 1988 presidential election. Many of the groups that formed the FDN would go on to establish the PRD.

Interest Groups

The decline of the PRI's monopoly on political power has created new opportunities for interests groups to gain access to policymakers, but it has also taken away the guarantee that important interest groups would have access to the state. Here, we shall examine how democratization has affected the fate of three important interest groups: organized labor, business, and emigrants. For labor, democratization has meant new opportunities to form independent unions—but it has also meant the end of privileged access to policymakers. As a result, while new unions have proliferated, the labor movement is now much weaker than before relative to the political influence of business owners. For business, the opening up of politics has been less disruptive. Business was never as integrated into the PRI's structure as labor, and business leaders have proved agile in gaining access to leaders in all political parties. Consequently, business is currently in a much stronger position to shape policy than labor. Last, important interest groups have recently formed around emigration. Millions of Mexicans have left the country in search of better opportunities north of the border. This group did not traditionally organize to press its demands on the state, but this situation too has changed since 2000.

Labor During the years of PRI dominance, labor was one of the pillars of the PRI's corporatist structure. Together with the PRI leadership, unions played an important role in managing economic policy and maintaining social stability. Labor leaders participated in wage negotiations, and representatives of labor were guaranteed a certain number of seats in the Legislature. In exchange, labor leaders used their influence to prevent workers from openly opposing the government's policies and from organizing unsanctioned strikes. Because they were guaranteed such benefits, labor leaders had no incentives to seek out new union members, and no interest in opposing the government's policies. This made unions under the PRI largely docile instruments of government power, designed to control workers rather than to represent their interests and press their demands on the state.

The combination of economic reform and increased political competition in the 1990s changed the nature of the relationship between the state and organized labor. The central element of these economic reforms was a reduction of the state's role in the economy. Privatization of state-owned enterprises in particular reduced the government's control over employment and wage levels. Cuts in government spending also reduced the resources the government could use to maintain the loyalty of labor leaders and the support of workers. PRI leaders also implemented a series of reforms that undercut the influence of labor within the party.

These changes had two different effects. On the one hand, they not surprisingly tended to weaken unions' power to mobilize workers and press for workers' interests. As the importance of unions declined both within the economy and within the party, so did their membership. Yet on the other hand, as the PRI's hold over unions declined, alternative independent unions began to emerge, taking advantage of the cracks in the corporatist organization of Mexican politics.

Independent unions had existed during the PRI's hegemony, but because the PRI did not recognize them as "officially sanctioned" unions, they had practically no access to the state's resources and so remained very weak. The context for labor mobilization changed substantially in the 1980s and 1990s, opening opportunities for labor unions that until then had remained closed. For example, in 1997 the National Union of Workers (*Unión Nacional del Trabajo,* UNT) was created as a competitor for the Labor Congress (*Congreso del Trabajo,* CT), an umbrella association of labor groups affiliated with the PRI. By 2002, the UNT was composed of more than 160 independent labor federations and unions, and it had formed a collaborative relationship with the leftist PRD that guaranteed UNT leaders spots on the party's slate of legislative candidates. The labor movement gained additional autonomy in 1999 when the Supreme Court ruled that government employees could join independent unions.

Although democratization, the decline of the PRI, and legal changes in the status of unions have given workers more options to organize and press their demands, labor's power remains limited in present-day Mexico. Employers frequently try to corrupt union leaders so that they will not faithfully represent their members' demands. In addition, high unemployment rates have left many formerly unionized workers willing to work for lower wages and without union representation. Finally, the opening up of opportunities for union organizing has caused bitter disputes within the labor movement, as unions vie for political credibility and membership. These divisions have served to weaken workers' voices and have limited the extent to which unions can meet the demand for workers' representation. In sum, recent developments have reduced workers' faith in new democratic institutions.

Business The organization of business interests had some similarities with labor under the PRI. On the one hand, the government mandated that employers and business owners had to be members of the association in their economic sector, such as the Confederation of National Chambers of Commerce (*Confederación de Cámaras Nacionales de Comercio,* CONCANACO) or the Confederation of Chambers of Industry (*Confederación de Cámaras de la Industria,* CONCAMIN). And like labor, the PRI also invited major business leaders to participate together with the government and labor in negotiations over major economic policy changes.

Yet, on the other hand, in contrast to the PRI's relationship with labor and peasants, business was never formally a part of the party's corporatist structure. This relative autonomy gave business leaders a certain degree of independence from the PRI. Thus, when the government needed big business' support—as when the PRI sought to pass NAFTA in 1994—it offered business leaders prominent roles in the negotiations. This tended to ensure that business' interests were protected. Yet when the government sought to enact policies that business opposed—for example, the government's takeover of large banks in 1982—business was also able to voice loud opposition. Such autonomy did not always translate into influence. However, the interests of the PRI and of business leaders most often coincided, and this gave business leaders few incentives to object to the PRI's policies.

A big change in the relationship between business and the government came in 1997, when the Supreme Court decided that compulsory membership in business interest groups was unconstitutional. Because many business owners felt that membership in a business interest group no longer offered any advantage in terms of being able to lobby the government, business interest group membership began to decline sharply. Interest groups were forced to innovate in terms of their activities and seek out new members. And after the PRI lost its legislative majority in 1997, business groups for the first time began directly lobbying the Mexican Legislature. With the increase in political competition, business leaders also saw opportunities outside of the PRI, and began to lobby other political parties as well, especially the center-right PAN.[28]

Since Mexico's transition to democracy, business has gained political influence, in particular relative to labor. In a country that has struggled with both slow economic growth and huge inequalities, this trend does little to reassure the population at large that the democratic system is effective in delivering policies and programs that will improve their economic and social situation.

Emigrants Between February 2008 and February 2009, it is estimated that more than 600,000 Mexicans migrated to the United States, though the number fluctuates with the state of the U.S. economy.[29] The migration is fueled mostly by the large wage disparity between the two countries, and strongly suggests that the Mexican government has been unable to effectively provide for many citizens. Mexicans who emigrate live in political limbo; among the Mexicans who reside in the United States, more than half are there illegally and, thus, have no political rights or representation in that country. And until recently, Mexican migrants also could not vote in Mexican elections either, unless they returned to Mexico to cast their vote. In contrast to labor or business, Mexican emigrants have not been very effective in organizing to press their demands on the Mexican state. The most obvious reason, of course, is that they are not in Mexico to do it, but also that they come from very different communities across Mexico and that they migrate to places all across the United States.

However, half of those Mexicans who leave the country eventually return to Mexico.[30] Moreover, emigrants in the United States send billions of dollars back to their families, and so have a huge impact on Mexico's economy. In 2008, for example, migrants in the United States sent back more than $25 billion—Mexico's second largest source of foreign exchange after oil! With the increase in political competition in recent years, the view towards migrants has also changed. Politicians from all parties realized that not only did returnees vote in elections at home but also that Mexicans abroad often have tremendous influence on how their family members vote. In order to attract this group of potential voters, policies were instituted geared at facilitating the re-insertion of migrants to life in Mexico and at utilizing the money that they send for development projects. The most prominent of these programs—the "3 × 1" program—was instituted by PAN president Vicente Fox in 2002. The program seeks to capitalize on remittances by matching funds provided by migrant associations for local infrastructure projects with funds from the federal, state, and local governments; migrant associations provide a fourth of the funds and the government provides the rest. Since migrant associations propose the projects and share the costs, the program has the potential of giving these organizations great influence and clout in their local communities. Additionally, migrants living in the United States were given the right to vote in

Mexican elections in 2005, thus explicitly recognizing them as active members of the political system. In the 2006 presidential election only about 32,000 Mexicans abroad voted, out of over 4 million who were eligible, limiting the potential impact and influence of this group on the election. However, it is yet too soon to judge the potential impact of these changes.

A strong civil society that can channel citizens' demands is a prerequisite for effective and legitimate government. During the PRI regime, the representation of societal interests was largely accomplished through the party's corporatist organization. This meant that few important interest groups existed independently of the state. In the last two decades, this situation has changed radically. The most obvious change has come at the level of political parties, where competition has increased between the PRI, PAN, and PRD. These three parties hotly contest elections, from the presidency on down to the local level.

Increased competition and pluralism has also helped the development of Mexico's civil society, allowing new social movements and interest groups to form. New workers' unions, independent of the state, now compete with older PRI-run unions for membership and influence. Business has also had to find new political allies and search for new members. Even migrants, who traditionally had no representation, have started to organize more formally to make their voice heard. Finally, a variety of non-governmental organizations have sprung up around issues that include everything from the environment to gay marriage to taxes. In short, new groups have challenged existing political practices, pushing the state to adopt more democratic practices.

However, the years of centralized, corporatist, interest representation still echo in Mexican politics, hindering the effectiveness of civil society in channeling citizens' demands. Many interest groups—especially those created during the PRI regime—retain a centralized structure that inefficiently represents members' demands. In the context of divided government, political parties have not been able to generate a consensus about the issues that Mexicans care about. In consequence, Mexicans have lost faith in parties and have instead turned to alternative forms of political expression. It is in part because of the inability of interest groups and parties to represent the interests of Mexicans effectively that social movements and non-governmental organizations have flourished in recent years. Where Mexicans perceive that the government fails (security, for example), they have turned to a variety of forms of protest (through social networks, for example).

CONCLUSION

At the height of its dominance, the PRI established what Peruvian writer Mario Vargas Llosa called the "perfect dictatorship"—a combination of democratic and authoritarian practices that guaranteed stable, effective government with minimal overt repression.[31] This dictatorship eventually revealed its imperfections, as the PRI's support gradually waned. The question that Mexico faces today, a decade after the transfer of power from the PRI to the PAN, is how to guarantee stable, effective, and legitimate government in a fully democratic context.

SUMMARY TABLE

Interests: Shaping Politics in a New Context

Interest Groups — During the years of one-party rule, unions, business associations, and other interest groups were very closely associated with the state. However, in a context of increased competition and pluralism, a variety of new and autonomous interest groups, including independent unions, emerged that push the state to adopt more democratic practices.

Political Parties — Although Mexican politics was dominated by a single party, the PRI, throughout the twentieth century, two other parties, the conservative PAN and the left-wing PRD, grew to occupy important spaces in the legislature as well as state and local politics. Today, these three parties share power and compete intensely for elected positions.

Social Movements — With the demise of the PRI as the chief venue for the expression of demands, social movements have emerged as a significant part of Mexican politics. Protests are organized around issues as diverse as teacher's rights, indigenous autonomy, and gay marriage. In recent years, people have also built organizations and arranged marches to protest against violence and the security situation.

Mexico has made huge advances since the days of the perfect dictatorship. Free and open political participation and vigorous contestation are now the rules of the game. Reforms have made political institutions more accountable. In particular, the legislature and the judiciary are no longer rubber-stamps, but are now independent institutions with the ability to check the power of other branches. Political reforms have also helped ensure that new political parties will be able to compete, and that voters who wish to express their political opinions will find an outlet for their voice. Elections today are highly competitive, and mostly free and fair. Finally, Mexican citizens today can express all sorts of interests and concerns through movements and groups that are no longer tethered to the state but are instead free to press their demands. In short, much has been done to guarantee limited government.

But limited government does not itself guarantee effective government—that is, it does not mean that the government can effectively solve the problems that citizens face. In the context of increased political and social pluralism, consensus in the legislature has been hard to come by, impeding action on a range of issues such as reform to the police and the energy sector, and has made rooting corruption out very difficult. For example, the police and judiciary are more independent, but both remain plagued by corruption. This has made it very hard to address the recent wave of violent crime. And although new paths for independent interest representation have opened up, some groups still find it difficult to make themselves heard. In particular, efforts at an inclusive citizenship will not be complete while indigenous groups continue to be marginalized economically and politically.

Perhaps an encouraging sign on the horizon is the growth of independent organizations and social movements in recent years, many of which have been formed to press the state to solve some of these issues. For example, the campaign for the annulment of the vote in the 2009 midterm election was prompted both by disillusionment with the way democratic institutions work in Mexico and by a strong sense that independent, democratically organized collective action might force political actors to listen to citizens' demands. ▲

KEY TERMS

Partido Revolucionario Institucional (PRI)   236
Tenochtitlán   237
criollos   240
mestizo   240
War of Independence   240
caudillos   240
Mexican–American War   240
Treaty of Guadalupe Hidalgo   240
Mexican Revolution   241
1917 Constitution   242
Corporatism   243
no-re-election clause   243
state-led economic development   244

Mexican Miracle   244
North American Free Trade Agreement (NAFTA)   246
Chamber of Deputies   246
Federal Electoral Institute (IFE)   247
National Action Party (PAN)   248
divided government   251
Senate   251
Supreme Court   252
mestizaje   259
Zapatista Army of National Liberation (EZLN)   262
Party of the Democratic Revolution   262
Frente Democrático Nacional (FDN)   268

REVIEW QUESTIONS

1. How did the PRI manage to stay in power so long?
2. Was the economy an important factor in the decline of the PRI?
3. Was civil society an important factor in the decline of the PRI?
4. Do you think that political elites (leaders of political parties, members of the government) played the leading role in Mexico's transition to democracy or were social movements and civil society more important?
5. Why do you think Mexicans express discontent with the way democracy works in Mexico?

SUGGESTED READINGS

Bethell, Leslie, ed. *Mexico since Independence.* Cambridge: Cambridge University Press, 1991. This edited volume brings together some of the most important scholars who have studied Mexico. Each chapter deals with an important phase of Mexican history, from independence to the formation of the PRI authoritarian regime.

Collier, Ruth Berins. *The Contradictory Alliance: State-Labor Relations and Regime Change in Mexico.* Berkeley: University of California Press, 1992. Analyzes the relationship between labor and the PRI and the importance of this relationship in the development of the PRI and the political history of Mexico.

Krauze, Enrique. *Mexico: Biography of Power*. New York: HarperCollins, 1997. Uses biographies of political leaders, particularly presidents but also revolutionary *caudillos* like Francisco Villa or Emiliano Zapata, to explain Mexican history.

Levy, Daniel, and Kathleen Bruhn. *Mexico: The Struggle for Democratic Development*. Berkeley: Univ. of California Press, 2002. This book focuses on contemporary Mexico. The authors explore the relationship between economic development and democratic development and how the tradeoff between stability and economic growth has shaped Mexico's development.

Magaloni, Beatriz. *Voting for Autocracy: Hegemonic Party Survival and Its Demise in Mexico*. Cambridge: Cambridge University Press, 2006. Explains how the PRI maintained power through a combination of patronage and elections.

Peschard-Sverdrup, Armand B., and Sara Rioff. *Mexican Governance: From Single-Party Rule to Divided Government*. Washington, D.C.: CSIS Press, Center for Strategic and International Studies, 2005. This edited book covers the transition from a single-party to a competitive, multi-party system. Each chapter analyzes the transformation of an institution, including the legislature, the judiciary, and the military.

Preston, Julia, and Samuel Dillon. *Opening Mexico: The Making of a Democracy*. New York: Farrar, Straus & Giroux, 2004. Preston and Dillon are journalists with broad experience in Mexico. This book includes anecdotes and firsthand accounts of important events in Mexico's political development and its path towards democracy, including the 1968 student movement, the 1985 earthquake, and the 1988 election.

NOTES

1. In December 2010, 54 percent of Mexicans thought that criminal organizations, and not the government, were winning the war against drugs. "Encuesta/ Perciben mas crimen," *Reforma*, published on December 1, 2010.
2. Rudiger Dornbusch, Alejandro Werner, Guillermo Calvo, and Stanley Fischer, "Mexico: Stabilization, Reform, and No Growth," Brookings Papers on Economic Activity, 1994, 1 (1994), 253–315.
3. For data on inflation, see Fabrice Lehoucq et al., "Political Institutions, Policymaking Processes, and Policy Outcomes in Mexico," Inter-American Development Bank, Research Network Working Paper #R-512, September 2005.
4. The official death toll was 32; however, most witnesses agreed that the number of victims numbered in the hundreds. See Kate Doyle, "The Dead of Tlatelolco," National Security Archive at the George Washington University, at http://www.gwu.edu/~nsarchiv/NSAEBB/NSAEBB201/index.htm.
5. Lehoucq et al. (2005).
6. "Encuesta / Ven mayor corrupción en Gobierno," *Reforma*, published on November 20, 2009.
7. http://www.transparency.org/policy_research/surveys_indices/cpi/2010/results.
8. Data reported in newspaper *Reforma*, from different sources including Encuesta Internacional sobre Criminalidad y Victimización, ICESI, CIDE, CIDAC, Fomento de Cultura Económica, SSP, Foro Económico Mundial.
9. http://www.icesi.org.mx/documentos/publicaciones/cuadernos/cuaderno_5.pdf, Instituto Ciudadano de Estudios sobre la Inseguridad (ICESI).
10. "Encuesta / Cuestionan bajas por guerra a narco," *Reforma*, published on September 1, 2010.
11. "Encuesta / Ven mayor corrupción en Gobierno," *Reforma*, published on November 20, 2009.

12. http://www.cartercenter.org/documents/278.pdf.
13. On the campaign finance system, see Eduardo Guerrero, "Fiscalización y Transparencia del Financiamiento a Partidos Políticos y Campañas Electorales: Dinero y Democracia," Serie: Cultura de la Rendición de Cuentas, Auditoría Superior de la Federación (2003). Campaign Finance Law, Electoral Competition, and Economic Policy. Ph.D. Dissertation, George Mason University, May 2006.
14. Eduardo Guerrero (2003).
15. Anne Doremus, "Indigenism, Mestizaje, and National Identity in Mexico during the 1940s and the 1950s," Mexican Studies / Estudios Mexicanos, Vol. 17, No. 2 (Summer 2001), 375–402.
16. Doremus (2001).
17. Guillermo De la Pena, "A New Mexican Nationalism? Indigenous Rights, Constitutional Reform and the Conflicting Meanings of Multiculturalism," *Nations and Nationalism*, 12 (2) (2006), 279–302.
18. See Deborah J. Yashar, *Contesting Citizenship in Latin America: The Rise of Indigenous Movements and the Postliberal Challenge* (Cambridge: Cambridge University, 1995); De la Pena (2006).
19. See Consolidating Mexico's Democracy. The 2006 Presidential Campaign in Comparative Perspective edited by Jorge I. Domínguez, Chappell Lawson, and Alejandro Moreno, The John Hopkins University Press, 2009.
20. See Joy Langston, "Rising from the Ashes? Reorganizing the PRI's State Party Organizations after Electoral Defeat," *Comparative Political Studies* 36, no. 3 (2003), 293–318.
21. See Kathleen Bruhn. *Taking on Goliath: The Emergence of a New Left Party and the Struggle for Democracy in Mexico* (University Park, PA: Penn State University Press, 1991).
22. See Joy Langston, "Strong Parties in a Struggling Party System; Mexico in the Democratic Era," in *Party Politics in New Democracies,* Paul Webb and Stephen White, eds. (Oxford: Oxford University Press, 2007).
23. "Encuesta / Ven mayor corrupción en Gobierno," *Reforma,* published on November 20, 2009.
24. Encuesta Nacional sobre el Sentir Ciudadano, conducted by IPN, Fundación Este País and ITAM, see http://www.desarrollopolitico.gob.mx/Portal/publicaciones/publicaciones_53.pdf.
25. See Matthew C. Gutmann, *The Romance of Democracy: Compliant Defiance in Contemporary Mexico*. (Berkeley, University of California Press, 2002).
26. See Guillermo Soberón, Julio Frenk, and Jaime Sepúlveda, "The Health Care Reform in Mexico: Before and After the 1985 Earthquakes," *American Journal of Public Health*, Vol. 76, No. 6 (June 1986).
27. See Diane E. Davis, *Urban Leviathan: Mexico City in the Twentieth Century* (Philadelphia: Temple University Press, 1994).
28. Business Politics and the State in 20th Century Latin America. New York: Cambridge University Press, 2004.
29. See http://pewhispanic.org/files/reports/112.pdf.
30. Gordon Hanson, "Illegal Migration from Mexico to the United States," *Journal of Economic Literature,* Vol. XLIV (December 2006), 869–924.
31. Vargas Llosa used this expression while participating on a televised panel in Mexico in August 1990.

Russia

Graeme Robertson

CHAPTER 8

Traditional dolls showing Russia's leaders from the communist era to today. Though much has changed since the

> **?** Why has Russia failed to consolidate democracy, remaining in many ways an authoritarian regime?

INTRODUCTION TO RUSSIA

Read and Listen to Chapter 8 at mypoliscilab.com

Study and Review the Pre-Test & Flashcards at mypoliscilab.com

In 1991, Russia was part of a larger country know as the Soviet Union, or more formally, the Union of Soviet Socialist Republics (USSR). A single-party communist regime, the USSR had been locked since the end of World War II in the Cold War, an intense political, economic, and military competition with the capitalist democracies in Western Europe, North America, and Japan. However, in the 1980s, the Soviet system entered a period of rapid change. Soviet president Mikhail Gorbachev cut the USSR's military capacity and worked with U.S. presidents Ronald Reagan and George H. W. Bush to end the Cold War. Gorbachev allowed democratic change to sweep across the formerly communist dictatorships in Eastern Europe and sought to bring political and economic reform to his own country. Gorbachev's reforms ultimately led to the Soviet Union itself falling apart, and, in 1991, Russia became a separate and independent country, led by a president, Boris Yeltsin, who promised prosperity and democratic government to his people.

Fast forward to 2007. That year, Western leaders accused then President Vladimir Putin of taking Russia down the path towards dictatorship. Putin was accused of stifling free speech, allowing the murder of muckraking journalists, monopolizing mass media channels, and manipulating elections. Yet, although Putin was unpopular—even feared—in the West, in Russia he was extremely popular. According to opinion polls, his approval rating consistently topped 70 percent. Thousands of young people demonstrated on Moscow's streets in support of their president and a Russian girl band even had a hit song about looking for "A Man Like Putin." His political party won 64 percent of the vote in parliamentary elections that year, though international observers condemned those elections as unfair.

What happened? Why has liberal democracy not taken root in Russia, and why does the current system that mixes elections with manipulation and repression seem so stable? When the Soviet Union collapsed in 1991, pessimists skeptical about Russia's prospects for building democracy were largely outnumbered by optimists who expected Russia to join the former communist states of Eastern Europe, such as Poland, Hungary, and the Czech Republic, which had already made great progress in the simultaneous introduction of capitalism and democracy. However, in the decades that have passed since then, the gap between the countries of Eastern Europe and the other former communist states such as Russia has grown larger, not smaller. In this chapter, we will explore the question of *why has Russia failed to consolidate democracy, remaining in many ways an authoritarian regime.* The main factors that account for Russia's turn toward non-democracy include a historical legacy of political centralization and non-democracy; contemporary political institutions that centralize power rather than promote limited government; the difficulty of maintaining order in a vast territory and diverse population; and the consequences of economic reforms implemented in the 1990s that led many Russians into poverty. Although Russia is now mostly stable and living standards have improved since the 1990s, Russian leaders have continued to focus on consolidating a powerful centralized government rather than building democracy.

This outcome is extremely important, and not just for Russia and the Russians. While Russia is no longer a global superpower, it remains an extremely important player in global affairs whose policies matter enormously to the United States, China, Europe, and others. For geographical and political reasons Russia's influence is strong in the United Nations and other global bodies, and it plays a crucial role in negotiations with potential and actual nuclear powers like North Korea and Iran. Moreover, Russia's own stockpiles of nuclear weapons dwarf those of any country except the United States. Russia is also central to efforts to limit the spread of drugs, organized crime, and political instability, especially in and around Afghanistan and the Middle East. Last, but by no means least, Russia's reserves of oil, gas, and key natural resources make it a vital economic partner, especially for Europeans.

HISTORICAL OVERVIEW OF RUSSIA

Russia is the largest country in the world—almost twice as big as the second largest country, Canada—stretching more than 4,000 miles and 11 time zones from its western boundary with Poland to its most eastern point on Ratmanov Island, only 2.4 miles from the United States. This immense country is also one of the world's most extreme in terms of climate. In summer, tourists flock to the sub-tropical beaches of Black Sea resorts like Sochi. Further north and further east lie some of the coldest inhabited places on earth, such as the village of Oymyakon in the Sakha Republic, with recorded winter temperatures below minus 90 Fahrenheit. Bounded by oceans to the north and east, and mountains and desert to the south, Russia is largely a flat land of forests, swamps, fertile farmland, and arctic tundra.

8.1 What are the historical precedents for democracy or authoritarianism in Russia?

Watch the Video "Churchill's Iron Curtain Speech" at mypoliscilab.com

Watch the Video "Nuclear Disarmament Under the INF Treaty" at mypoliscilab.com

Watch the Video "August 1991: The Collapse of the Soviet Union" at mypoliscilab.com

Geography and the Formation of the Russian State

The beginnings of the Russian state are traditionally traced back to the city of Kyiv (now the capital of Russia's neighbor, Ukraine) around the year 1000. However, Kyiv is located in the relatively open and flat grassland to Russia's south, and so was vulnerable to attack from nomadic warrior tribes. Consequently, the center of Russian politics gradually moved to a better-protected city to the north: Moscow. Through a mixture of marriage, trade, and violence, Moscow slowly achieved dominance over neighboring principalities, and in 1547, Ivan IV became the first Russian monarch to receive the title of tsar, or emperor. Ivan became known to history as "Ivan the Terrible" because he presided over an enormous expansion of Moscow's empire, subjugating nomadic tribes to the south and east, and slowly conquering Swedish-held lands to the north and west. Russian expansion continued with such remarkable success that by the beginning of World War I in 1914, the empire included most of present-day Ukraine, Belarus, Moldova, Finland, Estonia, Latvia, Lithuania, and parts of Poland to the west; Armenia, Azerbaijan, Georgia, and parts of Turkey to the south; and Kazakhstan, Kyrgyzstan, Tajikistan, Turkmenistan, Uzbekistan to the east. For a time, the Russian Empire even claimed Alaska.

RUSSIA

RUSSIA IN COMPARISON

	United Kingdom	Germany	France	Japan	India	Mexico	Russia	Nigeria	China	Iran
Freedom House Classification	Democracy	Democracy	Democracy	Democracy	Democracy	Partial democracy	Partial democracy	Partial democracy	Non-democracy	Non-democracy
Land Size (sq km)	243,610	357,022	643,801	377,915	3,287,263	1,964,375	17,098,242	923,768	9,596,961	1,648,195
Land Size Ranking	79	62	42	61	7	15	1	32	4	18
Population (July 2011 Estimate)	62,698,362	81,471,834	65,312,249	126,475,664	1,189,172,906	113,724,226	138,739,892	155,215,573	1,336,718,015	77,891,220
Population Ranking	22	16	21	10	2	11	9	8	1	18
Life Expectancy (Years)	80.1	80.1	81.2	82.3	66.8	76.5	66.3	47.6	74.7	70.1
Life Expectancy Ranking	28	27	13	5	51	72	162	220	95	146
Literacy Rate	99%	99%	99%	99%	61%	86.1%	99.4%	68%	91.6%	77%
GDP Per Capita (2010 Estimate)	US$35,100	US$35,900	US$33,300	US$34,000	US$3,500	US$13,800	US$15,900	US$2,500	US$7,600	US$11,200
GDP Ranking	36	32	39	38	163	85	71	178	126	100

How did Russia get so big? The growth and dominance of the Russian state was largely the result of its superior military and political organization, which allowed it to subjugate its neighbors. With each stage of expansion, Moscow's relative advantage in power grew, allowing further expansion. The region's physical geography also played a role in Russia's growth. The flat, open terrain and lack of natural borders between regions meant that the Russian state could expand almost limitlessly.

Russia's tremendous size has proven to be a double-edged sword. While the empire was truly vast, for most of its history Russia has been a relatively poor society. Much of the land is infertile, with enormous areas of forest and swamp that are unconnected by roads and situated in the vast cold north, with rivers that flow toward the North Pole rather than in an east–west direction, which would have facilitated commerce and trade. Russia's great size continues to hobble its economic development to this day: As recently as 2009, Russian president Dmitri Medvedev announced the planned completion of the first road system that would connect Russia completely from east to west.

Moreover, as the Russian Empire expanded, it incorporated a diverse array of different ethnic, language, and religious groups. Moscow's ability to impose its political will over these groups has fluctuated over time, and the difficulties such efforts involved have often pushed the country's rulers to prioritize effective over limited government—even though the result has sometimes been that government has been neither limited nor effective. Moreover, as the Russian Empire expanded, it increasingly came into conflict with the economically and politically more advanced Western European powers, and eventually with the United States. In these conflicts, the same geographical features that allowed the empire to expand also made Russia vulnerable to invasion, especially from its European neighbors to the west.

Over the centuries, the pressure to compete militarily and economically has caused recurring debates among Russian elites about what political direction Russia should follow. Three broad camps can be identified in these debates: liberals, conservatives, and radicals. Liberals have traditionally favored integration with Western Europe and the adoption of European political and cultural practices. The liberal camp is most famously associated with Emperor Peter the Great, who moved Russia's capital from Moscow to St. Petersburg in 1713 in an attempt to bring Russia closer to Europe. In recent years, liberals have supported the introduction of a market economy, integration into European institutions, and close cooperation with the United States and the other Western powers in foreign policy.

In contrast, conservatives in Russia have long argued against integration with the West, believing instead that Russia should follow its own distinct path, given its particular historical and cultural traditions. Historically, this group was associated with leaders of Russia's Orthodox Church and with wealthy landowners. In today's Russia, conservatism is associated with the Putin and Medvedev administrations, who favor a mix of state control and market economics, a distinctive national political system that is not consciously modeled on Western democratic institutions, and a foreign policy that cooperates and competes with the West on a case-by-case basis.

Finally, a radical group, influenced by Karl Marx and homegrown Russian thinkers, has argued in favor of various utopian schemes by which Russia could break out of its relative weakness. This third group, which brought together intellectuals in the major cities with the emerging urban working class in the early twentieth century, formed a faction known as the Bolsheviks and led the Russian Revolution in 1917. The Bolshevik faction was renamed the Russian Communist Party in 1918. In post-communist Russia, a small radical fringe remains, but it is isolated and largely invisible in mainstream politics.

The Russian Revolution and the Rise of the USSR

In 1914, World War I broke out in Europe involving Great Britain, Germany, France, Russia, and many others. Although the devastation resulting from the war hurt every country involved, the effects were felt perhaps most of all in Russia, where military defeat and economic crisis led to an almost total breakdown of political and social order. In the chaos that followed, an uprising in February 1917 in the imperial capital Petrograd (now known as St. Petersburg) led to the collapse of Russia's centuries-old monarchy. The tsarist regime was replaced by a provisional government, which was in turn overthrown by the Bolshevik Party led by Vladimir Lenin later the same year. The Great October Socialist Revolution, as this event was known, was followed by a civil war in which the Communists slowly established their control over most of the Russian Empire, founding the newly named Union of Soviet Socialist Republics (USSR) in 1922.

Having secured control of the state, the revolutionaries confronted the challenge of remaking Russian society along communist lines—a challenge compounded by the fact that Russia was still a largely agrarian society with a weak industrial base and had been devastated by nearly a decade of war. Lenin died in 1924 and Joseph Stalin steadily established himself as the primary leader of the Communist Party. Stalin set about constructing an entirely new economic and political system, quite different from the one that existed under Lenin. In economics, Stalinist-style communism came to mean state ownership of almost all productive assets, including land, industry, and infrastructure; a program of government-directed industrialization; collectively owned and operated farms; and the substitution of the market for setting prices and regulating supply and demand with a vast system of centralized economic planning.

Along with the centrally planned economy, the revolutionaries established a political system in which power was concentrated in the hands of the top leaders of the Communist Party of the Soviet Union. All other political parties were banned, and dissenting political opinions were repressed. During Stalin's rule (1926–1953), the state engaged in widespread human rights violations against millions of Soviet citizens. The worst came in a period known as the Great Terror (1936–1938) when torture, execution, and imprisonments in state detention centers, known as the "Gulag," were widespread. The repression touched many different kinds of people, including key officials in the Communist Party itself, and loyal Soviet citizens who were members of social groups deemed by the regime to be suspect.

For all its brutality and waste, the Stalinist model of communism brought considerable economic progress. By the late 1960s, despite suffering colossal losses during World War II, the Soviet Union was no longer an economic backwater. Communism had engineered astonishingly rapid industrialization, and during the Cold War, Russia was considered one of the world's great "superpowers," along with

communism ■ political doctrine that holds that the wealthy exploit workers and the poor under capitalist economic systems; that economic wealth should be redistributed as much as possible; and that a single, vanguard political party should direct the government and control the state.

Great October Socialist Revolution ■ Soviet name for the Bolshevik seizure of power in October 1917 that led to communist rule and the creation of the Soviet Union.

soviet ■ Russian word meaning "council," used for the main legislative assemblies of state in the USSR.

USSR ■ Union of Soviet Socialist Republics, also known as the Soviet Union. The name for the state officially formed in 1922 on the territory of the former Russian Empire.

the United States. The Soviet system successfully produced and distributed large quantities of products, dramatically improved living standards, and consolidated political control over the country's vast territory. The economy was transformed from one dominated by agriculture that had changed little in hundreds of years to one based on manufacturing, industry, and some amazingly advanced technologies. This once-backward state put the first satellite into orbit and the first human being in space, and built a military and nuclear arsenal to match even that of the United States. Furthermore, as a result of World War II, the USSR had overseen the imposition of communist rule across much of Eastern Europe, and many other countries around the world sought to copy the Soviet example as a way to industrialization and modernization. As a result, defenders of the Stalinist system might claim that it at least embodied "effective government," and one that represented a real challenge to the Western democratic model. In fact, for some in Russia today, the Stalin era remains a source of pride and some history textbooks in Russia today describe Stalin as "an efficient manager," much to the horror of human rights activists and former victims of repression.

However, the system had serious problems. In economics, while quantities of goods could be produced, quality was always a problem. Moreover, the communist economy, while good at concentrating resources on specific problems, had limited capacity to generate industrial and technological innovations and over time the return on investments made by the Soviet state began to decline. Politically, communist ideology and the government's reliance on centralized political control led to a very rigid political system that was unable to adapt quickly to changing circumstances. Moreover, the human rights violations of the Stalin era continued to be a feature of the communist system, albeit on a much smaller scale. This combination of repressive and artificially rigid politics along with clear economic problems led eventually to considerable disillusionment with communism, even among some senior party officials. Nevertheless, the Soviet political and economic system remained largely unchanged from 1945 to 1985.

Reform and the Collapse of the USSR

In 1985, there were few indications that change would come soon to the Soviet Union. Yet, in just seven years, Russia would hold free elections, launch radical economic reforms, and declare itself independent of its own former empire. While there were many factors affecting this process, the leadership of Soviet leader Mikhail Gorbachev, who ascended to power in 1985, played a large part.

Aware of growing economic inefficiencies, serious demographic problems related to low birth rates and high levels of alcoholism, and considerable disillusionment within the leadership with the path the USSR was on, Gorbachev was determined to reinvigorate Soviet communism both economically and politically. He began by trying to intensify the pace of planned development, but quickly turned to introducing partial elements of a market economy. This program of economic reforms he called *perestroika*, a Russian word meaning "restructuring." Some private business in the form of cooperatives was permitted, while state-owned companies were given more autonomy from government plans. However, the piecemeal introduction of market

perestroika ■
Russian word meaning "restructuring," used by the last Soviet president, Mikhail Gorbachev, as a slogan for his economic reforms.

reforms led not to increased growth but to hoarding of goods, shortages, and rampant stealing from the state. Instead of curing the chronic problems of the Soviet economy, Gorbachev's reforms induced a full-scale economic crisis and real fear of food shortages, even in the major cities.

With his economic reforms failing, Gorbachev accelerated his efforts to reform the Soviet political system. Abroad, he made it clear that the USSR would no longer act to support the communist regimes in Eastern Europe. At home, frustrated by what he saw as efforts from within the Communist Party to block his economic program, Gorbachev launched a series of increasingly radical political reforms, collectively known by the Russian word glasnost, meaning "openness." These reforms began with allowing the publication of previously banned books and art and free discussion of sensitive periods in Soviet history, such as Stalin's repressions. Soon, reforms also came to include competitive elections to new parliaments in Moscow and the regions.

However, once again, Gorbachev's efforts backfired. Abandoning the communists in Eastern Europe led to a wave of revolutions in 1989 that brought down the Berlin Wall and swept communists from power in Poland, Hungary, Czechoslovakia, East Germany, and elsewhere, and dealt a major blow to the credibility of the communist project. Moreover, freer discussion of the past did much to damage support for the communists' record in office in the USSR itself. The introduction of elections with real competition led to the defeat of Communist Party candidates in many places, including in the capital, Moscow. This was something Gorbachev had expected, and to a certain extent had intended. However, he did not anticipate that an end to prohibitions on public protest would lead to the outbreak of nationalist movements in the Baltic regions and ethnic conflicts in the republics of Armenia, Azerbaijan, Georgia, and Kyrgyzstan. What emerged was a tide of nationalism and separatist sentiment in various parts of the USSR that forced Gorbachev to try to negotiate a new relationship between the central government and its constituent regions.

The Soviet Union had, technically, been a federation, though power in practice was heavily centralized. Faced with a major renegotiation that looked likely to lead to independence for some parts of the USSR, hardliners in the regime launched a coup in August 1991. The leader of the Russian Republic, Boris Yeltsin, and a few thousand others resisted and the coup plotters quickly backed down. In a bid for power, Yeltsin quickly moved to humiliate and sideline Gorbachev. Together with leaders from Ukraine and Belarus, Yeltsin signed a new treaty dissolving the USSR. On December 31, 1991, the famous hammer-and-sickle flag of the Soviet Union was lowered for the last time over the Kremlin, the castle in central Moscow that houses the Russian government. Russia, also now officially called the Russian Federation, was an independent state once more.

Russia's contemporary borders are much smaller than they had been under the pre-1917 tsarist system, and its population of about 150 million people is half that of the USSR. The new independent Russia was led by Boris Yeltsin, who had been elected president in June 1991 as part of the political reform process. Yeltsin came to power with the enthusiastic support of—and promises of assistance from—the United States and all the Western European powers. The demise of the

glasnost ■ Russian word meaning "openness," used by the last Soviet president, Mikhail Gorbachev, as a slogan for his political reforms.

Soviet Union had brought a quick and relatively bloodless end to the Cold War that had dominated world politics since 1945. By the early 1990s, democracy and capitalism, it appeared, had won. However, as we will see in the next sections, things turned out to be more complicated than that. Russia had virtually no experience or history of democratic government. Moreover, the new Russia inherited

SUMMARY TABLE

Historical Overview: Political Leadership in Russian History

1000–1500	Eastern Slavic City-States	Emergence of Kyiv and other Slavic city-states.
1547–1917	Russian Empire	Moscow's ruler Ivan IV, Ivan the Terrible, first claims title of tsar as Russian Empire expands to cover much of Eurasia.
February–March 1917	Beginning of Russian Revolution	Romanov tsar abdicates, replaced by the Provisional Government.
October 1917	Great October Socialist Revolution	Lenin and the Bolsheviks overthrow the Provisional Government in the name of the Soviets.
1918–1922/3	Civil War	War ends as Soviet government reestablishes control over most of former Russian Empire.
1924	Death of Vladimir Lenin	First Soviet leader dies.
1926–1953	Stalin Era	Stalin gradually emerged as the dominant leader after Lenin and built a new political system until his death in 1953.
1953–1964	Khrushchev Era	Nikita Khrushchev presides over period of "de-Stalinization" until he is removed from office by a vote of the Communist Party Central Committee.
1964–1982	Brezhnev Era	Height of Soviet power and of the Cold War under Leonid Brezhnev. Brezhnev died in office in 1982.
1982–1984	Andropov Period	KGB head Yuri Andropov takes over after Brezhnev's death, but dies unexpectedly in office.
1984–1985	Chernenko Interregnum	Aged Konstantin Chernenko takes over from Andropov but dies in office.
1985–1991	Gorbachev Era	Gorbachev's reforms end in collapse of communism and of the USSR in 1991.

an economy that was in crisis and that would need major and painful surgery in order to rebuild, a task made much more difficult by the lawlessness and weakness of state institutions that had become pervasive under Gorbachev.

INSTITUTIONS IN RUSSIA

In the early 1990s, the Russian state faced the enormous task of rebuilding almost all of its political institutions, most of which were designed for a communist system and were ill-suited for democratic governance. Moreover, unlike some of the East European communist states, Russia had little useable earlier experience to fall back on. After all, in its modern history, Russia had known only monarchy until 1917 and Communism until 1991. Russia's leaders were pressed to act quickly to adopt new institutions, but this process proved to be a truly daunting task full of trial and error. In this section, we see how initial efforts in the 1990s to shape strong institutions were undermined by the political and economic weakness of the Russian state in the aftermath of the collapse of Soviet power. However, as the economy recovered since 2000, the state has recouped much of its authority, and presidents have used their extensive powers, granted by the constitution, to centralize control over Russia's far-flung regions and to tighten the incumbent party's grip over the electoral process. This has resulted in a system in which most key officials are appointed by the incumbent president and his closest allies and where elections increasingly act to rubber-stamp choices made behind closed doors.

8.2 How have Russia's state institutions shaped the distribution of power today?

Explore the Comparative "Federal and Unitary Systems" at mypoliscilab.com

Constitutional Crisis 1992–1993

Foremost on the minds of political leaders in 1992 was the economic crisis they inherited. Gorbachev's economic reforms had lead to the collapse of the state system, a burgeoning black market and hoarding of goods in anticipation of future price rises. Together, these elements meant serious shortages of basic goods, and the international community rushed to ship food aid to the collapsing superpower—chicken drumsticks have been known in Russia as "Bush legs" ever since, in honor of then U.S. president George H. W. Bush.

Because addressing the economic crisis took priority, the question of building a new set of political institutions to govern the country was put on the backburner. In light of the emergency situation, the Russian parliament granted President Boris Yeltsin extraordinary powers to rule by decree—that is, without parliamentary assent. This centralized political power in Yeltsin's hands, giving him the authority to rush through a package of anti-crisis measures, including the immediate freeing of prices and removal of restrictions on economic activity. However, the immediate effect of these measures was to set off a round of hyper-inflation in which prices rose to more than 25 times their previous level in one year and industry ground almost to a halt. As a result, many members of parliament came to regret their decision to grant Yeltsin such great powers, and they attempted to win back control. Not surprisingly, Yeltsin resisted, and by the summer of 1993 a showdown between the president and the legislature seemed inevitable. In an effort to end the crisis once and for all, Yeltsin unilaterally declared parliament to be dissolved. The head of Russia's Constitutional Court,

Constitutional Court ■ determines and interprets whether legislative acts and presidential decrees are constitutional.

the equivalent of the U.S. Supreme Court, declared Yeltsin's action unconstitutional, and parliament then voted to impeach Yeltsin and to put the vice president in his place. In response, Yeltsin dispatched police units to surround the parliament building. After an 11-day siege, members of parliament and their supporters who had been trapped in the building broke through the police cordon and attempted to seize key government buildings in Moscow. After several tense hours, Yeltsin persuaded the Russian military to support him and ordered tanks to attack the Russian parliament building, right in the middle of downtown Moscow. Yeltsin's opponents soon capitulated. When the siege was over, somewhere between 187 (according to the government) and 1,000 people (according to parliamentary supporters) had been killed. But Yeltsin now had a free hand to impose his preferred set of political institutions.

The Constitution: President, Prime Minister, and Parliament

The constitution that provides the current institutional structure of Russian government was approved in a national referendum on December 12, 1993, though the referendum results were tainted by allegations of fraud. The shape of the constitution was heavily influenced by Yeltsin and his advisors' recent experience of conflict with the parliament, and as a result power is heavily concentrated in the hands of the president. As we will see in this section, the Russian president has more power to act unilaterally—without legislative approval—than most other presidents around the world—far more than the president of the United States, for example. The president is elected by universal suffrage to a six-year term (increased from four years starting with the president elected in 2012), and no president can serve more than two consecutive terms. The constitution also created a legislature, called the Federal Assembly, consisting of an upper house—called the **Federation Council**, to which two representatives of each of Russia's regions are sent—and a lower house, called the **Duma**, which consists of 450 representatives popularly elected for five-year terms.

Technically, Russia's system of government is **semi-presidential**, resembling the constitutional structure of France. That is, in addition to the president, there is a prime minister and cabinet who manage government affairs and who are appointed by the president and accountable to the Duma majority. However, the Russian president enjoys far greater unilateral constitutional authority than does the president of France, and his accountability to the Duma is limited. Russia's president has the power to both appoint and dismiss the prime minister and all the cabinet ministers. Although the president's prime ministerial nominee must win the confidence of a Duma majority, the president has the final word. That is, Article 111 of Russia's constitution states that if the Duma rejects the president's prime ministerial nominee three times in a row, the president must dissolve the Duma and call new elections. Since Duma members would much rather avoid risking their jobs in a new election, in practice this rule means that the president can choose the prime ministerial candidate of his choice. Imagine how different U.S. politics would be if the president could dissolve Congress when it rejected one of his nominees!

As in many other semi-presidential systems, the constitution does give parliament the power to vote "no-confidence" in the prime minister and his or her

Federation Council ■ upper house of the Russian parliament, consisting of two representatives of each region, one appointed by the regional governor and one by the regional parliament.

Duma ■ lower house of the Russian parliament, consisting of 450 representatives elected via national list proportional representation.

semi-presidential ■ political system with a directly elected president and a government headed by a prime minister who is responsible to an elected parliament.

TABLE 8.1

Presidents and Prime Ministers in Post-Communist Russia

President		Prime Minister	
Boris Yeltsin	July 1991–December 1999	Yegor Gaidar (acting)	June 1992–December 1992
		Viktor Chernomyrdin	December 1992–March 1998
		Sergei Kirienko	March 1998–August 1998
		Viktor Chernomyrdin	August 1998–September 1998
		Evgenii Primakov	September 1998–May 1999
		Sergei Stepashin	May 1999–August 1999
Vladimir Putin	December 1999–May 2000 (acting) May 2000–May 2008	Vladimir Putin	August 1999–May 2000
		Mikhail Kasianov	May 2000–February 2004
		Viktor Khristenko (acting)	February 2004–March 2004
		Mikhail Fradkov	March 2004–September 2007
		Viktor Zubkov	September 2007–May 2008
Dmitri Medvedev	May 2008–May 2012	Vladimir Putin	May 2008–May 2012

government. But in contrast to most other constitutions, the Russian constitution does not specify what happens if such a vote passes. Article 117 (3) states that if the Duma votes no-confidence in a prime minister twice within three months, then the president can chose either to fire the prime minister and his or her government, or to dissolve the Duma and call new elections. This means, as in France, that even if the parliament votes to censure the president's prime minister, the president remains in office and can influence the formation and dissolution of both the incumbent government and the parliament itself. Table 8.1 lists the presidents and prime ministers who have served in post-Communist Russia.

The constitution also contains several provisions that concentrate power in the office of the president, rather than creating a system of checks and balances by dispersing power across branches of government. For example, the constitution accords the president the authority to issue decrees that have the immediate effect of law as long as they do not contradict the constitution or existing federal law. President Yeltsin used this decree power more than 1,500 times. Some of Yeltsin's decrees merely funneled government expenditures to particular projects his allies requested. However, many decrees change government policy dramatically. For example, the laws that transformed Russia from a communist system into a market economy in 1992 were all passed by decree and did not involve any legislative input. Presidential decrees also served as the basis for Russia's launching of warfare in Chechnya in December 1994.

Power is further concentrated in the presidency because, although the Russian constitution provides for an independent judiciary in theory, it also gives the president considerable influence over the judicial branch of government and essentially makes the national prosecutor's office and the courts tools of the presidency. The president has the power to nominate the prosecutor-general, who in turn appoints lower-level prosecutors. While these appointment powers are not necessarily excessive in themselves, in practice there has been little effective separation of the executive and judiciary, and partial subordination of the courts and the prosecutor's office to the executive branch. This has meant a politicization of prosecutions that was evident under Yeltsin, but that increased under President Putin. Prosecutions have been used to silence government critics and to renationalize state property that had been (often illegally) sold off to private-sector investors.

Despite this clear centralization of power, it is important not to exaggerate the extent to which the Russian constitution gives the president unilateral power. Without a parliamentary majority, the president will encounter roadblocks, because, in the end, legislation passed through the Federal Assembly can override presidential decrees. Members of the Federal Assembly, like the president, the government, and regional assemblies, have the right to initiate legislation, though finance bills can only be introduced with the agreement of the government. Draft laws are introduced into the Duma and can be passed by a majority of all deputies (not just those in attendance and voting). Laws are then passed to the Federation Council, where they can be approved or rejected by half of the deputies there. Laws that have not been taken up for consideration within 14 days are considered passed, and a veto by the Federation Council can be overturned by a two-thirds majority of the Duma. Laws then pass to the president for signature, who has 14 days to exercise a veto. Presidential vetoes can be overturned by a two-thirds majority of both houses of the Federal Assembly.

Federalism

Like most large and diverse countries—the United States, Canada, India, or Mexico for example—Russia is also a federal system. Although most federal systems are originally designed to balance effective national government with some degree of local autonomy, in Russia the system was inherited from the USSR without any clear sense of how power should be distributed between the federal government and the regions. As a result, the division of powers has been the subject of

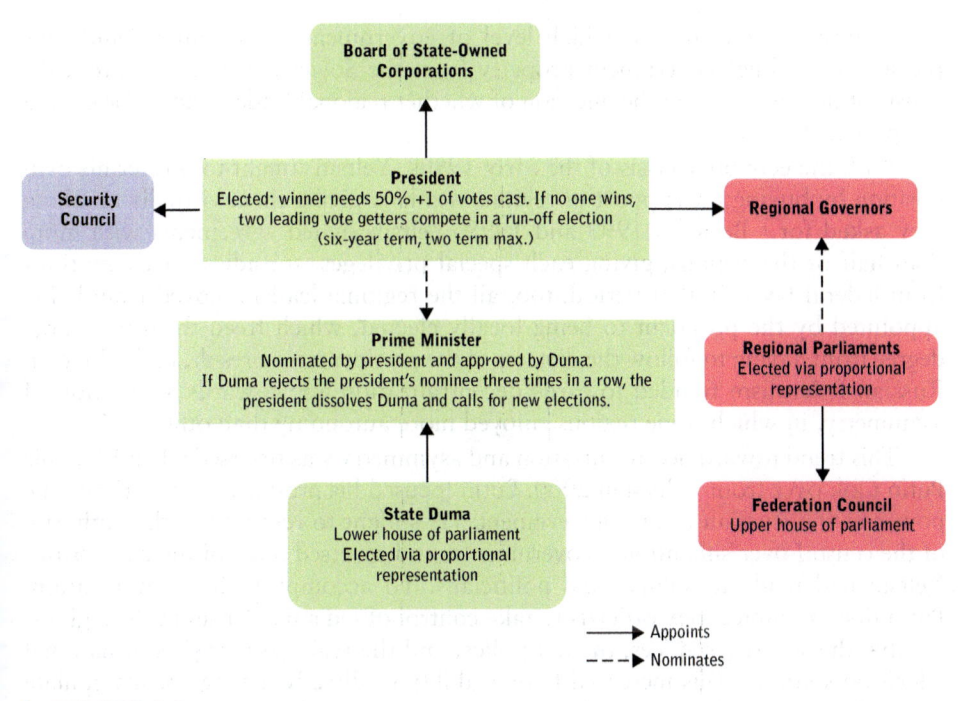

```
                    Board of State-Owned
                       Corporations
                            ↑
                            |
                        President
  Security       Elected: winner needs 50% +1 of votes cast. If no one wins,    Regional Governors
  Council    ←   two leading vote getters compete in a run-off election    →
                    (six-year term, two term max.)
                            |                                                        ↑
                            ↓                                                        |
                       Prime Minister                              Regional Parliaments
               Nominated by president and approved by Duma.       Elected via proportional
           If Duma rejects the president's nominee three times in a row, the   representation
               president dissolves Duma and calls for new elections.
                            ↑                                                        ↕
                            |
                       State Duma                                  Federation Council
                   Lower house of parliament                      Upper house of parliament
                   Elected via proportional
                       representation
```

⟶ Appoints
--▶ Nominates

FIGURE 8.1

The main institutions of government in Russia and patterns of appointment. Important parts of the Russian government are connected to one another by a system of appointments and nominations. This chart illustrates some of the main relationships. An arrow indicates, for example, that ultimate responsibility for appointing the prime minister lies with the state Duma but that the president also plays a key role by nominating (indicated by a line, not an arrow) the candidate for the prime minister's job.

continuing political debate and contestation. In contemporary Russia, the central government has come to dominate the sub-national units, resulting in an unusual degree of political centralization for a federal system of such size and diversity.

Russia inherited a federal structure from the Soviet Union that consists of 83 regions, each of which has status comparable to a state in the U.S. federal system. Under the Soviets, the system was federal mostly in name only, as the central government was generally able to impose its will over the regions through its power to hire and fire regional officials. When the USSR collapsed, it was not clear whether the Russian Republic's central government retained this authority or not, so leaders of Russia's subnational governments perceived an opportunity to seize more political power. Since 1992, Russia has witnessed a tug-of-war between the center and the regions over the balance of power in Russian federalism.

The 1993 constitution sought to centralize power. It enshrined the constitutional primacy of federal laws over provincial legislation (Article 4.2), as well as federal control over the entire judicial system (Article 71) and over foreign and defense policies (Article 71). However, the constitution was vague on important policy issues, including which level of government possessed the authority to tax natural resources such as oil, timber, or coal, and which level of government owned (and could thus profit from selling) government property from the Soviet era. Crucially, too, the constitution was silent on the question of whether regional leaders should be elected or appointed.

With the economic crisis of the early 1990s, Yeltsin sought to bolster his own position by buying the support of regional leaders, giving them virtually anything they asked for.[1] Between 1993 and 1998, Yeltsin signed agreements with more than half of the regions, giving each special privileges, subsidies, or exemptions from federal laws. In that period, too, all the regional leaders moved from being appointed by the president to being locally elected, which freed them to a large degree from having to follow the dictates of the president. As a result, under Yeltsin, Russian federalism trended towards decentralization and towards a situation of asymmetry, in which some regions enjoyed more autonomy than others.

This trend toward decentralization and asymmetry was reversed when Vladimir Putin took over from Yeltsin in 2000. Putin focused his presidency on restoring the power of the Russian central government. He sought to re-establish the authority of the central over subnational governments, and reversed most of the concessions Yeltsin had made to subnational politicians. To accomplish this centralization, Putin first appointed new officials to take control of federal agencies in the regions, notably the security services, the tax police, and the regional branches of national television stations. This increased Putin's ability to directly manage or manipulate political affairs in the regions. He then introduced legislation to reduce regional governors' influence over federal tax revenue, and to limit the proportion of taxes that governors controlled.[2] These changes meant that regional governors had to appeal directly to the president for funds to meet their budget obligations.

Putin also eliminated many of the special privileges that regions had obtained under Yeltsin. Regional governors lost their seats in the upper house of the Russian parliament—a privilege that had guaranteed them immunity from prosecution for corruption, for example. Then, in 2004, terrorists seized a school in the southern Russian city of Beslan, resulting in the deaths of hundreds of children. Local and regional officials bore the brunt of the criticism for the security failings that allowed the tragedy to take place. In response, Russia's parliament abolished direct popular gubernatorial elections and gave the president the power to nominate candidates for governor, who, in turn, would then be voted up or down by the regional legislatures. Since the president now essentially determined who would serve as governor in each region, the Russian central government's power was vastly increased. As evidence of the center's influence, between 2005 and April 2008, 25 of 79 elected regional governors who sought reappointment were fired.[3]

Because of these reforms, the central government—and, in particular, the president—has now emerged as the dominant political actor in Russian federalism. The president has control over the most important financial flows and can hire and fire governors. As a result, governors who want to stay in office follow the president's political orders. For governors who do not mind following these orders, the system serves their interests well, since they are now unaccountable to the local voters—a fact that has shielded many unpopular and corrupt governors from removal.

Elections

Since independence in 1992, Russia has had six parliamentary elections. Originally, elections to the Duma took place using a mixed electoral system. One half of the deputies were elected on single-member districts contested by candidates in the localities (much like U.S. House of Representative elections) and the other half were elected in a single national proportional representation (PR) election in which political parties determined the order of the candidates. All parties which gained at least 5 percent of the vote in the national PR election were guaranteed representation in the Duma. This system produced elections in which large numbers of independents or non-party candidates were elected. These deputies were a mixed bag, ranging from principled oppositionists to criminals seeking immunity from prosecution (which the constitution guarantees to sitting Duma members), but in general independents lined up behind the Yeltsin government on key votes. Nevertheless, in the Yeltsin era, the presidential administration had great difficulties mustering a parliamentary majority for legislation, because, as we see below, pro-presidential parties did extremely poorly on the party list side of the elections.

Under President Putin, the balance of forces changed somewhat, with strong pro-presidential parties being elected and much of the opposition initially coming from the independent deputies elected in single-mandate seats. In 2005, a new electoral law was passed instituting a single national list PR election for all 450 Duma seats, and the threshold for representation was increased to a minimum of 7 percent of the vote. Further legal changes mean that in the future, parties getting more than 5 percent but less than 6 percent will get one seat, and those receiving between 6 percent and 7 percent of the vote will get two seats. Stringent rules were also passed on party registration to ensure that only truly national parties with representation across the whole federation could contest elections. These rules have had the effect of significantly strengthening a small number of parties and making it much harder for new parties to enter the political contest.

The quality and fairness of elections in Russia has always been questionable. After independence in the 1990s, elections were not fair, in the sense that access to money and the media vastly favored incumbent politicians over their opponents. Moreover, there were frequent and credible allegations of fraud at all levels. On the positive side, however, national elections were at least highly competitive, incumbents often lost, and opposition parties frequently did well.

However, if Russia's elections were flawed from the beginning, over time they have become even less free, and less fair. Contemporary elections in Russia still do not meet the standards expected of democratic elections, due to lack of fair access to the mass media for opposition candidates and parties, vast infusions of illegal campaign contributions from businessmen and others trying to buy influence or seats in the legislature and simple ballot-stuffing. Moreover, since 2000, political competition has declined, partly due to the popularity of the incumbent administration and partly due to the Kremlin's increasing manipulation of the media and the electoral process. These changes in elections are a key feature of Russia's turn away from democracy in recent years.

The first post-communist parliamentary elections in Russia took place under the new constitution in December 1993. Despite Yeltsin's success in passing a new

Liberal Democratic Party (LDPR) ■ a nationalist party that has enjoyed a close relationship with the Kremlin throughout the post-communist era.

Communist Party of the Russian Federation (CPRF) ■ successor to the Communist Party of the Soviet Union. A leftist nationalist political party that has formed the principal opposition for most of the post-communist era.

Agrarian Party ■ leftist party that represented Russian peasants. Merged with the ruling United Russia Party in 2008.

Federal Security Service (FSB) ■ the principal domestic security agency in Russia. Analogous to the FBI in the United States.

Committee on State Security (KGB) ■ known by its Russian acronym, KGB, the Committee on State Security was responsible for both domestic and international security and intelligence. A massive organization analogous to the U.S. FBI and CIA combined.

constitution, Russia's deep economic crisis meant that he was very unpopular. As a result, his allies in parliament won only 15.6 percent of the seats (Table 8.2). Opposition parties—both the ultra-nationalist Liberal Democratic Party and the leftist Communist and Agrarian parties—gained seats at the government's expense, taking together more than 32 percent of seats.

Elections were held again in December 1995.[4] Combined with the ongoing economic crisis and a growing impression that the central government was losing control over Russia's territory, these elections weakened Yeltsin's government even further, as the opposition continued to gain ground. As Table 8.2 shows, by this year, the Communists and Agrarians together held nearly 40 percent of the seats, and pro-government parties only 14 percent.

The parliamentary results revealed Yeltsin's political weakness as his own presidential reelection campaign approached in 1996. At the start of the campaign, Yeltsin had the support of less than 2 percent of likely voters. However, by lavishing government spending on politicians who promised to deliver votes from their supporters and by unfairly dominating television, Yeltsin won 35 percent of the vote in the first round of voting. In the second round runoff, Yeltsin faced the Communist Party candidate. He framed his campaign as a referendum on the Soviet past, and ended up winning 54 percent of the vote—despite, it was later revealed, suffering a heart attack between rounds.

Yeltsin's health continued to weaken during his second term and the slow economic decline over which he presided turned into a full-scale economic collapse in the summer of 1998. This combination of ill health and unpopularity meant Yeltsin and his entourage needed to find a successor to run for the presidency in 2000. Yeltsin settled on a relatively unknown politician, Vladimir Putin. Putin, who had previously served as Yeltsin's chief of staff and head of the domestic security agency, the Federal Security Service (FSB), was appointed prime minister in September 1999. Putin was a former Committee on State Security (KGB) officer—the Soviet-era security agency equivalent of a combined CIA and FBI—with little political experience, and he was initially perceived as politically weak.

Putin's first challenge as prime minister was to lead the government's campaign in the 1999 parliamentary elections. The election campaign was dramatically affected by two serious national security crises. First, just as the campaign was getting underway, Islamist militants from the region of Chechnya attacked the neighboring region of Dagestan, as part of their effort to create an Islamic state in southern Russia. At the same time, three mysterious nighttime apartment bombings in the cities of Buynaksk, Moscow, and Volgodonsk killed some 300 sleeping civilians and terrorized the entire country. Putin responded with an aggressive and successful military assault on Chechnya, and promised to destroy the militants. Putin's tough tone proved enormously popular, and voters began to rally around the new prime minister.

Putin's new popularity helped boost the image of the party most closely allied with the Kremlin, the Unity Party. Newspapers and government-controlled TV and radio stations promoted Unity, and generous financial support appeared from businessmen who benefited from their close ties to the Kremlin. Every day the most popular media outlets spewed slander and innuendo at Kremlin opponents, accusing

TABLE 8.2

Seats as Percentage of the 450 Available in Russian Duma Elections: 1993, 1995, 1999, 2003, 2007

Party	1993	1995	1999	2003	2007
Parties of Power					
Our Home is Russia	-	12.2	1.6	-	-
Fatherland/All Russia	-	-	15.1	-	-
Unity/United Russia	-	-	16.2	49.3	70.0
Liberal Parties					
Russia's Choice	15.6	2.0	-	-	-
Union of Right Forces	-	-	6.4	0.7	-
Yabloko	5.1	10.0	4.4	0.9	
Party of Russian Unity and Accord	4.2	0.2	-	-	-
Democratic Party of Russia	3.3				
Centrist Parties					
Women of Russia	5.1	0.7	-	-	-
Nationalist Parties					
Liberal Democratic Party	14.3	11.3	3.8	8.0	8.9
Congress of Russian Communities		1.1	0.2	-	-
Motherland	-	-	-	8.2	-
Leftist Parties					
Communist Party of the Russian Federation	10.7	34.9	25.1	11.6	12.7
Agrarian Party	7.3	4.4	-	0.4	-
Fair Russia	-	-	-	-	8.4
Independents and Others	42.2	21.8	26.9	19.6	-

Source: www.russiavotes.org

them of crimes like murder and child molestation. The government's opponents responded in kind, but their access to the media was more limited. When the votes were counted, Unity had performed relatively well for a new party, taking 16.2 percent of the seats (see Table 8.2). Unity's success made Putin the clear favorite to succeed Yeltsin. In a surprise move, President Yeltsin then resigned on December 31, 1999, appointed Putin as acting president, and moved the presidential elections up four months, to February. This allowed Putin to capitalize on Unity's strong showing in the parliamentary elections. In the presidential election, Putin trounced the Communist Party candidate, winning in the first round with 53 percent of the vote.

Putin's victory ushered in an era in which both parliamentary and presidential elections have become markedly less competitive than they were under Yeltsin. After Putin's inauguration, Unity and its main opponent in 1999—Fatherland—merged to form the pro-Putin United Russia Party. United Russia dominated the 2003 Duma elections, in which it took first place with 49.3 percent of the seats, as well as the 2007 Duma elections, where it won a dominating 70 percent of seats. Putin himself won overwhelming re-election in 2004, winning in the first round with 71 percent of the vote.

What has made Russian elections so much less competitive since 2000? Part of the story is Vladimir Putin's popularity. Public opinion polls have found that Putin's political and economic successes brought him genuine popularity with many Russians.[5] With Putin so popular, few other political leaders were willing to risk their own political careers in order to challenge either him or his hand-picked successor, Dmitri Medvedev. Yet, Putin's popularity is not the only explanation for the decline of competitiveness in Russian elections. Also important is the strict control the government exerts over television and the elections themselves. All national channels cover the president and his government in positive, often fawning, terms, while opposition parties and leaders are often ignored or ridiculed. In addition, the Kremlin has shown itself willing to use the public prosecutor's office and other means to intimidate potential political opponents, while limits on the ability of other political forces to contest elections have also done much to foster the current dominance of pro-Kremlin parties.

United Russia Party ■ Russia's largest political party that includes most of the leading politicians and many other important figures in the country. A self-described conservative party that was formed in December 2001 through the merger of the two main pro-government parties in the Duma.

The "Tandemocracy" of President and Prime Minister

In 2008, Vladimir Putin's second term as president ended. Although a newcomer to national politics in 1999, by 2008 Putin had become a hero for many Russians. Many argued for a constitutional amendment to allow him to run for a third consecutive term as president. However, Putin resisted this temptation and a few months before the March 2008 presidential elections, he announced his support for Dmitri Medvedev, a long-time political associate from St. Petersburg. Putin's support immediately boosted Medvedev in the polls, and he ended up winning easily, with 70 percent of the vote in the first round.

The 2008 election appeared to represent a democratic and largely unsurprising transfer of political power: a popular president announced his support for one particular candidate, and universal suffrage in an open election determined the winner. Yet, although popular opinion played an important role in Russia's 2008 presidential

While formal power lay with Russian President Medvedev (center-left), many believed that it was Prime Minister Putin (center) who really called the shots. This view was confirmed when Medvedev agreed to stand down after only one term in office and announced his support for Putin's return to the presidency in 2012. This mismatch between formal and informal power is a recurrent feature of Russian politics.

election, the elections did not truly embody one of the other core principles of democracy, contestation. Putin's chosen successor enjoyed the enormous resources of the Russian government, and Putin and his allies used every means available to undermine Medvedev's opponents.

More importantly, although power formally passed from Putin to Medvedev, it was unclear whether power had really changed hands. Medvedev moved into the president's office, but he promptly appointed Putin as his prime minister, giving Putin continued control of day-to-day government operations, and allowing Putin to remain in the spotlight and take credit for many of the Medvedev administration's successes. The question of the balance of "real" power between these two leaders remained the focus of Russian politics after 2008.

There was much speculation over whether the two leaders actually worked in tandem—what commentators called, tongue-in-cheek, "tandemocracy"—or whether they represented different political philosophies and engaged in vigorous behind the scenes competition. The lack of clarity over who held power had the advantage of giving people of quite different political inclinations the sense that someone in the top leadership represented them. Liberals looked to Medvedev, while more conservative people admired Putin. Most questions about the nature of the Putin–Medvedev relationship were answered in September 2011, when Medvedev

SUMMARY TABLE

Russia's Constitution: Few Checks on Executive Power

President	Formally (and usually in practice, too) the most powerful official in Russia. Popularly elected in a two-round system in which the top two candidates proceed to a runoff if no candidate receives a majority in the first round.
Prime Minister	Appointed by the president but approved by the Duma. Appointment procedure heavily weighed in favor of presidential nominees, who are rarely rejected.
Federal Assembly	Consists of two houses. The lower house, or Duma, consists of 450 members elected according to a national list proportional representation system. Since 2001, the Russian president has enjoyed majority support in the Duma.
	The upper house, or Federation Council, consists of two representatives from each of Russia's 83 regions. These appointed officials rarely demonstrate much independence.
Judiciary	Constitutional Court decides on the constitutionality of laws and decrees brought to it by the president, the government, either house of the Federal Assembly, the Supreme Court, or one of the regional parliaments. Widely considered to exercise little independence.
Regional Governors	Regional leaders were elected up to 2005. Since then, they are appointed by the president.

announced that he would not seek a second term in office, but instead would support Putin's return to the presidency in the elections scheduled for March 2012. While the tandem was preserved when Putin in turn announced that he would appoint Medvedev to the prime ministership, it was clear that Putin remained the dominant partner. Nevertheless, the mismatch between who was constitutionally in control and who was actually in charge illustrates something important about the real nature of Russian politics. Despite the supposedly "super-presidential" constitution, for four years Russia had a prime minister who, while constitutionally subordinate to the president, actually wielded considerably more power thanks to informal relationships and networks. Such a mismatch between public politics and what goes on behind closed doors is a common feature of illiberal democracies in the contemporary world and one of the key features that separates them from long-standing democracies.

Looking at how institutions have evolved in Russia over the last two decades tells us a lot about why Russia has not become a liberal democracy, when many of its neighbors have. After the collapse of the Soviet Union, Russia was weak and although the constitution provided for a strong presidency, the central authorities in Moscow had great difficulty turning formal powers into real control over the vast country. However, over time as the economic situation began to improve, the control of the center over the regions and over electoral politics more generally, has increased. Reestablishing strong, effective central authority has been the number one priority for the leadership, with issues of democracy and governance being placed firmly on the back burner.

IDENTITIES IN RUSSIA

Many Russians were unhappy about the collapse of the Soviet Union in 1991. President Putin, for one, described the Soviet collapse as a catastrophe. As its largest component, Russia had always dominated the Soviet Union, and ethnic Russians had often held the top positions in the union's government and in the Communist Party of the Soviet Union. Consequently, the collapse of the USSR signified a tremendous loss of prestige for Russia, not to mention the loss of half its population. Many Russians believed that in the short span of two years, Russia had gone from one of the world's superpowers to "just another country." Moreover, during this period of weakness, many of Russia's ethnic minorities presented demands for greater political autonomy. Some observers supposed that such demands could lead to the breakup of Russia itself. Others believed that the collapse of the USSR would generate a backlash among ethnic Russians, sparking a growth of Russian nationalism that would target ethnic minorities within Russia itself.

However, these worst-case scenarios have not come to pass. With the important exception of the breakaway region of Chechnya, inter-ethnic relations have remained largely peaceful, and Russian nationalism, while not completely absent, has not become an important form of political identity. Similarly, economic class and religion have also failed to emerge as major mobilization identities in the post-Soviet era. In short, although Russia is very diverse, its ethnic, linguistic, and religious diversity has not translated into *political* diversity—the government has not had to struggle to overcome deep polarizing identity-based divisions within Russian society in its effort to reconsolidate the Russian state. The comparative lack of politicized identities in Russia helps explain why the Russian central government has managed to centralize power with relatively little opposition.

8.3 How have ethnic and other identities shaped post-communist politics in Russia?

Watch the Video "The South Ossetia Crisis" at mypoliscilab.com

Ethnic Politics

According to its 2002 census, Russia today is home to approximately 160 different ethnic groups. One way to think of these groups is to classify them according to language group and then ethnicity. The largest group in terms of population includes speakers of Slavic languages, who make up about 83 percent of the total population. Among the Slavs, ethnic Russians are the largest group (80 percent of the population), with Ukrainians (2 percent) and Belarusians (0.5 percent) making up most of the rest of Slavic speakers.

Non-Slavic ethnic groups make up the rest of the country's population. The largest group of non-Slavs consists of 5.3 million speakers of Tatar, a language related to Turkish (4 percent of Russia's total). About 5 million people (3.5 percent) speak Caucasian languages (from the Caucasus region in southwestern Russia), including ethnic Chechens, Avars, Karbardinians, Dargins, and Ingush. In addition, there are about 2.7 million speakers (2 percent) of Finno-Ugric languages, Samoyedic, Mongol, and several other languages.

In short, although Russians are the dominant ethnic group, about 20 percent of the population is not ethnically Russian, does not speak Russian as a first language, and often has different religious traditions from the Russian (Christian) Orthodox Church. Such ethnic groups are found in larger concentrations along the Volga River and in Russia's border regions. Given Russia's immensity, the presence of ethnic minorities on Russia's periphery far from Moscow suggests that Russia's government might face political challenges to central political control. How has Russia responded to the challenge of ethnic diversity since 1991?

Under the Soviet system, the central government could control potential ethnic unrest from the center through a combination of the "carrot" of economic development and the "stick" of repression. In the aftermath of the collapse of the Soviet Union, however, Russia's continued existence as a state was put into question. Across the country, regional leaders—and not just those in the ethnic republics—were claiming additional authority from the central government, even claiming the right to secede from the Russian Federation. Many adopted the symbols of independent states such as flags and national anthems, and a few regional leaders even discussed setting up an alternative currency to the Russian ruble. To many observers, it appeared that Russia might fragment into several additional independent states—reversing nearly 1,000 years of the consolidation of the Russian state.

However, with the exception of Chechnya and regions in the north Caucasus region, separatism never truly threatened the unity of the Russian state, and ethnicity, while socially important, has been a relatively unimportant form of political identity in most of Russia. Given the importance of ethnic mobilization on nearly every continent on the planet, this successful de-mobilization of ethnicity merits explanation. How has Russia managed to undercut ethnic political mobilization?

There are three answers to this question. First, although each ethnic republic bears the name of a particular ethnic group, the "indigenous" ethnic group is usually a minority within "its" own republic. In most ethnic republics, either Russians comprise the majority of the population or the population is fairly diverse. As a result, politicians in ethnic republics know that ethnic appeals can only go so far, and would be met with substantial opposition.

Second, non-Russians make up only 20 percent of the population and are fragmented into many small groups that themselves do not necessarily share political interests. As a result, non-Russians have been unable to find common ground to coordinate lobbying pressure on the government in Moscow for political concessions. For example, Tatarstan, a large region on the Volga River that has a Tatar-speaking Muslim majority, currently competes for leadership of Russia's Muslims with other regions, such as Chechnya, whose people are from a completely different ethnic group and speak a language that is not only different but from an entirely different family of languages.

Third, the central government has undertaken extensive and expensive efforts to purchase the support of ethnic groups in potentially troublesome regions. For example, as noted previously, President Yeltsin made deals with leaders of particular regions, giving them special rights and privileges. For example, in a secret agreement the diamond-rich eastern republic of Sakha was able to negotiate the right to retain 25 percent of gem-quality diamonds mined on its territory. While Putin reversed many of these arrangements using the threat of punishment for regional leaders who objected, local leaders are still granted extensive freedom of action on issues that are not of direct concern to the Kremlin. The remaining leeway continues to undermine the momentum for ethnic separatism by giving ethnic political leaders powerful incentives to cooperate with rather than fight against Moscow. As a result, ethnicity has actually lost salience as a form of political mobilization in recent years.

Chechnya and the Politics of the Caucasus

There is one major exception to the relative unimportance of ethnic identity to Russian politics: the ongoing conflict in Chechnya and the surrounding areas. The Caucasus Mountains mark the boundary between contemporary states of Russia, Georgia, and Azerbaijan. The Caucasus is a region of tremendous religious, ethnic, and linguistic diversity. Most of the 5.6 million or so people who live in the Russian part of the Caucasus are Sunni Muslim, with the Ossetians being the only large Orthodox Christian group. Diversity of political identities, combined with mountainous terrain and a strategic location between the historically important Russian, Iranian, and Turkish empires, has made the Caucasus a turbulent area for centuries.

Some ethnic groups in the Caucasus region have a long history of attempting to resist Russian political domination. During World War II, for example, some Chechens tried to take advantage of the war to revolt against the Soviet Union. In response, Joseph Stalin declared the entire population of Chechens to be Nazi sympathizers, and after the Soviet army pushed German forces from the Soviet Union in 1944, Stalin loaded approximately 500,000 Chechens on trains and shipped them hundreds of miles east to Kazakhstan. In some remote areas, the Soviet army simply massacred Chechens—perhaps 80,000 died overall—and most Chechens were unable to return home until after Stalin's death in 1953.

In November 1991, as the Soviet Union was collapsing, the Chechen regional parliament declared Chechnya's independence from Russia. President Yeltsin's initial response was weak: he declared a state of emergency in Chechnya and threatened to reestablish Russian control by force, but he did not follow through on this threat. However, Chechen leaders proved unable to encourage economic growth or impose law and order in their own territory, and their republic became a center of lawlessness and smuggling. In December 1994, Yeltsin opted to launch a full-scale military intervention in order to reestablish Russian control over Chechnya.

Chechnya ■ region in the north Caucasus area of Russia. Site of two wars in the post-communist era.

Caucasus Mountains ■ a range of steep mountains stretching from the Black Sea in the west to the Caspian Sea in the east. The Caucasus Mountains mark the border between the Russian Federation in the north and Georgia and Azerbaijan to the south. A region of tremendous ethnic, linguistic, and religious diversity.

Russian military forces vastly outnumbered Chechen resistance fighters, but they failed to establish control, and in 1996, the Russians agreed to a peace deal in which de facto Chechen independence was allowed. In 1999, however, a faction of Chechen militants associated with Islamic extremists invaded the neighboring Russian region of Dagestan in an attempt to expand the area under their control. This reignited the war, as Russia launched another full-scale invasion. This time, the Russians succeeded in gaining control, though they inflicted thousands of casualties and committed many human rights violations in doing so.

Losing the conventional war, Chechen fighters resorted increasingly to attacks on civilian targets outside the borders of Chechnya, such as the 2004 murder of 350 hostages at an elementary school in Beslan, North Ossetia, many of them young children. Other atrocities have included bombings of apartment buildings, airliners, subway trains, rock concerts, hospitals, trains, and markets. More than a thousand people have been killed in terrorist incidents in Russia since 1991, with some 600 killed in Moscow alone by 2007.[6] Though by 2010 Russia had largely defeated pro-independence Chechen militants and established a Chechen-led regime in power, acts of terrorism and violence have continued, especially in the North Caucasus region, though isolated incidents have also occurred elsewhere in Russia.

The Chechen conflict has also negatively impacted respect for media freedom and human rights in Russia. Individual Chechen civilians as well as Russian conscripts have been caught up in the brutality of a civil war. Famous, and not so famous, journalists and human rights campaigners have been killed, often in circumstances that led many to speculate about the involvement of the Russian army or security forces. Media freedom has suffered as limits on reporting about the conflict have been justified on grounds of state security. In Chechnya, peace has been restored at the cost of installing a repressive and often violent Chechen regime, while fear has also lead to reprisals against ethnic Chechens and other Caucasians living in Moscow and elsewhere in Russia. Tired of terrorist attacks, Russian citizens, for the most part, have been willing to support their government in actions that have frequently breached both democratic and human rights norms. In short, the bloody Chechen conflict has made the environment much more difficult for democracy in Russia.

Russian Nationalism

The collapse of the Soviet Union represented a "loss" in the Cold War. Any country that loses a war—hot or cold—suffers a serious blow its pride. Some observers worried that defeat in the Cold War would generate a reaction in favor of Russian nationalism, which would take the form of paranoia towards foreigners and minorities. Observers referenced a frightful historical analogy to draw attention to the dangers of Russian nationalism: the rise of fascism and Nazism after Germany's defeat in World War I and its subsequent economic collapse during the Great Depression.

However, with the exception of racist skinhead violence in some of Russia's larger cities and some marginal political groups, fears of a wave of violent nationalism sweeping Russia have so far proven unfounded. Politically, ethnic Russian nationalism has been a relatively unimportant source of mobilization at the ballot box. Patriotism and nationalist rhetoric have been used extensively by both government and opposition parties, and nationalist parties have enjoyed some electoral success, but much of the appeal to patriotism is designed to draw on loyalty to the Russian state rather than on an ethnic Russian identity. In fact, much of the mobilization of patriotism involves attempts to remind voters of the glories of the Soviet era, and in particular of the victory of the multi-ethnic Soviet army against fascist Germany in the Second World War. Indeed, one of Putin's first acts as president was to order new lyrics to the Russian national anthem that were set to music from the old Soviet national anthem, and to restore the communist-era Red Flag as the banner of the Russian army.

What Happened to Class Identity?

The 1917 Russian Revolution sought to mobilize workers and peasants based on their class identities—on the notion that a small elite exploited them economically and oppressed them politically. The central stated goal of the communist Soviet government was the elimination of economic class differences, and although economic inequality was never completely eliminated, the Soviet Union did succeed in eliminating the vast differences between rich and poor that had characterized pre-1917 Russia.

With the collapse of the Soviet Union, economic inequality increased with startling speed: in less than ten years, Russia went from being one of the most equal countries in the world to one of the most unequal. A small number of Russians quickly became powerful and wealthy. The most high profile of these was a small group known as the oligarchs who, by means both legal and illegal, managed to obtain ownership of much of Russia's vast natural resource wealth. The nickname "oligarchs" was given to them because they used their power to try to control Russian politics, and in particular the presidency of Boris Yeltsin. While a few people grew rich, many millions more were thrust into poverty as both the economy and the social safety net built in the USSR fell apart.

Nevertheless, despite 70 years of Soviet ideological indoctrination and despite the memories of what the Soviet system accomplished in terms of eliminating inequalities, no single party or candidate has proven able to dominate the mobilization of class-based identities. A significant proportion of the electorate votes for leftist candidates, but these candidates and messages are divided among a range of parties, both in government and in the opposition. The largest and most obviously leftist party, the Communist Party, continues to contest elections and in the 1990s was usually the largest single party. However, the communists were never able to mobilize more than about one-third of the electorate to support its presidential candidates and so have been largely excluded from power.

Part of the reason for the failure of the communists to take real power has been the success of pro-government parties in making leftist rhetoric part of their own domain. President Putin made much political capital out of criticizing the

oligarchs ■ the name given in Russia in the 1990s to a small group of businessmen who used connections to state officials to enrich themselves and then to take control of the state itself.

oligarchs and appealing strongly to "ordinary" Russians. Moreover, a number of political parties using leftist rhetoric have been sponsored by the Kremlin to draw support away from the communists and other leftist parties of opposition. Thus, no party has been able to monopolize or use class identities as a vehicle to gaining power. Moreover, as in the United States, personalities, evaluations of economic performance, party allegiances, and ideological positions on non-economic matters play an important role in voting decisions and in recent years these factors have played to the advantage of the incumbent Putin–Medvedev tandem.[7]

Religious Identity

If eliminating economic inequality was one goal of Communism, eliminating religion was also important. Marx argued that religion was the "opiate of the masses," and Soviet leaders agreed as they attempted to eliminate religion as a source of political identity—and, thus, as a source of political mobilization. For centuries, Russian Orthodoxy was Russia's dominant religion and the Orthodox Church had been closely allied with the Russian state. Under Communism, the government initially attacked the Church, confiscating its property, destroying churches, and persecuting priests. Over time, the Russian Orthodox Church endured, less by fighting Soviet power than by cooperating with it. Nevertheless, 70 years of official atheism meant that by the time of the Soviet collapse, the Russian Orthodox Church was greatly diminished. This perhaps explains the relative weakness of religious identity in contemporary Russia.

After the Soviet collapse, there were high expectations in some parts for a religious revival, but most evidence suggests this never occurred. Although both Presidents Yeltsin and Putin made considerable displays of their Orthodox faith, and the Orthodox Church claims 120 million Christians in Russia, these claims are based on Russian ethnicity, not on religious belief or practice. In opinion polls, between 55 and 85 percent of Russia's 145 million citizens describe themselves as "Orthodox." This compares with the 70 percent of respondents who tell pollsters they believe in UFOs and the 60 percent who believe in astrology.[8] In fact, international studies like the World Values Survey indicate that Russians are far less likely to attend religious services than are the citizens of many other countries. Only 2.5 percent of Russians reported attending religious services at least once a week, compared with 33.4 percent of Americans or 39.4 percent of Italians. Even in highly secular Great Britain, 13.6 percent reported attending religious services at least once a week.[9] These numbers represent an enormous transformation from pre-revolutionary Russia in which religion was a central part of life. In short, religion is not a powerful force for political mobilization among those who declare formal affiliation with the Russian Orthodox Church.

Something similar can be said for minority religions in Russia. Islam is Russia's largest minority religion. Islamic leaders in Russia claim to represent 20 million citizens, or 14 percent of the total population, but the influence of Muslim organizations has been limited. Compared with the tensions between Islam and other religions in places such as Israel/Palestine, India, Egypt, and Nigeria, for example, relations between the Russian state and Muslims have been generally stable and

Cleaning the floor in a vast new mosque built in the Chechen capital of Grozny. Russia's post-communist experience has been greatly shaped by violence and repression related to conflict in its Muslim majority south.

peaceful. In part, this is because Muslims in Russia are divided along economic, geographic, ethnic, and theological lines.[10] Moreover, Russian presidents have gone to considerable lengths to reach out to Muslim and other religious minorities by, for example, regularly appearing in public with the heads of all Russia's major religions.

This situation is complicated somewhat by the role of Islam in Chechnya. Although Islam is a key part of Chechen identity, most scholars argue that nationalism and clan loyalties have played a much bigger role in the conflict than religion, despite the influx of international jihadists who came to Chechnya to fight the Russians and to attempt to turn the conflict into a religious struggle between the Islamic Chechens and the Orthodox Christian Russians.[11] These attempts have largely failed, but the language of Islamic terrorism is still useful to militants and to the Russian authorities alike, especially given the continued use of terrorist tactics within Russia by Chechen groups.

In sum, neither Orthodox Christianity nor Islam has played a major role in the development of Russian politics since the end of the Soviet period. Both Orthodoxy and Islam are socially important, and extremists on both sides have sought to politicize religion and make Russia a venue for a religious clash. But so far, the Russian state has been able to contain these pressures and push political organizing away from religion or sub-national identities and generally in the direction of large, catchall political parties.

> **SUMMARY TABLE**
>
> **Identities: Ethnicity, Nationalism, and Religion**
>
> | | |
> |---|---|
> | **Ethnic Politics** | With 160 different ethnic groups and about 20% of its population of non-Russian ethnicity, Russia is a multi-ethnic federation that has generally handled inter-ethnic relations well. The major exception to this rule is the Caucasus region that has seen two wars in Chechnya, myriad other incidents and conflicts, and has been a major source of instability. |
> | **Russian Nationalism** | Aggressive forms of Russian nationalism exist but are generally limited to small groups and youth gangs and are marginalized from mainstream politics. State patriotism is a very strong part, however, of most successful Russian political parties' rhetoric. |
> | **Class** | While Russia is characterized by some of the sharpest inequalities of any country in the world, there is little evidence of sharp class divides in voting or political behavior. |
> | **Religion** | While most Russians describe themselves as Orthodox Christians, this is primarily an ethnic identity. Religious observance is generally low. Russia also has some 20 million Muslims and other religious minorities. |

INTERESTS IN RUSSIA

8.4 Which interests are most influential in Russia and how have these shaped post-communist politics?

Watch the Video "The Litvinenko Affair" at mypolscilab.com

Watch the Video "Russian Political Reform" at mypolscilab.com

Explore the Comparative "Interest Groups" at mypolscilab.com

A key issue in understanding how and why Russia has failed to consolidate democratic institutions is the way in which private interests, and in particular economic interests, have dominated the broader interests of the country in the formation of public policy. In particular, the ability of a small group of businessmen, known informally as the oligarchs, to use public policy and public resources to accumulate vast wealth and political power, at the same time as living standards collapsed for the vast majority of citizens, created enormous disenchantment with the political system and widespread demands for a strong hand in politics. In response, the government has reasserted control over previously privatized assets and used prosecutions and other judicial means to strip powerful individuals of influence and make others cooperate with the state. Rather than bringing public accountability and transparency, however, the reassertion of state control has led to a blurring of the line between private and state interests and rampant corruption at all levels of government.

In this section, we examine first how the process of privatization and economic reform was hijacked by a small group of men who went on to dominate Russian politics in the 1990s, while the rest of the population suffered one of the worst economic contractions in history. We then look at how Vladimir Putin capitalized on popular discontent to rein in the oligarchs and create a more corporatist approach to both business interests and labor. A similar pattern has been seen with political parties, where a wide array of mostly short-lived elite-driven parties have given way to a single dominant party. In this context, life has been difficult for social movements and NGOs trying to establish themselves on the Russian political scene, though as we will see, there has been considerable growth and diversification of social movement activity in recent years.

Economic Reform, Economic Collapse, and the Rise of the "Oligarchs"

At the end of 1991, Russian leaders faced the historically unprecedented task of transforming a communist economy into a capitalist one. In the Soviet communist economy, all companies were state owned, and production was organized not by the market but by state orders issued according to an economic plan drawn up by the government. Converting to capitalism meant that almost the entire economy had to be sold off to private owners, that new markets had to be established to buy and sell everything from apples to land to TVs to stocks and shares, and finally that many of the companies currently in operation and employing people had to be closed when the government stopped subsidizing them. How Yeltsin's government would accomplish these feats was far from clear.

Some felt that it was necessary to move gradually. Others, led by a young Russian economist, Yegor Gaidar, thought the process would be quite simple: lift government price controls and limits on trade to create a market, then sell off state-owned companies that had the potential to become efficient and productive, and close the rest down. This plan was known as **shock therapy** because privatizing and moving quickly to a market system "shocked" the weak and unprofitable parts of the economy into elimination, thereby strengthening remaining companies. The pain of forcing companies to restructure or go out of business would in itself be "therapeutic."

On January 1, 1992, prices were liberalized and by 1993 the first wave of privatization, focusing on small and medium-sized companies such as restaurants, shops, and small factories, was almost complete. In 1995, the second phase of privatization began. This wave covered large firms such as telecommunications and oil and gas companies that held the promise of enormous profits and also accounted for the bulk of the economy. As a result, between 1994 and 1997, the proportion of the Russian economy accounted for by private firms rose from 21 to 59 percent.[12]

However, instead of being efficient, the privatization process proved to be enormously corrupt, with company and government insiders helping themselves to ownership of the choicest companies at bargain basement prices, at the expense of the interests of the population at large. The most infamous case of this so-called **insider privatization**, perhaps, was the case with the so-called "Loans for Shares" scheme in which a small group of bankers were able to snap up shares in key energy, metallurgy, and telecommunications companies. These bankers and others then

shock therapy ■ a program of rapid economic liberalization intended to introduce market mechanisms in place of state control.

Insider privatization ■ the transfer of state-owned assets and companies into the hands of government or company insiders, often by illicit or underhand means.

went on to finance Yeltsin's 1996 re-election campaign, and to amass vast wealth and property that included all of the main mass media outlets. Those involved became known as the "oligarchs," a group of a dozen or so men with who came to dominate Russian political and economic life, particularly during the period of Yeltsin's second term, from 1996–1999.

While some used their newfound wealth to invest and develop longer-term business strategies, most oligarchs used their political power to slow or stop further market-enhancing reforms that might have introduced greater competition or efficiency. Enterprises were privatized, but no system emerged for bankruptcies or for making these newly private enterprises act as if they were operating in competitive markets. Russia became trapped in an economic situation that was no longer state dominated, but neither was it a market economy. Political economists call this a "partial reform equilibrium," in which the winners of reform, not the losers, ultimately sabotage the economic reform process.[13]

The result was not just the transitory recession that all post-communist countries experienced, but a prolonged economic slump. In 1999, some eight years after the reforms had begun, the IMF estimated that the size of the Russian economy had fallen to 45.1 percent of its 1989 level. In other words, a decade of transition had seen average incomes cut in half. Moreover, the economic crisis did not affect everyone equally. While some grew fabulously wealthy, World Bank estimates show that the poverty rate in Russia rose from about 2 percent in 1988 to 50 percent by 1995.[14] In other words, the number of people living below the poverty line increased from about 2.2 million to 72.2 million! Consequently, while there was plenty of "shock" for the majority of Russians, there was very little "therapy."

In the summer of 1998, the chronic decline of the Russian economy became an acute economic crisis. The lack of a properly functioning market meant that most Russian companies were going bankrupt, unable to pay their bills or their workers' wages. However, mass insolvency did not lead to widespread plant closures or mass layoffs. The government had no interest in forcing insolvent enterprises to close down or restructure. Instead, these companies resorted to using goods to pay their bills. Government statistics showed that about 15 percent of company sales were paid for in kind rather than money, an extraordinarily high proportion for an industrial economy. Moreover, by 1998, only 16 percent of all companies were paying their taxes on time, which, in turn, meant that the Russian government lacked money to pay its own employees as well. With neither private companies nor the government having money to pay workers, arrears in wages were rampant. By 1998, fully 64 percent of all Russian adults were owed at least four months' worth of back wages.

The situation was unsustainable, and in August of 1998, the government defaulted on its debts, and the Russian ruble collapsed. Though seen as a disaster at the time, the crisis was actually cathartic. The collapse of the ruble relative to foreign currencies made imports extremely expensive, rendering Russian-made products competitive once more. As a result, the economy started to grow for the first time since the late 1980s. This trend coincided with rising prices for oil and gas and other Russian exports, which helped the government to solve its budgetary problems, so state employees were paid their full wages. Economic growth averaged more than 6 percent per year between 1998 and 2007, and living standards improved dramatically. In 2000, Russian income per capita was $7,430. By 2008, it had risen to $15,630. Moreover, despite the widespread stories of the increasing number of Russian millionaires, the benefits have not been limited to the upper echelons alone: the percentage of the population living below the poverty line fell to 13.5 percent in 2008.

Much of this economic growth, however, has been driven by increases in prices for commodities, most notably oil and gas, that dominate the Russian economy. While the renewed growth is certainly welcome, heavy reliance on natural resource exports is not without its problems, both economically and politically. Economies that rely heavily on natural resources are vulnerable to price fluctuations that can be very damaging. The ruble collapse of August 1998 came at a time when world oil prices were at historic lows. Worse, natural resource economies often have difficulties developing internationally competitive industries in other sectors, due to the effect of natural resources on inflating the value of a country's currency. This makes diversification difficult.

More recently, there has been a lot of attention on the political downside of natural resource–based economies.[15] Some argue that governments that do not need to rely on taxation for revenue (because they have money from natural resource exports) can rule autocratically because they do not need the assent of the governed. Others maintain that natural resources provide easy money that can be used to buy off elites and to consolidate the control of one group, thus inhibiting democratic development. Arguments like these suggest that there is a **natural resource curse** that tends to make it difficult for democracy to emerge in countries that are heavily based on natural resources. While this view is not without its critics, the recent history of Russia does seem to lend support to the idea that natural resource dependence can have negative consequences for political development.

natural resource curse ■ the theory that countries with natural resources find it harder to develop economically and tend to be more authoritarian.

Putin, the Fall of the Oligarchs, and Business Interests

Vladimir Putin, who succeeded Yeltsin as president in 2000, understood the popular anger at the oligarchs and he quickly moved against them. Beginning with the arrest of media mogul Vladimir Gusinsky on charges of embezzlement, Putin expropriated the assets of, and then exiled or arrested, several of the most prominent oligarchs. Evidence of wrongdoing was not hard to find, not least due to the enormously complicated and often contradictory legislation that had been in place. In what was perhaps the highest profile campaign against the oligarchs, Putin arranged to bring Russia's largest oil company, Yukos, back under the control of Kremlin-allied companies and to send its owner and chief financial officer to prison in Siberia. This case demonstrated both the government's seriousness and its capacity to control the oligarchs if it wanted to. As a result, other oligarchs quickly fell in line with the Kremlin's political goals—and they have become significant financial supporters of Kremlin political projects.

However, neutering the oligarchs does not mean that business interests are no longer influential. Since the Russian state and key government officials now either own or are represented on the boards of major companies, the interests of Russia's largest companies now have a direct voice inside government policymaking. In addition to corporations having an inside voice in policymaking, state officials also have considerable influence over the behavior of corporations, leading to an incredibly complex intermingling of public and private interests. Whether this has been good for the corporations is a matter of some debate, but it undoubtedly has benefited state officials, making public office a direct route to considerable personal wealth.

Smaller businesses are represented, too, through an interest group, the Russian Union of Industrialists and Entrepreneurs (RUIE). This organization reflects the interests of a much broader lobby, and includes representatives of formerly state-owned companies as well as newer enterprises formed in the post-Soviet era. The RUIE has been instrumental in lobbying for the creation of a generally pro-business legislative framework, as well as representing the interests of large individual companies. For its part, the Russian government has generally welcomed the influence of the RUIE, inviting representatives to formal consultations and using the body as a key device for coordinating business interests.

Labor

In addition to its efforts to dominate big business, Russia's central government has gone to great lengths to control and/or co-opt organized labor. Moreover, in contrast to the purpose of such top-down corporatist arrangements in many European countries (see chapters on Germany and France, for example), most such efforts in Russia have come at the expense of workers' interests.

The reason the government has sought to control labor is that the economic restructuring that accompanied reform was bound to create job losses and unemployment. The Russian government, which had seen massive strikes in 1989, feared that workers' protests against unemployment would derail the reforms and destabilize the country.

As it turned out, controlling workers' protest has been easier than influential political scientists predicted at the time.[16] This is because state-controlled unions organized under the Soviet Union, now renamed the Federation of Independent Trade Unions of Russia (FITUR), have continued to dominate the representation of workers. These unions have strong incentives to cooperate with the Russian government. The FITUR inherited a vast network of Soviet-era organized unions in practically every workplace that existed before 1991, and as of 2009 still claims 26 million members. One might think this would offer the FITUR a position of considerable power but the government held a trump card: it can determine the rules governing the formation of unions. And so, in return for FITUR cooperation, the government passed legislation that has protected FITUR's monopoly and made it very difficult for alternative unions to form. As a result, with the exception of coal miners and a few other groups such as dockworkers and air-traffic controllers, independent unions have failed to establish a strong presence in Russia; by 2000, 5 percent of union members, at most, were in independent unions.

This system played an important role in ensuring social peace during the economic catastrophe of the 1990s, making it difficult for workers to find ways to press their demands outside of tame official channels. Nevertheless, there was plenty of anger and discontent that led to waves of strikes and regionally organized protest demonstrations. These tended to be focused in places governed by opponents of Yeltsin, who provided workers with assistance in protesting in the hopes of strengthening their negotiating position.[17]

Workers' strikes and independent unions played a major role in bringing down communism and the Soviet Union. However, the current lack of genuine representation for workers, either at the workplace or in politics, has contributed to the centralization of power by the Kremlin and inhibited the development of a democratic political system.[18] Nevertheless, tensions within the existing FITUR-dominated system seem to be creating pressure for more liberal legislation on union formation. Between 2006 and 2008, strikes, while still limited, once again began to spread across the country, affecting foreign and domestic investors, well-to-do industrial and natural resource enterprises, and infrastructure installations. So far, the government has been resolute in resisting pressure to allow alternative unions more voice and scope to organize, but pressure for more democracy in the workplace is unlikely to go away.[19]

Political Parties

Next we turn to political parties in Russia, which illustrate, perhaps most clearly, the turn from ineffective pluralism in the 1990s to a much more organized, controlled, quasi-corporatism in more recent years. Many observers currently view Russia as returning to a one-party political system. Whether this will be a democratic one-party system—as in Japan—or a non-democratic one—as under the Soviet Union—remains to be seen.

Mass Parties In the post-communist era, Russia has had only one mass political party on the scene. This is the Communist Party of the Russian Federation (CPRF), a successor party to the Soviet-era Communist Party. Under Yeltsin and Putin, the CPRF has played the role of a loyal opposition, contesting elections and winning seats, but never seriously threatening to take real power. The CPRF has drawn its supporters predominantly from older and poorer voters, as well as voters in rural areas. Paradoxically, the CPRF has had a harder time flourishing in the era of Vladimir Putin, a politician who often seems nostalgic for the communist era, than it did under the anti-communist Yeltsin. In part, this is because Putin's patriotic appeal and general popularity has drained voters away from the CPRF, but it also seems that Putin is impatient with the communists as a political force.

Government Parties By contrast, the remainder of Russia's political parties is better described by the concept of **elite parties**, which are essentially alliances of politicians created as vehicles for competing in elections. Most of the elite parties have been driven by attempts on the part of the Kremlin to either create a "virtual opposition"—that is, government-sponsored parties that use the same rhetoric as true opposition parties but are created specifically to draw votes away from the real opposition—or to create a "party of power" that could provide a legislative majority for the president.

elite parties ■
political parties that provide a vehicle to office for leaders without having a mass organization in the country.

The prototypical "virtual opposition" party is the Liberal Democratic Party (LDPR). The LDPR and its leader Vladimir Zhirinovsky emerged quite suddenly as a genuinely independent, and extremely angry, opposition voice in the Duma elections of 1993. Since then, the LDPR has been continuously represented in parliament and has run candidates for the presidency. However, the LDPR has gradually mellowed into part of the Russian political establishment. Political parties that run in elections to attract opposition or protest votes but support the government in parliament like the LDPR have become a common feature of Russian politics. The most famous examples are the Motherland Party, which took 9 percent of the party list vote in the Duma in 2003, and A Just Russia Party, which won 8 percent in 2007. Not unexpectedly, the contradictions of running as the opposition, then legislating with the government, have meant that such parties typically do not live long and are soon replaced by another party performing the same job.

The efforts of the Kremlin to create a lasting "party of power" to represent its wishes in the Duma initially were not much more successful. The first prototype for a "party of power," Russia's Choice, ran in support of the government's radical economic reform agenda in 1993 but only took 14 percent of the votes. Other efforts under Yeltsin to create a party of power suffered similar fates. Since the Putin era, things have changed considerably. The United Russia Party was created in December 2001, and right away Putin made it clear that this was the new "government" party for officials to join. Since then, United Russia has dominated elections, taking 37 percent of the vote in 2003 and 64 percent in 2007. In achieving this dominance, United Russia has benefited tremendously from its perceived closeness to Vladimir Putin, even though Putin himself ran for the presidency twice as an independent.

Iabloko ■ the leading left of center liberal political party in the post-communist era. The name is an acronym taken from the names of the party's founders and means "apple."

Right Cause ■ a leading right-wing political party in the post-communist era. Despite taking its name from a Stalin era slogan, Right Cause embraces a pro-business ideology has been closely associated with key oligarchs and pro-market factions in the Russian government.

Liberal Parties The other "family" of parties is the liberal parties, most notably the social democratic party **Iabloko** and the pro-business Union of Right Forces. Formed around a well-known liberal economist, Grigory Yavlinskii, Iabloko (an acronym meaning "apple" formed from the three founders' initials) has represented a primarily urban, well-educated, and socially liberal constituency since the early 1990s. Iabloko won representation in parliament in every election until 2007. However, largely deprived of television coverage in the 2007 elections, it failed to cross the high threshold of 7 percent of the vote needed for representation and has since struggled with internal splits.

If Iabloko is the "left" liberal party, **Right Cause** is the right-wing pro-business version. Formed in 2009 from a merger of other rightist parties, individual leaders within Right Cause have maintained close links with the government over the years even as the party itself often finds itself taking opposition stances on specific questions.

Party System One consequence of the relative lack of mass parties "on the ground" is that the dynamics of parties have been very closely tied to the incentives created by the electoral system. In fact, for most of the post-communist era, the institutions that shape political competition have been determined by the political interests of key politicians.

In the first decade of post-communism, political parties were very weak, largely because candidates could gain office either through the use of state resources, private wealth, or other "party substitutes."[20] This meant that some of the most powerful and influential politicians in Russia (including Boris Yeltsin and Vladimir Putin) gained office without even joining a political party.

Under Vladimir Putin, however, the lack of an institutionalized party system is increasingly seen as a political problem. To this end, a number of election law reforms were made with the aim of increasing the role played by parties. The reforms have had two main effects. One is to unite most of the political elite in one party, United Russia, backed by former President Putin and most of the other important office-holders in Russia. The second has been to make it harder for small or regionally based parties to participate in politics.

The main concern with Russian political parties now is not the lack of a party system, but rather a fear that Russia is reverting to a one-party system, under the domination of United Russia, which took two-thirds of the vote in the 2007 parliamentary elections. If true, this raises the further question of whether it is possible for Russia to have a one-party dominant political system and still be a democracy. As with the case of Japan, such an outcome is possible in theory, if other parties are allowed to compete fairly in elections. This does not seem to be the case in Russia, however. The party system is clearly manipulated to ensure Kremlin dominance, and serious opposition is sometimes refused access to the ballot. Moreover, state dominance of the media, and in particular television, is such that opposition parties are not fairly and equally covered. Thus, although other parties are allowed to compete in elections, the dominance of United Russia is one of the features that makes Russia an illiberal democracy at best.

Social Movements

Despite, or perhaps because of, the great social, economic, and political transformations that have taken place in Russia over the last two decades, there has been relatively little in the way of organized social movements. Political scientist Marc Howard argues that this is due to a combination of the economic crisis that makes people turn inward, a distrust of public organizations held over from the communist era, and a reliance on close personal networks rather than broader social organizations.[21] Nevertheless, it also seems to be the case that since the economy began growing again at the beginning of this century, there has been a dramatic growth in the number and range of civil society organizations and NGOs operating in Russia. This growth has led the government to innovate and improvise new ways of integrating these movements into the political system while preventing them from becoming a source of true political opposition.

One of the first major organizations to gain prominence was the League of Committees of Soldiers' Mothers. Initially inspired by problems with the military draft and the brutal hazing to which draftees to the Russian army are often subject, the league has grown in both size and prominence due to the war in Chechnya, and now has thousands of members and activists all over Russia. The league has taken explicitly anti-war positions, campaigned for the release of more truthful information about the nature of the war and its casualties, and even negotiated with Chechen militants for the release of prisoners. While often a thorn in the side of the Russian authorities, a combination of moral weight and a strong international reputation has largely shielded the league from the kinds of harassment the Russian government has inflicted on other anti-war groups.

Pensioners have also been in the vanguard of the resurgence of social movement activity in the Putin years. Pensioners' protests in 2005 against changes that would have significantly reduced social benefits led to large-scale mobilizations all across Russia. Over the course of a few weeks, senior citizens demonstrated an ability to mobilize large numbers onto the streets and to engage not just in marches and demonstrations, but also in road blockades and other forms of civil disobedience. Faced with this mobilization, the Russian government very quickly made changes to the benefits legislation and began to re-think its strategy toward civil society.

The pensioners' protests were followed by a proliferation of youth activism, inspired both by the pensioners and by the example of mass mobilizations against authoritarian rulers elsewhere. While pensioners were filling Russian streets in January 2005, just the previous month in Ukraine, a broad coalition dominated by young people filled the squares of Kiev, brought the government to its knees and engineered the so-called Orange Revolution. Russians both in and out of government were well aware of the Ukrainian events in interpreting the pensioners' protests. For

Leftist youth unfurl a banner calling for an end to the Putin–Medvedev "tandem." Despite government repression, both opposition and pro-government demonstrations can frequently be seen on Russia's streets.

the opposition, the experience of the protests suggested the limits of then President Putin's power and forged a new sense of solidarity and tolerance among different factions. Eventually this led to the creation of a united opposition movement, **Other Russia**, which brought together political parties, youth groups, independent trade unionists, and liberal politicians like Boris Nemtsov and the former world chess champion Garry Kasparov.

This new civic opposition represented a major change in Russian politics. It is clear that the variety of protests and protest participants in today's Russia is much greater than at any time since Boris Yeltsin stood down in 2000. For example, in March 2006, an estimated 125,000 demonstrators gathered in more than 360 cities and towns to protest increases in utility prices and rents, while on February 12, 2006, thousands of car owners rallied in 22 cities to protest the jailing of a motorist hit by the speeding car of a prominent Russian politician. Moreover, in early 2007, activists across Russia organized a series of high-profile demonstrations called Dissenters' Marches in Nizhnyi Novgorod, St. Petersburg, and Moscow. These events were just part of more than 2,900 different protest events attended by more than 800,000 people in 2007 alone.

The Kremlin administration of presidents Putin and Medvedev also seems to have recognized that a new phase of politics in Russia began with the pensioners' protests. Having ensured the cooperation of the largest parts of organized labor, and having "tidied up" political parties and the electoral arena, the administration recognized that its primary challenge now came from the emergent civic opposition. In fact, in the years since the events of January 2005, the government has shown an increasing preoccupation with the opposition in general, and the NGO sector in particular. To deal with this challenge, the government employed repression of opponents, curtailing freedom of assembly and expression. Demonstrators now find it harder to get licenses to demonstrate and are often beaten or shepherded away from the areas in which they would like to gather. Protesters are regularly harassed, and frequently arrested, especially in the run-up to major political occasions. In addition to repression, the government has helped to create funding and institutional incentives for NGOs and civil society groups to cooperate with the government, and engaged actively in the creation of social organizations—in particular youth groups—friendly to the Kremlin.[22] The most prominent of these is the youth movement, *Nashi* (Ours), that has acted almost as the personal mobilizing wing of Vladimir Putin. These measures to control social movements are part of the reason Russia is now seen as an illiberal democracy. If Russia, however, is to start opening up again politically, it seems likely that social movements, probably in alliance with discontented factions within the current elite, would play a major role.

Taken together, what we have seen over the last decade in Russia is the deep intermingling of state interests and public officials in many key aspects of life in Russia. Government officials run major corporations, cooperate closely with state-sponsored labor unions, play a key role in the creation and functioning of political parties, and even sponsor the creation of supposedly nongovernmental organizations. Such mixing of public and private functions happens to a degree in all countries, even the most democratic. Nevertheless, the extent to which the public interests of the state and the private interests of officials, businessmen,

Other Russia ■
a loose alliance of opposition parties and movements ranging from neo-fascist to liberal opponents of the existing political system in Russia. Closely associated with former World Chess Champion Garry Kasparov.

Nashi (Ours) ■
a state-sponsored national patriotic youth movement closely associated with former Russian President Vladimir Putin.

> **SUMMARY TABLE**
>
> **Interests: Mobilizing, Channeling, and Shaping Politics**
>
> | | |
> |---|---|
> | **Interest Groups** | While government is no longer dominated by a small group of businessmen ("oligarchs"), big business and government remain closely intertwined. The government has also sought to control labor unions, though some independent voices representing labor are starting to be heard. |
> | **Political Parties** | Russian politics is dominated by a pro-government catchall party, United Russia, and a number of smaller pro-government parties. Among the opposition, only the Communist Party has substantial representation. |
> | **Social Movements** | In recent years, social movements have emerged as a significant part of Russian politics. Protests defending the rights of groups as diverse as pensioners, motorists, and youth are common. To combat them, pro-government youth movements have been created that mobilize young people in support of state priorities. |

and others have become entwined with one another is extraordinary in contemporary Russia. This has meant that although civil society and the private economy are both more developed than at any time since the end of communism, transparency, accountability and the rule of law have remained elusive. Interest representation continues to be something that takes place out of the public eye and access to power is restricted to small groups with little effective public pressure for more democratic procedures.

CONCLUSION

In this chapter, we have seen how Russia's post-communist experiments with rapid privatization and political pluralism led to economic crisis, a disintegration of constitutional federalism, and the domination of the state by a small group of oligarchs. Russia has many of the forms of democratic politics, but little of the content. In the 1990s, Russia had elections and political competition, but the capture of the Russian state by private interests, the disintegration of constitutional order across the vast expanse of Russian territory, and a dramatic economic collapse made it impossible to describe Russia as a democracy.

Since 2000, many of these problems have been alleviated. In particular, a single constitutional order has been reestablished across the whole country and the economy has, for most people, turned around dramatically. However, the line between private interests and the state remains extremely fuzzy, with state office and self-enrichment perhaps even more closely associated with one another than ever. Moreover, while elections continue to be held with competing candidates and even turnover at the highest political levels, the extreme centralization of power and the weakness of independent parties mean that there is little accountability. Russia may have acquired more stability and kept some democratic forms, but building a genuinely democratic system seems far off the political agenda.

Why have the hopes for democratic transition been disappointed? As we have seen in this chapter, there are many reasons. Russia and most of the former Soviet states had no history or experience with democracy to fall back on and most of the institutions inherited from the Soviet period made democratization harder, not easier, to achieve. Moreover, by the time Russia gained its independence in 1991, it faced extreme economic crisis, a disintegration of its territory and state, and the need build a democratic system at the same time. This so-called "triple transition" has proven very difficult to navigate.

In trying to deal with the political problems of the post-communist era, Russian leaders have settled on institutions that tend to centralize power, emphasizing effective over limited government. How effective the government is, as we have seen, is a matter of debate—but few would argue that government in Russia is limited. An over-powerful executive, a system that is federal in name but highly centralized in practice, and elections that allow only very limited competition have all made it less likely that liberal democracy will emerge in Russia in the near future.

Fascinatingly, the homogenized identities created by decades of communist rule have been relatively slow to change. There is little evidence of class or ethnic voting, though Russian nationalism clearly plays a role. Fears of ethnic separatism, outside of Chechnya at least, have not been realized, though the ongoing crisis in Chechnya has created serious problems of instability, especially in the Caucasus region.

The process of economic reforms, which produced great concentration of wealth and mass impoverishment, also have made it harder to achieve progress in democratization. While business interests and those of the state have become increasingly hard to distinguish, labor and other social interests have been pushed to the margins. Outsiders in the political process have little voice and political parties have either become closely integrated with the government or have faced marginalization.

Study and Review the Post-Test & Chapter Exam at mypoliscilab.com

KEY TERMS

communism 283
Great October Socialist Revolution 283
soviet 283
USSR 283
perestroika 284
Glasnost 285
Constitutional Court 287
Federation Council 288
Duma 288
semi-presidential 288
Liberal Democratic Party 294
Communist Party of the Russian Federation 294
Agrarian Party 294
Federal Security Services (FSB) 294
Committee on State Security (KGB) 294
United Russia 296
Chechnya 301
Caucasus Mountains 301
Oligarchs 303
shock therapy 307
insider privatization 307
natural resource curse 309
elite parties 311
Iabloko 312
Right Cause 312
Other Russia 315
Nashi 315

REVIEW QUESTIONS

1. Why do you think Russia has had more difficulty consolidating democracy than some of the other post-communist countries?
2. How has Russia's inheritance from the Soviet Union shaped its post-communist path?
3. Many people think that Russia's strong president has been bad for democracy—do you agree?
4. To what extent has the Russian government been justified in using force to keep Chechnya part of the Russian Federation?
5. To what extent has the privatization process of the 1990s made it harder for Russia to develop a functioning market economy and a liberal political system?

SUGGESTED READINGS

Beslan, Timothy Phillips. *The Tragedy of School No. 1*. Granta, 2007. A moving journalistic account of the events surrounding the hostage-taking and massacre that greatly influenced Russian politics in the Putin era.

Goldman, Marshall I. *Petrostate: Putin, Power and the New Russia*. Oxford University Press, 2008. Engaging explanation of the rise of Vladimir Putin and analysis of the nature of power in Russia today.

Hale, Henry E. *Why Not Parties in Russia*. Cambridge University Press, 2006. An analysis of why Russia has not developed stable political parties in the post-communist era.

Lieven, Anatole. *Chechnya: Tombstone of Russian Power*. Yale University Press, 1998. A highly readable story of the politics of the Caucasus and why Russia failed to win the first war in Chechnya.

Robertson, Graeme B. *The Politics of Protest in Hybrid Regimes*. Cambridge University Press, 2011. An account of how political protest on the streets shaped the design of Russia's political institutions and parties under Putin.

Taylor, Brian D. *State Building in Putin's Russia: Policing and Coercion after Communism*. Cambridge University Press, 2011. An impressive assessment of the revival of the Russian state under Putin.

NOTES

1. Daniel Treisman, *After the Deluge* (Ann Arbor: University of Michigan Press, 1999).
2. Peter Reddaway and Robert W. Orttung, eds. *Dynamics of Russian Politics: Putin's Reform of Federal-Regional Relations*, 2 vols. (Lanham: Rowman & Littlefield, 2004).
3. Graeme B. Robertson, "Sub-national Appointments in Authoritarian Regimes," (Midwest Political Science Association, Chicago, (2010).
4. The 1993 constitution provided for a two-year term for the first Duma and four-year terms thereafter.
5. Timothy J. Colton and Henry E. Hale, "The Putin Vote: Presidential Electorates in a Hybrid Regime," *Slavic Review*, 68, no. 3 (Fall 2009), 473–503.
6. Brian D. Taylor, *State Building in Putin's Russia: Policing and Coercion after Communism* (New York: Cambridge University Press, 2011), 82–88.
7. Timothy J. Colton and Henry E. Hale, "The Putin Vote: Presidential Electorates in a Hybrid Regime," *Slavic Review*, 68(3) (Fall 2009), 473–503.
8. For details on religiosity in Russia, see S. B. Filatov and R. N. Lunkin, "Statistics on Russian Religiosity: The Magic of Numbers and the Ambiguity of Reality," http://www.ecsocman.edu.ru/images/pubs/2006/05/04/0000276258/35-Filatovx2c_Lunkin.pdf.

9. http://www.worldvaluessurvey.org/
10. Shireen Hunter, *Islam in Russia: The Politics of Identity and Security* (Armonk, NY: M.E. Sharpe, 2004), 272.
11. Valery Tishkov, *Chechnya: Life in a War-Torn Society* (Berkeley: University of California Press, 2004).
12. Stanley Fischer and Ratna Sahay, *The Transition Economies After Ten Years* (Washington, DC: IMF, 1999).
13. Joel Hellman, "Winner Takes All" (*World Politics*, 50(2): 203–234 (1998).
14. Branko Milanovic, *Income, Inequality, and Poverty During the Transition from Planned to Market Economy* (Washington, DC: World Bank Regional and Sectoral Studies, 1998).
15. Richard M. Auty, *Sustaining Development in Mineral Economies: The Resource Curse Thesis* (London: Routledge, 1993).
16. Adam Przeworski, *Democracy and the Market: Political and Economic Reforms in Eastern Europe and Latin America* (Cambridge University Press, 1991).
17. Graeme B. Robertson, "Strikes and Labor Organization in Hybrid Regimes," *American Political Science Review*, 101(4): 781–798 (November 2007).
18. On workers and the collapse of communism, see Alain Touraine et al., *Solidarity: The Analysis of a Social Movement: Poland 1980–1981* (New York: Cambridge University Press). On workers and the collapse of the USSR, see Paul Thomas Christensen, *Russia's Workers in Transition: Labor, Management, and the State under Gorbachev and Yeltsin.* (DeKalb, Northern Illinois University Press, 1999).
19. Samuel A. Greene and Graeme B. Robertson, "Politics, Justice and the New Russian Strike," *Journal of Communist and Post-Communist Studies*, 42(4): 73–95 (December 2009).
20. Henry Hale, *Why Not Parties in Russia?* (New York: Cambridge University Press, 2006).
21. Marc Howard, *The Weakness of Civil Society in Post-Communist Europe* (New York: Cambridge University Press, 2003).
22. Graeme B. Robertson, "Managing Society: Protest, Civil Society and Regime in Putin's Russia," *Slavic Review*, 68(3): 528–547 (Fall 2009).

CHAPTER 9

Nigeria

Alexandra Scacco

A worker cleans up a spill from an abandoned Shell oil well in the Niger Delta. Nigeria's oil wealth has contributed little to the oil-producing region's development, and the Niger Delta has borne a disproportionate share of the costs associated with oil extraction.

> **What factors account for Nigeria's poor economic and political performance since independence?**

INTRODUCTION TO NIGERIA

On October 1, 1960, when Nigeria officially gained independence from Great Britain, the new country's economic and political future looked bright. A Nigerian diplomat recalls standing among the crowds in Lagos as Nnamadi Azikwe was declared the independent nation's first Nigerian governor-general:

> I was privileged to have been there when the Union Jack was finally lowered at midnight on that historic day and the new Nigerian flag of green, white, green, hoisted in its place . . . Independence had been achieved without violence or any bloodshed . . . The country had been making steady economic progress even in the last years of British colonial rule. All this was before the oil boom.
> (Ambassador Dapo Fafowora, *The Nation*, October 8, 2009)

The international press was equally positive, citing sound economic infrastructure, what appeared to be a strong agricultural sector, and vast proven oil reserves in the Niger Delta. Politically, the British had left the country on good terms with Nigeria's independent government, and the new nation's first constitution had been negotiated over more than a decade between the British and the leaders of Nigeria's three main political parties. *Time* magazine went so far as to call Nigeria an example of "democracy's workability in Africa."[1] Yet despite this initial optimism, within the next six years, Nigeria's prime minister was assassinated, a military government installed, and the country collapsed into a brutal civil war. Five decades later, Nigeria is one of the most poorly governed countries in the world, and economic development has fallen far short of expectations at independence.

For much of the post-independence period, Nigeria's economy has not simply stagnated, but actually contracted. According to the World Bank, Nigeria's per capita gross domestic product (GDP) declined from US$1,113 in 1970 to US$1,084 in 2000. By 2008, GDP per capita had risen to just over US$1,400. This figure places Nigeria below the average for sub-Saharan African countries.

While the economy has deteriorated, poverty levels have risen. The percentage of Nigerians living on less than US$2 per day has drastically increased from 36 percent in 1970 to nearly 70 percent in 2007. Nigeria currently ranks 158th out of 177 countries on the United Nations' Human Development Index (HDI), worse than many African countries without oil wealth.[2] As of 2007, only 47 percent of the country's population had access to a safe source of drinking water, well below the sub-Saharan country average of 58 percent. Even more astonishing, life expectancy at birth in Nigeria is only 48 years.

The capacity and integrity of the Nigerian government is closely linked with the disappointing state of the country's economy. Nigeria's public officials are consistently ranked among the most corrupt in the world.[3] Compared to other Africans, in 2005 Nigerians were twice as likely to have to pay a bribe to a public official to do his or her job.[4] The weakness and corruption of the Nigerian government have contributed to the decay of public infrastructure over time. All but the country's largest federal roads are poorly maintained, while hospitals and schools in much of the country lack basic equipment and even access to electricity.

The quality of democracy in Nigeria today is generally as poor as the government's record of providing basic public goods—goods or services like national defense that, once provided, are accessible to all residents of a country—to its citizens. Since the transition from military to multi-party rule in 1999, four rounds of national elections have been held—the founding elections in 1999, and subsequent elections in 2003, 2007, and 2011. All but the most recent elections were marred by widespread observable fraud, and the 2003 and 2007 elections were so poorly organized, and even violent in some parts of the country, that the major international election monitoring bodies decided not to declare them free or fair.

The government enjoys little legitimacy in the eyes of ordinary citizens. Nigerians have the lowest level of trust in their government of any Africans surveyed by the *Afrobarometer*. In 2005, only 26 percent of Nigerian survey participants said that they trusted the president, and only 22 percent trusted members of the national legislature. We can compare these numbers with those for Ghana, another West African country with a British colonial legacy. In 2005, 75 percent of Ghanaians surveyed said they trusted the president, and 68 percent trusted the legislature. Even Zimbabwe, a country that has witnessed extreme abuses of power by its government in recent years, fared better, with 31 percent trusting the president and 35 percent trusting the legislature.

At first glance, Nigeria's underperformance seems puzzling, given what appeared to be such promising signs at independence. However, just below the surface, the real picture was much less rosy. This chapter asks the question: *what factors account for Nigeria's poor economic and political performance since independence?* A number of key features of Nigeria's political history and underlying ethnic demography raise red flags: (1) the British legacy of exploitative colonial rule, (2) the impact of long military government, and (3) the country's high level of ethnic diversity.

Niger Delta ■ an oil-rich region in the south of Nigeria, which has suffered from severe pollution related to the extraction of oil and years of fighting between insurgents and government forces.

Above all, however, Nigeria's vast natural resource wealth sets it apart from many of its neighbors. In 1956, oil was first discovered in the southeastern wetlands of Nigeria, called the Niger Delta, during the final years of colonial rule, and extraction began in 1958. Today, Nigeria is sub-Saharan Africa's largest and the world's 15th largest oil producer, with an output of 2.1 million barrels per day.[5] Yet, rather than generating wealth and stability for the nation, Nigeria's oil wealth has created or exacerbated problems that similarly diverse but resource-poor African countries have been better able to confront since independence.

resource curse ■ the observation that countries with an abundance of natural resources often perform worse in terms of economic development and good governance than countries without these resources.

Nigeria is a classic case of what has come to be known as the resource curse—the observation that countries rich in natural resources like oil, diamonds, or natural gas often perform worse in terms of economic development and good governance than do countries without these resources. The example of Ghana is once again a helpful point of comparison. Ghana's mineral resources, including gold and diamonds, are minimal in scale compared with Nigeria's oil reserves. However, Ghana outperforms Nigeria in GDP per capita, life expectancy, and on many measures of democratic quality. Drawing on comparisons like these, this

TABLE 9.1

A Comparison of Sub-Saharan African Countries, 2009

Country	Total population (in thousands)	GDP per capita (2009 US$)	Natural resource rents (Percent of GDP)	Life expectancy at birth	Population below poverty line of US$1.25 per day	Primary school enrollment/attendance	Freedom status	Corruption Perception Index (worst is 0, best is 10)	Former colonial power
Angola	18,498	4,081	39%	48	54%	58%	Not free	1.9	Portugal
Botswana	1,950	5,885	4%	55	31%	87%	Free	5.6	UK
Ghana	23,837	1,098	9%	57	30%	77%	Free	3.9	UK
Nigeria	154,729	1,089	23%	48	64%	61%	Partly free	2.5	UK
Rwanda	9,998	526	3%	51	77%	86%	Not free	3.3	Belgium
Senegal	12,534	1,020	2%	56	34%	58%	Partly free	3.0	France
Sub-Saharan Africa	841,364	1,134	15%	53	53%	65%	Partly free	2.8	

Sources: World Development Indicators, UNICEF State of the World's Children, Freedom House, and Transparency International. All data are for 2009, except for population below poverty line (1994–2008) and primary school enrollment (2005–2009).

chapter will use the Nigerian case to help explain the paradox of why having an abundance of natural resource wealth can in fact be a "curse" for a country's economic and political health.

HISTORICAL OVERVIEW OF NIGERIA

Nigeria's history and politics help to explain its disappointing economic development and poor governance since independence. This section will lay the foundation for our argument that the country's ethnic diversity, colonial legacy, and problematic civil-military relations are all overshadowed by the politically divisive impact of oil.

9.1 How has Nigeria's history informed its performance as a democracy?

The Pre-Colonial Period: A Diverse Territory

Prior to the arrival of the British in the mid-1800s, some estimate that more than 200 distinct tribal groupings inhabited the territory that would become Nigeria. However, the region was dominated by three large, regionally concentrated ethnic

Explore the Comparative "Governments and Public Opinion" at mypoliscilab.com

NIGERIA

NIGERIA IN COMPARISON

	United Kingdom	Germany	France	Japan	India	Mexico	Russia	Nigeria	China	Iran
Freedom House Classification	Democracy	Democracy	Democracy	Democracy	Democracy	Partial democracy	Partial democracy	Partial democracy	Non-democracy	Non-democracy
Land Size (sq km)	243,610	357,022	643,801	377,915	3,287,263	1,964,375	17,098,242	923,768	9,596,961	1,648,195
Land Size Ranking	79	62	42	61	7	15	1	32	4	18
Population (July 2011 Estimate)	62,698,362	81,471,834	65,312,249	126,475,664	1,189,172,906	113,724,226	138,739,892	155,215,573	1,336,718,015	77,891,220
Population Ranking	22	16	21	10	2	11	9	8	1	18
Life Expectancy (Years)	80.1	80.1	81.2	82.3	66.8	76.5	66.3	47.6	74.7	70.1
Life Expectancy Ranking	28	27	13	5	51	72	162	220	95	146
Literacy Rate	99%	99%	99%	99%	61%	86.1%	99.4%	68%	91.6%	77%
GDP Per Capita (2010 Estimate)	US$35,100	US$35,900	US$33,300	US$34,000	US$3,500	US$13,800	US$15,900	US$2,500	US$7,600	US$11,200
GDP Ranking	36	32	39	38	163	85	71	178	126	100

groups: the Ibo in the southeast, the Yoruba in the southwest, and the Hausa in the north of the country. These three groups governed themselves very differently from each other. The Ibo were organized into many relatively small city-states, with no centralized political authority in the region. In the southwest, the Yoruba lands were divided into small, often warring, states—such as the Oyo and Benin empires, and later city-states such as Ijebu and Ibadan.

In contrast, from as early as the eleventh century, the Hausa territories were ruled through a series of highly centralized monarchies, known as emirates, in what would become northern Nigeria. By 1804, most of the Hausa territory had been brought under the control of a single monarchy, the Sokoto Caliphate. Thus, by the time Nigeria became part of the British Empire, in 1900, the Hausa region had been ruled as a distinct state for nearly a hundred years.

The population of Nigeria's territory was also divided along religious lines. In the 1500s, Islam reached the Hausa states via trans-Saharan trade and migration networks. By the early nineteenth century, as the result of the wars of the "jihad" in the northern region, the overwhelming majority of the Hausa population had converted to Islam. In contrast, residents of the south of the country practiced diverse indigenous religious traditions prior to colonial rule.

This underlying ethnic and religious diversity has often been blamed for Nigeria's contemporary governance woes. However, on its own, the country's ethnic and religious composition cannot easily explain why the Nigerian government is worse at providing public services when compared with similarly diverse West African countries such as Ghana or Cameroon. The pre-colonial ethnic landscape is still important to consider, though, because the British thought about these divisions as they designed colonial institutions that would shape political competition after independence.

Colonial Nigeria: Unequal Regional Development

In the late 1800s vast stretches of West African territory came under British influence, as European powers extended their colonial empires in what is known as the "Scramble for Africa." In 1886, the British chartered the Royal Niger Company, which unified British commercial interests in the lower regions of the Niger River. In 1900, the territory was added to the British Empire when Nigeria officially became a British protectorate.

Britain ruled the country much as its other colonies were administered, with the primary goal of extracting natural resources—such as palm oil, cocoa, and groundnuts—rather than promoting local development. When they established their protectorate, the British divided the territory into northern and southern regions and governed them as separate administrative units under different leadership and governance rules. The British attempted to apply indirect rule—a strategy that deliberately used local and native political institutions to carry out colonial administration—in all areas but with very different levels of success. In the north, the British governed through the Hausa emirs, who retained some political power of their own in exchange for accepting British authority. As part of this bargain, the British agreed to limit the spread of European culture in the northern region,

Colonial administrators meet with tribal representatives in Lagos, 1910. While southern Nigeria was under direct British rule, the north of Nigeria was ruled indirectly. These distinct strategies of rule contributed to different levels of political participation and economic development in the two regions.

closing the entire area to Christian missionaries and severely limiting the possibility for local children to attend English-style schools.

In contrast, Christian missionaries and English schooling were permitted in the southern region. Within several decades, much of the south's population was converted to Christianity, and major investments in education were made across the southern protectorate. Yet compared to the north, indirect rule worked less smoothly in the south, particularly in the southeastern Ibo region, where the British encountered more popular resistance and had difficulty finding a stable leadership through which to govern.

These different approaches to colonial rule, particularly with respect to religion and education, led to uneven political and economic development in the north and the south. By 1950, several hundred southerners had completed university degrees, while only one person from the north was a university graduate.[6] As a result, southerners were far more likely to work within the colonial administration than northerners, and their exposure to European cultural influences encouraged southerners to take a more active role in politics. For example, by the 1920s, nationalist pro-independence movements had emerged in the southwestern colonial capital of Lagos, and local candidates ran in municipal elections. In contrast, the emirs discouraged political and nationalist activities in the north, where the first political parties did not emerge until the late 1940s. These north–south differences became increasingly contentious as the colonial government began to negotiate the terms of independence with Nigerian political elites.

By the early 1950s, political parties had emerged to represent each of the three major ethnic groups: the Hausa were represented by the Northern People's Congress (NPC), the Yoruba by the Action Group (AG), and the Ibo by the National Council of Nigeria and the Cameroons (NCNC). The party leaders from each region competed vigorously to retain their ethnic autonomy and influence what would become Nigeria's first independent political institutions.

In 1957, the southeastern (Ibo) and southwestern (Yoruba) regions became formally self-governing. Leaders of the northern (Hausa) region initially refused self-governance, because they feared the two southern regions would control Nigeria's independent government and discriminate against their region's Islamic traditions. The northern emirs agreed to self-government in 1959, but only after obtaining key political concessions from the British, including guarantees that the north would receive at least half of the seats in the new central House of Representatives, and that the allocation of all government tax revenue, including oil revenues, would be based on population. This last item was particularly important for two reasons. First, the 1952 census determined that the population of the north was significantly larger than that of the southern regions combined and, second, because oil was discovered in southern Nigeria in 1956.[7]

By 1958, it was clear that the revenues from oil would be vast. This fact, in combination with the strong ethno-regional cleavages described above, quickly reduced Nigeria's politics to a fight over the way in which oil revenues would be divided and distributed. As the size of the potential national "cake" increased, so did the rewards for controlling the central government.

Nigeria since Independence: Political and Economic Crisis

Nigeria became formally independent in October 1960, and the question of how diverse ethnic groups might work together to distribute revenues from oil production remained at the heart of its politics after independence. Already by this point, political competition centered on a three-way competition over control of the central government and access to the rapidly increasing oil revenues. During Nigeria's first experiment with democracy, between 1960 and 1966—what would later come to be known as the First Republic—national-level politics were defined by a series of increasingly bitter disagreements between the main regional political parties.

In 1966, a group of mostly Ibo military officers seized power in a coup d'état. When northern officers regained power by overthrowing them, the Ibo seceded from Nigeria and declared themselves the independent Republic of Biafra. Nigeria collapsed into a civil war, known as the Biafran War, which lasted from 1967 until 1970, when Biafra was defeated. It is estimated that at least a million people died, many from disease and starvation, and the war devastated the economy in the southeast. The coup in 1966 and the ensuing civil war resulted in more than a decade of military rule, ending democracy in Nigeria for many years.

Following the end of the civil war, the 1970s began a period of economic optimism in Nigeria. In 1973, and then again in 1979, the price of oil soared, resulting

---

House of Representatives ■ the more powerful of the two chambers of the National Assembly, it has 360 directly elected members.

First Republic ■ Nigeria's first period of democratic governance, from 1960 to 1966. Characterized by intense regional disagreements, it ended in a coup and was followed by more than a decade of military rule.

Republic of Biafra ■ a majority Ibo state in the southeast of Nigeria that seceded from the remainder of the country in 1967; it was reabsorbed into Nigeria in 1970, after a brutal civil war that killed more than a million people.

in a massive influx of oil revenues to the central government. In response, the government began to spend lavishly on large-scale infrastructure projects. A detailed investigation of Nigerian economic development during the oil boom reveals that, between 1973 and 1980, Nigeria's capital stock grew at an average rate of 14 percent per year, leading to an astonishing tripling of Nigeria's capital stock in only eight years.[8]

In spite of high levels of government spending, Nigeria emerged from the decade with little to show in the way of economic productivity. By the end of the 1970s, manufacturing had begun to stagnate. Capacity utilization in manufacturing, a sector largely owned by the government, declined from an average of 77 percent in 1975 to less than 40 percent by the mid-1980s. Thus, the gap between the potential output that could be generated with existing infrastructure and the actual output produced became much wider during this period. It is difficult to escape the view that much of the government's investment of oil revenues was wasted.[9]

An infamous example of unproductive government investment is the Ajaokuta steel complex, located in central Nigeria. Since construction began in the late 1970s, more than US$1 billion of government funds has been allocated to the project. Yet more than 30 years later, the mill still has not produced a single piece of steel! Today, the plant sits virtually empty, with the exception of a small, underutilized staff, even though it was initially meant to employ as many as 10,000 workers. Although it is difficult to prove, conventional accounts of the project suggest that sizeable sums of money were siphoned off into private hands.[10] What is clear is that this type of investment in industry contributed little to the country's economy.

In 1979, the military government, then led by Yoruba army officer General Olusegun Obasanjo—who would later become Nigeria's president from 1999–2007—relinquished power. Nigeria adopted a new constitution, this time modeled after the United States rather than Great Britain. National elections were held in 1979, ushering in what came to be known as the Second Republic. These elections marked the first peaceful transfer of power since independence, and expectations for the new government were high.

Unfortunately, the new democratic system was doomed to fail, partly because the oil boom ended abruptly when the price of oil fell in 1981. Between 1980 and 1982, oil revenues declined by 53 percent. The government's inability to manage the economic crisis encouraged the military to seize power again in December 1983, followed by another military coup in 1985. Military rule continued throughout the 1980s and 1990s, with the exception of an abortive effort to reestablish democracy in 1993 that lasted for less than two weeks.

During the 1980s and 1990s, military leaders redrew Nigeria's political institutions, concentrating power in the hands of the central government and gutting the authority of regional legislatures. The military also sought to destroy Nigeria's main political parties. In 1989, the military ruler at the time dissolved all existing parties and replaced them with two parties created by the military.[11] Moreover, during this period, the government became more repressive, taking control of the press, banning all popular political activity, and sanctioning widespread human rights abuses.

Olusegun Obasanjo
■ military ruler from 1976 to 1979 and elected president in 1999 until 2007.

Second Republic ■ the democratic institutions in place between 1979 and a military coup in 1983; the regime was modeled on the American system of government.

Sani Abacha ■
Nigeria's most repressive military dictator, who assumed power in a coup in 1993 and ruled until his death in 1998.

Fourth Republic ■
Nigeria's current political regime, in place since the adoption of the 1999 constitution.

In June 1998, the opportunity for democracy re-emerged when General Sani Abacha, Nigeria's most autocratic military ruler to date, died suddenly of a heart attack. Less than a year after Abacha's death, former military head of state Olusegun Obasanjo was elected president in multi-party elections in April 1999. These elections ushered in Nigeria's Fourth Republic. Given Nigeria's history of failed attempts to transition to democracy, it is important to ask how such a repressive leader's death could lead so quickly to the holding of elections.

The nature of Abacha's rule had led to intense domestic and political pressure for a genuine transition to democratic politics. Following Abacha's takeover in a coup in 1993, his government became notorious at home and abroad for its human rights abuses, particularly its brutal repression of any political dissent, and its staggering corruption, even by domestic standards. Some estimates suggest that Abacha and his family personally stole as much as $3 billion from the state during his rule.[12] Abacha's abuses caused many countries to restrict diplomatic relations and curtail their development aid to Nigeria. By 1995, domestic and international pressure for a return to multi-party politics pushed Abacha to promise a democratic transition within three years.

A few months before he died, Abacha oversaw carefully scripted elections, during which all five parties allowed to participate nominated him as their only candidate for president. The public reaction was swift and violent, including demonstrations, riots, and even anti-government bombings.[13] During his time as head of state, Abacha centralized power to such a great extent that he left behind no clear successor when he died. It also quickly became clear that many members of his officer corps supported the transition to civilian rule. Abacha's excesses discredited military rule to such an unprecedented degree that the public was able to force a rapid transition to multi-party elections.

Nigeria's Fourth Republic began with the country's deep economic crisis, with decaying infrastructure, and weak political institutions. During Obasanjo's years as president (1999–2007), civil liberties improved and several major macroeconomic reforms were credited with reducing inflation and attracting higher levels of foreign investment.[14] Yet Obasanjo's government performed far less well in curbing government corruption and improving living standards for ordinary Nigerians, and perhaps his most enduring legacy will be his questionable commitment to free and fair political competition, discussed in the next section.

Several underlying features of Nigeria's politics and demographics have hindered the country's progress toward a stable and prosperous democracy. On the eve of independence, political competition had already taken the form of a struggle between three large ethno-regional political blocs with semi-autonomous political institutions vying for control over the central government and access to the country's increasing oil wealth. Civil war, military rule, staggering corruption, and mismanagement of the economy were the major legacies of Nigeria's first four decades of independence. Although political freedoms have improved since the transition from military rule in 1999, it remains to be seen whether the Nigerian government today can escape its legacy of economic crisis and governance failure.

SUMMARY TABLE

Historical Overview: Colonization and Regime Change in Nigeria since the Nineteenth Century

1800s	Indigenous states and empires (e.g., the Sokoto Caliphate in northern Nigeria)	Ended with British conquest
1886–1899	Royal Niger Company in operation	Ended with transfer to imperial Britain
1900–1913	British protectorates of northern and southern Nigeria	Ended with merger
1914–1960	British protectorate	Ended with Nigeria's independence
1960–1966	First Republic	Ended with military coup by Ibo officers
1966–1979	First period of military rule	Ended with election of civilian government
1979–1983	Second Republic	Ended with military coup after contested election
1983–1993	Second period of military rule	Ended with presidential election
1993	Third Republic	Aborted when military government annuls election results
1993–1999	Third period of military rule	Ended with death of Abacha and transition to civilian rule
1999–present	Fourth Republic	

INSTITUTIONS OF NIGERIA

Nigeria's contemporary government institutions contribute to the country's poor political and economic performance. In theory, Nigeria's institutions should promote "good government." However, the formal rules are rarely put into practice. Instead, most of Nigeria's state institutions are too weak to function as they are supposed to, according to their description in the constitution. We will consider three explanations for Nigerian institutional weakness: (1) the legacy of colonialism, (2) the experience of post-independence military rule, and (3) the distorting impacts of oil on the country's politics and economy. As we shall see, although all three explanations have merit, the impact of oil best helps to explain Nigeria's institutional weakness in comparison with other sub-Saharan African countries.

9.2 To what extent can the weakness of Nigerian state institutions be explained by its oil abundance, as opposed to its historical experiences with colonial or military rule?

Nigeria's Political Institutions in Theory

Explore the Comparative "Subnational Governments" at mypolscilab.com

Before we can understand some of the shortcomings of Nigerian governance today, we need a basic understanding of the country's political system, as laid out in the constitution.

Like the United States, Nigeria is a *federal system.* The country is carved into 36 states, each with its own house of assembly, governor, and bureaucracy. What makes the country federal is the fact that several areas of policy are made by states, without the involvement of the central government. Nigeria has been a federation since the end of the colonial period, a decision made by the British in an attempt to respond to long-standing ethnic divisions in the colonial territory. Federalism in Nigeria is supposed to decentralize political power.

As are most countries in Africa, Nigeria is a *presidential system,* which means that vast powers in the central government are concentrated in the hands of the president. Nigeria's current constitution was modeled after the American political system in a number of important respects. The president is directly elected through a popular vote and, unlike in parliamentary systems, the legislature—the National Assembly—does not have the power to dismiss him. The only routine way for a president to be removed from office is through the ballot box, since impeachment requires at least two-thirds of the votes of members of the National Assembly. The Nigerian president is powerful in the same way that the American president is powerful, due to the system's "separation of origin" (the president is directly elected, not chosen by the legislature) and "separation of survival" (the president cannot be dismissed by the legislature).

National Assembly ■ Nigeria's national legislature, modeled after the U.S. Congress. The body is composed of a Senate with equal representation for all of Nigeria's states, and a House of Representatives with representatives apportioned in proportion to each state's population.

In terms of the second way politics is structured, the electoral system, Nigeria can be considered strongly *majoritarian.* Electoral districts for all elections always have a magnitude of one, meaning that only one candidate from each constituency can win office. This is obvious in the case of the presidency, but for other political offices, this is an important fact. Races for the national legislature or the state houses of assembly can be described as "winner take all" elections, in that candidates who come in second or third, even if the race is close, do not gain any position in government. In addition, the electoral system operates under the *plurality rule,* meaning that the candidate who wins the most votes gains office, even if he or she does not capture more than 50 percent of the vote.

federal character principle ■ the constitutional requirement that a candidate must win not only the most votes but also a quarter of the votes in at least two-thirds of Nigeria's states in order to win the presidency.

The plurality voting system in Nigeria operates with an important twist for presidential and gubernatorial elections. In these races, under what has been dubbed the federal character principle, candidates must not only win the most votes, but must also win at least one-quarter of the vote in at least two-thirds of the states (for the president) or local government areas (for the governor) that they will preside over when in office. This means that, for example, a presidential candidate is forced to appeal to voters across regions, since no single region—north, southeast or southwest—contains two-thirds of Nigeria's states. The federal character system has been in place since Nigeria's second experiment with democracy (the Second Republic, founded in 1979), and was created with the goal of undermining the inter-regional conflict that contributed to the Biafran War.

In theory, Nigeria also has a relatively autonomous judiciary. Chapter IV of the Nigerian Constitution includes an expansive set of provisions designed to ensure individual liberties and protect civil rights. In principle, the constitution also allows for judicial review of legislative decisions and executive actions. However, Nigeria's judicial system is complex because it combines three codes of law: Nigerian statute law, customary law, and Sharia law (Islamic law). Nigeria's statute law is heavily influenced by English law, and empowers state legislatures to pass laws on any subject that is not exclusively reserved for the federal government. This "Exclusive Legislative List" includes laws relating to defense, foreign policy, and the use of natural resources. Each of Nigeria's 36 states has a high court. Nigeria's highest court is the Supreme Court, which is presided over by the Chief Justice of Nigeria and up to 21 justices. The Supreme Court was created to hear appeals from the state high courts.

Sharia law ■
religious Islamic law, which has been adopted in several northern Nigerian states.

Customary law in Nigeria is designed to reflect indigenous customs and practices. It can vary by locality and is administered by customary courts, usually led by traditional tribal rulers and applied to areas like domestic disputes and requests for divorce. Finally, under the Fourth Republic, several states in the northern region have made the contentious decision to adopt Islamic law. Advocates of Sharia claim that it applies only to Muslim Nigerians, but non-Muslim minorities in the north have argued that this is difficult to effect in practice, citing restrictions on the sale of alcohol and mixed gender public buses as examples. Ambiguities in the constitution about the legality of Sharia continue to fuel the debate in Nigeria today.

In sum, although the president is powerful, Nigeria's political institutions—including federalism, the separation of powers and an independent judiciary—are, in theory, designed to disperse rather than concentrate political power. As a democracy, government should in theory protect individual and group rights while also promoting law and order. Moreover, by forcing candidates to appeal to Nigerians on a basis other than ethnicity, the presidency is supposed to serve as a unifying force, in an effort to overcome the divisive impact of Nigeria's long-standing ethnic divisions.

Nigeria's Political Institutions in Practice

On paper, Nigeria's political institutions should provide both limited and effective government. In practice, Nigeria's institutions have never lived up to that promise. Although Nigeria is technically a federal system, the central government is by far the senior partner in the federation, while the states have far less autonomy over important policy issues than state governments do in the United States. The federal government is exclusively in charge of all taxation decisions and tax collection, all election rules, the military, regulation of the financial sector, corporations, labor unions, trade, and the police. As such, if a large-scale riot or protest breaks out in a particular state, it is up to the central government to decide when and how to respond. States are in charge of building and maintaining non-federal roads, zoning laws, waste management, and the structure and content of primary and secondary education. With respect to schooling, however, a closer look at the constitution reveals that the National Assembly has the power to set "minimum standards" of education at all levels. In practice, this means that the central government intervenes in education policy, an area that many state officials feel should be their responsibility.

Beyond the *formal* weakness of the states, as written into the constitution, state governments are further handicapped in practice by frequent failure of the central government to distribute funds in full and on time to states. It is widely acknowledged that state budgets are smaller in reality than they should be according to the law, due to rampant corruption at the highest levels of government. The imbalance in power between the central government and the states have led prominent scholars to label Nigerian federalism as "hollow" or "sham" federalism.[15]

The description of the electoral system in the previous section also sheds light on the way that political competition *should* take place, if all worked according to the constitution. In reality, however, the relationship between the popular vote and which candidates ultimately take up office in important elections like gubernatorial races and the presidential contest has become increasingly tenuous since political competition returned in 1999. Obasanjo was re-elected in controversial elections in 2003 and his favored candidate, Umaru Yar'Adua (also from the People's Democratic Party), was elected president in 2007.

Umaru Yar'Adua ■ president of Nigeria from 2007 until his death in 2010.

In 2003, international observers across the country observed irregularities at polling stations across the country, including outright intimidation and violence by armed militias, particularly in the Niger Delta region. In 2007, the irregularities were sufficient that election monitors, including the EU observer mission, claimed that the electoral outcomes, for both presidential and governor races, in many states most likely did not reflect the will of the majority of voters.[16] As a result, Nigeria's democracy rankings by the Freedom House organization declined following the 2007 elections. Its scores since 2003 in the areas of political rights and civil liberties have never risen above 4 on a scale from 1–7, where 1 describes a democratic process that is "fully free" and 7 one that is "not at all free." In 2009, Nigeria's political rights score slipped from 4 to 5, partly because of new evidence on the flawed nature of the 2007 national elections.[17] The 2011 elections came much closer to being free and fair, but even so, the quality of electoral competition over the past decade suggests we should be cautious about calling Nigeria a democracy, much less a consolidated democracy.

More generally, an analysis of formal political institutions is probably not the best way to study Nigerian politics. The weakness of many of Nigeria's institutions makes it difficult for other branches of government to function in the way they were intended. For example, the judicial branch is a relatively independent arm of government, but it often takes years for court decisions to be reached and for rulings to take effect. Although they began investigations in April 2007, it was only in February 2009 that election tribunals were able to overturn seven of the most questionable results of the most recent gubernatorial elections. Examples like these reflect the pervasive weakness of many Nigerian political institutions, with the notable exception of the office of the president. The rest of this section will describe this weakness in more detail and will offer explanations for the low levels of state capacity we observe in Nigeria today.

A "Critically Weak" State

One of the clearest manifestations of the gap between the promise and the reality of Nigerian government is the weakness of the Nigerian state. Put most simply, Nigeria's state does not perform some of its most basic functions. Although

Nigeria is not a failed state—a country in which the government cannot maintain effective political control over the national territory—the Nigerian government struggles to perform many of the core functions we expect from a state. In 2009, the Fund for Peace published its annual "Failed States Index," ranking 177 countries according to the stability and effectiveness of their governments. Somalia, a country that has been without a functioning central government since 1991, was ranked as the weakest state, while Norway, a prosperous welfare state and consolidated democracy, was listed as the most sustainable state. Nigeria was ranked as the 15th weakest state in the world, performing worse than the majority of sub-Saharan African countries. The index rated several of Nigeria's main political institutions, including the police, the judiciary, and the civil service, as among the weakest in the world.[18] Two important dimensions of state capacity are (1) a government's ability to maintain order within its borders, and (2) its capacity to provide other basic public goods to citizens. Several concrete examples will help highlight Nigeria's weakness along these two dimensions.

Most critically, the Nigerian government has difficulty maintaining law and order within the state's borders. Since the return to multi-party politics in 1999, Human Rights Watch estimates that as many as 10,000 people have been killed in hundreds of localized violent conflicts, ranging from religious riots between Christians and Muslims in northern Nigerian cities, to conflicts between herders and farmers in rural areas, to violence between government and insurgent groups in the Niger Delta region. Many of these violent conflicts started out small in scale, but quickly spiraled out of control because the police lacked the manpower, training and resources to stop them.

Large-scale conflicts between Christians and Muslims have become both more common and more deadly in the past decade. In perhaps the best-known cases, riots in the northern towns of Kaduna and Jos in 2000 and 2001, respectively, killed at least 2,000 civilians and displaced thousands more. In both cases, police forces were quickly overwhelmed and the violence continued for several days before military intervention ended the fighting. Riots in dozens of other towns followed a similar pattern.[19] The virtual non-presence of police in urban areas has led to the rise of vigilante security groups—in some cases deliberately sanctioned by state and local governments—to carry out the crime-fighting duties of the police.

The absence of law and order represents the most egregious, but by no means the only obvious, failure of the Nigerian state. Public service provision is also notoriously poor across most of Nigeria. Perhaps the most emblematic failure in Nigeria today is the central government's inability to maintain the national electricity grid. In a country of massive oil deposits, it is estimated that only 36 percent of Nigerians have regular access to electricity from the national electricity monopoly, the National Electric Power Authority (NEPA)—which Nigerians dryly refer to as "Never Expect Power Again." Most Nigerians experience daily power outages, disrupting productive activity and causing those who can afford them to invest in expensive private generators. In 2009, parts of Lagos, the capital city, went without power for an entire month, and many rural areas go without power for days or even weeks at a time. Nigeria's electricity generation capacity is one tenth of South

Africa's, a country with one-third of Nigeria's population. Indeed, many analysts consider the lack of stable, affordable electricity the most important immediate cause of Nigeria's slow economic growth.[20]

As limited as the central government's capacity to deliver public goods has been, lower tiers of government perform far worse. On paper, local governments are responsible for administering a range of local public goods, including building and maintaining sanitation systems, local roads, health clinics, and public schools. In practice, local governments across the country lack the capacity to fulfill these tasks. This is not surprising, however, as they have virtually no independent sources of income and rely entirely on disbursements from the central government that often simply do not arrive. The limited authority granted to local officials hampers policymaking on the ground and contributes to poor outcomes. For example, the Nigerian police force is largely controlled by the central government and, because of decisions taken during military rule, police offers are often assigned to work in locations far from home. Police officers, therefore, commonly lack local knowledge and may not even speak the local language fluently, making it difficult to effectively carry out their duties.[21]

The Colonial Legacy and State Weakness   How can we explain the fact that Nigeria, Africa's most populous country and its largest oil exporter, is saddled with such feeble infrastructure and such weak institutions? One commonly made argument for poor economic and political outcomes in sub-Saharan Africa focuses on the legacy of colonial rule in the region. Because their main goal was the extraction of natural resources, rather than promoting local development, European colonizers in Africa did not build strong and legitimate political institutions with the interests of local populations in mind. Instead, colonial authorities invested just enough coercive power to prevent local unrest, and only developed infrastructure if doing so would help them extract resources.

Due to the nature of decades of colonial rule, upon independence in the mid-1900s, most new African states confronted especially unfavorable conditions for building effective states. The British ruled Nigeria as they did other "extractive" colonies, and it did not enjoy the benefits of robust representative political institutions or guaranteed private property rights before independence. Investments in railway infrastructure and roads were made primarily to facilitate the export of local natural resources, including tin, cotton, cocoa, groundnuts, and palm oil. Other aspects of Nigerian colonial administration were also less than ideal, including the administration of the northern and southern regions in isolation from one another until relatively late in the colonial period.

Nigeria's low level of economic development today cannot be understood without reference to its colonial past. However, the Nigerian experience was not as pernicious as the worst forms of extractive rule in Africa. The transfer of power from British to Nigerian rule offers a useful example. Decolonization in Nigeria did not happen overnight, as in many cases in Africa. The British negotiated the terms of independence for more than a decade with politicians from each of the three major ethno-regional groups before departing in 1960. Similarly, the adoption of a federal constitution in 1954 was a deliberate attempt to accommodate patterns of ethnic diversity that pre-dated colonial rule. At the very least, Nigeria's colonial experience was not sufficiently negative to distinguish it from other African countries with a legacy of colonial rule which have performed far better since independence.

Another argument that is difficult to fit with the Nigerian experience focuses on *which* European power ran the colonial administration. Many scholars have argued that a legacy of British rule is associated with more effective and more representative post-colonial institutions than that of rule by other European countries.[22] In sub-Saharan Africa, 19 countries are former British colonies. The quality of governance today varies widely across these countries, with Botswana, Ghana, and South Africa generally considered top performers, and Eritrea, Sudan, and Nigeria performing worse on standard measures of economic development and governance. The fact that Nigeria performs worse than most other former British colonies suggests that a legacy of British rule cannot on its own account for Nigeria's underperformance.

Military Rule and State Weakness Another possible explanation for the low level of state capacity we observe in Nigeria today is its long experience with military rule since independence. Authoritarian rule has been common throughout Africa. Scholars have associated military rule with poor governance outcomes through several different channels. For example, military involvement in politics has been associated with higher levels of corruption and less competent economic policymaking than other forms of government. Other cross-national research has shown that military coups increase the likelihood of *future* coups, an argument that fits with Nigeria's turbulent politics of the 1980s and 1990s. The instability in politics associated with coups has been linked to poor economic development, such as low levels of economic growth.[23]

Military governments have ruled Nigeria for 29 of its 50 years of independence. However, there is no clear relationship between the prevalence of military rule in Africa and government performance on political and economic indicators. A number of countries with relatively long histories of military rule, including Ghana (23 years) and Benin (21 years), are relatively strong economic performers, and have relatively effective and legitimate states. Conversely, several poor performers have had only short experiences with military rule, including Sierra Leone (six years) and Liberia (four years).

Similarly, the case for a "military curse" does not hold up if we compare periods of democracy to non-democracy in Nigeria since independence. In a recent study, Carl LeVan shows that the Nigerian government performed no better on important policy outcomes during democratic rule than during periods of military government. For example, the government's budget deficits were no worse during the years of military rule, and civilian governments were no better in terms of improving education outcomes or in terms of improving the efficiency of the judicial system.[24] On balance, Nigeria's experience with military rule is not sufficient to explain its poor government performance since independence.

TABLE 9.2

Heads of State since Independence

1960–1966	Nnamdi Azikiwe	Appointed governor-general, elected president	Deposed
1966	Johnson Aguiyi-Ironsi	Assumed power in military coup	Assassinated
1966–1975	Yakubu Gowon	Assumed power in military coup	Deposed
1975–1976	Murtala Mohammed	Assumed power in military coup	Assassinated
1976–1979	Olusegun Obasanjo	Succeeded Mohammed upon his death	Transfer to civilian rule
1979–1983	Shehu Shagari	Elected president	Deposed
1983–1985	Muhammadu Buhari	Assumed power in military coup	Deposed
1985–1993	Ibrahim Babangida	Assumed power in military coup	Resigned
1993	Ernest Shonekan	Appointed by Babangida	Deposed
1993–1998	Sani Abacha	Assumed power in military coup	Died in office
1998–1999	Abdulsalami Abubakar	Succeeded Abacha upon his death	Transfer to civilian rule
1999–2007	Olusegun Obasanjo	Elected president	Stepped down after two terms
2007–2010	Umaru Yar'Adua	Elected president	Died in office
2010–present	Goodluck Jonathan	Assumed power when Yar'Adua fell ill, elected president in 2011	

Oil Dependence and State Weakness

The most important factor explaining Nigeria's institutional weakness and poor political and economic performance is the government's heavy reliance on oil revenues. Evidence for a resource curse is strong, both in global studies and when one limits the analysis to African countries. For example, scholars have found that between 1960 and 1990, GDP per capita in countries rich in mineral resources increased at an annual rate of 1.7 percent, compared with a growth rate of between 2.5 and 3.5 percent in countries without mineral resources.[25]

On average, natural resource–dependent countries in Africa, including Nigeria, Angola, Sudan, Cameroon, and the Democratic Republic of Congo, have been less democratic and less prosperous than countries lacking natural resources, including Benin, Mali, and Senegal.[26] Among African countries classified as rich in natural resources, only Botswana, which is rich in diamonds, managed to achieve both high levels of long-term investment (greater than 25 percent of GDP) and an annual per capita GDP growth rate of more than 4 percent per year.[27]

More than any other natural resource, oil dependence has been linked to a range of other problems in economic development. Oil-exporting countries exhibit strikingly high levels of poverty, economic inequality, poorer education and health indicators, higher levels of corruption, higher levels of intra-state violence, and delayed or incomplete democratization.[28] In sum, research makes clear predictions about the effects of overreliance on oil, but we know less about *why* oil dependence is so harmful. A number of possible causal mechanisms link the presence of oil wealth with poor economic and political outcomes through the channel of institutional weakness.

Oil and Weak Bureaucratic Capacity

In theory, states that sit atop vast oil reserves should be rich, and should be able to use that wealth to develop a strong, effective state. Paradoxically, however, oil abundance seems to have had harmful effects on the Nigerian economy. One reason for this is that states that have access to revenues from the sale of oil are not forced to raise revenue by taxing their own citizens.[29] Oil eliminates the need for direct linkages between citizens and the state that political scientists have long argued are crucial for the formation of strong states. The "easy money" from oil flows in such great quantities that the Nigerian government virtually ceased investing in other sectors of the economy such as agriculture or industry.

Instead, government actors spend much of their time engaged in rent-seeking—trying to manipulate political rules in order to capture profits—for example, from the sale of oil on international markets. Moreover, because the oil industry is unusually capital intensive rather than labor intensive, it generates relatively few jobs. Those jobs that are available are usually filled by foreigners because the Nigerian education system has generally not been able to produce a sufficient number of skilled workers.

Oil also tends to weaken state institutional capacity because its production is relatively easy to tax. This means that political leaders have powerful incentives to

rent-seeking ■ manipulating the economic environment in order to capture economic "rents," created when the state directly receives income from selling goods, like oil, at levels above their production costs.

invest in the oil industry and to maintain political control over the oil industry, and weak incentives to spend time and money up front in developing the bureaucratic capacity to tax citizens in other ways. Taxing is not simply about getting people's money—governments need highly educated, trained, skilled personnel to administer the tax bureaucracy, modern computer systems to manage all the data, a legal system to adjudicate contentious tax cases, and personnel with police powers to pursue cases of tax evasion. Oil, however, is easy to tax: its extraction and refining cannot be hidden from the view of government, and it is very difficult to smuggle large quantities of oil under the nose of government authorities, in contrast to money, guns, or drugs. Therefore, states that can tax oil production often do not seek to fully develop the government institutions necessary to administer other forms of taxes.[30]

This situation is compounded in post-colonial states like Nigeria. In early-forming states, government bureaucracies evolved and consolidated over centuries, often in response to popular demands for public services. In contrast, many ex-colonies had extremely weak bureaucracies upon independence. These bureaucracies had not been designed with the local population in mind. Instead, colonial authorities designed them with their own interests in mind—interests that involved extracting and exporting raw materials such as gold, rubber, or ivory. The discovery of oil did not generate incentives for Nigerian leaders to develop strong and legitimate government institutions after independence—quite the contrary. Since independence, tax collection beyond the oil industry has been minimal in Nigeria. The government has never invested much in developing either tax-collecting capacity or the administrative capacity to spend government revenue effectively on public services such as education, infrastructure development, or health care. In short, oil revenues give government leaders few incentives to invest in developing bureaucratic capacity.

Oil and the Absence of Government Accountability The cause of weak state capacity in oil-rich countries is not simply about taxing, it is also about spending. When states tax their citizens, citizens typically demand something in return: they want decent public services and they want to hold their leaders to account if the government fails to provide those services. Because citizens are not taxed heavily in oil-rich states, they tend to complain less about poor government services. In this way, oil wealth short-circuits the mechanisms that tend to lead to more effective and legitimate government.

When citizens are not taxed, they have relatively weak interests in mobilizing to demand better government services, because such mobilization would, in effect, be demanding both higher taxes and better services, not just the latter. In an environment where the government demands little of citizens but also promises little in return, citizens are likely to be less engaged in politics and will pay less attention to the way in which public resources are used. The absence of taxation eliminates an important source of citizen oversight and accountability: without pressure from citizens, the nation's individuals, media, and interest groups in civil society will not actively seek to hold government power-holders accountable.

Thus, oil dependence tends to weaken incentives for citizens to hold the government to accounts, and allows corruption to run rampant. A brief discussion of the way that oil revenues are distributed in Nigeria illustrates this dynamic at work. As in many other oil economies, in Nigeria multinational corporations bid for contracts to extract and export oil. Revenues flow directly from these multinationals into a central government fund based on how much oil the multinationals extract. In theory, the central government is then supposed to distribute resources to states and cities. However, as noted above, the institutions do not work as they are described on paper. Instead, politicians with sticky fingers manage to get their hands on much of the oil revenues and use those monies for their own purposes, to enrich themselves and their friends, or to fund their own campaigns or campaigns of their political allies.

The description above links oil wealth to poor governance outcomes through the channel of weak institutions, which have allowed government activities at all levels to be dominated by a vicious cycle of corruption that further weakens the state. The ease of access to oil revenues weakens politicians' interests in the hard work of developing state administrative institutions that might effectively deliver public policies and improve state legitimacy. Without oversight from citizens or government institutions themselves, politicians prioritize obtaining access to oil revenues rather than advocating particular policy positions that might improve citizens' lives or improve the economy. And in a low-tax environment, citizens have few interests in protesting against government mismanagement of public funds. In the end, the reliance on oil has enriched a tiny segment of Nigeria's population while actually leading to higher levels of unemployment and poverty for ordinary Nigerians.

In theory, Nigeria is a federal system in which power is dispersed widely at various levels of government. It has an autonomous judicial branch and holds elections in which, according to the federal character principle, power cannot be concentrated in the hands of one ethnic group at the expense of another. States and the federal government are tasked in the constitution with providing a range of public goods—such as functioning schools, a stable supply of electricity, and serviceable roads. In practice, the Nigerian state is incapable of carrying out many of its obligations.

As the table on the next page indicates, there are many possible explanations for the weakness of Nigeria's formal institutions compared to other developing countries. Although the extractive nature of colonial rule and Nigeria's long history of military rule have been less than ideal for Nigerian economic and political development, here we have argued that Nigeria's oil wealth has been the most important contributor to Nigeria's weak state institutions. Since the 1960s, the central government's increasing reliance on oil revenues has "hollowed out" the ministries that form the executive branch. By offering a constant stream of revenues that does not depend on tax collection from ordinary citizens, oil has also radically reduced the accountability of Nigerian politicians to their constituents. As we will see in the next section, the discovery of oil in southern Nigeria has also had a devastating impact on the country's already complex identity politics.

> **SUMMARY TABLE**
>
> **Institutions in the Fourth Republic: Nigeria's Resource Curse**
>
> | | |
> |---|---|
> | **Formal Institutions** | A federal, presidential, and majoritarian system with an independent judiciary modeled on the United States. The president and governors are elected with a plurality of votes, but they must receive votes from a diverse set of regions (the "federal character" principle). |
> | **Institutional Weakness** | Institutions other than the presidency are weak. States and local governments have few powers and are hampered by misappropriation of funds at higher levels. Elections are frequently rigged. Corruption is rampant. Public services (e.g., local police and the electricity grid) are lacking. |
> | **Oil and State Capacity** | Nigeria's oil wealth means politicians have little incentive to build bureaucratic and economic capacity to raise non-oil revenue. The resulting low-tax regime means citizens are less likely to demand accountability from their leaders. |

IDENTITIES IN NIGERIA

9.3 What role has Nigeria's ethnic diversity played in contributing to its history of violent conflict?

Ethnic and regional identities play a large role in Nigerian politics. Religion has also become increasingly politicized over time, particularly in northern Nigeria. This section considers the extent to which ethnic and religious divisions influence Nigeria's government performance. We shall see that, on its own, the diversity of political identities cannot easily explain poor government performance. Instead, it is the combination of Nigeria's cultural landscape and the presence of oil that has been particularly harmful.

Watch the Video "Shell Oil in Nigeria" at mypoliscilab.com

Ethnic Diversity: Is Nigeria Too Diverse to Govern?

High levels of diversity in Africa are said to be a stumbling block for economic development because members of a particular ethnic group may be reluctant to work for the betterment of society as a whole, as opposed to working only to improve the welfare of their own group. For example, diversity may lead to reluctance by some groups to pay taxes for government spending that benefits other groups. In the end, African governments may remain weak because citizens tend to hold strong attachments only to their ethnic group and weak attachments to the entire national community.[31]

This argument predicts that a country as diverse as Nigeria should have difficulties developing.[32] With more than 250 ethnic groups, along with a host of

FIGURE 9.1

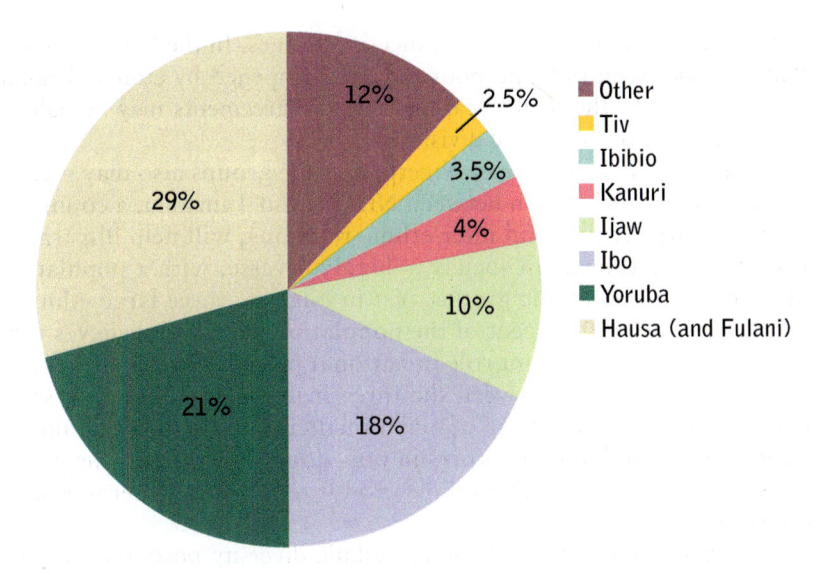

Ethnic Groups in Contemporary Nigeria

This figure shows the ethnic composition of Nigeria's population. More than two-thirds of Nigerians belong to one of the country's three largest ethnic groups—the Hausa-Fulani, the Yoruba, and the Ibo. The rest of the population belongs to more than 100 smaller ethnic communities.

- Other: 12%
- Tiv: 2.5%
- Ibibio: 3.5%
- Kanuri: 4%
- Ijaw: 10%
- Ibo: 18%
- Yoruba: 21%
- Hausa (and Fulani): 29%

regional and religious divisions, Nigerian society is astoundingly complex. Several features of the ethnic landscape have the potential to polarize society and complicate governance. First, the population of each of the three main ethnic groups is regionally concentrated. The Hausa dominate the north, the Ibo the southeast, and the Yoruba the southwest. Such geographic concentration of different ethnic groups in different regions within one country tends to be associated with violent conflict.

Second, in Nigeria, religious divisions between Christians and Muslims tends to accentuate ethnic divides rather than weaken them, because both Christianity and Islam are also regionally concentrated, with Islam dominant in the north of the country and Christianity dominant in the south. This means that both ethnicity *and* religion divide the Hausa from the Ibo and many other southern ethnic groups.

Religion and ethnicity in Nigeria are what is known in political science as **reinforcing social cleavages**—divisions in society that overlap one another—which further destabilize politics by intensifying disagreements between groups. Imagine a country where social class closely overlaps ethnic identity, such that members of one ethnic group are much poorer on average than members of another ethnic group. Now imagine a country where ethnicity and income divisions are

reinforcing social cleavages ■ divisions in society, such as ethnic, religious, or economic distinctions, which coincide with one another. For example, ethnic and religious identities coincide to a great extent in northern Nigeria.

cross-cutting social cleavages ■ social divisions which do not generally coincide with one another. For example, members of the Yoruba ethnic group in Nigeria are divided nearly equally between Muslim and Christian religious affiliations.

unrelated, a case of **cross-cutting social cleavages**. In the latter example, conflicts that arise between rich and poor may be dampened by ethnic allegiances across social classes. In the former case, ethnic disagreements may actually exacerbate disputes based on economic divisions.

Third, the relative size of Nigeria's ethnic groups also may increase the risk of conflict. A comparison between Nigeria and Tanzania, a country with a history of relatively peaceful inter-ethnic relations, will help illustrate this point. Like Nigeria, Tanzanian society is highly diverse, with a population made up of more than 100 ethnic groups. Yet in Nigeria, three large ethnic groups account for nearly 70 percent of the population, and each believes it has enough weight to play a dominant role in national politics. This makes for highly contentious competition between the three main groups. In contrast, Tanzania's ethnic landscape is made up of much smaller groups, such that no one group is large enough to dominate others in political competition. This provides incentives for Tanzania's smaller ethnic groups to work together in order to govern the country.

There is no doubt that Nigeria's ethnic diversity poses serious challenges for peace, stability, and economic prosperity. But are political identities sufficient to explain Nigeria's poor government performance? Comparisons against other African countries suggest otherwise. Sub-Saharan Africa contains some of the most diverse countries on earth, but they vary widely in terms of their levels of stability, conflict, and the quality of governance. For example, although South Africa is among the most diverse countries on the continent, it outperforms most of the region on economic and governance indicators. Similarly, Somalia and Zimbabwe are among the least diverse, but these countries rank toward the bottom in terms of measures of government quality and economic prosperity.

A comparison with Ghana—another West African country—further illustrates the problem of using the diversity of political identities to predict economic development or government performance. Both Nigeria and Ghana share a legacy of British colonialism. They even share some of the same ethnic groups—and, as in Nigeria, membership in one of the larger ethnic groups in Ghana strongly predicts how an individual will vote. Ethnic groups in Ghana are regionally concentrated and Ghana also has three major ethnic groups that comprise more than 70 percent of its population. Despite all these similarities, Ghana has outperformed Nigeria in terms of economic development and political stability in recent decades. This comparison suggests that although we cannot rule out the notion that Nigeria's diversity has made governing the country difficult, diversity of political identities is not enough to explain Nigeria's disappointing political and economic trajectory since independence.

We cannot entirely rule out the argument that Nigeria's ethnic composition has made governing the country more difficult than a country like Tanzania. Looking at Nigeria's history since independence, the *combination* of politicized ethnicity and valuable natural resources has been particularly harmful to development and good governance. In Nigeria, the discovery of oil exacerbated distributional conflict between the country's major ethnic groups. Nigeria thus performs worse than countries that have either a difficult ethnic demography *or* large-scale mineral resources, but not both.

Why are deep ethnic divisions and natural resources such a difficult combination? As the amount of resources available to the central government increases, so does the value of gaining control over the central government, which typically (and especially when the resource is oil) has first access to the country's natural resource wealth. Under these conditions, politics soon becomes a battle over the control of state resources more than anything else. In Nigeria, this dynamic has had many negative consequences for the economy and governance.

Ethno-regional distributional conflict has directly affected government performance by crowding out productive activities, as politicians are distracted by the constant fight over resource allocation. At the state and local levels of government, the fact that the central government has access to such vast resources has angered politicians and bureaucrats who feel they are not receiving their fair share. Oil revenues have also distorted patterns of government investment, with investment in the oil industry replacing investment in other sectors, particularly agriculture. Aside from the normal risks involved in becoming a single commodity economy, this shift of investment focus has meant that, outside of the oil industry, the government itself has become one of the country's major employers. This has made competition over government jobs particularly fierce, a struggle that often occurs along ethnic lines, heightening tensions between groups.

Ethnicity, Oil, and Violent Conflict

In addition to distributional wrangling inside the government, the combination of politicized ethnicity and oil dependence in Nigeria has directly contributed to a series of violent conflicts between various ethnic groups and the state, with profoundly negative consequences for Nigeria's economic and political development. Here we discuss two of these conflicts: (1) the secessionist Biafran War (1967–1970) and (2) a series of smaller-scale violent episodes in the Niger Delta region since the 1990s.

The Biafran War: Oil and Secession Many scholars have pointed to the importance of oil in understanding the causes of the Biafran War. The majority Ibo territory of Biafra in the southeast included the oil-rich region of the Niger Delta, where the vast majority of Nigeria's oil deposits are located. The potential revenues from oil made violent conflict more likely in at least two ways. First, oil made it more likely that Biafra could be economically viable as a state independent from Nigeria, making secession a more attractive option for regional leaders. Second, oil was already seen as a vital source of revenue for the central government, making Biafran secession unacceptable, and increasing the government's willingness to fight over the territory.

The long-term causes of the Biafran War are rooted in ethno-regional competition and the politics of uneven regional development during the colonial period. The decision by the British to govern Nigeria first as two and then as three largely autonomous regions complicated the process of decolonization and amplified the already high levels of mistrust between the three major ethnic groups. The relative underdevelopment of their region made northern leaders wary of independence, fearing southern domination. In order to convince them to accept self-rule, the British preserved the colonial boundaries between the regions that gave the north the largest territory and the majority of the country's population. In newly independent Nigeria, the northern region was allocated the majority of seats in the federal legislature, producing grievances in the southeastern and southwestern regions.

Intense ethno-regional competition over control of the central government undermined Nigeria's First Republic, resulting in a coup in January 1966 by a group of mostly Ibo junior officers. Several months later, northern officers carried out a counter-coup. During this period, ethnic tensions and uncertainty about the country's future spiraled out of control, culminating in the massacre of tens of thousands of ethnic Ibos living in the northern region.

The massacres intensified Ibo grievances and made the idea of secession attractive to many Ibos. Yet, Nigeria's richest oil reserves are found in the Niger Delta, an area nested in Nigeria's southeast. Without access to the region's vast oil reserves, the central government's revenues would have vastly contracted. Thus, throughout the 1960s, the country's politics was dominated by competing claims on the Niger Delta's oil reserves. Following the northern officers' 1966 coup, southeasterners feared that the resources from their region would be used exclusively to benefit the northern region.

The southeastern region, including the Niger Delta, seceded as the Republic of Biafra in May 1967. The Biafran War began two months later and lasted until January 1970, when the Nigerian army, with British support, defeated the separatist state. Few states had recognized or given material support to the Biafrans, the Nigerian's victory was decisive and, under the leadership of Nigeria's military leader Yakubu Gowon, the southeast was quickly re-incorporated into the Nigerian state. The war's consequences for the country as a whole were staggering. More than a million, and possibly as many as three million, people died as a result of the war, most due to disease and starvation.

The war was particularly harmful for the Ibos. The southeast's economy was shattered and had to be rebuilt by the state governments in the region. Infrastructure was recovered relatively quickly, due to the oil boom beginning in 1973, but middle-class Ibos suffered long-term hardship for several reasons. First, many Ibos were unable to reclaim pre-war jobs in the Nigerian government, and pervasive discrimination against hiring Ibos in the public sector lasted for decades after the war had ended. Second, the Nigerian government changed the country's currency in 1968 from Nigerian pounds to naira, rendering Nigerian pounds owned by residents of Biafra virtually worthless. Further, Ibos who had exchanged their Nigerian pounds for Biafran currency lost all of their savings, as Biafran pounds were never recognized by the Nigerian government and were not exchangeable.[33] In sum, although the economy as a whole recovered relatively quickly during the 1970s, negative consequences of the war for Ibos persisted for many years.

As we have seen, before the outbreak of civil war in 1967, Nigeria's federal system contained three large regions, each dominated by a single ethnic group: the Hausa-Fulani in the north, the Yoruba in the southwest, and the Ibo in the southeast. Partly to avoid another war between any of these three groups, during the period of military rule after the war, and during the Second Republic that began in 1979, the federation was split into an increasing number of smaller states. By 1976, Nigeria was divided into 19 sub-national states and, by 1996, the federation contained 36 states. This institutional change made political competition at the federal level much more complex, and dampened competition between the three largest ethnic groups over control of the central government. Now, smaller ethnic groups became majorities in some of the newer states, bringing a more diverse set of groups to positions of power in government.

Some argue that the creation of new states made conflict at the national level less likely (as the Ibo, Yoruba, and Hausa were now divided across many smaller states) while, at the same time, shifted the locus of political conflict to the *state* level, with new groups competing over state-level offices and resources.[34] Conflicts in the Niger Delta beginning in the 1990s conform in some ways to this pattern. These conflicts involve competition over access to oil revenues, but involve a set of much smaller non-Ibo ethnic groups who also live in the most oil-rich region of the country.

Conflicts in the Niger Delta Beginning in the 1990s, disagreements over the distribution of oil revenues led to several smaller-scale violent conflicts in the Niger Delta between a set of relatively small ethnic groups and the government. In spite of the vast wealth generated from the region's oil, ordinary residents have realized few material benefits. Economic development has lagged far behind local expectations, and most of the region's population lives in extreme poverty. At the same time, the process of extracting oil has produced severe environmental degradation. Grievances about the lack of economic development and inter-group competition over oil rents have fueled scores of violent conflicts in the region since the 1980s, many fought explicitly along ethnic lines.

Violence in Ogoniland Perhaps the best-known conflict in the Niger Delta peaked in the early 1990s in the territory in the southeast region of the Delta basin where the ethnic Ogoni minority is concentrated. Ogoniland includes the city of Port Harcourt, the most important oil town in the region, and has been a center of conflict over land rights and oil production since the 1980s. Conflict in the area markedly increased in the wake the controversial Land Use Act passed in 1978, and its incorporation into Nigeria's 1979 constitution. The act made clear that the federal government exclusively owned all minerals, including oil and gas, found on Nigerian territory. The law also explicitly vested ownership of all land within a state in the hands of the state governor, and allowed the state government to expropriate land in exchange for nothing more than the value of crops or buildings on the land at the time of government seizure.[35] As residents of the Niger Delta were quick to realize, this rate of exchange falls far below the actual value of land in an oil-rich region.

Land confiscation by the government in the Ogoni territories increased rapidly during the 1980s. At the same time, environmental pollution in the region became visibly worse after Royal Dutch Shell and Chevron began large-scale oil extraction on lands seized by the government. In 1990, a group of Ogoni political activists, including the writer Ken Saro-Wiwa, formed an organization called the Movement for the Survival of the Ogoni People (MOSOP) to raise awareness of living conditions in their region and to protest the activities of the government and the international oil companies.

Ken Saro-Wiwo ■ Nigerian author and one of the founders of the Movement for the Survival of the Ogoni People (MOSOP); executed by the government in 1995.

Movement for the Survival of the Ogoni People (MOSOP) ■ a group founded in 1990 by Ogoni political activists to oppose land expropriation and pollution resulting from oil extraction in the Niger Delta.

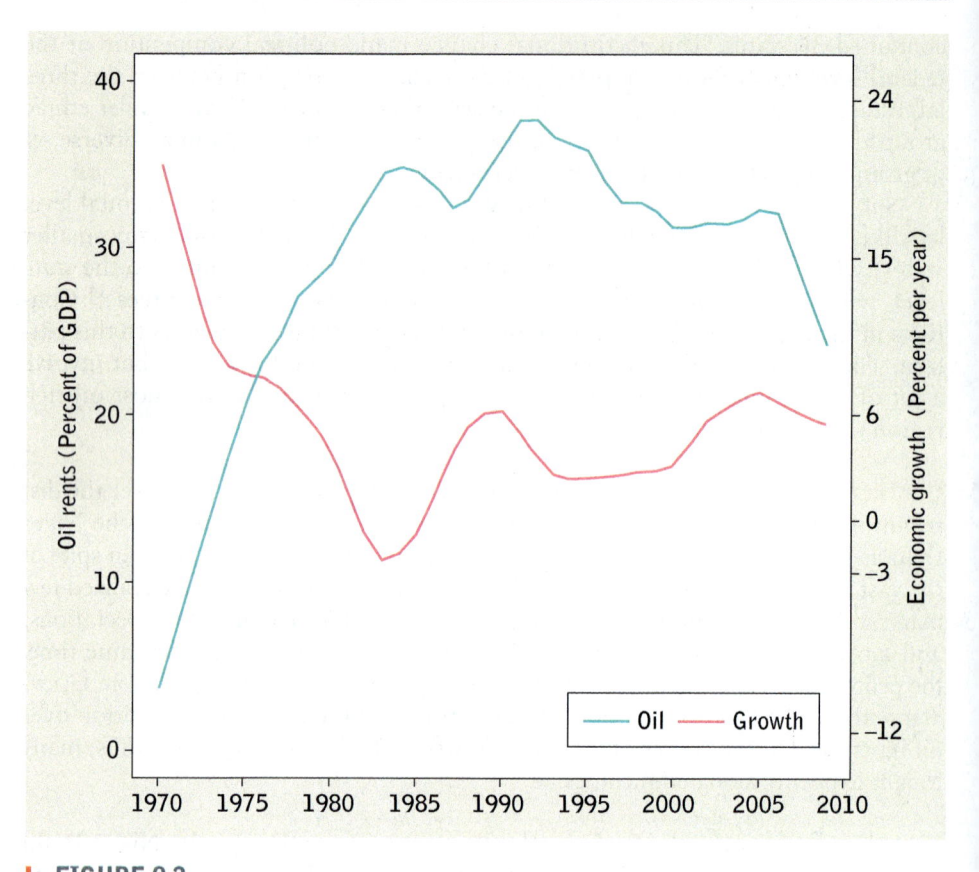

FIGURE 9.2

Oil Rents and Economic Growth in Nigeria, 1970–2010

This graph shows oil revenues as a proportion of GDP (the line starting at the bottom, with axis on the left) and growth rates (the line that starts at the top, with axis on the right) over time. Although oil revenues become increasingly important to Nigeria's economy, this does not lead to higher growth rates.

By 1992, less than two years after MOSOP's founding, violence sharply escalated between the Ogoni movement and the government. When the government remained unresponsive to Ogoni protests, MOSOP shifted its strategy from targeting government officials to directly sabotaging privately owned oil infrastructure. Oil extraction slowed considerably during this time, to the alarm of the government, which then swiftly resorted to repression, eventually calling in the military to combat MOSOP in 1994. The crisis culminated in the execution by the government of nine Ogoni activists, including Saro-Wiwa, in 1995, to the outrage of domestic and international human rights organizations.[36] This government action effectively ended the conflict in Ogoniland in 1995.

Government confiscation of land became a fact of life in the Niger Delta during the 1980s and 1990s, enraging a local population already angry about the appall-

Ogoni villagers protest against oil extraction in the Niger Delta in 2008. Ogoniland has suffered severe environmental degradation since oil extraction began several decades ago.

ingly low levels of development in their area. The form that resistance has taken is relevant for a discussion of identity in Nigerian politics. It is no accident that major resistance movements in the Delta have developed along ethnic lines. Ethnic networks facilitated mobilization for MOSOP, as well as other resistance groups and local militias. This form of resistance has been much easier to coordinate than a pan-ethnic movement. Ethnic divisions were already well developed before oil was found in the region. Since its discovery, local ethnic conflicts have intensified and proliferated.

Ethnic Conflicts in Warri Another case from the Niger Delta that highlights the potentially explosive interaction between ethnic divisions and oil is a set of conflicts between members of the Ijaw and Itsekiri ethnic groups that escalated in the late 1990s. The Ijaw are the largest ethnic group in the Delta region, and the Itsekiri are a much smaller group. Prior to and during the colonial period, Itsekiri dominated local trade with Europeans. As a consequence, they became a relatively wealthy minority group in the region. Itsekiri affluence is particularly visible in the city of Warri, the second largest city in the region. This economic differential has long been a source of tension with the Ijaw and the groups have struggled for political control of Warri for decades.

The Ijaw–Itsekiri conflict intensified after the discovery of oil in the 1950s, increasing competition over land and scarce jobs in the oil industry. Conflict between the Ijaw and the Itsekiri became violent in late 1990s, shortly before the return of local electoral competition during the transition from military to civilian rule in Nigeria. Disputes over the relocation of one of the area's local government headquarters from an Ijaw area to an Itsekiri area sparked deadly rioting over a period of several weeks in 1997 in the run-up to local elections in 1998. Several hundred people were reported to have been killed on either side of the conflict. Control over the local government in Warri was sought after because of the promise of political patronage in the form of government jobs and access to government revenue. Though never on a scale equivalent to the 1997 crisis, disputes have repeatedly flared up between the two groups over access to government positions and jobs in the oil industry. Ethnic tension in Warri remains high to this day.[37]

The conflicts described here peaked in the 1990s, but the Niger Delta region has seen a host of other conflicts emerge between local militant groups and the government since 2000. The region remains heavily militarized, in spite of an amnesty signed between Umaru Yar'Adua and Niger Delta militants in 2009. Violent conflict is likely to remain a feature of the region's politics.

Poor governance in the region—including the failure to promote local development, protect the environment, or provide public goods in resource-rich areas—has been an important contributor to violence in the Niger Delta. In addition to its direct humanitarian consequences, conflict in the region has had observable consequences for the national economy. The U.S. Energy Administration estimated Nigeria's crude oil production in 2008 at 1.94 million barrels per day, well below the country's estimated total production capacity of 2.7 million barrels per day. Political instability, violence, and theft were cited as the main reasons for below-capacity production.[38]

In sum, as the table on the next page summarizes, ethnic divisions that predate colonial rule remain relevant for Nigerian politics today. When combined with the potent allure of control over the south's rich oil wealth, ethno-regional competition has contributed to violent conflict, and even outright civil war. The concentration of the country's oil reserves in the Niger Delta, a territory that initially fell within the Ibo-dominated southeastern region, encouraged the Biafran secession in 1967. The region's oil abundance meant that it was simply too valuable for the Nigerian government to lose, and the country was plunged into a costly war.

Decades later, in the wake of institutional changes that divided Nigeria's three regions into a series of much smaller states, groups indigenous to the Niger Delta mobilized violently against the state and the oil companies operating in the region. The government's failure to manage the country's diversity and oversee the redistribution of oil revenues in a transparent and fair way has stoked ethno-regional grievances, with deadly consequences. Even today, we cannot understand the logic of political mobilization in Nigeria without considering its ethnic landscape.

> **SUMMARY TABLE**
>
> **Identities: Compounding the Resource Curse**
>
> | | |
> |---|---|
> | **High Levels of Ethnic Diversity** | Nigeria is home to more than 250 ethnic groups, with three large groups that are regionally concentrated: the Hausa in the north, the Ibo in the southeast, and the Yoruba in the southwest. Religious and ethnic cleavages typically reinforce each other. |
> | **Ethnic Diversity and the Resource Curse** | Other African countries are also diverse, but the discovery of oil heightened ethnic tension as politics became a battle over the control of state resources. |
> | **Violent Conflict** | This distributional conflict has underpinned two episodes of brutal violence: the Biafran War (1967–1970) and the fighting that erupted in the oil-rich Niger Delta in the 1990s. |

INTERESTS OF NIGERIA

In contrast to the central role of identities, many of the interest groups we think about when we study advanced democracies, such as social classes, economic sectors, or even political parties, are not the most important actors in Nigerian politics. If they participate in politics at all, these groups tend to work outside of the government in ways that typically do not directly affect the political outcomes we care most about, like who wins elective office or how state resources are distributed. Classical interest groups in contemporary Nigeria are not dominant political actors. However, two groups—ethno-regional blocks and the military—are crucial to understanding the country's politics.

9.4 Can Nigeria's poor government performance be explained by the weakness of traditional interest groups that play a role in politics in developed democracies?

Political Parties

Nigerian elections since the end of military rule in 1999 have been dominated by competition between the ruling **People's Democratic Party (PDP)** and several smaller regionally based parties. However, unlike the Democratic and Republican parties in the United States, political parties in Nigeria today are best thought of as loose coalitions of powerful individuals rather than strong organizations with an independent effect on political outcomes.

Without question, the PDP is the dominant party in Fourth Republic Nigerian politics. PDP presidential candidates have won all four presidential elections—in 1999, 2003, 2007, and 2011. The party has also won majorities in the National Assembly in each election, and the majority of governorships. If we look simply at election results, the PDP's dominance has actually increased during the three rounds of national elections since 1999. Even if we grant that the 1999 and 2003 elections were complicated by widespread fraud, experts typically agree that, at least in these

People's Democratic Party (PDP) ■ Nigeria's dominant party since the reestablishment of democratic elections in 1999; its candidates have won all four presidential elections since then and have continuously held a majority in the National Assembly.

Watch the Video
"Go Slows in Lagos"
at mypoliscilab.com

Nigeria's current president, Goodluck Jonathan, after casting his vote in the 2011 election. Jonathan, formerly the governor of Bayelsa state, is the first Nigerian president to come from the Niger Delta region.

All Nigeria People's Party (ANPP) ■ one of Nigeria's largest opposition parties, it draws most of its support from the predominantly Muslim north of the country. It fielded the runner-up in the 2003 and 2007 presidential elections, former military ruler Muhammadu Buhari.

elections, Olusegun Obasanjo, the PDP's presidential candidate, is likely to have won, even without fraud.[39] The case for the victory of Umaru Yar'Adua, a Hausa from northern Nigeria and Obasanjo's chosen successor in the 2007 elections, is less clear.

The PDP can be thought of as a "coalition of national elites" which distinguishes it from smaller, regionally based parties.[40] The PDP is a self-described centrist party that generally favors liberal economic policies, though it is difficult to find real distinctions on economic or other areas of policy in comparison with other parties. The main feature that distinguishes Nigeria's parties is the distribution of their support base across regions. In the 2003 and 2007 presidential and National Assembly elections, the PDP won with a clear margin in all states except those in the far north of the country and several states in the southwestern region. In the 2011 elections, the PDP lost support in additional northern states, but it remains the party with the most geographically diverse support base.

The party with the second-largest support base is the All Nigeria People's Party (ANPP), by far the largest opposition party. ANPP draws the majority of its supporters from states in the extreme north of the country. In the 2007 elections, the ANPP won seven out of 36 governors' races, all in northern, Muslim-majority states, including Kano, the state with the largest population in the northern region. In both 2003 and 2007, the ANPP fielded former military leader General Muhammadu Buhari as its presidential candidate. Buhari's campaigns in both 2003 and 2007 were based around scathing critiques of government corruption and PDP misconduct. In 2003, Buhari won 32 percent of the vote in the presidential race, finishing second after PDP's Obasanjo, and in April 2007 he won 18 percent of the vote, according to official results. The ANPP initially challenged Yar'Adua's victory, filing a petition to nullify the results due to widespread fraud across the country. After negotiations in June 2007, however, a segment of the ANPP leadership agreed to join Yar'Adua's government, a decision that Buhari himself denounced.[41]

After the ANPP, the party with the next largest share of the vote in the presidential race in April 2007 was the Action Congress of Nigeria (ACN), whose candidate, Atiku Abubakar, was vice president under Obasanjo from 1999 to 2007. Abubakar received just over 7 percent of the vote. The ACN was formed in a merger of several smaller opposition parties in 2006. The party's strongest following is in the Yoruba states in southwestern Nigeria, and the ACN's candidate, Babatunde Fashola, won the governor's race in Lagos state in April 2007. The ACN has been described as the successor party to the Action Group (AG), the southwest's major political party during the First Republic, but it has yet to articulate a clear set of substantive ideas in its platform.

Action Congress of Nigeria (ACN) ■ a political party with strong support in Lagos and other parts of southwest Nigeria.

Like the three parties described above, most parties in Nigeria are difficult to distinguish along programmatic or ideological lines. For example, the PDP is strikingly similar to its major competitor, the ANPP, on issues of macroeconomic and foreign policy. When stated programs *do* differ, they often bear little resemblance to parties' behavior when in office. Nigerian parties are typical in their weak organizational structures of many political parties in Africa. Most of Nigeria's parties lack the resources and the bureaucratic capacity to do little more than engage in political patronage—distributing state resources to voters in exchange for their support—on a small scale (for example, handing out bags of rice or t-shirts) during election campaigns. Some of the weaker party bureaucracies exist only temporarily, operating in the months leading up to an election and dissolving once the campaign ends.[42]

political patronage ■ the distribution of state resources, such as government jobs or private goods, to ordinary citizens in exchange for their political support.

Perhaps the most striking feature of political parties in Nigeria's Fourth Republic is how *personalized* they tend to be. The personalities and interests of powerful politicians dominate discussions of political parties in the media. This is partly because parties usually lack a broad resource base, since they are often not strong enough to systematically raise money through contributions by ordinary members, but instead rely on large donations from a small number of wealthy individuals, who either become politicians themselves or sponsor someone to run on their behalf. Nigerian parties are also highly factionalized: power struggles and splits within parties receive as much attention in the media as competition between parties, another reflection of the weakness of parties' formal bureaucratic structures.

Nigerian politics is dominated by individual personalities, while party loyalty among ordinary voters is weak. To illustrate this point, we can imagine what would happen if Olusegun Obasanjo, one of Nigeria's most well-known and influential politicians, who won the presidential elections in 1999 and 2003 by a clear margin, had decided to abandon the People's Democratic Party (PDP) when he ran for reelection in 2003. Although it would have made things more difficult for him, it is conceivable that Obasanjo could have defected from the PDP by joining another party, or creating his own party, and retained much of his popular support. Political parties as autonomous organizations that can influence political outcomes simply do not exist in Nigeria today.

Where Is the Working Class?

An interesting puzzle for social scientists who study sub-Saharan Africa is the virtual absence of class cleavages—divisions among voters along lines of social class. Some scholars of African politics have gone so far as to say that social classes in Africa, particularly lower classes, are not fully formed as self-conscious interest groups.[43] The Nigerian case fits into this general pattern. Since independence, Nigerians have not systematically voted along class lines, and class-based identities are weaker than identities based on region, ethnicity, or religion. There is little evidence of class-based mobilization by elites in politics or even in civil society.

To gauge the role of class-based politics in Nigeria, we can look first at formal institutions of competition, such as political parties. Strikingly, there have been almost no labor parties—political parties explicitly advancing the interests of workers—with more than a fringe following in the country since independence. There are only two examples of labor-oriented political parties gaining attention in recent elections. The Democratic Socialist Movement (DSM) is a subsection of the National Conscience Party (NCP) that formed in 1998, during the transition from military to multi-party rule. The DSM has had little impact on Nigerian politics, however, and has never contested a national election. Further, the NCP party of which it is a part receives little support from the electorate at any level. In the 2007 presidential elections, the NCP candidate received only .02 percent of the national vote, and the party did not win any seats in the legislature.

Similarly, the newly formed Labor Party (originally created in 2002 as the Party for Social Democracy) competed in the 2007 federal elections and won only one seat out of 360 in the House of Representatives and no seats in the Senate. The Labor Party's only major win since the transition from military rule in 1999 was in the 2007 governor's race in Ondo state, in the southwestern region, after a legal battle over evident fraud by the ruling People's Democratic Party (PDP) candidate brought Labor candidate Olusegun Mimiko to power. The extent to which the party has actually mobilized workers is limited, however. The party's organization is so weak that it is unclear whether they will be able to contest future elections, and the party currently revolves largely around the personality of Mimiko himself.

Looking beyond the party system to civil society, the evidence is similar. There has been no discernable workers' movement with more than a small following since the 1960s. Nor has organized labor played an important role in economic life in Nigeria. Today, there are only four labor unions with nationwide reach in the country. The largest union, the Nigerian Labor Congress (NLC), reports a membership of 4 million. If accurate, this would make the NLC one of the largest trade unions on the continent. The figure is less impressive, however, when we consider that Nigeria's total population is more than 140 million. More importantly, the NLC has struggled over the past several decades to achieve core objectives, such as wage increases for workers and preventing hikes in the price of fuel. The NLC and other unions faced particularly tough challenges during the later, more repressive, years of military rule. To date, none of Nigeria's labor unions has been strong enough to effect meaningful changes for workers.

More generally, the idea of a working class with common interests or a shared identity is absent from Nigerian politics, and appeals to class identity have played little role in the political discourse surrounding most elections in the post-independence period. The question of *why* class cleavages have not been exploited more systematically in Nigerian politics, or in most of Africa, is a difficult one to answer, but several features of African economies work against class-based political competition.

For one thing, it may be the case that most of sub-Saharan Africa is simply *not industrialized enough* to produce clearly demarcated social classes with competing political parties. Aside from South Africa, it is difficult to find examples of genuine industrial revolutions in most African states. Even today, most of the continent's economies are based in predominantly agrarian societies. Particularly in rural areas, where the majority of Africans still live, the main occupation is small-scale farming for family subsistence, rather than commercial agriculture. Most rural farmers, thus, have little contact with the capitalist market. As such, we should not be surprised that class politics characteristic of fully capitalist, industrialized societies is largely absent in Africa. Even Karl Marx did not expect class struggle to feature prominently in rural societies.

Nigeria is an interesting case to consider, since the country is relatively urbanized by African standards, with 48 percent of the population living in urban areas. Although detailed employment data are difficult to come by, it is clear that wage laborers account for only a small proportion of Nigeria's urban workforce. In fact, the formal sector in urban areas is dwarfed by the informal economy, the mass of unprotected workers who are not monitored or taxed by the government. Most of Nigeria's informal urban workers are extremely poor, and many work as temporary workers, unpaid apprentices, or family laborers. The informal sector has grown over the past few decades largely because formal sector employment has been outpaced by the rate of urbanization.[44]

With so many laborers working as subsistence farmers in rural areas, and in the informal economy in the cities, Nigeria's economy lacks a sufficiently large pool of wage laborers to form a distinct working class. Absent a working class, it is unlikely that political mobilization along class lines would be successful. This could be true for several reasons. Perhaps most importantly, the structure of the economy makes collective action more difficult from the workers' point of view. For example, like most other sub-Saharan African economies, Nigeria lacks a large mass of factory workers, who are easier to mobilize into a labor movement than members of the occupational groups that dominate Nigeria's urban economy. Unskilled laborers who work as apprentices, for example, often live and work in the home of their employer, in relative isolation from other workers. The simple fact of small-scale work settings makes it much more difficult to organize a political movement of apprentices, self-employed traders, or other types of informal urban workers than to coordinate workers on a factory floor.

informal economy ■ the sector of an economy that is not monitored or taxed by the government. In many developing countries, the informal economy can be larger than the formal sector.

The same thing could be said of the rural economy. As we discussed previously, when considering the adverse effects of oil on government investment in different sectors of the economy, commercial agriculture in Nigeria today remains woefully underdeveloped. Most Nigerian farmers are smallholders—people who farm a plot of land that they own in order to feed their family, not to produce cash crops. Again, it is more difficult for so many small-scale farmers to organize collectively than we would expect it to be for workers on large-scale commercial farms. In sum, coordination problems make it less likely that we will see parties organizing around identities like the "agrarian poor" or "informal urban workers."

Turning from the difficulties workers face to the incentives of political elites, conditions are equally unfavorable for class-based politics. In Nigeria, politicians compete vigorously to gain office in part because office-holders have preferential access to state resources. To put it simply, Nigerian politicians and bureaucrats benefit from the oil wealth to a much greater extent than do ordinary Nigerians. Seen in this light, politics in Nigeria is centered on issues of controlling access to state resources. Politicians want to gain office, but they also want to do so by relying on as few voters as is absolutely necessary, so they don't have to redistribute benefits too widely. Politicians are not likely to be attracted by the possibility of a political party whose support base was the mass of poor Nigerians rather than a smaller group. Given that social classes in Nigeria are not sufficiently differentiated to generate smaller groups, politicians have fewer incentives to organize along class lines.

Finally, it may be the case that ethnic identities are simply so strong in Nigeria that they trump other identities like social class when ordinary people are forced to make choices during elections. In the early 1960s, Nigerian labor leaders attempted, without success, to form a Nigerian labor party. Although many workers 1964 expressed some support for a labor party, as the elections neared, they overwhelmingly shifted their support toward parties that appealed to their ethnic rather than class-based identities. This suggests that Nigerian laborers are caught between their identities as workers and as members of a particular ethnic group.[45]

Economic Interest Groups

Similar arguments explain the absence of interest-group politics by different sectors of the economy in Nigeria today. In developed countries, economic sectors often play a role in politics through pressure groups, like the agriculture and telecommunications lobbies in the United States. In Nigeria, these groups are typically neither large enough nor organized enough to exert much influence over policy-making or in mobilizing voters. As we have discussed, Nigeria's oil wealth has had the perverse effect of reducing the government's attention to other sectors in the economy. Government investment in commercial agriculture and manufacturing has sharply declined since the 1970s and, as a result, the size and power of these sectors have deteriorated. Since so few Nigerians work in the manufacturing industry, and since most farmers are smallholders rather than workers on large-scale commercial farms, collective action in the form of lobbying the government on behalf of one's occupational group is extremely difficult.

Given the importance of oil wealth for Nigerian politics, one might expect workers in the oil industry to have organized politically to defend their interests. One feature in particular makes political mobilization of oil workers unlikely, however. As noted earlier, oil production is a capital-intensive rather than a labor-intensive industry, meaning that a relatively small number of skilled workers is required, rather than a large number of unskilled workers. In practice, this means that the oil industry has created few jobs for Nigerian workers. In fact, many of Nigeria's oil workers have been brought in by oil companies from abroad and therefore are not voters. This reduces incentives for politicians to attempt to explicitly mobilize oil workers.

Ethno-Regional Groups

If classical interest-advancing groups such as social classes, interest groups rooted in different economic sectors, and even political parties are all relatively weak, what sort of interests are at the center of Nigerian politics? Which are the groups that must be considered if we are to understand who wins elections on the national stage, or how the state's resources are distributed? As should be clear by now from our earlier discussions of institutions and identities, regionalism remains strong in Nigerian politics today. Voters pay close attention to the ethnic and regional identities of political candidates at all levels of government. In contrast to political party platforms, which do not differ in meaningful ways, politicians' identities offer at least some basic information to voters about how a candidate might behave once in office, even if the basic expectation is simply that a politician will favor his own identity group when deciding where to allocate resources.

At the national level, the "federal character" principle we discussed in the institutions section, where a presidential candidate must win not only the most votes but also a quarter of the votes in at least two-thirds of Nigeria's states, is a crucial feature of political competition. In practice, this means that, in order to win office, presidential candidates must be acceptable to a sizeable share of at least two of the country's three main ethnic groups, and it is in their interest to appeal to smaller ethnic groups as well. Attracting sufficient support from Nigeria's ethno-regional blocs is essential for a candidate to be successful at the national level. Less formally, both voters and political elites have come to expect some degree of alternation in the regional identity of the president. For example, after Obasanjo, a southerner, spent two terms as president, many political pundits and opinion leaders suggested that it was the northern region's "turn" to win the office in 2007, something that happened with Yar'Adua's victory. This expectation can be seen as an important, albeit informal, institution of power-sharing between regions.

The Military

One of Nigeria's major achievements since 1999 has been the withdrawal of the military from formal involvement in politics. Our discussion of the chaotic and fraudulent 2007 elections, however, illustrates how fragile Nigerian democracy remains today. The weakness of the country's political parties and other institutions of political competition, such as the widely discredited electoral commission, leave open the threat of military coup in practice and in the minds of ordinary Nigerians. Events at the end of 2009 and in early 2010 offer an example. In late November 2009, President Umaru Yar'Adua left Nigeria for Saudi Arabia to seek medical treatment for a serious, possibly life-threatening heart condition. For several months, he was not seen in public and his absence was destabilizing at the highest levels of government. Neither Yar'Adua nor his advisors publicly announced his illness, and they left no plan in place for the transfer of power when he left for Saudi Arabia. On February 9, 2010, the Senate appointed Vice President Goodluck Jonathan as acting president, amid popular protests in response to Yar'Adua's disappearance, and widespread public rumors that the political crisis would result in a military takeover.[46] Yar'Adua eventually returned to Nigeria in late February 2010, but did not resume official duties, and he died in May 2010.

Even without the formal return of military rule, experts are quick to note that the military plays an important informal role in political competition at the national level.[47] Nearly all of the presidential candidates with a serious chance of winning office since 1999 have come from military backgrounds, including Obasanjo and Muhammadu Buhari, both of whom were previously military heads of state. In the 2003 race, all four of the main presidential contenders were retired generals. In addition to Buhari, former military ruler Ibrahim Babangida ran for the presidency in 2007. Retired military officers are also among the wealthiest groups in the country. Under military rule, high-level officers served as chairmen of government-owned companies, including the Nigerian National Petroleum Company, the state-controlled company that regulates Nigeria's oil industry.[48] As a result, between the 1970s and the 1990s, the military produced more millionaires than any other occupational group in Nigeria. This wealth has been translated into political influence in the Fourth Republic. The conventional view among ordinary Nigerians is that, even today, no candidate can become president without at least the tacit support of the military.

As the table on the next page indicates, many of the interest groups that mobilize political actors in developed democracies are simply absent from Nigerian politics. As in most African countries, social classes (such as the working class) are not well defined and the political groups that often mobilize them (such as labor unions or workers' parties) have played a limited role in Nigerian elections. This may be because Nigeria is not industrialized enough for class-based politics, or because the government's focus on extracting as much revenue as possible from the oil industry has inhibited the development of effective sector-specific interest groups. Even political parties, which typically play a crucial mediating role between the interests of ordinary citizens and a country's political elite, are little more than loose coalitions of powerful individuals. Loyalty to even the largest political parties is weak, as both voters and politicians shift from party to party across elections.

In contrast, although the "federal character" requirements in Nigeria's constitution have helped insure that no single ethnic group can determine who is elected to the highest state- and national-level offices, politicians remain keenly aware of the ethnic composition of their constituencies and ethnic cleavages remain cru-

SUMMARY TABLE

Interests: Nigeria's Lack of Strong Classical Interest Groups

Class Cleavages	Remain relatively unimportant in Nigerian politics. Labor is only weakly organized, and almost no parties that advance workers' interests have been formed.
Economic Interest Groups	Non-oil sectors of Nigeria's economy rarely mobilize for political action.
Political Parties	Contests between candidates of the People's Democratic Party (PDP) and several smaller regionally based parties have dominated political competition. But programmatic differences between parties are small and parties' organizational structures are weak.
Ethno-Regional Groups	Regional identities remain a powerful and sometimes divisive force in Nigerian politics. Many voters expect that the office of the president should rotate among regions.
The Military	Has had a tremendous impact on Nigerian politics both directly through coups and military rule and indirectly through supporting particular civilian governments. Most Nigerian heads of state have come from a military background.

cial for political mobilization and redistribution both before and after elections. Finally, although the military is no longer formally in control of the government, former military officers play an important informal role in politics—either as wealthy backers of civilian politicians, or as candidates themselves. A quick look at the list of Nigeria's heads of state, even during periods of civilian rule and multiparty competition, confirms this.

CONCLUSION

To many observers, Africa's most populous country seemed poised to achieve great things at independence. Looking more closely at the initial political and demographic conditions Nigeria's newly independent government faced in 1960, this chapter has made the case that Nigerian economic and government underperformance should not be surprising. Even beyond the difficult ethno-regional landscape and its experiences under colonial and military rule, the discovery of oil has been particularly devastating for Nigeria.

To better understand how Nigeria has become such a poorly governed state, we have analyzed the interaction between Nigeria's history, institutions, and its relevant identity and interest groups. During the colonial period, Nigeria was ruled as two separate protectorates, each with different systems of government and different education systems. The powerful, centralized Hausa states in the north were able to convince the British to rule indirectly in their region, and to restrict the spread of English education. In the southern protectorate, the British invested more much more heavily in education and allowed Christian missionary schools to operate. By the eve of independence, this historical divergence in policy contributed to severe inequalities in development across the northern and southern regions, undermining Nigerians' sense of a common national fate, and setting the stage for the inter-regional conflict that has defined much of Nigeria's post-independence politics.

Five decades later, after a large-scale civil war and a series of smaller violent conflicts, many of the fundamental issues of how to manage Nigeria's ethnic diversity and its oil wealth remain unresolved. At the core of Nigeria's governance problems lies the weakness of its formal institutions, which are unable to carry out many of the most basic tasks—such as providing minimum levels of law and order—laid out in the country's most recent constitution.

More than any other feature of its history or politics, Nigeria's oil wealth has contributed to its institutional weakness. The easy availability of vast oil revenues to the central government since the 1970s has skewed the interests of politicians and other government officials away from providing public services that benefit citizens, away from building a competent bureaucracy, and away from investing in other sectors of the economy.

At the same time, the highly centralized nature of the oil industry, in which revenues flow directly from foreign companies to the central government, has enabled staggering corruption at its highest levels, even under civilian rule. In combination with the country's long-standing ethnic and ethno-regional divisions, the country's oil wealth has further destabilized the country by directly contributing to violent conflicts, including the secessionist Biafran War and smaller-scale rebellions by ethnic groups indigenous to the Niger Delta region. Less dramatically, oil has reduced routine political competition and the process of governance itself to an entrenched struggle over state resources rather than a productive activity.

Unlike the central role played by identity groups in Nigerian politics, classical interest groups such as social classes, economic sectors, and even political parties have had relatively little impact on political competition in Nigeria. Most political parties have been unable to command consistent loyalty from voters, and have been able to exert little leverage over their own politicians. The military remains an important, if ominous, exception to Nigeria's institutional weakness. Although Nigeria's most recent presidential elections suggest this may be changing, the military remains one of the few formal institutions with the potential to affect the outcome of elections.

In sum, Nigeria's oil wealth has proven to be more of a misfortune than a blessing in its impact on the country's post-independence political development. More than any of the other features of Nigeria's history and politics we have considered, the discovery of vast oil resources has exacerbated Nigeria's already fraught ethno-regional relations. Crumbling industry, empty government ministries, irregular electricity, and widespread poverty remain the visible legacies of Nigeria's resource curse.

KEY TERMS

Niger Delta 322
resource curse 322
Ibo (Igbo) 326
Yoruba 326
Hausa 326
Sokoto Caliphate 326
Scramble for Africa 326
indirect rule 326
House of Representatives 328
First Republic 328
Republic of Biafra 328
Olusegun Obasanjo 329
Second Republic 329
Sani Abacha 330
Fourth Republic 330
National Assembly 332
federal character principle 332
Sharia law 333
Umaru Yar'Adua 334
rent-seeking 339
reinforcing cleavages 343
cross-cutting cleavages 343
Ken Saro-Wiwo 347
Movement for the Survival of the Ogoni People (MOSOP) 347
People's Democratic Party (PDP) 351
All Nigeria People's Party (ANPP) 352
Action Congress of Nigeria (ACN) 353
political patronage 353
informal economy 355

REVIEW QUESTIONS

1. In what ways did British administrative policies during the colonial period differ between northern and southern Nigeria? What effects did these differences have on economic and political development in the two regions?
2. Can you think of examples where oil wealth has been helpful for a country's economic prosperity and citizen quality of life? What are the key ways in which these countries differed from Nigeria prior to the discovery of oil?
3. Is ethnic diversity necessarily an obstacle for a country's economic development? If not, what are the conditions that make it more or less problematic?
4. In what ways has Nigeria's oil wealth led to violent civil conflict between regional or ethnic groups?
5. The chapter described several arguments linking oil revenues to poor economic development through the channel of weakening political institutions. Can you think of other ways that oil or other natural resource income could be harmful for a country's economy?

SUGGESTED READINGS

Acemoglu, Daron, Simon Johnson, and James Robinson. "The Colonial Origins of Comparative Development." *American Economic Review* 91:5 (2001), 1369–1401. A highly influential article written by development economists, which argues that the disease environment European colonizers faced as they attempted to build their empires in Africa shaped the type of institutions they built which, in turn, shaped prospects for economic development today.

Auty, Richard. *Sustaining Development in Mineral Economies: The Resource Curse Hypothesis*. New York: Routledge, 1993. Auty's book is now seen as the classic work on the potentially detrimental effects of oil dependence on economic development.

Karl, Terry Lynn. *The Paradox of Plenty: Oil Booms and Petro-States.* Berkeley: CA, University of California Press, 1997. Karl's book builds on Auty's idea of the resource curse, but adds an in-depth discussion of the ways in which oil dependence can weaken political institutions. The book draws on detailed case studies from Venezuela to illustrate the argument.

Osaghae, Eghosa E. *Crippled Giant: Nigeria Since Independence.* London: C. Hurst and Co., 1998. An engaging history of contemporary Nigeria, Osaghae's book describes the origins of uneven economic and political development in northern and southern Nigeria during the colonial period, and makes the case that this inequality has been a destabilizing force in post-colonial politics.

Ross, Michael. "Does Oil Hinder Democracy?" *World Politics* 53: 3 (2001), 326–361. An important work in the literature on the resource curse, Ross finds that increases in oil exports inhibits democratization across countries, but especially in countries that are already poor.

Suberu, Rotimi. *Federalism and Ethnic Conflict in Nigeria.* Washington, DC: United States Institute of Peace Press, 2001. Suberu's book has become a classic for students of Nigerian politics. He argues that the Nigerian government's increasing reliance on oil revenues since the 1970s has "hollowed out" Nigeria's federal system, gradually centralizing authority and weakening government accountability.

NOTES

1. Quoted in Michael Crowder, "Whose Dream Was It Anyway? Twenty-Five Years of African Independence," *African Affairs*, 86 (1987), 7–24.
2. Nigeria receives a worse ranking than 21 sub-Saharan African countries, including the Democratic Republic of the Congo, Sudan, Eritrea, and Zimbabwe, in the UN 2008 Human Development Index (HDI).
3. Since 2000, Nigeria's ranking in Transparency International's Corruption Perception Index (CPI) has never risen above 120th out of a total of 180 countries included in the index.
4. The Afrobarometer is an independent research organization that has conducted surveys in 12 African countries since 1999 and 20 countries since 2009.
5. CIA World Factbook: https://www.cia.gov/library/publications/the-world-factbook/geos/ni.html. Nigeria is the largest oil producer in sub-Saharan Africa. The next largest oil producer in the region is Angola, another country that performs well below average across economic and political indicators when compared with other sub-Saharan African countries.
6. The case for uneven economic and political development between the northern and southern regions is made persuasively by Eghosa E. Osaghae in *Crippled Giant: Nigeria Since Independence* (London: C. Hurst & Company, 1998).
7. Population figures are highly controversial in Nigeria, and experts typically agree that no fully reliable census has been conducted in recent years. As a rough estimate, however, we can consider the most recent census results from 2006, in which the total population was counted at just over 140 million, with more than 75 million people living in the north and just fewer than 65 million living in the south.
8. Xavier Sala-i-Martin and Arvind Subramanian, "Addressing the Natural Resource Curse: An Illustration from Nigeria," Working Paper 9804 (National Bureau of Economic Research, 2003).
9. Sala-i-Martin and Subramanian.

10. "Nigeria Confronts Corruption," *BBC World News: Africa,* November 11, 1999.
11. Larry Diamond, Anthony Kirk-Greene, and Oyeleye Oyediran, eds., *Transition Without End: Nigerian Politics and Civil Society under Babangida* (Boulder, CO: Lynne Rienner, 1997).
12. "Sani Abacha," Encyclopedia Britannica, *Encyclopedia Britannica Online.* Accessed online: June 12, 2011. http://www.britannica.com/EBchecked/topic/701368/Sani-Abacha.
13. "Observing the 1998–1999 Elections: Final Report," The Carter Center Democracy Program and the National Democratic Institute for International Affairs, Summer 1999: http://aceproject.org/regions-en/countries-and-territories/NG/reports/Final%20Report%20Nigeria-1998-99.pdf.
14. Abdul Raufu Mustapha, "Nigeria since 1999: Revolving Door Syndrome or Consolidation of Democracy," in Abdul Raufu Mustapha and Lindsay Whitfield, eds., *Turning Points in Africa Democracy* (Suffolk, UK: James Currey, 2009).
15. Rotimu Suberu, *Federalism and Ethnic Conflict in Nigeria* (Washington, DC: United States Institute of Peace Press, 2001).
16. European Union Election Observation Mission, Federal Republic of Nigeria: available online at: http://eeas.europa.eu/human_rights/election_observation/nigeria/final_report_en.pdf. The condensed press release is available at: http://www.europarl.europa.eu/meetdocs/2004_2009/documents/dv/nigeriapressrelease/nigeriapressreleaseen.pdf.
17. "Freedom in Retreat: Is the Tide Turning?" Freedom House Report 2008. Available online at: http://www.freedomhouse.org/uploads/fiw08launch/FIW08Overview.pdf.
18. The only institution considered "moderately" effective was the military, which has been active in peacekeeping operations throughout West Africa.
19. Alexandra Scacco, *Who Riots? Explaining Participation in Ethnic Violence,* manuscript. (Columbia University, 2010).
20. Agwara John Onyeukwu, *The Resource Curse in Nigeria: Perceptions and Challenges* (Budapest, Hungary: Open Society Institute, 2007); "Nigeria Moves to Address Chronic Power Outages," *The Wall Street Journal,* April 25, 2009; "Nigerian People Seeing Little Benefit from Record Oil Revenues," *New York Times,* July 21, 2008.
21. Chief J. M. Olanipekun, *Local Government in Nigeria* (Lagos, Nigeria: Africa Leadership Forum 1998). For a discussion of the Nigerian police, see Scacco (2010).
22. Jennifer Widner, *Economic Change and Political Liberalization in Sub-Saharan Africa* (Baltimore: Johns Hopkins University Press, 1994).
23. Harold Crouch, "Patrimonialism and Military Rule in Indonesia," *World Politics,* 31(4) (1979): 571–587; Kurt Weyland, "The Politics of Corruption in Latin America, Journal *of Democracy,* 9:2 (1998), 108–122; Alberto Alesina et al., "Political Instability and Economic Growth," *Journal of Economic Growth,* 1 (June 1996), 189–211.
24. Carl LeVan, *Dictators, Democrats and Government Performance in an African Country,* Ph.D. dissertation manuscript (University of California, San Diego, 2006).
25. The classic work on the resource curse is Richard Auty, *Sustainable Development in Mineral Economies: The Resource Curse Thesis* (London and New York: Routledge, 1993). See also Erika Weinthal and Pauline Jones-Luong, "Combating the Resource Curse: An Alternative Solution to Managing Mineral Wealth," *Perspectives on Politics,* 4:1 (2006), 35–53.
26. Nathan Jensen and Leonard Wantchekon, "Resource Wealth and Political Regimes in Africa," *Comparative Political Studies,* 37:7 (2004), 816–841; and Olomola Philip Akanni, "Oil Wealth and Economic Growth in Oil Exporting African Countries," AERC Research Paper 170 (Nairobi, Kenya, 2007).

27. Thorvaldur Gylafson, "Natural Resources, Education, and Economic Development," *European Economic Review*, 45 (2001), 847–859.
28. Michael Ross, "Does Oil Hinder Democracy?" *World Politics*, 53 (2001), 325–361; and Macartan Humphreys, Jeffrey D. Sachs, and Joseph E. Stiglitz, *Escaping the Resource Curse* (New York: Columbia University Press, 2007).
29. Terry Lynn Karl, *The Paradox of Plenty* (Berkeley: University of California Press, 1997).
30. Karl, (1997).
31. Habyarimana, James et al. "Why Does Ethnic Diversity Undermine Public Goods Provision?" *American Political Science Review*, 101(4) (2007), 709–725.
32. William Easterly and Ross Levine, "Africa's Growth Tragedy: Policies and Ethnic Divisions," *Quarterly Journal of Economics*, 112(4) (1997), 1203–1250; Alberto Alesina and Elina La Ferrara, "Ethnic Diversity and Economic Performance," *Journal of Economic Literature*, 43:3(4) (2005), 762–800.
33. I. I. Upkong, "Economic Recovery in the Eastern States of Nigeria," *Issue: A Journal of Opinion*, 5(1), 45–53.
34. Donald Horowitz, *Ethnic Groups in Conflict* (Berkeley, CA: University of California Press, 2000), 603–605.
35. For exact wording, see "Land Use Act, Chapter 202, Laws of the Federation of Nigeria," available online at www.nigeria-law.org.
36. "The Price of Oil: Corporate Responsibility and Human Rights Violations in Nigeria's Oil Producing Communities" (Washington D.C., Human Rights Watch, 1999).
37. "The Price of Oil," 100–103.
38. "Nigeria Country Analysis Brief" (U.S Energy Information Administration, 2009). Available online at http://www.eia.doe.gov.
39. Darren Kew, "The 2003 Elections: Hardly Credible, but Acceptable," in Robert I. Rotberg, ed., *Crafting the New Nigeria: Confronting the Challenges* (Boulder, CO: Lynne Rienner, 2004), 139–173.
40. Richard L. Sklar, *Nigerian Political Parties: Power in an Emergent African Nation* (Trenton, NJ: Africa World Press, 2004), Introduction.
41. "Nigeria Opposition Move Condemned," *BBC World News: Africa,* June 28, 2007.
42. Gero Erdmann, "Party Research: The Western European Bias and the 'African Labyrinth,' *Democratization*, 11(3) (2004), 63–87.
43. James R. Scarrit and Shaheen Mozaffar, "The Specification of Ethnic Cleavages and Ethnopolitical Groups for the Analysis of Democratic Competition in Contemporary Africa," *Nationalism and Ethnic Politics*, 5(1((1999), 82–117.
44. Vali Jamal and John Weeks, "The Vanishing Urban–Rural Gap in Sub-Saharan Africa," *International Labour Review*, 127(3) (1998), 271–291.
45. Robert Melson, "Ideology and Inconsistency: The 'Cross-Pressured' Nigerian Worker," *American Political Science Review*, 65(1) (1964), 161–171.
46. "Nigerians Wonder: Could a Military Coup Help Us?" *Time,* January 31, 2010.
47. Mustapha and Whitfield (2009), "Elections in a Fragile Regime," *Journal of Democracy*, 14:3 (2003).
48. Joseph P. Smaldone, "National Security," in Helen Chapin Metz, ed., *Nigeria: A Country Study* (Washington, D.C.: Federal Research Division, Library of Congress, 1991).

CHAPTER 10

China

Andrew Mertha

As the People's Republic of China enters its seventh decade, growing wealth, spectacular parades, and increasing nationalism mask the momentous challenges faced by China's leaders and its people.

> **?** How has China's authoritarian regime managed to build and consolidate state strength in just 60 years?

INTRODUCTION TO CHINA

On October 1, 2009, China celebrated the 60th anniversary of the People's Republic. On that same date in 1949, Chairman **Mao Zedong**—the hero of the revolutionary army and the leader of the Communist Party that had overthrown the Nationalist government—stood on the podium before the Gate of Heavenly Peace in Tiananmen Square in Beijing, and conveyed the unmistakable message that "The Chinese people have stood up." His was not empty rhetoric: over the previous century China's power had declined due to weak political leadership in the face of European imperialism, and the rise of neighboring Japan. A massive portrait of Mao remains aloft on Tiananmen Gate. Mao's face also graces China's currency, and every year millions of Chinese visit Mao's embalmed body in a Beijing mausoleum.

The principal reason Mao remains such an important figure decades after his death is because he is widely regarded as *the* founding father—the individual who united China after decades of dissolution and anarchy. Since the late 1800s, China's leaders had sought wealth and power to develop China's economy, to provide China's citizens a high standard of living, to resist foreign invasion, and to stand up for their interests on the global stage. However, for the century prior to 1949, China was largely unable to attain these goals. Mao's great achievement was to provide the prerequisite—a unified Chinese state—for achieving wealth and power.

Since the death of Chairman Mao in 1976 and the gradual shift to a market-based economy that began two years later, China has also become richer than ever. Its economy has experienced double-digit growth most of the past 30 years, as China has become a manufacturing powerhouse and the world's largest exporter. Per capita income went from 379 *renminbi* (RMB) to 48,353 RMB (about $7,600) in 2010. To be sure, China remains poor by U.S. standards. However, because income is very unequally distributed and because China's population is about 1.3 billion, economic development has brought literally hundreds of millions of people from abject poverty into the middle class. In short, since 1949 the Chinese state has reversed course, moving from "weakness" to "strength."

What explains this rapid transformation? If we wish to understand contemporary Chinese politics, we must begin with the question, *how has the Chinese government managed to build and consolidate state strength in just 60 years?* Some answer this question by pointing to the non-democratic nature of Chinese government: a few key members of the **Chinese Communist Party (CCP)**—the only political party in the country (except for eight decorative parties subservient to the CCP)—control every facet of Chinese politics. After the collapse of the Soviet Union in 1991, many now see China as the last of the world's great communist dictatorships.

Mao Zedong ■ born in 1893, the son of a well-to-do peasant, Mao, more than any other individual, personified the Chinese Communist Party, which he helped found in 1921 and led until his death in 1976.

Read and Listen to Chapter 10 at mypoliscilab.com

Study and Review the Pre-Test & Flashcards at mypoliscilab.com

Chinese Communist Party (CCP) ■ the single-party apparatus and single most powerful institution in China since 1949.

Connecting the emergence of effective government in China with the iron fist of a highly centralized dictatorship seems logical. Politics in a democracy are often messy and often inefficient; many argue only a dictatorship could create effective government in a diverse society of more than 1.3 billion people—four times the population of the United States. Indeed, many observers marvel at the central government's ability to regulate the behavior of individual Chinese citizens—even their most intimate personal choices, for example by limiting the number of children each family can have.[1] This "One Child Policy," which is aimed at limiting China's population growth, seems every bit as totalitarian as Nazi Germany or the Soviet Union under Stalin.

However, focusing on the One Child Policy as an example of China's state strength would mislead us to believe the state is more powerful than it really is. The government is able to implement such draconian measures within the area of population policy because China's overpopulation presents a very real challenge to the country's continued stability. Few issues are as critical to China's future economic, political, and societal development as managing population growth and the One Child Policy receives an inordinate amount of attention and state resources from Beijing. It is an exception to the rule. Indeed, a view of Chinese politics that relies upon the heavy hand of the authoritarian government leaves many, indeed most, political puzzles unexplained. Like many governments around the world, China's central government actually exhibits traits of state *weakness*: lack of sufficient well-trained personnel and sufficient budgetary resources to implement its chosen policies, politicization of the policy process, and massive corruption.

How can we answer this chapter's main question—China's transformation from an ineffective to a strong state—given the paradoxically relatively weak state of China's central government? The answer is that the consolidation of state strength in China over the last 60 years is possible due to the combination of "control when necessary" from the center with "decentralization when possible" of political power to provincial, municipal, and county government authorities. China's national leaders reason that local decision making will generate more effective government on most issues than would centralized control from Beijing. China's rise is evidence that such an approach has worked in practice. However, although the central government relies on local authorities to implement its will, local politicians frequently clash with and even ignore the central government's dictates. If Chinese politics were simply about the imposition of authority "from above," such political outcomes would be inexplicable.[2]

This chapter begins with an historical overview of the modern Chinese state. We will look at China's state institutions, particularly the Chinese Communist Party, the government, and the People's Liberation Army (PLA). This will be followed by a discussion of Chinese identities, including the shared historical experiences that contribute to contemporary Chinese nationalism, but also looking at two other competing sets of identities, those of the Tibetan and Uyghur minorities. The final section looks at the exponentially rising number of competing interests in China from state institutions as well as from society and the fourth estate, the media.

CHINA

CHINA IN COMPARISON

	United Kingdom	Germany	France	Japan	India	Mexico	Russia	Nigeria	China	Iran
Freedom House Classification	Democracy	Democracy	Democracy	Democracy	Democracy	Partial democracy	Partial democracy	Partial democracy	Non-democracy	Non-democracy
Land Size (sq km)	243,610	357,022	643,801	377,915	3,287,263	1,964,375	17,098,242	923,768	9,596,961	1,648,195
Land Size Ranking	79	62	42	61	7	15	1	32	4	18
Population (July 2011 Estimate)	62,698,362	81,471,834	65,312,249	126,475,664	1,189,172,906	113,724,226	138,739,892	155,215,573	1,336,718,015	77,891,220
Population Ranking	22	16	21	10	2	11	9	8	1	18
Life Expectancy (Years)	80.1	80.1	81.2	82.3	66.8	76.5	66.3	47.6	74.7	70.1
Life Expectancy Ranking	28	27	13	5	51	72	162	220	95	146
Literacy Rate	99%	99%	99%	99%	61%	86.1%	99.4%	68%	91.6%	77%
GDP Per Capita (2010 Estimate)	US$35,100	US$35,900	US$33,300	US$34,000	US$3,500	US$13,800	US$15,900	US$2,500	US$7,600	US$11,200
GDP Ranking	36	32	39	38	163	85	71	178	126	100

HISTORICAL OVERVIEW OF CHINA

10.1 How has China's long imperial past informed the country's current state strength?

China's dramatic decline as a global power from the mid-nineteenth century to 1949—its Century of Humiliation (*bainian guochi*)—acts as both a warning and as an inspiration. It warns against sliding into political dissolution and anarchy. At the same time, preoccupation with China's very survival inspired Chinese intellectuals, politicians, and common citizens to figure out how to reclaim the mantle of greatness that their country lost when it was invaded by European imperial powers throughout the nineteenth century and Japan in 1931.

Century of Humiliation (*bainian guochi*) ∎
A period between the mid-nineteenth to the mid-twentieth century, during which China suffered repeated military defeats from a number of European colonial powers and Japan, which resulted in several foreign "spheres of influence" on Chinese soil.

▶ Watch the Video "China's New Rich" at mypoliscilab.com

▶ Watch the Video "U.S.–China Trade Tensions" at mypoliscilab.com

✳ Explore the Comparative "Development" at mypoliscilab.com

The Chinese Empire

China has been famously described as "a civilization pretending to be a state."[3] Indeed, Chinese civilization has existed for far longer than a modern Chinese state. For much of the past 2,000 years, China was a fairly cohesive empire, having been unified by Emperor Qin Shi Huang Di in 221 BCE. Although the Qin Dynasty barely lasted a generation, the China it consolidated lasted until the early twentieth century.

China's leaders traditionally measured their power by their kingdom's cultural strength, and considered their kingdom to be at the center of the world. The Chinese word for "China" (*Zhongguo*) literally translates into "central state," or more commonly (but less accurately) "Middle Kingdom," indicating China's place at the center of all political, social, and political activity. Societies and cultures far from the empire's capital were deemed irrelevant and subservient, and the people inhabiting those regions dismissed as "barbarians" who lacked culture—*Chinese* culture.[4]

This view of China as positioned at the center of the world was possible because of China's physical environment: it is surrounded by some of the most inhospitable topography in the world. The northeast is bordered by the frozen wastelands of Siberia, the northwest is bounded by the inhospitable Gobi Desert, the west is buttressed by the impassable Himalaya mountains, and the southwest extends into the malaria-infested jungles of Burma, Laos, and Vietnam.

China's immediate neighbors—Japan, Korea, and several kingdoms in Southeast Asia—grudgingly acknowledged China's centrality by agreeing to be "vassal states" of China. Under this system, leaders of neighboring states were compensated financially for adopting key elements of Chinese political identity, such as the Confucian approach to statecraft, and the Chinese writing system. In many ways, China's leaders had good reason to believe they occupied the "Middle Kingdom."

The imperial government apparatus was remarkably limited in scope—a fact that will prove telling in identifying the source of China's state strength today. There were only six central government ministries (then called "Boards"), encompassing the universe of government functions: Personnel, Revenue, Rites, War, Punishments, and Public Works—and the central government's authority only penetrated to the county (*xian*) level. Below that, cities, towns, and villages were self-governing and life flourished in the absence of substantial central government involvement.[5]

How is it possible for such a huge country to be governed if the government itself did not penetrate down to the municipal, township, or village level? A large part of the answer is that the Chinese state and Chinese society were bound together and regulated by a complex set of relationships and obligations designed to maintain harmony and avoid chaos—Confucianism. Confucius (Kongzi) was a scholar who lived from 551 to 479 BCE, during a time of civil war. He and his followers looked back to a mythical "Golden Age" when China was imagined to have been unified and free of conflict. Confucius advocated a way to return to such a situation of stability. His teachings advocated maintenance of a society in which people were not equal; rather, each individual was part of a status network set according to family, profession, or other attributes. An individual's relationships to superiors and subordinates were governed by a complex set of obligations and responsibilities. Superiors could expect subordinates to fulfill obligations—but they also had to discharge their own clearly mandated responsibilities to their subordinates.

Confucianism held that social stability would be maintained by upholding particular codes of conduct towards one's superiors, one's subordinates, and to the community at large. For example, a particularly effective institution was the *baojia system*, in which family members were collectively held responsible for all members' behavior. If one family member was accused of violating the law or behavioral norms, the punishment—even execution—could be meted out to a specified number of generations of the individual's family, including several degrees of cousins. In the absence of extensive central government involvement in local affairs, this and other Confucian measures effectively overcame the potential for political chaos in Imperial China—even though it clearly came at the cost of suppressing individual freedom.

The Confucian system went far beyond the family: the very same sets of obligations and responsibilities extended to the relationship between the emperor and his subjects, as well as between the Middle Kingdom and its vassal states. As long as the emperor and his dynasty remained strong and cohesive, the idea of social hierarchy that was central to Confucian cultural identity generated tremendous political cohesion throughout the empire. As a result, China exhibited far less social and political unrest than was the case in Europe—even though the Chinese state was not "strong," according to our modern definition of state strength. This form of cultural identity directly shaped Chinese politics for almost 3,000 years, from the mid-seventh century BCE. until 1911.

However, the durability of China's Confucian political and social order was premised on maintaining a certain degree of isolation from the rest of the world. Encroachment by European imperial powers in the nineteenth century proved too much for this system to bear. In the late 1700s, the Chinese emperor could dismiss Great Britain's requests for trade, asserting that "[we have not] the slightest need of your country's manufactures."[6] China, thus, insisted that Great Britain pay in silver for the tea and other goods sold to British merchants, rather than trade it for British imports. Yet in making this demand, China's leaders put the British in an untenable economic position—one that threatened to deplete England's silver reserves merely to satisfy the English consumer's insatiable thirst for tea.

Confucianism ■ the basic philosophy and organizing principle of traditional China in which "right conduct" was the most important goal for individuals and representatives of the state.

baojia system ■ a system of social accounting whereby extended families undertook the responsibility of preparing its members to serve society and state as a whole, and in which entire families were held accountable for individual transgressions of its members.

China's leaders believed they could ignore the rapidly expanding global trade economy in the 1800s. However, because China had isolated itself from the world for so long, the country was unable to withstand the changing international military context. By that time, China's military capability lagged far behind European powers, such as Great Britain. The British government, thus, exploited already existing demand for opium in China by expanding the supply and lowering the price. Given opium's addictive qualities, demand for the drug in China increased rapidly. Commissioner Lin Zexu's destruction of a vast quantity of opium in 1839 provided the pretext for the first of the Opium Wars between China and the UK, which resulted in China's defeat. The UK forced China to open up to foreign trade and to cede Hong Kong.[7] The decades that followed saw China divided up by various Western countries into separate "spheres of influence" (China was never "colonized" per se; it was too big). The southwest went to France; the southeast to Great Britain; the northeast to Germany and, increasingly after 1895, Japan; parts of Manchuria and Mongolia to Russia; and Shanghai and other trading ports were managed by a consortium of European imperialist powers.

While China was being dismantled from the outside, it was also rotting from the inside. Mark Elvin describes an efficient, stable, and well-organized economy by the late imperial period, but one in which China's rapidly expanding population created not only cheap labor, but required production be used exclusively for the basic sustenance of the people. As a result, there existed no incentive for innovation, and China stagnated in the fields of engineering, mathematics, and science, areas in which it had previously been centuries ahead of Europe and the rest of the world.[8]

At the top of the political system, the situation was even more alarming. For centuries, Chinese imperial dynasties that had degenerated into weakness and corruption were eventually overthrown and replaced by a new dynasty. However, given the ease with which Western powers had demeaned China, by the late nineteenth century, many Chinese scholars and politicians began to wonder whether the imperial system itself needed to be scrapped and replaced with different political institutions.[9]

Chinese Republic ■ established in 1912 to replace the imperial system, ruled by the Nationalist Party. When Nationalist forces fled the mainland following their defeat by the Communists in 1949, it was reestablished on the island of Taiwan.

Sun Yat-sen ■ the first president of the Republic of China and founder of the Nationalist Party.

Nationalist Party (*Guomingdang* or *Kuomingtang*) ■ the ruling party of the Chinese Republic until 1949, after which members fled to Taiwan.

The Chinese Republic

In 1911, the Qing Dynasty—which had ruled China since 1644—collapsed. This marked the end of the Chinese Empire. In its place rose the Chinese Republic—a civilian-led regime. However, it quickly became clear that the main source of power lay with the armed forces, or, more specifically, with one individual—Yuan Shikai—who was in charge of reforming the armed forces. Under Yuan, the republic quickly devolved from an incipient parliamentary democracy into a dictatorship. But when Yuan unexpectedly died in 1916, the entire system collapsed. Given this power vacuum, central power disappeared overnight and the country fragmented into hundreds of military fiefdoms ruled by warlords.[10] By 1916, China's once-vaunted unity and cohesion was no more.

Yuan's predecessor as president of the republic, veteran Chinese nationalist Sun Yat-sen, retreated to the southern province of Guangdong in order to build up an army of his own and reunify China under the banner of his Nationalist Party (or

Guomindang). Although Sun died in 1925, within two years his successor, Chiang Kai-shek, managed to unify large parts of China through a patchwork of political alliances between rival warlords. However, Chiang confronted other players besides the warlords.

In 1919, the Versailles Treaty following the end of World War I stipulated that Chinese territory taken by Germany would be given to Japan instead of back to China (both China and Japan were on the Allied side). This caused disillusionment in China with the West, and opened up a tremendously creative wellspring of introspection (referred to as the May Fourth Movement, referring to the date in 1919 when the Chinese took to Tiananmen Square to protest the treaty) among Chinese reform-minded intellectuals as to how China might evolve in a way that was not vulnerable to Western insincerity. This context helps us make sense of the embrace of communism by some Chinese as both "Western" (i.e., not traditionally Chinese, and therefore, disreputable) and as "anti-West" (i.e., not corrupted by Western duplicity).

Established in 1921, the Chinese Communist Party and the Nationalists were political allies up until 1927, at which point Chiang attempted to literally kill all the Communists off. Chiang failed, allowing the Communists to scatter across the countryside and regroup. This failure to decisively defeat the Communists would later come back to haunt Chiang and the Nationalists.[11]

China's fragmentation and weakness presented its neighbor and former vassal state, Japan, with the perfect opening to act upon its own imperial ambitions. After defeating the Chinese navy in 1895, Japan gradually increased its presence in northeast China and annexed the Chinese province of Manchuria outright in 1931. In 1937, it declared war on China as the first stage of its attempt to conquer resource-rich areas in Southeast Asia and to establish what it called the "Greater Asia Co-Prosperity Sphere" under its leadership. The War of Resistance against Japan—the Chinese moniker for World War II—continued until Japan surrendered to the Allies in August 1945. The war was a particularly brutal experience for the Chinese, because Japan committed numerous atrocities, including the Rape of Nanjing during which the Japanese army massacred up to 300,000 Chinese, and the infamous Unit 731 in which Chinese civilians and POWs were subject to gruesome experiments such as vivisection, amputation, and exposure to biological weapons.[12]

After the war, the rest of the world sought to rebuild. However, China experienced another four years of violent civil war between the Nationalists and the Communists, resulting in 1.2 million casualties and culminating with the defeat of the Nationalists and the establishment of the People's Republic of China on October 1, 1949. At that time, the remaining Nationalist forces retreated to the island of Taiwan (Formosa) where they reestablished the Republic of China. China has regarded Taiwan as a renegade province ever since.

Consolidating the People's Republic of China

Between 1911 and 1949, China experienced the collapse of a centuries-old monarchy, a failed attempt to create a democratic form of government under the republic, fragmentation under numerous warlords, foreign invasion, occupation, and years of bloody civil war. In 1949, few observers expected the Communists

Chiang Kai-shek ■ Sun Yat-sen's successor as leader of the Nationalist Party from 1925 until his death in 1975. Chiang represented the more conservative, military wing of the Nationalist Party and was a staunch anti-communist.

May Fourth Movement ■ mobilization of Chinese seeking to increase China's wealth and stature on the world stage; so called because on May 4, 1919, students, intellectuals, and others filled Tiananmen Square to protest the ceding to Japan of several Chinese territories hitherto held by Germany.

Rape of Nanjing ■ the mass murder and torture of between 200,000 and 400,000 Chinese civilians by the Japanese during WWII in Nanjing; the event continues to strain Sino-Japanese relations today.

People's Republic of China ■ the current regime of China, led by the Chinese Communist Party.

to successfully overcome the political chaos that had plagued China for decades. This returns us to the main question of this chapter: in the aftermath of decades of chaos, how has the Chinese Communist Party managed to consolidate its authority while building up state strength?

The CCP benefited from several sets of circumstances. First, the People's Liberation Army (PLA), under the command of the CCP, enjoyed a series of military victories. During the Korean War (1950–1953), the PLA fought United Nations forces led by the U.S. military to a stalemate—which, given China's previous record of defeats at the hands of far less-powerful opponents, was regarded not unjustifiably as a victory. In 1962, the PLA also soundly defeated India's military in a series of battles along their disputed border deep in the Himalaya Mountains. The PLA also detonated China's first nuclear weapon in the Lop Nor desert in 1964.[13] These victories gave the PLA and CCP leaders tremendous legitimacy and helped the party consolidate its rule.

Second, the CCP benefited from international perceptions. The CCP was able to convince other countries that China was more powerful than it actually was, and that it was not to be trifled with. Mao expertly played up U.S. perceptions of China's strength so that U.S. leaders overestimated Chinese military capabilities and by extension Beijing's international influence. All this provided China was a degree of military security that it had not enjoyed since before the arrival of the British in the early 1800s. And this freedom from international invasion and/or influence gave the CCP breathing room to consolidate its hold on power.

Third, the CCP's effort to establish authority over Chinese territory benefited from China's geographic environment. Although surrounded on the east by its Cold War ideological enemies—Japan, South Korea, and Taiwan—the PRC also had formidable buffer zone along its northern, southern, and western borders. For example, China and its northern neighbor the USSR—sharing a 4,380-kilometer-long border—were allies until the 1960s. Chinese military projection was also key in preventing Tibet from breaking away from China in 1950 and again in 1959, and in defeating India during the Sino-Indian war.

Finally, the CCP benefited from the domestic economic environment, which was finally improving after decades of stagnation or decline. Land reform brought the dream of property ownership to millions of peasants who had hitherto worked under the yoke of the landlord class. In the cities, the new government established an industrial program that within the space of a few years made China a viable economic power. Thus although in 1949 China had very little modern economic infrastructure to speak of, within ten years it has established an impressive heavy industrial base modeled on the Soviet Union's. The planned economy—in which CCP government bureaucrats and not market forces made economic decisions ranging from what to manufacture, how to distribute it, to what prices to set—consolidated the economy under the centralized control of the state.

In sum, victory in Korea, the first sustained domestic peace in over a century, and fulfillment of promises to make China economically strong reinforced feelings of nationalism and support for the communist regime. Indeed, within the first several years after 1949, China's leaders had amassed an extraordinary amount of social and political capital that allowed them to transform society in ways that weaker states could only dream of. This laid the base for the eventual emergence of a strong Chinese state. However, China's government would first have to pass through two difficult decades.

Mao's Attack on the State

In an ironic and tragic twist, much of the new state's accomplishments of the early to mid-1950s were halted and even reversed by a series of policy choices undertaken by Chairman Mao and several key individuals in the top CCP leadership. The economic development program that China adopted from the Soviet Union in the early 1950s successfully helped China industrialize. However, the command economy could not be sustained in the long run, for several reasons. First Soviet assistance was in the form of loans, which by the late 1950s China had to pay back. Second, this industrial program benefited people in the cities but imposed significant costs on rural peasants, who received artificially low prices for their agricultural output but were forced to pay artificially high prices for fertilizer and other necessities.

Third, reliance on the centralized Soviet economic model meant that central-government bureaucracies were growing extremely powerful. To Chairman Mao, this was an unacceptable "selling out" of the revolutionary ideals of equality and shared sacrifice. Mao could not stomach this institutionalization of the revolution. He wanted to achieve a state of *permanent* revolution, in which people would rise up against what he saw as the evils of a stable political system that valued routines and predictability above all else. Indeed, Mao believed that the Soviet Union exhibited these tendencies, and he grew increasingly suspicious of the USSR and eager to establish a uniquely Chinese socialist path towards economic development.[14]

Mao's suspicions were confirmed by two events that took place in 1956. In February, at the Communist Party of the Soviet Union's 20th Party Congress, Nikita Khrushchev denounced his predecessor, Josef Stalin. Mao interpreted this as a personal attack on his vision for the Chinese revolution. The second event was the anti-Soviet revolution that took place in Hungary in late October and early November, which was quashed by Soviet tanks. Mao felt that the Soviet system lacked a pressure valve through which its citizens could criticize and suggest ways to reform the system. In response, he launched the **Hundred Flowers Movement** in the spring of 1957, in which he exhorted citizens to "let one hundred flowers bloom and one hundred schools of thought contend." Although it took some time for understandably cautious Chinese to respond, once they did, the criticisms escalated to the point of demanding that Mao step down and that the CCP be dismantled. Only weeks after the "Hundred Flowers" began, it was unceremoniously halted and immediately replaced by an **Anti-Rightist Campaign**, which targeted those who had criticized the regime under the "Hundred Flowers." More than half a million people were persecuted as "Rightists," lost their jobs, went to prison, or were sent to perform hard labor for the next two decades. Since most "rightists" were among the educated class, intellectuals and other experts were effectively expelled from society, severely curtailing China's further technical development for the next several decades.

Mao's political concerns and policy goals merged into what is known as the **Great Leap Forward (GLF)** of 1958 to 1961. The GLF was a policy that aimed

Hundred Flowers Movement ■ a short-lived movement in which Mao offered Chinese citizens a channel to articulate grievances ("let a hundred flowers bloom and let one hundred schools of thought contend"). When critics began to call for dismantling the CCP and for Mao to step down, the movement was quickly quashed.

Anti-Rightist Campaign ■ in response to the Hundred Flowers Movement, those who had criticized the regime were labeled "rightists" and forced out of their jobs, imprisoned, or forced into hard labor for the next two decades.

Great Leap Forward ■ Mao's attempt to transform China into an agricultural exporter and industrial powerhouse in three years by combining traditional and modern industrial techniques simultaneously in the cities and in the countryside. The political pressure for subordinates to inflate production figures led to widespread famine and starvation in which 30 million people died.

to make China a major industrial and agricultural power by using its huge labor pool to pursue industry and agriculture simultaneously in both the cities and in the countryside. Thus, urban areas saw the planting of "victory gardens" wherever there was space to do so, while the countryside was illuminated by "backyard steel furnaces," by which peasants could smelt steel when they were planting and harvesting in the fields. An overly ambitious utopian vision, the GLF sought to eclipse the growing power of central government ministries by giving local party officials the task of mobilizing hundreds of millions of Chinese workers and peasants. The central government defined success by how much local officials could "produce," and, thus, local officials soon began to inflate their production figures in their quest to rival neighboring locales. In many cases, local officials claimed to have produced five times or more than what they had actually produced. Yet, when the central government calculated what it would take to redistribute, it based its figures on these wildly inflated figures: if it took 20 percent from an area that had inflated its output figures fivefold, the result was that the state ended up taking all the grain and leaving the peasants with nothing. The result was the worst famine in world history, in which more than 30 million people died.[15]

Mao, suffering from his association with the GLF disaster, retired from active politics for a few years. Yet, rather than humbling him, this experience only reinforced

CHINESE GOVERNMENT AND PARTY OFFICIALS PUBLICLY HUMILIATED DURING THE CULTURAL REVOLUTION

By the mid-1960s, Mao felt that the country was slipping from his grasp and moving in the direction of the Soviet Union, which had, in his mind, extinguished its revolutionary flame. The Cultural Revolution was Mao's attempt to destroy the party apparatus that he spent his whole life creating, resulting in the death, torture, imprisonment, and public humiliation of thousands of Chinese officials.

his belief that China's central government was becoming anti-revolutionary. His next—and final—political act would seek to destroy the very institutions he had help establish.[16] This was the Great Proletarian Cultural Revolution (1966–1976), in which Mao sought to put China back on the revolutionary track that he had devoted his life to pursuing. In particular, Mao felt that the Communist Party itself was the source of "revisionism," a regression back to the bad old days before the revolution, and would end up a lifeless, oppressive, fascist regime, just like the Soviet Union. In addition to a number of new policy initiatives, particularly in culture and in the arts, the Cultural Revolution was also distinguished by the purging and killing of many top leaders, and the closing of schools and mobilization of students to be Mao's "shock troops"—the "Red Guards"—to destroy whatever vestiges of the old society remained. The result was that political institutions, particularly the party and the government, were so weakened that the People's Liberation Army—the only viable political institution left standing—was called in to restore order and to effectively run the state. The government and the party continued to function, but both had been severely weakened. Still, the final irony of Mao's attempts at establishing a utopian socialist state was that his weakening of Chinese political institutions *aided*, rather than hindered, much of the subsequent political and economic reform and made the current shape and structure of China possible.

The Emergence of the Contemporary PRC

Chairman Mao died in 1976. After a brief power struggle, a reform coalition led by Deng Xiaoping gained control in December 1978 and began to turn China away from a planned economy and towards market-based capitalism. Deng had been a close follower of Mao since the 1930s and had held some of the highest positions in the CCP before being purged twice during the Cultural Revolution. When Deng returned to power in 1977, his faith in communism was not shaken, but his faith in *Maoism* was. During the next decade-and-a-half, Deng would work tirelessly to adapt China's economic system to his goals of opening up to the outside world (through massive infusions of foreign direct investment, FDI) and reforming China's economic system. In this sense, Deng was as much a revolutionary as Mao had been. At the beginning, the reforms were modest: after fulfilling their much-reduced production quotas, peasants were allowed to sell surplus produce in unofficial markets at prices set by supply and demand (the household responsibility system in agriculture). This experiment, given the artificially low baseline for improvement due to Mao's disastrous policies, led to a dramatic increase in production and improvements in peasant income all over the country.

As economic reforms proceeded, China's leaders recognized that a considerable pool of their population's workforce resided in the countryside. Therefore, Chinese leaders made it easier for laborers to relocate to cities to work in urban factories for relatively low wages by relaxing the onerous residency (*hukou*) restrictions. This was the beginning of China's rapid economic growth in recent decades, as millions of peasants began to enter a huge mobile labor pool. Encouraged by government incentives, factories sprang up all over the country, producing all sorts of cheap goods for export. In many instances, local government leaders built and

Great Proletarian Cultural Revolution ■ Mao's final attempt to counteract what he saw as the bureaucratization of the revolution, by purging and killing many top leaders and training a new generation of revolutionary successors known as the Red Guards.

Deng Xiaoping ■ A close follower of Mao from earliest days of the revolution. By the late 1950s, he was in charge of the day-to-day business of the entire CCP apparatus. Twice purged during the Cultural Revolution, Deng presided over the next two decades of reform. Deng is acknowledged as the "architect" of the reform era which continues into the present day.

hukou ■ a means of population control through residency permits that originated during the Mao era. Housing, medical benefits, and food purchases are all tied to residency permits, thereby making it impossible for non-*hukou*-wielding citizens to live in the cities. Although the restrictions eased in the 1980s to allow labor markets to flourish, certain benefits (such as public education) are still tied to the *hukou*.

managed these factories according to economic considerations, increasing both local revenue and personal wealth. At the same time, urban workers who had worked for decades for minimum wages in exchange for job security, free housing, health care, and other benefits (the iron rice bowl) found these benefits quickly disappearing before their eyes, setting the stage for unrest.

More and more cities in China were given the right to work directly with foreign investors, which curtailed the central government's ability to subsequently rein in local officials. As China moved away from a planned economy in the mid-1980s, local officials no longer relied on decision makers in Beijing to provide them with the money, resources, and production targets required by the state plan. Local officials found themselves making an increasing number of economic decisions independently from Beijing. Decisions such as what crops to grow, what factories to build, what markets to sell to—all of these became local decisions. With this economic decision-making power came a certain degree of political decision-making power that had hitherto been monopolized by Beijing.

But why would Beijing consciously give up such a degree of power to local state officials? There are at least three reasons. First, by the late 1970s, it had become increasingly clear to veteran revolutionaries that Maoist policies would not make China rich, or by extension, powerful. China would have to take another path and CCP leaders could see that capitalism was working well in Japan, Korea, and Taiwan, China's archenemy. Second, CCP authorities needed the help of local

iron rice bowl (tian fanwan) ■ in pre-reform China, workers received very low wages but were promised minimum benefits that kept them from starvation. Benefits included housing, medical care, education, and other basic services. In the 1980s and 1990s, new workers were hired at higher wages but without "iron rice bowl" benefits.

SUMMARY TABLE

Historical Overview of China

1793	Macartney Mission to the Qing Court
1839–1842	First Opium War
1911/1912	Fall of the Qing Dynasty and establishment of the Republic of China
1916	Death of Yuan Shikai and start of the Warlord Era
1919	May Fourth Movement
1921	Establishment of the Chinese Communist Party
1937–1945	The War of National Resistance against Japan
1937/1938	The Nanjing Massacre
1945–1949	The Civil War
1949	Establishment of the People's Republic of China
1956	Khrushchev's Secret Speech and the Hungarian Uprising
1957	The Hundred Flowers Movement
1957–1958	The Anti-Rightist Campaign
1958–1961	The Great Leap Forward
1966–1976	The Cultural Revolution
1976	The Death of Mao Zedong
1978	Deng Xiaoping and the Reform Coalition takeover

governments to implement their reform agenda, because entrenched interests in central-government bureaucracies opposed the loss of power that dismantling the planned economy would bring. Finally, the leadership in Beijing felt that the CCP's and PLA's coercive apparatus could provide a check on excesses that might result from the transition to a market economy. They were largely right, but to understand how the state has been able to handle this transition from communism to capitalism, we must analyze the contemporary Chinese state with regard to institutions, identities, and interests.

INSTITUTIONS OF CHINA

China is an authoritarian regime, although in the first years after the Communist Revolution it was closer to a totalitarian regime. In recent decades, the government has moved away from the emphasis on coercion, total control of society, and ideological indoctrination that define totalitarianism, and it has begun to experiment with new ways to provide economic opportunities to its citizens, and even to allow for greater social freedoms. In fact, the communist regime has undertaken economic reforms and allowed somewhat greater social freedoms precisely to maintain political control. In this section, we first explain why China can be classified as a one-party authoritarian rather than totalitarian regime. And, second, we describe the institutions of China's national governing apparatus, exploring the intimate relationship between the Chinese Communist Party and government institutions. Third, we then explain how the Communist Party allows for some degree of local and regional government policy experimentation—particularly in economic policy, even as it exercises ultimate final political authority. This combination of central control by the Communist Party with local and regional experimentation helps answer this chapter's question of how China has found the right political recipe for rapidly strengthening its state.

Chairman Mao's most-quoted aphorism is, "Political power grows out of the barrel of a gun. . . ." yet most people forget the more important part of the couplet, ". . . but the party must always control the gun." The Chinese Communist Party is the most important political institution in the country. It sets the ideological "tone" of the state, guides government policy, and controls the military. However, given the vast network of Communist Party members—somewhere around 80 million people—China is not simply an oligarchy. It is, instead, a single-party authoritarian regime. Let us explore how the CCP manages politics in China by both maintaining monopoly control at the national level, but also allowing some experimentation at the sub-national level of government.

10.2 What are the mechanisms that constrain as well as allow Chinese leaders to wield power?

Explore the Comparative "Civil Liberties" at mypoliscilab.com

China's Elite Institutions

To understand how Chinese politics works—and how China has developed a strong state relatively rapidly—we must first understand the relationship between the Chinese Communist Party and government institutions at the national level.[17] The CCP permeates all Chinese institutions, but we can also distinguish the CCP from those institutions.

Political Bureau (Politburo) ■ the top organizational group in the CCP and thus the highest-ranking institution of the Chinese state. It includes the head of the party (the general secretary), the head of the government (the premier), and the most important individuals in the Chinese state. Its standing committee is the highest deliberative body in the land.

State Council ■ the highest government institution in China, consisting of the premier, several vice premiers, and a similar number of more policy-oriented state councilors, that manages China's gargantuan network of ministries, commissions, bureaus, and other governmental institutions at the national level.

Politburo Standing Committee ■ the most important CCP leaders, makes China's most important political decisions.

reciprocal accountability ■ government officials are accountable to the party leaders who hire and promote them, but party leaders are also accountable to the government officials in the Central Committee selectorate who choose them.[20]

At the top of all Chinese national institutions are the two most important state organs, the Political Bureau (Politburo) of the Chinese Communist Party and the State Council. Members of the Politburo lead the CCP, and the State Council is the executive branch of government. However, because China is a single-party regime, final political authority ultimately rests with the leaders of the CCP who sit on the Politburo, particularly its Standing Committee.

There are usually about 25 members of the Politburo. Over the years, between five and nine of its members sit on its Politburo Standing Committee. These are the most important CCP leaders, and as such they are the most important of China's political leaders. These leaders include the general secretary, or head of the Communist Party; the premier, who is the head of the government; the chairman of the National People's Congress; and a few other top provincial leaders and the heads of the more important national ministries. The Standing Committee meets weekly and makes the most important political decisions.

Joining the party is not a simple matter. The application process is rigorous and invasive, and intensive reevaluation continues throughout a party member's career. Membership imposes constraints and intense responsibilities while also opening up political and other doors not available to non-party members. Indeed, as a person ascends the career ladder within the government, they reach a certain point in which the only way they can continue to advance is if they join the party.

The government apparatus in China consists of functional commissions or ministries (and their lower-ranking counterparts such as bureaus, offices, or sections), as well as a legislative apparatus, the National People's Congress (the judiciary is not a separate branch of government). The highest government organ is the State Council, functionally equivalent to the executive branch. It is headed by the premier, who is assisted by several vice premiers and state councilors. Already we can see the tight connection between the CCP and the institutions of government in China: when we think of China's leader, we think of its premier—currently Wen Jiabao. However, Wen ranks lower than Party Secretary Hu Jintao in terms of seniority on the Politburo. The State Council manages the day-to-day operation of the institutions of government, which include the central ministries, commissions, bureaus, and offices. It is also important to note that the People's Liberation Army (PLA) does not report to the government, but to the *party,* because Hu Jintao is both Party Secretary as well as chairman of the Military Affairs Commission, the equivalent of the US president's role as "Commander in Chief."

Although in the past top leaders' terms were open-ended, top leaders today are bound by a two-term limit of five years each.[18] The process for choosing members of the Politburo and the State Council is shrouded in secrecy, although they are announced with great fanfare at the CCP Party Congresses and the full National People's Congress meetings, which occur every five years. Some argue that top leaders are selected (and removed) through the mechanism of reciprocal accountability via the selectorate.[19] The selectorate in China is the Central Committee of the CCP, which is a group of about 300 officials in the government, the military, and the CCP apparatus (that is, full-time party members) who are led by a Standing Committee of about 100 who meet at regular intervals to discuss and often vigorously debate policy as well as selecting China's leaders. Others, like Joseph Fewsmith, argue that selection to top posts is a function of personal relationships

CHINESE CITIZEN LOOKING AT POSTERS OF PAST PRC LEADERS

As China moves farther away from the eras of Mao Zedong (1949–1976), Deng Xiaoping (1978–1995), and even Jiang Zemin (1989–2002), the head of state (Hu Jintao, at far right and his putative successor Xi Jinping, not pictured) is less likely to rule by sheer personal will and political power. Rather, he will be bound increasingly by the complex network of institutions comprising the Chinese state.

and factional struggles for power within the CCP—meaning that the "selectorate" does very little actual "selecting." This is an ongoing debate, but what is important to underscore is the degree to which participation in the political process has been limited to top members of the CCP and closed to ordinary citizens—until very recently.

It is when we move beyond the very top of the system that the selectorate mechanisms begin to show some teeth. The top positions (*nomenklatura*) in all government institutions, from ministers to county officials and below are filled with personnel chosen by the party. As one official put it to me, "the government lays out the 'chairs' while the party chooses the 'hats.'" A powerful committee called the *Bianwei,* comprised of officials from the State Council, Ministry of Personnel, Ministry of Finance, and most important among them, the CCP Organization Department, chooses how many personnel slots each ministry, bureau, and office receives, while the party by itself chooses the individuals who occupy the topmost positions. And this mechanism, like most national government and party institutions, is replicated all the way down to the county level. Thus, it is through personnel appointments, more than anything else (perhaps short of controlling the military), that the party is able to exercise and maintain its control. Indeed, as in other one-party states such as Saddam Hussein's Iraq, there is a sort of a "glass ceiling" in China, where in order to be promoted beyond a certain position, whether in a school, a hospital, or a bank, an person must become a party member.

The legislative branch of government is the National People's Congress (NPC), which has evolved from a "rubber stamp" to an organ that, in a consulting and coordinating capacity, and under its mandate to promulgate China's increasing body of laws, is becoming increasingly consequential, albeit not terribly powerful. For

nomenklatura ■ the appointment system of leading officials, demonstrating the monopoly power of the CCP Organization Department in putting politically reliable cadres into positions of power throughout the state apparatus.

the past generation, the chairmanship of the National People's Congress has been held by some of the most powerful people in China, who have used their own personal and professional authority to empower the NPC. Additionally, given the skyrocketing number of laws in China, the NPC as a legislative body has seen its own relevance increase dramatically. Legal and policy questions are often hotly debated and NPC drafting committees actively seek out non-governmental, even foreign, expertise on complicated questions of substance. As far as appointment confirmation functions are concerned, the NPC has no role akin to the U.S. Congress. In this sense, it is distinct from the Central Committee (which is a CCP organ), in that it is concerned with lawmaking and policy, not human resources and appointments, which, as noted above, are handled ultimately by the party.

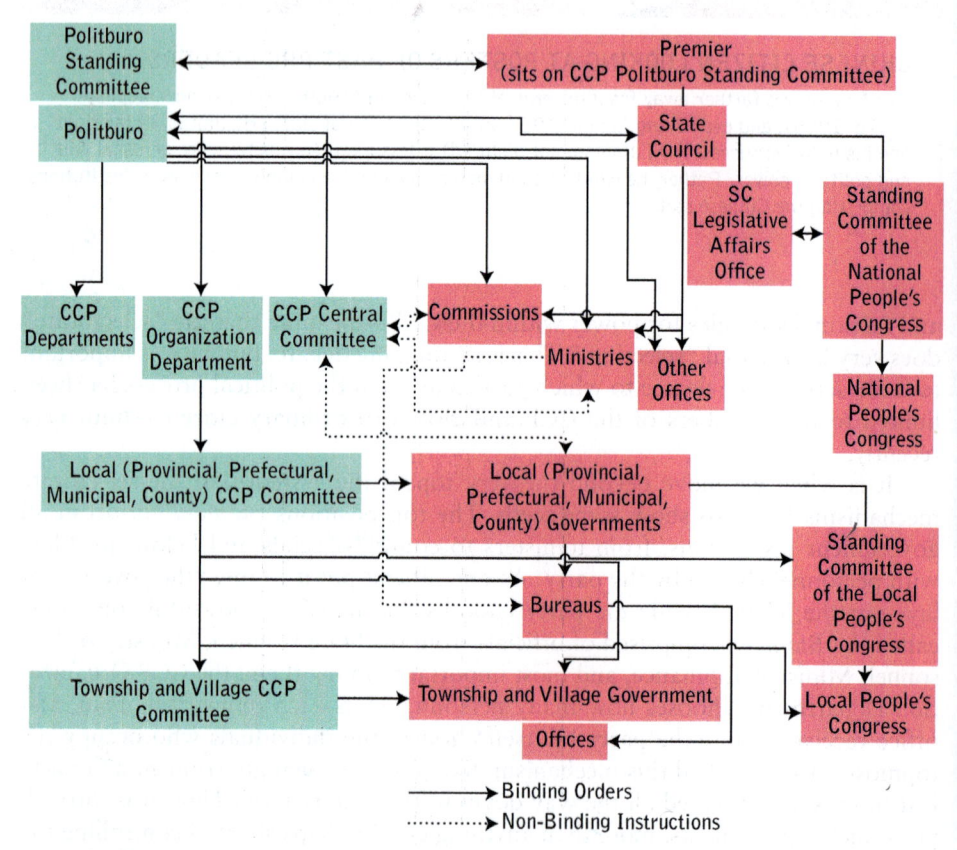

FIGURE 10.1
CCP and Government Structure of China

The Politburo Standing Committee led by the general secretary of the Communist Party is the top decision-making body in the country, but its decisions are enshrined in policy and in national laws and subsequently implemented and enforced by a dizzying array of party (in green) and government (in red) institutions, all of which have their own interests not always aligned with the top leadership. This extends geographically all the way from the Politburo and State Council in Beijing down to a million township and village government offices.

The national government bureaucracy is made up of more than 30 ministries, commissions, and bureaus that handle everything from economics to the arts, from agriculture to infrastructure, and from education to national security. These organs have evolved over time and have taken on often-conflicting responsibilities as well. Very few of them are capable of managing a distinctive policy area (which have grown far more complex than during the Mao era) on their own and they often have to coordinate with one or more of their counterparts. When differences arise—as they inevitably do—and when these differences cannot be resolved among the agencies themselves, they are bumped up to the State Council and/or to individual State Council members (state councilors or vice premiers) in their functions as leaders of ad hoc coordination offices—leadership small groups—which bring together clusters of ministries and other agencies in order to work together to achieve a particular policy goal; these clusters are collectively referred to as *xitong*. For example, the anti-pornography *xitong* includes the ministry of public security, the ministry of education, the press and publications administration, the administration for industry and commerce, and other government units that might not otherwise naturally come in contact with one another and is led by the "anti-pornography leadership small group." Figure 10.2 illustrates the way *xitong* work.

leadership small groups ■ groups of top State Council and other officials that head a given *xitong*. These groups often step in to make decisions when *xitong* are unable to resolve a problem that arises between their member bureaucracies. Some leadership small groups are more fluid, while others have become increasingly institutionalized over time.

xitong ■ clusters of related bureaucracies that are lumped together in pursuit of a specific set of policy goals. In recent years, *xitong* has been used more loosely to refer to any kind of bureaucratic system in China.

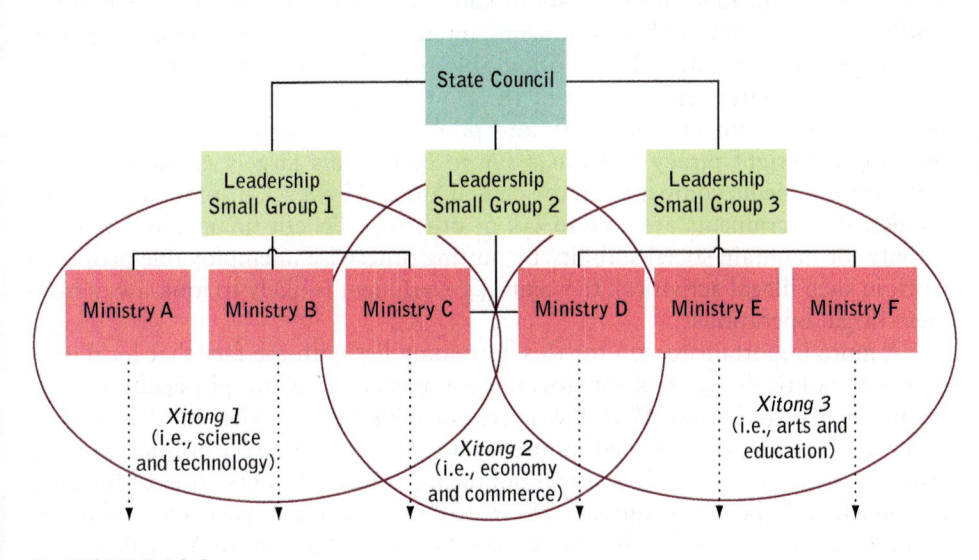

FIGURE 10.2

Policy Coordination: Leadership Small Groups and *Xitong*

As is increasingly the case, when policy does not fit neatly into the domain of a single bureaucracy in China, the relevant bureaucracies are clustered together into what is called a *xitong*. Each *xitong* has its own leadership, which coordinates policy and resolves conflicts between two or more bureaucracies within the *xitong*. In recent years, *xitong* have become more fluid and often members of one *xitong* in one policy area also belong to another *xitong* governed by another policy area. Thus, "Ministry D" could be the Ministry of Culture, which is in charge of arts and education (*Xitong* 3), as well as the commercial market for value-laden merchandise (*Xitong* 2), such as books and movies. *Xitong* do not appear on formal organizational charts, but they are the organizing principle through which government bureaucrats in China approach their institutional responsibilities.

Even "retail-level" units embedded throughout Chinese society are often the lowest-ranking offices in a national government bureaucracy. The office where one buys train tickets is part of the Ministry of Railways, bookstores are managed by the government's Ministry of Culture and the CCP's Propaganda Department, and registering one's name at a hotel means sending it to the local office of the Ministry of Public Security.

Local State Government

The structure of government at the national level is replicated across China's 31 provinces, 17 prefectures (an administrative division below a province including a large city and the surrounding area), 652 cities, and 2,861 county governments (and to add to the confusion, these numbers are constantly in flux). That is, most local government agencies are counterparts to ministries in Beijing. For example, the Ministry of Agriculture has its own bureaus of agriculture in every province, city, and county, which oversee more than a million townships and villages scattered throughout China.

Yet, even though they have the same institutional structure as the national government in Beijing, the interests of sub-national Chinese governments often conflict with the national government's interests. And despite China's authoritarian system, local officials are often able to at least partially ignore central-government dictates and implement their own preferred policies. For example, the central government has loudly and publicly proclaimed its commitment to reducing copyright piracy in China, due to complaints largely emanating from software and media companies in the United States. However, insofar as county or municipal governments are able to tax or otherwise benefit financially from this activity (or maintain social stability by putting otherwise unemployable people to work in such illegal activities), the central government is likely to look away from these illegal operations.

A more important reason for this autonomy lies with the fact that local governments politically control the government agencies that are physically located within their jurisdictions. With few exceptions (such as the General Administration for Customs), the national ministries do not exercise direct political control down to the local level. Sub-national politicians control the allocation of budgets, personnel, and operating equipment (cars, computers, office space, etc.). Thus for example, if there is a policy disagreement between the Ministry of Agriculture and a provincial government, the provincial agricultural bureau will tend to comply with the provincial government leaders, and not with the national Ministry of Agriculture, because the provincial agricultural bureau has only non-binding relations with its national-level ministerial counterpart. This trend extends down as far as the county level.

Such sub-national political autonomy seems puzzling in a single-party authoritarian regime. How does the central government in Beijing ensure that localities at least partially comply with national policy? The key is the relationship between the government and the CCP; the Communist Party monopolizes control over

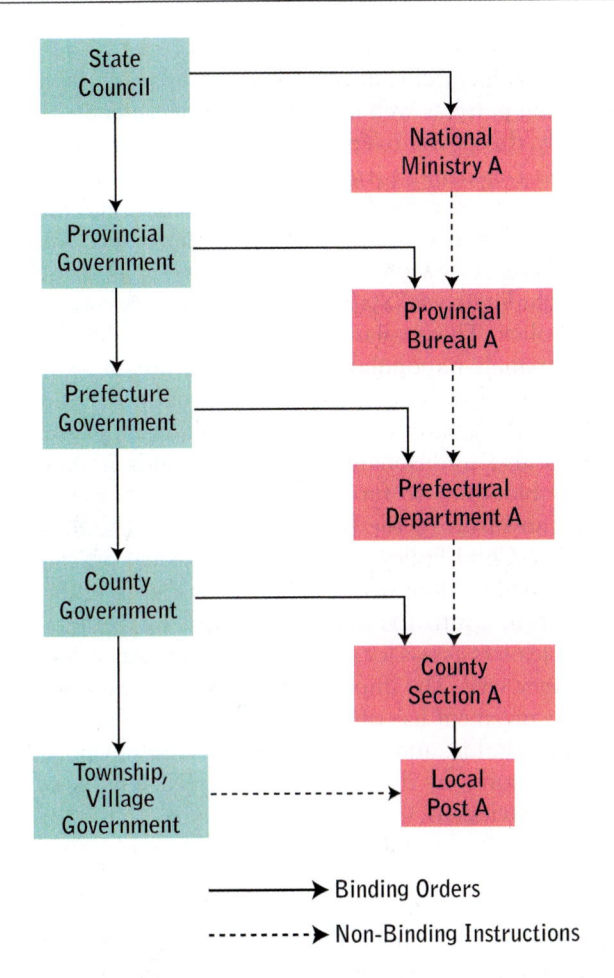

FIGURE 10.3
Decentralized Authority Relations

Each bureaucratic unit in China has non-binding, consultative relations with a number of other units, but it only has binding, leadership relations with one superior unit. For the vast majority of government bureaucracies in China, their superior unit is the government at the same administrative level as the unit in question. For example, local functional bureaucracies, such as the provincial bureaus of agriculture, are under the direct control of the provincial government, and not the national Ministry of Agriculture. It is for this reason that policy implementation in China often reflects local rather than national priorities.

appointment of the most senior personnel in any government organization—at both the national *and* sub-national level. That is, the CCP appoints the top people in *every* government agency, from national-level cabinet ministers and vice ministers to provincial governors and vice-governors all the way down to manager and vice manager of government-owned factories in a small town in the interior.

All such appointees must be party members and in order to advance one's career within China's political hierarchy, government officials literally must join and seek to move up within the party as well as within the government.

As noted already, this power over appointments and promotions gives the CCP and its Organization Department (*zuzhi bu*) immense political power.[21] With this power, the CCP connects its own definition of "the national interest" to Chinese politicians' professional goals—to move up the career ladder. And career advancement is based on careful review of local party leaders' implementation of CCP priorities (typically including social stability, economic development, and adherence to the One-Child Policy). This explains why we often see local officials enforcing policies that are extremely unpopular.[22] The most dramatic example of this is the One-Child Policy. Chinese citizens, particularly those in the countryside, retain a traditional belief that the greater the number of children, the greater their security in old age. Families also traditionally favor male children, who are expected to carry on the family bloodline to future generations—a couple's inability to have a son is viewed as an insult to the family's ancestors. The national government implemented the One-Child Policy, but left it up to local officials to enforce. It is not difficult to imagine how intensely local officials dislike enforcing this policy—but because population control is among the most important criteria by which national-level party leaders assess local officials' performance, local officials tend to enforce the policy very well. The importance of carrying out the One-Child Policy to cadres' career advancement has often led to forced sterilization, exorbitant fines levied on errant households, and a generation of children born "in secret" who are treated as "nonpersons" by the state and who receive none of the benefits and rights of other Chinese citizens.

The Military

It is often remarked that the Chinese revolution was a peasant revolution. It was also a military one. From the very beginning, when Mao Zedong was fashioning a form of rural communism in the mountains of Jiangxi Province, the military was an integral part of Chinese communism. Many of China's first generation leaders who did not have military portfolios after 1949 had spent much of their time on the battlefield as political commissars (officers in charge of maintaining the ideological orientation of the troops).

The two goals of the PLA are to defend China from outside invasion and to protect the Chinese Communist Party—not the government—from attack. Thus, the military has always been subordinate to the CCP. This node of authority is readily identifiable in the chairmanship of the **Military Affairs Committee (MAC)**. Only Mao Zedong, Hua Guofeng, Deng Xiaoping, Jiang Zemin, and Hu Jintao have chaired this committee, and all of them, with the exception of Deng were also the head of the CCP, either as chairman (Mao and Hua) or general secretary (Jiang and Hu). So, even if there is no military general on the Politburo Standing Committee, the army's interests are represented at the very least by the most powerful member on that body. We will discuss the military again below.

Military Affairs Committee (MAC) ■ the group through which the party controls the military. The chairman of the MAC is (with the one exception of Deng Xiaoping in the 1980s) the CCP general secretary.

The gradual, liberalizing tendencies described above and below represent the Chinese state's recognition that it can no longer micromanage every aspect of social, economic, and even political behavior in China. But it also suggests a degree of maturity among China's leaders: they are beginning to accept the reality that they cannot—but also take comfort in the fact that they *need* not—undertake such micromanagement in order to maintain their authority and pursue the twin goals of wealth and power. How do these new developments impact the CCP's ability to control politics? To answer this question, we must turn to a discussion of identities and interests in contemporary China.

SUMMARY TABLE

China's State Institutions

The Chinese Communist Party	Founded in 1921, and currently numbering 80 million, the CCP formulates the general policy line of the country. The CCP holds a Party Congress every five years to renew or replace leadership positions and introduce the latest CCP platform. CCP members always hold top government positions, which results in CCP domination of the entire Chinese state.
The Government	China's government is in charge of substantive policymaking and implementing government—and CCP—policy. Led by the premier, who manages the State Council, the government is made up of dozens of commissions, ministries, bureaus, and other offices that handle the myriad aspects of governance. The government apparatus is replicated geographically (though the apparatus is increasingly streamlined at lower points in the system) at the various local administrative levels in China.
The National People's Congress	While the National People's Congress has long served merely as a legislative rubber stamp for CCP initiatives, it has become increasingly significant as a forum for debating the complex and ever-expanding processes of lawmaking in China.
Local Governments	The functional bureaus that are the local counterparts of national ministries are often under the direct control of local officials. While local officials are monitored by the CCP apparatus, they are able to exercise a considerable degree of autonomy in economic and even political behavior that diverges from the spirit and sometimes even the letter of national policy. Such decentralization is necessary because national level authorities recognize that the central government in Beijing cannot manage a country as vast as China.
The People's Liberation Army	Charged with protecting the country from invasion and protecting the CCP from insurrection, the PLA reports to the party and not to the government.

IDENTITIES IN CHINA

From Totalitarian to Authoritarian Identities

10.3 How have Chinese identities changed in the past 60 years?

Watch the Video "China's Tibet Policy" at mypoliscilab.com

Explore the Comparative "Civil Rights" at mypoliscilab.com

China is not a democracy. But what sort of non-democratic regime is it? One might think that because the Communist Party has held power for 60 years, China must necessarily be a totalitarian regime rather than merely an authoritarian regime. However, while it is understandable how such a point of view might arise, such a view is fundamentally wrong.

More often than not, our view of China is colored by what we see on the television or read in newspapers and magazines. We tend to be bombarded with stories and descriptions that are "newsworthy"—the military crackdown on pro-democracy protesters in 1989, recent demonstrations by and the incarceration of Tibetan (2008) and Uyghur (2009) protesters, and the show trials and arbitrary prison sentences handed out to dissidents. These events certainly describe important aspects of contemporary China, but such a description is incomplete and focuses on aspects of Chinese politics that are peripheral to the lives of most Chinese citizens.

During the Mao era, from the mid-1950s onwards, some aspects of China's political system could be described as totalitarian.[23] First, in this era there was little, if any, societal or political pluralism outside of state control and monitoring. Since the Communist Revolution, opposition parties have been banned (except as window dressing), and in the early decades the government brutally repressed real and imagined opposition movements. Party leadership would target the suspected demographic group or class by mobilizing a majority of citizens who were often motivated by fear of being—and relief at not having been—similarly identified as an enemy of the state. But most state control was far more benign: society was organized into "work units" (*danwei*) which were an extension of the workplace (factory, ministry, etc.) and which provided the "iron rice bowl": "womb to tomb" welfare benefits ranging from schooling, medical care, housing, and food. The work unit's permission was required for travel, marriage, and even family planning. Thus, although one can argue that Chinese citizens' lives were more strictly controlled than those of their counterparts in the Soviet Union, China never had a secret police force like Russia's KGB. It didn't need one: the state could do much of its monitoring of its citizenry through the microscope of the work unit.

In contrast, in China today there are genuine—albeit limited—opportunities for individuals and groups outside the formal state apparatus to help shape policy. The state has receded from the day-to-day lives of ordinary citizens, just as the work unit itself has largely withered away. In ordinary conversations, in print, and even in blogs, discussion of formerly taboo subjects has increased, in no small part because the state lacks the ability to monitor all such discussions.

Although citizens clearly do protest government decisions publicly, the rules and regulations governing freedom of assembly have changed little over time, and enforcement of these laws has remained strict. That is, although Chinese authorities are now somewhat more lenient towards "spontaneous" protesters, the state permits no *organized* political protest. The government remains vigilant against any type of

danwei ■ the *danwei*, or "work unit" was traditionally the lowest form of government in China, as well as a way to organize the populace. *Danwei* were made up of the workers and their leaders in a given factory, school, etc. It was the *danwei* that issued the *hukou* and "iron rice bowl" benefits. In terms of organizing society in China today, the role of *danwei* have declined dramatically.

organized event that the authorities do not control. This limit on political pluralism is characteristic of authoritarian regimes.

Second, under Mao the government frequently coercively mobilized citizens to support its policy goals. For example, government campaigns sought to mobilize ordinary citizens in political witch-hunts to attack "counter-revolutionary" groups such as intellectuals, landlords, and former capitalists, many of whom were stripped of their jobs and property and sent to "reeducation camps" in the wilderness, or killed outright. Fearing the repressive power of the state, citizens rarely sought to oppose such programs. During the Cultural Revolution, Chairman Mao even closed schools and mobilized high school and college students to purge supposedly counter-revolutionary elements within the government and the CCP. Students donned Red Guard armbands and military uniforms and were put under extraordinary emotional pressure to bear witness against or even kill disgraced officials, intellectuals, and eventually members of other, rival Red Guard groups—even if they had been friends before the onset of the Cultural Revolution—under the hideous logic that "if we kill one today, there will be fewer of them that might kill us tomorrow."

In other cases—during Mao's era—as in the tree-planting and literacy campaigns—the goals were more benign. However, citizens did not have the choice over whether to participate in these campaigns; they risked severe punishments if they chose not to take part. Individuals even felt compelled to compete with their friends and neighbors. For example, students were forced to compete with each other to exceed their government-mandated quotas in the "Exterminate the Four Pests" campaign in the late 1950s—which sought to kill off mosquitoes, rats, flies, and sparrows (which were thought to eat valuable grain seeds), or else they and their families would fall under a dark political cloud. Under such conditions, even benign campaigns assumed an uncomfortable degree of coercion.

Such government campaigns are largely a thing of the past. They do occur from time to time, but they are no longer coercive in terms of punishments meted out for non-compliance. Recent campaigns include promotion of cleanliness in China's major cities (to discourage jaywalking, littering, and the national pastime of spitting) and public awareness campaigns about preventing the spread of SARS and HIV. Prior to the 2008 Olympics, mass mobilization was utilized to clear up the algae around Qingdao in preparation for boating events. And while at times it is true that the government does mobilize nationalistic protests, such protests arguably tap into genuine reservoirs of nationalistic sentiment, which are not under state control. Such contemporary mobilization is certainly not coercive in the way campaigns were undertaken in Mao's time.

Indeed, the most recent large-scale citizen mobilization had no coercive dimension at all: efforts to assist the victims of the massive Wenchuan earthquake of 2008. Much like in the United States immediately after 9/11, when volunteers descended on New York City to provide support and assistance, citizens from all over China abandoned their family and work responsibilities to travel (sometimes a great distance) to Sichuan Province to help dig people out from rubble, aid those survivors they found, and console those who had lost family and loved ones in the earthquake. In fact, in this case the speed, depth, and effectiveness of spontaneous popular mobilization outpaced the government's rescue efforts.

Finally, under Mao, the government engaged in extensive efforts at ideological indoctrination. The government's efforts were so extreme that citizens could be imprisoned and even executed for "improper thought."[24] Indoctrination began early in school and was frequently reinforced. Even if people saw the lie behind these ideological exhortations, they realized that they had to appear to believe them. Given these efforts at indoctrination, up through the 1980s, intellectuals adhered to two different vocabularies—one "official" the other "non-official"—depending on the context in which they found themselves. At work, they would automatically shift into the opaque, stilted "official" vocabulary that was rife with double meanings and sophisticated wordplays. Yet at home or with friends, they would relax and shift into speaking about what was really on their minds.[25]

Today, the government has abandoned most—but by no means all—efforts at ideological indoctrination (ideology does remain an important part of party members' lives). Chinese people speak more freely in professional, social, and even political contexts in which they find themselves, although they remain far from being able to engage in full free expression without threat of retribution. Even during Chinese Communist Party meetings, members are as likely to discuss business management techniques or mundane public policy issues as they are likely to discuss ideological matters (or even text each other dirty jokes).

In sum, contemporary China is an authoritarian regime, not a totalitarian one. The CCP is the most important political institutions in the country. It sets the ideological "tone" of the state, guides government policy, and controls the military. However, given the vast network of Communist Party members—80 million people—China is not an oligarchy. It is, instead, a single-party authoritarian regime.

But the costs of maintaining power with only sticks and not with carrots is prohibitive. There needs to be some sort of "ideology" to encourage people to act in ways beyond their immediate self-interest.[26] In the past, Marxism-Leninism-Mao Zedong Thought fit this bill. But things have changed since the death of Mao. Perhaps the most significant of these has been the frantic search on the part of China's leaders to replace discredited and anachronistic Marxist ideology with another way to maintain the normative legitimacy of the state. After its victory in the 1949 Revolution and well into Mao's tenure, the CCP could claim legitimacy and rationalize its hold on power by claiming to have ended class-based economic exploitation and to have started China down the road to a socialist utopia. The party enjoyed considerable support in this regard, and was able to mobilize the population into meeting a vast array of policy goals. Yet by the early 1970s, popular support was wearing thin. People were coming to realize that they had worked, struggled, and sacrificed for very little gain—the only ones who had truly gained were the political elites within the party. China in the 1970s enjoyed domestic peace that had not characterized the decades prior to 1949, but the Revolution seemed to have replaced one form of inequality with another—and China remained impoverished.

In sum, after Mao's death in 1976, the leaders of the party realized that they could no longer mobilize the great masses of Chinese citizens with ideological exhortations alone. Communist ideology was gradually tossed aside in favor of efforts to achieve economic wealth through market capitalism and national power on the world stage. By reshaping the way in which it sought popular legitimacy—focusing on making China rich and powerful—and by succeeding on both of those dimensions—the CCP has maintained itself in power. The party still calls itself the Chinese *Communist* Party, but it has all but jettisoned its traditional ideological core. This raises the question of precisely how the CCP mobilizes identity in support of its regime. In the material that follows we focus on how the CCP constructs nationalistic sentiment among the Chinese population, and on how it manages ethnic and religious minorities to maintain political stability.

Nationalism as a Unifying Force

As China's leaders look to economic performance—the means to wealth and power—as their yardstick for legitimacy among Chinese citizens, the CCP confronted a dilemma. Its leaders realized that they needed to discard the ideology and policies of communism if they wanted to remain in office and achieve their goals of national wealth and power. However, they also understood that were they to simply announce, "We are no longer communists," and say nothing more, many citizens would not merely be flabbergasted at the ideological about-face, but would also search for a replacement for the ideology that had motivated their political beliefs and actions for decades. That is, China's leaders recognized that in abandoning communism, they would create an ideological vacuum—and that citizens' search for alternatives might include forms of political identity of which the regime would not approve, such as religion, a demand for democracy, or widespread anti-regime cynicism or even anger. The most dramatic example of this was the protests in the spring of 1989 all over China, which led to the military crackdown of June 4, 1989, in Beijing and Chengdu, in which hundreds, possibly even thousands, of people were killed.

To fill this ideological void, the party has turned to nationalism. It has connected its self-serving self-portrait as China's national savior to the construction of a stronger sense of Chinese national identity. The CCP's emphasis on strengthening nationalism is not without merit. After all, just over 60 years ago, China had been in a state of domestic decay and then civil war for nearly a century. The party did, in fact, unify and bring peace to the country, and it has staunchly defended China's national sovereignty since 1949. Cultivating such a national identity is an important tool for the state to construct and maintain national unity, particularly given citizens' inability to hold government to account for its actions and performance. That is, because China is an authoritarian system, it lacks the "safety valve" of free and fair elections. Without elections, China's leaders have powerful incentives to put the blame for poor policy performance on foreigners to deflect potential blame that may fall in their laps.

From a very early age, Chinese students, like students everywhere, are inculcated with national narratives that explain their, and China's, place in the world. These narratives draw on China's rich history, but pay special attention to China's experience at the hands of foreign imperialists. It is not surprising, therefore, that many Chinese sometimes view globalization and China's international interactions with ambivalence, suspicion, and some degree of defensiveness. It is certainly in Beijing's interests to underscore how bad things were before 1949, and to focus on the establishment of the PRC in order to enhance its own legitimacy in the face of an increasingly non-ideological and materialistic society.

These nationalist narratives have been a part of China's popular culture for decades, including film, books, and even ballet and opera. Recent expressions have taken on a different form, that of China finally (re)taking its rightful place in the world as a global power. Filmmaker Zhang Yimou, long vilified by many nationalist-leaning Chinese for making art-house films critical of China but lapped up by foreign audiences, choreographed perhaps the most dramatic example of this new nationalism in the opening ceremonies of the 2008 Beijing Olympics (while another famous Chinese artist, Ai Weiwei, who helped design the famous "Bird's Nest" stadium, was temporarily detained by authorities in April 2011). Possibly the most spectacular opening ceremonies yet, they reflected and instilled a tremendous degree of national pride among vast segments of its Chinese audience (tellingly, the foreign reaction was one of wonderment mixed with a healthy dose of trepidation).

Thus, encouraging national pride has the short-term effect of aligning citizens' interests (living in a country that is rich and powerful) with the party's interests (running a country that is rich and powerful). However, cultivating nationalism can also be a double-edged sword—because protests against perceived slights to China's national honor can get out of control.[27] For example, in 2005, when citizens called for a boycott of Japanese goods because of Japan's unwillingness to admit responsibility for its wartime record in China, the government disavowed the protests because it feared damaging its important economic relationship with Japan.[28] Likewise, in 2008, when citizens demanded a boycott of the French supermarket chain Carrefour because pro-Tibet protests occurred when the Olympic torch passed through France, the government made it difficult for protesters to organize too effectively, for similar reasons.[29]

To promote its interests, the government can mobilize its citizens. Yet to prevent nationalistic protest from getting out of line and threatening the regime's political supremacy, the government also puts its coercive apparatus on alert, and even mobilizes instruments of repression against its own citizens if protests and demonstrations do not wind down according to the state's timetable. In May 1999, for example, U.S. warplanes bombed the Chinese embassy in Belgrade, Serbia, during the Balkan War. Although the United States immediately apologized for what it said was an accident that occurred due to outdated maps, Chinese demonstrators attacked the U.S. embassy in Beijing, as well as consulates throughout the country—the U.S. consul's house in the city of Chengdu was burned to the ground. Foreigners were intimidated by roving gangs of visibly angry citizens, and it was impossible to even suggest the idea that the bombing was a mistake, much less discuss the situation objectively with Chinese citizens.

Yet a month later, such nationalistic fervor had all but disappeared: Chengdu residents wondered why tourism was down, and merchants selling anti-American t-shirts in Beijing were ordered to stop or risk punishment. In the wake of these protests, many Chinese felt that although their nationalism was genuine, the government had cynically manipulated their anger. This underscores the high risks involved in attempting to construct a form of political identity like nationalism to substitute for the discredited and discarded socialist ideology—nationalism moves average people to take political action—but average people may not understand (or may understand but object to) the government's interests and tactics used to achieve those interests.[30] In sum, abandoning communist ideology and replacing communism with nationalism has benefits and potential costs. The benefit includes identifying the regime with China's ability to stand up to foreigners, something that pre-1949 governments could not credibly say. The potential costs, however, include accusations of "selling out" Chinese interests when the government backs away from anti-foreign protest.

Ethnicity and Religion as Potentially Divisive Forces

China's rulers also confront the issue of ethnic and religious diversity in their quest to consolidate power and build up China's strength. At first glance, China might appear to resemble its ethnically homogenous neighbors such as Japan and Korea. Indeed, 92 percent of China's population belongs to the dominant Han ethnic group. However, the other 8 percent of the population include some 55 minority groups, whose levels of assimilation and ability and/or willingness to coexist with the Han vary greatly. And in the Chinese context, it is important to remember that 8 percent of the population is about 100 million people—more than the population of all but a few countries in the world! Most of these minority groups are concentrated in China's border regions, which amplifies the challenges and potential threats that the CCP confronts to maintaining China's political integrity. In this section, we focus on how the central government manages two such minority groups, the Tibetans and the Uyghur.

Tibetans Tibetans[31] are different from Han Chinese in terms of language, cultural background, the type of Buddhism they practice, and even the clothes they wear and the food they eat. For centuries, the Kingdom of Tibet was allied with but formally independent of the Chinese Empire. In 1950, Tibet became a part of the People's Republic of China, officially designated as an "autonomous region." However, this autonomy was largely in name only and had more to do with the fact that the population was not ethnically Han than with real political autonomy. Tibetans attempted to resist the CCP's annexation, but negotiations between Chairman Mao and Tibet's political and religious leader, the 14th and current Dalai Lama Tenzin Gyatso, only led to an uneasy truce. This truce broke down in 1959 as Tibetans took to the streets against Chinese domination. The PLA then invaded Lhasa, Tibet's capital, and the Dalai Lama fled to northern India, where he continues to live today as the head of Tibet's government-in-exile. Tibetans suffered a great deal over the next two decades, particularly during the Cultural Revolution, when many Buddhist monks were defrocked and imprisoned and their monasteries destroyed.

At the beginning of the reform era (1978–present), the general secretary of the Chinese Communist Party, Hu Yaobang, sought to ease Beijing's draconian policies towards Tibet. However, after Tibetans protested again against Chinese rule in March 1989, the central government imposed martial law and reasserted its political control over the region. The government initially handled protests marking the

19th anniversary of the imposition of martial law in March 2008 with moderation. However, the protests quickly expanded in size and scope, and the central government once again cracked down harshly, imprisoning dozens or even hundreds of monks, and reinstituting harsh repressive policies.[32]

China's central government maintains that by bringing economic development and modernization to the region, it is liberating the Tibetan people from a backward social structure and a religion that practiced slavery and tolerated terrible income inequalities. Many Tibetans respond that infrastructure projects Beijing touts as evidence of modernization are in truth designed to consolidate China's military control over Tibet. They also claim that economic development programs are targeted at the Han Chinese residing in Tibet, while the native population has been largely left behind. The population of Tibet is just under 3 million—minuscule when compared to China's overall population—and estimates of the Han population vary wildly: the Chinese government claims it is only 3 percent of the total, while Tibetan groups claim it is more than half of the province's population.[33]

The Dalai Lama remains the most visible face and the most authoritative voice regarding Tibetan interests. While not advocating independence, he does seek

> **THE REACH OF THE CHINESE STATE**
> Beijing does not bother with subtleties when it comes to demonstrating its political reach. It is not accidental that the Tibetan script (top row) of this sign is in an even smaller font than the English translation of the dominating Chinese characters, underscoring that this temple complex may be culturally Tibetan, but it is located within *Chinese* territory and is, therefore, Chinese.

greater autonomy for Tibet. However, he does not limit this to Tibet's current borders, but rather to "traditional Tibet," which comprises parts of Xinjiang, Qinghai, Sichuan, and Yunnan provinces, fully one-third of China. China's current president Hu Jintao, once Tibet's CCP secretary, has so far seemed unwilling to use his former hard-line credentials (it was under Hu's tenure that martial law was imposed in 1989) to resolve the problem. The fear among many is that once the Dalai Lama passes from the scene, more hard-line advocates for Tibetan independence will take over and the chances for resolution of the conflict will become even more elusive than they are now.

China will never voluntarily cede its control over Tibet, for geopolitical reasons. Tibet is located at the origins of four of Asia's major rivers (the Salween, Mekong, Yangtze, and Yellow rivers), the basins of which provide water for one-quarter to one-third of the world's population. Tibet is also the source of rare minerals necessary for China's nuclear energy and weapons programs. Finally, Tibet forms a formidable natural boundary with China's western neighbors, some of which (e.g., India) Beijing views with suspicion. It is difficult to imagine any country willing to part with such an effective strategic buffer zone.

The Uyghur Much of the same geopolitical concerns shape government policy toward the Uyghur[34] minority in the **Xinjiang Uyghur Autonomous Region (UAR)** in northwestern China. Because their ancestors migrated to the region long ago from an area near Turkey, the Uyghur look more like Middle Easterners or Europeans than Han Chinese. They are also Muslim, and as such they look to a spiritual center—Mecca, in Saudi Arabia—that exists physically outside China, and to some extent identify with the Islamic community around the world, something that can dampen their nationalistic identification with China.

The ethnic and religious dimensions of identity influence China's ability to assimilate the Uyghur, and also influences how the Uyghur are portrayed in the international media. As in Tibet, many Han Chinese have migrated to the Xinjiang UAR: as of 1998, 47 percent of Xinjiang was Uyghur, while 41 percent was Han; 75 percent of the population of the region's capital city Urumqi is Han. And as in Tibet, the lion's share of economic opportunities has been awarded to the Han, at the expense of the Uyghur. More concretely, there are dwindling opportunities to use the Uyghur language, effectively equating Han assimilation with economic and political success and threatening Uyghur culture with extinction within the next few generations.

In July 2009, tensions erupted as the Uyghur took to the streets and riots broke out in Urumqi and the city of Kashgar. Although it is unclear who instigated the violence, almost 200 people ultimately died and destruction of property was widespread. Chinese President Hu Jintao even cut short an important foreign trip to return to China to deal with the political crisis in Xinjiang. The region was put under curfew and news (and Internet) blackout. More than 1,000 people were arrested or detained in connection with the riots, and more than two dozen people received death sentences for instigating the unrest.[35]

The government's response suggests that in the case of Xinjiang, it is willing and able to meet challenges to its authority with force. For other non-Han groups,

Xinjiang Uyghur Autonomous Region (UAR) ■ established in 1955, a provincial-level unit with a large percentage of the Uyghur minority group. Geographically, the Xinjiang AR is the largest single administrative region in all of China.

> **SUMMARY TABLE**
>
> **Identities in China**
>
> | | |
> |---|---|
> | **Totalitarian to Authoritarian Governance** | In a totalitarian system, identities are indistinguishable from the state. In authoritarian regimes, the identities of its citizens are a constant challenge for the regime, endlessly negotiated and renegotiated. There is more freedom, but there is also an increased sense of uncertainty as to what the parameters of this freedom—at any given place or time—might actually be. |
> | **Nationalism** | As Maoism became discredited after the excesses of the Cultural Revolution and as economic incentives replaced moral and normative ones, China's leaders sought something that would satisfy the non-material concerns of its citizens. Increasingly, nationalism has been used to fill this void. But nationalism can mobilize Chinese citizens in ways that authorities may not be able to control. And nationalism is not easily reconciled with ethnic pluralism. |
> | **Ethnicity** | Although only 8 percent of China's population are not of the Han majority, a number of China's 55 minority groups reside along border areas and other locales that make governance from Beijing difficult. Moreover, these places often border unstable areas in central Asia. Beijing has sought to place these areas under control, but in doing so, has further alienated many of these groups, particularly the Tibetans and the Uyghur. |

the government has yet to take such draconian steps. Groups such as the Mongols (5 million) and Manchus (9 million) have more easily assimilated into Han Chinese culture. The Hui (who, along with the Tibetans, Uyghur, Mongols, and Zhuang, have their own autonomous region in lieu of a standard "province") are also Muslim, but they are otherwise indistinguishable from the Han. Other provinces, such as Yunnan and Guizhou, have dozens of minority groups that generally seek accommodation with the Han majority. Thus, although some tensions exist, most groups have been able and largely willing to work within existing institutions.[36]

INTERESTS IN CHINA

10.4 Who wants what in China, and how do they get the state to provide it for them?

For much of the Mao era, individual interests were subsumed under the goals of the state, while unofficial interest groups were non-existent. This is no longer the case. In the past few years, barriers of entry into the political process have been reduced for certain non-traditional groups—media groups, non-governmental organizations, and domestic and foreign policy experts—resulting in an increase in the pluralization of the policy process. This is a very fragile development. It is not always (or even often) successful and these non-traditional groups must not be seen by the state as threatening. But these groups have been able to shape policy, ironically, by carefully allying themselves with bureaucrats who share their policy goals. This is a form of political pluralization as distinct from democratization because of the continuing lack of leaders' accountability to their constituents.[37]

Indeed, although certain mechanisms of state repression remain relatively unchanged, the state as a whole is moving in a more politically liberalized direction, albeit very slowly. There are, for example, a growing number of arenas—through the media, petitioning authorities (*xinfang*),[38] and by taking to the streets—in which citizens can, and do, engage in contestation. In 2005, there were 87,000 protests in China, as reported by the State Security Bureau (because these are official figures, the actual number is likely to be much higher).[39] In response to the anger that many officials felt over having been ordered to shoot and kill civilians during the 1989 Tiananmen Square crackdown, there are even extensive discussions within the coercive apparatus about using less force and more persuasion.[40]

State Organizations: The Case of the Military

At first glance, it seems strange to imagine that the state has to fight with itself in the policy-making process. However, once we recognize that the state is, in fact, thousands of discrete interests, understanding Chinese politics as a "state of nature" among an ever-growing number of bureaucratic actors begins to make sense. The interest within the state that best illustrates this competition for power and influence in recent years has been the Chinese military.

Traditionally, the PLA has sought to stay out of domestic politics, although it has been forced to intervene at critical moments in the past, such as curbing the anarchy of the Cultural Revolution in 1968–1970 and cracking down on students and citizens in Beijing and other cities in 1989, largely against its will.[41] The PLA's goal is in establishing a world-class modern military. This follows decades of atrophy and neglect: for example, from the early 1980s to the late 1990s, the PLA was responsible for raising much of its budget and was, thus, forced into commercial activity (i.e., running hotels, selling dual-use technologies to allies, dabbling in real estate, etc.) that undermined its ability to function as a modern military. The first Gulf War, with its reliance on "smart" weaponry, demonstrated to Chinese military leaders just how hopelessly backward China was in relation to the seemingly infinitely more advanced United States. In 1998–1999, the military was forced to give up ownership of its hotels, real estate holdings, and commercial activities in exchange for increases in its operating budget. These increases appear quite dramatic because of the unsustainably low baseline budget that had forced the PLA into commercial activity in the first place.[42]

More recently, the PLA has engaged in curious, even seemingly self-destructive, behavior in waters off China's coast, including harassing the *USS Impeccable* in 2009, and in ratcheting up anti-U.S. rhetoric in 2010 and 2011, following other instances of assertive Chinese maritime behavior. Although it is difficult to state with certainty what is actually taking place, it seems fairly clear that this assertiveness is less a symptom of China's international strength than it is one of China's domestic weakness. China's military does not have direct representation on the highest policymaking bodies in China today and, therefore, uses other means to leverage its goals and interests in the policy process. The fact that it has been acting out in such a way signals the weakness of the Hu-Wen leadership in reining in military "adventurism." Seen differently, however, what we are witnessing is simply Chinese bureaucratic interest politics being played out on the international stage.

Local Governments

Traditional center-local relations in China are captured in the saying, "The mountains are high, and the emperor is far away." Today, this dynamic is reflected in the couplet, *shang you zhengce xia you duice* ("above they have their policies, below we have our counter-measures"). In the old days, when China still had a planned economy, Beijing was able to exert leverage over local governments by threatening to deny them important economic benefits, but as the planned economy was phased out during the 1980s and the 1990s, Beijing found itself in a situation where it had to take local government considerations increasingly into account in order to expect its policies to be implemented locally.

But local governments do not simply manipulate orders from on high; more recently, local governments have become increasingly aggressive in influencing the policy *process*. In Beijing, there are an ever-growing number of local government liaison offices in which representatives of local governments can monitor and influence the decision making that occurs in the capital. Moreover, local governments (and their constituents) from the interior are becoming increasingly vocal, particularly those that largely missed out on the economic boom of the 1990s.

The Media

Despite the common perception that the media is tightly controlled in China, China's citizens often have access to a great deal of information, although official censorship continues to limit certain type of information from getting through. Although it is important to avoid overstating the growing parameters of acceptable discourse in China, newspapers, magazines, and television broadcasts have provided a platform for journalists to pursue stories that match their own increasingly progressive interests and agendas. There are 2,000 newspapers and 7,000 periodicals in China and the government simply cannot control all of them. Moreover, during the reform era, media outlets have been increasingly responsible for their own bottom lines and can no longer depend on state budgetary allocations to cover their operating costs. As a result, they must rely on advertisers and, thus, they now carry stories that people are interested in consuming. Very often, this means an increasing focus on controversial subjects, including government injustice, civil protest, and the like.[43] The simultaneous publication of articles on these media websites ensures an even wider audience.

"Maverick" publications (i.e., *Southern Weekend*) as well as traditional CCP mouthpieces (such as the *China Youth Daily*) have also become quite assertive in following and reporting on politically sensitive stories. Magazines such as *Caijing* (*Finance*) are sanctioned by the government because they have been better able to ferret out corruption than the government's own efforts! Although the government continues to constrain search engines like Google and Yahoo, has pressured Apple into eliminating any apps that reference the Dalai Lama,[44] and attempts to censor websites that focus on one of the "three T's"—Taiwan, Tibet, and Tiananmen—there is a vibrant blogosphere in China that is becoming increasingly difficult for the authorities to manage, let alone control.

Industrial and Professional Groups

Industrial and professional groups that seek to influence policy are also often consulted by the government during the law- and policymaking process. These include multiple industry groups in sectors as diverse as steel, consumer electronics, and computer software. Many business associations that lobby the Chinese government can point to some modest successes in influencing policy, or, at the very least, are now able to sit in on the policymaking process,[45] much like K Street in Washington, D.C. That being said, "lobbying" is a very politically charged term in China, and it is never used to describe what is going on, even though that is exactly what it is.

Non-Governmental Organizations

Non-governmental organizations (NGOs) have also proliferated in China. Although the actual numbers are impossible to determine accurately (in part because there are many NGOs that are still waiting to be official approved but which nonetheless operate in anticipation of such approval), a figure of 500,000 distinct NGOs is probably fairly accurate. Given that China is a one-party authoritarian state, this is an astonishingly high number. These associations run the gamut from foreign and domestic business groups in Beijing and Shanghai that seek better intellectual property protection, to rural-based environmental NGOs in the backwoods. One particularly important node of the media's power is the close relationship it shares with many Chinese non-governmental organizations, and one thing that accounts for the successes of NGOs in Chinese politics is that a large percentage of their officers and staff members were trained as journalists or editors, giving them especially close access to the media. Legal institutions also have abounded with lawyers and other legal specialists working together with the Chinese government (and particularly the National People's Congress, China's legislative body) to establish laws and regulations as well as to educate Chinese officials.[46]

Chinese Citizens

There are 1.3 billion (and growing) Chinese citizens. They are as diverse as the human condition allows. Insofar as they can be organized into groups, they are more likely to pursue their interests in today's Chinese political process. There are a number of (not necessarily mutually exclusive, nor exhaustive) groups that get the attention of the leadership, including migrant workers, laid-off state workers, poorer denizens of China's interior, and Chinese youth.

Migrant Workers Under Mao, it was easy to prevent peasants from flooding into the cities. With the easing of local registration systems in the 1980s in order to create an export-oriented labor force and to build bridges and roads all over the country, there has been an influx of internal migrant workers that currently hovers around 150 million strong. Although they have no rights, they have begun to push back against many of the injustices they face. This, combined with the resentment and suspicion that urbanites have towards these migrants, make them a political tinderbox.

Laid-Off State Workers Likewise, many workers from Mao-era state-owned enterprises, who were promised lifetime security but were forced into early retirement or retained to do menial jobs for a fraction of their original salary, are deeply resentful of the government for this about-face. In anticipation of this, the Chinese government has been very strategic in terms of how it sequences the closing down of these factories, in order to minimize the possibility of protest by this disenfranchised group.[47]

Denizens of the Interior There continues to be a tremendous income gap as well as divergent levels of and opportunities for achieving wealth between citizens located along the rich coastal provinces, such as Jiangsu, Zhejiang, Shanghai, Fujian, and Guangdong, and those located in the interior. Some of these divergences in income levels have been somewhat softened by the Hu Jintao administration in response to the exuberant search for wealth at the expense of equitable distribution under Jiang Zemin. Specifically, the "Develop the West" (*xibu da kaifa*) campaign is an all-out attempt to ease these inequalities by investing in infrastructure in the underdeveloped areas in western China. Nevertheless, inequalities in income and opportunities between provincial capitals in the interior and the towns and countryside over which they administer have actually risen in the past decade. Thus, the "contradiction" between coastal and interior development, identified by Mao Zedong himself, continues to challenge the Chinese leadership.

China's Youth China's younger generation knows no other environment than reform and it has no way to appreciate how much an improvement life in China is today from 30 or even 20 years ago. Given the relative youth of China's population combined with the dramatic pace of change within their lifetimes, these interests are likely to be far more demanding on China's top leaders in the short to medium term.[48]

As the table on the following page summarizes, it is no longer possible for Beijing to mandate that policy be implemented without question. Nor is it the case that any variation of the policy as formulated in Beijing is due solely to *state* agencies, which alter the policy to meet their own interests. Increasingly in contemporary China, state policy is also shaped by non-state actors, something that was impossible only a decade or so ago.

It is in this context in which we should assess and evaluate the behavior of the Chinese state. On the matter of interest articulation, although it is difficult to make sweeping generalizations about political liberalization, it is equally difficult to argue that the state remains unresponsive to societal interests. China remains authoritarian, and although it is liberalizing, it is doing so at its own measured pace.

But it is not doing so uniformly. In the last few years of the past decade, particularly from 2007 up to the present day, China has slowed down or even halted some of the liberalizing trends described previously. Part of this was foreseeable because of the lead up to the Beijing Olympics of 2008. China wanted the games to go without a hitch in order to ensure there were no flies in the ointment of China's international "coming out party," signified by its long-sought-after goal of hosting the Olympics (it had previously lost its bid to host the 2000 Olympics when Sidney was chosen in 1993). But part of the slowdown in liberalization had to do with events that occurred in the months just prior to the Olympics, particularly the crackdown on Tibetan protesters in March 2008. These trends were partially mitigated by the Wenchuan earthquake which hit Sichuan Province two months

SUMMARY TABLE

Interests in China

The Military	Increased government spending to develop a world-class army capable of fighting a high-tech adversary and maintaining the status quo with Taiwan.
Local Governments	In addition to traditionally adapting central policies to suit their needs, local leaders are increasingly entering the policy process itself.
The Media	Although media liberalization has suffered a setback from the mid-2000s, many Chinese journalists continue to test the limits of state tolerance not simply through writing and broadcasting but also by engaging directly or indirectly in policy activism.
Industrial and Professional Groups	"Lobbying" remains a politically suspect idea in China, but industrial and professional groups have created a vast network of influence vis-à-vis government–business relations.
Non-Governmental Organizations	Numbering as many as half a million, NGOs have become a widespread, if not quite influential part of Chinese governance. Yet, the government has shown a remarkable willingness to delegate certain responsibilities to these organizations as long as they are not deemed a threat to the system.
Citizens	There are any number of cleavages that run across the Chinese body politic: generational, economic, geographic. Each of these categories exhibits a loose but nonetheless discernable set of interests that continue to challenge the authorities.

later, in which the domestic and international news media (National Public Radio just happened to be in broadcasting that week from Sichuan) were provided a great deal of access to some dimensions of the story, but denied access to others. As recently as the summer of 2010, government control over the media remains in place, as evidenced by the most recent crop of arrests of journalists, the Google controversy, and the continued blocking of Facebook. At the same time, China's English-language news sources, particularly the *China Daily* and the *Global Times*, have become quite outspoken and over the past several years and have run an increasing number of stories that are often quite critical of Chinese policies.

CONCLUSION

The question posed at the beginning of this chapter was: how has the Chinese government managed to build and consolidate state strength in just 60 years? On the one hand, one can argue that China at the time of the fall of the last imperial dynasty a century ago was a blank sheet of paper upon which anything could be written. On the other hand, such an assessment, as Mao found to his chagrin, ignores the historical context through which Chinese institutions, identities, and interests continue to be refracted.

The revolutionary victors of the Chinese civil war created a vast network of government institutions to administer the continent-sized country they had inherited. Many of these institutions—the Politburo, the State Council, various ministries, to name a few—still stand today. Others have had their names changed over the years, and they have amassed an ever-growing set of responsibilities to meet the challenges of a rapidly changing, globalizing world, but the overall structure remains little changed. By weakening these institutions in the 1960s, Mao may have made them even more durable than they had been before, because his actions actually made Chinese institutions more flexible and adaptable. The experience of China since the beginning of the reform era in 1978 has shown that its institutions can meet the demands and challenges of an increasingly complex world.

Second, during the Mao era, much of the glue that held these institutions together was provided by the heavy ideological climate of political campaigns, mass mobilization, and the promises of socialism. When these ideological exhortations were no longer tenable, they were replaced by appeals to nationalism, which provided crucial legitimacy to the state, but which also threatened the stability of the state by reigniting nationalist impulses among various minority groups that increasingly resented central-government domination.

Study and Review the Post-Test & Chapter Exam at mypoliscilab.com

And, of course, it is the satisfaction of these societal interests that ensures the continued legitimacy of the Chinese state. China's ability to continue managing and building state strength for the next 60 years may well rest on how well it meets the ever-growing universe of interests among its own people and institutions. It is true that political institutions must evolve at a rate that enables them to absorb, manage, and provide for the social demands that emerge from economic development. Otherwise, rather than moving closer to achieving its twin goals of wealth and power, China will risk courting instability, disorder, and crisis.

KEY TERMS

Mao Zedong   366
Chinese Communist Party (CCP)   366
Century of Humiliation (*bainian guochi*)   370
Confucianism   371
baojia system   371
Chinese Republic   372
Sun Yat-sen   372
Nationalist Party (*Guomingdang or Kuomingtang*)   372
May Fourth Movement   373
Rape of Nanjing   373
People's Republic of China   373
Hundred Flowers Movement   375
Anti-Rightist Campaign   375
Great Leap Forward   375
Great Proletarian Cultural Revolution   376
Deng Xiaoping   376
hukou   377
iron rice bowl (*tian fanwan*)   378
Political Bureau of the Chinese Communist Party (Politburo)   380
State Council   380
Politburo Standing Committee   380
leadership small groups   383
xitong   383
Military Affairs Committee (MAC)   386
danwei   388
Xingjiang Uyghur Autonomous Region (UAR)   395

REVIEW QUESTIONS

1. What are some of the important similarities in terms of political processes and outcomes that we find in China and in democratic regimes?
2. What are some of the key differences in these processes and outcomes that we see in China from those in other authoritarian regimes?
3. Would China be stronger or weaker, or would it be more or less effective in realizing its long-term goals, if the national government had better control over local governments; that is, if it was more centralized? Why?
4. How important is China's recent history (the past 150 years) to understanding contemporary Chinese politics?

SUGGESTED READINGS

Lieberthal, Kenneth G. *Governing China: From Revolution Through Reform* (2nd ed.). New York, NY: Norton, 2003. A richly-detailed and informed introduction to the contemporary Chinese state, emphasizing its institutions and policymaking functions.

MacFarquhar, Roderick, ed. *The Politics of China: The Eras of Mao and Deng* (2nd ed.). New York, NY: Cambridge University Press, 1997. Perhaps the best single history of the People's Republic of China with individual chapters written by the preeminent scholars of Chinese politics.

Gries, Peter Hays, and Stanley Rosen, eds. *Chinese Politics: State, Society and the Market*, New York and London: Routledge, 2010. An edited volume that looks at the many different dimensions in evolving relationship between the state and society in China today.

Perry, Elizabeth J., and Mark Selden, eds. *Chinese Society: Change, Conflict and Resistance* (3rd ed.). New York and London: Routledge, 2011. An edited volume, now in its third edition, that expertly analyzes the nodes of tension in contemporary Chinese society.

Pye, Lucian W. *The Spirit of Chinese Politics* (new ed.). Cambridge, MA: Harvard University Press, 1992. A classis study of the Chinese "political mindset" that still remains as thought provoking today as when it was first published almost 50 years ago.

O'Brien, Kevin J., and Lianjiang Li, *Rightful Resistance in Rural China*. New York, NY: Cambridge University Press, 2006. An important book that demonstrates how the powerless in China nonetheless seek to demonstrate injustice by invoking official laws and showing how local leaders deviate from them.

NOTES

1. Tyrene White, *China's Longest Campaign: Birth Planning in the People's Republic, 1949–2005* (Ithaca, NY: Cornell University Press, 2006); and Susan Greenhalgh and Edwin A. Winckler, *Governing China's Population: From Leninist to Neoliberal Biopolitics* (Stanford, CA: Stanford University Press, 2005).
2. The best recent book on decentralization is Pierre F. Landry, *Decentralized Authoritarianism in China: The Communist Party's Control of Local Elites in the Post-Mao Era* (New York, NY: Cambridge University Press, 2008).
3. Lucian W. Pye, *The Spirit of Chinese Politics* (new ed.) (Cambridge, MA; Harvard University Press, 1992), 235.
4. Samuel S. Kim, *China, the United Nations, and World Order* (Princeton, NJ: Princeton University Press, 1979), Chapter 1.
5. See G. William Skinner, *Marketing and Social Structure in Rural China* (Ann Arbor, MI: The Association for Asian Studies, 2001); and Di Wang, *Street Culture in Chengdu: Public Space, Urban Commoners, and Local Politics, 1879–1930* (Stanford, CA: Stanford University Press, 2003).
6. Kenneth G. Lieberthal, *Governing China: From Revolution Through Reform* (2nd Ed.) (New York, NY: Norton, 2003), 6.
7. Hsin-pao Chang, *Commissioner Lin and the Opium War* (New York, NY: Norton, 1964).
8. Mark Elvin, "The High-Level Equilibrium Trap: The Causes of the Decline of Invention in the Traditional Chinese Textile Industries," in W. E. Willmott, *Economic Organization in Chinese Society* (Stanford, Calif., Stanford University Press, 1972), 137–172.
9. Benjamin Schwartz, *In Search of Wealth and Power: Yen Fu and the West* (Cambridge, MA: The Belknap Press of the Harvard University Press, 1964).
10. Ernest P. Young, *The Presidency of Yuan Shih-kai: Liberalism and Dictatorship in Early Republican China* (Ann Arbor, MI: University of Michigan Press, 1977).
11. For a fictional account that perfectly captures the mood and tenor of these events, see Andre Malraux, *Man's Fate (La Condition Humaine)* (New York, NY: Vintage, 1990).
12. Iris Chang, *The Rape of Nanking: The Forgotten Holocaust of World War II* (New York, NY: Penguin, 1997).
13. John Lewis and Xue Litai, *China Builds the Bomb* (Stanford, CA: Stanford University Press, 1988).
14. Kenneth G. Lieberthal, "The Great Leap Forward and the Split in the Yan'an Leadership, 1958–65," in Roderick MacFarquhar, ed., *The Politics of China: The Eras of Mao and Deng*, 2nd Ed. (New York, NY: Cambridge University Press, 1997), 87–147.
15. Jasper Becker, *Hungry Ghosts: Mao's Secret Famine* (New York, NY: Holt, 1998).
16. Roderick MacFarquhar and Michael Schoenlhals, *Mao's Last Revolution* (Cambridge, MA: Belknap Press of Harvard University Press, 2008).
17. See Susan L. Shirk, *The Political Logic of Economic Reform in China* (Berkeley, CA: University of California Press, 1993).
18. Melanie F. Manion, *Retirement of Revolutionaries in China: Public Policies, Social Norms, Private Interests* (Princeton, NJ: Princeton University Press, 1993).
19. Shirk, *The Political Logic of Economic Reform in China*.

20. Shirk, *How China Opened its Door: the Political Success of the PRC's Foreign Trade and Investment Reforms,* (Washington, DC: Brookings Institution Press, 1994, 19).
21. John P. Burns, *The Chinese Communist Party's Nomenklatura System: A Documentary Study of Party Control of Leadership Selection, 1979–1984* (Armonk, NY: M.E. Sharpe, 1989); and Kjeld Erik Brodsgaard and Zheng Yongnian (eds), *The Chinese Communist Party in Reform* (London: Routledge, 2006).
22. Kevin J. O'Brien and Lianjiang Li, "Selective Policy Implementation in Rural China," *Comparative Politics*, Vol. 31, No. 2 (January, 1999), 167–186.
23. Juan Linz and Alfred Stepan, *Problems of Democratic Transition and Consolidation: Southern Europe, South America, and Post-Communist Europe* (Baltimore, MD: Johns Hopkins University Press, 1996).
24. See "Chairman Mao Is a Rotten Egg," in Chen Jo-his, *The Execution of Mayor Yin and Other Stories from the Great Proletarian Cultural Revolution* (Bloomington, IN: Indiana University Press, 1978).
25. Perry Link, *Evening Chats in Beijing: Probing China's Predicament* (New York, NY: Norton, 1993).
26. Douglass North, *Structure and Change in Economic History* (New York, NY: Norton, 1982).
27. Peter Hays Gries, *China's New Nationalism: Pride, Politics, and Diplomacy* (Berkeley, CA: University of California Press, 2004).
28. http://www.chinadaily.com.cn/english/doc/2005-04/23/content_436720.htm.
29. http://www.nytimes.com/2008/05/02/world/asia/02china.html?_r=1.
30. Gries (2004), chapter 7.
31. Barry Sautman, June Teufel Dreyer (ed.), *Contemporary Tibet: Politics, Development, and Society in a Disputed Region* (Armonk, NY: M.E. Sharpe, 2005).
32. http://www.savetibet.org/media-center/ict-news-reports/new-measures-reveal-government-plan-purge-monasteries-and-restrict-buddhist-practice.
33. http://www.asianpacificpost.com/article/all-hans-deck-tibet.
34. S. Frederick Starr, ed., *Xinjiang: China's Muslim Borderland* (Armonk, NY: M.E. Sharpe, 2004).
35. Le, Yu (26 January 2010). "China Sentences Four More to Death for Urumqi Riot." Reuters. http://uk.reuters.com/article/2010/01/26/uk-china-xinjiang-idUKTRE60P3HM20100126, Retrieved December 12, 2011.
36. I am grateful to Ian Smith for this insight.
37. Andrew C. Mertha, *China's Water Warriors: Citizen Action and Policy Change* (Ithaca, NY: Cornell University Press, 2008).
38. Carl F. Minzner, "Xinfang: Alternative to Formal Chinese Legal Institutions," 42 *Stanford Journal of International Law* 103 (2006), 103–179.
39. Minzner (2006), 153.
40. Murray Scot Tanner, "Rethinking Law Enforcement and Society: Changing Police Analyses of Social Unrest," in Neil J. Diamant, Stanley B. Lubman, and Kevin J. O'Brien, eds, *Engaging the Law in China: State, Society, and Possibilities for Justice* (Stanford, CA: Stanford University Press, 2005), 193–212.
41. Ibid.
42. James Mulvenon, *Soldiers of Fortune: The Rise and Fall of the Chinese Military-Business Complex, 1978–98* (Armonk, NY: M.E. Sharpe, 2001).
43. Daniel C. Lynch, *After the Propaganda State: Media, Politics, and "Thought Work" in Reformed China* (Stanford, CA: Stanford University Press, 1999).
44. http://www.theinquirer.net/inquirer/news/1567047/apple-joins-persecution-dali-lama.
45. Scott Kennedy, *The Business of Lobbying in China* (Cambridge, MA: Harvard University Press, 2005).

46. Dorothy J. Solinger, *Contesting Citizenship in Urban China: Peasant Migrants, the State, and the Logic of the Market* (Berkeley, CA: University of California Press, 1997); and Li Zhang, *Strangers in the City: Reconfigurations of Space, Power, and Social Networks within China's Floating Population* (Stanford, CA; Stanford University Press, 2002).

47. William Hurst, *The Chinese Worker after Socialism* (New York, NY: Cambridge University Press, 2009).

48. See Samuel P. Huntington, *Political Order in Changing Societies* (New Haven, CT: Yale University Press, 1968).

CHAPTER 11

Iran

Arzoo Osanloo

rotestors gather around Tehran's Azadi (Freedom) Tower. In June 2009, post-election protests rocked major ties in Iran. Hundreds of thousands of protestors demanded accountability for unexpected results that conferred e presidency to incumbent Mahmoud Ahmadinejad by a 2 to 1 margin. For many, the manifestations were a ferendum on the entire system of the Islamic republic.

> **?** How does a dynamic civil society survive under repressive non-democratic governments in Iran?

INTRODUCTION TO IRAN

On June 12, 2009, Iranians went to the polls to elect the tenth president of their 30-year-old Islamic republic. For weeks before the election, the candidates conducted energetic campaigns, held televised debates, took part in town hall style meetings, and used hard-hitting TV and radio ads and Internet campaigns.

Mir-Hossein Mousavi and Mehdi Karroubi—two reformist candidates who opposed the incumbent president Mahmoud Ahmadinejad—rallied voters with a promise to enact widespread political change. Their campaigns echoed the concerns of Iran's youthful population, two-thirds of which is under the age of 30. Many of Iran's voters expressed dissatisfaction with the government's management of the economy, its confrontational foreign policy, and widespread corruption. A vocal women's movement also called for changes to discriminatory policies.

The hard-fought campaigns generated considerable excitement, and the opposition candidates appeared to gain supporters. The extent to which Iranians participated in the political process surprised observers the world over. Such robust participation is rarely seen in the Middle East or, for that matter, anywhere in the world. The campaigns sparked debate about whether Iran—which international organizations do not classify as a democracy—could change government through elections, and whether such change could also bring about major reforms in government policies.

Just hours after the polls closed, the state-controlled media announced President Ahmadinejad the definitive winner. Almost immediately, the opposition candidates and their supporters denounced the results as fraudulent and insisted on a recount. Hundreds of thousands of people took to the streets in protest, insisting that the government release details on the vote count in disputed regions. Pro-government counter-protestors retaliated, calling the demonstrators *monafeqin* or traitors. After days of protests and demands for action, the government's religious leader—Ayatollah Ali Khamenei—warned activists that they would be arrested and tried for threatening the security of the nation, a crime against God that carries the death penalty. Yet protestors continued to demonstrate for several more months, even in the face of increasing violence, arrests, show trials, torture, and risk of death.

Ahmadinejad's government sidestepped the movement's demands, and he was inaugurated for a second term. Protests against the government continued under heavy censorship and repression. Many Iranians still believe that the government stole the election and point to the mounting use of repressive tactics as evidence that the government's claim of fair elections is untrue.

The 2009 election exposed the tension at the heart of contemporary Iranian politics: the country's *society* and *culture* are diverse, yet its government refuses to concede any ground to demands for greater *political* diversity—for democracy. In this chapter, we attempt to answer the following question: *how does a dynamic civil society survive under repressive non-democratic governments in Iran?* The answer will lead us to consider the nature of Iran's Islamic republic and to examine the tension between its democratic appearance and the non-democratic reality that seems to be unfolding. This chapter will examine the major factors that lead up to what, in some assessments, is a novel form of republic, while in other respects, operates as an authoritarian regime, especially since the June 2009 elections.

HISTORICAL OVERVIEW OF IRAN

For almost 3,000 years, the country we now call Iran was called Persia. In ancient Persia, we see inklings of modern political concepts such as democracy, limited government, and human rights. By the seventh century, Arab invaders brought Islam to much of Persia, but because of the richness of their own civilization, Persians integrated it with their own culture and practices. This is critical because Persians, who are not Arab, acceded to and elaborated the branch of Islam that fit within their own traditions, Shi'ism. Characterized by the historic battles against oppression and injustice, today's Shi'i in Iran also see themselves struggling for a more just society, with different factions battling over ownership of what this legacy means for contemporary society. By the fifteenth century, the Safavid Dynasty used the common religion to consolidate their rule, although later rulers gave religion lesser importance as they attempted to emulate Western forms of modernization. The discovery of oil in 1908 and its exploitation by the West led to a national consciousness that has provided the backdrop for all Iranian politics since. In the first half of the twentieth century, the Pahlavi Dynasty aimed to modernize the country, but used repressive tactics that led to both a religious and nationalist backlash, and eventually the 1979 revolution. In the aftermath of the revolution, Iranians constructed a new form of governance, drawing from a heritage doubly characterized by the pursuit of justice: Islam and democratic governance. Today's struggles are deeply entrenched in these two legacies and, for many Iranians, are complementary.

11.1 How does the memory of ancient Persian civilization inform and influence the struggles for democracy and nationalism in Iran?

Watch the **Video** "The Iran-Iraq War" at **mypoliscilab.com**

Ancient Persia: From the Achaemenids to Sassanids

Iranians trace their history back to the Achaemenid Empire (550–330 BCE). At the height of their power, the Achaemenids ruled over 33 nations, and their dominion encompassed parts of India, Central Asia, Europe, and North Africa—the largest empire in ancient history. The Achaemenid's founder was Cyrus the Great who reigned from 559 to 529 BCE. Although Cyrus the Great established and built a great empire through military conquest, historians since antiquity have also noted that he freed oppressed peoples from tyrannical rulers as well.

Cyrus the Great introduced the idea of freedom of worship among the diverse populations he incorporated into his empire. For example, when the Babylonian emperor Nebuchadnezzar II conquered and destroyed Jerusalem in 597 BCE, he forced the Jewish people into exile in Babylon, in contemporary Iraq. When Cyrus invaded Babylon in 539 BCE, he allowed the Jews freedom of worship and granted them the right to return to Jerusalem.

IRAN

IRAN IN COMPARISON

	United Kingdom	Germany	France	Japan	India	Mexico	Russia	Nigeria	China	Iran
Freedom House Classification	Democracy	Democracy	Democracy	Democracy	Democracy	Partial democracy	Partial democracy	Partial democracy	Non-democracy	Non-democracy
Land Size (sq km)	243,610	357,022	643,801	377,915	3,287,26	1,964,375	17,098,242	923,768	9,596,961	1,648,195
Land Size Ranking	79	62	42	61	7	15	1	32	4	18
Population (July 2011 Estimate)	62,698,362	81,471,834	65,312,249	126,475,664	1,189,172,906	113,724,226	138,739,892	155,215,573	1,336,718,015	77,891,220
Population Ranking	22	16	21	10	2	11	9	8	1	18
Life Expectancy (Years)	80.1	80.1	81.2	82.3	66.8	76.5	66.3	47.6	74.7	70.1
Life Expectancy Ranking	28	27	21	5	51	72	162	220	95	146
Literacy Rate	99%	99%	99%	99%	61%	86.1%	99.4%	68%	91.6%	77%
GDP Per Capita (2010 Estimate)	US$35,100	US$35,900	US$33,300	US$34,000	US$3,500	US$13,800	US$15,900	US$2,500	US$7,600	US$11,200
GDP Ranking	36	32	39	38	163	85	71	178	126	100

Cyrus is also remembered for commissioning Cyrus's Cylinder, a tube-like stone carving inscribed in cuneiform that details his conquest of Babylon and elaborates his values. Some scholars consider Cyrus's Cylinder to be the first "human rights declaration," because it affirms Cyrus's respect for Babylonians' religious and political traditions. The Achaemenid Empire eventually grew to be the largest empire in the ancient world, and this achievement remains a source of nationalistic pride for contemporary Iranians.

The Greco–Persian Wars brought about an end to the expansive Persian Empire. With the demise of the Achaemenids the remaining groups persisted under the rules of various empires, including the Seleucids and the Parthians, and then scattered into various tribes, until the rise of the Sassanid Empire, which was the final pre-Islamic dynasty, lasting from 224 BCE through 641 AD. For Iranians, this period signifies the flourishing of pre-Islamic Persian civilization prior to the Arab conquest of the seventh century.

The frontiers of the Sassanid Empire reached roughly the same territories as those of the Achaemenids, with the capital in Ctesiphon in modern-day Iraq. Strong state centralization, elaborate city planning, and agricultural and technological development characterized Sassanid rule. They cherished literature, music, art, poetry, sciences, and sports, and for these reasons, the Sassanids are an important source of the Iranian national imaginary for instituting "civilizational values" that led to a renaissance of the Persian Empire. Their empire eventually gave way to Arab conquest, but conversion of the Persian population to Islam took place gradually, particularly as Persian-speaking elites attempted to gain positions of prestige under Muslim rule.

The Safavids and the Spread of Islam

After the Sassanids succumbed to Arab conquest, in the seventh century, foreigners ruled Iranian territories for the next 900 years: first Arabs and Turks until the early thirteenth century, and then Mongols—led by Genghis Khan—until about 1500. At that point, a native dynasty again rose to power—the Safavids.

The Safavid Empire is particularly important for two reasons: first, it consolidated Persian identity, as distinct from Arab identity. With the onset of a new religious authority, through invasion, the Persians were unique in re-adapting the Islam of the Arabs to their own existing cultural practices. Conversion of most of the population to Islam took more than a century. In spite of conquest, Persians integrated Islam into Persian culture. While this is too early to be speaking of "nationalism," this strong foundation of "Persianness" informs the nationalism of the modern era. Under the Safavids, Persian arts and culture flourished, including poetry, literature, architecture, and art. In large part, the Safavid legacy defines what it means culturally to be an Iranian today.

Second, the Safavids shaped and centralized Shi'i Islam as a state religion. Islam is divided into two main sects: Shi'i and Sunni. About 10–20 percent of Muslims around the world are Shi'i, and around 40 percent of all Shi'i live in Iran. The Safavid rulers imposed Shi'i Islam, centralized control over religious worship, and gave Shi'i religious authorities a role in governing their empire.

Shi'i ■ the second largest denomination in Islam that follows the succession of the Prophet Mohammad through family members.

Sunni ■ the largest denomination in Islam that asserts the succession of the Prophet Mohammad through consensus among the community of believers.

The state-sponsored and centralized Islam of the Safavids was a precursor to later debates about the state and governance, including the role of the *ulama*, Muslim legal scholars, who were empowered by the centralization of religion by the Safavid state. The inclusion of the *ulama* in governance, moreover, set the stage for the later alliance between religious groups and the *bazaari*, merchant classes. This deliberate mixing of religion and state continues to reverberate throughout Iranian politics and culture to this day.

ulama ■ Muslim legal scholars.

bazaari ■ merchant classes.

Between the eighteenth and nineteenth centuries, different dynasties, Afsharid and Zand, ruled over Iran, with the final house, the Qajar, reigning over much of the nineteenth century. Between 1796 and 1925, the Qajar rulers saw their form of dynastic leadership waning as the colonial powers, especially Great Britain and Russia, sought and gained land and influence in the region. The Qajar rulers ceded much of the northwestern territories to Russia and split the province of Azerbaijan between themselves and their Russian counterparts, dividing the Azeri Turks between Persian and Russian territories.

By the late nineteenth century, already destabilized Qajar rulers suffered a series of internal rebellions by the merchant classes over tobacco and sugar prices, due to Qajar imports from Europe, particularly Great Britain. The *ulama*'s expressed disapproval of the government during prayer meetings also took a heavy public toll on the leaders. The *bazaari* and the *ulama* rallied for a shift in governance that led to a new era. Between 1906 and 1911, a series of popular uprisings resulted in the Persian Constitutional Revolution that changed the form of government in Iran forever. While the Qajar *shah* remained in power, the establishment of a constitutional monarchy gave the people, for the first time, a constitution limiting the exercise of state power and popular representation in the form of the country's first parliament, *Majlis*, which convened in October 1906.

Persian Constitutional Revolution ■ the revolution in Iran that provided the basis for representative government by establishing a parliament and reducing the power of the monarchy—the first of its kind in Asia.

The implications for Iranian politics were profound: although the Qajar shah remained in power, for the first time in its long history, Iran was moving away from absolute monarchy and toward democracy. The political alliance between the *bazaari* and the *ulama* brought new societal groups into politics and energized a vibrant movement for a new form of government. However, as we will see below, this political alliance has also proven highly problematic throughout the course of the twentieth century.

shah ■ title of an Iranian monarch.

Majlis ■ parliament in Iran.

Oil and the Rise of Nationalism in the Twentieth Century

At the start of the twentieth century, three developments shaped the Iranian political landscape: (1) foreign involvement, (2) the discovery of oil, and (3) cooperation between the merchant classes and the religious leadership. Foreign meddling generated a consistent reaction: nationalism and a desire for strong, independent leadership.

In 1908, a London millionaire, William Knox D'Arcy, discovered oil in Iran and formed the Anglo-Persian Oil Company (APOC), a company known today as British Petroleum (BP). Iranian oil entered the world market in 1913 with the construction of a massive oil refinery at Abadan, on the Persian Gulf. Around the same time, APOC negotiated a deal to supply the British Navy with oil. This access proved crucial to Britain's victory in World War I, and the British government realized that access to Iranian oil was of vital long-term importance to its national security. Britain and Russia competed for various interests in Iran and divided the country into **spheres of influence**, with the Russians holding sway over northern Iran and Britain having control over the southern, oil-rich areas. While neither power ever formally colonized Iran, foreign domination challenged the legitimacy of Iran's rulers, and the influence of foreign corporations and governments would provide the primary source of growing nationalism among Iranians during in twentieth century.

In the early 1920s, a military officer named Reza Pahlavi led a coup to depose the last Qajar shah and instituted himself as the first leader of the Pahlavi Dynasty. The first Pahlavi administration was characterized by its iron-handed rule. With the onset of World War II, the Allies needed to secure the flow of oil. When Germany invaded the Soviet Union in June 1940, the British grew fearful that the Germans would have a direct route to the oil through the **Persian corridor**, a railway supply line connecting the southern Soviet Union to Iran. To prevent this, British and Soviet forces invaded and defeated Iranian forces. The British forced Reza Shah into exile in South Africa, and his son, the crown-prince, Mohammad Reza Shah, succeeded him. Reza Shah became an autocratic leader, but at the same time, he is attributed with beginning to develop the country's infrastructure and is credited with having supported Iranian nationalism, women's education, and Iran's entry into the international economy. He also sparred with religious leaders, whose role in governance was greatly reduced. Reza Shah followed the example of Kemal Ataturk (of Turkey) in seeking to instill a secular nationalism in Iran. In addition, he instituted a number of programs that focused on women's entry into public life, through increased education and employment.

Reza Shah also changed the name of the country from Persia to Iran in 1935, signaling that the term "Persian" referred to the people of Fars province, or just one of numerous ethnic groups that make up the country. He noted that the term Iranian is more inclusive, as it includes all the regions and peoples that came from the Caucasus to live in the Iranian plateau.

With the access of the merchant classes to parliament and the improvement of civil institutions, the population was now increasingly aware of the importance of oil resources to the nation. And, they were gaining more knowledge about the deeply inequitable division of profits from those resources. The government gained only 16 percent of the oil company's net profits, and much of that was earmarked to pay foreign debts incurred by the Qajar rulers. The area covered by the British concession, moreover, was so vast that it prevented Iran from seeking additional investors. In addition, the horrible working conditions for Iranian laborers, the lack of sufficient infrastructure for the maintenance of the refinery, and the failure to train Iranians in the skilled components of refinement brought great disdain for the British controlling interests among the Iranian populace.

Deepening resentment over the oil concession agreement sparked discussions on the subject of nationalizing the country's main resource, oil. As a result, in 1951, *Majlis* voted to nationalize Iranian oil, and shortly thereafter elected Mohammad Mossadeq, a European-trained lawyer, statesman, and staunch supporter of na-

---

spheres of influence ■ division of control between Russia and Great Britain over Iranian territory in early twentieth century.

Persian corridor ■ the railway supply line connecting the southern Soviet Union to Iran during World War II.

tionalization, as their prime minister. Nationalization during the Cold War gave the British an easy target to call for an international boycott of Iranian oil. The oil company (now the Anglo-Iranian Oil Company or AIOC) withdrew from Iran, thus closing the world's largest oil refinery, and the Abadan Crisis ensued. In July 1951, Mossadeq ended dealings with AIOC when it threatened to pull its employees out of Iran. When the shah attempted to replace Mossadeq as prime minister, Mossadeq grew even more popular.

The United Kingdom, still weakened by World War II, now sought international support for an invasion of the oil-rich regions of Iran, and requested the help of U.S. President Harry Truman. The American government, mired in the Korean War, opposed invasion, and helped the United Kingdom to seek a diplomatic profit-sharing solution, but both Iran and the United Kingdom rejected the proposal.

In 1953, under President Eisenhower, the United States mounted its first covert coup, Operation Ajax. The goal of the operation was to oust Prime Minister Mossadeq and re-instate the shah. American and British leaders justified their actions by claiming that nationalizing oil would bring the Iranians dangerously close to communism. This and subsequent support of the shah led the Americans to eclipse the British as the core Western influence in Iran.

The success of the coup left Mossadeq under house arrest for life, and Mohammad Reza Pahlavi was restored to power. By the mid-1970s, oil revenues reached their highest point, and Iran enjoyed a period of modest economic growth, but with little room for political dissent and an increasingly autocratic leadership. Using the profits from the oil receipts, the shah funded vast army and military expenditures. In 1963, he launched a series of modernizing reforms, named the White Revolution, ostensibly aimed at helping the peasantry by re-distributing feudal lands, but also seeking to thwart the influence and power of large-scale landowners by creating a base of support among the working classes.[1] Alongside land reforms, the shah's government established social programs for workers, women, and urban and rural poor, including literacy, education, and health care. In 1963, women gained the right to vote. These reforms were presumably also aimed at modernizing Iran's economy and strengthening the industrial sectors.

Although the reforms of the White Revolution were voted on by a referendum, there was little doubt about the power structure of the Iranian state at this time, as political parties were strictly monitored and professional associations severely limited. Ironically, the reforms of the White Revolution increased the number of people who had historically opposed the monarchy: working classes and intellectuals. With little meaningful political participation, such groups went underground and became allied with another historical foe of the regime, the religious leadership of the country. The White Revolution incensed many members of the *ulama,* not only because they found the social programs and government control of resources anti-Islamic, but also because their landholdings were often the base of their own income and endowments. Thus, the rural peasantry and urban poor who often looked for guidance to the *ulama* felt increasingly uneasy about the seemingly un-Islamic programs the shah was implementing.

Abadan Crisis ■
the result of Iran's decision to nationalize oil resources in 1950. In response, the British oil company AIOC closed the world's largest oil refinery in the city of Abadan, withheld key resources from Iran, and withdrew their employees to keep Iran from refining its oil.

Operation Ajax ■
1953 CIA covert coup d'état that toppled Iran's Prime Minister Mohammad Mossadeq, who was responsible for nationalizing Iran's oil.

White Revolution ■
a series of land reforms instituted by the shah in 1963, aimed at redistributing feudal land holdings among the peasantry to gain favor. Also included were economic and social reform policies aimed at modernizing the economy.

The 1979 Iranian Revolution

The shah's White Revolution alienated many individuals, and at the same time closed off possibilities for protest by tightly controlling political and professional mobilization through the use of the secret police, SAVAK. As a result, citizens increasingly turned toward the one arena over which the shah had less control, the *ulama*. One of the greatest critics of the shah's modernization policies was Ayatollah Ruhollah Khomeini, who, in June 1963, publically denounced the shah's policies as anti-Islamic. His speeches marked a shift in the orientation of the bookish religious scholar toward more political pursuits. His outspokenness resulted first in his arrest, and later, in April 1964, in exile in Najaf, the Shi'i religious center in Iraq. Khomeini's exile sparked days of anti-shah rioting in the city of Qom.

Among Khomeini's criticisms were of the shah's brutal crackdowns on student protests and the Status of Forces Agreements, a set of treaties between the United States and Iran that granted diplomatic immunity to Americans living in Iran. These laws, which were not reciprocated by the United States, guaranteed that U.S. military personnel and their dependents who committed crimes in Iran would be sent home for processing by military courts instead of standing trial in Iran. Khomeini was not alone in such criticisms. A tide of anti-shah protests was emerging, as well, from leftist, secular, and nationalist groups. Such groups also pointed to the harsh tactics of political suppression and called on the shah to respect human rights. Furthermore, criticisms by international human rights organizations and even U.S. President Jimmy Carter gave domestic groups credibility and leverage.

In 1978, pressure mounted as anti-shah protests spread throughout the country. After meager efforts at political and economic reform, the opposition pressed for the shah's ouster. On January 16, 1979, the shah stepped on a plane to leave Iran for, what his aides claimed was a vacation. But he would never return. Just two weeks later, on February 1, 1979, Ayatollah Khomeini emerged from exile and returned to Iran to lead the establishment of a new leadership, under a novel form of governance, an Islamic government, Hookoomat-e Islami.

In the immediate aftermath of the shah's overthrow, it was unclear how revolutionary forces would work together to form a new state. The various groups which had come together to overthrow the shah disagreed on the composition of the new polity. Initially, some of the disparate groups envisioned a power-sharing arrangement. Nationalists and intellectuals, including Mehdi Bazargan, the prime minister of the newly formed provisional government, argued for a democratic republic with multiple parties. Ayatollah Khomeini and his supporters, however, wanted an Islamic mode of statehood, even rejecting the use of the word "democracy" in the name of the new state.[2]

A key event that tipped the scale was the takeover of the U.S. embassy in Tehran on November 4, 1979. An Islamist student group entered and occupied the embassy, and held 52 Americans hostage for 444 days. The Islamists stated that they would release the hostages only if the United States were to return the shah—who had fled into exile, first to Egypt and then to the United States—to

---

Status of Forces Agreements ■ a set of agreements between Iran and the United States that granted immunity from prosecution to American military personnel and their dependents who committed crimes in Iran against its citizens or property.

Hookoomat-e Islami ■ Islamic government; a theory of Islamic governance put forth by Ayatollah Khomeini.

Iran to face trial (he died before the hostage crisis ended). Religious leaders rallied Iranians to their side, drawing on nationalist enmity against the United States, which intensified as secret embassy documents connecting Iranian secular nationalists and leftists to the United States were released around the country. The student group claimed that U.S. embassy officials were attempting a coup, reminiscent of 1953, to re-install the shah. The hostage crisis and embassy takeover gave Khomeini the advantage over nationalists and leftists. Bazargan, among others, vehemently disagreed with holding the Americans, and when Khomeini would not intervene to free them, Bazargan tendered his resignation.[3] Khomeini further leveraged the rampant anti-Americanism to consolidate power.

Even with the weakening of nationalist and leftist forces, the effort to consolidate the revolution was not easy. The *ulama* were divided among themselves, while the provisional government that took control in the immediate aftermath of the revolution carried out arbitrary arrests, forced disappearances, show trials, and mass executions.

Profiting from the instability in Iran, in 1980, Iraq, led by Saddam Hussein, invaded Iran to gain port access to the Persian Gulf, through the *Shatt al-Arab* waterway, breaching a previous treaty, the Algiers Accords, that established Iran's right over the area. The resulting eight-year war, known to Iranians as the Imposed War or the Sacred Defense, was devastating for Iranians and their economy. American-supplied chemical and conventional weapons destroyed the lives of hundreds of thousands of people.[4] Massive casualties plagued both sides. In 1988, after a U.S. missile shot down an Iranian passenger plane that killed all 290 civilians aboard, Khomeini agreed to sign United Nations peace accords aiming to end hostilities. The length and brutality of the war, including the U.S. support of Iraq, permitted the conservative religious leaders and their supporters to further consolidate their power and to justify repression of their people.[5]

Khomeini's repressive tactics had two main goals. The first was to secure Iran against outside aggression, which was predominantly tied to UK interference in the late-1800s to mid-1900s, and U.S. meddling since the 1953 coup. The second was the consolidation of Islamic governance, driven by a theory of the justness of Islamic jurists. This theory held that in the absence of their final prophet, Shi'i Muslims needed a final arbiter of Islamic principles. Thus, the Islamic state would have an office devoted to the *Velayat-e Faqih*, or Guardianship of the Jurist whose role would be to determine whether state policies were in conformity with Islamic principles. However, the day-to-day operations of this body were left unclear.

Although there were many groups debating this issue, two distinct interpretations of this Islamic body have emerged: hardliner and reformist. Hardliners believe that the office of the Velayat-e Faqih has authority to intervene and override actions that transgress its interpretation of Islamic principles. This is important because it also evinces a monopoly on religious interpretation of Islam's holy scriptures. Hardliners seek to bring to fruition "true" Islamic government that Khomeini envisioned, one that does not answer to the people, but to God. Thus, they push for an institutional structure that prioritizes non-elected over elected bodies.

Shatt al-Arab (Arabic) or Arvand Rud (Persian) ■ a river whose southern end flows into the Persian Gulf and forms the border between Iran and Iraq.

Velayat-e Faqih (Guardianship of the Jurist) ■ theory of Islamic governance set forth by Ayatollah Khomeini, in which the just Islamic society is led by the highest religious jurist who is the final arbiter on all matters of governance.

Hardliner ■ one who believes that government should be beholden to a strict interpretation of Islamic principles. Hardliners push for institutional structures that prioritize non-elected over elected bodies and see social control as the key element in bring about a moral order.

Reformist ■ one who believes that government should consider many possible forms of governance, including, but not limited to Islamic principles. Reformists support institutional bodies of elected officials over non-elected bodies, and aim to limit the power of the state in shaping social relations.

fiqh ■ Islamic jurisprudence derived from sacred sources, such as the Quran.

The reformists, on the other hand, believe that the Velayat-e Faqih would be a body that lay politicians consult on matters of Islamic jurisprudence or *fiqh*. They emphasize the state's structure as an Islamic republic, with direct popular representation that answers to the people, and a government structure with separate branches that serves as a system of checks and balances. Reformists, thus, aim to allow elected bodies to have more power at the expense of non-elected bodies. Reformists also seek to limit the power of the state in shaping social relations, while hardliners see social control as the key element in bringing about a moral order. To date, this debate has in large part been won by the hardliners, but the role of Islam and the nature of the state are the key issues at the heart of current political struggles, including the 2009 post-election protests.

Khomeini died in 1989 without leaving a successor. Hardline factions were concerned that a power vacuum would undermine their authority. As a consequence, they aggressively sought to weaken opposition groups. In addition, they used the state's security apparatus to enforce morality codes, thus further defining the state through Islamic principles. For example, in the early 1990s, arrests, imprisonments, and floggings for immodesty, defined through public dress and behavior codes, increased dramatically. To the hardline *ulama* in power, the alleged flouting of Islamic dress codes was an act of defiance to the state. Women were (and are) more often cited for improper dress, although there are also dress codes for men. The hardline *ulama*, as the self-appointed arbiters of Islamic principles, used the issue of public comportment to legitimize their broader authority in Islamic governance. The reformist factions sought to develop and expand the political and legal institutions of the republic, thus placing more power in the hands of voters. But by 1997, the political climate was such that even opinions that were ostensibly sanctioned by the government's reformist factions could lead to arrest, imprisonment, or other harsh measures.

Khatami and the Limits of Reform, 1997–2005

In this environment of increasing religious conservatism, Mohammad Khatami, a Muslim religious authority and former minister of Culture and Islamic Guidance who had campaigned on a reformist platform, shocked Iran's conservative political establishment by winning the 1997 presidential election with 70 percent of the vote. Khatami gained the allegiance of youth, urban professionals, and secular Iranians who wanted less religious interference in everyday life, and women. One of his first acts as president was to announce relaxations of enforcement of the morality codes. Khatami brought a more open style to his administration, invited average Iranians to participate in government, and allowed Iranians greater leeway in their personal lives. Observers soon reported a dramatic increase in the number of satellite dishes popping up on rooftops, even though they were illegal. Newspaper and magazine circulation also flourished, and numerous Internet cafes opened. The international media began referring to signs of change in Iran, and to political openings.

However, Khatami's popularity and policies threatened the hardliners in the regime, who responded by questioning reformists' loyalty to revolutionary aims, including opposition to Western interference. The Revolutionary Guards or *pasdaran* threatened to enforce the regulations on public comportment, including restrictions on Western forms of dress. The point of such threats was to demonstrate that despite Khatami's landslide election, the elected president was not in charge. Instead, unelected religious leaders held final authority.

In 1999, the Islamic republic of Iran entered its twentieth year. During that time, the government was facing a disillusioned populace. Detractors were growing as economic hardship spread. Many were beginning to see that, despite overwhelming popular support, the president was unable to change laws in step with what the vast majority of people seemed to want—jobs and greater social and political freedoms.

The limits of Khatami's presidential powers were also becoming apparent to his constituents as his initiatives were overridden by unelected officials, sometimes by violent and illegal means, such as the attacks on students, who, in July 1999, protested the closing of a popular reformist newspaper. Thus, it was not until Khatami's landslide victory, and then his inability to enact reforms, that Iranians realized the limits of their "republican" side of the Islamic republic.

The massive groups of disgruntled young people posed a particular problem for the regime's leadership, as this growing segment of the population questioned the legitimacy and authority of the unelected political officials, and makes up over half the electorate. Strict control on economic, social, and political matters by unelected government officials engendered further discontent, so much so that the reform-minded Khatami won 77% of the votes cast at his 2001 re-election. This election was widely seen as a mandate for reforming the institutions of the state.

Khatami's elections and their aftermath brought about a greater understanding of how the Islamic republic works. In the wake of student protests, public discussions revealed a deeper knowledge of the state, the limits of popular governance, and the failure of reformist politicians to enact the changes they had promised. The reformist administrators adopted the language of freedom, justice, and equality, but the fractious political situation felt, to many Iranians, more stifling than ever before.

Pasdaran ■ military force formed after the revolution to prevent dissent and preserve the aims of the revolution by assisting in the enforcement of the post-revolutionary government's morality laws.

Ahmadinejad and Conservative Reaction, 2005–Present

Today, the conduct of Iran's hardline officials is enacted in part in the context of an ideological power play that emerged in reaction to Khatami's 1997 victory. However, the renewed power and seemingly free hand of the conservatives to direct policies today is also connected to geopolitics, including the events of 9/11 and the U.S. invasions of Afghanistan and Iraq.

In March 2000, prior to the 9/11 attacks, the Clinton administration publicly apologized to Iran for the 1953 CIA-sponsored coup and partially lifted sanctions against Iran. Many in Iran who wished for rapprochement saw this as an opening. This era was also accompanied by an attempt at diplomacy from Iran's reformists, which included President Khatami's U.N. initiative, Dialogue among Civilizations. After the U.S. World Trade Center was attacked on September 11, 2001, the Iranian people, led by their president, sent condolences and even supported the U.S. overthrow of the Taliban.

Despite Iran's support, President George W. Bush's 2002 State of the Union speech designated Iran as part of the "Axis of Evil," which sounded the death knell for the reform movement. The hardline clerics in Iran used the label as an illustration of how Khatami's conciliatory attempt at dialogue with "The Great Satan" brought Iran no closer to resolving its disputes with the United States.

The surprising June 2005 election of Tehran's relatively unknown mayor, Mahmoud Ahmadinejad, to the presidency came about from the widespread frustration at the reformists' inability to produce economic and political change. The 2005 elections also saw a decline in voter turnout, due to an election boycott by reformists who rebuked the limits to reform forced upon them by hardline factions. The leading clerics, moreover, wanted to have in place a president whose views were more in tune with the hardline foreign policies espoused by Ali Khamenei, who had replaced Khomeini upon the latter's death, especially toward the United States. Ahmadinejad initially pledged that there would be no changes to the social relaxations that had come about under Khatami, and vowed to make changes to benefit the poor. However, his close personal relationship with the hardline clerics, though he himself is not a cleric, promised greater unity of purpose and a tougher stance toward the United States. Thus, the hardline government's actions must be understood today in the renewed fight against perceived western aggression.

The February 2006 announcement by then U.S. Secretary of State Condoleezza Rice of $75 million dollars to "promote democracy" in Iran was seen by Iranian officials as an attempt to finance Iranian dissidents and opposition groups, in hopes of spurring regime change. The announcement triggered a harsh reaction by hardliners against those deemed to be sympathetic to the West. Despite previous promises of maintaining the relaxed social controls, the spring of 2006 saw the beginnings of crackdowns on the least empowered segments of the population—women, ethnic and religious minorities, and student groups.

As the table on the next page suggests, Iran's ancient yet diverse culture provides a strong foundation for nationalism that led to the overthrow of absolute monarchy and a Constitutional Revolution in the early twentieth century. European meddling matched by monarchical mismanagement of the country's resources inspired the political conscience of the merchant classes. Merchants, along with religious leaders, rose up against the foreign interference and the threat of colonialism. The discovery of oil intensified popular demands for national control. Government under the Pahlavi Dynasty was characterized by repression on the one hand and modernizing programs on the other. Such modernizing efforts benefited some sectors of society, including women, but the repression alienated both secular Iranians and Iran's Islamic clergy. Massive popular opposition exploded in 1979, toppling the shah and his entire regime. Today, both secular Iranians and moderate clergy feel left out of politics. To understand how religious authorities have gained the upper hand within Iran's Islamic republic, it is necessary to understand the state institutions created since the 1979 revolution.

Historical Overview of Iran

SUMMARY TABLE

Historical Overview: Political Authority from Ancient Persia to the Islamic Republic

550–330 BCE	Achaemenid Empire	Ended with invasion by Alexander the Great.
334–224 BCE	Seleucid and Parthian rule	Ended with Sassanid Empire.
224 BCE–641 AD	Sassanid Dynasty	Ended with Arab Conquest. Introduction of Islam in Persia.
641–962	Arab rule	Ended with Turkic rule.
962–1220	Turkic rule	Ended with Mongol conquest with invasion of Genghis Khan.
1220–1501	Mongol rule	Ended with Safavid rise to power.
1501–1736	Safavid Dynasty	Ended with Afsharid and Zand rule.
1736–1795	Afsharid and Zand dynasties	Ended with Qajar Dynasty.
1795–1925	Qajar Dynasty	1906–1911 Constitutional Revolution ends absolute monarchical rule by introducing Iranian parliament. Qajar rule ends when Prime Minister Reza Khan is declared shah in 1925.
1925–1941	Pahlavi Dynasty: Reza Shah	Occupying powers force Reza Shah's abdication in 1941. His son is chosen as successor.
1941–1979	Pahlavi Dynasty: Mohammad Reza Shah	Ended with Iranian revolution and establishment of Islamic Republic of Iran.
1979–1989	Islamic Republic: Ayatollah Ruhollah Khomeini, Supreme Leader	Ended with Khomeini's death in 1989.
1989–present	Islamic Republic: Ali Khamenei, Supreme Leader	

INSTITUTIONS OF IRAN

11.2 What are the institutions of the Islamic republic and how do they contribute to the simultaneous development of both repressive governmental tactics and popular mobilization?

shari'a ■ Islamic legal principles.

Watch the Video "Iran's Hybrid Regime" at mypoliscilab.com

Explore the Comparative "Constitutions" at mypoliscilab.com

When the shah's government fell on February 14, 1979, the leaders of the revolution, comprised of members of the *ulama* and the nationalist opposition, formed the Council of the Islamic Revolution. The council dissolved *Majlis* and supervised the transformation of all political and legal institutions. On April 1, 1979, Iranians voted in a referendum to declare Iran an Islamic republic—98 percent voted "yes." That summer, a provisional government, which was appointed by the council, drafted a new constitution, with the lay Muslim nationalist, Mehdi Bazargan, the prime minister of the provisional government, at the helm. Iranian voters approved, again by an overwhelming margin, the referendum of October 24, 1979, that established the constitution of the Islamic republic of Iran.

As the name implies, Iran's constitution combines elements of republican governance—a system of government without a monarch that allows for popular representation in a unicameral parliament, with Shi'i Islamic principles, or *shari'a*, both integrated into law and guiding on matters not directly addressed by existing laws. This combination resulted from a political compromise that emerged immediately after the shah's overthrow. At that time, the diverse groups that had united in battle against the shah could not agree on the form Iran's new government should take. Secular leaders wanted a multi-party democracy, while Ayatollah Khomeini and his influential followers among the *ulama* wanted an Islamic state. One of the main factors that brought the disparate groups together was the common opposition to foreign domination, and thus, the constitution specifies the anti-imperialist and anti-colonialist stance for the country.

Although Khomeini did not completely eliminate the republican aspects of the new constitution, in order to implement his theory of Islamic government, he pushed *Majlis* to ratify several constitutional articles that granted greater power to religious authorities. In this section, we will describe the combination of republican and Islamic institutions that make up Iran's system of government, and explain how the Islamic face of the state came to dominate the republican institutions. An important question that arises is how the relationship between Islamic principles and republican institutions both produce the possibilities of dissent and reform, but also make possible the repression and crackdowns on dissent seen since the post-election protests of 2009.

Republican Institutions

The Iranian government has a set of institutions that should sound familiar to anyone taking this course. Iran's government is a republic characterized by direct representation, in which candidates to the presidency and parliament are popularly and directly elected by the citizens. Universal suffrage begins at the age of 18. The "republican" aspects of Iran's government consist of three branches: the executive, the legislative, and the judiciary. The 1906–1911 Constitutional Revolution paved the way for the framework for the state. The drafters of the post-1979 constitution had different political interests, but pieced together a constitution that implemented elements of Iran's earlier constitution, the constitution of France's Fifth republic, and principles of Islamic governance.

The constitution promises legal protection to all citizens, both women and men, and provides equality before the law. It expresses the inviolability of dignity, life, property, rights, residence, and livelihood of individuals, and promises equal protection under the law for all ethnic groups or tribes, no matter their race, color, or language. In addition, the constitution promises equal protection of non-Shi'i Muslims and other recognized religious groups.[6] Each recognized religious minority elects a representative to parliament. The number of representatives is determined by the population. For instance, there are currently two parliamentarians representing Christian Armenians, one for Assyrians, one for Jews, and one for Zoroastrians. The specificity of constitutional protections for minority groups in the Iranian context is distinct from the U.S. Constitution, which does not specify gender, race, or religion.

Iran's constitution protects basic human rights and civil liberties, press freedom, the right to organize and demonstrate, and the right to an attorney and to appeal a legal decision. The constitution also provides negative freedoms, such as the right to be free from arbitrary arrest, torture, surveillance, including wiretapping, and *habeas corpus* or being held without charge. It also includes promises of pension, disability pay, adequate housing, and free education, both primary and secondary. These populist entitlements were inspired by the common concern of both the merchant classes and the *ulama* of the monarchy's waste and hoarding of the country's vast resources. They highlight, moreover, the popular nature of the revolution. Finally, the constitution memorializes the religious and anti-imperialist values of the revolution and makes the carrying out of its aims a persistent goal of the government.

The President The president heads the executive branch and is charged with implementing the constitution. As chief executive, the president is responsible for matters related to national planning, the state budget, and signing legislation into law. The president also represents Iran to foreign countries, and signs treaties and other international accords. He is Iran's representative to the United Nations. However, in a significant departure from the U.S. model, the president in Iran is not the commander in chief of the armed forces.

Presidents are directly elected through popular vote by an absolute majority, for a maximum of two consecutive four-year terms, but unlike U.S. presidents, who can serve a maximum of two terms, presidents in Iran may run for re-election in one non-successive term after having served two consecutive terms. The president's qualifications include being an Iranian-born citizen and member of the Shi'i faith. While the constitution does not specify the gender of candidates for president, when women have submitted their candidacy for approval, the official vetting body, the Council of Guardians, a non-elected group of legal experts discussed below, has rejected them.[7]

The president appoints a cabinet and vice presidents to aid in serving out his duties. The current president has a cabinet of 21 ministers and ten vice presidents.

Majlis must approve his nominees, but only after they have been vetted for government service.

Parliament Members of Iran's parliament come to power through direct popular elections and serve four-year terms with no term limits. There are currently 290 members of the Iranian parliament. Members of parliament are charged with carrying out the laws of the Islamic republic and representing the interests of the *mellat,* or nation. Women are permitted to run for parliament and have held up to 5 percent of seats at any one time. Like candidates for president, candidates for parliament must be approved by the Council of Guardians (see below).

The Iranian parliament occupies a distinctive role in national politics, in that since the 1906–1911 Constitutional Revolution it has given lay citizens a role in government, after more than 2,500 years of absolute monarchy in Iran. When Khomeini first entered the scene, however, one of his first acts after setting up his Council of the Islamic Revolution was to dissolve the nation's parliament, stating that Iran did not need manmade laws because God's laws were sufficient. The new parliament was to serve simply as a planning body. Parliament continues to battle to establish its purpose clearly. To this day, many of the elected members of parliament struggle to pass laws responsive to the needs of their constituents, rather than just provide the regulatory framework for implementing laws. All laws that parliament passes must also be approved by the Council of Guardians. At various junctures, members of parliament have taken a stand against the interpretations of Islamic principles offered by the Council. Such standoffs had deleterious effects on the government's ability to carry out its mission. Thus, in 1988, the Iranian constitution was amended to create a new body, the Expediency Council, which would oversee disagreements between parliament and the Council of Guardians.

The Judicial Branch Iran's judiciary is the least republican of the three branches. Although the Iranian constitution states that the judiciary is an independent branch of government, it is not. This is because the judiciary is housed within the office of the supreme leader, the country's highest authority on Islamic jurisprudence. The judiciary is comprised of civil and criminal courts, as well as the Islamic Revolutionary Court, which hears cases brought against people accused of defying the values of the Iranian Islamic revolution; a Special Court for the Clergy, which deals only with members of the *ulama*; and a Press Court, which hears cases brought against newspaper editors and journalists accused of transgressing the press laws. The head of the judiciary is responsible for drafting legislation and selecting all judges. He must be a member of the *ulama*, with training in Islamic jurisprudence and civil law and procedure, and is appointed by the supreme leader to serve a five-year term.

In addition to the head of the judicial branch, the executive branch also has a Ministry of Justice. The justice minister works closely with the judiciary, but in a different capacity. The justice minister is responsible for the day-to-day administration of courts, financial affairs, and employment of personnel other than judges.

The head of the judiciary selects the minister of justice from a list of nominees presented by the president.

Iran's history of revolt against injustice, including the 1979 revolution, led to the establishment of the republican elements of Iran's constitution, which seek to prevent a return to the tyranny of the shah's rule. However, the founding republican principles were created in tandem with Islamic values. That is, the constitution also states that the country is founded on a belief in the Shi'i *ummah*, or community of religious believers, the oneness of God, and divine revelation. What ultimately became an overriding factor in the constitution of the Islamic republic was the line that read: *"all laws must conform to the principles of Islam."* For some, it was just a convention, but for others, this phrase became the codification of the rule of *ulama* and *shari'a* over the elected bodies of government and the civil and constitutional laws. It is in this principle that we see the explanation for the dominance of the Islamic over the republican elements of Iran's constitution.

ummah ■ for Muslims, the community of believers.

Islamic Institutions

The Islamic institutions of the Iranian government highlight the non-democratic nature of governance in Iran. This is because the republican elements of Iran's constitution—its popularly elected president and parliament—do not have the final say in politics, and do not provide effective checks and balances on the Islamic elements of Iran's constitution. Instead, unelected authorities or government officials who gain office through controlled elections have final political authority. Let us consider the complex relationship between the three key Islamic institutions of Iran's government: the supreme leader, the Assembly of Experts, and the Council of Guardians.

Supreme Leader Iran's highest political and religious authority—more powerful than the president—is known as the supreme leader. The supreme leader's authority derives from Shi'i theology as interpreted by Ayatollah Khomeini in the notion of *Velayat-e Faqih*, Guardianship of the Jurist, and is so stated in the constitution of the Islamic republic. The supreme leader, as Iran's highest religious authority, judges whether the operations of government are in accordance with Islamic law, and has the final word in all foreign and domestic policy, particularly in terms of whether government policies conform to Islamic principles. Ayatollah Khomeini was the Islamic republic's first supreme leader. The second, and current, is Ayatollah Ali Khamenei.

supreme leader ■ Iran's highest political and religious authority. The first supreme leader was Ayatollah Khomeini.

According to Iran's 1979 constitution, the supreme leader is commander in chief of the armed forces, appoints all senior military and police commanders, and has the power to declare war and peace. He also selects the highest-ranking members of Iran's judiciary, the head of the national radio and television networks, the leaders of Iran's major religious organizations, and the members of Iran's National Security Council, which controls all matters pertaining to internal security, defense policy, and foreign affairs—including Iran's nuclear policy. The supreme leader also appoints six of the 12 members of the Council of Guardians. The constitution

PRESIDENT MAHMOUD AHMADINEJAD ADDRESSES AUDIENCE DURING COMMEMORATION OF AYATOLLAH KHOMEINI'S DEATH

Photos of religious leaders, including the supreme leaders, Ayatollah Khamenei (left) and Ayatollah Khomeini, adorn city walls, offices, and public gathering places, serving as constant reminders of the revolutionary aims to overthrow the monarchy and instill Islamic values.

also empowers the supreme leader to create advisory bodies. On July 25, 2011, the supreme leader, Ayatollah Khamenei, appointed a new committee, the Supreme Council of Arbitration and Adjustment of Relations between the Three Branches of Government. This body of five members is appointed for a term of five years and reports only to the supreme leader. The creation of this body is rumored to address failures of the Expediency Council in carrying out its mandate. How this body operates and its level of influence over the leader and the branches of government remain to be seen.

Assembly of Experts The supreme leader is Iran's highest political authority—but he is theoretically accountable to the Assembly of Experts—a group of 86 senior Islamic scholars who select, oversee, and can dismiss the supreme leader. Members of the Assembly of Experts are elected through direct popular elections for eight-year terms, but they meet relatively infrequently, for a minimum of four days per year.

To date, the Assembly of Experts has exercised its appointment power only once, when Ayatollah Ruhollah Khomeini died in 1989.[8] The assembly elected

Assembly of Experts
■ a group of 86 senior Islamic scholars who select, oversee, and can dismiss the supreme leader.

TABLE 11.1

Supreme Leaders, Presidents and Prime Ministers of the Islamic Republic of Iran

Supreme Leader	President	Prime Minister
Ayatollah Ruhollah Khomeini, 1980–1989	Abolhassan Banisadr, 1980–1981	Mohammad-Ali Rajai, 1980–1981
	Mohammad-Ali Rajai, 1981–1981	Mohammad Javad Bahonar, 1981
	Ayatollah Ali Khamenei, 1981–1989	Mir-Hossein Mousavi, 1981–1989
Ayatollah Ali Khamenei, 1989–present	Ayatollah Akbar Hashemi Rafsanjani, 1989–1997	Position of prime minister abolished in 1989
	Seyyed Mohammad Khatami, 1997–2005	
	Mahmoud Ahmadinejad, 2005–present	

Ayatollah Ali Khamenei, who has served as supreme leader ever since that year. The Assembly of Experts meets in secret; thus, it is not known whether or to what extent it actually oversees the supreme leader's activities.

Council of Guardians The Council of Guardians is a group of 12 senior scholars of Islamic jurisprudence and civil law who determine whether the laws and actions of government officials are in conformity with Islamic principles. The Council of Guardians vets and must approve all candidates for president, *Majlis*, and the Assembly of Experts, and can dismiss the president under certain conditions. It supervises elections, and has veto power over bills passed into law by *Majlis*. The supreme leader appoints the six religious members of the Council of Guardians, and the head of Iran's judicial branch (himself appointed by the supreme leader) nominates the six legal scholars, subject to approval by *Majlis*.

In recent years, the council has taken a more active role in vetting candidates for elected office, disqualifying many reform-minded and liberal candidates as not sufficiently dedicated to its particular interpretation of Islamic values. For example,

Council of the Guardians ■ a group of 12 senior scholars of Islamic jurisprudence and civil law who determine whether the laws and actions of government officials are in conformity with Islamic principles.

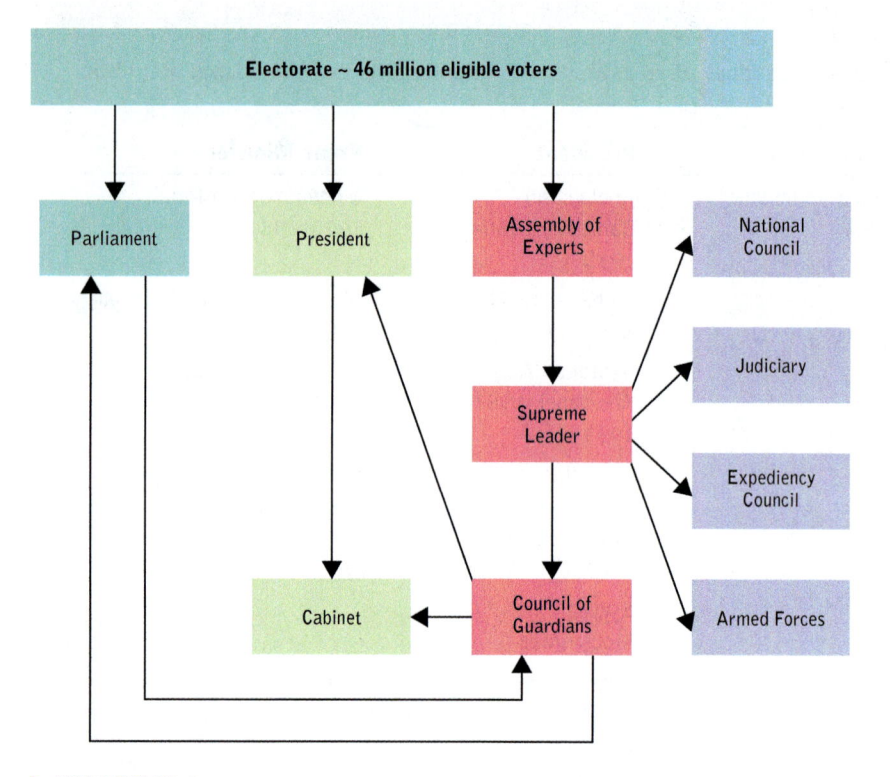

FIGURE 11.1
The Iranian State

The Islamic republic of Iran is comprised of elements of a republic, including the three branches of government: legislative, executive, and judicial. Iran's republic is placed in check by the powers of the supreme leader, the highest religious authority in the country, who determines that government act in accordance to the strictures of Islam. The arrows note the source of power or appointment for each office. For instance, the President's source of power is the electorate, but the Council of Guardians vets all candidates for the presidency.

in a show of force, the council rejected the applications of 3,500 candidates for the presidential elections of 2005, and found only a handful had the necessary qualifications to run for the office. In 2000, the council rejected the Iranian parliament's ratification of CEDAW, the United Nations Convention on the Elimination of Discrimination against Women.

In sum, as described in in the table on the next page, Iran's constitution combines both republican and Islamic elements. On the one hand, this hybrid form allows Iranian citizens to create spaces in which they can express themselves politically, such as in direct elections for the country's legislative representatives. On the other hand, unelected Islamic religious authorities clearly have the final word in politics, not elected officials accountable to the public. Moreover, conservative religious authorities have in recent years increasingly used the military, police, and the *basij*—paramilitary forces—to control the population and repress dissent.

basij ■ a volunteer civilian paramilitary group.

SUMMARY TABLE

Institutions of the Islamic Republic of Iran

Executive — Made up of president and his cabinet of ministers. President is directly elected by a majority every four years. Failure of a single candidate to gain majority triggers a runoff election. President is not the commander in chief. Candidates vetted by Council of Guardians.

Legislature — Currently 290 members. Members of parliament are directly elected every four years, with no term limits. Abrahamic faiths (Judaism, Christianity, and Islam) and Zoroastrianism have designated representative seats. Candidates vetted by Council of Guardians.

Judiciary — Not an independent branch of government, but rather part of the offices of the supreme leader. Consists of civil, criminal, revolutionary, press, and clerical courts. Head of the judiciary drafts legislation and selects the country's judges. Head of the judiciary must be a member of the *ulama*, with training in Islamic jurisprudence and civil law and procedure, and is appointed by the supreme leader to serve a five-year term.

Supreme Leader — Highest political and religious authority—more powerful than the president. Supreme leader's authority derives from Shi'i theology as interpreted by Ayatollah Khomeini in the notion of *Velayat-e Faqih*, Guardianship of the Jurist.

Assembly of Experts — A group of 86 senior Islamic religious scholars who select and oversee supreme leader. Can technically dismiss the supreme leader as well. Members are elected through direct popular elections for eight-year terms. They meet infrequently.

Council of Guardians — A 12-member council made up of six religious legal scholars who are chosen by supreme leader and six legally trained professionals chosen by parliament. Vets all candidates for election and laws passed by parliament.

Expediency Council — Created in 1988 to preside over intractable disputes between Council of Guardians and parliament. Members appointed by supreme leader every five years. Role expanded to advisory body to the supreme leader in 2005.

Arbitration Committee — Newest body, created in 2011, to preside over disputes between different branches of government. Comprised of five members, appointed by and report to the supreme leader for a period of five years.

IDENTITIES OF IRAN

11.3 How do the diverse groups that make up the "Iranian" people participate in the system of Islamic republican government?

In this section, we consider the relevance of some of Iran's most prominent ethnic, religious, and other organized groups. The enduring legacy of these identities may help shed light on the puzzle of massive protest and appeals to democracy in the face of increasing authoritarianism. We will explore how the Islamic republic can and must allow diversity of religious, and to some extent, ethnic viewpoints, although not secularism. Given Iran's diversity, however, we will also see how the state must constantly balance perceived threats through control, negotiation, incorporation, and where necessary, violence.

Watch the *Video* "Youth in Iran" at mypoliscilab.com

Pre-Islamic "Persian": Achaemenids to Sassanids

Among Iranians, the legacy of the Achaemenids is an important and enduring memory of the deep respect their ancestors had for humanity, which exists today. According to historian Richard Frye, the image of Cyrus the Great has emerged as "the epitome of the great qualities expected of a ruler in antiquity, and he assumed heroic features as a conqueror who was tolerant and magnanimous as well as brave and daring. His personality influenced the Greeks and Alexander the Great, and, because he also influenced the Romans, his rule continues to influence our thinking even now."[9] For many contemporary Iranians, Cyrus embodies justice, tolerance, courage, and intelligence, or, *javanmardi*, which many see as qualities native to the Iranian character, and which they seek to embody.

In contemporary times, some Iranians reference Cyrus as an indigenous source for religious and ethnic tolerance and democratic governance. While some Iranians connect their identities to the pre-Islamic period of Cyrus the Great, a broad range of backgrounds and social classes also figure in Iranians' multi-faceted national identity.

Ethnic Identities

Iranians are comprised of mixed ethnicities. As noted earlier, the old name for the country, Persia, referred to the people of the Fars province in the southwestern region, and did not represent the country's diverse range of peoples. For this reason, Reza Shah changed the name of the country to Iran. In addition to Persian and Turkic ethnic groups, Iranians also consist of tribal and/or nomadic groups, such as Baluchis, Qashqais, Bakhtiaris, Kurds, and Lurs, and other minorities, including Arabs, Armenians, Assyrians, and Jews.

Persians, Kurds, and speakers of other Indo-European languages in Iran are descendants of the Aryan tribes that began migrating from Central Asia into what is now Iran in the second millennium BCE. Those of Turkic ancestry are also from Central Asia and are descendants of tribes that arrived in the territory from about the eleventh century AD. The Arab minorities are settled predominantly in southwestern Iran, Khuzestan, and trace their descent from the Islamic conquests of the seventh century. Many of the smaller minority groups, including Armenians and Jews, also locate their settlement in the region to ancient times.

More recently, Iran has served as a place of refuge for Afghans escaping persecution from the persistent conflicts in their country, starting with the 1980 invasion of Afghanistan by the Soviet Union. Iran is host to the second-largest Afghan refugee population, almost 2 million; a larger group finds refuge in Pakistan. While Afghans of many backgrounds live in Iran, today, most of Iran's Afghan refugees are primarily Shi'i Hazara, a minority ethnic group.

Over the past 100 years, Iran has standardized mechanisms of integration and control in order to prevent uprisings, including the institution of the state's official language as the Persian language, *Farsi*.

This means that some ethnic groups, such as the Sunni Kurds, face both direct and indirect discrimination, ranging from mass killings to restrictions on their language. The government's aim has been to put down separatist movements while encouraging integration. However, Sunni Kurds in Iran, unlike their counterparts in Turkey, have their own province, Kurdistan, in which they are free to practice their religion, speak their language, and practice their cultural traditions. There are also Shi'i Kurds in Iran, *Kermanshahi Kurds*, who make no claim to an independent state.

Still, no matter the group in power, Iran's central government has been intolerant of ethnic uprisings that challenge its authority or legitimacy. For example, during the 1979 revolution, Kurds rallied in support of the shah's ouster, but in the post-revolutionary era, Ayatollah Khomeini called the concept of ethnic minority contrary to Islamic doctrines. He also accused those "who do not wish Muslim countries to be united" of creating the issue of nationalism among minorities, views shared by many in the clerical leadership. More recently, members of a Kurdish separatist group known as The Free Life Party of Kurdistan (PJAK), were arrested, tried, and executed on charges of being *moharebeh*, or an enemy of God.

Religious Identities

The official state religion of Iran is *Ithna 'Ashari* or Twelver Shi'i Islam, in which the faithful follow the Prophet Mohammad's line of succession. Twelver Shi'i Muslims believe that the final messenger of God, the *Mahdi* (Guided One), is hidden in occultation, and will not emerge until the Day of Judgment. Twelver Shi'i believe in a hereditary line of imams, all descendants of Prophet Mohammad. There have been 11 such imams, with the twelfth being the Mahdi.

The Iranian constitution does recognize and afford political representation and, hence, some degree of protection and participation for all religions of a "book," that is to say, all religions that are monotheistic and possess a holy book. This includes the three Abrahamic religions, Judaism, Christianity, and Islam, as well as Zoroastrianism.

Zoroastrianism was the world's first monotheistic religion and is indigenous to Iran. Zoroastrians may trace their heritage back to the time of the first Persian Empire in antiquity, the Achaemenids or the Sassanids. Today, the Zoroastrian population in Iran is estimated to be as low as 20,000. The center of their faith is in the city of Yazd, where the eternal flame and their holy book, the *Avesta,* can be found. Iran also claims the second-largest Jewish population in the Middle East, after Israel. Although the population has dwindled since the revolution, the Iranian

Jewish population is well respected and successful. Iranian Jews trace their heritage back to the destruction of Jerusalem in the fifth century BCE, when Cyrus the Great afforded them refuge and protection.

Christians in Iran similarly have a heritage of refuge and exile. The vast majority of Christians in Iran is of Armenian background.

An estimated 95 percent of Iranians are Muslim, and about 89 percent are believed to be Shi'i. The small Sunni Muslim minority is found among ethnic groups, such as Kurds, Arabs, and others.

The Safavid era produced a different form of Islam with Persian-nationalist underpinnings in Shi'ism. With Savafid centralization, Persia adopted a significantly different path to faith through Shi'ism and centralization. Thus, it is here that we begin to see the emergence of a distinct "Irano–Islamic" religion. While the history of the Sunni–Shi'i split has a religious version, there is also a nationalist and ethnic layer to the Safavid Shi'i state.

The contemporary Iranian Shi'i state, however, draws more directly from the historical fissures that brought about splits within the Muslim community. In this history, it is the Battle of Karbala that dominates the narrative of Iranian Shi'i as mourners and martyrs for the righteous cause of justice. The Prophet Mohammad died without designating a successor. One group believed in successive leadership chosen by the Prophet's companions, while another group believed that those who best knew the Prophet were his blood-relatives and they should emerge as his heirs through inherited succession. The latter group believed that Ali, Mohammad's cousin and son-in-law, should be the Prophet's successor, and became known as the Partisans of Ali, or Shi'i. After a series of battles, Ali was murdered in 661 AD while in the midst of prayers. Later, his son, Hossein, was martyred at the Battle of Karbala. Hossein is honored by the Shi'i as a martyr who fought tyranny because he refused to pledge allegiance to Yazid, the Umayyad (Sunni) caliph. Hossein sought to create a state that would restore a true Islamic leadership instead of the rule of the unjust Umayyads. The anniversary of his martyrdom is called Ashura, and is a day of mourning for Shi'i Muslims. An especially important holiday in Iran, the state uses Ashura annually to commemorate injustices against the Shi'i today.

While Shi'i await the day of judgment for the emergence of the final imam, the Baha'i believe he arrived in the mid-nineteenth century. For this reason, they are considered heretics by the Islamic state. The Baha'i faith was conceived in Iran around the mid-nineteenth century. In 1844, a man from Shiraz, Seyyed Mirza Ali Mohammad, claimed that he was the hidden prophet of Shi'i Islam. He was executed in 1850, but his followers remained. From this time, followers of the Baha'i faith have been denounced as heretics.

Today, Article 4 of Iran's constitution holds, "All civil, penal, financial, economic, administrative, cultural, military, political, and other laws and regulations must be based on Islamic criteria." While the state recognizes Christianity, Judaism, and Zoroastrianism as official religions and affords their devotees the freedom to worship, apostasy is a crime and Baha'is are technically guilty *a priori*, and could potentially face the death penalty.

In short, although Iran has several religious minorities and although its constitution guarantees freedom of belief, various laws place restrictions on religious freedoms. Article 513 of the Penal Code defines an "insult to religion" as an offense punishable by death or prison terms of between one and five years. Articles 6 and 26 of the Press Code forbid writings "containing apostasy and matters against Islamic standards [and] 'the true religion of Islam.'"

Social Classes

During the period of industrial growth and development in the 20th century, urban intellectuals and leftists demanded accountability for the government's harsh autocratic practices. Meanwhile the less industrialized sectors of society, the rural and urban poor, began to see a trickling of benefits from the state coffers emerge in the form of infrastructure, education, and health care. Also at the time, religious elite, who were traditionally responsible for charitable endowments, felt the sting of the bureaucratic state taking control of their projects. Meanwhile, the primary sources of their vast endowments, land tracts from which they received taxes and in turn used for charity, were expropriated. Tensions between mosque and state remained at the core of the collapse of the last Iranian monarchical dynasty, the Pahlavi.

At the time of the 1979 revolution, the class structure shifted. Many landed elites were either forced to leave the country or lost their resources through government expropriation. Some private lands were turned over to public use. During the war with Iraq, families were displaced to the urban centers in search of shelter and jobs. As the country's economic woes worsened, more rural farmers moved to the cities in search of opportunity. Meanwhile, the Islamic republic worked to build roads, schools, and housing throughout the country, but especially in the regions swelling with urban growth and those devastated by the war. Additionally, secular or leftist elites in government service were replaced by employees devoted to the aims of the revolution, both spiritually and politically. The results included greater overall education and employment for the population that had been neglected or undermined by the Pahlavi government and the establishment of new urban and middle social classes that include former rural peasants, poor, and traditional religious classes.

Post-Revolutionary "Hybrid" Identities

An unintended consequence of the post-revolutionary state's merging of Islamic principles with those of a republic is that it has brought about *hybrid* identities, where individuals identify at once with seemingly "traditional" communal Islamic values and also the individual identities of citizens endowed with rights.[10] This is sometimes both a burden and a boon for Iranians, who make individual claims on the state but at the same time adhere to the principles deemed to be part of their faith. With the Shi'i principles of justice-seeking, however, many political activists draw from religious examples for intellectual or theological justification, while appealing to the institutions of the state for procedural reforms. This has been the basis for challenges by reformers to the system, including the current Green Movement for Reform, but also, on a more daily basis, by individuals seeking public redress for private matters, especially women in the context of familial conflicts.

Another effect of the liberalizing tendencies emerging from the "republicanization" of Islamic principles is the increasing call for a Muslim state that distinguishes public administration and governance from the private matters of religion. This is not to suggest a secular movement is afoot, although some political actors and activists are making such demands.

Women in the Vanguard

Just after the 1979 revolution, a powerful cleric, Ayatollah Taleghani, declared that women in Iran should voluntarily take up the *chador* because, "we want to show that there has been a revolution, a profound change." At that time, the clerical elite signaled the politicization of women in Iran. The dress code serves as a social marker of a woman's virtue and is a key measure of the post-revolutionary state's own virtue and legitimacy. A significant aim of the revolution was to cleanse the Iranian nation of corrupt Western values. Western decadence came to be embodied in the image of the miniskirt-clad Iranian woman. The new image of the chador-attired woman became a symbol of modesty and virtue, and for some, of an "authentic" Islamic Iranian vision of women. It was also symbolic of the religious ethos of the Shi'i mourners. Thus, images of Iranian women dressed in black chadors depicted the state's success in ridding Iran of Western influences, and offered a basis for its legitimacy—virtuous citizens. As women became virtuous, they also reflected the virtuousness of the state. The need for the state to discipline the women, who were measures of the state's own goodness, was an essential

chador ■ a long tent-like garment, usually black, that covers a woman from head to toe, leaving only the face and hands exposed. Today, it is the dress of some conservative women.

WOMEN AT A BUS STOP IN TEHRAN
Women, as key figures in the moral rehabilitation of the country, have used the state's own discourse of improvement to seek changes in discriminatory laws.

starting point for state-building at the inception of the Islamic republic. Public statements, prayers, and speeches were replete with discussions about women's morality and the importance of women's modesty in raising honorable sons and daughters, and in guiding the family. Since the family is said to be "the fundamental unit of society," (Iranian Constitution 1989), the ultimate success of the family, and hence the nation, depends on women's moral virtue. For this reason, women's honor is not a private matter, but one of public concern and in need of surveillance and intervention. By recognizing women's roles in nurturing the nation and its citizens, the state also acknowledges women's political roles.

The revolutionary aim of improving society through the rehabilitation of women also gave women some unexpected social and political power. After the revolution, increased attention to women led to large improvements in rates of women's health, literacy, education, and labor force participation.[11] Some two-thirds of university students in Iran are females.[12] In addition, women's groups have used the focus on their actions, roles, and comportment to make specific de-

SUMMARY TABLE

Identities in the Islamic Republic of Iran

Pre-Islamic "Persian"	Embodies justice, tolerance, courage, and intelligence, as qualities native to the Iranian character. In contemporary times, some Iranians reference Cyrus the Great as an indigenous source for religious and ethnic tolerance, democratic governance, and respect for human rights.
Social Class	With oil wealth and industrialization, class struggles emerged between the landed gentry and aristocrats of monarchical times, and working classes. Religious elites believe they have a duty to redistribute wealth by providing charity from monies received through religious taxes.
Ethnic	Iranians consist of multiple ethnic groups, primarily Persian and Turkic. Many identify with tribal and/or nomadic groups, such as Baluchis, Qashqais, Bakhtiaris, Kurds, and Lurs. Other minority groups include Arabs, Armenians, Assyrians, and Jews.
Religious	State religion of Iran is defined as Shi'i Islam. There are also Sunni Muslims, Jews, Christians, and Zoroastrians. There are also Baha'is, who are seen by state law as apostates.
Hybrid	Hybrid identities emerge as a consequence of the post-revolutionary state's merging of Islamic principles with those of republican governance, where individuals identify at once with seemingly "traditional" communal Islamic values and the individual, rights-based identities of citizens endowed with rights.
Women	Often the focus of state disciplining policies, women's groups have tapped into the preoccupation with their status and roles to maneuver for greater legal rights and demand equality.

mands for legal redress, especially in the context of family laws and their calls for an end to gender discrimination.[13]

Nevertheless, when state authorities or vigilantes attack women for not abiding by dress codes, they see themselves as protecting the nation. A woman's style of dress, moreover, is thought to be a political statement about her attitude toward Islam and the Islamic republic. Women believed to have defied social regulations are routinely stopped, arrested, interrogated, fined, imprisoned, and verbally and psychologically abused. Such a course of action might befall a woman for as little as wearing lipstick, revealing her hair, or polishing her nails. When viewed in the larger current political context, moreover, we also see that women who are politically active are more likely to be arrested, tried, and imprisoned for immodest dress. The watchful eye of government officials takes something as seemingly apolitical as lipstick as an act of political defiance.

INTERESTS IN IRAN

11.4 What are the competing interests of the various stakeholders that lead to civil unrest and protest in the face of a repressive state?

Watch the Video "Iran's Nuclear Ambitions" at mypoliscilab.com

Explore the Comparative "Media and Interest Articulation" at mypoliscilab.com

Let's look back to our main question, how do groups in a seemingly authoritarian state find room—social, legal, and political—for direct challenges to the leadership? To explore this question, we examine some interest groups that have emerged since the 1979 revolution. The effects of the war and the history of popular uprisings against injustice are important, as are the shared national memories of individual justice-seekers, both from the pre-Islamic Iranian national memory, such as Cyrus the Great, as well as the Shi'i figure of the martyr Hossein. The contemporary period is filled with daily references to these national memories. For instance, the collective memory of the Iran–Iraq War serves as a present-day allusion to the martyrdom of Ali, Hossein, and other noble Shi'i fighting for justice. This section will examine the motivations of various groups.

Military Interests

Since the start of the Iran–Iraq War in 1980, several groups have emerged with great political and social leverage, especially the Revolutionary Guards (*Pasdaran e Enqelab*) and the *basij*, a volunteer civilian paramilitary unit, under their control.

The Revolutionary Guards (RG), also known as the Army of the Guards (*Sepah e Pasdaran*), formed a distinct and separate branch of Iran's military, and during the war were known for their courage and strategic missions. They consist of a combined military force with its own army, navy, air force, intelligence, and special forces (the *Qods* force), and today are charged with controlling Iran's borders. The RG is recognized as a component of the Iranian military under the constitution, separate from but matching with the other arm of Iran's military, the *Artesh*, or army. The RG is now a military-based business enterprise with holdings in oil and gas, telecommunications, and agriculture, and many other economic sectors, and thus wields considerable economic and political influence, as well.

The *basij* is a volunteer-based paramilitary force, with 90,000 regular soldiers and 300,000 reservists. *Basij* forces have become increasingly important in securing, regulating and repressing the civilian population.

The jurisdiction of these different groups officially resides with the supreme leader, who controls all the branches of military and security services. Today, the Revolutionary Guard has moved beyond a military purpose, and supports its ever-widening functions under the auspices of the leader's protection.

The relationship between the military, the oil economy, and the state is important to disentangle. One question that emerges is whether, in a state where the military is so heavily involved in economic activities, popular sovereignty can exist. If the answer is no, then why have we seen such a high level in protest in Iran?

Political Interests

Iran has a strong history of both anti-government political mobilization and repression of opposition groups. As we have seen, opposition groups often with myriad interests have aligned with each other for a specific goal of overthrowing a monarch or repressive ruler, as in the 1906–1911 Constitutional Revolution or in the 1979 revolution, but then struggled for ultimate power rather than power-sharing in the post-revolutionary era.

After the revolution, political parties emerged as part of the long list of political institutions to be rehabilitated after the demise of the shah. Indeed, the 1979 constitution supports the freedom of association and organizing. However, given the caveat that requires all activities to conform to Islamic principles alongside an unelected clerical monopoly on the interpretation of the meaning of "conformity" and "Islamic principles," post-revolutionary leaders aiming to isolate opposition have narrowly defined those terms.

In the immediate post-revolutionary period, numerous political parties emerged that spanned the field from secular leftists, including communists to conservative clerical groups. Over time, nationalist and secular parties were prohibited and deemed anti-Islamic, including the *Tudeh*, or Communist Party, which had operated in Iran since 1941, but faced suppression under Mohammad Reza Shah's regime. After the 1979 revolution, Ayatollah Khomeini systematically purged the Tudeh Party. The National Front, a coalition of secular democratic parties that supported Prime Minister Mossadeq's oil nationalization in the early 1950s, also faced suppression, both under the shah and the Islamic republican leadership. Many of its supporters have fled the country.

In the years since the revolution, numerous political parties emerged and then were restrained by state forces. The political parties that have staying power have a strong Islamic platform, but many include democratic ideals and human rights in their policies, as well. Thus, even as they are Islamic, political parties in Iran today can be divided along a spectrum with reformists at one end and hardliners at the other. For instance, one leftist party, the Freedom Movement of Iran (FMI), which formed in 1961, was made up of the more religiously oriented members of the National Front and was popular with leading intellectuals. In the 1960s and

Tudeh ■ the Iranian Communist Party.

National Front ■ a coalition of parties that support secular democracy and nationalization of oil.

1970s, FMI members operated primarily outside of the country, as political dissent was met with severe penalty. After the revolution, FMI members formed part of the provisional government, including Mehdi Bazargan, one of FMI's founders. FMI was initially active in the post-revolutionary government, but with the consolidation of power of the conservative Muslim groups, FMI members, who protested the role of the *ulama* in government, resigned.[14] By mid-1989, FMI was the only non-religious party operating in the country. That same year, its members were refused permission to run for office. In 1991, FMI was officially banned, although its existence was tolerated. FMI was active up to the summer of 2009, when, after its condemnation of the elections, its leader Ebrahim Yazdi and other members were imprisoned. Still, FMI continues to operate, but mostly underground or outside the country.

The Islamic Republican Party (IRP) was established after Khomeini's return to Iran. Although Khomeini himself was never a member, the IRP supported the establishment of a religious state. Members of the IRP were sometimes referred to as followers of the "line of the imam," signifying loyalty to Khomeini. Because the party so closely associated itself with Khomeini and his theory of state, its members were elected to a majority in the first Assembly of Experts that drafted the constitution and its first parliament. The party was disbanded in 1987 over factionalism that grew from disagreement over the Iran–Iraq War. Two other important political groups that formed after the fall of the shah were the moderate Muslim People's Republican Party, associated with the Grand Ayatollah Mohammad Kazem Shariatmadari, and the secular leftist *National Democratic Front*. Both parties fought for power with the IRP, but were eventually eliminated by the pro-Khomeini groups.

After the regime had eliminated secular and centrist Islamic parties, the main opposition to the IRP was the *Mujahedin-e Khalq (MEK)* or the *People's Mujahedin*. The MEK was a liberal Shi'i Islamic party made up primarily of religious youth, but who were not themselves members of the *ulama*. When the group formed in 1965, its platform consisted of Marxist, nationalist, and Islamic values. Its goal was to thwart the shah's government through an armed uprising. During a ten-year period, it carried out militant attacks, including the assassination of a U.S. military adviser. By 1975, the MEK had been suppressed for the most part. It re-emerged in 1979 and competed for a role in the post-revolutionary government. The MEK quickly found itself in conflict with the IRP because its adherents rejected Khomeini's theory of Islamic government. The MEK believed that individuals were qualified to interpret sacred religious texts for themselves and were not beholden to the *ulama*. In the summer of 1981, the MEK again attempted an armed rebellion against the government. More than 7,500 MEK supporters were killed during the conflict, and again the MEK was defeated.

The MEK's leaders, particularly Massoud Rajavi, fled to France with the impeached first president of the Islamic republic, Abolhassan Banisadr, and together they created the first non-monarchist exile resistance party, The National Council of Resistance. Bani Sadr broke with Rajavi in 1984, due to the latter's support for direct contact with Iraq. The MEK is still active and for many years was designated as a terrorist organization by the United States and other Western governments. In

---

National Democratic Front ■ leftist political party founded in 1979 to offer secular opposition to Islamic parties, went underground in 1981.

Mujahedin-e Khalq (MEK) or People's Mujahedin ■ Marxist, nationalist, Islamic political party, mounted armed rebellion, banned and in exile.

1985, Rajavi accepted an invitation from Saddam Hussein to establish the MEK's base in Iraq, with military training camps near the war front. The MEK fought Iranians seemingly on the side of the Iraqis. For this reason, despite their defiance of the current Iranian government, they are despised by a majority of Iranians today.

Given the exodus of almost 10 percent of the country's population since the revolution, other opposition groups and political parties in exile also exist, many active in organizing both inside and outside of Iran. In addition to the MEK, the People's Fedayeen and the Kurdish Democratic Party of Iran (KDP) both represent banned parties operating outside of Iran. The People's Fedayeen, a Marxist organization, like the Tudeh Party, was crushed in the early 1980s. Its surviving members retreated to Europe and reemerged as an exile group, eventually joining the exiled members of the Tudeh Party in Germany.

Like many of the other political parties, the KDP advocated for a democratic form of government alongside some socialist values. In addition, the KDP espoused political and cultural rights for the Kurdish ethnic minority within the centralized Iranian government. Since 1979, the KDP has been struggling against the Iranian government. By early 1986, KDP militants had been driven out of the Iranian state of Kurdistan, but continue some minimal military attacks against Iranian army units from bases in Iraqi and Turkish Kurdistan.

Organized Interests

Since the 1950s, Iranian labor groups have asserted their rights to form unions or syndicates, agitating for greater pay, work conditions, and pensions. The constitution of the Islamic republic, moreover, protects the rights of labor groups to form unions. Although a large part of the discourse on the 1979 revolution was to tend to the rights of the oppressed and to redistribute the wealth of the nation to the people, the rights of workers to unionize and collectively bargain for a greater share of the nation's wealth have been met with vehement resistance by government forces.

Inasmuch as the Iranian constitution protects workers' rights, the constitution also states its "fierce" opposition to communism, which, it maintains, is at odds with Islamic values. Thus, although many natural resources, such as oil, are nationalized, the distribution of the revenues from sales is justified on other principles. For example, during the revolution, aid to the poor was justified on the Islamic principle of charity, while during the war with Iraq, government officials stated that rationing was a public necessity. Finally, in the fall of 2010, the government terminated wartime subsidies in line with more liberalizing economic policies, and justified it with the claim that general subsidies are no longer needed. Instead, government agencies now determine which families are in financial need and distribute funds directly to them.

A comprehensive Labor Law covers the spectrum of labor relations and is generally favorable to employees. In theory, workers in Iran have the right to form labor unions, but no system of recognition or protection for unions exists. Workers are represented by a state-sponsored institution, Workers' House, which disputes unfair state labor policies.

In addition to the Labor Law, workers' councils, in the spirit of an Islamic council, started to form soon after the revolution. This system, along with most unions, was disbanded in 1985. A private sector growth and liberalization program began in the early 1990s, which gave greater license to employers to issue workers' contracts, including short-term and temporary. Today, the government endorses a system of individual rather than collective bargaining. As a result, workers who have attempted to roll back or protest the government's liberalization have been met with severe police repression.

Since the early 2000s, the government has launched economically liberalizing policies, and despite the labor protections embedded in the Iranian constitution and the labor laws, it has put down workers strikes and jailed union leaders, such as Mansour Osanloo, of the Tehran's bus drivers' union.

Nuclear and Scientific Interests

The pursuit of scientific knowledge through research is a foundational principle within the Islamic republic's constitution and harkens to a civilizational principle derived from antiquity where Persians made important contributions to math, physics, chemistry, algebra, and medicine. Thus, one source of pride that remains constant throughout numerous repressive governments is Iranian scientific research as part of the nation's heritage. Each year, the Iranian government prides itself on sending local youth to international math and science competitions. In 2010, a report by the Canadian research firm, Science-Metrix, gave Iran the world's highest ranking in growth of scientific output.[15]

Iran scientific and security aims converged when it ratified the Nuclear Non-Proliferation Treaty (NPT) in 1970. Mohammad Reza Shah introduced his intention to produce nuclear power in Iran as early as 1973, when he established the Atomic Energy Organization (AEO) of Iran. The goal of the organization was to construct a network of more than 20 nuclear power plants. By 1978, two nuclear reactors, both near Bushehr, on the Persian Gulf, were near completion and scheduled to begin operation in the beginning of 1980. The provisional post-revolutionary government, however, temporarily ended the program before the launch. The AEO is now engaged in nuclear research and, with Russian and Chinese aid, is constructing several medium-size nuclear power reactors, as well as support facilities for producing and refining uranium into fissile material.

With Iran's entry into the NPT, it makes its nuclear activities open to the verification of the International Atomic Energy Agency (IAEA), created under the auspices of the treaty. The NPT has three main aims: non-proliferation, disarmament, and the right to peaceful use of nuclear technology. The NPT has dual objectives: for countries like Iran, the NPT creates guarantees to technology and requires transparency of nuclear activities and scientific development. For the five signatory countries that have publicly declared they possess nuclear weapons, the United Kingdom, France, Russia, China, and the United States, the NPT creates obligations to transfer technology.

Since the revelation in 2002 by the head of an Iranian resistance group in exile that Iran was making nuclear weapons in two secret underground locations, international tensions have flared at Iran's ostensible violation of the NPT. Iran, however, maintains that its research and technology are for peaceful purposes and, hence, was not required by the NPT to disclose any material. Reading the NPT differently, critics of Iran, especially the United States, have asked that Iran be required to prove it is *not* trying to develop nuclear weapons. Iran, however, counters that the signatories with the technology are, themselves, in violation of the NPT for refusing to transfer nuclear technology.

A number of factors make the nuclear issue an important one both strategically, for the government of Iran, and nationally for the people. Strategically, Iran's leaders see the injustice of their neighbors who have not signed the Non-Proliferation Treaty having available nuclear weapons, including Israel, Pakistan, and India. In this sense, development of nuclear power, some think, would serve as a deterrent.

In a meeting of the NPT on May 29, 2010, the 189 member states unanimously voted on steps toward nuclear disarmament and making the Middle East free of atomic weapons. This, however, would require Israel, not currently a party to the NPT, to join the treaty, disclose its holdings, and disarm. This it has unequivocally refused to do, with the support of the United States.

In the midst of negotiations and threats to sanction Iran a fourth time, the United Nations Security Council suggested a deal with Iranians whereby the peaceful use of technology could be managed if Iran did not develop the scientific knowhow for refining uranium, but rather sent it to a third country, likely Austria or Russia, which would then return the enriched materials that could be used in medical and scientific research, but nothing further. On May 24, 2010, Iranians concluded a similar agreement with Turkey, but it did not satisfy the United States and its allies, which then issued the next round of sanctions.

The issue of scientific development is an important one for Iranians, whose heritage claims many scientific advances and a history of support of inquiry, research, and discovery. With the refusal of the United States and the European powers to recognize Iranian cultural and scientific history, the attempts to prevent Iran from developing nuclear materials for scientific and medical research have backfired as Iran has time and again argued that sanctions are politically motivated and hypocritical.

Examples of Protest

While the 2009 post-election protests stunned the world, a study of the history and social organization of Iran, including the existing institutions, identities, and interests, gives a more detailed vantage point from which to understand a history of protest and social mobilization, particularly in the face of unjust leaders, whatever the form of the state. In this section, we will explore two historical examples of protest to better understand the sources of more recent protests that took place in the summer of 2009.

Tobacco Protests   The Tobacco Protests of 1890–1891 presaged the Constitutional Revolution of 1906–1911 that finally placed limits on the rights of the shah. At the same time, they highlight key actors in social movements, such as the merchants and religious leaders, and the institutions created to allow for dissent, protests, and, in some cases, revolution.

In 1890, the Qajar shah, Nasser al-Din, granted a tobacco concession to a British company, the Imperial Tobacco Corporation of Persia. In exchange for a meager payment and a 25 percent net share in future profits, the British company would hold a complete monopoly on the production, domestic sale, and export of all tobacco products in the country for a period of 50 years. In addition, Iranian tobacco farmers and merchants were prohibited from the individual cultivation, sale, and export of their tobacco. This decision threatened the livelihoods of more than 200,000 people working in the domestic tobacco industry. This concession to a foreign power came on the heels of others like it, which left Iranian merchants unable to compete with the economic advantages granted to foreigners.

When the shah announced the details of the concession to the public, immediate country-wide condemnation followed. The first to protest the concession were the Russians who, in September 1890, balked at the concession as a violation of a regional trade agreement. News of the concession also spread throughout the country, and by spring 1891 massive protest rallies were taking place Iran's large cities: Tehran, Tabriz, and Shiraz. Initially, the protestors were merchants who were not permitted to sell their goods and were forcibly being driven out of business. They soon found common cause among the *ulama,* who were equally troubled by the economic monopoly handed to foreigners.

By December 1891, a member of the religious elite, Ayatollah Mirza Hassan Shirazi, issued a *fatwa*, an Islamic legal ruling, prohibiting the use of tobacco. Throughout the country, people obeyed the *fatwa*. They disposed of all their tobacco paraphernalia and set fire to stores selling tobacco products. Within days, a boycott of tobacco had set in. Protestors gathered in front of the shah's home and demanded he revoke the tobacco concession. Initially, he reacted with force and gave his soldiers orders to shoot the unarmed civilians. Despite numerous injuries and deaths, the protests continued. Under the mounting pressure, the shah revoked the concession. He then pardoned the leaders of the boycott and compensated the families of the dead. Several days after the revocation of the concession, Ayatollah Shirazi lifted the tobacco ban.

The tobacco protests highlighted the role of the religious elite, who, alongside merchants, came together under their common indignation for unfair competition and forced the shah to abrogate a foreign concession. The tobacco protests, moreover, shed light on the shah's untrammeled power and underscore the beginnings of a wider movement to rein in the shah's power while giving political voice to the people, and led to the Constitutional Revolution of 1906–1911.

fatwa ■ an Islamic legal ruling.

1999 Closing of *Salaam* Newspaper and Student Uprising   The summer of 1999 in Iran saw the violent culmination of the government's inter-factional sparring and, at the time, led to the greatest protest against the state since the 1979 revolution. On July 8, students from all over the country spent a day protesting the closure of one of the country's reformist newspapers, *Salaam*. One day later, in the middle of the night, special armed forces broke into University of Tehran dormito-

A STUDENT PROTESTS WHILE ARMED GOVERNMENT FORCES STAND READY

The 1999 student protests were the first major demonstrations since the 1979 revolution. Challenges to the government's treatment of the press and student protesters revealed cleavages within the government and power structures, as well as the limitations of the popularly elected president's powers.

ries, where they beat and killed a number of students. Riots broke out throughout Iran for several days afterwards, as students demanded accountability for these attacks.

At the height of the riots in downtown Tehran, students stood undaunted before masses of armed forces as they demanded President Khatami come before them and explain and thus take responsibility for what had happened. Khatami, however, did not appear. Rumors circulated that he was afraid, because apart from his personal bodyguards, the president of the Islamic republic of Iran had no security forces of his own—which turned out to be true. Khatami's failed public appearance made apparent the weakness of the elected bodies of the Islamic republic. Unlike in the United States, the president of the Islamic republic of Iran is not the commander in chief of the armed forces. The unelected religious leaders, who did not obtain power from the voters, possess military might. While Khatami, the president, might have had popular support, with no military backing, Iranians began to question the power of the president and hence, their representative republic.

The situation was important for what it revealed about the political system. The 1997 reformist victory had brought hope to people who advocated for greater political change. But the news of the riots, especially Khatami's failure to quell the violence and meet the students' demands, dismayed reformists. Newspaper accounts explained that the president of the Islamic republic was powerless without the support of the unelected religious political leaders, such as the Council of Guardians, despite having received the popular vote—not to mention that Khatami was, himself, a member of the *ulama*. Further angered and frustrated, moderates and their supporters among the working classes began to ponder the meaning of republic if elected leaders were not free to act and if unelected government officials could kill with impunity.

After days of rioting, the situation finally calmed down. In nationwide speeches, Khatami spoke to the students. He promised to address their grievances, but also appealed to the students to cooperate with his administration and to seek redress through legal channels and the political process. Reactions were mixed. What the people came to observe during these months was that the will of the electorate was diminished by the power of unelected government officials. After

SUMMARY TABLE

Interests in the Islamic Republic of Iran

Military	Revolutionary Guards emerged as elite forces protecting Iran during the war with Iraq. After the war, they assumed activities parallel to Iran's official armed forces, but today have interests in Iran's economic, telecommunications, and banking sectors. Paramilitary groups, *basij*, monitor civilians.
Political	Through centuries of struggle with repressive governments, political organizations grew as an important civilian tool to rein in Iranian leaders. After the 1979 Iranian revolution, political parties once again emerged, but those that challenge the Islamic republic's leaders have been prohibited.
Organized Labor	Labor organizing is officially protected by the constitution, but vehement intolerance of communism alongside liberalizing economic policies have diminished prospects for unions and collective bargaining. Officials have put down strikes and imprisoned labor leaders.
Nuclear and Scientific	Pursuit of science is defined as a national interest. As part of this, the Iranian government supports nuclear exploration. Iran's foes claim that Iran's program to develop nuclear technology is a quest for a weapon and in violation of Iran's obligations under the Nuclear Non-Proliferation Treaty. The Iranian government posits that it is abiding by its responsibilities under the NPT and those countries failing to share technology with Iran are in violation of the treaty.

the riots, the president's addresses often referred to the people's power through the political process. In one speech, Khatami stressed that, "a kind of mobilization of public opinion has been created which should not be taken as a minor achievement." Khatami noted that, "it is important to guide this national consensus toward more fundamental affairs such as institutionalization of the system within the framework of law and safeguarding the people's rights and observing freedom and security with the objective of the society's progress and consolidation of the system."[16]

Significantly, Khatami located that power in law, and he spoke as much to reformists as to the hardliners. Khatami's addresses, constantly locating government and popular action in the rule of law, were part of a political agenda that aimed to expand the legitimacy of elected government officials with an emphasis on civil law and institutions, as the future of popular power and the Islamic republic.

The 1999 riots showed Iranians that President Khatami was decidedly not authorized with police powers, but they also showed a young populace willing to fight for republican principles and democratic processes, and that these values were not incompatible with Islam. Ten years later, in 2009, many young Iranians would die protesting against the injustices they felt they had been dealt by the elections. One of the aims of this chapter has been to examine the historical and political context, the identities, and interests through which both the sense of injustice and entitlement came about.

CONCLUSION

Soon after questions of election fraud were deflected or cast aside by the leadership, Iranians and Iran observers strove to place the protests of 2009 into a larger historical context. The years after the revolution have been difficult for Iranians, contending with war, strict religious discipline, and harsh economic conditions. The process of consolidation of the Islamic republic that was simultaneously taking place during the 30 years since the revolution, has also forced Iranians to make accommodations to the state. The mass protests of June 2009 demonstrated a shift; Iranians have come to better understand the operations of the state and have placed expectations on it in tandem with the promises made at the time of the revolution: justice.

The aim of this chapter has been to try to understand the seeming contradictions in Iran's state form, a theocratic Islamic republic which appears to produce an authoritarian and repressive government while at the same time creating a populace that has mobilized massive protests against governmental aggression with calls for transparency and accountability. In this chapter, we have considered factors that shed light on the peculiar nature of protest in Iran. With a shared national and historical imaginary that extends beyond religion to pre-Islamic groups and beyond ethnicity to include non-Persians, Iranians have many sources from which to make claims on the state. What we have seen is that it is precisely the contradictions of this strange state form, an Islamic republic, which allow Iranians to push ideas of democracy into the national consciousness, and from which Iranians seek justice and accountability from their leaders.

Study and Review the Post-Test & Chapter Exam at mypoliscilab.com

KEY TERMS

Shi'i   412
sunni   412
ulama   413
bazaari   413
shah   413
Persian Constitutional Revolution   413
Majlis   413
spheres of influence   414
Persian corridor   414
Abadan Crisis   415
Operation Ajax   415
White Revolution   415
Status of Forces Agreements   416
Hookoomat-e Islami   416
Shatt al-Arab (Arabic) or *Arvand Rud* (Persian)   417
*Velayat-e Faqih (*Guardianship of the Jurist)   417
hardliner   417
reformist   417
fiqh   418
Revolutionary Guards or *Pasdaran*   418
shari'a   422
mellat   424
ummah   425
supreme leader   425
Assembly of Experts   426
Council of the Guardians   427
basij   428
chador   434
Tudeh   437
National Front   437
National Democratic Front   438
Mujahedin-e Khalq (MEK) or People's Mujahedin   438
fatwa   442

REVIEW QUESTIONS

1. How do the republican elements of the Islamic republic of Iran differ from republican states in Europe and North America?
2. Iranian history precedes the advent of Islam. Are there elements of Iran's pre-Islamic history that contribute to the social movements for popular governance and calls for democracy today?
3. Similarly, what are the elements of Iranian Shi'i Islam that allow for protest and support popular movements for change?
4. Give an example of how diverse interest groups come together to call for change.
5. How are minority groups, especially women, politically mobilized by Iran's government?

SUGGESTED READINGS

Abrahamian, Ervand. *Iran Between Two Revolutions*. Princeton, NJ: Princeton University Press, 1982. This study of the period between the Constitutional Revolution and the Iranian Revolution of 1979 details the political, social, and economic forces that led to deep divisions among the Iranian people.

Afary, Janet. *The Iranian Constitutional Revolution, 1906–1911: Grassroots Democracy, and the Origins of Feminism*. New York: Columbia University Press, 1996. This book offers a detailed study of the Constitutional Revolution with insights to the grassroots nature of the uprisings and the role of women.

Arjomand, Said Amir. *After Khomeini: Iran Under His Successors*. Princeton, NJ: Princeton University Press, 2009. The author provides an examination of governance in post-revolutionary Iran after the death of its founder.

Katouzian, Homa. *The Persians: Ancient, Medieval and Modern Iran*. New Haven, CT: Yale University Press, 2010. Integrating a literary and cultural history of Iran, this book explores the mechanisms of absolute power since ancient times.

Keddie, Nikki. *Modern Iran: Roots and Results of Revolution.* New Haven, CT: Yale University Press, 2006. This book provides a historical analysis of the foundations of the Iranian revolution and assesses its consequences.

NOTES

1. Ervand Abrahamian, *Iran Between Revolutions* (Princeton, NJ: Princeton University Press, 1982).
2. In an interview with Italian journalist, Oriana Fallaci, Khomeini explained that "Islam does not need adjectives such as democracy... Islam is everything." *New York Times*, October 21, 1979.
3. Whether Khomeini knew about or was involved with the student embassy takeover and hostage crisis is disputed.
4. Barry Lando, *Web of Deceit: The History of Western Complicity in Iraq, from Churchill to Kennedy to George W. Bush* (New York: Other Press, 2007).
5. Ray Takeyh, *Guardians of the Revolution: Iran and the World in the Age of Ayatollahs* (Oxford: Oxford University Press, 2009).
6. The Iranian constitution recognizes religious groups that are monotheistic and emerge from the Abrahamic tradition; that is, Judaism, Christianity, and Islam. Iranians also recognize Zoroastrianism, the first-known monotheistic religious tradition.
7. The constitution specifies that candidates for the office of the president must by *rejal*, a word with an Arabic root. Iranian officials interpret this word to mean "male." The meaning of this word, however, has been disputed by women running for president and others, who suggest that the word refers to the quality of being reasonable or possessing reason, and thus permits women to hold the office of president.
8. In 1985, the Assembly of Experts selected a successor for Khomeini, Ayatollah Montazeri, but in 1989, just months before his passing, Khomeini dismissed Montazeri as his replacement.
9. Richard N. Frye, *The Heritage of Persia* (New York: World Pub. Co., 1963).
10. Arzoo Osanloo, *The Politics of Women's Rights in Iran* (Princeton, NJ: Princeton University Press, 2009).
11. Louise Halper, "Law and Women's Agency in Post-Revolutionary Iran." *Harvard Journal of Law and Gender*, 28 (2005), 6, 85–142.
12. Frances Harrison, "Women Graduates Challenge Iran," *British Broadcast News*, September 19, 2006. http://news.bbc.co.uk/2/hi/middle_east/5359672.stm. Accessed July 19, 2011.
13. Arzoo Osanloo, "Islamico-Civil 'Rights Talk': Women, Subjectivity, and Law in Iranian Family Court," *American Ethnologist*, 33(2) (2006), 191–209.
14. H. E. Chehabi, *Iranian Politics and Religious Modernism: The Liberation Movement of Iran Under the Shah and Khomeini* (Ithaca, NY: Cornell University Press, 1990).
15. Science-Metrix, "30 Years in Science: Secular Movements in Knowledge Creation," 2010, 7. http://www.science-metrix.com/30years-Paper.pdf. Accessed, July 19, 2011.
16. *Iran News,* July 13, 1999.

GLOSSARY

1917 Constitution   created a federal system, checks and balances between the executive and legislative branches of government, and an independent judiciary in Mexico. It also included extensive labor rights and a system of communal land ownership.

1935 Government of India Act   the last and most substantial decentralization of power by the British administration before independence, this act transferred major areas such as agriculture and policing to elected Indian provincial governments, although the British still held ultimate control. Many of its provisions were later voluntarily adopted by India in the 1950 Constitution.

1947 Constitution   the constitution that the Western powers imposed on Japan after World War II and that has governed Japan ever since.

Abacha, Sani   Nigeria's most repressive military dictator, who assumed power in a coup in 1993 and ruled until his death in 1998. Abacha was notorious for brutally repressing political opponents and stealing billions of dollars in government funds.

Abadan Crisis   the result of Iran's decision to nationalize oil resources in 1950. In response, the British oil company AIOC closed the world's largest oil refinery in the city of Abadan, withheld key resources from Iran, and withdrew their employees to keep the country from refining their own oil.

Action Congress of Nigeria (ACN)   a political party with strong support in Lagos and other parts of southwest Nigeria.

Agrarian Party   leftist party that represented Russian peasants. Merged with the ruling United Russia Party in 2008.

All Nigeria People's Party (ANPP)   one of Nigeria's largest opposition parties, it draws most of its support from the predominantly Muslim north of the country. It fielded the runner-up in the 2003 and 2007 presidential elections, former military ruler Muhammadu Buhari.

Amakudari **(descent from heaven)**   practice in which bureaucrats retire from government jobs to high-paying jobs in the industries they had regulated.

Ancien Régime   a term coined during the French Revolution to refer derisively to the "old regime," or the time prior to 1789 when kings ruled with absolute power and where the clergy and nobility were also strong forces in French society.

Anti-Rightist Campaign   in response to the Hundred Flowers Movement, those who had criticized the regime were labeled "rightists" and forced out of their places of work, imprisoned, or forced into hard labor for the next two decades. In one fell swoop, up to 300,000 of China's intellectual class were expelled from politics and society.

Article 9   article in Japan's postwar constitution that eliminated Japan's military and renounced Japan's right to wage war.

Article 48   The article in Germany's Weimar Constitution that allowed the president to bypass the Reichstag and rule by decree during "emergency situations," the nature of which were never properly defined.

Assembly of Experts   a group of 86 Islamic scholars in Iran who select, oversee, and can dismiss the supreme leader.

authoritarian regime   a non-democratic regime that focuses on controlling political pluralism through coercion.

backbenchers   the rank and file Members of Parliament in the UK who do not have a position in the government or a leadership role in an opposition party. Backbenchers literally sit on the back benches in the House of Commons, with the government and lead opposition members sitting in the front benches.

Backward Castes   the broad group of castes in between the upper castes and the untouchables, with around 40–45 percent of the Indian population. Substantial Backward Caste movements have emerged in many states since the 1960s, helped by constitutional

449

provisions that allow job and educational reservations to be set aside for them.

bakufu the central government led by the shogun during the Tokugawa era in Japan.

banlieues literally "suburbs" in French, but more accurately, a shorthand for depressed zones on the peripheries of major cities that have high rates of joblessness and lawlessness, and that are often associated with an elevated population of ethnic minorities.

baojia **system** a system of social accounting in China whereby extended families undertook the responsibility of preparing its members to serve society and state as a whole, and in which entire families were held accountable for individual transgressions of its members.

Basic Law West Germany's founding constitutional document, as well as the constitutional document of contemporary Germany.

basij a volunteer civilian paramilitary group in Iran.

bazaari merchant classes.

Bharatiya Janata Party successor party to the Hindu Nationalist Jana Sangh, which opposed the Congress party in India from the 1950s until it entered the Janata coalition in 1977. The BJP was founded as a separate party in 1980, after the Janata coalition broke up. In the late 1980s, it rapidly increased in influence and it is now the main opposition party to the INC. It headed the NDA coalition governments in New Delhi from 1998–1999 and 1999–2004. It stands for a strong, assertive policy of emphasizing *Hindutva*, or "Hinduness" in politics, and is often seen as hostile to minorities.

Bill of Rights drawn up in 1688 following the "Glorious Revolution"—restricted the monarch and granted English citizens right to elect representatives, carry arms, and be free of royal taxation.

Bismarck, Otto von Prussian leader who first unified Germany and served as chancellor for more than two decades in the Second Reich.

Bundesrat the upper house of the German parliament that represents the interests of the 16 federal states.

Bundestag the lower house of the German parliament. Its members elect the chancellor.

Burakumin Japan's largest minority group (approximately 2–3 million people). Somewhat like the old "untouchable" castes in India, Burakumin—despite looking exactly like other Japanese—tend to face significant discrimination in Japan.

Cabinet the ministers of the government of the UK, chosen by the prime minister from Members of Parliament. The Cabinet takes collective responsibility for all decisions of government.

caste system word for the hierarchical Hindu social and religious system, through which Hindus are split up into broad caste categories of priests, warriors, merchants, and those who serve them, as well as hundreds of smaller occupational and ritual castes (*jati*) within each of these categories. The system has many local and regional variations, and also exists also among the Muslim, Christian, and Sikh minorities, even though those religions formally renounce caste inequalities.

Caucasus Mountains region named for a range of steep mountains stretching from the Black Sea in the west to the Caspian Sea in the east. The Caucasus Mountains mark the border between the Russian Federation in the north and Georgia and Azerbaijan to the south. A region of tremendous ethnic, linguistic, and religious diversity.

caudillos the name given to strongmen whose power was based on control of a personal army.

Century of Humiliation (*bainian guochi*) A period between the mid-nineteenth and the mid-twentieth century, during which China suffered repeated military defeats from a number of European colonial powers and Japan, which resulted in several sovereign "spheres of influence" by foreigners on Chinese soil.

chador a long tent-like garment, usually black, that covers a woman from head to toe, leaving only the face and hands exposed. Today, it is the dress of some conservative women and government officials in Iran.

Chamber of Deputies lower house of the legislature in Mexico. It is composed of 500 members directly elected by the citizens; 300 of them are elected in single-member districts and 200 are elected through proportional representation.

Chartist movement a nineteenth-century social movement demanding political and social rights for workers that engaged in peaceful mass protest.

Chechnya region in the north Caucasus area of Russia. Site of two wars in the post-communist era.

Chinese Communist Party (CCP) the Leninist single-party apparatus and single most powerful institution in China since 1949.

Chinese Republic established in 1912 to replace the imperial system, ruled by the Nationalist Party. When Nationalist forces fled the mainland following their defeat by the Communists in 1949, it was reestablished on the island of Taiwan.

Church of England the established state church, with the monarch as its head. Created by Henry VIII in a split from the Roman Catholic Church. In contrast to the separation between church and state in the United States, in Britain there is an official church.

civil war armed combat within the boundaries of a sovereign state between parties that are subject to common authority at the start of hostilities.

class-consciousness an individuals' self-awareness of the political implications of belonging to a particular economic class.

coalition governments governments comprised of more than one political party, each of which holds at least one cabinet ministry.

co-determination German law requiring that companies with more than 500 employees allow workers to be represented on their board of directors.

cohabitation when the president and the majority in the National Assembly of Mexico (and, thus, the prime minister) come from political parties on opposite sides of the political divide.

collective action problem a situation wherein each individual has incentives not to participate in an action that benefits all members of the group.

Committee on State Security (KGB) known by its Russian acronym, KGB, the Committee on State Security was responsible for both domestic and international security and intelligence. A massive organization analogous to the U.S. FBI and CIA combined.

communism a political doctrine which holds that the wealthy exploit workers and the poor under capitalist economic systems; that economic wealth should be redistributed as much as possible; and that a single, vanguard political party should direct the government and control the state.

Communist Party of the Russian Federation (CPRF) successor to the Communist Party of the Soviet Union. A left nationalist political party that has formed the principal opposition for most of the post-communist era.

comparative method an approach to building arguments that involves comparing and contrasting cases (a set of countries, for example) that share attributes or characteristics but differ on the outcome you're exploring—or that have a variety of attributes but experience the same outcome.

comparative politics the systematic search for answers to political questions about how people around the world make and contest authoritative public choices.

Confucianism the basic philosophy and organizing principle of traditional China in which "right conduct" was the most important goal for individuals and representatives of the state.

Conservative Party emerging from the Tory Party in 1834, the Conservative Party has long been associated for supporting the monarch and the Church of England. A party long supported by traditional elites, it generally advocates for lower taxes and smaller government.

conservative political interests an attitude that favors preserving things the way they are, or even reversing recent political changes.

Constitutional Council the body of the judiciary tasked with reviewing legislation (when requested) to ensure that it conforms to the constitution.

constitutional dictatorship strong rule by one or more leaders who are nominally constrained by a written constitution approved by the people through their representatives.

constitutional monarchy a democratic system in which a king, queen, or emperor serves as head of state, symbolically embodying the culture and values of a state's citizens and history, yet operates under the rules and constraints imposed by a written constitution.

constructivism assumes that political identities are malleable, even if they often appear to be primordial, and suggests that we think of identity as an evolving political process rather than as a fixed set of identity categories.

constructive vote of no confidence parliamentary vote that can withdraw confidence in, and thereby terminate, a government only if a prospective successor has majority support.

corporatism a pattern of interest group mobilization in which the state plays an active role in organizing and mediating between groups.

Council of the Guardians a group of 12 senior scholars of Islamic jurisprudence and civil law who determine whether the laws and actions of government officials are in conformity with Islamic principles.

criollos word used to describe those born in New Spain or Mexico, from Spanish parents.

cross-cutting cleavages social divisions which do not generally coincide with one another. For example, members of the Yoruba ethnic group in Nigeria are divided nearly equally between Muslim and Christian religious affiliations.

cultural identity attachments based on non-economic associations, based on a understanding of common heritage.

Dalits literally, "the oppressed." A modern and more politically acceptable name for the ex-untouchable Scheduled Castes, this term is used especially by SC activists and politically aware scholars and activists.

danwei the *danwei*, or "work unit" was traditionally the lowest form of government in China, as well as a way to organize the populace. *Danwei* were made up of the workers and their leaders in a given factory, school, etc. It was the *danwei* that issued the *hukou* and "iron rice bowl" benefits. In terms of organizing society in China today, the role of *danwei* have declined dramatically.

decolonization the process of peaceful abandonment of the British Empire, permitting colonies to become independent states. Most immigrants to Britain post–1945 came from these colonies.

democracy a political regime that allows for government accountability to all citizens through institutionalized participation and contestation.

Democratic Party of Japan (DPJ) Japan's leading opposition party after 1997. Defeated the LDP in the 2007 House of Councillors election and the 2009 House of Representatives election.

devolution the process of creating parliaments in Scotland, Wales, and Northern Ireland, with their own elections, and some tax-setting powers. Can legislate in all areas not reserved to the UK Parliament.

Diet Japan's parliament.

dirigisme an economic strategy that involves the state providing significant leadership in the capitalist economy through policies such as indicative plans and selective support for favored industries.

divided government a situation where the legislature and the executive are held by different parties, making agreement across party lines necessary in order to pass any legislation.

Duma lower house of the Russian parliament, consisting of 450 representatives elected on a single national list proportional representation basis.

early-forming state a state that managed to consolidate sovereignty centuries ago.

East India Company (EIC) private British trading company established in 1600, which expanded through conquest and British military support after the 1750s to administer most of India. As a result of the 1857 mutiny and rebellion, its charter was ended and Indian administration was taken over directly by the British government.

economic development sustained increase in the standard of living of a country's population, resulting from changes and improvements in education, infrastructure, and technology.

electoral system the political institutions that translate citizens' votes into legislative seats and/or control of a directly elected executive.

electorate a group of citizens eligible to participate in the election of government leaders.

elite parties political parties that provide a vehicle to office for leaders without having a mass organization in the country.

Estates-General a meeting of representatives from the clergy, the nobility, and the middle classes in the *Ancien Régime*, it was last convoked in 1789 by Louis XVI in an effort to stave off resistance to higher taxes.

ethnicity a group of people who share an understanding of a common heritage based on religion, language, territory, or family ties.

failed state a state where sovereignty has collapsed or was never effectively established.

fascism a totalitarian ideology often based in racist principles that glorified militarism, violence, nationalism, and the state over individual interests and identities, and that emphasized the importance of charismatic individual political leaders.

fatwa an Islamic legal ruling.

federal character principle the constitutional requirement that a candidate must win not only the most votes but also a quarter of the votes in at least two-thirds of Nigeria's states in order to win the presidency.

Federal Constitutional Court The highest court in Germany, established by the Basic Law and responsible for judicial review.

Federal Electoral Institute (IFE) institution created in 1990 that is in charge of organizing elections in Mexico and guaranteeing their fairness.

Federal Republic of Germany (FRG) The official name for both West Germany during the period of German division, and for unified Germany after 1990.

Federal Security Service (FSB) the principal domestic security agency in Russia. Analogous to the FBI in the United States.

federal system a state in which the constitution grants two or more governments overlapping political authority over the same group of people and same piece of territory.

Federation Council upper house of the Russian parliament, consisting of two representatives of each region, one appointed by the regional governor and one by the regional parliament.

Fifth Republic the current political regime of France, established by the Constitution of 1958.

fiqh Islamic jurisprudence derived from sacred sources, such as the Quran.

First Employment Contract the 2006 proposal in France to make it easier for employers to fire young workers during the first two years of their employment; designed to encourage firms to hire more workers, it instead sparked tremendous opposition that resulted in massive demonstrations and eventually the repeal of the law.

First Republic Nigeria's first period of democratic governance from 1960 to 1966. Characterized by intense regional disagreements, it ended in a coup and was followed by more than a decade of military rule.

foreign direct investment the purchase or creation of assets in one country by an individual, firm, or government based in a different country.

Fourth Republic Nigeria's current political regime, in place since the adoption of the 1999 constitution.

Fourth Republic the French political regime that lasted from 1946–1958. It was characterized by leadership by political parties, and by great political instability. It launched France's postwar economic recovery and fostered good relations with Germany and Europe, but fell due to its inability to deal with colonial crises, such as the Algerian War.

Free-market principles an economic system in which private individuals and firms (rather than the government) own and have rights to make all decisions about buying and selling property.

French Communist Party (PCF) France's main party of the far left. Its fortunes have declined precipitously since its heyday in the immediate post–World War II era. Even though it has moderated its platform significantly, it has received well less than 10 percent of the popular vote in recent years and holds only a handful of seats in the National Assembly.

***Frente Democrático Nacional* (FDN)** coalition of left-wing parties and movements that got together to support the candidacy of Lázaro Cárdenas in the 1988 presidential election. Many of the groups that formed the FDN would go on to establish the PRD.

Gandhi, Mohandas K. the inspirational architect of non-violent resistance to colonial rule, this often unpredictable leader helped transform Congress into a mass party in the 1920s, and was the conscience of the nationalist campaign until his assassination by a Hindu nationalist militant in January 1948.

Gandhi, Indira daughter of Jawaharlal Nehru, she became prime minister in 1967 three years after her father's death, but her conflicts with party leaders led to a major split in the party in 1969. After her crushing electoral victory in 1971, she led the Congress Party and the country from 1971–1977 and 1980 until her assassination in 1984. But, despite her many successes, her rule is associated with the "emergency" of 1975–1977, during which her political opponents were arrested and detained without trial. Gandhi was not related to Mahatma Gandhi: Indira Nehru became Indira Gandhi on her marriage to Feroze Gandhi.

Gandhi, Sonia current president of the Congress Party and the chairperson of the United Progressive Alliance (UPA) coalition, which Congress leads.

gender a concept used to distinguish the social and cultural characteristics associated with femininity and masculinity from the biological features associated with sex, such as male or female reproductive organs.

German Democratic Republic (GDR) The official name of East Germany, the communist state that existed from 1949 to 1990 before the fall of the Berlin Wall.

glasnost Russian word meaning "openness," used by the last Soviet president, Mikhail Gorbachev, as a slogan for his political reforms.

globalization the increase in the scope and extent of political, economic, and cultural connections between governments, organizations, and individuals across state borders.

Government the organization that has the authority to act on behalf of a state, and the right to make decisions that affect everyone in a state.

grandes écoles the elite, highly selective, specialized universities in France that train many of the country's upper echelon of civil servants, politicians, and business leaders.

Great Leap Forward (1958–1961) Mao's attempt to transform China into an agricultural exporter and industrial powerhouse in three years by combining traditional and modern industrial techniques simultaneously in the cities and in the countryside. The political pressure for subordinates to inflate production figures led to widespread famine and starvation in which 30 million people died.

Great Proletarian Cultural Revolution (1966–1976) Mao's final attempt to counteract what he saw as the bureaucratization of the revolution, by purging and killing many top leaders, training a new generation of revolutionary successors known as the Red Guards. The latent violence erupted at the very beginning, causing events to spiral increasingly out of control until Mao had to bring in the military to restore order.

Great October Socialist Revolution Soviet name for the Bolshevik seizure of power in October 1917 that led to communist rule and the creation of the Soviet Union.

Green Revolution term used to describe the introduction of high-yield varieties (HYVs) of wheat and rice in the 1960s, especially in Punjab and Haryana. These new varieties, together with the increased use of fertilizer, mechanization, and irrigation, led to India becoming self-sufficient in these important foods.

guestworkers (*Gastarbeiter*) Workers from southern Europe and Turkey who, as part of government policy, were invited to settle temporarily during the economic boom of the 1950s and 1960s. Many stayed permanently, and thereby changed the ethnic complexion of German society.

hardliner one who believes that the government of Iran should be beholden to a strict interpretation of Islamic principles and that government should inform the people of their rights and duties accordingly. Hardliners push for institutional structures that prioritize non-elected over elected bodies and see social control as the key element in bring about a moral order.

Hausa one of Nigeria's three main ethnic groups and the dominant group in the north of the country.

Head of state the symbolic embodiment of the culture and values of a state's citizens and history, typically a monarch or appointed honorary president who has little authority.

Hinduism majority religion in India, with 81 percent of the population. Drawing inspiration from Sanskrit and Pali texts thousands of years old, this religion is polytheistic and highly diverse in terms of its leadership and regional differences in theology and practice.

Hookoomat-e Islami Islamic government; a theory of Islamic governance put forth by Ayatollah Khomeini.

House of Commons the lower chamber of Parliament in the UK. Currently comprised of 650 Members of Parliament. Has power to legislate, amend, and pass bills. The party with the most seats in Parliament forms government.

House of Councillors (HC) the upper house of the Japanese Diet. Members serve fixed six-year terms.

House of Lords the upper chamber of Parliament in the UK. Comprised of appointed and hereditary members. Has lost power to veto bills and now can only delay legislation.

House of Representatives the more powerful of the two chambers of the National Assembly in Mexico, it has 360 directly elected members.

House of Representatives (HR) the lower (and more powerful) house of the Japanese Diet. Members of the HR serve four-year terms, although elections may be called anytime during those four years.

hukou a means of population control through residency permits that originated during the Mao era in China. Housing, medical benefits, and food purchases are all tied to the *hukou*, thereby making it impossible for non-*hukou*-wielding citizens to live in the cities. Although the restrictions eased in the 1980s to allow labor markets to flourish, certain benefits (such as public education) are still tied to the *hukou*.

Hundred Flowers Movement a short-lived movement in which Mao sought to provide Chinese citizens a channel to articulate their grievances ("let a hundred flowers bloom and let one hundred schools of thought contend"). When criticisms began to call for the dismantling of the CCP and for Mao to step down, the movement was quickly and unceremoniously quashed in June 1957.

Iabloko the leading left of center liberal political party in the post-communist era. The name is an acronym taken from the names of the party's founders and means "apple."

Ibo (Igbo) one of the country's three main ethnic groups and the dominant group in the southeast of Nigeria. The majority Ibo territory of Biafra declared independence in 1967, but was defeated in 1970.

Indian Administrative Service (IAS) the most elite and prestigious all-India civil service, the IAS staffs virtually all the most senior positions in state and central governments, as well as many state enterprises. It is recruited mainly through a national and very competitive annual examination, though some places in each state's IAS "cadre" are also reserved for promotees from the state's own civil service.

Indian National Congress the dominant political party in India from 1885 until the present. Founded as an elite organization devoted to greater Indian representation in government, it was transformed by Gandhi and Nehru in the 1920s into a mass organization demanding self-government for India, and in the late 1930s into a mass political party that won independence in 1947.

Indian Police Service (IPS) the elite all-India Police Service, which parallels the IAS, staffing the most important police positions in the states and at the Centre.

indirect rule a form of colonial governance, most commonly used by the British, in which traditional leaders are incorporated into the system of colonial administration.

industrial policy Japan's governmental approach to promoting economic growth and internationally competitive businesses. Especially in the 1950s and 1960s, the Japanese government bureaucracy shifted resources and provided regulatory advantages to specific firms in industries that it wanted Japan to become internationally competitive.

informal constitution the collection of statute law, treaties, precedent, custom, and legal interpretations that constitute the UK's equivalent of the formal legal constitution. The absence of a formal constitution allows for effective government.

informal economy the sector of an economy that is not monitored or taxed by the government. In many developing countries, the informal economy can be larger than the formal sector.

insider privatization the transfer of state-owned assets and companies into the hands of government or company insiders, often by illicit or underhand means.

interest groups organized groups of citizens who seek to ensure that the state enacts or follows particular policies.

interventionist state the central government allocates resources, sets prices, makes investment decisions, and owns most of the country's productive industries and/or resources.

iron rice bowl (*tian fanwan*) in pre-reform China, workers received very low wages but were promised minimum benefits that kept them from starvation. Benefits included housing, medical care, education, and other basic services. In the 1980s and 1990s, workers were asked to part with many of these benefits while new workers were hired at higher wages but without "iron rice bowl" benefits.

ius sanguinis policy of determining citizenship through ancestry rather than through birthplace.

ius soli policy of determining citizenship by birthplace, rather than through ancestry.

Jammu and Kashmir India's only Muslim-majority state. Formerly ruled by a Hindu maharajah, the state delayed joining India or Pakistan in 1947, precipitating a Pakistani attempt to take the state by force. India rushed troops to Kashmir in October 1947 when the maharajah hurriedly decided to accede to India, leading to the first India–Pakistan conflict. India has held on to most of the state since then, but it has faced periodic political unrest and militant campaigns in the state, supported by Pakistan, and conflicts between India and Pakistan have led to declared war three times and to undeclared fighting on several more occasions.

Janata Party the loose coalition of parties that came together to defeat Indira Gandhi in a massive rebuke to her "emergency" rule after elections were called in 1977. One part of this coalition survived as the Janata Party after the coalition broke up in 1979, as a center-left coalition representing especially the middle and lower castes. This party subsequently split several times.

Japan Socialist Party (JSP) Japan's largest opposition party from 1955 through 1993.

Jinnah, Mohammad Ali the dominant leader of India's Muslim community from the early 1930s, the president of the All India Muslim League, and the first leader of Pakistan, which he led until his death.

judicial review the ability of a country's high court to invalidate laws that the legislature has enacted by declaring them unconstitutional.

junta a group of leaders of a military regime.

Kai-shek, Chiang Sun Yat-sen's successor as leader of the Nationalist Party from 1925 until his death in 1975. Chiang represented the more conservative, military wing of the Nationalist Party and was a staunch anti-communist.

keiretsu a network of interlocking firms that share their own central bank.

kōenkai Japanese politicians' personal support organizations that mobilize support for individual candidates.

Labour Party founded in 1895, the Labour Party advocated on behalf of the newly enfranchised working classes and the poor in Britain. By 1945, it had replaced the Liberals as the main opposition party to the Conservatives. It advocates extensive social policies and a powerful role for government.

laïcité secularism, or the principle of separation of church and state in France.

l'alternance literally "the alternation" in French; the shift in power from the right to the left that took place for the first time after the 1981 elections; left parties accepted the political institutions of the Fifth Republic once they came to power.

late-forming state a state that only consolidated sovereignty in recent decades.

leadership small groups groups of top State Council and other officials in China that head a given *xitong*. These groups often step in to make decisions when *xitong* are unable to resolve a problem that arises between their member bureaucracies. Some leadership small groups are more fluid, while others have become increasingly institutionalized over time.

Liberal Democratic Party (LDP) political party that dominated Japan's government for all but 11 months from 1955 until 2009.

Liberal Democratic Party (LDPR) nationalist party that has enjoyed a close relationship with the Kremlin throughout the post-communist era.

Liberal Party emerging form the Whig Party in 1859, the Liberal Party represented urban interests and the middle classes in Britain. It advocated social reform and for the extension of political rights. It is a predecessor to the contemporary Liberal Democrats.

liberal political interests an attitude favoring gradual political change.

Länder the 16 political units, or states, that form the Federal Republic of Germany (FRG).

Magna Carta the original "constitutional" document of British government. Signed in 1215 between King John and barons, setting out limits on the monarch and establishing civil rights.

Majlis parliament in Iran.

majority rule an electoral system which requires candidates to win an actual majority of 50 percent +1 of the votes in an electoral district to win.

malapportionment in Japan, many rural districts got more representation than they deserved according to population and other urban districts got less representation than they deserved. Under SNTV electoral rules in Japan, some urban districts held five times as many voters per seat than some rural ones, but this was reduced substantially in the new system.

May Fourth Movement refers to the mobilization of Chinese citizens seeking ways to increase China's wealth and stature on the world stage; so called because on May 4, 1919, Chinese students, intellectuals, and others filled Tiananmen Square to protest the ceding to Japan (instead of the returning to China) of several Chinese territories hitherto held by Germany.

Meiji oligarchs small group of men who directed the emperor and played the central role in the Japanese government in the aftermath of the Meiji Restoration.

Meiji Restoration 1868 revolution led by samurai who "restored" power to Emperor Meiji and created a new governmental system centralized around him that exerted power throughout the country.

mellat nation.

Members of Parliament (MPs) typically, refers to members of House of Commons in Britain, each elected as the single representative of a geographical constituency through "first past the post" voting.

mestizaje project espoused by the Mexican government that promoted the integration of Mexico's Indians into national life and suggested that all Mexicans belonged to a single, *mestizo* race.

mestizo word used to describe those of mixed Indigenous and Spanish descent.

Mexican–American War armed conflict between Mexico and the United States over the territory of Texas, which was annexed by the United States in 1845. The conflict started in 1846 and ended in 1848 with the Treaty of Guadalupe Hidalgo.

Mexican Miracle term used to refer to the years between 1940 and 1970 when the Mexican economy grew at 6 percent per year on average, based on a strategy that called for heavy state intervention in the economy.

Mexican Revolution after Porfirio Díaz reneged on his promise to hold free elections in 1911, Francisco Madero led a revolt against his dictatorial rule. The armed insurrection included a diversity of groups and demands, including a mostly peasant movement in the south, as well as armies in the north that fought for labor rights and political reform.

Military Affairs Committee (MAC) the Military Affairs Commission is the group through which the Chinese Communist Party controls the military. The chairman of the MAC is (with the one exception of Deng Xiaoping in the 1980s) the CCP general secretary.

military regime a non-democratic system ruled by top members of the armed forces. In such systems, the selectorate is typically limited to the highest ranks of the officer corps.

mixed electoral system an electoral system that combines a plurality or majority electoral rule to elect some members of the national legislature, while a proportional representation electoral rule is used to elect the remainder.

monarch the king or queen of England. Before 1688, had near absolute power to collect taxes, raise armies, and dissolve Parliament. Since that date, the monarchs have been limited by the Bill of Rights and their powers today are negligible.

monarchy a non-democratic system in which rulers assume power via birthright and are not removed from power until they die.

Movement for the Survival of the Ogoni People (MOSOP) a group founded in 1990 by Ogoni political activists to oppose land expropriation and pollution resulting from oil extraction in the Niger Delta. Abacha's government executed nine of its leaders in 1994, drawing widespread international condemnation.

Mughal Empire founded by Babur in 1526, the Mughal territories expanded to incorporate most of South Asia, and the empire reached its peak from the mid-sixteenth to the late-seventeenth centuries, before declining rapidly after the death of Emperor Aurangzeb in 1707 and breaking up in 1720.

***Mujahedin-e Khalq (MEK)* or the People's Mujahedin** Marxist, nationalist, Islamic political party, mounted armed rebellion, banned and in exile.

multinational corporations (MNCs) firms that are headquartered in one country but that have operations and employees in many others.

Muslim League established in 1906, this elite-run association and later political party promoted Muslim interests and, from the early 1940s under its leader M. A. Jinnah, the formation of the state of Pakistan as a solution to the problem of how to protect Muslim interests in a Hindu-majority country.

Nashi (Ours) a state-sponsored national patriotic youth movement closely associated with former Russian President Vladimir Putin.

nation a form of political identity—a cultural grouping of individuals who associate with each other based on collectively held political identity.

National Action Party (PAN) founded in 1939 by a group of conservative businessmen and intellectuals, in part as a reaction to the left-wing policies of President Lázaro Cárdenas (1934–1940). In 2000, a member of the party, Vicente Fox, was elected president of Mexico.

National Assembly the lower house of parliament in France; its members are directly elected by the citizens; it supports but can also vote to remove the prime minister.

National Assembly Nigeria's national legislature, modeled after the U.S. Congress. The body is composed of a Senate with equal representation for all of Nigeria's states, and a House of Representatives with proportional representation.

National Democratic Front Iranian leftist political party founded in 1979 to offer secular opposition to Islamic parties, went underground in 1981.

National Front In Iran, a coalition of parties that support secular democracy and nationalization of oil.

National Front (FN) France's most significant far-right party. Founded in 1972, it rose dramatically in influence beginning in the mid-1980s. Led until 2011 by Jean-Marie Le Pen, it is staunchly anti-immigrant. Although not a force in the National Assembly, it receives significant percentages of the vote in a number of regions and local communities and has had a significant impact on the national political discourse.

Nationalist Party (*Guomingdang* or *Kuomingtang*) the ruling political party of mainland China until 1949, after which members fled to Taiwan.

Natural resource curse the theory that countries with natural resources find it harder to develop economically and tend to be more authoritarian.

Nazism The ideology of the Adolf Hitler and the Nazi Party. A racial version of Fascism that places the "Aryans" at the top of the racial hierarchy and demands that they conquer and eliminate lesser races in their quest for more living space.

Nehru, Jawaharlal one of the major Congress Party leaders in the fight for freedom, and independent India's first prime minister from 1947 to his death in 1964.

Neighborhood effect The positive impact on the probability of a regime change to democracy of having a geographic neighbor that is a democracy.

Niger Delta an oil-rich region in the south of Nigeria, which has suffered from severe pollution related to the extraction of oil and years of fighting between insurgents and government forces.

nomenklatura the appointment system of leading officials in Leninist systems, *nomenklatura* appointments demonstrate the monopoly power of the Party Organization Department in putting politically reliable cadres into positions of power throughout the state apparatus.

Non-democracy a system in which rulers are not accountable to the ruled because rulers restrict political participation and contestation.

no re-election clause the 1917 Constitution prohibited the re-election of the president and a reform in 1933 extended this prohibition to include members of the legislature and elected officials at the state and local levels.

North American Free Trade Agreement (NAFTA) an agreement signed in 1994 that sought to remove most barriers to trade and investment, including tariffs, quotas, and licensing requirements, between Mexico, the United States, and Canada.

Obasanjo, Olusegun military ruler of Nigeria from 1976 to 1979 and elected president in 1999 until 2007, he oversaw the country's first peaceful transition of power in 1979, though his commitment to free and fair political competition was questioned during his time as president.

oligarchs the name given in Russia in the 1990s to a small group of businessmen who used connections to state officials to enrich themselves and then to take control of the state itself.

oligarchy a non-democratic system of "rule by the few." The selectorate consists of a small social, economic, or political elite. Criteria for membership are often informal, as are the group's rules for leadership selection.

Operation Ajax 1953 CIA covert coup d'état that toppled Iran's Prime Minister Mohammad Mossadeq, who was responsible for nationalizing Iran's oil.

Other Russia a loose alliance of opposition parties and movements ranging from neo-fascist to liberal opponents of the existing political system in Russia. Closely associated with former World Chess Champion Garry Kasparov.

panchayat previously referred to representative village assemblies, now refers mainly to elected local governments, to which many development tasks have been decentralized since the passage of constitutional amendments in the 1990s.

Parliamentary sovereignty principle that all power in the UK comes from Parliament. In actuality, this means that the majority party in Parliament has sovereignty and can legislate and execute policies at will.

parliamentary supremacy a democratic system in which the legislature holds supreme political authority—no court can overrule legislation that it passes.

parliamentary system a democratic constitutional design in which voters only elect a legislature, and in which the legislature (parliament) itself elects the executive to head the government.

Partido Revolucionario Institucional (PRI) founded in 1929 in the aftermath of the Mexican Revolution and would grow to dominate Mexican politics throughout the twentieth century. Although it lost the presidency in 2000, it remains an important player in state and national politics.

Party of the Democratic Revolution left-wing party founded in 1989 in Mexico by a group of dissident members of the PRI. Although it has never won the presidency, the party governs several states and is, with the PRI and the PAN, one of the three largest parties in Congress.

party system the typical pattern of political competition and cooperation between parties within a state.

pasdaran see Revolutionary Guard.

Patel, Sardar Vallabhbhai the "Iron-Man" of the Congress Party organization and independent India's first home minister in charge of law and order at the federal level. Together with Gandhi and Nehru, one of the main three leaders of the Congress Party during the final days of the independence struggle.

People's Democratic Party (PDP) Nigeria's dominant party since the reestablishment of democratic elections in 1999; its candidates have won all four presidential elections since then and have continuously held a majority in the National Assembly.

People's Republic of China   the current regime of China which is led by the Chinese Communist Party.

perestroika   Russian word meaning "restructuring," used by the last Soviet president, Mikhail Gorbachev, as a slogan for his economic reforms.

per capita gross domestic product (GDP)   the average citizen's yearly income.

Persian Constitutional Revolution   the revolution in Iran (1906–1911) that provided the basis for representative government by establishing a parliament and reducing the power of the monarchy—the first of its kind in Asia.

Persian corridor   the railway supply line connecting southern Soviet Union to Iran during World War II.

personalistic regime   a non-democratic system built around the glorification and empowerment of a single individual. The key characteristic of personalistic regimes is a lack of clear rules governing politics.

personal vote   for years, most politicians (especially from the LDP) in Japan drummed up electoral support through their personal popularity and individual efforts to aid constituents, rather than on ideological or policy appeals.

pluralism   in which interest group mobilize and organize societal interests freely, in a decentralized fashion.

plurality rule   an electoral system in which the candidate who receives the largest share of the votes in the electoral district wins the seat, even if that share is less than a majority of 50 percent +1 of the votes.

Political Bureau of the Chinese Communist Party (Politburo)   the highest-ranking institution of the Chinese state, which includes the head of the party (the general secretary), the head of the government (the premier), and the most important individuals in the Chinese state. Its standing committee is the highest deliberative body in the land.

political cleavage   a salient dimension of political conflict and competition within a given society, such as religion, ethnicity, or ideology.

political economy   the study of the relationship between economics and politics.

political party   a group of people who have organized to attain and hold political power.

political patronage   the distribution of state resources, such as government jobs or private goods, to ordinary citizens in exchange for their political support.

political violence   the use of force by states or non-state actors to achieve political goals.

post-materialism   a set of values that emphasizes goals such as personal freedom, environmental preservation, aesthetics, and anti-racism over material values such as economic and national security.

postwar settlement   collection of tacit and official agreements between labor and capital that were designed to ameliorate the class cleavage and that underpin postwar Germany's economic system.

prefecture   Japan's largest administrative subunit (akin to states in the United States, but with much less independent power).

president   the chief executive in a presidential system, directly elected by the voters.

presidential system   a democratic constitutional design in which voters directly elect a legislature as well as an executive.

President's Rule   emergency clauses in the Indian Constitution giving the central government the right to suspend state governments and administer states in case of financial or security emergencies. These controversial clauses were widely abused in the 1960s, 1970s, and 1980s, but in recent years, except in Kashmir, they have been used much less often.

prime minister   the chief executive in a parliamentary system, elected by the members of parliament.

Prime Minister's Questions   a weekly occurrence in the UK while Parliament is in session during which the prime minister must face questions on policy from both the opposition and their own party.

primordialism   assumes that identity is something people are born with or that emerges through deep psychological processes in early childhood, given one's family and community context.

proportional representation   an electoral system that gives legislative seats to parties in proportion to the votes they receive in each district.

Rape of Nanjing   the mass murder and torture of between 200,000 and 400,000 Chinese civilians by the Japanese during WWII in Nanjing; the event continues to strain Sino-Japanese relations today.

Raj   literally rule, administration, but often used as a general term for the period of British rule in India from 1757–1947.

reciprocal accountability government officials are accountable to the party leaders who hire and promote them, but party leaders are also accountable to the government officials in the Central Committee selectorate who choose them.

Reform Acts a series of acts between 1832 and 1928 that increased the voting franchise of the UK from less than 5 percent of men to all adults over the age of 18.

reformist one who believes that government should consider many possible forms of governance, including, but not limited to, Islamic principles, and which answers to the needs of the people. Reformists support institutional bodies of elected officials over non-elected bodies, and aim to limit the power of the state in shaping social relations.

regime change a transition between democratic and non-democratic forms of government.

Reichstag The term for the legislative assembly under both the Second Reich and the Weimar Republic.

reinforcing cleavages divisions in society, such as ethnic, religious, or economic distinctions, which coincide with one another. For example, ethnic and religious identities coincide to a great extent in northern Nigeria.

rentier state state in which revenues do not accrue from the citizens, but rather from rents paid by external client states on use and exploitation of natural resources.

rent-seeking manipulating the economic environment in order to capture economic "rents," created when the state directly receives income from selling goods, like oil, at levels above their production costs.

republic a form of government that relies on rule by the people through their representatives.

repertoire of collective action the most common type of protest actions undertaken within a country in a given time period.

Republic of Biafra a majority Ibo state in the southeast of Nigeria that seceded from the remainder of the country in 1967; it was reabsorbed into Nigeria in 1970, after a brutal civil war that killed more than a million people.

reservations system the proportional system through which lower castes and tribals are allocated jobs and educational positions in government employment. The system was significantly expanded in the 1990s to include Backward Castes and some religious minorities, as well as the Scheduled Castes and Scheduled Tribes, for whom it had been established in 1950.

resolution of no-confidence initiated by the National Assembly of France, a successful resolution of no-confidence involves a majority of the members voting against the government and requires the government to fall.

resource curse the observation that countries with an abundance of natural resources often perform worse in terms of economic development and good governance than countries without these resources.

Revolutionary Guard or *Pasdaran* branch of military founded after the revolution in Iran to advance Islamic revolutionary principles and to prevent internal dissent by enforcing moral codes.

revolutions armed conflict between insurgents and forces of a state in which the insurgents win and impose wholesale political change.

Right Cause a leading right wing political party in the post-communist era in Russia. Despite taking its name from a Stalin era slogan, Right Cause embraces a pro-business ideology has been closely associated with key oligarchs and pro-market factions in the Russian government.

samurai warriors who ultimately became bureaucrats during the Tokugawa era in Japan.

Saro-Wiwo, Ken Nigerian author and one of the founders of the Movement for the Survival of the Ogoni People (MOSOP); he was one of the "Ogoni Nine" executed by the government in 1995.

Scheduled Castes those castes included on central and state "schedules" (lists) of the most discriminated against castes, those traditionally treated as "untouchable" by upper-caste Hindus. Castes listed as SC are eligible for special reserved places in government employment, schools, and colleges.

Scheduled Tribes tribal peoples recognized by the government in schedules similar to those for the SCs and, like the SCs, eligible for special reserved places in government employment, schools, and colleges. Unlike SCs, who are spread across the country, tribals are heavily concentrated in a few states, such as Jharkhand, Orissa, and states in the northeast of the country.

Scramble for Africa the extension of European colonial empires throughout Africa in the late nineteenth and early twentieth century.

Second Republic the democratic institutions in place between 1979 and a military coup in 1983 in Nigeria; the regime was modeled on the American system of government.

selectorate small subset of the national population that chooses and removes the leader or leaders.

self-defense forces Japan's de facto military.

semi-presidential political system with a directly elected president and a government headed by a prime minister who is responsible to an elected parliament.

semi-presidential system a democratic constitutional design in which the president and prime minister share executive authority.

semi-presidentialism the organization of political power in Fifth Republic France; a democratic constitutional design in which the president and parliament enjoy separation of origin but only the president enjoys separation of survival.

Sénat the indirectly elected upper house of parliament in France; it can delay but cannot block legislation and cannot remove either the president or the prime minister.

shah title of an Iranian monarch.

Shari'a Islamic legal principles.

Sharia law religious Islamic law, which has been adopted in several northern Nigerian states source of tension that has resulted in religious riots in a number of northern towns.

Shatt al-Arab (Arabic) or Arvand Rud (Persian) a river whose southern end flows into the Persian Gulf and forms the border between Iran and Iraq.

Shi'i the second largest denomination in Islam that follows the succession of the Prophet Mohammad through family members.

shock therapy a program of rapid economic liberalization intended to introduce market mechanisms in place of state control.

shogun generalissimo or supreme military ruler who led Japan (1603–1868).

Sikhism founded by Guru Nanak (1465–1539) in the Punjab, and formalized by nine subsequent leaders, Sikhism is a monotheistic religion that combines elements of Hinduism and Islam, and whose male adherents—all named "Singh" or lion—typically signify their membership through practices such as wearing their hair uncut (under a turban), wearing a steel bangle, and carrying a small knife (*kirpan*).

Singh, Manmohan Oxford-trained economist who initiated India's economic reforms as finance minister in the 1990s, and was chosen by Sonia Gandhi after Congress' victory in 2004 to become prime minister. Reelected as a result of the Congress–UPA victory in 2009.

single non-transferable vote (SNTV) system in multi-member districts: Japan's House of Representatives electoral system from 1947–1993. Voters cast ballots for individual candidates in electoral districts. Most districts held three, four, or five seats. In each district, those candidates (up to the number of seats in the district) who received the most votes were awarded the seats.

single-party regime a non-democratic system in which one political party dominates all government institutions and restricts political competition to perpetuate itself in power.

Social Democratic Party One of Germany's largest political parties, founded in 1860 to represent the interests of the working class.

Socialist Party (PS) the biggest center-left party in France. Its long-time leader François Mitterrand was the first left-of-center president in the Fifth Republic. The election of the PS in 1981 has been called *l'alternance*.

social movement organized, sustained, and collective efforts that make claims on behalf of members of a group.

society all formal and informal organizations, social movements, and interest groups that attempt to (1) remain autonomous from state control and (2) articulate their own economic, cultural, and/or political identities and interests.

Sokoto Caliphate founded in 1809, following the Fulani Jihad, it was a powerful, relatively centralized empire in northern Nigeria before British rule.

sovereignty supreme legal authority over people within a certain territory.

soviet Russian word meaning "council," used for the main legislative assemblies of state in the USSR.

spheres of influence division of control between Russia and Great Britain over Iranian territory in early twentieth century.

state a political-legal organization with sovereign power over a particular geographic territory and the population that resides within that territory.

State Council the highest government institution in China, consisting of the premier, several vice premiers, and a similar number of more policy-oriented state councilors, that manages China's gargantuan network of ministries, commissions, bureaus, and other governmental institutions at the national level.

state-led economic development strategy of economic development that gives the government a central role as the promoter of capital formation. The government rather than the market decides where to direct investment resources.

Status of Forces Agreements a set of agreements between Iran and the United States that granted immunity from prosecution to American military personnel and their dependents who committed crimes in Iran against its own citizens or property.

Sunni the largest denomination in Islam that asserts the succession of the Prophet Mohammad through consensus among the community of believers.

Supreme Court the head of the judicial branch in Mexico. It is made up of 11 judges (*ministros*) whose term lasts 15 years. Judges are elected by the Senate from a list of three names proposed by the president.

supreme leader Iran's highest political and religious authority. The first supreme leader was Ayatollah Khomeini.

Taisho Democracy growth of democracy—in the form of greater political and social rights and emergence of political parties—in the first decades of the twentieth century. Named after the Emperor Taisho who reigned from 1912–1926.

Tenochtitlán city-state founded in what is now Mexico City; capital of the Aztec Empire.

theocracy a non-democratic regime in which leaders who claim divine guidance hold the authority to rule.

Tokugawa era (1603–1868) period in which Japan's central government was led by the shogun.

totalitarian regime a non-democratic regime that attempts to shape the interests and identities of its citizens through the use of ideological mobilization, coercion, and limitation of political and social pluralism.

Treaty of Guadalupe Hidalgo this treaty, signed in 1848, put an end to the Mexican–American War, recognizing Mexico's loss of Texas and other territory that corresponds to present-day California, Nevada, and Utah, as well as most of Arizona, New Mexico, and Colorado to the United States.

Tudeh the Iranian Communist Party.

ulama Muslim legal scholars.

ummah for Muslims, the community of believers.

Union for a Popular Movement (UMP) the main center-right party in France. It evolved out of the Gaullist Rally for the Republic Party (RPR) in 2002, and both presidents since that time have been elected as representatives of the UMP.

unitary system a state in which the constitution grants the central government exclusive, final authority over policymaking across the entire national territory.

United Russia Russia's largest political party that includes most of the leading politicians and many other important figures in the country. A self-described conservative party that was formed in December 2001 through the merger of the two main pro-government parties in the Duma.

untouchability practice of treating members of the traditionally "unclean" Hindu castes who dealt with animal and human death or waste as "untouchable." This discrimination can take several forms: not going near these castes, not wanting to have them as friends or marriage partners or neighbors, or discriminating against them in terms of employment, housing access, or access to temples. Although made illegal by the 1950 Constitution, many discriminatory practices survive today.

USSR Union of Soviet Socialist Republics, also known as the Soviet Union. The name for the state officially formed in 1922 on the territory of the former Russian Empire.

***Velayat-e Faqih* or Guardianship of the Jurist** theory of Islamic governance in Iran set forth by Ayatollah Khomeini, in which the just Islamic society is led by the highest religious jurist who is the final arbiter on all matters of governance.

Vichy regime the Nazi-sympathizing puppet state set up in the southern part of France from 1940–1944, following France's World War II defeat at the hands of Germany.

vote of confidence a vote held in the British Parliament to discover whether the government of the day has the confidence of Parliament. If the government fails, it must hold new elections.

wall in the head :refers to the difference in mentalities between people living in West and East Germany.

War of Independence in 1810, the people of Mexico took arms to fight for their independence from Spain. The War of Independence lasted until 1821, when Spain recognized Mexico's independence.

Weimar Republic Germany's first democratic regime that was founded in 1919 after World War I and lasted until 1933, when it was destroyed by the Nazis.

welfare state the term used to describe the role states play in protecting the economic and social well-being of all its citizens through redistributive taxing and spending programs.

White Revolution a series of predominantly land-based reforms instituted by the shah in Iran in 1963, aimed at redistributing feudal land holdings among the peasantry to gain favor. Also included were economic and social reform policies aimed at modernizing the economy.

Xiaoping, Deng born in Sichuan, Deng was a close follower of Mao throughout the earliest days of the revolution. By the late 1950s, he was in charge of the day-to-day business of the entire CCP apparatus. Twice purged during the Cultural Revolution, Deng re-emerged to preside over the next two decades of reform before his death in 1997. Much as Mao is credited with unifying China, Deng is acknowledged as being the "architect" of the reform era which continues into the present day.

Xinjiang Uyghur Autonomous Regions (UAR) established in 1955, a provincial-level unit with a large percentage of the Uyghur minority group. Others autonomous regions include the Guangxi Zhuang AR, the Tibetan AR, the Inner Mongolian AR, and the Ningxia Hui AR). Geographically, the Xinjiang AR is the largest single administrative region in all of China.

xitong clusters of related bureaucracies that are lumped together in pursuit of a specific set of policy goals. In recent years, *xitong* has been used more loosely to refer to any kind of bureaucratic system in China.

Yar'adua, Umaru president of Nigeria from 2007 until his death in 2010; left a power vacuum and raised fears of a coup when he went abroad for medical treatment in 2009.

Yat-sen, Sun the first president of the Republic of China and founder of the Nationalist Party.

Yoruba the dominant ethnic group in Nigeria's southwest, and one of the country's three main groups.

Zapatista Army of National Liberation (EZLN) insurgent armed group based in the state of Chiapas and organized in defense of the rights of indigenous communities. After an uprising in January 1994, the group has mostly pressed its demands through nonviolent means such as marches and protests.Case Studies in Comparative Politics

Zedong, Mao born in 1893, the son of a well-to-do peasant, Mao, more than any other individual, personified the Chinese Communist Party, which he helped found in 1921 and led until his death in 1976.

CREDITS

Page 1: Reuters/Corbis; **page 12:** Lv Mingxiang/Corbis; **page 18:** AFP/Getty Images; **page 33:** AFP/Getty Images; **page 39:** Reuters/Corbis; **page 44:** Time and Life Pictures/Getty Images; **page 50:** Steve Easton/Hulton Archive/Getty; **page 62:** Hulton Archive/Getty Images; **page 77:** Oliver Multhaup/AP Photo; **page 84:** Carl Weinrother/Art Resource; **page 86:** Robert Wallis/Corbis; **page 100:** David Turnley/Corbis; **page 114:** AFP/Getty Images; **page 121:** Gamma-Rapho/Getty Images; **page 129:** Phillipe Wo Jazer/Corbis; **page 145:** AFP/Getty; **page 150:** AFP/Getty Images; **page 162:** Corbis Wire/Corbis; **page 184:** Image Bank/Getty; **page 185:** Everett Kennedy Brown/Corbis; **page 194:** Pallava Bagla/Corbis; **page 202:** Walter Bosshard/Corbis; **page 210:** Ahmitt Bhargava/Corbis; **page 223:** Parth Sanyal/Corbis; **page 235:** Alfredo Estrella/Getty; **page 248:** Gregory Bull/AP Photo; **page 255:** Marco Ugarte/AP Photo; **page 261:** Eduardo Verdugo/AP; **page 277:** Denis Sinyakov/Corbis; **page 297:** Natalia Kolesnikova/AFP/Getty; **page 305:** Dmitry Kostyukov/Getty; **page 314:** Natalia Kolesnikova/AFP/Getty; **page 320:** Ed Kashi/Corbis; **page 327:** Hulton Archive/Stringer/Getty; **page 349:** Austin Ekeinde/Corbis; **page 352:** Pius Utomi Ekpei/Stringer/Getty Images; **page 365:** Tao Ming/Corbis; **page 376:** Contact Press; **page 381:** Peter Parks/AFP/Getty Images; **page 394:** David Gray/Corbis; **page 407:** Corbis News/Corbis; **page 426:** Valda Moaiery/Corbis; **page 434:** Alexandra Boulat/Corbis; **page 443:** AP Photo

SUBJECT INDEX

References to figures and tables are in *italic* text.

Numbers
1979 Iranian revolution, 416–418
1986 French education reform protests, 144
2005-2006 French protests, 144–146

A

Abacha, Sani, 330
accountability of government
 oil dependency and, 340–341
 of Second Reich, 79
 taxation and, 340
Achaemenid Empire, 409–412
Act of Toleration (UK), 44
Act of Union (UK), 45
Action Congress of Nigeria (ACN), 353
activism. *see* protests; social movements
African countries, comparison of, *323*
Agrarian Party (Russia), 294
Ahmadinejad, Mahmoud, 408, 420
Ajaokuta steel complex, 329
Algerian war for independence, 122
Algiers Accords, 416
All Nigeria People's Party (ANPP), 353
amakudari, 175
America. *see* United States
Ancien Régime, 118. *see also* France, history of

Anglo-Persian Oil Company (APOC), 413
Anti-Rightist Campaign (Maoist China), 375
anti-Semitism in prewar Germany, 96
aristocracy. *see* class identity
Article 9 of Japanese Constitution, 158
Article 48 of Weimar Constitution, 83–84
Article 49-3 of the Constitution of the Fifth Republic, 125
Assembly of Experts in Iran, 426–427
asylum law in Germany, 100
authoritarian regimes
 defined, 22
 vs. totalitarian regimes, 84–85

B

backbenchers, 53
Backward Castes, 214
bakufu, 154
banlieues, 144
baojia system in China, 371
Basic Law (German constitution), 88–91
basij (Iran), 437
bazaari, 413
Beijing Olympics of 2008, 402
Berlin Wall, 86–87
Bharatiya Janata Party (BJP), 214
Biafran War, 328, 345–347
Bill of Rights (UK), 44

Bismarck, Otto von, 79–82
Blair, Tony, 48–49
Britain. *see* United Kingdom
British Petroleum (BP), 413
Bundesrat, 79, 89, 91–92
Bundestag, 88–91
Burakumin, 176
bureaucracy, Japanese, 173–175
business associations in UK party system, 68–70
business interests, Russian, 309–310

C

cabinets
 shadow Cabinets, 58
 in United Kingdom, 53
Calderón, Felipe, 262
campaign laws
 in Japan, 168–169
 in Mexico, 256
Cárdenas, Cuauhtémoc, 268
Cárdenas, Lázaro, 242
caste system in India, 217–219, 222–224
 Backward Castes, 214, 217
 caste discrimination, 218–219
 caste reservation system, 214, 222–223
 defined, 200
 Scheduled Castes, 210, 218
Catholicism, in France, 136
Caucasus Mountains, 301
caudillos, 240

cell phones, Indian adoption of, 230
Century of Humiliation (China), 370
chador, 434
Chairman Mao. *see* Mao Zedong
Chamber of Deputies (Mexico), 246, *247*, 268
chancellors of Germany, *107*
chapter framework for book, 11–12
Chartist movement, 71
Chechnya, 301–302
  ethnic identities in, 301–302
  Islam in, 305
  mass murder of by Stalin, 301
  Russian war against, 290, 294, 301–302
Checkpoint Charlie (Berlin Wall), 86
checks and balances
  in French politics, 130
  in German politics, 91–93
  in Mexican politics, 252
Chiang Kai-shek, 373
China
  as authoritarian regime, 379, 388–391
  baojia system, 371
  Beijing Olympics of 2008, 402
  Chinese Communist Party (CCP), 366, 379–383
    factors supporting rise of, 374
    importance of, 379
    political power of, 384–386
    structure of, *382*
  comparison to other countries, *369*
  Confucianism, 371
  cultural identity, 370–371
  danwei work units, 388
  as dictatorship, 366–367
  economic growth, 366, 377–378
  economic inequality, 366, 400
  electoral system, 380–381
  elite institutions, 379–383
  ethnic conflicts, 393–396
  geography of, 370, 374
  history of, 370–379, *378*
    Century of Humiliation, 370
    Chinese Empire, 370–372
    Chinese Republic, 372–373
    contemporary, 377–379
    Great Leap Forward, 375–376
    Mao takeover, 375–377
    People's Republic of China, 373–375
    World War II, 373
  household responsibility system, 377
  introduction to, 366–367
  iron rice bowl, 378
  leadership small groups, 383
  legislative branch, 381–382
  local governments, 384–386
  map of, 368
  military, 386–388
  mobilization of citizens by, 389–390
  One-Child Policy, 367, 386
  overpopulation in, 367
  People's Liberation Army (PLA)
    military victories by, 374
    political participation by, 397–398
  Politburo, 380
  political identities, 388–396
    change from totalitarian to authoritarian, 388–391
    ethnicity and religion, 393–396
    nationalism and, 391–393
  political institutions, 379–388, *387*
  political interests, 397–402, *401*
    citizens, 400–402
    industrial and professional groups, 399
    local state government, 398
    mass media, 398–399, 402
    military organization, 397–398
    non-governmental organizations (NGOs), 399–400
  State Council, 380
  Taiwan and, 373
  Tibetans in, 393–395
  Uyghur in, *396*
  weak central government, 367, 384–386
Chinese Communist Party (CCP), 366, 379–383
  factors supporting rise of, 374
  importance of, 379
  Politburo, 380
  political power of, 384–386
  structure of, *382*
Christian Democratic Union, 105–106
Christianity
  in Iran, 432
  in Nigeria, 327, 343–344
Church of England, 64
citizenship law in Germany, 101–102
civil rights. *see also* gender issues
  in India, 229–231
  in United Kingdom, 46
civil society
  in India, 201
  in Mexico, 268
  in United Kingdom, 71–72
civil wars, 33
class identity
  in France, 134–135
  in Iran, 433
  in Japan, 177–178
  in Nigeria, 354–356
  in Russia, 303–304
  in United Kingdom, 60–62

Subject Index

class-consciousness, 25
cleavages. *see* political cleavages
coalition governments, 32, 48
co-determination law in Germany, 104
coercive mobilization of citizens, 389
cohabitation in French politics, 124–125
Cold War, 278
collective action, 28–32, 133. *see also* interest groups; political parties; protests; social movements
collective action problem, 12
colonial legacies, 14. *see also* decolonization
   Indian, 203–207
   Mexican, 237–240
   Nigerian, 326–328, 336–337
Committee on State security (KGB), 294
communism
   1989 revolutions and, 285
   defined, 22
   in Iran, 437
   in Soviet Russia, 283–284
Communist Party in post-war France, 134, 141–142
Communist Party of China. *see* Chinese Communist Party (CCP)
Communist Party of the Russian Federation (CPRF), 294
comparative method, 6
comparative politics, 3–6
   contemporary issues, 32–36
   defined, 3
   questions asked by, 10–11
confidence vote, 54
Confucianism, 371
Conservative Party (UK), 46, 69
conservative political interests, 29

Constitutional Council (France), 127–128
Constitutional Court (Russia), 287–288
Constitutional Courts, 20
constitutional dictatorships in France, 119
constitutional monarchies, 22–23
   defined, 23
   in French history, 119
   United Kingdom as, 44
constitutions, 298
   German (Basic Law), 88
   Indian, 205–207
   Iranian, 422–423
   Japanese, 158
   Mexican, 241–242
   Russian, 288–290, 298
   United Kingdom (unwritten), 40–41, 51
constructive vote of no confidence, 89
constructivism, 27, 28
contemporary issues in comparative politics, 32–36
corporations, multinational (MNCs), 16
corporatism, 30, 243
corruption
   in Indian politics, 215–217
   in Mexico, 252–253
   in Nigeria, 321–322
Cortés, Hernán, 237
Council of Guardians in Iran, 427–428
countries included in book, selection criteria for, 6–11
country comparison overview, 5
coups d'état, 119
Criollos, 240
cross-cutting social cleavages, 344
cultural identities, 26

D

Dalits, 210, 218
danwei work units, 388
de Gaulle, Charles, 120, 123
decolonization, 14. *see also* colonial legacies
   of India, 201–208
   of Nigeria, 336–337
   by United Kingdom, 46–47
defense spending by Japan, 158
democracy, 17
Democratic Party of Japan (DPJ)
   2009 win, 151, 161
   2011 tsunami response, 161–162
democratic regimes, 19–21, 88–91
   constitutional formats, *19*
   electoral systems in, 20
   list of, *18*
   political institutions in, *17*, 19–21
   Weimar Republic as, 83
democratization, 46. *see also* regime change
Deng Xiaoping, 376–377
devolution, 48. *see also* decolonization
Díaz, Porfirio, 240–241
dictatorships, China as, 366–367
Diet (Japan), 166–167, 179
dirigisme, 121
discrimination
   caste-based, 218–219
   gender-based. *see* gender issues
divided government, 251, 266
drug trafficking violence in Mexico, 253–254, *253*
Duma, 288, 293

E

early-forming states, 14, 17
East Germany
   reunification, 98–99

East Germany (*continued*)
  as totalitarian regime, 86–87
East India Company, 198–200
economic class. *see also* class identity
  cleavage based on, 26–27
  political identity based on, 25
economic development
  defined, 33
  free market vs. intervention, 34
  gender identities and, 28
  state-led, 244
economic globalization, 15–17
economic inequality
  in China, 366, 400
  defined, 34
  in Mexico, 237
Edict of Nantes, 118
education
  in Germany, 97
  in Japan, 178
  in Nigeria, 332
effective government
  in Germany, 94
  in Japan, 166
  vs. limited government, 6
  in Mexico, 244
  parliamentary sovereignty and, 51–52
  two-party system and, 56, 69
  in United Kingdom, 40, 49, 51–56, 69
  USSR as, 284
Election Commission (EC) in India, 215–217
election results in United Kingdom, 55
electoral systems, 20–21
  in China, 380–381
  in France, 128–132, *128*
  in Germany, 89–91
  in India, 209–211
  in Japan, 167–173
  majoritarian, 54–56
  in Mexico, 246–248, 255–257

in Nigeria, 332–333
in Russia, 293–296
in United Kingdom, 54–56
electorate, 22
electricity failures in Nigeria, 335–336
elite parties, 311
England. *see* United Kingdom
environmental groups
  in Germany, 108
  in Japan, 181–183
  in Mexico, 266
Estates-General, 118–119. *see also* French Revolution
ethnicity
  cleavages based on, 27
  defined, 26
  in France, 135
  in Germany, 99–103
  in India, 217, 225–227
  in Iran, 430–431
  in Japan, 175
  in Mexico, 240, 260–261
  in Nigeria, 342–345, *343*
  political identity based on, 26
  in Russia, 299–301
  in United Kingdom, 64–65
Euro currency, 92
European Court of Justice (ECJ), 52
European Union
  formation of, 92–93
  French participation in, 121, 128
  German participation in, 92–95
  United Kingdom participation in, 59–60
executive branch
  in France, 124–125, 130
  in Japan, 167
  in Russia, 288, 292
  in United Kingdom, 52–53
executive-legislative balance of power, 19
executives, 19

F

failed states, 14
Failed States Index, 335
farmers as interest group in India, 227–228
fascism, 22
fatwas, 442
federal character principle in Nigeria, 332
Federal Constitutional Court (Germany), 91
Federal Electoral Institute (IFE) in Mexico, 247
Federal Republic of Germany (West Germany), 86
Federal Security Service (FSB), 294
federal systems, 19
federalism
  in Germany, 91–92
  in India, 208–209
  in Mexico, 254–255
  in Nigeria, 332
  in Russia, 290–292
Federation Council (Russia), 288
Federation of Independent Trade Unions of Russia (FITUR), 310
Fifth Republic (France), 123–125, 130
financial crisis of 2008 in Germany, 110
financial sector (UK), 70–71
First Employment Contract (France), 145
First Republic (Nigeria), 328, 346
Foreign Direct Investment, 16
foreign-born citizens. *see* immigration
formation of states, early vs. late, 14, 17
Fourth Republic (France), 121
Fourth Republic (Nigeria), 330
Fox, Vicente, 247–248

Subject Index

France
  2007 presidential election, 129
  cohabitation, 124–125
  colonial uprisings against, 121–122
  comparison to other countries, *117*
  democracy in, 123
  electoral system, 128–132, *128*
  ethnic diversity in, 135
  European Union participation, 121, 128
  government system, *126*
  grandes écoles, 125
  history of, 118–123
    19th-century regime change, 120
    French Revolution, 119–120
    Middle Ages to *Ancien Régime*, 118–119
    modern era, 120–123
  immigration to, 135
  interest groups, 139
  introduction to, 115–118
  l'alternance, 140
  map of, 116
  nationalism in, 135
  political identities, 132–138
    class identity, 134–135
    post-materialist identity, 137–138
    religious identity, 136
  political institutions, 123–132, *132*
    electoral systems, 128–132
    executive branch, 124–125
    judicial branch, 127–128
    legislative branch, 126–127
  political interests, 138–147
  political parties, 124, 135, 140–142
  presidents and prime ministers, *131*
  protests
    analyzing, 115–118
    examples of, 142–147
    likelihood of, 132–133
    reasons for, 131–132, *137*
  regime change, 119, *122*
  semi-presidential system, 124–125
  state interests, 142
Free Democratic Party, 106–107
Freedom House classifications, 5
Freedom Movement of Iran (FMI), 437–438
freedom of the press in India, 229–231
free-market principles, 34
French Communist Party (PCF), 141–142
French Revolution, 119–120
Frente Democrático Nacional (FDN), 268

G

Gandhi, Indira, 212–214
Gandhi, Mohandas K., 201–202
Gandhi, Rajiv, 214
Gandhi, Sonia, 214
GDP (gross domestic product)
  annual yearly growth rate, *35*
  comparison of, *5*
  defined, 33
  Nigerian decline in, 321
  per capita in 2009, *34*
gender identities, 28
gender issues. *see also* civil rights
  in Iran, 434–435
  in Japan, 179
  in United Kingdom, 65–67
  women's suffrage, 72
geography
  Chinese history and, 370, 374
  Russian history and, 279–283
German Communist Party, ban on, 91
German Democratic Republic (East Germany)
  incorporation of, 98–99
  as totalitarian regime, 86–87
Germany
  asylum law, 100
  challenges to economic/political model, 110–111
  chancellors of, *107*
  comparison to other countries, *81*
  constructive vote of no confidence, 89
  division and reunification of, 85–88, 98–99
  education system, 97
  electoral systems, 89–91
  ethnicity in, 99–103
  Grand Coalition, 94, 106
  history of, 78–88, *88*
    late formation of, 79
    Nazi regime, 83–85
    postwar era, 85–88, *110*
    Second Reich, 79–82
    Weimar Republic, 78, 82–83
  Holocaust views, 98
  immigration and, 99–103
  introduction to, 78
  judicial review, 91
  legislature in, 89
  map of, 80
  military in, 92, 97
  political identities, 95–103, *102*
    post-war, 96–98
    pre-war, 95–96
  political institutions, 88–95
    chancellor democracy, 88–91
    European Union, 92–95
    federalism, 91–92
    judiciary, 91
    NATO, 92
  political interests, 103–111
  political parties, 105–110, *109*

Germany (*continued*)
  Christian Democratic Union, 105–106
  far left, 109–110
  far right, 108–109
  Free Democratic Party, 106–107
  Greens, 107–108
  second votes gained by, *90*
  Social Democratic Party, 106
  postwar settlement, 103–105
  religious cleavage in, 79
  social movements, 108
  wall in the head issue, 98
  as welfare state, 103–104
glasnost, 285
globalization, 15–17
Glorious Revolution of 1688, 44
Good Friday Accord, 48
Gorbachev, Mikhail, 284–285
government institutions. *see* political institutions
Government of India Act, 203
governments, 13
grandes écoles, 125
Great Britain. *see* United Kingdom
Great Depression, 82–83
Great Leap Forward, 375–376
Great October Socialist Revolution, 283
Great Proletarian Cultural Revolution, 376–377
Green Revolution in India, 227
Greens (Germany), 107–108
Grundgesetz (German constitution), 88
guestworkers (Germany), 99–100

H

habeus corpus, 41
Hausa tribe, 323–326. *see also* Nigeria
head of government, 13
head of state, 22–23
Hidalgo, Miguel, 240
Hinduism, 217, 226
history
  of China, 370–379, *378*
    Century of Humiliation, 370
    Chinese Empire, 370–372
    Chinese Republic, 372–373
    contemporary, 377–379
    Great Leap Forward, 375–376
    Mao takeover, 375–377
    People's Republic of China, 373–375
    World War II, 373
  of France, 118–123
    19th-century regime change, 120
    French Revolution, 119–120
    Middle Ages to *Ancien Régime, 118–119*
    modern era, 120–123
  of Germany, 78–88, *88*
    late formation of, 79
    Nazi regime, 83–85
    postwar era, 85–88, *110*
    Second Reich, 79–82
    Weimar Republic, 78, 82–83
  of India, 198–207, *205–206*
    British Empire colonization, 200–207
    colonialism, 203–207
    Mughal Empire, 198–200
  of Iran, 409–420, *421*
    1979 revolution, 416–418
    Abadan Crisis, 415
    Ahmadinejad regime, 419–420
    ancient Persia, 409–412
    discovery of oil, 413–415
    Iraq war, 417
    Khatami regime, 418–419
    protests, 441–445
    Safavid Empire, 412–413
    White Revolution, 415
  of Japan, 154–165, *163–165*
    1990s, 160–161
    2000s, 161–165
    Koizumi reforms, 187–189
    Meiji era, 155–156
    postwar era, 158–159
    pre-war era, 156–157
    Tokugawa era, 154–155
  of Mexico, 237–250, *249–250*
    1910 revolution, 241–242
    colonial, 237–240
    independence, 240–241
    modern era, 244–250
    one-party rule, 242–243
    PRI hegemony, 243–244
  of Nigeria, 323–331, *331*
    Biafran War, 328
    colonial, 326–328
    independence, 321, 328–330
    pre-colonial, 323–326
  of Russia, 279–287, *286*
    collapse of USSR, 284–287
    expansion of empire, 279–282
    geography and, 279–283
    Russian Revolution, 283–284
  of United Kingdom, 41–49, *49*
    contemporary, 47–49
    establishment of state, 41
    Indian colonialism, 200–203
    limited government emergence, 44–46
    twentieth-century, 46–47
Hitler, Adolf, 84. *see also* Nazi regime
Holocaust issue in contemporary Germany, 98
homogeneity of Japan, 175–177
Hookoomat-e Islami, 416
House of Commons (UK), 41
House of Councillors (Japan), 166–168
House of Lords (UK), 41
House of Representatives (Japan), 166–167
House of Representatives (Nigeria), 328
Hu Jintao, 380

Subject Index

hukou restrictions in Maoist China, 377
human rights
 in Iranian constitution, 423
 Persian history of, 412
 USSR violations of, 283–284
Hundred Flowers Movement, 375

I

Iabloko party (Russia), 312
Ibo tribe, 323–326, 328, 345–347. *see also* Nigeria
immigration
 to China, 400
 to France, 135
 German political parties opposing, 108
 to Germany, 99–103
 to Japan, 176–177
 from Mexico, 271–272
 to United Kingdom, 64–65
Imposed War (Iran-Iraq 1980-1988), 417
income inequality. *see* economic inequality
India, 194–232
 castes, 217–219, 222–224
  Backward Castes, 214, 217
  caste discrimination, 218–219
  reservations system, 214, 222–223
  Scheduled Castes, 210, 218
 civil society, 201
 comparison to other countries, 197
 constitution, 205–207
 decolonization of, 201–208
 electoral system, 209–211
 ethnic conflicts, 203
 freedom of the press, 229–231
 Green Revolution, 227
 Hindu-Muslim conflict, 203–204
 history of, 198–207, *205–206*
  British Empire colonization, 200–207
  colonialism, 203–207
  Mughal Empire, 198–200
 introduction to, 195–198
 languages in, 208–209, 219–220, *220*, 223–224
 map of, 196
 martial classes, 211
 political identities, 217–225, *225*
 political institutions, 207–217
  civil-military relations, 211
  Election Commission (EC), 215–217
  federalism, 208–209
  judiciary branch, 211–212
  parliament, 209–211
 political interests, 225–231, *230*
  business interests, 228–229
  ethnic and minority, 225–227
  mass media, 229–231
  poor citizens, 228
  rural, 227–228
  voters, 227
 political parties, 201, 212–215, *215*
 politicians' criminal records, 215–217
 President's Rule clause, 207–208, 212
 prime ministers, *216*
 religion in, 198, 220–222, *220, 226*
 state creation, 208–209, 223–224
 tribes, 210
 voter turnout, 227
 voters' concerns, 224
Indian Administrative Service (IAS), 209
Indian National Congress, 201, 212–215
Indian Police Service (IPS), 209
indirect rule in Nigeria, 326–327
individual reluctance to benefit group. *see* collective action problem
industrial policy of Japan, 159
Industrial Revolution in United Kingdom, 45, 61
inequality, economic. *see* economic inequality
informal constitutions, 51
insider privatization, 307
institutions. *see* political institutions
interest groups
 characteristics and formation of, 30
 in France, 139
 in Mexico, 269–273
 in Nigeria, 356–359
 pluralism, 68
 vs. political parties, 30
 protests and, *146*
interests. *see* political interests
International Government Organizations (IGOs), 15
International Non-Governmental Organizations (INGOs), 15
interventionist states, 34
Iran
 2009 election, 408
 Afghan refugees in, 431
 American involvement with, 415–416, 419–420
 Assembly of Experts, 426–427
 comparison to other countries, *411*
 constitution of, 422–423
 Council of Guardians, 427–428
 ethnic conflicts, 431
 government structure, *428*
 Guardianship of the Jurist office, 417–418
 history of, 409–420, *421*
  1979 revolution, 416–418
  Abadan Crisis, 415

Iran (continued)
  Ahmadinejad regime, 419–420
  ancient Persia, 409–412
  discovery of oil, 413–415
  Iraq war, 417
  Khatami regime, 418–419
  protests, 441–445
  Safavid Empire, 412–413
  White Revolution, 415
  introduction to, 408–409
  Islam in
    early spread of, 412–413
    founding principles of, 425
    Guardianship of the Jurist office, 417–418
    Mujahedin-e Khalq (MEK), 438–439
    as official religion, 431
    political institutions of, 425–428
    Shi'i state, 432
  judicial branch, 424–425
  language of, 431
  leaders of, 427
  map of, 410
  naming of, 414
  Nuclear Non-Proliferation Treaty (NPT) participation, 440–441
  parliament of, 424
  political identities, 430–435, 436
    ethnic identities, 430–431
    post-revolutionary hybrid identities, 433–434
    pre-Islamic Persian, 430
    religious identities, 431–433
    social classes, 433
    women's rights, 434–435
  political institutions, 422–429, 429
    Islamic, 425–428
    republican, 422–425
  political interests, 435–445, 444
    labor unions, 439–440
    military, 436–437
    nuclear and scientific, 440–441
    political parties, 437–439
    president of, 423–424
    protests, 441–445
    religious identities, 431–433
    Revolutionary Guards (pasdaran), 418–419, 436–437
  shah, 413
  Sharia law, 422
  spheres of influence over, 414
  supreme leader, 425–426
Ireland, religious identity in, 64. see also United Kingdom
iron rice bowl, 378
Islam, 417–418. see also Sharia law
  in Iran
    early spread of, 412–413
    founding principles of, 425
    Guardianship of the Jurist office, 417–418
    Mujahedin-e Khalq (MEK), 438–439
    political institutions of, 425–428
    Shi'i state, 432
  in Nigeria, 326, 343–344
  in Russia, 304–305
  Shi'i and Sunni sects of, 412
  ummah (community of believers), 425
Islamic Republican Party (IRP) of Iran, 438
Islamic Revolutionary Court of Iran, 424

J

Japan
  1947 Constitution, 158
  1994 electoral reform, 171–173
  campaign laws, 168–169
  class identity, 177
  comparison to other countries, 153
  defense spending, 158
  Democratic Party of Japan (DPJ), 151
  economy of
    1990s decline, 160–161
    bureaucracy and, 173
    economic miracle, 159
  education in, 178
  electoral system, 167–173
  gender issues, 179
  history of, 154–165, 163–165
    1990s, 160–161
    2000s, 161–165
    Koizumi reforms, 187–189
    Meiji era, 155–156
    postwar era, 158–159
    pre-war era, 156–157
    Tokugawa era, 154–155
  homogeneity of, 175–177
  immigration to, 176–177
  industrial policy, 159
  introduction to, 151
  Koreans in, 176–177
  labor unions, 177
  Liberal Democratic Party (LDP), 151
  lost decade, 160
  malapportionment, 170–171
  map of, 152
  military, 158
  nationalism in, 156–157
  political identities, 175–180, 179, 180
  political institutions, 165–175, 174
    bureaucracy, 173–175
    judiciary, 173
    parliamentarism, 166–167
    unitarism, 165
  political interests, 180–189
    environmental groups, 181–183
    modern vs. traditional, 183–187

Subject Index

political interests *(continued)*
　postwar, 181
　rural vs. urban, 170–171, 189
political parties, *182*
pre-war economic growth, 156–157
prime ministers, 167
property values in, 160
religion in, 175–176
single-party nature of, 165–173
social status, 177–178
Taisho Democracy, 157
tsunami of 2011, 161–162
xenophobia, 154–155
Japan Socialist Party (JSP), 158–159
Jinnah, Mohammad Ali, 195, 203–204
judicial branch
　in France, 127–128
　in Germany, 91
　in India, 211–212
　in Iran, 424–425
　in Japan, 173
　in Mexico, 252–254
　in Nigeria, 332–333
　in Russia, 290
judicial review
　defined, 20
　in France, 127–128
　in Germany, 91
　in United Kingdom, 52
juntas, 24

K

Kaduna and Jos riots of Nigeria, 335
Khatami regime in Iran, 418–419
Khomeini, Ayatollah Ruhollah, 416–418
kieretsu, 158
kinship bonds, 27
koenkai, 169
Koizumi, Jun'ichiro, 161–162

Koreans in Japan, 176–177
Kurds, 431. *see also* Iran

L

labor unions
　in France, 139
　in Iran, 439–440
　in Japan, 177
　in Mexico, 269–270
　in Nigeria, 355
　in Russia, 310–311
　UK party system and, 68–70
Labour Party (UK), 46, 69
laïcité, 134, 136
l'alternance, 140
land size comparison between countries, 5
Länder, 91–92
languages
　in India, 208–209, 219–220, *220,* 223–224
　in Iran, 431
late-forming states, 14, 17, 78–79
Le Pen, Jean-Marie, 141
legislative-executive balance of power, 19
legislatures
　in China, 381–382
　defined, 19
　in France, 126–127
　in Germany, 89
　in Japan, 174
　in Mexico, 254, *258*
　in Nigeria, 332–333
　in Russia, 288–290
　in United Kingdom, 53–54
Liberal Democratic Party (LDP) of Japan, 188–189
　2009 loss, 151, 161, 188–189
　challenges to, 182–183
　dominance of, 151, 159, 165–173
　rural vs. urban support for, 183–187

Liberal Democratic Party (LDPR) of Russia, 294, 312
Liberal Party (UK), 46
liberal political interests, 29
life expectancy comparison between countries, 5
limited government
　vs. effective government, 6
　factors supporting, 56–60
　in Germany, *94*
　in Japan, 165
　in Mexico, 241, 250, 255
　terrorism and, 48
　in United Kingdom, 40, 44–46, 56–60, 70
literacy rate comparison between countries, 5
lobbyist groups in China, 399
Lok Sabha (House of the People), 209–211
lost decade in Japan, 160

M

MacArthur, Douglas, 158
Madero, Francisco, 241
Magna Carta, 40, 41, 44
Majlis (Iranian parliament), 413
majority rule, 20
　defined, 21
　in France, 128
malapportionment, 170–171
Mao Zedong. *see also* China
　Anti-Rightist Campaign, 375
　coercive mobilization by, 389
　Great Leap Forward, 375–376
　Great Proletarian Cultural Revolution, 376–377
　Hundred Flowers Movement, 375
　importance of, 366
　state takeover by, 375–377
maps
　China, 368
　France, 116
　Germany, 80
　India, 196

maps (continued)
  Iran, 410
  Japan, 152
  Mexico, 238
  Nigeria, 324
  Russia, 280
  United Kingdom, 42
  world, 4
Marx, Karl
  economic class theories, 25
  vs. Max Weber, 26
mass media
  in China, 398–399, 402
  in India, 229–231
  in Russia, 296
  in United Kingdom, 72–73
May 1968 protests, 143–144
May Fourth Movement, 373
Meiji era in Japan, 155–156
  Meiji oligarchs, 156
  social status and, 178
Members of Parliament (MPs), 51
mestizaje project, 258–260
Mestizos, 240, 258–259
Mexican-American War of 1846, 240
Mexico, 235–274, 272
  1985 earthquake, 267–268
  campaign laws, 256
  civil society, 268
  comparison to other countries, 239
  constitution of 1917, 241–242
  corruption, 252–253
  divided government, 251, 266
  drug trafficking violence, 253–254, 253
  economic crisis, 244–246
  economic growth, 245
  economic inequality, 237
  electoral systems in, 246–248
  emigration from, 271–272
  ethnicity in, 258–260
  executive branch power, 257
  history of, 237–250, 249–250

  1910 revolution, 241–242
  colonial, 237–240
  independence, 240–241
  modern era, 244–250
  PRI hegemony, 243–244
  single-party rule, 242–243
  indigenous identities, 260–261
  indigenous population, 263
  interest groups, 269–273
  introduction to, 236–237
  labor unions, 269–270
  limited government in, 241, 250
  map of, 238
  Mexican Miracle, 244
  nationalism in, 263
  no-reelection clause, 243
  North American Free Trade Agreement (NAFTA), 246
  plurality rule, 256
  political identities, 258–263, 263
    cleavages in, 262–263
    ethnic diversity and, 260–261
    indigenous, 260–261
    mestizaje project, 258–260
  political institutions, 250–258, 257–258
    electoral systems, 255–257
    executive-legislative relations, 251–252
    federalism, 254–255
    judiciary branch, 252–254
  political interests, 264–273, 272
  political parties, 242–243, 264–266
  presidential succession, 243
  PRI (*Partido Revolucionaro Institucional*), 265
    decline of, 244–250
    ethnicity and, 258–260
    hegemony of, 243–244
    ouster of, 236
  separation of powers, 254
  social movements, 266–268

  state-led economic development, 244
  taxes paid by, 248
middle class. *see* class identity
militant democracies, 91
military
  in China, 386–388
  in Germany today, 92, 97
  in India, 211
  in Iran, 418–419, 436–437
  in Japan today, 158
  in Nigeria, 329, 358–359
  in Second Reich, 82, 96
Military Affairs Committee (MAC), 386
military regimes
  defined, 24
  in Nigeria, 337
Mitterand, François, 140
mixed electoral systems, 21
mobile phones, Indian adoption of, 230
mobilization. *see also* collective action; protests
  coercive, 389
  primordialism and, 27
monarchies, 22–23
  defined, 23
  United Kingdom as, 40, 51
Movement for the Survival of the Ogoni People (MOSOP), 348
Mughal Empire, 198–200
Mujahedin-e Khalq (MEK), 438–439
multi-member districts (MMDs), 21
multinational corporations (MNCs), 16
Muslim League in India, 204
Muslims. *see* Islam

N

National Action Party (PAN), 247

National Assembly (France), 124, 126–127, *130*
National Democratic Front (Iran), 438
National Electric Power Authority (NEPA) in Nigeria, 335
National Front (FN) party, 135, 141
National Front (Iran), 437
National People's Congress (China), 381–382
National Socialist German Workers Party. *see* Nazi regime
nationalism
  in China, 391–393, *396*
  in contemporary Germany, 95, 97
  in France, 135
  in Japan, 156–157
  in Mexico, 263
  Nazism and, 85
  in Russia, 302–303
  in Second Reich, 95
  in United Kingdom, 63
Nationalist Party of China, 372–373
nations, 13. *see also* political identities
NATO, 92
natural resource curse, 309. *see also* oil
natural resources
  economies based on, 309
  oil. *see* oil
Nazi regime
  contemporary attitudes toward, 98
  in German history, 83–85
  ideology of, 85
  nationalism and, 95
  as totalitarian regime, 85
  Vichy regime and, 120
Nehru, Jawaharlal, 195, 201–202, 221
neighborhood effect, 24

neo-corporatism, 104
newspapers. *see* mass media
Niger Delta, 322
Nigeria, 321–361
  Ajaokuta steel complex, 329
  comparison to other countries, 325
  comparison to sub-Saharan countries, 323
  corruption in, 321–322
  economy of, 321, 330, 339–340
  education in, 332
  election fraud, 334
  electoral system, 332–333
  ethnic conflicts, 342–350
  ethnic groups in, *343*
  GDP decline, 321
  heads of state, *338*
  history of, 323–331, *331*
    Biafran War, 328, 345–347
    colonial, 326–328
    independence, 321, 328–330
    pre-colonial, 323–326
    tribes in, 323–326
  informal economy of, 355–356
  introduction to, 321–323
  judicial branch, 332–333
  labor unions, 355
  map of, 324
  oil dependence, 322
    conflicts caused by, 345–350
    economic growth and, *348*
    state weakness and, 339–342
  political identities, 342–351
  political institutions, 331–342, *342*
    in practice, 333–334
    in theory, 332–333
  political interests, 351–359, *359*
    economic interest groups, 356–357
    ethno-regional groups, 357–358
    military, 329, 358–359

  political parties, 328, 351–354
  political patronage in, 353
  public service failures, 335–336
  religion, 326, 327
    religion in, 343–344
    Sharia law in, 333
  violent conflicts in, 335
  weakness of, 334–337
    colonial legacy and, 336–337
    military rule and, 337
    oil dependence and, 339–342
  working class in, 354–356
nomenklatura appointments, 381
non-democracy, 17
non-democratic regimes, 21–24
  China as, 388–391
  comparison of, *23*
  list of, *18*
  pre-war Japan as, 154
  Second Reich as, 79
  selectorate comparison, *23*
non-governmental organizations (NGOs), 399–400
no-reelection clause in Mexican constitution, 243
North American Free Trade Agreement (NAFTA), 246
nuclear and scientific Iranian interests, 440–441
Nuclear Non-Proliferation Treaty (NPT), 440–441

O

Obasanjo, Olusegun, 329–330
Ogoniland violence, 347–349
oil
  in Iran, 413–415
  Nigerian dependence on, 322
    conflicts caused by, 345–350
    economic effects, 329
    economic growth and, *348*
    state weakness and, 339–342

oligarchies, 23
  defined, 23
  Meiji era in Japan, 156
One-Child Policy in China, 367, 386
Operation Ajax, 415
oppositionalism in United Kingdom, 57–58
organized labor. *see* labor unions
Other Russia, 315

P

Pakistan, 195, 204–205
panchayat assemblies, 208
Parliament (UK)
  debate in, 57–58
  Members of Parliament (MPs), 51
  oppositionalism in, 57–58
  origin of, 41
  prime minister role in, 51–54
  sovereignty of, 51–52
  vote of confidence, 54
parliamentary sovereignty, 51
parliamentary supremacy
  defined, 20
  in United Kingdom, 51–52
parliamentary systems
  defined, 19
  in Germany, 88–91
  in India, 209–211, *215*
  in Iran, 424
  in Japan, 166–167
parties. *see* political parties
Party of the Democratic Revolution (PRD) in Mexico, 262
party systems, 31, *31. see also* political parties
  in Russia, 313
  in United Kingdom, 68–70
People's Democratic Party (PDP) of Nigeria, 351–353
People's Liberation Army (PLA), 386–388

military victories by, 374
political participation by, 397–398
People's Republic of China. *see* China
perestroika, 284
Persian Constitutional Revolution, 413
Persian corridor, 414
personalistic elections in Japan, 168–169
personalistic regimes, 24
pluralism, 30, 68
plurality rule, 20
  defined, 21
  in Mexico, 256
  in Nigeria, 332
policy communities, 70–71
Politburo of Chinese Communist Party, 380
political cleavages, 26–27
  cross-cutting, 344
  defined, 26
  in France, 132–138
  in Mexico, 262–263
  reinforcing, 343–344
political economy, 33
political identities
  cleavages in. *see* political cleavages
  culture-based, 26
  defined, 25
  economic class-based, 25
  in France, 132–138
    class identity, 134–135
    post-materialist identity, 137–138
    religious identity, 136
  in Germany, *102*
    post-war, 96–98
    pre-war, 95–96
  in India, 217–225, *225*
  in Iran, 430–435, *436*
    ethnic identities, 430–431
    post-revolutionary hybrid identities, 433–434
    pre-Islamic Persian, 430

religious identities, 431–433
social classes, 433
women's rights, 434–435
in Japan, 175–180, *180*
Marx vs. Weber on, 26
in Mexico, 258–263, *263*
  cleavages in, 262–263
  ethnic diversity and, 260–261
  indigenous, 260–261
  mestizaje project, 258–260
  nations as, 13
  in Nigeria, 342–345
  primordialism vs. constructivism, 27–28
  in Russia, 299–306, *306*
    Chechnyan, 301–302
    class identity, 303–304
    ethnic identities, 299–301
    religious identity, 304–305
    Russian nationalism, 302–303
  sources of, 27–28
  in United Kingdom, 60–67, *67*
political institutions, 17–25, 287–299
  in China, 379–388, *387*
    elite institutions, 379–383
    local state government, 384–386
    military, 386–388
    Politburo, 380
    State Council, 380
  in democratic regimes, *17*, 19–21
  in France, 123–132, *132*
    electoral systems, 128–132
    executive branch, 124–125
    judicial branch, 127–128
    legislative branch, 126–127
  in Germany, 88–95
    chancellor democracy, 88–91
    European Union, 92–95
    federalism, 91–92
    judiciary, 91
    NATO, 92
  in India, 207–217

Subject Index

civil-military relations, 211
Election Commission (EC), 215–217
federalism, 208–209
judiciary branch, 211–212
parliament, 209–211
in Iran, 422–429, *429*
Islamic, 425–428
republican, 422–425
in Japan, 165–175, *174*
bureaucracy, 173–175
judiciary, 173
parliamentarism, 166–167
unitarism, 165
in Mexico, 250–258, *257–258*
electoral systems, 255–257
executive-legislative relations, 251–252
federalism, 254–255
judiciary branch, 252–254
in Nigeria, 331–342, *342*
in practice, 333–334
in theory, 332–333
in non-democratic regimes, 21–24
power concentration of, *21*
in Russia, *291*
constitution, 288–290, *298*
elections, 293–296
federalism, 290–292
president and prime minister, 296–299
United Kingdom, 49–60, *59*
European Union, 59–60
longevity of, 56–57
majoritarian electoral system, 54–56
oppositionalism, 57–58
parliamentary sovereignty, 51–52
prime ministerial government, 52–54
regional governments, 58–59
political interests, 28–32. *see also* interest groups; political parties; social movements
in China, 397–402, *401*

citizens, 400–402
industrial and professional groups, 399
local state government, 398
mass media, 398–399
military organization, 397–398
non-governmental organizations (NGOs), 399–400
in Germany, 103–111
in India, 225–231, *230*
business interests, 228–229
ethnic and minority, 225–227
mass media, 229–231
poor citizens, 228
rural, 227–228
voters, 227
in Iran, 435–445, *444*
labor unions, 439–440
military, 436–437
nuclear and scientific, 440–441
political, 437–439
in Japan, 180–189
environmental groups, 181–183
modern vs. traditional, 183–187
postwar, 181
rural vs. urban, 170–171, *189*
liberal vs. conservative, 29
in Nigeria, 351–359, *359*
economic interest groups, 356–357
ethno-regional groups, 357–358
military, 358–359
in Russia, 306–316, *316*
business interests, 309–310
economic reform and collapse, 307–309
labor unions, 310–311
in United Kingdom, 67–73

political participation. *see* interest groups; protests; social movements
political parties. *see also* party systems
alternation of, 7–8
characteristics of, 30–32
defined, 30
in France, 124, 135, 140–142
in Germany, *90,* 105–110, *109*
in India, 201, 212–215, *215*
vs. interest groups, 30
in Iran, 437–439
in Japan
Democratic Party of Japan (DPJ), 151
Japan Socialist Party (JSP), 158–159
Liberal Democratic Party (LDP), 151
in Mexico, 242–243, 264–266
in Nigeria, 328, 351–354
parliamentary sovereignty and, 52–53
protests and, *146*
in Russia, *295,* 311–313
in United Kingdom, 46, 58–59
in Weimar Republic, 83
political patronage, 353
political protests. *see* protests
political violence, 32
Poll Tax (UK), 49–50
population
in China, problem of, 367
comparison of, 5
post-materialism in France, 134, 137–138
poverty
globalization and, 16–17
in Nigeria, 321
prefectures in Japan, 166
presidential systems, 19
President's Rule in Indian constitution, 207–208, 212
Press Court of Iran, 424

PRI (*Partido Revolucionaro Institucional*), 265
  Chamber of Deputies seats held by, 247
  decline of, 244–250
  ethnicity and, 258–260
  hegemony of, 243–244
  response to 1985 earthquake, 267–268
prime ministers
  defined, 19
  in India, *216*
  in Japan, 167
  in Russia, *289*
  in United Kingdom, 52–54
Prime Minister's Questions (PMQ), 57
primordialism, 27
proportional representation
  defined, 21
  in Weimar Republic, 83
Protestant Church of England, 41
protests. *see also* social movements
  in China, 388–389, 397
  in colonial India, 202–203
  in France, 142–147
    analyzing, 115–118
    examples of, 142–147
    likelihood of, 132–133
    reasons for, 131–132, *137*
  in independent India, 221
  in Iran, 441–445
    1999 student uprising, 442–445
    Tobacco Protests, 441–442
  in Japan, 182–183
  leadership of, 146
  in Mexico, 267, 268
  as state failure, 142
Prussia, 79–82
public services
  in China, 378
  in Iran, 415
  Nigerian failure to provide, 335–336
public works spending in Japan, 169
Putin, Vladimir, 292, 296–298, 309–310

R

race, 26
Raj, 198
Rajya Sabha (House of the States), 209–211
Rape of Nanjing, 373
redistribution of wealth, 35, 36. *see also* welfare states
Reform Acts (UK), 45–46
regime change, 24–25. *see also* revolutions
  defined, 24
  French, 119, *122*
  Nigerian, *331*
regional parties in UK politics, 58–59
regionalism, 63
Reichstag, 79
religion
  in France, 136, 137–138
  in Germany, 79
  in India, 198, 220–222, *220*, *226*
  in Iran, 431–433. *see also* Islam
  in Ireland, 64
  in Japan, 175–176
  in Nigeria, 326, 327, 343–344
  in Russia, 304–305
  in United Kingdom, 64
rentier states, 437
rent-seeking economic behavior, 339
repertoires of collective action, 133
Republic of Biafra, 328, 345–347
republics, French, 119
resolution of no-confidence, 125
resource curse, 309. *see also* oil
reunification of Germany, 87–88, 98–99
Revolutionary Guards (*pasdaran*), 418–419, 436–437
revolutions, 32–33. *see also* regime change
  1989 wave, 285
  French Revolution, 119–120
  Iran in 1979, 416–418
  Mexico in 1910, 241–242
  Russian Revolution, 283–284
Right Cause party (Russia), 312
rural economy of Nigeria, 356
Russia, 278–317. *see also* USSR
  centralization of power, 292
  comparison to other countries, 281
  constitutional crisis of 1992-1993, 287–288
  economic growth, 308–309
  economic privatization, 307–309
  electoral systems, 293–296
  executive branch power, 288, 292
  geography of, 279
  history of, 279–287, *286*
    collapse of USSR, 284–287
    expansion of empire, 279–282
  geography and, 279–283
  independence, 285
  Russian Revolution, 283–284
  introduction to, 278–279
  map of, 280
  mass media, 296
  oligarchs, 307–308, 309
  party system, 313
  political identities, 299–306, *306*
    Chechnyan, 301–302

class identity, 303–304
ethnic identities, 299–301
religious identity, 304–305
Russian nationalism, 302–303
political institutions, 287–299, *291*
  constitution, 288–290, *298*
  elections, 293–296
  federalism, 290–292
  judicial branch, 290
  president and prime minister, 296–299
political interests, 306–316, *316*
  business interests, 309–310
  economic reform and collapse, 307–309
  labor unions, 310–311
political parties, *295*, 311–313
political schools of thought in, 282–283
presidents and prime ministers, *289*
religion in, 304–305
semi-presidential system, 288–290
size of, 279–282
social movements, 313–316

S

Sacred Defense (Iran-Iraq war), 417
Safavid Empire, 412–413
Salinas, Carlos, 245–246
samurais, 154, 155
Sarkozy, Nicolas, 140
Saro-Wiwa, Ken, 348
Sassanid Empire, 412
Scheduled Castes, 210, 218
schooling. *see* education
Scramble for Africa, 326
Second Reich, 79–82
  militarism in, 96
  nationalism in, 95

Second Republic (France), 120
Second Republic (Nigeria), 329
secularity in France, 136
selectorate. *see also* non-democratic regimes
  in China, 380–381
  comparison of, 23
  defined, 22
self-defense forces in Japan, 158
semi-presidential systems, 19–20
  defined, 20
  in France, 124–125
  in Russia, 288–290
Sénat, 125–127
Senate (Mexico), 251–252
separation of powers
  in Mexico, *254*
  in Russia, 288
shadow Cabinets, 58
shah of Iran, 413
Sharia law. *see also* Islam
  in Iran, 422
  in Nigeria, 333
Shi'i Islam, 412, 432, 438
Shinto religion, 175–176
shoguns, 154
Sikhism, 203, 214
Singh, Manmohan, 215
Single Non-Transferable Vote (SNTV) system in Japan, 168
single-member districts (SMDs), 20, 21
single-party regimes, 23–24
  defined, 23
  Mexico, 1917-1940, 242–243
social classes. *see* class identity
Social Democratic Party (Germany), 79–82, 106
social movements. *see also* protests
  characteristics and formation of, 29
  in Germany, 108
  in Mexico, 266–268
  in Russia, 313–316

in United Kingdom, 71–72
social programs. *see* public services
Socialist Party (PS) in France, 140–141
Socialist Reich Party, ban on, 91
societies
  defined, 13
  vs. governments and states, *14*
Sokoto Caliphate, 326
sovereignty
  defined, 12
  European Union and, 92
  globalization and, 15–17
Soviet Union. *see* USSR
Special Court for the Clergy in Iran, 424
State Council (China), 380
state institutions. *see* political institutions
state interests of France, 142
state-led economic development, 244
states
  defined, 12
  vs. governments and nations, *13*
Status of Forces Agreement, 416
student movement in Mexico, 267
Sun Yat-sen, 372–373
Sunni Islam, 412
Supreme Court (India), 211–212
Supreme Court (Mexico), 252
Supreme Court (UK), 52

T

tabloid newspapers. *see* mass media
Taisho Democracy, 157
Taiwan, 373

taxation
   administering, 339–340
   government accountability and, 340
television broadcasting. *see* mass media
Tenochtitlán, 237
terrorism, impact on limited government, 48
Thatcher, Margaret, 47
   exclusion of policy communities, 70
   Poll Tax scheme, 49–50
theocracies, 24. *see also* Iran
Third Reich. *see* Nazi regime
Third Republic (France), 120
Tibet, 393–395
Tokugawa era in Japan, 154–155
Tokyo stock market crash, 160
totalitarian regimes
   vs. authoritarian regimes, 84–85
   defined, 22
   East Germany as, 86–87
   examples of, 22
   Nazi regime as, 85
Treaty of Guadalupe Hidalgo, 240–241
Tudeh party (Iran), 437

U

ulama, 413
Union for a Popular Movement (UMP) party, 140
unions. *see* labor unions
unitary systems
   defined, 19
   in Japan, 165
   United Kingdom as, 51–52
United Kingdom
   civil society, 71–72
   class identity in, 60–62
   comparison to other countries, 43
   constitution, unwritten, 40–41, 51
   decolonization by, 46–47
   election results, 55
   ethnic identities in, 64–65
   European Union participation, 59–60
   gender issues, 65–67
   history of, 41–49, 49
      contemporary, 47–49
      establishment of state, 41
      Indian colonialism, 200–203
      limited government emergence, 44–46
      twentieth-century, 46–47
   immigration to, 64–65
   introduction to, 40–41
   limited government in, 40, 44–46, 56–60
   map of, 42
   mass media, 72–73
   as monarchy, 40, 44
   naming conventions for, 40–41
   Parliament, 41
   party system, 61, 68–70
   policy communities, 70–71
   political identities, 60–67, 67
   political institutions, 49–60, 59
      European Union, 59–60
      longevity of, 56–57
      majoritarian electoral system, 54–56
      oppositionalism, 57–58
      parliamentary sovereignty, 51–52
      prime ministerial government, 52–54
      regional governments, 58–59
   political interests, 67–73
   regional identities in, 63
   religious identities in, 64
   social movements, 71–72
   welfare state emergence, 47
   women's suffrage, 72

United Russia party, 296
United States
   Iranian involvement, 415–416, 419–420
   Japanese occupation, 158
Unity Party (Russia), 294–295
untouchables. *see* Scheduled Castes
USSR. *see also* Russia
   collapse of, 284–287
   economic development in, 283
   founding of, 283
Uyghur in China, 395–396

V

Versailles Treaty, 82
Vichy regime, 120
violence. *see* political violence
vote of confidence, 54
voting systems. *see* electoral systems

W

Warri violence, 349–350
wealth inequality. *see* economic inequality
wealth redistribution, 35, 36
Weber, Max
   vs. Karl Marx, 26
   theories of, 26
Weimar Constitution, 83
Weimar Republic, 78, 82–83
welfare states. *see also* redistribution of wealth
   defined, 34
   Germany as, 82, 103–104
   spending by, 36
   United Kingdom, development of, 47
Wen Jiabao, 380
West Germany, 86
Whig Party (UK), 45
White Revolution in Iran, 415

Subject Index

women's rights. *see* gender issues
working class. *see also* class identity
 in Mexico, 242–243
 in Nigeria, 354–356
world map, 4
World War I, and Russia, 283
World War II
 China in, 373
 France in, 120–121
 Germany after, 85–88

X

xenophobia. *see also* immigration
 in early Japan, 154–155
 in German society, 102, 108
Xingjiang Uyghur Autonomous Regions (UAR), 395
xitong groups, 383

Y

Yar'Adua, Umaru, 334, 358
Yeltsin, Boris, 285–286
Yoruba tribe, 323–326. *see also* Nigeria
Yuan Shikai, 372–373

Z

zamindars, 227
Zapatista Army of National Liberation (EZLN), 260
Zedillo, Ernesto, 252
Zoroastrianism, 221, 431

NAME INDEX

A

Abacha, Sani, 330, *331*, 338, 348
Abubakar, Abdulsalami, 338
Abubakar, Atiku, 353
Adenauer, Konrad, 105, *107*
Advani, L. K., 226
Aguiyi-Ironsi, Johnson, 338
Ahmadinejad, Mahmoud, 407–408, 419–420, 426, *427*
Ai Weiwei, 392
Alexander the Great, *421*, 430
Ali (son of Prophet Mohammad), 432
Alí' Mohammad, Seyyed Mirza, 432
Álvarez, Luis Echeverría, 245
Andropov, Yuri, 286
Ansell, Ben, 7
Art, David, 7
Ataturk, Kemal, 414
Attlee, Clement, 47
Aurangzeb (emperor), 198–199
Azikwe, Nnamadi, 321, 338

B

Babangida, Ibrahim, 338, 358
Babur, 198
Bahonar, Mohammad Javad, 427
Balladur, Edouard, 131
Banisadr, Abolhassan, 427, 438
Barre, Raymond, 131
Bayrou, François, 129
Bazargan, Mehdi, 416–417, 422, 438
Béland, Daniel, 142

Bérégovoy, Pierre, 131
Bismarck, Otto von, 79, 95, 103, 106
Blair, Tony, 48, 69
Bleich, Erik, 7
Bonaparte, Napoleon, 240
Bové, José, 137
Brandt, Willy, 106, *107*
Brezhnev, Leonid, 286
Brown, Gordon, 48, 69
Buhari, Muhammed, 338, 353, 358
Bush, George H. W., 278, 287
Bush, George W., 48, 420

C

Calderón, Felipe, 245, 252, 254, 262
Calles, Plutarco Elías, 242
Camacho, Manuel Ávila, 244, 245
Cameron, David, 13, *13*, 39, 48, 54, 56, 72
Cárdenas, Cuauhtémoc, 265–266, 268
Cárdenas, Lázaro, 242–244, 245, 247, 265, 268
Carter, Jimmy, 416
Chaban-Delmas, Jacques, 131
Charles I (king), 41, 44, *49*, 60
Chernenko, Konstantin, 286
Chernomyrdin, Viktor, 289
Chiang Kai-shek, 372–373
Chirac, Jacques, *131*, 140–141, 146
Churchill, Winston, 46–47, 203
Clinton, Bill, 419

Confucius, 371
Cortés, Hernán, 237, *249*
Cortines, Adolfo Ruiz, 245
Cresson, Edith, 131
Cromwell, Oliver, 41, *49*
Cromwell, Richard, 49
Cyrus the Great, 409, 412, 430, 432, 435

D

da Silva, Luiz Inácio (Lula), 1
D'az, Porfirio, 240–242
de Gaulle, Charles, 120, 123–124, *131*, 135, 140, 143
de Murville, Maurice Couvre, 131
de Villepin, Dominique, 131
Debré, Michel, 131
Deng Xiaoping, 376–377, *378*, 381, 386
Desai, Moraji, 216
Descartes, 119
d'Estaing, Valéry Giscard, *131*, 140
Díaz, Porfirio, 249
Diderot, Denis, 119
Din, Nasser al-, 442

E

Eisenhower, Dwight, 415
Elvin, Mark, 372
Erhard, Ludwig, *107*

F

Fabius, Laurent, 131
Fafowora, Dapo, 321

485

Name Index

Fashola, Babatunde, 353
Fewsmith, Joseph, 380
Fillon, François, *131*
Fox, Vicente, *245*, 247–248, *250*, 252, 262, 271
Fradkov, Mikhail, *289*
Frye, Richard, 430

G

Gaidar, Yegor, *289*, 307
Gandhi, Indira, *206*, 212–214, *216*, 226
Gandhi, Mohandas K. (Mahatma), 201, *206*, 207–208, 212
Gandhi, Priyanka, 214
Gandhi, Rahul, 214
Gandhi, Rajiv, 214, *216*, 228
Gandhi, Sonia, 194, 214
Gingrich, Jane, 7
Gorbachev, Mikhail, 278, 284–285, *286*, 287
Gowda, H. D. Deve, *216*
Gowon, Yakubu, *338*, 346
Gujral, I. K., *216*
Gusinsky, Vladimir, 309

H

Hall, Peter, 71
Hatoyama, Yukio, 150
Henri IV (king), 118
Henry VIII (king), 64
Herz, Bertrand, 77
Hidalgo, Miguel, 240, *249*
Hindenburg, Paul von, 84
Hitler, Adolf, 7, 22, 78, 82–85, 87, 91, 96–98
Hossein (grandson of Prophet Mohammad), 432, 435
Howard, Marc, 312
Hu Jintao, 380–381, 386, 395, 398, 400
Hu Yaobang, 394

Hua Guofeng, 386
Huang Di, Qin Shi, 370
Hurtado, Miguel de la Madrid, 245
Hussein, Saddam, 381, 417, 438

I

Inglehart, Ronald, 134, 137
Ivan IV (tsar), 279, 286

J

Jahan, Shah, 199
James II (king), 44
Jiang Zemin, 386, 400
Jinnah, Mohammad Ali, 195, 204–205, 207
John I (king), 41, 44
Jonathan, Goodluck, *338*, 352, 358
Jospin, Lionel, *131*
Juppé, Alain, *131*

K

Karroubi, Mehdi, 408
Kasianov, Mikhail, *289*
Kasparov, Garry, 315
Khamenei, Ali, 408, *421*, 425–427, *427*
Khan, Genghis, 412, *421*
Khan, Reza, *421*
Khatami, Mohammad, 418–420, *427*, 443–445
Khomeini, Ruhollah, 416–418, *421*, 422, 424–426, *427*, 429, 431, 437–438
Khristenko, Viktor, *289*
Khrushchev, Nikita, *286*, 375, 378
Kiesinger, George, *107*
Kirienko, Sergei, *289*
Knox D'Arcy, William, 413

Kohl, Helmut, 93, 98, 106, *107*
Koizumi, Jun'ichiro, 161–162, *165*, 187–190

L

Le Pen, Jean-Marie, 129, 135, 141
Le Pen, Marine, 141
Lenin, Vladimir, 283, *286*
LeVan, Carl, 337
Lin Zexu, 372
Louis XIV (king), 118
Louis XV (king), 118
Louis XVI (king), 118–119, 122

M

MacArthur, Douglas, 158
Madero, Francisco, 241
Maino, Sonia, 214
Major, John, 48
Mao Zedong, 366, 374–377, *378*, 379, 381, 383, 386, 388–391, 393, 397, 400, 402–403
Marier, Patrik, 142
Martínez-Gallardo, Cecília, 8
Marx, Karl, 25–26, *26*, 28, 282, 304, 355
Mateos, Adolpho López, 245
Mauroy, Pierre, *131*
Maximilian, Ferdinand, 249
Medvedev, Dmitri, 282, *289*, 296–298, 304, 314–315
Meiji (emperor), 155
Merkel, Angela, 77, 106, *107*
Mertha, Andrew, 9
Merz, Friedrich, 102
Messmer, Pierre, *131*
Miliband, Edward, 69
Mimiko, Olusegun, 355
Mitterrand, François, 93, 124, *131*, 140

Name Index

Mohammad, 412, 431–432
Montesquieu, Baron de, Charles-Louis de Secondat, 119
Morelos, José María, *249*
Morgenthau, Henry, Jr., *95*
Mossadeq, Mohammad, 415, 437
Mountbatten, Louis, 205
Mousavi, Mir-Hossein, 408, 427
Murtaia, Mohammed, *338*

N

Nanak, 203
Nanda, Gulzarilal, *216*
Napoleon, Louis, 120, *122*
Napoleon Bonaparte, 119–120, *122*
Nebuchadnezzar II, 409
Nehru, Jawaharlal, 195, 198, 201, 205, *206*, 207–208, 211, 213, *216*, 217, 221, 223, 231
Nemtsov, Boris, 315
North, Douglas, 390

O

Obama, Barack, 77
Obasanjo, Olusegun, 329–330, 334, *338*, 353–354, 357
Obrador, Andrés Manuel López, 262
Ordaz, Gustavo Díaz, *245*
Osanloo, Massoud, 440
Ozawa, Ichiro, 187, 189

P

Pahlavi, Reza, 414, 415, 420, 433
Patel, Sardar Vallabhbhai, 201–201, 205, 208–209

Peter the Great, 282
Petraeus, David, 386
Pompidou, Georges, *131*
Ponce de León, *245*
Portillo, José López, *245*
Primakov, Evgenii, 289
Putin, Vladimir, 278, 282, *289*, 290, 292–294, 296–299, 301, 303–304, 306, 309, 311–315

R

Raffarin, Jean-Pierre, *131*
Rafsanjani, Akbar Hashemi, 427
Rajai, Mohammad-Ali, *427*
Rajavi, Massoud, 438
Rao, P. V. Narasimha, *216*, 226, 228
Rao, P.V. Narasimha, 214
Reagan, Ronald, 93, 278
Reza, Mohammed, 414, 430, 437, 440
Rice, Condoleezza, 420
Robertson, Graeme, 9
Rocard, Michel, *131*
Rousseau, Jean-Jacques, 119
Royal, Ségolène, 129

S

Sadr, Bani, 438
Safavid, *421*
Salinas, Carlos, 245–246, *245*, 250, 260
Sarkozy, Nicolas, 129–130, *131*, 140
Saro-Wiwo, Ken, 348
Sassanid, *421*
Scacco, Alexandra, 9
Scheiner, Ethan, 7–8
Schmidt, Helmut, 97, *107*
Schroeder, Gerhard, 92, 101, 106, *107*, 108

Shagari, Shehu, *338*
Shariatmadari, Kazem, 438
Shastri, Lal Bahadur, 213, *216*
Shekhar, Chandra, *216*
Shirazi, Mirza Hassan, 442
Shonekan, Ernest, *338*
Singh, Charan, *216*
Singh, Manmohan, 194, 210, 214–215, *216*
Singh, V. P., *216*
Stalin, Joseph, 283–284, *286*, 301, 367, 375
Stepashin, Sergei, *289*
Sun Yat-sen, 372–373

T

Taisho (emperor), 157, *163*
Taleghani, 434
Tanaka, Kakuei, 184
Tenzin, Gyatso (Dalai Lama), 393, 395
Thatcher, Margaret, 47, 49, 51, 69, 70, 72, 93
Thiers, Adolphe, 120
Tilly, Charles, 133
Tokugawa, Ieyasu, 154
Truman, Harry, 415

V

Vajpayee, Atal Bihari, *216*
Valdés, Miguel Alemán, *245*
Vargas Llosa, Mario, 273
Vasconcelos, José, 259
Voltaire (François-Marie Arouet), 119

W

Weber, Max, 26, *26*
Wen Jiabao, 380, 398
Wiesel, Elie, 77
Wilkinson, Steven, 8

William (king of Holland), 44
William I (William the Conqueror), 41, *49*

X
Xi Jinping, 381

Y
Yar'adau, Umaru, 334, *338*, 350, 353, 358
Yavlinskii, Grigory, 312
Yazdi, Ebrahim, 438
Yazid, 432
Yeltsin, Boris, 278, 285, 287–288, *289*, 290, 292–294, 301, 303–304, 307–309, 311–313, 315
Yuan Shikai, 372, *378*

Z
Zedillo, Ernesto, 252
Zhang Yimou, 392
Zhirinovsky, Vladimir, 312
Zubkov, Viktor, *289*